LEONARD ARRINGTON AND THE WRITING OF MORMON HISTORY

LEONARD ARRINGTON
AND THE
WRITING of MORMON
HISTORY

GREGORY A. PRINCE

THE UNIVERSITY OF UTAH PRESS
Salt Lake City

THE TANNER TRUST FUND
Salt Lake City

Copublished with
the Tanner Trust Fund,
J. Willard Marriott Library

 The Defiance House Man colophon is a registered trademark of
the University of Utah Press. It is based on a four-foot-tall
Ancient Puebloan pictograph (late PIII) near Glen Canyon, Utah.

20 19 18 17   3 4 5

Library of Congress Cataloging-in-Publication Data

Name: Prince, Gregory A., 1948– author.
Title: Leonard Arrington and the writing of Mormon history
  / Gregory A. Prince.
Description: Salt Lake City : University of Utah Press, 2016. |
  Includes bibliographical references and index.
Identifiers: LCCN 2015050433| ISBN 9781607814795 (cloth : alk. paper) |
  ISBN 9781607814801 (ebook)
Subjects: LCSH: Arrington, Leonard J. | Church of Jesus Christ of Latter-day Saints—History. |
  Mormon Church—History.
Classification: LCC BX8695.A77 P75 2016 | DDC 289.3072/02—dc23
LC record available at http://lccn.loc.gov/2015050433

All photos courtesy of Susan Arrington Madsen

Printed and bound by Edwards Brothers Malloy, Inc., Ann Arbor, Michigan.

Frontispiece: Formal portrait of Leonard Arrington by William Whitaker, 1998.

This book is dedicated to all who believe
"that truth has got to be preserved"—even inconvenient truth.

CONTENTS

PREFACE

In March 2005, *David O. McKay and the Rise of Modern Mormonism* was published by the University of Utah Press. It represented a decade of hard work that was sandwiched into whatever gaps I could find in a schedule that included being a husband, a father of three children including an autistic son, and CEO of a biotechnology corporation. It also represented a labor of love because my coauthor, Wm. Robert Wright, and I decided to forego all royalty income in return for a higher quality publication and a lower price point. Within weeks of the book's publication my wife, JaLynn, asked, "What's next?" I said, "I don't have a clue, but I know it will find me." I didn't have to wait long.

Several months after the McKay book was published, I was invited to speak on it in the Logan Tabernacle. After my speech, a woman approached the podium and introduced herself. "I'm Susan Arrington Madsen." She asked if I was returning to Salt Lake City that night. I said I wasn't returning until the following day, whereupon she requested that I meet her at a local restaurant for breakfast.

The breakfast lasted for three hours. She said she had read the McKay biography and had then discussed with her two brothers, James and Carl, the possibility of my writing their father's biography, to which they readily agreed. I was both honored and overwhelmed at the invitation—the same way I had felt when Bob Wright asked me, a decade earlier, if I would write the McKay biography. Given the choice of writing biographies of any two Mormon figures of the twentieth century, I would certainly have included both men on my short list, and it is probable that David O. McKay would have been first and Leonard Arrington second. Both were towering figures in their fields—McKay as church president and, in my opinion and the opinion of many people both in and out of the LDS Church, the most important Mormon of the twentieth century; and Arrington as the only professional historian ever to serve as LDS church historian and arguably the most important figure in twentieth-century Mormon historiography.

There was a parallel between the two projects that made both irresistible: the quantity and quality of manuscript material that was made available to me. In the case of David O. McKay it included some forty thousand pages of diaries kept for him by his secretary Clare Middlemiss, and over one hundred thousand additional pages of scrapbooks and speeches, almost none of which had ever been accessible to scholars. And in the case of Leonard Arrington it included some twenty thousand pages of diaries, none of which had yet been made available for scholarly research, and the remainder of the astounding 319 linear feet of Leonard's papers at the Merrill-Cazier Library at Utah State University. By rights given her by her father as trustee of his estate, Susan gave me unrestricted access to the diaries several years before they were opened to the public.

The Arrington diaries are a hybrid of several types of documents. Generally the most valuable are the real-time entries that he either typed himself or dictated to his secretaries. Although most such entries are descriptive, occasionally Leonard wrote reflectively, particularly in his years as church historian. The real-time entries are most plentiful during the church historian years, and drop off quite drastically after 1982.

He wrote to Grace daily during his three years of military service and included copies of many of the letters in the diaries. The diary record of those years is comprised almost entirely of those letters.

Leonard wrote weekly letters to his children, usually addressing all three in the same letter. Although the real-time diary entries dwindled after 1982, these letters continued through the final years of his life, and he inserted copies of them in the diaries. They therefore constitute the most useful record of the last seventeen years of his life. While Leonard occasionally included in his diaries letters to and from correspondents besides his children, the vast majority of those letters are in the correspondence files of the Leonard J. Arrington Historical Archive.

On occasion, usually in the years after he became church historian, Leonard included in the diaries retrospective sketches of his earlier life and the lives of his ancestors. These occur in random order, giving the sense that he visited episodes whenever the thought occurred to him.

Supplementing these primary sources are several privately published biographies and autobiographies written for family and close friends. An early attempt at autobiography turned into a biography written by Rebecca Cornwall in 1976. Cornwall collaborated with Leonard the following year in editing the autobiography of Grace Arrington. Shortly after Grace's death in 1982, Lavina Fielding Anderson completed a three-volume history of Leonard's decade as church historian, *Doves and Serpents: The Activities of Leonard Arrington as Church Historian, 1972–1982*. It depends almost exclusively on his diaries and was commissioned by him. Beginning in the early 1990s, Leonard published a series of illustrated autobiographical and ancestral monographs.[1]

Finally, as detailed in chapter 30, Leonard wrote a memoir that was published by the University of Illinois Press in 1998, a year before his death. He focused primarily on the church historian years—hence the title, *Adventures of a Church*

Historian—and included in the introduction a disclaimer: "This is not an auto-biography, a personal life that begins with birth and proceeds to the date of writing without omitting significant events and influences. It is a memoir—a rehearsal of a portion of my life that was particularly intense and meaningful."[2]

Taken together, these voluminous unpublished and published records give an unusually detailed accounting of Leonard's life—almost an embarrassment of riches for a biographer. Very few significant gaps appear in the most important years of his career—his years as church historian—and so I have been able to rely both on Leonard's voice and the later voices of interviewees to tell most of the story, rather than providing the kind of filler material that generally accompanies biographies. My task has been to assemble the source materials, look for the important stories that comprise each chapter, and then tell those stories in the words of the participants, wherever possible, providing context and reflection while attempting to stay in the background.

My approach to the writing of this book is similar to that of the McKay book in two ways. First, I have organized it topically, rather than taking the strictly chronological, cradle-to-grave format of many biographies. And second, I have supplemented the rich documentary record with contemporary interviews of those who knew Leonard well. The passage of time has allowed these interviewees to gain a perspective not possible at the time the events were happening, and the reader will readily appreciate the texture that the interviews have given to the book. By the time I had conducted one hundred interviews for the McKay book, I felt that I had a good perspective on his life and times—that there were no surprises left to discover. I also conducted one hundred interviews for this book and came to the same conclusion. In all instances, I made complete transcripts of the recorded interviews, so all quotations are accurate.

One difference in the two books is that I never met David O. McKay, even though all of my formative years in the LDS Church were dominated by his presence. I was three years old when he became Church President, and had just returned from a proselytizing mission to Brazil when he died in 1970. By contrast, I met Leonard on several occasions, usually at an annual meeting of the Mormon History Association but once on a more intimate level when I met him at his home and recorded his reminiscences of President McKay. Moreover, I served in the Brazilian South Mission at the same time as his son James.

The writing of all three of my books—the other being *Power from on High: The Development of Mormon Priesthood* (1995)—was, in a strange way, deeply influenced by Leonard, albeit indirectly. As the reader will see, Leonard created an atmosphere that was very welcoming of amateur historians—what he called "history buffs," people with a deep interest in Mormon history but no formal training in historiography. I suspect that this had much to do with the fact that he himself received no formal training in the writing of history, instead earning a PhD in economics. Although he became church historian of the LDS Church, some historians never fully accepted him as one of their own, and it appears to me that he wanted to give in a way that he did not receive.

One beneficiary of his acceptance of amateurs was Lester Bush, a physician with no formal training in historiography. As the reader will see in chapter 21, Leonard's encouragement of Lester's efforts, particularly his seminal article on blacks and priesthood, was deeply affirming, and Lester went on to become a major player in Mormon history, in part because of Leonard.

By chance, not having met Lester previously, JaLynn and I bought a home in the same ward (congregation) as Lester and Yvonne Bush when we moved to Maryland in 1975. Lester and I quickly became close friends and he became a role model to me of how one might write Mormon history without having the usual credentials—I had degrees in dentistry and pathology. Those first years were when Lester served as associate editor of *Dialogue: A Journal of Mormon Thought*. They also coincided with the headiest days of "Camelot," the nickname often given to the History Division during Leonard's tenure as LDS church historian, as well as, with deeper nostalgia, the years during which the division was disassembled and shipped to Brigham Young University. Because of Lester's editorship, he was a nexus of information coming from all points of the Mormon compass, much of it directly from Leonard and his closest associates. The weekly, and sometimes daily debriefings that I received from Lester put me into close virtual proximity of Leonard and his franchise and showed me how authentic Leonard's reach was to the history buffs.

A four-year term (1977–1981) as elders' quorum president in my ward led me to research deeply the early years of Mormon priesthood; and with the direct mentorship of Lester and the indirect mentorship of Leonard, I wrote *Power from on High*. Then, the McKay biography beckoned.

When I was still in the early years of the McKay project, Leonard published his autobiography, *Adventures of a Church Historian*. I read it in its entirety during one memorable Sunday afternoon and then sent him a letter of appreciation that included a description of some of the minor bruises I had taken in encounters with some members of the LDS Church hierarchy over issues of history— bruises that paled in comparison to what he had experienced. Several weeks later—six months before his death—I received a handwritten letter from him, on stationery bearing the profile of a chicken as a letterhead:

17 Aug., 1998
Dear Greg,

Your warm and informative letter was most welcome. I very much
admire you and wish you the best—on the McKay project and the
[Paul] Dunn project.

I got well acquainted with Elder Dunn & Jeanne when I was
invited to go to the Far East Area meetings in 1975. My wife and I
often ate dinner with them and we liked them very much. I too
think he is fully worthy of a biography and hope you will persevere.
It is satisfying and sufficient that people you regard as faithful servants approve. We felt that way with approval from the First Presidency and a majority of the Apostles.

Blessings on you!

Leonard

The letter, and particularly its two concluding sentences, gave me the extra
measure of energy needed to complete the decade-long McKay project, and it has
hovered over the current decade-long project continually, always reminding me
of why it is worth the effort. Only upon completing the writing of Leonard's
biography, however, did I fully appreciate the meaning to him of those concluding sentences. Blessings on you, too, Leonard!

Acknowledgments

This book grew from a request from the children of Leonard Arrington—James, Carl, and Susan—that I be their father's biographer. They gave me access to his voluminous papers, including his diaries, years before these documents were available to other researchers. In addition, all three gave me rich, candid interviews that provided unique insights into their father and mother. This book would not exist without their support.

Cory Larson provided the essential role of research assistant in going through the extensive correspondence in Leonard's papers at Utah State University. Alicia Kimball scanned and typed into the computer thousands of pages of Leonard's diary entries and other documents. The work of both individuals was crucial in facilitating the project.

The staff of the University of Utah Press has repeated its amazing performance in publishing my prior book, *David O. McKay and the Rise of Modern Mormonism*. I could not have asked for better, more professional editors.

Finally, my wife, JaLynn, provided encouragement and patience as I worked through my third decade-long process of writing a book.

Prologue

Following the death of Joseph Smith Jr. in 1844, the church that he founded split into several factions. The two largest were the Church of Jesus Christ of Latter-day Saints (LDS), led by the Quorum of the Twelve Apostles (and then Brigham Young) and with headquarters ultimately in Salt Lake City, Utah; and the Reorganized Church of Jesus Christ of Latter Day Saints (RLDS), led by Joseph Smith III and with headquarters ultimately in Independence, Missouri. For over a century, the two churches sparred, attacking each other's truth claims on the one hand, and seeking to convert each other's flocks on the other. Thus, the two men walking arm-in-arm in 1974 through the green streets of reconstructed Nauvoo, the city founded by the Mormon prophet, were an unsettling sight, for they were the official historians of the two churches that many presumed still to be at war.

The LDS Church, by far the larger of the two, still smarted from the refusal of Joseph Smith's mother, sisters, wife, and children to leave Nauvoo after Smith's death and follow Brigham Young to the Great Basin in 1847. The formation of the RLDS Church in 1860, with Smith's oldest son as its prophet and president, deepened the animosity.

The RLDS Church, stung by persistent and credible allegations that Joseph Smith had secretly practiced polygamy, sought to distance itself as far as possible from the Utah church whose identity *became* polygamy. "What did I know about who I was when I was growing up?" Robert Flanders, the first RLDS professional historian to analyze the Nauvoo period, summarized. "All I knew about who I was, was that I was *not* Mormon. That was the mantra. 'Bob, you are *not* Mormon.' I'm not exaggerating about this. I knew *nothing* about my religious tradition, except that Joseph Smith was our founder and we were not Mormon."[1]

The two men who were walking the streets together also worked together. Indeed, they were principal engineers of rapprochement between the two traditions. Richard P. Howard, RLDS church historian since 1966, had launched an effort in 1967 to convince leaders of both churches to exchange microfilm copies of crucial manuscripts that would illuminate the earliest days of Mormonism. His own leaders immediately approved the proposal, but LDS leaders declined. The 1972 decision by LDS leaders to professionalize their Historical Department included the calling of Leonard J. Arrington to the office of church historian.[2] In the spring of 1974, shortly before the Mormon History Association held its first meeting in Nauvoo, and a few months before the conspicuously leisurely and amiable stroll of the two historians, Arrington and his coworkers renewed the request to the LDS First Presidency.[3] A month later they met with that body and won approval.[4] Diplomacy at the level of the historians initiated lasting peace between the two churches at all levels, and Arrington was the LDS diplomat-in-chief.

There was irony in the fact that Arrington's relationship with the RLDS Church was smoother than that with his own. Although 1974 was a good year for Mormon historians—a coworker later referred to the period nostalgically as "Camelot"—storm clouds hovered just beyond the horizon. Within two years, the tempest began. By 1982, the decade-long professionalization of the Historical Department came to an end—and with its ending came the beginning of a decade-long battle between the LDS hierarchy and Mormon intellectuals which culminated in the high-profile excommunication of the "September Six" in 1993.

Camelot died, but Arrington's benevolent influence did not. Perhaps the highest compliment he could have received came from Paul M. Edwards, a descendant of Joseph Smith and a member of the RLDS hierarchy. While noting that the LDS theology allowing for humans to progress to godhood was a bit much for the RLDS to swallow, Edwards said to me, in a casual conversation many years ago, "If such a thing is possible, I would like Leonard Arrington to become my God."[5]

A word about the dedication to this book: In 1973 writer Carol Lynn Pearson met with Leonard Arrington, who consoled her following an incident when her cover story for the LDS Church magazine, the *Ensign*, was pulled at the last minute because of her support of the Equal Rights Amendment. In her diary she wrote, "He said that he has been in my position before. In fact, he said he is enough of a realist that he makes two copies of his journal—one that stays in his office, and another that goes home with him. He said that no matter what happens to him, he wants his true story to be preserved. I told him that I also write down all of these details in my diary, and we were in agreement that truth has got to be preserved, whatever the cost."[6]

1

ANCESTRY

STRAIGHT FROM THE SOIL

TENNESSEE

The American South in the late nineteenth century was hostile territory for Mormon missionaries, with many being persecuted and some killed.[1] In the 1890s two Mormon missionaries working in eastern Tennessee were charged with violating the law and brought before the squire—a combination of sheriff, judge, district attorney, and justice of the peace—for trial. Upon hearing the case, Squire LeRoy Arrington found them innocent. However, rather than placing them in harm's way by releasing them immediately in the hostile environment, he invited them to stay in his home for several days until tempers cooled. Impressed by their sincerity, Arrington befriended them and their successors. Eventually he, his wife, and most of his children converted to Mormonism.[2]

OKLAHOMA

The Oklahoma Land Rush of 1889 has been immortalized in print and film, but it was only the first—and not the largest—of several land rushes and land lotteries in the Oklahoma Territory that extended into the early years of the twentieth century. A land lottery in 1901 attracted over 160,000 registrants who hoped to draw for parcels totaling 3.5 million acres—nearly double the size of the 1889 rush. Among the lucky registrants was the Corn family, which relocated from Indiana. Four years later the Arrington family, which had stopped briefly in Georgia after leaving Tennessee, purchased a farm adjoining that of the Corns—both farms being in the center of what later became the Dust Bowl.

Noah Arrington grew up farming, attending school only as the seasons allowed. While sufficiently adept at mathematics to keep up with the business side of farming, he had only rudimentary skills in reading and writing. Edna Corn, five years Noah's junior, was the younger sister of a schoolteacher and received eleven full years of schooling, graduating from high school.

In 1911 and 1912, Frank J. Cannon, disaffected son of Mormon apostle George Q. Cannon and former U.S. senator from Utah, went on a lecture tour to publicize his book, *Under the Prophet in Utah*, which was highly critical of his former church. One of his stops was in Lawton, Oklahoma, near the Corn farm. Because their daughter Edna had a romantic interest in a Mormon, the parents attended Cannon's lectures and came away persuaded that Mormonism was evil. Knowing that her parents would never approve of her marriage to a Mormon, Edna eloped with Noah in 1913, shortly after her graduation.[3]

IDAHO

Three of Noah Arrington's brothers left Oklahoma in 1906 to work on the construction of the Salt Lake and Los Angeles Railroad—later part of the Union Pacific. Two of the three subsequently settled in Twin Falls, Idaho. On their recommendation, Noah and Edna moved to Twin Falls, where they spent the remainder of their lives. Within a year of their move, Edna converted to Mormonism.[4]

For several years, Noah worked as a hired hand on a nearby farm, putting in ten-hour days and then returning home to work twenty acres of leased farmland using a one-horse walking plow. By 1920 he had purchased the land and concentrated on farming it. In 1925, at age thirty-five, he was called to serve a two-year proselytizing mission to the southern states.[5] He moved Edna, who was four months pregnant, and their four children into Twin Falls, the nearest town, and leased his farmland for six hundred dollars a year—the sole source of financial support for his family during his two-year absence. He relied on the generosity of his two sisters to pay for his mission expenses.[6] While he never complained of the hardships caused by his mission, his granddaughter noted, "I have some pictures of Noah when he was on his mission, and he looks depressed in quite a few of them. Think about it: he left behind Edna and five children!"[7]

Despite his scant formal education, Noah demonstrated sufficient leadership skills to serve as a conference president—roughly the equivalent, in the fledgling southern LDS Church of the 1920s, of today's stake president—in Virginia, North Carolina, and Florida.[8] One incident related by his son-in-law captured the seriousness with which he wore the mantle of missionary:

> I'll tell you a story that has stuck with me for years. When he was on his mission, he and his companion had all the mission records in his valise, which is a style of briefcase. He laid it down by his feet to buy

the train tickets. When he went down to pick it up, it was gone. His companion didn't have it. So they went into a secluded corner by themselves and prayed about it and when they got through praying, he said, "I know just where it is." He went down a long dark hallway and down the stairs and down a long dark hallway to the furnace room and it was behind the furnace.[9]

Noah returned to farming in 1927 and expanded his franchise by purchasing a forty-acre parcel at an inflated price, on credit. Then came the Great Depression. Potatoes that had sold for $1.75 a bushel soon were selling for $0.10 per hundred pounds. "He managed to hold on while many others didn't," wrote Leonard in a diary entry. "He persuaded bankers and capitalists to reduce loans, postpone demand for payment, forgive interest, and so on. He never told us anything about all this, but we know about it in general. Edna, of course, cooperated by being a good frugal housewife and mother and helper."[10] Frugality was a constant. "Mom was very anxious to keep the light bill down to only $1 [per month], so the use of electricity was very sparing."[11] "Once a year Dad would buy a new dress for my mother—usually gingham and rather plain. There was no consideration to style or color, but simply something that would cover and last. My mother never complained of this."[12] For his own part, Noah was equally thrifty. "Not until 1936, after he had been farming for twenty-two years, did Dad buy a tractor and begin to enter into mechanized farming."[13] By the time of his death in 1968, Noah was a prosperous farmer with five hundred acres of prime farmland.

Noah: A Hard-Working Farmer

Although Noah Arrington was industrious and successful at farming, his lack of formal education constricted his world. From his mission field in Florida, Noah wrote a 1926 letter to nine-year-old Leonard that portrays his limitations in spelling and syntax: "I suppose that you have all plans made for you and I to go into the chicken buisness. You wanto figer what kind of chickens we want. also about how many we should buy to start with. also what we should feed them in order to get the most eggs. . . . The Elders taken my picture yesterday and I may send home next week. Love Daddy."[14]

"My father," wrote Leonard decades later, "said 'he done' and 'he seen,' but my mother always insisted we speak correctly."[15] Noah's church duties—he served as a high councilor from 1919 until he was called as a bishop in 1936—included delivering sermons on a monthly basis. "His sermons were interesting: filled with Tennessee mountaineer expressions and pronunciations," recalled Leonard. "They were based on the Bible to some extent, but mostly on his own experiences. They were down-to-earth."[16] And they reflected the limited scope of his reading: the scriptures, primarily the Latter-day Saint canon; a few church books; the *Twin Falls News*; and the *Idaho Farmer.* "Not being educated, he talked like a country farmer. He was not at home in any discussion of ideas."[17] Unless he felt that talk was necessary, he was likely to remain silent. "One could work all day beside him and he'd never say a word. He was a silent workman and thought talking took your mind off your work."[18] If he was introspective, he never let on. "He never told anyone his innermost secrets, if he had any."[19]

Parsimonious in his verbal communication, Noah let his actions do his speaking. "He gave more than he was required to give. The neighbors respected him, as did his hired hands. He got a lot of work out of them, but they liked him because he was fair, paid them promptly and without quibbling, and paid them well."[20] "If one of them wanted his pay in advance to take care of a doctor's bill Dad would give him not only the pay in advance but a little donation besides."[21]

Noah's kindness to strangers, demonstrated through actions rather than words, was notable. In the 1930s, with the Great Depression in full swing, Noah converted an apple orchard into a potato field, in the process harvesting sufficient firewood for several years' use. Leonard later wrote of his responsibility with the wood: "One of my chores, as a boy, was to chop enough kindling to use for the night, to start the fire in the morning. . . . Every evening after school or work I spent about half an hour getting kindling and stove wood." One night Noah, hearing a noise in the yard, went out to the woodpile.

> [He] saw a fellow taking some pieces of wood. The fellow said he needed the wood to keep his family warm and didn't have any money—it being depression and all. He was convincing, so N.W. [Noah] asked him if he needed food. Upon his affirmative, N.W. went to the cellar and took out a bag of potatoes and a bag of apples. Kenneth and Wayne were sleeping out in the shed across the lot and he woke them and had them get the apples and potatoes out. When the fellow was about to leave, N.W. said, "Next time, when you need something, don't come at night like this when I'll have to wake the boys; come in the daytime when it won't be any trouble for us to help you."[22]

He was also openhanded to the LDS Church, perhaps to a fault. Leonard remembered him being "very generous with the Church but being very tight with his own family," giving money to the church to purchase organs "at a time when we thought he should have bought a piano for the family. He bought land for the

Church Welfare Program at a time that we thought he should have fixed up the house, but that is the way he was."[23]

Indeed, his relationship with his own family often stood in sharp contrast to his dealings with outsiders. Leonard recalled many instances where his father served as a willing, impromptu counselor to neighbors and members of his congregation, withholding judgment and offering help. "He was a wise person and his wisdom was evident to people who had experience with him." Yet, paradoxically, his children saw him as unwilling, or perhaps unable, to extend the same courtesy to them.

> It is strange that his children did not go to him with their problems, that is, the real problems of growing up and meeting life. They saw other people doing it but did not feel free to go themselves. We asked ourselves why this was and we decided that we thought he would consider us weak and vacillating if we went to him with problems. He expected us to solve these ourselves; not that he told us this but somehow he didn't appeal to us as the warm kind of personality that would be sympathetic. We didn't feel to trust him by telling him confidential things.[24]

While there was no question in his childrens' minds that he was a caring father, they did not consider him a "pal." "He never took us fishing, though he sometimes said he would when he had time. He never had time. . . . He was not cold and forbidding; he was warm and receptive, but not like a pal."[25]

While Noah's financial generosity toward outsiders increased with his gradually improving prosperity, he remained penurious towards his family. Leonard reminisced, "His propensity to consume was mightily low. By that I mean, he spent very little on the family. Whatever he earned he put into land and farm equipment and livestock. He always invested productively, not consumptively." That meant utilitarian clothing for the children, bedrooms without heating, no electricity, telephone, radio, or automobile until well after all of the neighbors had them, no visits to the dentist, and not even to the doctor unless it was clear that they had an infectious disease. "Everything into land, into building up property. No investment in the children or their education. . . . We did not take vacations; a holiday was a day of work on the farm, as was Saturday." Leonard recalled his father speaking often "about going to the hills to lie under the pines. But somehow there was always too much work to be done."[26]

In Leonard's view, Noah's paradoxical generosity towards outsiders and parsimony towards his children devolved from a simple, though questionable, logic: "Dad would not help out his sons because he thought it would spoil them."[27]

Leonard's relationship with his own children stood in sharp contrast to that with his father.

Noah's calling as bishop in 1936 placed him in a different ecclesiastical posture than his prior calling as high councilor: he was now a line officer, instead of staff, and instead of visiting a different flock each month, he had personal responsibility for one flock—his own congregation. He worked by instinct, not by the book, and while his style was atypical and sometimes unorthodox, it was often remarkably effective, as illustrated by an incident when he needed a new assistant. He felt strongly that Jay Merrill, a businessman who had recently moved to Twin Falls, was the man for the job. But there was one catch: "Jay smoked cigars and everybody knew it." When Noah proposed his choice to the stake president, the reply was expected: "You can't do that; everybody knows that Jay Merrill smokes big black cigars." But Noah was ready with a rebuttal: "He's quit." When? "The minute I asked him to be my counselor he quit." Noah won the argument, and likely changed a life in the process. "Jay became his counselor, later his first counselor, later counselor in the stake presidency, and the first Mormon elected to the state House of Representatives representing Twin Falls County."[28]

Noah's approach to selecting a new president of the Relief Society (the women's organization within the church) was similarly unorthodox. Seeing that only the older women had been involved in the society, he caught everyone by surprise by choosing Harriet Sorensen, a young woman who only recently had moved, with her husband, into the congregation—his thought being that a younger president would attract younger women into the group. As had been the case with Jay Merrill, Noah's choice was at first dismissed out-of-hand by the stake president. "You can't choose her; she's only twenty-seven years old. The older women wouldn't accept her. She could never function." Noah again was persistent, and again he won his case, thus beginning "a new era in the Twin Falls Relief Society." In dealing with her, Noah demonstrated something of a sixth sense, a trait that others in his congregation also witnessed.

> Once my Dad told her he wanted her to go to the temple, and requested her to wait in line and get a temple recommend.[29] . . . She said she didn't want to interfere with others who were getting their recommends. He argued with her a little, but she didn't remain to get hers. When she got home she received a telephone call from her sister Alice saying she was getting married in the Salt Lake Temple and wanted her (Harriet) to be present. Harriet then needed the recommend. She telephoned the bishop's office. Jay Merrill answered the telephone. Harriet explained that she had turned down the bishop

about getting a recommend and now discovered she needed one. . . . She said, "How did the bishop know that I needed one?" Jay said: "When you've served Bishop Arrington as long as I have, you know you don't need to ask that question."[30]

EDNA: A MOTHER'S INFLUENCE

Noah and Edna Arrington's marriage of forty-seven years ended with Edna's death in 1960. The marriage, while durable, was often difficult for her, as Leonard sympathetically recalled:

> Mom felt very much hurt during the early years of her marriage that Dad did not confide in her, talked rather brusquely to her, and always regarded her interests and desires as far below those of the farm. I saw her secretly crying a few times when I was just a child. I realize Dad had problems, but I do think he should have been more sympathetic with Mom's needs. My Dad was the real authority in the home, and always had the last word. He was rather an authoritarian or patriarchal figure. I'm sure he loved Mom and that she loved him, and that somewhat tempered his patriarchal attitude which no doubt came from his father, who was even more so.[31]

Although Edna never challenged Noah's patriarchal dominance, she exerted a strong influence on her children—and even on Noah. Leonard obviously respected both parents highly: "She was good with words, spelled very well, knew 'sophisticated' words, read widely in novels, short stories, and assorted church literature. She knew a good deal of history, geography, and literature. She knew poetry, music. She had catholic interests." And because she was more literate than Noah, she became his scribe and bookkeeper. "She is the one who kept him from going to jail because of income tax."[32]

Edna encouraged her children to gain the formal education that their father lacked, including college. Leonard noted, "This did not work out in some cases: LeRoy was not interested in academic achievement, nor Marie; but I and some of the younger brothers were."[33]

2

A CHILDHOOD
WITH CHICKENS

Leonard James Arrington—who went by the nickname of "Jimmy" until he began his academic career in his thirties—was born in an unpainted frame house measuring only ten-by-fifteen feet, near Twin Falls, Idaho, on July 2, 1917. Typical for the time and place, Edna was assisted in the delivery by a midwife, Mary Ann Swenson, rather than a physician.[1] Although he began as a healthy baby, Leonard's life almost came to a premature end during his second year.

In 1918 a novel strain of influenza virus caused a pandemic that persisted for a year and killed between 50 and 100 million people worldwide—far more than all battlefield fatalities of World War I. Restrictions on public meetings and travel, combined with strict quarantines of infected households, were implemented in an attempt to limit the spread of the disease. However, all of the restrictions were temporarily suspended on November 11, 1918, to allow for public celebration of Armistice Day—the end of the war. Cases of influenza in Twin Falls peaked a short time thereafter, and all members of the Arrington family were infected. Leonard's illness was grave, and the doctor didn't mince words about the prognosis. "When Doctor Cloucheck said I had pneumonia, he told my father, also down with the flu, that I would die within twenty-four hours. My father seemed resigned to it (having previously lost Thelma [a daughter]), but my mother was not." Rising up from her sick bed, against the strong objections of the doctor, Edna summoned a friend, Hannah Bowen, and with her joined in ministering to Leonard in a manner generally done only by the male, lay ministry, "anointing me, blessing me, and praying for me. Their blessing was efficacious. . . . My mother always believed that God had saved me for a special purpose. As I achieved in school and in other activities, she believed I was vindicating God's saving gift to her."[2]

Perhaps weakened by his bout with influenza, Leonard experienced serious illnesses—smallpox, diphtheria, and typhoid fever—before his fourth birthday. In the case of smallpox, as with influenza, he credited women's spiritual ministrations for his recovery. "According to my mother, the midwife, Anna Swenson, came, tended to me, and prayed with my mother over me. . . . My mother always said that the Lord preserved me to do an important work—she didn't know what."[3]

Noah's proselytizing mission to the southern states hastened Leonard's maturation. Only seven years old when his father departed, he worked at his uncle's dairy, delivering milk twice a day and washing bottles, for $0.35 a day. "I sometimes think I brought in more money than any one else in the family. When Uncle Glenn would pay me at the end of a month I would take it in and give it to mamma and say, 'You can now buy some groceries.' It was usually $10.35."[4] Less regular was income derived from a semipro baseball league, as he nostalgically wrote to his wife, Grace, when he was in Italy in the U.S. Army. "I'd go to town in the summer to help Grandma sell vegetables & then stop by the ball game. For every pop bottle I could pick up, I was given 1 penny. The first game I went to (I slipped in free) I picked up 60 bottles & walked home with 60¢ in my pocket." Money, rather than any athletic prowess, drew him to the game, and he went as often as he could, sometimes making "an extra nickel picking up [a] gentleman's hat that he had dropped below the bleachers."[5]

Noah's return eased the financial strain on the family, but only enough to let it weather the Great Depression two years later. The Arrington sixty acres supplied plenty of food—"we had pigs, sheep, chickens, an orchard, and grew a variety of crops"—but cash was tight. "We had only such meat as [Dad] killed and butchered right on the place—hogs, sheep, cows, chickens. . . . We never had beef animals during the time I was growing up."[6]

The family spent winter evenings gathered around the wood-burning stove, then snuggling down with siblings under inadequate bedding for the night, in bedrooms lacking heating. "I remember us sleeping four in a bed; three lengthwise and one crosswise at the foot of the bed. We always had bed partners. Roy and I and Marie when she was little; then Roy and I; then Roy and I and Kenneth; and so on. We didn't have adequate room or beds or bedding until about the time I went to College."[7]

Leonard did well in school, although his later proficiency in spelling—he often won spelling bees—came from much remedial work. In a letter written to his father shortly after Noah left for his mission, Leonard tipped his hand on words that had *not* been on his recent spelling test: "I have a good teacher. And yesterday I got a hunderd in spelling. I have got my rubbers they fit me good. Leroy is wasing bottls for ucle glen. I get in the coal and kinding. Keneth is feeling good."[8]

He had no regrets about the education he got outside the sphere of Mormon influence. He recorded in his diary favorable impressions of Twin Falls's public schools. "The teachers seem to have been of high quality, and well prepared. Knowing, as I do now, of some of the inadequacies of schools in Utah, I can be grateful I was born and raised in a non-Mormon town." At no time during his elementary and secondary education did he have a Mormon teacher—"by deliberate policy there were no Mormon teachers in Twin Falls"—and he later saw this as a distinct advantage. "My present impression is that Mormon communities placed such stress on right thinking and right behavior that they did not always insist upon academic excellence and intellectuality. The people of Twin Falls insisted upon right behavior, perhaps, but did respect training and intellect and obtained some of the finest graduates of colleges and universities."[9]

While all five brothers generally gravitated to fieldwork on the farm, Leonard's preference was chicken farming. Noah made good on his missionary promise to partner with Leonard, building a henhouse shortly after his return. The enterprise prospered on one level but was a great disappointment on another, for Leonard gave far more than he got. By the time of Leonard's senior year in high school, his flock consisted of four hundred laying hens and two thousand baby chicks, of which he was sole caretaker. However, "my father insisted that all of the income go to him, and so he did all the financial business. This was perhaps why I had never developed any training or experience in business methods, and, for that matter, developed no interest. It was wrong of my father; he should have worked as my 'pardner.'" When Leonard returned to the farm from his first year of college, "there was virtually nothing left of the enterprise. From my father I received nothing for the time I had invested and the disposal of the properties." Nonetheless, an adult Leonard put the issue into a perspective that escaped him as a youth:

> When I recall that all of this took place during the depression of the 1930s when my father and mother had a family of nine children to provide for with very little cash income, I can understand that they really needed the cash income which the sale of eggs, the sale of fryers, and the sale of cull hens provided. It may have been the principal cash income of the farm during the terrible years of 1933 and 1934 when potatoes brought as low as ten cents for a 100-pound bag. My father was too proud a man to admit this, however, and thus could not have been expected to explain it to me.[10]

Despite his financial disappointment with chickens, they became a theme that lasted for decades in Leonard's life. The letterhead on his personal stationery was a chicken in profile; and when a stepson produced a seven-foot fiberglass chicken in the 1980s, Leonard proudly positioned it in his front yard, much to the consternation of his Salt Lake City neighbors. More significantly, however, chickens allowed him to hone a skill that served him well throughout his later career. His sister Marie recalled: "He preached more times to those chickens, whenever he had to give a talk in church or in school or in the FFA [Future Farmers of America]. That was his place to go and practice it. He'd stand in there at the front of the building and have these two hundred chickens. He would spend hours out there practicing his speeches."[11]

Leonard's own recollection confirms that of his sister. "That was about the time my voice was changing, and I was not satisfied with my new voice. All the Arrington voices were high-pitched, maybe a little whiny." When a teacher suggested that speaking "from our abdomen" would make his voice deeper, more solid and more resonant, the chicken coop became his laboratory. "I spent many hours in the chicken house orating to the chickens, where there was already a certain amount of noise with which I had to compete. By practicing day after day, week after week, this 'Chicken Coop Demosthenes' developed a stronger and deeper voice than most of the Arringtons. I was proud that I succeeded in learning to sing bass in the ward choir."[12]

Leonard never got over his fondness for chickens. "I loved the chickens and never once had the feeling that I would be glad to be rid of the responsibility, time-consuming as it was. I was fascinated by chickens, engrossed and enchanted. And there was a sense of fruition in living through each year's cycle." But for all of its earlier utility, chicken ranching was a passing fancy for Leonard. "I eagerly left it all behind—the henhouse, the chickens, the pedigreed cocks, to pursue 'higher learning.' My primary focus became economics, politics, literature, philosophy, and religion. I gladly embraced a new vocation, the world of scholarship—teaching and writing."[13]

3

ENCHANTED BY ECONOMICS
THE UNIVERSITY OF IDAHO

Higher education was not an Arrington family priority. Leonard's older brother LeRoy may have considered college, but opted instead to serve a proselytizing mission for the LDS Church and then devote his life to farming. Noah, whose own education amounted to little more than elementary school, saw no value in a college education. A man of few words, he never explained his position, but his sons knew that he wanted them to follow in his farming footsteps. Even without him spelling it out, they would have had no problem deducing that he saw college as a path leading away from the farm. Edna, with a high school diploma, appreciated the leavening influence of education but saw a college degree in the middle of the Great Depression as impractical. Of Leonard's extended family, only Noah's Aunt Bessie Arrington consistently encouraged Leonard to go to college.

In Leonard's mind, however, there was no ambivalence as to the *what*—only the *where*. He did not know where his determination to seek a college degree came from, but it was definitely there. As he approached graduation, he applied for and was awarded a one-hundred-dollar Union Pacific scholarship intended for use at the University of Idaho. Leonard responded to the urging of someone, "perhaps my father," and wrote to BYU, which offered him "a $200 working scholarship. This meant that they promised me $200 worth of work at the rate of 35 cents per hour. I think I never did seriously consider going." Still able to work and earn additional funds under the University of Idaho arrangement, Leonard concluded the "$100 workless scholarship seemed to be superior to a $200 work scholarship."[1]

Noah's contribution to Leonard's college education as a freshman consisted of a single $5 bill (in spite of Leonard's sweat equity in the family poultry business, Noah retained all of the profits), a handshake, and three words: "Be a man." Edna secretly gave him "as much as $15," Aunt Bessie "probably $5."[2]

THE UNIVERSITY OF IDAHO

Leonard did not own a car. Even a Greyhound bus ticket was beyond his means. He would ride his thumb the 650 miles to Moscow. "I was picked up on the highway to Filer, where my brother left me, by the Idaho Superintendent of Public Instruction, Brother [John W.] Condie, who said he would be driving all the way to Moscow—what a lucky development!"[3]

A decade prior to Leonard's arrival at the University of Idaho, the LDS Church had constructed its first-ever Institute of Religion adjacent to the Moscow campus. The program was something of an experiment—an effort to see if classes in Mormon history, theology, missionary preparation, and courtship/marriage instruction would be successful on the college level, supply social activities that would let young Latter-day Saints meet in suitably supervised activities, and meet the spiritual challenges of the college experience that all too frequently left religious convictions in fragments. These weekday and evening classes were housed in a multipurpose building near a campus that could also serve as a chapel for Sunday and MIA meetings. Three LDS professors teaching in academic departments at the University of Idaho made the proposal and, in 1926, church president Heber J. Grant appointed J. Wyley Sessions, a former mission president, to launch the program. He taught the first classes in the fall of 1927 to a Mormon student body of fifty-seven, and Charles W. Nibley dedicated the first institute building in September 1928. The experiment was so successful that other institutes quickly sprouted near Utah State University, Idaho State University, the University of Utah, and the University of Southern California. By 1950, it numbered at least a dozen programs in four states, and the program has continued to thrive.[4]

The seven-year-old institute building that welcomed Leonard included classrooms for religious instruction, but also dormitory space for two dozen LDS students. (The concept of having institute buildings double as dorms was phased out during the 1960s.)[5] He was already familiar with it since, as a senior in high school, he had attended a Future Farmers of America convention on campus, visited the institute, met George Tanner, who had replaced Sessions as director in 1931, and made arrangements to occupy one of its dorm rooms and participate in an unusual food cooperative.

In 1932, with the Depression making a college education less affordable, Tanner had initiated a food cooperative for the LDS students. By pooling their financial resources and supplying most of the labor for food preparation and clean-up, they could greatly reduce the cost of meals. After a successful first year, Tanner went to the university president and proposed expanding the arrangement to include non-LDS students. The president approved. Eventually it became the second largest student cooperative system in the United States.[6] This arrangement was beginning its third year in 1935–1936 when Leonard became a farm-skilled and hard-working participant. He recalled how it worked:

> The idea was that a mature student would be appointed business manager for the co-op and do all the buying, a full-time cook would be employed to make up the menus and do the cooking, and student committees would then take turns helping the cook, carrying out the food, washing dishes, and so on. Each person took his turn. About seventy students living in Ridenbaugh [Hall] and about twenty-five living at the LDS Institute were in the co-op. Buying our food in this manner at wholesale prices and doing our own work without having to pay anything to the university for overhead insured that we could get by on our meals very cheaply. As a matter of fact, we were able to get by for $11 per month for our meals. This seems unbelievable, but anyone who saw what we ate would understand how it was possible—lots of potatoes, very little meat, small helpings.[7]

The expense side of Leonard's ledger included $11 per month for food, $8 for rent, a little for books and an occasional movie, and two novelties that he had not previously experienced or even heard of in the isolated world of the family's Twin Falls farm: milkshakes and Coca-Cola.[8] The income side included the $5 from his father, the few dollars that his mother and aunt had scraped together for him, and $75 from the Union Pacific scholarship. He should have received the remaining $25 the second year; but when Leonard switched out of an agricultural economics major, he forfeited the sum. His last source was a grant from the National Youth Administration that paid $0.35 an hour for forty-three hours of work per month—a total of $15.05.[9] The two sides balanced, but campus life was not idyllic for Leonard. He recalled ruefully and without nostalgia:

> I must have been a pretty smelly, unkempt fellow. I simply did not have any money and could not afford to spend for anything unnecessary. I washed my own clothes in the basement of the Institute. My recollection is that I wore one pair of socks for a full week, a shirt for a full week, and I wore one set of underwear for a full week. I often wore my ROTC uniform and do not recall that I ever washed or ironed one. I recall getting an occasional haircut—waiting until the hair was long and then telling the man to cut it real short.[10]

He did not recall having a date for his first two years at the university, in part because he could not afford it and in part because few LDS women attended the

university. He was chair of the Junior Parade Committee, so he "felt an obligation" to attend the Junior Prom, but did not even include his date's name in his
memoirs of the event.[11]

Leonard had focused on agriculture in high school and declared agricultural
economics as his major at college, perhaps because he genuinely felt drawn to the
field and perhaps to ease Noah's apprehensions. What he envisioned, however, did
not match academic reality. "I thought I was going to learn how to farm," he confessed, and it was a shock when he realized that "a person did not go to college
to become a better farmer." Instead, their college courses trained them "in agricultural science," and job prospects steered them into careers "for the government—
for the Department of Agriculture or for state extension service or for some
agricultural company—McCormick Deering Seed Company or something on that
order."[12]

He spent his first year taking two semesters of chemistry, math, and English,
and a semester apiece of botany and zoology. "I enjoyed the English and zoology
but none of the other courses." He earned a solid "B" for both semesters in chemistry, but "did not understand it, had no interest in it, and could not see that it
had any relationship to farming." He tried to negotiate with advisors in the College of Agriculture to avoid a second year of chemistry, but when they refused to
consider his plea, he looked at other options. Among them were English and two
fields that had not previously occurred to him, law and economics. An English
professor responded to an autobiographical writing assignment by seeking out
Leonard to tell him, "I should think you might be interested in going to law
school. You look to me like you would make a fine lawyer in an agricultural region." Leonard visited the dean of the law school and asked his advice on prelaw
curriculum. The dean recommended, "Take some history, lots of English, and take
all the economics you can stand."[13]

Leonard was already interested in history and English, but economics was a
delightful surprise. "I was completely enthralled," he recalled. "I read not only
the regular text but other texts as well. I read every bit of reading matter that the
professor suggested plus other books and articles that I found in the library." The
unexpected enchantment did not wear off, and he ended up with a new major.[14]

And what of history, the field that eventually drew him in, gave him his career,
and established him as the founding father of an unlikely subspecialty? It was
an ironic experience. On his advisor's insistence, he took European history from
Frederick C. Church, "who was, by all odds, the dullest teacher in the university.
One class was on the French Revolution, the other was Europe in the first half of
the nineteenth century." He was tortured at the time, but in looking back, it was
"amusing . . . to recall that the only boring classes I took at the university were

those two courses in history, and that I took no courses at all in American history, the field in which I later became a national authority."[15] Leonard's ultimate gateway to a career in history was economics, but several years elapsed before his choice of a dissertation topic in economic history placed him solidly on that road.

INTELLECTUAL STRUGGLES

The most daunting challenge that Leonard faced during his freshman year was not the decision to change his major. Rather, it was the world of ideas that shook the provincial mindset of his Twin Falls upbringing. "I didn't have any intellectual struggles until I went to the University of Idaho," he recalled in a 1995 interview,[16] but during the first semester biological evolution challenged his intellectual innocence. Although the LDS Church did not—and still does not—have an official doctrinal position on evolution, influential church authorities who claimed a lock on doctrinal orthodoxy were unrestrained in condemning it in the strongest terms, not bothering to label their statements as personal opinion rather than official policy. Even though other General Authorities such as scientists James E. Talmage and Joseph E. Merrill worked hard to present a more nuanced picture, Apostle Joseph Fielding Smith, who was the son of a church president, the church historian, and the author of an authoritative series of essays on gospel questions that appeared monthly in the church magazine, wrote and spoke vehemently in opposition to evolution. As a result church members, particularly in rural regions, often absorbed the belief that organic evolution was not only incorrect, but evil—a direct challenge to the foundational belief that human beings were the result of God's special creation. (So persuasive were Smith and his like-minded colleagues that in 2009, the bicentennial year of the birth of Charles Darwin, Mormons ranked second only to Jehovah's Witnesses as evolution deniers, with only 22 percent agreeing "that evolution is the best explanation for the origins of human life on earth.")[17]

By mid-November, following lectures on evolution and "several big arguments" outside of class, Leonard arrived at a position that seemed to reconcile scientific teaching with his religious belief: "I formulated the theory of organic evolution among lower forms of life[,] and man starting on a separate sphere, changing and evolving into what he is at present."[18] In fact, his formulation was not novel at all, and represented what generally is termed "special creation." Although this new certitude relieved his anxiety, it was short-lived—five days, to be precise. The following Sunday he wrote: "Went to church in the evening & Rev. Purdy of the Methodist Church gave a splendid sermon on the earth and we as God's creations. During a moment of abstraction I found a terrible flaw in my solution to the problem of evolution, so I have to start all over again."[19] His next step was to consult George Tanner, director of the LDS Institute of Religion.

He could not have chosen a better counselor. Tanner had been part of a bold, one-time initiative by the LDS Church that came at the instigation of Church Commissioner of Education Joseph F. Merrill. Merrill, who subsequently was called to the Quorum of the Twelve Apostles and remained there until his death in 1952, was a scientist by training and the first native Utahn to receive a PhD from Johns Hopkins University. With a deep appreciation of the value of a liberal education, he arranged leaves of absence for several church employees to attend the University of Chicago Divinity School and earn graduate degrees. Some earned doctoral degrees; others, including Tanner, earned master's degrees.[20] Upon completing his degree in 1931, Tanner was assigned to the LDS Institute of Religion at the University of Idaho, where he remained until 1960. Leonard praised both his professional and his personal expertise:

> He attempted to expose us to the very best religious scholarship and learning, and his superiors gave him complete freedom in determining the course of study and the most useful textbooks and readings. . . . Above all, he wanted us to realize that deep religious faith can be perfectly consistent with genuine academic scholarship. His policy was one of intellectual openness, one fully supported by Elder Merrill and, at that time, by Elder [John A.] Widtsoe and the First Presidency. George was a "liberal" and not afraid to declare it. "Liberals," he said, "are people who are not afraid to think independently, even though this thinking may lead in a little different direction from orthodox Mormon teaching."[21]

Tanner's independent thinking was evident in his thesis, "The Religious Environment in which Mormonism Arose." Acknowledging in the introduction that "on the question of bias and prejudice there seems to be about an equal amount exhibited in the pro-Mormon and anti-Mormon books," he relativized Mormon exceptionalism by placing it squarely in the context of its times. Its claim that "the original gospel had been restored with all its spiritual gifts, did not find itself in an entirely hostile world. There were several societies already in existence which made similar claims." The Mormon "Word of Wisdom" embodied conventional thought that had been most popularly conveyed in the *Journal of Health* beginning in 1830, "condemning the use of liquor, tobacco, tea and coffee, and excessive meat eating. . . . The 'Word of Wisdom,' which was given as a revelation by the Prophet [Joseph Smith] to his people, gave religious sanction to a movement already prominent in America." In summary, "If the doctrines and practices selected for treatment here can be taken as an index of the whole, it would appear that most of the Mormon doctrines were to be found in the contemporary churches."[22] Such a candid—and well-documented—appraisal of Mormonism's origins that nonetheless preserved respect for its truth claims was almost unprecedented in the Mormonism of eight decades ago, and its author was perhaps uniquely qualified to guide Leonard across the minefield of paradigm-changing thought.

Tanner became Leonard's spiritual mentor on December 4, 1935, the date of their first meeting in his office after Leonard matriculated at the university. The meeting was memorable for both men—indeed, in a 1976 interview Tanner recalled it in remarkable detail: "I remember very distinctly one afternoon I was sitting in the office at the LDS Institute and Leonard Arrington came in, and I could see he was definitely agitated. He came in and wanted to know if he could talk with me awhile. I said, 'You bet, that's exactly why I'm here. I'm very anxious to talk with students that would like to have me talk with them.'"

The eighteen-year-old student confided that one of his classes had presented some "very upsetting" information. He blurted out his problem and, in essence, "wanted me to tell him all about evolution in one short lesson, which isn't easy to do—it's quite a big subject." Leonard queried, "Just what is the score on this? Just what is there about evolution?"

Tanner's first task was to reassure him by providing him with peers and, second, to authorize him to postpone judgment. "That was forty years ago," mused Tanner, "but I remember that conversation very vividly."

> I said, "Now Leonard, you're not the first of our young men to come up here and get upset, and you certainly won't be the last to come. . . . There will be so many of the courses you take that evolution will simply be taken for granted, and for someone to completely try to dodge the question of evolution is just quite out of the question and can't be done. . . . So why don't you go ahead and study here . . . and when you're through with it, you'll be so much better prepared then to decide whether evolution is good than to pre-judge it. . . . If you don't want to believe it, that's up to you."[23]

The lesson took. The following semester, in a paper for his freshman English class entitled "Two Arringtons," Leonard wrote a manifesto that set him apart not only from his age peers, but also from the vast majority of his coreligionists both then and now:

I am not the same Leonard Arrington I used to be. I can now make that statement with fairness both to my former self and to my present self. It would be well to compare these two selves at this stage of my college career—the Leonard Arrington that left his hopeful parents for college, and the Leonard Arrington that will go back home for the first time this June after almost a year of college influence and training. . . .

The major change has come about through my acceptance of much of the teachings of science in preference to some of the doctrines of fundamentalists. I now accept the main outlines of the theories of evolution and behaviorism, both of which I formerly violently opposed.[24]

In addition to helping Leonard deal with the physical world of evolution, Tanner assisted him in dealing with the spiritual world:

Brother Tanner and my major professor, Dr. [Erwin] Graue, also introduced me to George Santayana's *Reason in Religion*. I do not say that I fully understood it, but the book gave me a concept that has been helpful ever since—that truth may be expressed not only through science and abstract reason, not only through scriptural texts, but also through stories, testimonies, and narratives of personal experience. Not only through erudite scholarship, but also through poetry, drama, and historical novels. Santayana used the term "myth"—a term well understood in recent religious literature—to refer to the expression of religious and moral truths in symbolic language. . . . Because of my introduction to the concept of symbolism as a means of expressing religious truth, I was never overly concerned with the question of the historicity of the First Vision or of the many reported epiphanies in Mormon, Christian, and Hebrew history. I was prepared to accept them as historical or as metaphorical, as symbolical or as precisely what happened.[25]

BACK AT THE FARM

Leonard's freshman year at college was the most significant transformational period of his entire life, shaping his subsequent careers and his ability to grapple with complex intellectual and theological issues. However, his return to the farm for the summer of 1936 was a return to the world of farm work—and a temporary departure from the daunting and yet exhilarating world of ideas. "Our home was a home of work and the dinner table conversations always related to our work assignments, not to such speculative things as our futures."[26]

Nonetheless, one conversation related to what his parents hoped would be his near-term future: an LDS proselytizing mission. The expectation was apparent, as older brother LeRoy recently had served in the Southern States Mission. Leonard, however, sidestepped his father's question by stating he did not want to interrupt his schooling yet.

The conversation, while postponed, was not concluded. Leonard recognized Noah's anxiety to have him serve, and his father accepted Leonard's departure for a second year of college "without a great deal of fuss." But when Leonard returned to Twin Falls after his sophomore year, Noah became "quite insistent" about Leonard's mission, while Leonard was even more reluctant than the prior summer. "By that time I was so excited about economics that I didn't want to interrupt it and felt that I should continue with my university education," he explained.

Hoping that a higher ecclesiastical voice would succeed where his had failed, Noah arranged for Leonard to meet with Charles Callis, Noah's former mission president who then was an apostle. To Leonard's surprise, Callis was sympathetic. "He simply mentioned the advantages of going on a mission, but he really did not try to argue me out of going back to school." When Noah inquired about the interview, Leonard "told him that Brother Callis thought I should do what I thought was best. My father seemed to accept that."[27]

Perhaps stiffening Leonard's resistance to a mission was the element that had dominated the family's entire life: money. Leonard had lived on pennies at college, hand-washing his clothes in the institute basement and working what amounted to a full-time job for thirty-five cents an hour. He found it troubling that Noah

> seemed to be prepared to send me on a mission but had insisted he could not afford to send me any money to help me at the university. I probably did not receive more than $15 or $20 from him during my first year and probably not more than that during my second year at the university. And he was willing to sign that he could not afford to send me to college, so that I could receive the NYA [National Youth Administration] help. How then could he find the $50 or $60 necessary each month to support me on a mission?

Noah's generosity with neighbors and the church, paid for by the parsimony with which he treated his wife and children, had taught Leonard an important lesson through the contrast. He felt firmly that if his father could support him on a mission, he could help him through college. Not doing so made Leonard less dependent and less anxious to accede to his father's wishes.[28]

Senior Year

Once he settled into an economics major, Leonard did well in school. Although never receiving straight As in a single semester—he always came up short either in physical education or ROTC, both of which counted towards his GPA—he made Phi Beta Kappa during his senior year.[29]

By his own account, "the single most important thing that happened" during his senior year was a "Religion in Life" week sponsored by the university. A dozen prominent speakers represented the major religious denominations, including Jewish and Buddhist, but Dr. Benjamin Mays, dean of religion at the African American Howard University in Washington, D.C., struck Leonard as "the most distinguished and most eloquent."

> Dr. Mays gave . . . perhaps the single most eloquent talk I have ever heard. Dr. Mays went on to become president of Morehouse College, a black university in Atlanta founded at the end of the Civil War. The son of sharecroppers, Mays once told his students, "They can make you sit in the back of the streetcar, but no one can confine a mind." One Morehouse graduate who took that advice to heart was the Reverend Martin Luther King Jr., who called Mays "my spiritual mentor and my intellectual father." Mays gave the eulogy at King's funeral. Hearing Dr. Mays was an important experience for me, not only for his manner of presenting religion and Christianity, but also because he was the first black educator I had encountered.[30]

The cumulative effect of the week was to demonstrate to Leonard how religious questions could be discussed in a public setting in a frank, open, and informative way, without dogmatism or animosity:

> They [the week's speakers] listened, were respectful of students and their questions, and discussed religious questions in a manner that was serious, meaningful, and sometimes eloquent. They did not avoid difficult problems, were willing to express personal opinions, and were skilled in utilizing humor to maintain interest and good feeling. There was no attempt to convert, no downgrading of dissenting opinions, no attempt to play on the emotions.[31]

Leonard modeled his own presentations in church and writing on religion after the speakers, and though he did not say so explicitly, the succession of distinguished spokesmen who could blend religious beliefs and intellectual rigor became an unforgettable template for how to approach difficult questions within his own spiritual tradition.

GRADUATE SCHOOL

As had been the case with undergraduate studies, by his senior year the question for Leonard was not the *what*, but the *where* for graduate school. Encouraged by his major professor, he applied for a Rhodes scholarship. The first choice for Idaho's nomination, he went to Spokane, Washington, for the regional competition, where a gap in his undergraduate economics education became his undoing. "Each of the candidates had to answer questions in front of fifteen people. My interview went fine until one of the persons present asked me about Keynesianism." He was baffled by the question. None of his economics courses, embraced so enthusiastically, had even mentioned "Keynesian economics, although the General Theory had been published in 1936." It was clear that he "was ignorant on the subject." Due to his unsatisfactory answers, and perhaps for other reasons of which he was unaware, he was not chosen as one of the regional awardees.[32]

While a Rhodes scholarship would have been an honor, it would have been an empty one: within months of Leonard's graduation from the University of Idaho, World War II began in Europe, and Rhodes scholars were reassigned to universities in the United States.

He applied to a dozen universities for graduate studies in economics, received scholarship or fellowship offers from half of them, and accepted a Kenan teaching fellowship at the University of North Carolina—the ancestral state of the Arrington family—that offered a stipend of $500 a year and a tuition waiver. This arrangement made it possible for him to cover his expenses without any additional income, and so he eagerly made preparations to return to the location where Arringtons had lived for almost two centuries and where his father, as a missionary, had spent a year as president of the North Carolina conference.[33]

4

Idaho Boy in Graduate School

The summer of 1939 was good for Leonard. On the advice of a fellow student he took a pass on the farm work that had never agreed with him anyway, and went to summer school between his junior and senior years. He also took correspondence courses so that by the beginning of his senior year he was only four credit hours shy of completing his bachelor's degree. This process qualified him to take graduate-level courses during that year and enter the University of North Carolina as an "advanced" graduate student.[1] With a leg up on graduate school and a light work load at the farm—"more or less full-time irrigating all summer"—he had time for leisure reading that included Vardis Fisher's *Children of God*, a novel about the history of the Mormons that won the 1939 Harper Prize in fiction.

At the end of the summer of 1939, he took a bus to Oklahoma to visit relatives before continuing to Chapel Hill, North Carolina. While in Oklahoma, he heard news of an interesting but distant catastrophe. His sleep on the floor of the front room of his aunt's house was interrupted at about three a.m. by yelling in the street. "I got up and looked out and saw a boy selling newspapers. He was yelling something very loudly that I couldn't quite make out. I saw other people in their pajamas and nightgowns getting papers from him and I got one as well. Huge big headlines said 'Germany Invades Poland. War Declared.'" This was how Leonard learned of the outbreak of World War II, but at the time he had no comprehension of what lay ahead for the world, and no idea that he would be a soldier in the war. "I don't recall giving any serious consideration to whether or not this might change my life."[2]

Initially, the war did not change his life nor, for that matter, did it have much effect on the lives of most Americans. The country was strongly pacifist, not at all eager to be drawn into another European war. Had Leonard received a Rhodes scholarship, the invasion of Poland would have changed his life immediately, for all Rhodes scholars were promptly sent back to the States. As it was, his plans remained intact and he boarded the bus as planned, headed for Chapel Hill, North Carolina.

UNIVERSITY OF NORTH CAROLINA

The University of North Carolina celebrated the sesquicentennial of its charter during Leonard's freshman year. Enrollment was small by today's standards— about three thousand students—and Chapel Hill itself was "a lazy little country village" that nonetheless possessed a long and prestigious cultural tradition fueled by prominent faculty and bright students—a sharp contrast to the insularity of Twin Falls that had shielded Leonard from milkshakes and Coke. His cultural and intellectual horizons expanded quickly to include weekly lectures by prominent professors, live drama at the Carolina Playhouse, concerts, art galleries, and art films.[3]

Always a voracious reader, he was freed from the time-consuming drudgery of his thirty-five-cents-per-hour job and read far beyond economics, recalling his delight in absorbing "dozens of books, about evenly divided between economics on the one hand, and religion, philosophy, and literature on the other."[4]

Still smarting from his ignorance of Keynesian economics, to which he had attributed his failure to obtain a Rhodes scholarship, he devoted his first fall quarter to remedying the deficiency. "I was completely absorbed in Keynes and his work. . . . I read the *General Theory*, nearly everything else by Keynes, a lot of reviews of his book, and indeed got such an understanding of Keynesian theory that I did a little tutoring of other graduate students on Keynes."[5]

His religious horizons also broadened. After some prodding from his older brother LeRoy, a returned missionary like their father, Leonard had accepted ordination as an elder in the LDS lay priesthood shortly before leaving Idaho. In North Carolina, he attended a small Mormon congregation in nearby Durham and was surprised to learn that his father had organized that very branch as a missionary in 1925. However, erratic and inconvenient bus connections between Chapel Hill and Durham made regular attendance impractical, so Sunday mornings usually found him at the Presbyterian Church in Chapel Hill.

His graduate studies proceeded smoothly, with no repeat of the intellectual crisis that had underlain his freshman year in Moscow, Idaho. His fellowship, which paid $500 a year and was renewed for a second year, required him to teach beginning classes in economics to undergraduate students, an experience that he greatly enjoyed.

North Carolina State University

Leonard returned to Idaho for the summer between his first and second year. Thanks to his overachieving in his final year at the University of Idaho, he was only twenty-two when his sophomore year at Chapel Hill rolled around. Early in January 1941, when the regular instructor in economics at nearby North Carolina State University suffered a heart attack and had to quit teaching, Leonard's graduate advisor recommended him for the job. It was a temporary but fulltime position, meaning that he had to put his own graduate studies on hold, but the teaching experience seasoned him. He was paid the princely sum of $800 for the remainder of the academic year, and UNC agreed to allow him to pursue a minor in agricultural economics at NC State. In January 1941, he moved to nearby Raleigh, where his teaching was sufficiently satisfactory that he was hired to teach for the full 1942–1943 academic year with a salary of $2,000. As at the University of Idaho, he went on only one date at UNC, so his financial needs remained modest. For the first time in his life, he had money in the bank.

The World of Mormon Studies

Although he was raised in a Mormon home, had attended classes at the LDS Institute of Religion at the University of Idaho, and had read Vardis Fisher's *Children of God*, Leonard's knowledge of the Mormon landscape, particularly at the level of academically sound studies, was scant. Writing decades later to Lowry Nelson, he acknowledged his naiveté as part of a thumbnail autobiography:

> I grew up on a farm in Twin Falls County, Idaho. . . . The Twin Falls area had not more than thirty or forty families who were LDS. The community as a whole was generally unfriendly toward Mormons, which means that all of my friends, associates, teachers, and so on were non-LDS—in fact, if anything, anti-LDS. So I never did realize there was such a thing as a Mormon subculture until I was introduced to that concept by T. Lynn Smith, yourself, and others. Mormonism was just a church one went to every Sunday—or at least every Sunday that it was convenient for us to go.[6]

NC State became the port-of-entry into the field that eventually defined Leonard's career and his life. Part of his minor studies in agricultural economics was readings in rural sociology, one of which cited Lowry Nelson's pivotal work, *The Mormon Village*. He read it with "enormous interest," followed by an article by Juanita Brooks in *Harper's*, and still more publications in the national press by

Bernard DeVoto. Then, he plunged deeply into the academic literature on Mormon history, economics, and sociology, including works by Lowell Bennion, G. Homer Durham (who later became his nemesis), William Mulder, Ralph Chamberlin, Heber Snell, Franklin S. Harris, Harold Christensen, Parley Christensen, and William R. Palmer. Extending his reading into church periodicals and manuals, he took particular note of a cadre of Mormon intellectuals who had moved into the ranks of LDS General Authorities, including John A. Widtsoe (who later shaped his career), James E. Talmage, B. H. Roberts, Orson F. Whitney, Richard R. Lyman, and Joseph F. Merrill—men who provided a counterbalance to the fundamentalism that was the prevailing philosophical thread of Mormonism.

By the end of a year and a half of intense reading, he concluded "that the Mormon experience was a subject worthy of scholarly endeavor; that the scholarly study of LDS history, culture, and thought [was] receiving the encouragement of our General Authorities; and that educated non-Mormons would regard a scholarly interpretation of Mormon history and policy with respect."[7]

As an aspiring economist, Leonard was particularly interested to find an article by Richard T. Ely, published in *Harper's Monthly Magazine* in 1903, titled, "Economic Aspects of Mormonism."[8] This almost-four-decades-old article provided an entrée when "I happened to meet Ely in the annual convention of the American Economic Association in Philadelphia in December 1941, and mentioned to him how much I enjoyed that article. He then gave me a personal lecture on the importance of the Mormons in American history and their praiseworthiness as a people. It was all a heady brew for an aspiring graduate student who happened to be an Idaho Mormon chicken farmer."[9]

5

A Woman Named Grace

Leonard discovered something besides Mormon studies during his two years at North Carolina State University: Grace Fort.

Dating had been a low priority up through his second year at Chapel Hill— only one date in that small town as in Moscow, Idaho—but graduate school had broadened his horizons socially as well as intellectually. He was in a looking mood. On his occasional Sunday trips to Durham to attend the small LDS branch, he became acquainted with Idell Savage, whom he dated several times. "Although she had pretty blue eyes and was pleasant and full of fun, I really did not see her as a prospective bride," was his friendly memory more than thirty years later. Upon moving to Raleigh in January 1941 to begin teaching at NC State, he found an even smaller LDS congregation that met in the Independent Order of Odd Fellows hall on Main Street. There were only seven members, of which three were single women. Leonard scrutinized all three but "did not see any of the girls as prospective wives."[1]

Then, in the fall of 1941 when he was beginning his second semester of teaching, Leonard was invited to a birthday dinner in honor of a new PhD student at NC State, Nyle Brady, who had just graduated from Brigham Young University. The dinner was scheduled for Saturday evening, but Leonard's attention focused on the afternoon, when he escorted "a young lady whose name I don't remember" to a football game in Chapel Hill. He made no comment on how well the team did; but his own record was dismal. When he asked if his date would like to take a drive and then get some refreshments, she said she would rather go home. She had, with erroneous politeness, not told him that her steady boyfriend had just come back from the army. Deflated, Leonard took her home and went off to dinner on his own, forgetting the birthday celebration until he just started on dessert. Hastily, he went to the Brady home where he encountered an acquaintance, Ruth Partridge, who had brought with her "a fine friend," Grace Fort. Ruth had planned for Leonard to partner with Grace at the birthday dinner, "but no-body told me that at the time and I was so dumb I didn't realize it."[2]

Decades later, in her autobiography, Grace gave her side of the story:

> Ruth had invited Kenneth and Christine Spencer, some young Mor-mon friends of the Brady's; "Jimmie" Arrington, who was intro-duced as a bright young professor at State College; and myself to a birthday dinner party at her house. It was to be Saturday night, Oc-tober 25, 1941. When I got to Ruth's house we waited and waited. "Jimmie" just didn't come. Finally, after an hour or more of delay he showed up. I was not at all impressed, first because he was late, and second because he was so little.[3] Anyway, I was half scared to death because of what I had heard about his brilliance. I thought, Golly Pete, I don't know whether I can talk to that guy or not. Any-way, we ate dinner and afterwards we played some games. When the time came to go, this "Jimmie" didn't even see me to the car. We went and got in our own cars. Ruth was so angry with him that she could have killed him. She said, "Here I was telling you what a nice guy he was, and he treated you like you were nothin'!"[4]

Grace shared Ruth's dismay and was still cool when "Jimmie" called her up a week later on October 30 and invited her to the LDS branch's Halloween party. Grace excused herself—her Bible class was meeting that night. He pressed: "What time do you get out?" "I don't get out 'til about 8:30." "Well, that'll be early enough," he said. "I'll pick you up at your house at a quarter to nine."[5]

Grace had nothing against either Mormons or Halloween parties, so she agreed, though with little enthusiasm that may have evaporated completely had she known that she was Leonard's third choice. "I phoned one of the Tilton girls and she had a date, I phoned the other one and she accepted. Then the afternoon I was to pick her up she said she wanted to go, but she wanted to go with another friend, which turned out to be her boyfriend, so I tried to think of somebody I could take. I suddenly remembered Grace."[6]

Decades later Leonard asked and answered the question, "What was there to attract Leonard to Grace? . . . There were, first of all, the physical things. Grace was lovely—had lovely greenish eyes, a lovely fair skin, lovely light brown hair, dressed nicely, and had a 'nice shape.' She was just the right size for Leonard—some three inches shorter than he. Grace was intelligent, energetic, self-assured, expe-rienced, had a going business and a car, had a wide friendship, and a captivating personality."[7] She was also three years his senior, a fact that mattered to neither of them.

While Leonard's social awkwardness and short physical stature initially got in the way of the relationship, surprisingly his religion did not. Although Mormons were even scarcer in Raleigh than they had been in Twin Falls, and although the South—particularly the Presbyterian South[8]—had for nearly a century viewed Mormons with general derision, Grace, a Presbyterian, had developed a sympathetic view of Mormonism by reading the *Reader's Digest* condensed version of Vardis Fisher's *Children of God*. "I had never previously heard of the Mormons nor of their faith. I had never met one. I mentioned to Ruth that I had been impressed with their history and religion, as portrayed in *Children of God* and I would like to meet one." No wonder Ruth had been furious when Leonard's ineptness had failed to pick up on the cues that would have introduced Grace "to a real, live Mormon." A religious woman herself, twenty-seven-year-old Grace respected Fisher's achievement in telling the Mormon story in terms "that would help non-Mormon readers to understand the intensity of faith and devotion which accounted for Mormonism's strength."[9] Few Mormons appreciated his prize-winning efforts, finding his naturalistic explanations insufficiently reverent. But Grace was the perfect reader.

Religion became a shared interest. Leonard, who had been a regular at the Chapel Hill Presbyterian Church for two years, cheerfully attended Grace's Presbyterian Bible class, and Grace, equally cheerfully, attended the LDS Mutual Improvement Association class. They dated frequently during the fall, the romance blossomed quickly, and shortly before Christmas they started looking at engagement rings. Leonard chose the perfect moment to present it: "I went with her to midnight mass at the Roman Catholic cathedral in Raleigh. While the choir in the balcony was singing 'O Holy Night' I took her hand and slipped the ring on her finger."[10]

He waited until her birthday in January for the formal proposal. Perhaps to his surprise, given how swimmingly the relationship had developed, "she did not accept," instead saying that "she wanted to see if she thought she was the best person for me to marry."[11] From Grace's perspective, the issue was a bit more complex. Most critically, the nation was now at war, the Japanese bombing of Pearl Harbor having occurred the prior month. Was it the right time to begin a marriage? Or, contrariwise, was it their only chance to begin a marriage? Grace later confessed that she had pored over "all this stuff in the papers and in magazines about whether one should get married during the war. Is it really wise to marry? I had all these reservations in my mind. Right now, they seem foolish. But they were vital to me then because I was making a lifetime decision." Yet there was something even deeper that caused Grace to pause: "I was at the point that I felt that I simply couldn't make another mistake in marriage."[12]

The story of Grace's failed first marriage and of Grace and Leonard's decision to conceal it from their own children became an important chapter of family history. It was, in fact, by accident that the children first learned of Mr. and Mrs. Michael Thompson. At age fourteen, daughter Susan developed an interest in family history and traveled to Idaho for a week of tutoring from Leonard's sister Marie Davidson, the family genealogist. While thumbing through Edna Arrington's family record book, Susan froze. Marie recalled that Edna received in the mail the formal card "that Mr. Ford and Mrs. Ford announce the engagement of their daughter Grace Thompson to Leonard Arrington. Well, my mother sat right down and wrote 'Grace Thompson' in her book." This was the detail that froze Susan. "I will never forget how white Susan turned."[13] Marie had no idea that this first marriage was news to Susan. Susan recalled:

> My mom . . . was Grace Fort, that was her maiden name, but it said Grace Thompson. I said, "Grace Thompson? Why does it say that?" Marie said, "Well, you know, that was her first marriage." "First marriage?" And all of a sudden, my aunt just went white. "Did you know that your mother had been married before?" I said, "No." You can imagine how she felt. I lay awake all night thinking, "Why didn't they tell us?" And she was awake all night, feeling badly because I discovered this, and my parents had kept it a secret.

Marie must have telephoned Grace at the first opportunity, for as soon as Susan returned home, even before she asked the question that was consuming her, Grace took her aside and said, "Look, I wanted to tell you, and Daddy didn't want to. I could never get permission to tell you guys yet." Her parents divorced and she was unhappy at home, so she got married young, at sixteen, and didn't finish high school. Grace had gotten rid of all her pictures of Michael Thompson, a policeman by profession. There were no children. He turned out to be an alcoholic.

Grace was already so unhappy that she was threatening to leave him. When he came home drunk one night, she announced, "I can't take this anymore." He pulled his revolver and tried to fire it at her. Fortunately, the safety was on, saving her life. There was no question that the marriage was over. She left on the spot. Susan was still baffled by Leonard's reticence, however. Had he been concerned that the children would think less of Grace? Susan didn't see it: "How do we feel about her divorcing him? Wonderful! She should have."

Susan was the youngest child and felt that her brothers Carl and James, both also in their teens, "were plenty old enough to know this." She didn't understand why Leonard was still keeping the family secret. Grace called Leonard into the room, and Susan thought he "looked kind of hang-dog." Grace announced, "Susan thinks that we need to tell Carl and James tonight." Susan recalled, "He kind of sat there and acted kind of funny, and pretty soon he said, 'Do you want a piece of apple pie? I've got some pie in the kitchen.' And he walked out. This is what happens when you get into their personal territory."[14]

Perhaps Leonard found himself falling back on Noah's silences at this moment of family crisis. Despite Susan and Grace's willingness to share the family secret, Leonard held out. Carl learned the fact when he was twenty-one, including the detail that Grace had stuck with the abusive and threatening marriage for eight years. "The secrets within the family were just so bizarre," he mused. His immediate reaction was: "Wow! You're a historian, and this doesn't come out?" His second, more reflective reaction was, "I think that was a part of Dad. He was a keeper of secrets. He was a keeper of the Church's secrets, and he was a keeper of the family's secrets."[15]

More than three decades after the divorce, and after her three children heard the story from her, Grace put it on the record in her autobiography, in a section she titled "My Ill-Fated Marriage." Leonard, who "asked me to dispose of all my photos of Mike and to talk no more about him and my former marriage," left no mention whatsoever of Mike Thompson in any of the hundreds of documents he produced. Grace concluded the saga by writing, "We both agree that the decision to put it out of our minds was wise; we also agree that now is the time and the occasion to present to the children my full story."[16]

Grace and Leonard continued to date throughout 1942, but she still hesitated, her reservations about marriage not completely resolved. Leonard was ready to plunge forward without delay and discounted his mother's concerns, contained in a letter to him (the text of which has not survived), that he would be marrying a non-Mormon.[17] In July 1942, after his second year of teaching at North Carolina State, he sent Grace the letter from Edna. Leonard attempted to soften the impact by accompanying it with his own reassurances in writing, which had the double advantage of letting him compose the letter carefully for maximum effect and also of giving Grace the opportunity to absorb both letters in private. But it also meant that he—and therefore Grace—had to deal with these epistles in solitude, lacking each other's company; and it was indicative of the difficulty that he had throughout his life in dealing with deeply emotional issues. He presented his mother's concerns as valid but downplayed them significantly, suggesting "that you should not worry over what Mother has written, because it isn't as important to her as she makes out. . . . As long as we are happy together and love each other, and have a grand home and family and respect her feelings, that is all she will require." Noting that Edna would have preferred that he go on a mission, get married in an LDS temple, and "make a lot of money," none of which happened (although he and Grace were "sealed" in an LDS temple ceremony after her subsequent conversion to Mormonism), "she will feel almost as good without those things." Then, he played his trump card, one that virtually guaranteed that Edna (and Noah) would bear no hard feelings if they were to get married: "We are going to do what suits us best, just as Mother did when she ran away to get married, and married without the consent of her parents, and didn't join the Church till after her third child."[18]

Indeed, when Leonard's family finally met Grace, "they were affectionate, kind, [and] enthusiastic." Describing the encounter in third-person, he praised how his work-focused Idaho parents and siblings "made her feel a member of the family . . . that they felt Leonard had really got himself a prize. This was not only true of Mom and Dad, but the rest of the family as well. . . . She grew to feel closer to Mom than to her own mother."[19] (Grace's mother, nicknamed "Nana," later became a constant part of Leonard's life when she moved in with them in Logan, Utah, and remained with them until her death years later.)

Even with Leonard's reassurances and their continuing courtship, Grace remained indecisive through the spring of 1943. She was wearing his ring, but Leonard described their relationship as "going steadily." He "felt certain that when I received the draft notice we would be married. That call came in March, 1943, and I reported for induction at Fort Bragg, North Carolina." Despite his conviction that induction would break the emotional log-jam, "Grace was [still] doubtful."[20] But a month later, events coincided to help her resolve her insecurities.

Stationed at Fort Bragg and unable for several weeks to obtain a pass, Leonard had to rely on occasional visits to the base from Grace. Finally, "The lieutenant told me Friday afternoon that I could get a pass. I phoned up Grace Friday evening and asked her if we could get married the next day. She said 'I'll try; I'm willing.'" Leonard immediately had a mandatory blood test done at the base infirmary, while Grace scrambled in Raleigh to arrange the wedding. Having recently converted to the Baptist faith, she approached her minister, who agreed to perform the ceremony. Next, she persuaded the county clerk in Raleigh to make a special trip to the office on Saturday morning and open it just to issue their marriage license. Then, within a few hours, she telephoned her friend Chloe Hodges, who agreed to sing "Because"; arranged for a woman to play the organ; contacted Leonard's colleagues at the Office of Price Administration, who agreed to be ushers; arranged for a barber to cut Leonard's hair and a tailor to press his pants; and somehow got the word out to enough of her friends to result in an audience of about two hundred people—all done before Leonard arrived from Fort Bragg.

Leonard "arrived at Raleigh on the bus about nine o'clock in the morning. Grace whisked me to the county clerk, to the barber, to the pants presser, to a store which would sell me a military cap suitable for marriage, and perhaps other things I don't recall." At two p.m. they were married in the Hayes-Barton Church. The whirlwind of events made for some fuzziness in Leonard's memory bank, but he clearly recalled, "As we walked down the aisle after the ceremony, I suppose I looked a little tired from all the excitement. Anyway Grace looked up at me, smiled her prettiest and said, 'Smile big for my friends,' and so I did." Their honeymoon, in Fayetteville, lasted slightly longer than twenty-four hours, and "Monday morning I was back at Ft. Bragg at 6:oo a.m. for bugle call."[21]

A Portrait of Grace

Grace and Leonard were a study in contrasts and complements. In terms of formal education they were poles apart: he was three years into his PhD program when they met; she had dropped out of high school in the ninth grade at age fourteen, worked for the telephone company for a while, then took a beautician course and worked with her divorced mother, also a beautician, at the Hayes-Barton Beauty Shop in Raleigh. Initially intimidated by Leonard's intellectual prowess, Grace came to admire it greatly. "She just loved hearing him talk about his life and his interests," recalled daughter Susan. "She always had lots of questions, and she said, 'We'd drive around, and it was so wonderful to talk to somebody who never had to say, "I don't know." ' "[22] Leonard, in turn, was a tutor who always played to the sensitivities of his audience.

With unfeigned warmth, Grace lavished appreciation and affection on Leonard, always grateful for the respect that he showed to her. "In all our married life he has never once done or said anything demeaning or disparaging or in any way caused me to feel that I was less educated, less smart, or less intelligent than he." His benign effect on her was passive, not active, "not by anything he said, but by being good, sweet, and kind his influence spilled over onto me. Not once has he ever suggested I change in any way what I was doing." Even on the touchy issue of religion, he held back from exerting any pressure to convert to Mormonism. "He never even asked me to join the Church. He would answer questions I asked, but he did not preach to me or put any pressure on me. When I wanted to be baptized into the Church and go to the Temple, he said, 'If you are sure that's what you want, it's fine with me.' "[23]

In her turn, Grace became Leonard's tutor on the essentials of life that are not learned in the classroom. "Grace," Leonard wrote, "is natively a remarkably intelligent person. . . . She is very knowledgeable on things she might have learned from conversations in the beauty shop, or from lectures, or from reading from what might be called light literature, or from personal conversations."[24] By the time they met, Grace was a woman of culture and refinement, and those were qualities that Leonard, by his own account, desperately needed. "I had grown up in a house without any of the amenities. We used an outside toilet, our culinary water came from a pump to a cistern that was filled with water from an irrigation ditch, we ate essentially what we grew—fruits, vegetables, grains, milk, and cream." It is likely that his personal habits, which while he was in college included wearing underwear for a week between changes, had not improved markedly in the move to North Carolina, and so Grace had her work cut out. "So she helped me learn to dress, to eat, to make small talk."[25]

Leonard was a willing, though needy student. A later coworker noted, "I never realized how far he had come so much as when he told me that when he married Grace, she taught him that you didn't wear the same pair of socks all week. You had to change your socks every day. She civilized him."[26]

Because of her lack of formal education, Grace's real talents were not always evident. Shortly after her death in 1982, Grace's daughter-in-law wrote to Leonard of her often underappreciated qualities:

> At first I underestimated Grace. She seemed so sweet and innocent and uncritical that I wondered how discerning she was. But then one night I sat in the kitchen with Susan and Grace talking late at night, and she told me some of the things she had discerned—her children's strengths and weaknesses, the nature of their relationship to you and some things about politics in the church hierarchy. Her insights were keen and pointed, even while they were still loving. She could really read people, and I soon learned that she didn't tell all she read in them. I never underestimated her after that.[27]

CLEARING THE PATHWAY

One of Grace's "keen and pointed" insights was that Leonard had enormous potential professionally but that, if he was to reach that potential, she would have to take care of details that otherwise would derail him. Susan recalled, "My mother was as responsible for his success as a historian as anybody else. She removed every stone from his path, as far as his personal life. She took care of the yard, she designed the house, she had it built, she took care of the kids." There is a proverb that states, "A burden that one chooses is not felt," but although Grace willingly chose to offload Leonard's burdens onto her own shoulders, those shoulders sometimes sagged. Susan continued,

I think my Mom spent some lonely time, because he was gone so much, particularly when we were small. You read in this book about how he spent his summers in Salt Lake, going through the Journal History of the Church, and how that got him so engrossed in Church history. I read that with a different eye, thinking, "He's going down there and spending all week, coming home on the weekend, and Mom is home with three little kids." I admire her for it. She was supportive, but I think she silently bore a pretty heavy burden. She didn't know how heavy it was going to be until it was upon her. But that was the generation—Dad goes and does this, and Mom's in charge of this.[28]

Their son James agreed, adding that Grace had confided to him the choice that she made early in the marriage. "She was going to clear the path for him. She told me that. She said, 'I made a decision. I could see that . . . if I could clear the path for him, that he would become a great man.' So without him even knowing—I don't think she ever sat down and said, 'I'm going to clear the way for you'—she just did it selflessly, and she cleared the path." That meant not only taking care of all routine household chores, but also decorating the house—"If my father had to decorate something, he'd put out a folding chair, in no particular location"—and making sure that family milestones were celebrated in style. "On birthday parties, she would make these elaborate cakes. I mean, make them from scratch! They were just these fabulous, elaborate cakes, and we would have these big parties with the kids, and my father would attend. But other than that, he was reading and typing away on his Olympic."[29]

6

WORLD WAR II
THE VOLUNTEER NOBODY WANTED

People remembered for the rest of their lives where they were when they heard of the surprise attack on Pearl Harbor that brought the United States into World War II. For Leonard, it was a random bit of news after a dull Sunday. He had dated an LDS girl in Goldsboro—a first but "not an exciting date," so he had not minded when the date ended in the late afternoon:

> I left her about five o'clock or so and drove back to Raleigh in my old Plymouth (my first car). Driving into Raleigh I noted that my gas tank was about empty (those were the days I would buy two or three gallons at a time). As the station attendant was putting in the gas I heard the radio playing, and just news. I asked the attendant, very laconically, "Anything in the news worth noting?" He said very excitedly, "They say Pearl Harbor has been attacked." It didn't dawn on me right off. "Where's Pearl Harbor?" I asked. He said, "Hawaii." Then added, "Sounds like war." . . . It hardly seemed real nor did I even think of the implications.[1]

In the short term, the implications for Leonard were, in fact, minimal. He continued teaching his classes at North Carolina State. The gas station attendant was right that it meant war, but it hardly seemed like Leonard's war. He did not mention in his memoirs listening to Franklin D. Roosevelt's galvanizing "Day of Infamy" speech, note the beginnings of rationing and restrictions, or mention the setting up of draft boards. Unlike a generation later, when men often went to great lengths to escape military service during the Vietnam War, the culture in 1942 created a positive pressure toward patriotism and serving one's country. Leonard felt the groundswell of loyal nationalism. "[I] became increasingly anxious to become involved in the war effort" as the spring wore on and the male students in his class joined the war effort. However, he made a firm resolve:

"Whatever I was going to do, I was not going to volunteer for the Army."[2] This was not an unusual feeling. The navy, in particular, was seen as treating (and feeding) its servicemen better; and perhaps Leonard and others felt that chances of survival increased if one served in a branch other than the army. Indeed, survival rates were better in the Army Air Force and far better in the navy, but far worse in the Marines.

An acceptable alternative developed during the spring of 1942 when the Department of Agriculture offered him the summer job of "checking cotton acreage."[3] Cotton production was tightly controlled, and farmers who exceeded their allotted acreage were fined, while those willing to withdraw some acreage from production to allow the soil, depleted by repeated crops, to remain fallow for a season or two were rewarded with federal payments. Much of his job consisted of riding through the North Carolina countryside on a bicycle, stopping at each farm to measure cotton acreage. "This was one of the most pleasurable summers of my life," he recalled, "filled with work, to be sure, but association with interesting people, people of a different culture, people who seemed to be serene and close to the earth."[4] If it reminded him of his Idaho boyhood, he did not say so in his memoirs; and in fact, it seems likely that it did not. North Carolina moved at a slower pace, and he was, for the most part, a welcome visitor rather than a son working, without enthusiasm, in the fields of Idaho under the orders of a labor-oriented father.

When the summer ended and Leonard returned to Raleigh, the motivation to volunteer had intensified into a strong enough feeling that he started taking steps to engage formally in the war effort, with almost comic effects. First, he tried the navy, with all going well until the physical examination. "They finally turned me down because I was too short. Their rules permitted them to take persons who were no shorter than 5'6". I had been under the impression all along that I was 5'6", but I was half an inch shorter." Since only his height disqualified him, the recruiting officials gave him a series of exercises that were intended to add the half-inch that he lacked, with instructions to return in a month and try again. "Well, I went back in a month or so but still couldn't quite make it."[5]

Next he tried the Army Air Force, which did not have the same height requirement, but was turned down because of a history of asthma that developed after his move to North Carolina. Then the Marines—same result.

Still resolved to avoid the army, Leonard applied for work with a war agency, the North Carolina Office of Price Administration, which regulated consumer prices on the home front. His credentials in economics found a welcome audience, the Raleigh OPA office hired him, and NC State gave him a leave of absence. Assigned to set local prices on firewood, commercial laundries, and dairy products, he traveled throughout eastern North Carolina and occasionally to the regional OPA office in Atlanta, Georgia. "I had a very pleasant assignment there, and very pleasant people to work with," he recalled. "It was a wonderful opportunity to gain experience in public service."[6] Best of all, it was providing a comfortable financial cushion for his marriage and future family—a thousand dollars above his annual salary at NC State of $2,200. Appreciative of his work, his boss at OPA filed a request that Leonard be exempted from the draft, but the request was denied. Leonard and Grace must have felt frustrated at the repeated thwartings of Leonard's efforts to find the best niche for his talents; but both seem to have accepted without question—or even comment—that contributing to the war effort was a patriotic duty that they could and would shoulder without complaint.

Still enjoying his work at OPA, Leonard planned with his boss on an alternative strategy to stay with the office. During that summer, Leonard had been called to preside over the LDS branch in Raleigh. Although it was a congregation of only eight or ten families and his religious duties were only part-time, they qualified him for draft-exempt 4D status, which came through toward the end of 1942. During the winter of 1942–1943, however, he became uneasy with the arrangement. He confessed, "I thought it was not patriotic, I did not think it was just or fair for me to have a 4D classification when I was not a full-time minister. So I wrote my draft board and told them to remove that classification and classify me however I should be classified." His request was quickly approved, and he was reclassified as 1A and drafted in February of 1943, with orders to report for duty in March of 1943 at Fort Bragg, North Carolina. "I was drafted about the same time as other persons my age were. Nearly everybody who went to Fort Bragg at the time I did was about the same age—26."[7]

BASIC TRAINING

Leonard's introduction to army life began on a cheerful note. He wrote delightedly to Grace, "My preliminary interviewer turned out to be a former student while I taught at Chapel Hill—and he majored in economics—so that was a break. . . . My classifier was Prof. Wynne of State College. After he found I could type & take dictation (he gave me two letters) he classified me as follows: 'Administrative non-commissioned officer.'" Because he scored exceptionally well on the intelligence test—"2nd highest out of 500 taking it here and among the highest 10th in the Army"—he was told to expect an imminent invitation to attend

Officer Candidate School.[8] But four days later he wrote ruefully, "Those of us that stayed were put again on special detail. Five of us were assigned to cleaning latrines. We are the best latrine cleaners in the Reception center, according to reports."[9] The invitation to OCS never came, and so in spite of his superb grades and preparation he spent the next three years in mostly ordinary assignments, rising only to the rank of corporal.

After a month at Fort Bragg—capped by his impromptu marriage weekend—he traveled by troop train to Fort Custer, Michigan, headquarters of the Military Police Division. There he received orders that bore no relationship to his education or intelligence. "I was assigned to a prisoner-of-war processing company. This company was to process enemy prisoners of war and was divided into three platoons. . . . I was assigned to the Italian unit, the 442nd prisoner-of-war processing platoon."[10]

Three decades later, he mused wryly on his experiences with the nation's largest bureaucracy during its greatest emergency—and correspondingly, its largest-ever talent search. "Of all the branches of the service the Army was the least desirable. Of all the branches of the Army the least desirable was the MP's [Military Police]. Of all the branches of the MP's the least desirable were those assigned to look after enemy prisoners of war. Of all the branches of those assigned to look after enemy prisoners of war the least desirable were those assigned to look after Italians. That, dear reader, is my testimony of the important status I was given in the Army."[11] What he did not mention, and perhaps what he did not even comprehend at the time, was that such an assignment virtually guaranteed that he would remain out of harm's way, situated far behind the front-line action that took the lives of hundreds of thousands of American troops.

After a nine-day furlough during which he and Grace traveled to Twin Falls to meet Noah, Edna, and most of Leonard's siblings, he prepared for overseas deployment.

NORTH AFRICA

Leonard's platoon traveled from Fort Custer to Camp Patrick Henry, near Norfolk, Virginia, where they spent the latter part of July awaiting the arrival of their transport ship. They were under strict orders to remain incommunicado. For the whole ten days, they were forbidden to leave camp, to make phone calls, send wires or letters, or otherwise communicate with the outside world. It was "one hell of a camp," as the usually mild-mannered Leonard put it, and it set the stage for the ocean voyage.

The ship was a converted Canadian passenger liner, formerly called the *Empress of Japan* but understandably renamed the *Empress of Scotland*. Refitted to accommodate three thousand troops, it became temporary home to more than double that number for the week-long ocean crossing. Men slept wherever they could—on deck, on stairs, on top of each other. Only two meals a day were served—British food, which was "some kind of fish." Leonard's digestion—possibly aided by mild seasickness—did not take kindly to the fare, so he survived primarily on oranges.

Allied forces did not yet have control of the sea lanes, so adding to homesickness, boredom, and the uncertainties of what awaited them was the constant threat of encountering the enemy. "When we saw ships on the distant horizon we had no way of knowing whether they were enemy or friendly ships" and naturally tried to avoid them, Leonard recollected. Such maneuvers came on top of the "zigzag course" they took "all the way across to prevent detection from any submarine. We saw submarines on two occasions but had no way of knowing whether they were friendly or not."[12]

The enlisted men were given no information regarding their destination, nor did their first port answer the question. They docked in the middle of the night, at two a.m., where they recognized some signs as posted in French while still others were in a language "that looked Arabic." In his memoirs, Leonard, tongue tucked firmly in his cheek, praised, "What romance," for their port of disembarcation was Casablanca. The "romance" began when "we were loaded immediately into trucks and carried about 20 or 30 miles out into the desert to a place which we were told was called Ber Rachid but which Americans in the area had been calling 'Bear Shit.'" Pitching their tents on the sand, they slept until the sand fleas attacked and awakened them rudely. "We woke up and peeked outside of our pup tents and saw off in the distance caravans of camels, donkeys, biblical men with turbans in a steady stream going to market."[13]

Prisoner of War Camp 101 at Ber Rachid contained twenty-five thousand German and twenty thousand Italian prisoners. Leonard's platoon was assigned to "process" the prisoners, not to guard them. Guard duty fell to "trigger-happy" Moroccans; and although "an average of one [prisoner] would get shot a night trying to escape,"[14] life for the American troops was boring, with their duties rising only occasionally to irritating. The passage of time cast no glamorous haze over the experience for Leonard.

> The whole idea of these processing platoons was a complete waste. The camp administrations already had sufficient records of these prisoners already taken shortly after capture. . . . The lieutenant was a

coward—a physical coward—and did not want to admit that we were useless and that we ought to be put into some useful work like fighting. So he stalled us along doing one little job and another and thus he and we kept out of the war zone and war activity. Ultimately, one by one, members of our platoon began volunteering for other things and he reluctantly allowed us to go.[15]

Only rarely was there a break in the monotony, such as when Leonard and his colleagues were allowed to leave to visit a nearby town where they had lunch at its "finest European restaurant. . . . They furnished us a set meal, except we had a choice between pork and lamb. There was lots of everything & a big variety. Also well cooked. I meant it was a real meal," he wrote to Grace. "Wine was served automatically. It was excellent, dry, French wine. The whole meal cost each of us 70¢—about what the wine alone would have cost in America."[16]

But those rare pleasures stood in stark contrast to the harsh reality of everyday army life for the enlisted man. He shared the details candidly with Grace:

Allen says that the latrine (it's an outdoor wooden toilet) stinks so much that we can't get settled long enough to pick up a good rumor.

The newest addition to our happiness is a wooden bed apiece, made by prison carpenters. They are hard but we are off the ground. Before we were bitten by sand fleas (sort of like mosquito bites). As Deupree says, all we have to worry about now are termites.

We take Atabrine tablets 5 days a week to guard against malaria. We sleep under mosquito nets.

It is very hot right now. Ward took out a 100 Franc note ($2.00) and said he'd offer every bit of it for a cold Coca-Cola. He isn't the only one either. Our water is not exactly cold & heavily chlorinated.[17]

Griping about chow, the enlisted man's traditional privilege since at least the days of the Roman army, was enthusiastically carried on by the American GI's. Spam, a mainstay of enlisted men's diet, drew particular scorn, and Leonard described a telling detail for Grace: "In the Red Cross bldg. in town there is a big cartoon drawn on the wall entitled 'Our final victory.' It shows a bomber soaring over a Spam factory & the soldier gleefully throws down tons & tons of bombs on it."[18]

Leonard saw opportunity amid the boredom and, against regulations, began to enter the camp and interact with Italian prisoners. "I felt a strong desire to learn Italian after finding out how poorly our Italian-American interrogators spoke Italian. I acquired an Italian grammar book, and made arrangement with an Italian Lieutenant prisoner to teach me. Strictly speaking, this was illegal. But nobody paid any attention to what privates did." He traded cigarettes, which otherwise he would not have consumed, and chocolate, which he would have consumed enthusiastically, for the language lessons. Before very long, despite his having learned the language through illegal means, "they allowed me to interrogate the prisoners and fill out the forms on the typewriter. I continued to improve my knowledge of Italian and this became very useful when I was later sent to Italy."[19]

After four months in Morocco, Leonard's platoon was transferred to a camp in Bizerte, Tunisia, where they continued to process Italian prisoners-of-war. He continued to hone his skills in Italian, read many books including Gibbons's classic history *Decline and Fall of the Roman Empire*, and, for the first time, dipped into the camp library's Russian literature: Dostoevsky's *The Brothers Karamazov* and Tolstoy's *War and Peace* and *Anna Karenina*. He also had his introduction to Italian opera when he first heard the exquisite soprano solo "Un bel di," from Puccini's *Madame Butterfly*.

Two other events broke the monotony. After sixteen months of military service, he was promoted to the rank of corporal; and he visited his brother Wayne who had joined the navy, and whose ship briefly put into port. Such a meeting would have been highly unlikely, since troop locations were considered classified— hence the common heading of a letter to the States, "Somewhere in Europe," or "Somewhere in the Pacific"—but Leonard and Grace had worked out a "secret code" before his deployment, and she was able to pass along his location to Wayne, who was on a destroyer escort.[20] "It was no trouble at all for him to get in touch. We've been together all afternoon. He showed me all over his ship, & we had supper on it—with real American ice cream. The first I've had since we've been over."[21]

Leonard's third and final stop in Africa was Oran, Algeria, where he transferred to the Army Finance Corps. "We were prepared for the southern France invasion, but at the last moment [French General Charles] DeGaulle said he didn't want military government troops—he would handle all of that himself. So we were sent to Italy instead."[22]

ITALY

Leonard arrived in Begnoli, Italy, in September 1944. His delight with his new, but still-Spartan accommodations underscored how miserable living conditions had been in North Africa. "We have cots to sleep on, electric lights in the orderly room, & some desks & chairs. So you see, we're pretty comfortable."[23]

While stationed in Begnoli, Leonard got a pass to visit Rome. By a sheer fluke, he met His Holiness, Pope Pius XII, an encounter he described excitedly to Grace. "The Pope was borne in on a hand-carriage or litter, borne by 6 colorful Swiss attendants." Wanting a good view of the proceedings, Leonard worked his way to the edge of the stage where the Pope's throne sat. After exiting his litter, the Pope greeted high-ranking American army officers, and then spoke to the crowd through a microphone. "He said a few words in Latin then in English, then in French. His English was pretty broken. I could have understood better if he had spoken in Italian. His French was pretty good. . . . He said he blessed us all & wished all of us would stay near to God & do as He wished us to do."

Upon concluding his remarks, the Pope spoke with other officers, and then began to mingle with enlisted men close to the stage. "When he came to me he blessed the beads I held. As I shook his hand I told him I was an American from the west. I bowed as I shook his hand but did not kneel or kiss the ring."[24]

During his time in Begnoli, Leonard "saw that we were headed for positions to fill places on the Italian front joining troops who were fighting under General Mark Clark against [German General Albert] Kesselring." The combat was ferocious, with each yard up the Italian peninsula a bloody contest. Leonard's conversations with those in a position to know provided ample evidence that there was nothing either glamorous or glorious about this phase of the war. "All of those with whom [I] conversed persuaded us that this whole campaign was a useless blood bath. I am more certain now than then that this was the case. There was never a more stupid general than Mark Clark." At the first opportunity, Leonard got a pass to go into Rome and introduced himself to the civilian administrator of the Allied Commission, Harlan Cleveland. "He was an economist that was about as close to the Ph.D. as I was and about the same age, and here he was the equivalent of a Major General and I was a [corporal]. I told him of my training and capabilities and asked if he could use me in the Allied Commission. He said he would have me transferred the next day and I would serve him as an economic assistant."[25]

Cleveland was good for his word. Instead of facing German bullets and artillery, Leonard, still a corporal, was now "Allied Controller of the Italian Census Bureau." His job was "to get statistics of interest to the Italian government, the Allied Commission, and the Allied armies; also to publish such statistics with appropriate presentations in both English and Italian." With a personal staff of thirty, he was the equivalent of Undersecretary of Commerce of the United States in charge of statistics.[26] Instead of living in a pup tent with other troops slugging their way northward through Italy, he was suddenly living in comparatively luxurious surroundings with a dazzling array of resources. "I shall have a large big office all to myself. The office at one time was occupied by a big Fascist. It has a private elevator. A private bathroom with hot steaming water, a private room for taking a nap, etc., large chandelier, a conference table, a wonderful hand carved desk & every other luxury," he announced wonderingly to Grace. "I am to take over tomorrow or next day unless the orders are changed."[27]

A week later, stunned by his sudden change in fortunes, Leonard confided to Grace his self-consciousness. "I occupy the President's office & have every person & facility at my disposal. . . . The Italians all know this old & young, they rise when I enter a room, all the ushers & secretaries, etc. say 'Good morning' & 'Good evening' to me as I come in or go out. At my slightest desire they all jump." To a Western American farmer who grew up on the edge of poverty, it was all a bit much to digest. "I can't put on my coat or hang up my hat. I can't sharpen my pencils or open my door. I can't call a cab, my usher must do it." Although the deference of his Italian hosts made him uncomfortable, he understood and accepted that more than politeness underlay it. "Their job depends on it. If I did these things myself, as I want to, they wouldn't have any job. They're too old to try something else. They've worked here 20 years & expect to work till they die." He concluded with an assessment that drew on his modest upbringing: "I love my *job* because of the service I'm performing the Allied Commission, but I don't relish my *position*, if you get the distinction."[28]

Self-conscious though he was, he learned to relish some of the perks of his temporary office. His first exposure to Puccini was the beginning of a lifelong love affair with opera, and he rejoiced to learn that, given his new position, the entire season was in his reach. "The errand boy stood in line for me all day to get me general admission tickets to the opera," he recalled, "and in the weeks that followed I went to 54 different operas in the Royal Opera House in Rome."[29] And all on a salary of sixty-seven dollars a month.

After the Allied troops pushed northward through Italy, Leonard was transferred to Milan for his last army assignment, the Committee of Price Control of North Italy. "We arrived in Milan in time to see Mussolini and his mistress Clara Petacci hanging by their heels from the roof of a service station," he wrote somberly. "It was perhaps three or four days after they had been shot."[30]

V-E Day occurred on May 7, 1945, less than a week after Leonard's arrival in Milan. With the end of the war in Europe he, like every other American soldier, was eager to head home. Two obstacles lay before him. The first was "points." In an attempt to impose some sense of fairness on the order in which troops would be brought home, the army assigned points for total time of military service, time served overseas, medals earned, combat stars, casualties suffered, and family size.

At war's end, eighty-five points were required to qualify for discharge. Leonard had just over half that number: forty-six.

The other obstacle was Japan. For months, Allied troops had been massing on several Pacific islands and were in training for an invasion of Japan, an invasion that experts estimated would result in at least one million Allied casualties, and far more among Japanese troops and civilians. Even women and children in Japan were being issued sharp sticks in lieu of more effective weapons to defend their homeland. American prisoners of war had suffered from frequent maltreatment: starvation, beatings, random executions, lack of medical care, and many other violations of the Geneva Conventions and Red Cross agreements. Even grimmer, as Leonard later discovered, "there were 100,000 American prisoners of war in Japan. Japanese officers had issued an order that every one of them was to be killed in the event of an invasion."[31]

Instead of returning to the States, many American troops in Europe were reassigned for redeployment to the Pacific Theatre. Leonard recalled estimates published in the newspapers that it "would take 8 million troops to invade Japan, of which 2 million would come from troops in Europe." He and his colleagues "supposed we would be among those transferred to the Pacific front. Considering Okinawa, we supposed the casualties would be heavy."[32]

Then, American forces dropped two atomic bombs on Japan in August 1945, and the war abruptly ended. The day after the bombing of the second city, Nagasaki, Leonard wrote to Grace a letter of remarkable sensitivity and anguish, considering how desperately he wanted the war to end:

> You have also probably been thinking of the atom bomb. It is really a terrible thing to contemplate. The papers report it killed 150,000 people in Hiroshima and probably almost as many in Nagasaki. It is horrible from that point of view. But if it has shortened the war by 6 months or a year, it has proved well worthwhile. It was the Japanese who started the war, and they asked for it. I'm sure if any of us, if we had to make the decision as to whether or not to use the bomb, would have said "Yes." However, we must realize it was a horrible choice and that the U.S.A. has lost a great deal of prestige among the peoples of the world. It has been a psychological loss that we were the first nation to use such a destructive power. We can redeem ourselves only by using it for the well being of the world from now on.[33]

Four months later in December 1945, the army revised its discharge guidelines. Leonard, in part because of a "disability . . . incurred or aggravated during your war service"—asthma—qualified for discharge. He was honorably discharged on January 4, 1946, and on January 5 began to draw a disability pension of $11.50 per month.[34]

In the aftermath of the first Gulf War in 1991, Leonard, in a letter to his children, reflected on the differences between two homecomings:

> It is interesting to watch the news broadcasts—filled with homecomings of soldiers and outbursts of patriotism. I was just thinking of my own homecoming. The war ended in August 1945, but they didn't get around to sending me home until January 1946. And when we landed, no band, no placards, no meeting of the ship by the President or the General of the Army, nor anybody. They took us to a port office where we were all duly registered and checked off (after 2 days wait). Then we were told to go to our home the best way we knew how.

Then, with prescient words, he described what likely lay ahead for the new cadre of veterans. "I'm glad the soldiers are home, and I'm glad people are showing their appreciation for them, but how long can it last? Take the soldiers who come home six months from now—what kind of appreciation will be shown to the sad sacks like I was?"[35]

The two most important things that awaited Leonard were Grace, who delayed her own Christmas for two weeks so they could celebrate together; and the Servicemen's Readjustment Act. With encouragement from President Franklin D. Roosevelt, the bill passed both houses of Congress early in 1944, and Roosevelt signed it into law. Commonly called the G.I. Bill, it made possible the higher education of millions of veterans including Leonard—in those days seventy-five dollars a month for a married veteran with family was good income—and also provided them with low-interest mortgages, a benefit that made buying a comfortable home possible for Leonard and Grace when they moved to Logan, Utah, in mid-1946.[36]

Having put his life on hold for more than three years, and with the financial backing of the G.I. Bill, Leonard returned to his doctorate studies, more motivated than ever not to waste a moment.

7

BECOMING DR. ARRINGTON

The slow pace of his duties in North Africa had given Leonard many hours to think about his future career. Within weeks of arriving in Morocco, he signaled to Grace his intention not to make permanent use of Dean Benjamin Brown's offer of a professorship at North Carolina State. "I'd try to get some sort of work in Salt Lake City and would use spare time in getting together material for my dissertation."[1] Having grown up in the West, he had no desire to settle permanently at an eastern university; since there were no colleges in Twin Falls, Salt Lake City was close enough. Grace's positive response to the idea quickly led to more definitive plans. But having been part of the greatest conflict in the world's history, he was in no mood to return immediately to fulltime studies. "During times of change like this, one wants to be in there pitching, using whatever talents he has in a desirable way. One definitely does not want to sit in a library studying & observing while others are moving the world. At least, not me." His plan was to spend three or four years in the workforce to achieve financial stability, and then return to Chapel Hill to complete his doctorate degree within "a year or two."[2]

His initial thought was to focus on the LDS Church Security Plan for his dissertation topic. Initiated by Harold B. Lee, president of a stake in the Salt Lake Valley, in the midst of the Great Depression as a grassroots initiative to supplement federal assistance to unemployed church members, it was adopted by the central church in 1936 and later renamed the Church Welfare Plan.

In the aftermath of V-E Day, Leonard wrote to LDS apostle John A. Widtsoe, a former university president who held an undergraduate degree from Harvard and a PhD from the University of Göttingen (Germany), asking for advice about three potential dissertation topics: (a) economic aspects of the Church Security Plan, (b) economic doctrines of the LDS Church, and (c) the business connections of the LDS Church. "Could you give me advice as to whether these fields have already been covered, whether the literature is adequate for a Doctor's dissertation, whether the research would have to be done entirely in Salt Lake, and whether the Church would cooperate in giving material for research."[3]

Leonard sent a copy of the letter to Grace—still a Baptist—who wrote back with total support:

> It is a nice letter and I am sure you will get an encouraging letter from Apostle Widtsoe soon. I would think they would be very proud to have you do your dissertation on some aspect of the Church. I wish the church was more anxious to let the world know more about it. Most people know absolutely nothing about the church except that it once (and as far as they know still believe) in polygamy. They know nothing of its wonderful faith and doctrine. It's such a pity they know only the one dark spot in the history of the church.[4]

Widtsoe, who had never met Leonard, wrote by return mail the thoughtful and encouraging response that Grace predicted. One day after the bombing of Hiroshima made the end of the war a near certainty, he advised, "If you desire to write a thesis dealing with some phase of the economics of the Latter-day Saint Church, you have a field at your command. Very little has been done in that field." With magnanimity, especially considering that he was writing to a man of whom he knew nothing, Widtsoe signaled his willingness to become a facilitator: "After you make up your mind as to one or two themes, it might be well to write me again, and I will be glad to present them to the Authorities of the Church for their inspection and willingness to give the assistance you need, by providing material in the archives of the Church."[5]

Leonard returned to North Carolina in January 1946 and immediately began teaching at NC State and Meredith College. The following month he sent Widtsoe a second letter sketching the couple's plans: "In June my wife and I plan to come to Utah and Idaho for the summer. Perhaps it would be possible for us to see you a few minutes, if your workload would permit it. . . . I am anxious to write on a Western topic, preferably a Church one . . . Another economist would probably not be a liability either to the Church or to the Intermountain Region."[6]

Widtsoe's friendly and encouraging reply, which invited the couple to visit with him, came four weeks later: "You will be able to find ample material for your doctor's dissertation under the title 'Economic Aspects of the Mormon Church Security Program.' When you get here, I think you will be able to pick up very quickly a very great amount of printed or typewritten material on the subject."[7]

By April, Leonard secured a teaching position in the West, not in Salt Lake City as he had originally hoped, but at Utah State Agricultural College (USAC, now Utah State University) in Logan. Although it was in pre-freeway days and

Logan was eighty miles from Salt Lake City, Leonard was well situated for intense research in and around the LDS Church Archives. He began teaching economics classes during the summer of 1946, with the full support of his dean to continue work on his doctorate degree with the University of North Carolina. "He hoped I could get it in a couple of years."[8]

LDS CHURCH ARCHIVES

Leonard's arrival at the LDS Church Archives coincided with the excommunication of Fawn McKay Brodie, niece of David O. McKay, second counselor in George Albert Smith's First Presidency and future church president. A year earlier, Brodie had published *No Man Knows My History*, a scholarly but unsympathetic biography of Mormonism's founder, Joseph Smith. While critically acclaimed nationally—it has remained in print continuously to this day—the book scandalized church members, who hastened to denounce her as lacking faith in Joseph Smith's prophetic mission. The church had taken the tack, after the death of B. H. Roberts in 1933, of usually ignoring critical or anti-Mormon works rather than engaging in two-fisted debates and "Bible bashing," but it made an exception for Brodie. An unattributed review, running to an astounding 160 column-inches, appeared in the *Church News*, blasting it as "a composite of all anti-Mormon books that have gone before."[9]

Some have assumed that Brodie's book poisoned the well for other scholars attempting to use the Church Archives; but Leonard, although he must have been alarmed at the reaction to Brodie, set the record straight: "The two things wrong with this assertion are that (a) Fawn Brodie's material is from anti-Mormon collections in the New York Public Library and elsewhere, and if she had used the materials in the Church Archives (which she did not) her book would have been very different; (b) my own experience demonstrates that the policy of restriction was not applied in 1946 or 1947, after Brodie's book appeared, but in 1951–52 when the deluge of graduate students from BYU occurred."[10]

Leonard's enthusiasm notwithstanding, there is no question that the archival staff during those years was generally unfriendly to scholars. Though unstated, the real problem appeared to be that the staff, including Church Historian Joseph Fielding Smith, felt that the history that emerged from the archives should continue to be written the way it had been written for decades: uncritical and celebratory of the triumphs of an exceptional, God-favored people. Anything short of that—including scholarly history that attempted to be data-driven and unbiased—was viewed as aiding the enemy. It is possible that Leonard, who managed to fly under the radar, failed to appreciate the importance of that attitude in 1946; it is certain that he underestimated it a quarter-century later.

Leonard's nascent relationship with the astute and pro-scholar Apostle Widtsoe quickly became the key that opened the archives to him. Widtsoe counseled
in a disarmingly candid manner:

> You'll have to do most of this work in the archives of the Church.
> Let me give you some practical advice. Now don't go in there and
> say, "I want everything you have on Mormon economic enterprises."
> You go in there and tell them that you're interested in studying Mor-
> mon culture and Mormon history. Begin by asking for some printed
> books about Mormon history—doesn't matter if you've seen them
> before or not. Ask for some printed books. Spend a day or two look-
> ing at them. Then, ask for some old newspapers. They'll bring them
> out and you'll look at them for two or three days. Then ask them
> what their basic source of material on Mormon history is. Now they'll
> say, "The Journal History of the Church." You'll say, "May I look at
> the first volume?" They'll bring it to you and you'll use that. When
> you finish that, go back and get the second volume, the third vol-
> ume, and stay there until you finish the Journal History of the
> Church. Considering things like they are in the Church archives, you
> have to be like the camel which poked his head in the tent and grad-
> ually moved along until gradually it carried the tent away with it.[11]

Leonard followed Widtsoe's advice to the letter, beginning with a memorable meeting with Joseph Fielding Smith in July 1946. After getting nowhere with
Assistant Church Historian A. William Lund, who "gave the impression that Joseph Fielding Smith very seldom assented" to requests for access to archival material, Leonard asked for an appointment with Smith. "I opened the door and walked
in and said, 'Elder Smith, may I see you for a few moments?' He did not look up,
did not say anything, didn't even grunt." After an embarrassingly long silence,
Smith said, "Well?" Leonard then stated his case, dropping Widtsoe's name as
having endorsed his research topic. Smith replied simply, "I guess there would be
no harm in that, but . . ." He never finished his sentence, instead refocusing his
attention on documents on his desk.

Unsure of what to do next, since Smith had not given explicit approval, he
improvised. "I then went to Brother Lund and told him that Brother Smith had
given his OK. 'Did he really?' said Brother Lund. I said, 'Yes, he did.' I am sure
that I talked more positively than I felt, but Brother Lund accepted it and showed
me a desk in the library and said, 'You may work at this place.'" Lund then led
him down the road that Widtsoe had predicted. "You ask for one item at a time

from the library and we will give it to you. When you have finished with that, ask for another and in that way you may have one document with you at the table at any time."

Working his way up the food chain as his mentor had suggested, Leonard soon arrived at the Journal History of the Church, a massive collection of scrapbooks chronicling the church's history as contained both in manuscript and published materials. He worked for four summers to complete his survey of the Journal History through 1905, which roughly coincided with the 1900 stopping point of his dissertation. "Then I began to examine other documents and manuscripts in the Archives. At no time was any document refused me and at no time were my notes ever examined or asked for. I did see much material which today is considered classified. The librarians even allowed me during the third summer to go through files in the library archives and to check out and pick out things that seemed important." Since the primary mission of the archives had been to collect material, rather than study it, it was not surprising to Leonard that he "discovered many things which they did not know existed and which I did not call to their attention." By being "as inconspicuous as possible," he worked with no interference. "This was the period when there was no censoring of notes and no restriction of material, or if there was, there was none on my work."[12] And he proved Widtsoe's prediction to be correct—indeed, insofar as his research subject was concerned, he "carried the tent away."

Although his research in the Church Archives was essential, he cast a broader net that sometimes included the *creation* of historical records. In 1988, at a banquet commemorating the thirty-year anniversary of the publication of *Great Basin Kingdom*, he read a list of historical figures and historians with whom he spoke—a virtual Who's Who of Mormon contemporary history and historiography that included William Wallace, a pioneer in Utah irrigation who told Leonard of accompanying his father to a private consultation with Brigham Young; Charles C. Richards, ninety-six years of age, who told him "about some financial dealings of the Church I wouldn't have otherwise known about"; LeRoi C. Snow, youngest son of church president Lorenzo Snow; and historians Ephraim Ericksen, Joseph Geddes, Feramorz Y. Fox, Preston Nibley, Dale Morgan, Wilfrid Poulson, T. Edgar Lyon, Leland Creer, A. C. Lambert, and Juanita Brooks.[13]

RETURN TO CHAPEL HILL

With four years of research under his belt, Leonard took an unpaid leave of absence from USAC during the 1949–1950 academic year, packed up his family—which now included year-old son James—and returned to the University of North Carolina. Grace and James lived in Raleigh, where Grace again worked with her mother in her beauty shop. Leonard hitchhiked to Chapel Hill during the week, returning to Raleigh on the weekend. He had set himself a rigorous goal: to complete all of the remaining requirements for his PhD, except for writing the dissertation. "This meant: (1) passing the examination in French, which I did on the first go-round, even though a very difficult examination; (2) taking a full course load each of three quarters and passing all courses; (3) taking a series of written examinations on course work done as a graduate student; (4) and taking the preliminary oral examination, which accepts or rejects the student as a candidate for the Ph.D."[14]

Of the four requirements, the preliminary oral examination was by far the most daunting. Designed to test the limits of the candidate's knowledge on a broad array of subjects, and not necessarily limited to his field of study, it consisted of sequential interrogation, in a venue open to faculty and graduate students, by the faculty members comprising the candidate's doctoral committee. Less than two weeks prior to the exam, Leonard's department chair informed him that it would last two and a half hours and would include questioning on public policy, economic history, public finance, agricultural economics, rural sociology, economic theory, resource economics, labor economics, and, most petrifying to Leonard, statistics—and that from Dudley Cowden, a noted national authority on the subject.

In reminiscing about the exam, Leonard described himself as having been "terrified" of what Cowden might do to him during his interrogation, to the point of obsessing. "The night before the exam—the one night I must have a good sleep in order to be alert and articulate at the examination, I tossed and turned, slept hardly at all, tried to prepare in my mind answers to hypothetical questions Cowden might ask." Then, almost providentially, "around 10 p.m. a mockingbird stationed himself on a tree outside our bedroom window and began to sing. Although it seems incredible, he sang all night! What a comforting thought, what a consolation, what a pleasant diversion! I have felt partial to mockingbirds ever since."[15]

The exam went fine until "the moment of terror," when Cowden took his turn: "'Mr. Arrington, have you ever taught a course in statistics?' Of course I had. 'What text did you use?' Before I could respond, Dr. Forster objected. It was an unfair question, he said. But Cowden knew what he was doing. 'What text did you use?' While Forster continued to murmur, I smiled a little and said I had used Croxton and Cowden, *Applied General Statistics.* Cowden grinned and said, 'You showed very good judgment; I pass.'"

COMPLETING THE DISSERTATION

Leonard returned to Logan for the 1950–1951 academic year and began one of the most productive periods of his career. In slightly over a year he wrote seven significant articles that were accepted for publication in regional and national professional journals, all of which were in preparation for the writing of his dissertation. The actual writing of the dissertation was something of an anticlimax. Beginning in January 1952, nearly thirteen years after he started his graduate work at UNC, Leonard wrote the 449 pages in just ten weeks.[16] He returned to Chapel Hill in March, defended the dissertation—"Mormon Economic Policies and Their Implementation on the Western Frontier, 1847–1900"—in April, turned in the approved copy in May, and returned to Logan in June. His PhD was awarded on August 22, 1952.[17]

8

GREAT BASIN KINGDOM
SAGA OF A SAGA

Without George Ellsworth, there likely would have been no *Great Basin Kingdom*. Instead, there may well have been only a series of well-researched and interesting articles about the economic life the Mormons created in their half-century domination of the Intermountain West. But largely due to George Ellsworth, seventeen years of effort produced a landmark event—the almost poetically named saga of the creation of a society. Their religious focus and almost inhuman self-discipline and sacrifice confirmed, stabilized, and allowed to flourish the vision of Zion that Joseph Smith had partially articulated before his murder in the Midwest. It was a story marred by the bloody crime of Mountain Meadows, demands for self-mastery that sometimes did not stop short of oppression, submission to a marital system that broke hearts and ennobled those who could and would treat it as God's will, and an institutionalized paranoia where the rest of the United States was concerned whose roots grew strong but twisted from the rich, black soil of Ohio and Missouri. While other religious movements in the United States had claimed that God spoke to them through their prophets, Mormons gave the claim a unique twist by moving across the continent and colonizing a barren desert in response to his voice.

More than an economic history, *Great Basin Kingdom* portrayed the saga of nineteenth-century Mormonism from a data-based, nonpolemical perspective—a sharp contrast to the many histories that preceded it. Thus, it established Leonard Arrington as a premier scholar of his generation, who set the bar for others who found in Mormon studies their love of profession. And yet, quite possibly it never would have come into being without George Ellsworth.

Ellsworth was the *yang* to Leonard's *yin*. A brilliant historian fresh out of a doctorate program at the University of California, Berkeley, Ellsworth joined the faculty of Utah State Agricultural College in 1950, four years after Leonard.

Insistent on the importance of narrative—that history needed to tell a *story*—and the necessity of precise prose, he held Leonard's feet to the fire and became the counterbalance enabling the transformation of a dry, data-laden economics dissertation into a compelling historical narrative and the reshaping of an economist into a historian. Leonard recalled their first meeting, at a faculty Christmas dinner and dance, as an unforgettable encounter: "I was the chairman of this Christmas dance, so I got a chance to meet everybody. As soon as he said, 'I'm George Ellsworth,' I said, 'I want to talk to you.' So, we traded dances even though his wife [Maria] was twice as tall as I am."

The Arringtons soon invited the Ellsworths to their house, where Leonard suggested to George, "You know, we ought to get people like us together to write papers and present them." That was the beginning of the Church History Club, initially composed of the Arringtons, Ellsworths, Eugene and Beth Campbell, and Wendell and Pearl Rich.[1]

Although Leonard's interest in Mormon history had begun a decade earlier as a graduate student and faculty member at North Carolina State, his training was in economics, not history, and the classes he was hired to teach at Utah State University were in his field of training. The first courses he taught were principles of economics, economic problems, and small business. The Church History Club allowed him a change in emphasis. Meeting once a month, the group read and critiqued each other's manuscripts. Ellsworth's influence was particularly important to Leonard. In addition to their informal monthly meetings, a teacher-student relationship developed when Leonard enrolled in two seminars in Mormon history and historiography taught by Ellsworth. "George was just the person to tutor me in the intricacies of Mormon history, literature, and historiography," Leonard praised. "What I learned from him was indispensable in writing *Great Basin Kingdom.*"[2]

In taking the initiative to form the group, Leonard foreshadowed his later success as an "entrepreneur" of history—a term that he used to describe himself. More than a mere promoter, Leonard invested in history the way other entrepreneurs invested in business ventures. He fostered interactions between historians whose inclinations likely would have led them to seclusion rather than socialization; he brought new scholars into the field; he raised and spent money to finance projects and degrees; and he even gave freely of his own voluminous research files—largesse almost unheard of in a field where scholars jealously hoarded their research notes.

TRANSFORMING A DISSERTATION

Leonard's doctoral committee at the University of North Carolina had been sufficiently impressed with his dissertation for his advisor, Dr. Milton Heath, to suggest that he consider revising it for publication. The Committee on Research in Economic History, part of the Economic History Association, had grant money from the Rockefeller Foundation to publish several volumes on American economic history, and Heath felt that a revised version of Leonard's dissertation would be a good addition to the series. On Heath's recommendation the committee gave Leonard a grant, and he set to work, sandwiching the additional research and writing between his teaching and research, the Arringtons' active engagement in their local church congregation, and the raising of three children. James was three when Carl was born in 1951, and Susan, their only daughter, was born in 1954, the same year in which Leonard's labors of revising and expanding his dissertation came to fruition in an eight-hundred-page manuscript. He sent a completed draft to Dr. Arthur H. Cole, chairman of the Committee on Research in Economic History, president of the Economic History Association, and a professor of business at Harvard. Lewis Atherton of the University of Missouri served as the manuscript reader, and wrote a six-page critique that encouraged publication but "also expressed some concerns"—concerns that Leonard's diary entry did not delineate.[3]

Leonard spent another year polishing "Building the Kingdom: The Economic Activities of the Latter-day Saints." In 1955 when he was ready to send it back to the committee, he felt generally satisfied with it, but Ellsworth took a harder look and gave him a candid assessment: "a wonderful piece of research from which a splendid history could be written."[4] The critique was withering, and it reoriented Arrington's vision of his work: "Suddenly I realized that it was a dry book." Comprehensive and detailed, it was also "a one-fold treatise." Ellsworth convinced his student that "I was going to have to quit thinking of myself as an economist writing an economics book, and [begin] thinking of myself as a historical writer trying to tell a fascinating story of a fascinating people."[5]

THE HUNTINGTON LIBRARY

Leonard was entitled to a sabbatical leave from Utah State and, with the blessing of his department chair, he applied for and received two six-month fellowships, the first from the Henry Huntington Library in San Marino, California, and the second from Yale University. Both institutions had excellent collections on nineteenth-century Mormon history, which was the dimension that "Building the Kingdom" lacked. In the fall of 1956, Leonard and Grace packed up their three children and moved to California. At the Huntington Library, the director, John E. Pomfret, invited Arrington to describe his research to a meeting of Southern California historians. Apparently impressed, Pomfert, "on the drive home . . . told me that he would be glad to give me a full 12-month fellowship to remain at Huntington—together with a private workroom of my own across from that of Allan Nevins—if I would remain there. I happily agreed to do so and wrote Yale to cancel my arrangement there." He then began blocking out a schedule for revising the manuscript chapter by chapter.[6]

He wrote seven pages the first day as a down payment and then, while immersing himself in "the indescribably rich and complete Western collection of the Huntington Library,"[7] undertook a rigorous schedule of writing one chapter each month. Unlike his later years as church historian, when he had an impressive staff to assist him, "it should be emphasized that this was strictly an individual project." He had no research assistants to help him nor any Xerox machine for duplication. "Everything had to be copied out laboriously on the typewriter."[8]

Leonard completed the manuscript in the fall of 1957 and sent it to the Committee on Research in Economic History, which accepted it with minimal changes and forwarded it to Harvard University Press. He summarized: "After eleven years of research and writing, without the aid of research assistants but with the critical comments and suggestions of George Ellsworth, I finished the book."[9] *Great Basin Kingdom* was published in the fall of 1958, while Leonard was on a Fulbright Fellowship in Italy. He did not receive a copy until the week after Christmas. Ellsworth paid him a high compliment by noting that what had been a treatise on economics was now an economic history. "And that was true. It was. So I began to see myself as a historian."[10] For the rest of his life, Leonard credited George Ellsworth for the mentorship that resulted in a shift in his professional identity.

CANDID HISTORY

The central theme of *Great Basin Kingdom* and of the dissertation from which it emerged, "the consistent applications of antebellum policies in the Great Basin while the nation was adopting a more individualistic and freewheeling capitalism," does not invoke expectations of a historical page-turner.[11] And indeed, the book never became a bestseller, though its sales were certainly respectable. One colleague noted, "There were never more than 7,500 copies of the hardbound sold. Later when it was put out in paperback it sold more, but it isn't a book that an awful lot of people have read."[12] However, its influence far outweighed its print run, and it marked a turning point in the telling of Mormon history. It built on the tradition of Juanita Brooks's landmark *Mountain Meadows Massacre*, a book published eight years earlier by a practicing Mormon, that told a dark story without bias. Where Brooks made her contribution through the intensity of her focus on Mormonism's most difficult episode, Arrington made his through his breadth in covering the history of Mormonism over its foundational half-century in Utah.

The literary backdrop before which *Great Basin* stood began in 1830 with the publication of the Book of Mormon by the church's founder, Joseph Smith. Four years later Eber D. Howe colonized the opposite pole of the world of Mormon polemics when he published the first anti-Mormon book, *Mormonism Unvailed*.[13] For more than a century thereafter, virtually all of the books and pamphlets relating to Mormonism were based on one of two assumptions: (1) Mormonism is not only a true religion, but *the* True Religion—indeed, the one and only true and living church upon the face of the Earth; or (2) Mormonism is not only false, but evil and dangerous.

In the introduction to *Great Basin*, Leonard wrote unapologetically to both sides about the daunting task of occupying a middle ground:

> To be sure, much of what may be called "the Mormon myth" has been unacceptable to social theorists. The writer's view is that ultimate truths are often, if not always, presented artistically or imaginatively in a way suited to the needs and exigencies of the living community of persons. While the Mormon story may not appeal to the rational faculty of the majority as an objective picture of the world about us, there can be no doubt that, somehow or other, it tapped immense creative forces in those believing it, and that it inspired a whole commonwealth of converts to make the desert blossom as the rose.
>
> Finally, a word to Mormon readers who will be troubled about my naturalistic treatment of certain historic themes sacred to the memories of the Latter-day Saints. The church holds, of course, that it is based on divine revelation. . . . [However,] it is impossible to separate revelation from the conditions under which it is received: "We have this treasure in earthen vessels." Or, as Brigham Young expressed it, "The revelations which I receive are all upon natural principles." The true essence of God's revealed will, if such it be, cannot be apprehended without an understanding of the conditions surrounding the prophetic vision, and the symbolism and verbiage in which it is couched. . . . A naturalistic discussion of "the people and the times" and of the mind and experience of Latter-day prophets is therefore a perfectly valid aspect of religious history, and,

indeed, makes more plausible the truths they attempted to convey. While the discussion of naturalistic causes of revelations does not preclude its claim to be revealed or inspired of God, in practice it is difficult, if not impossible, to distinguish what is objectively "revealed" from what is subjectively "contributed" by those receiving the revelation.[14]

Occupying middle ground involved canvassing available data, letting data rather than dogma or animus define the story, and then telling the story within a compelling narrative framework. "I did not start my study with the assumption that church authorities were a bunch of rascals; neither did I start with the assumption that church authorities were angels. I hunted for all the evidence I could to determine the facts, and then presented them," Leonard explained to a correspondent in 1959. The orientation stood him in good stead over the next four decades of his very productive life.[15]

The basic narrative of the Mormon colonization of the Great Basin was already well understood and generally acknowledged by all sides: Beginning with the entry in 1847 of the vanguard of Mormon expatriates driven from their previous homes at gunpoint, the Mormons prevailed against considerable obstacles, including a harsh natural environment and a hostile U.S. government intent on obliterating polygamy, and established a stable society that became one of the United States a half-century later. Context and meaning were where the two sides differed.

For a believing Latter-day Saint to write of the Mormon pioneers was nothing novel, and Leonard did not hesitate to give praise where it was due—indeed, successfully farming what was largely a desert with little precipitation and scant natural resources was a noteworthy accomplishment. However, he tempered his praise in a way that few previous authors had done, in essence declining to have God speak from each bush along the way. The "natural principles" of which Brigham Young spoke factored into most of the saga, and Leonard wove them into the narrative, a narrative that comprised both marked successes and heartrending failures.

Great Basin pays particular attention to the first decade of colonization, when an economic foundation was built from scratch. Feeding the population was, of course, the primary concern; but basic infrastructure and buildings required either a manufacturing base or the importation of manufactured goods—the latter being far less desirable since it would require the export of scarce cash or commerce based on a virtually nonexistent locally produced surplus. Three important commodities—sugar, iron, and lead—were among the first to be targeted for self-sufficiency.

While sugar cane cultivation was not a possibility, sugar beets provided an acceptable source of sucrose, and the land proved amenable to their growth. But growing sugar beets was the easier task; converting the vegetable into sugar was another story. The first crop of "22,000 bushels of beets were ground into molasses, but the production of sugar was 'a complete failure.' To add to the difficulties, the sugar beet crop failed in 1855 and 1856 because of drought and grasshopper destruction of the seed." The church's First Presidency sought divine intervention "that no failure of the kind will again thwart our wishes, and that we shall soon be able to furnish, from the beet, sugar sufficient for home consumption," but to no avail. The sugar factory was closed and the equipment scavenged for other purposes. The direct loss to the church and the investors was $100,000.[16] It was not until the late 1880s, with the development of new technology for extracting sucrose from sugar beets and the subsequent formation of the Utah Sugar Company (later the Utah-Idaho Sugar Company), that sugar production in Utah reached commercial scale.

The discovery of iron-rich ore in mountains three hundred miles south of Salt Lake City led to the formation of the Iron Mission in 1851. With a crew of energetic and initially enthusiastic "missionaries" who knew little about iron or steel production, mission leaders began to mine a mountain containing 200 million tons of 52 percent iron ore. Eight years later, after the direct expenditure of approximately $150,000 of scarce currency, the iron works were closed, having produced "nothing more than a few andirons, kitchen utensils, flat irons, wagon wheels, molasses rolls, and machine castings."[17]

The "Lead Mission," established near present-day Las Vegas, suffered a similar fate: "The ore was yielding only twenty to thirty per cent lead; there were many impurities which caused much of the lead to burn up during the smelting, and washing was impractical since the nearest stream was twelve difficult miles away; provisions and forage for the animals had to be hauled 230 miles over a difficult road; and the Indians were giving trouble." Those missionaries abandoned the place and returned to Salt Lake City in March 1857 "with only sixty tons of ore having been mined."[18]

Had failure been restricted to a single enterprise, one might have written it off to bad luck. The failure of multiple, strategic industries, however, called for a more fundamental explanation, and Leonard supplied it forthrightly:

> That in each case the church eventually assumed responsibility and
> control was due partly to the lack of private capital, and partly to the
> belief that all institutions in Mormondom ought to be under the influence of the Priesthood. While this assured a concentration of

efforts in building the Kingdom, it also involved the danger of tying the hands of the "experts" who were engaged in the active management of these enterprises. Brigham Young and his appointed lay leaders were outstanding colonizers, and there can be no doubt that they were dedicated to the Kingdom, but the more the specialists depended on them for leadership, the more the specialized industries were apt to suffer from inexpert direction. . . .

It is quite possible that the sugar, iron, and lead enterprises, and perhaps others, would have been more successful if knowledgeable private interests had been allowed a freer hand in the day-to-day direction, and a stronger voice in the making of basic decisions.[19]

Stated differently, economic principles had (and have) no respect for priesthood. The failure of church leaders to understand this and to make appropriate adjustments was pervasive throughout the latter half of the nineteenth century, and particularly during the crucial first decade of colonization. The expenditure of labor and capital on the failed industries meant less could be applied to agricultural improvement—"the construction of additional irrigation works, barns, corrals, and the purchase of farm equipment"—which would have generated tradable commodities. Again, Leonard spelled out the implications: "The development projects required tremendous investment in industrial machinery, equipment, supplies, and transportation, which absorbed most of the exchange potential of the Mormons without adding anything to it, thus creating an unfavorable balance of trade." That worsened as the trade provided in early years by Gold Rush traffic declined. Without the failed industrial investments, that temporarily lucrative exchange with migrating forty-niners could have been used by Mormons "to import blooded livestock, agricultural machinery, nails, and tools."[20]

The church hierarchy responded to the failures—and to the consequent privations caused by them—by blaming the people rather than the flawed economic system that the leaders themselves had established: "the failure of the people to do what they had been commanded; namely, cease to patronize the [non-Mormon] merchants and establish home industries."[21] Well-intentioned Mormons, most notably William Godbe and E. L. T. Harrison, tried to persuade church leaders, both in person and in print, that "the development of mining, 'foreign trade,' and cooperation with Gentile [i.e., anything not Mormon] and capitalistic enterprise were the way of the future. . . . It was apostasy, they were told, 'to honestly differ with the Priesthood' on such important matters of temporal policy. One might as well expect 'to differ honestly with the Almighty!' "[22] Economic policy was a matter of dogma and thus was above criticism. Although Godbe, Harrison, and others had acted with the intent of moving the church and the people to a better economic position, they were excommunicated in 1869.

By 1900—the end of the period covered in *Great Basin Kingdom*—arable land had long been in private hands and most was being farmed. The new immigrants kept pouring in because of the church's longstanding policy of "gathering to Zion," but they were unwelcome in rural, agrarian communities that had already absorbed close to their maximum. As a result, these newcomers tended to settle in the cities. As Leonard summarized: "With 'outsiders' attracted in ever greater numbers to Utah, and with Mormons settling in increasing numbers in non-Mormon communities and neighborhoods, the days of the proud, isolated, self-sufficient Kingdom were at an end."[23]

The culture region constituting the aptly named "Great Basin Kingdom" was a success when measured in terms of becoming a vibrant culture with high religious and moral values and a strong emphasis on education, but in economic terms it fell far short of the potential it might have reached if it had been guided by sound and modern economic principles, rather than backward-looking policies increasingly couched in the language of dogmatism. In fact, it was "gentiles" who moved into the Great Basin who took advantage of the economic opportunities that the Mormons ignored and achieved such potential. Although by 1900 the vast majority of Utah's population was still Mormon, 90 percent of the state's millionaires were non-Mormons.[24]

RECEPTION AND REVIEWS

The initial reaction to the publication of *Great Basin Kingdom*, at least in Salt Lake City, was silence. Leonard wrote, "As far as I am aware, not a word about it was said in any of the Salt Lake newspapers."[25] Perhaps the silence was not surprising, for Leonard grew up outside of Utah, had never lived in Salt Lake City, and was out of the country when the book was released. Furthermore, Harvard University Press had no experience in marketing books on Mormonism to a Utah readership. Indeed, its only known prior title on the subject, a 1922 book entitled *Communism Among the Mormons*, was hardly the making of a best-seller to that audience.

In many quarters, both then and later, the book presented a conundrum. For more than a century, readers who picked up a "Mormon" book had seen little more than polemics. Yet this one did not begin from a preselected menu of attitudes; rather, it made a new demand of the reader: suspend judgment. Leonard Arrington's name was largely unknown, and neither his name nor the content of the book offered clues about who he was—Mormon or non-Mormon? One graduate student in Canada who later became a coworker recalled, "My major professor had read Leonard's book. . . . He said, 'Bruce, it is a very comprehensive book. It is a very good book. It's favorable to the Mormons, but Leonard Arrington is not a Mormon.' "[26] Leonard was amused that people could not identify his religious affiliation on the basis of the book, but even he may not have realized that he was creating a middle ground that had not existed before. As the book began to circulate among historians, the range of responses, as he reflected thirty years later, brought him obvious glee:

> I began to get letters, complimenting me on the book and then asking me, ever so timidly, ever so obliquely, whether I was a Mormon. They suggested that they had been unable to determine my religious affiliation by reading the book. If I was a Mormon, why wasn't the treatment more faith-promoting; if I was a Gentile, how could it be so even-handed and fair? . . .
>
> A professor at BYU assigned the book to the forty students in his History of Utah class and required them to write a review of it. Then, on the final exam, he asked them to assess whether the author of the book was a Mormon. . . . Roughly half of them concluded I was a Mormon, the other half that I was not. This was perhaps the supreme compliment that a book like this could have been given.[27]

Edward C. Banfield, author of *The Moral Basis of a Backward Society*, traveled the long distance to Logan from the University of Pennsylvania to determine whether Leonard was a faithful Mormon.[28] Perhaps the greatest compliment, though a back-handed one, came from the cataloguers in the LDS Church History Archives. After Leonard became church historian in 1972, he checked the card catalog to determine if the church even had a copy of *Great Basin Kingdom*. It did, but he noticed a little "a" in the corner of the card. Asking the librarian the meaning of the letter, he was told that it meant "anti-Mormon."

> "Why would it have been classified as anti-Mormon?" I asked.
>
> "Well," one person replied, "it was a scholarly book, which meant it wasn't designed to be faith-promoting; and if it wasn't *for* the Church, then, by classification, it had to be against. Moreover, it didn't go through a Church reading committee, which meant it wasn't approved. And if it wasn't approved, then, by definition, it must be . . ."
> Well, you get the story.[29]

The church's ambivalence in classifying the book was matched by its ambivalence in selling it through its wholly owned publisher, Deseret Book. Everett

Cooley, director of the Utah State Historical Society, recalled meeting with the company's representative, who informed him the book was not selling and discovering that they had kept it under the counter, concerned over its representation of Mormon history. The president of the historical society's board of trustees scolded the representative, "You don't recognize what a great book this is, and how it will benefit the Church for the treatment Leonard has given it, rather than making everything so miraculous. There is a logical explanation for much of it."[30]

Perhaps the most memorable review of *Great Basin Kingdom* came from one of Leonard's nephews, a high school student who was "induced" by his father to read the book: "Dear Uncle Leonard, I think you were a pretty good writer not to make the book no duller than it was. Your loving nephew, Farr."[31]

Published and verbal reviews were almost uniformly positive. Two LDS General Authorities, Hugh B. Brown of the Quorum of the Twelve Apostles and Levi Edgar Young of the First Council of Seventy, wrote congratulatory letters. Howard Lamar, a towering figure in Western American history and president of Yale University, called *Great Basin Kingdom* "one of the great books on the West in the 20th century."[32] The book was placed in the president's library in the White House, "the only book dealing with the history of the Mountain West and one of four books on the history of the American West as a whole."[33]

But the review that mattered the most to Leonard came from a man who would be instrumental in his being called as church historian and would become LDS Church president just two months after that: "President Harold B. Lee assured me that '*Great Basin Kingdom* was a monument to LDS history, the finest thing on LDS history since B. H. Robert's *Comprehensive History* was first published beginning in 1906.' "[34]

IMPACT

The impact of *Great Basin Kingdom* extended—and continues to extend—well beyond the reviews and even beyond the content of the narrative. It has the distinction, reserved for only a few classics, of remaining in print today, more than a half-century after its initial publication. For one thing, Leonard's skill and persistence in the archives showed the way for generations of subsequent scholars. Gary Topping, an insightful literary biographer of Utah historians, pointed out: "Arrington's quiet persistence in working his way into and through the archives of the Mormon Church opened our eyes to the rich depths of the sources it contained, sources that no previous scholar had been able to exploit that thoroughly. For many years one of the most valuable parts of the book was its elaborate documentation, which called attention to previously unknown sources and suggested promising paths for future research."[35]

Of even greater value has been its role as a model of research and writing spanning the entire field of Mormon studies. Douglas L. Alder, a history professor at Utah State University, a president of the Mormon History Association, and an influential president of Dixie College perched on the southern border of the state, praised "the model of going to a major university, producing this stuff for a non-Mormon faculty, submitting it to a first rate press, getting it accepted and then . . . practicing on the premise that you work from documents and let the chips fall where they may. You're not defending, you're not promoting, you're not attacking. And of course all these other guys were going to do the same thing. Bill Mulder was doing it and Gene Campbell was doing it but they didn't have the national impact."[36] John Hughes wrote Leonard his own evaluation of *Great Basin Kingdom*'s long-term achievement. The book has, he commented, " 'in the fullness of time' achieved a tremendous victory in liberating the minds of young Mormons. They now know they have a heritage, and they know what it means. It is perfectly obvious that *GBK* has given them the intellectual framework, and they are building on it."[37]

Two decades after the publication of *Great Basin Kingdom*, George Ellsworth invited several colleagues to nominate the all-time best books of historical writing in the field of Utah and Mormon studies. While not a scientifically designed survey, it did garner the votes of thirty-five people in the field. Ranked first, by a considerable margin, was *Great Basin Kingdom*.[38]

9

THE ACADEMIC YEARS AND THE MOVE TO GREENER PASTURES

Children dream of their futures, of the place they will eventually occupy in the adult world. Leonard dreamed large. "Since I was a freshman in college, I have had visions, at various times, of becoming president, Church apostle, U.S. Senator, or the author of a great and lasting book on economics." But shortly after he arrived at graduate school in the fall of 1939, everything had changed. To a friend he wrote in a pessimistic tone rarely seen in his later life: "These dreams have all vanished into thin air. It would be intellectually, physically, and financially impossible for me to become any of these. You taught me to dream and you encouraged me, but now I know too much of the world—its cruelties, disappointments, and necessities—to dream."[1]

Four years later, and weeks after arriving in North Africa, he wrote to Grace of his scaled-down but remarkably detailed ambitions for life as a college professor. He wanted to settle in a medium-sized town of perhaps 25,000 to 125,000 inhabitants (for which Logan fit the bill). He wanted "a nice home & farm on the outside of the city." While he never acquired the farm, his dream of the nice home came true. He wanted to be "where there are some fine LDS people, who are intellectually inclined" (something that the presence of Utah State Agricultural College made possible). Finally, he wanted to be "where we can give our children the best opportunities & the happiest childhood." He also wanted to live in Idaho, and the city that came closest to his wish list was Boise.[2]

Leonard's inclination toward Boise was a combination of attraction to it on the one hand, and repulsion from other cities on the other. In Boise, "I feel we will be so much freer to do & say as we wish, with no external compulsion. . . . We are far enough removed from Salt Lake to be able to do and say as we please. Our living will not be controlled by the Church." Provo would be another option, but even though Leonard had never lived in Utah, he knew enough about the intellectual atmosphere to dread the prospect of living in the home city of Brigham Young University. "I'm afraid the intellectual atmosphere there would be stifled by the dogmatists of the Church. If the Church disapproves of certain portions of a book, we wouldn't use it for a textbook, etc. We would be criticized for not being true LDS, not having faith, etc."[3]

His enthusiasm about Boise began to wane, however, as he encountered LDS servicemen with whom he discussed the idea. In October 1944, he spoke with a lieutenant from Utah. "He thought I shouldn't teach at BYU, tho even there a teacher is much freer than is commonly thought—so he said. He thought A.C. [Utah State Agricultural College] in Logan would be swell, or if we preferred a large city, Salt Lake would be better & teach at U. of U [University of Utah]." Although the lieutenant had never been to Boise, he knew schoolteachers and professors there were very poorly paid and he saw little likelihood that their salaries would go up. "All in all, he could see little economic opportunity for progressive young people in Idaho. . . . Logan is an agricultural center & would be splendid for an agricultural economist & economist mixed. Also it would be a wonderful place for our country home. . . . [But] it will be hard to root me out of our plans for going to Idaho."[4]

Following up on that conversation, Leonard tracked down a Boise newspaper two weeks later. "I read it over very carefully . . . & its policy & items gave me the feeling that my ideas might not be welcome there, that maybe we'd be better off in Logan, Salt Lake, Ogden or some place a little less Provincial."[5]

A short time thereafter, he spoke with a Lieutenant Smith, "a dramatics teacher in Ogden," who strongly advised Leonard, "Don't settle in Boise or Pocatello, Idaho. The schools are only 2-year schools & are on very meager budgets. I'd never be able to advance far or support a family of 4. I'd have to be hustling for money all the time. There isn't much culture in those towns & I probably wouldn't be very happy." The lieutenant recommended Provo and Brigham Young University, but Leonard, in a letter to Grace, repeated his reservation about that university, that "this factor of freedom in teaching is important to me so I probably shouldn't teach there." That narrowed his top choices to Logan and Salt Lake City.[6]

Finally, he met an LDS chaplain in Italy just a month prior to V-E Day—"the first time since I've been overseas I met an L.D.S. chaplain." This unnamed chaplain "was a great big husky fellow formerly an All-American football player. He used to be with Utah State at Logan. He says Logan is a town of only about 12,000 and that most of the Professors have small farms. The climate is swell, he says, and most everything is grown in the valley. He says the college doesn't pay much but that it is growing. And besides the cost of living is very low."[7] Although Grace's letters of response have not survived, apparently she was uniformly encouraging and supportive and, as a southern woman, did not have a personal favorite among the western towns Leonard was mulling over. Had she known of the severity of Logan winters in comparison to the mild climate of North Carolina, she may not have been as supportive.

Leonard hedged his bets by applying to ten colleges and universities, including Boise Junior College and Brigham Young University, and two long shots in Stanford and the University of California–Berkeley. Given that he had only a bachelor's degree, it is not surprising that he was not offered a position at either California school. Four of the remaining eight offered him a job, the best of which was Utah State, which offered him an assistant professorship and a starting annual salary of $3,000. "I accepted the USAC offer, although I had never been in Logan and did not know anybody who lived there."[8] It was a practical decision and, as it turned out, a fortunate one.

Six months after returning from the war, Leonard drove with Grace across the country. "We drove through Sardine Canyon into Cache Valley on July 1, 1946. The valley was lovely, colorful, cherries showing red. Neither of us had been in Cache Valley before. We looked at each other and said, 'This is our valley!'" Housing was scarce in the immediate aftermath of the war. On the day they arrived, they looked at the only three homes in Cache Valley that were on the market. The following day they purchased one for $6,500. "We got a $5,000 GI loan and paid the rest down. Payments would amount to $50 per month for ten years. In 1956 we had it all paid off."[9]

LIFE AT UTAH STATE

Leonard settled in quickly, teaching a heavy load of at least sixteen hours per week on a campus and to a student body quite different than what he had seen before the war. The campus was cramped, as the G.I. Bill had doubled the prewar enrollment. There were not enough classrooms, laboratories, teachers, or beds. To address the demand, "USAC and other colleges brought in Quonset huts and surplus barracks. My first class was in an old barracks." But perhaps the greatest change was in the student body. "Some college traditions were suspended: the freshman beanie skullcap worn by entering freshman was unthinkable for veterans. No 25-year-old-freshman who had gone through the Battle of the Bulge and had a wife and two kids was going to put on a beanie cap." The veterans, eager to launch careers after the hiatus of the war, were model students. "Grade-point averages went up. Flunk-outs and absenteeism hit an all-time low. Classrooms and labs were used all day, even on Saturdays."[10]

Another marker of what was appropriate—or, in this case inappropriate—was Leonard's nickname. His boss felt that "Jimmie" was "not dignified enough" for a professor. In about 1947–1948, his second year of teaching, Dean William Wanlass instructed him to start using "Leonard." Wryly, Noah Arrington, though for reasons unknown, "also gave me $20 to go back to Leonard."[11]

Grace was still a Baptist when they reached Logan. There was no Baptist congregation in Cache Valley, but the rural city had both a community church and a Presbyterian church. Leonard and Grace easily worked out what seemed to be a reasonable and fair compromise, alternating between the LDS ward and one of the other two churches. "Reverend Miner Bruner [the Presbyterian] was o.k., but we had the impression that he and his congregation were more anti-Mormon than they were pro-Christian." After attending LDS services for two months, Grace announced her decision to convert. They drove to Twin Falls in September, where Noah Arrington, then an LDS bishop, performed the baptism. "We were in a kind of Shangri-la," Leonard wrote of their life in Logan. "It was precisely what I had hoped for and dreamed for. A rather simple, pleasant, informal life."[12]

Leonard's teaching duties covered the spectrum of economics: "advanced economic theory, income and employment, labor economics, money and banking, American economic history, history of economic thought, advanced monetary theory seminar, and several sections of principles of economics."[13] He taught in an era preceding student evaluations of faculty, so the verdict on his teaching performance came from later recollections: "He wasn't the most exciting teacher in the world," recalled Max Evans, later an employee in the Church History Department and also a future director of the Utah State Historical Society. "But you know what they say about economics, the 'dismal science.' So given the topic, he was pretty good. I've had better."[14]

It was clear to some that although he thrived on the overall academic experience, teaching was not his first love. Ross Peterson, a student and later a stalwart in USU's History Department, director of its Mountain West Center, biographer of Stuart Udall, and future president of Deep Springs College, recalled a class that was daring for the day: "I did take a class from him called 'Communist Economics.' We had about 25 or 30 in the class. He assigned two of us for one country, and then we had to give a 50-minute presentation on that country. I remember Leonard gave maybe the first lecture and the last lecture. I did Bulgaria. And that was the class. You learned a lot, but I think Leonard had a project going at the time. My impression of him, at first, was that teaching wasn't really his passion; especially teaching a course like that."[15]

Peterson's appraisal was astute. Leonard's passion lay in research and writing, activities relatively new to a land-grant college that did not become a university (renamed Utah State University) until 1957, more than a decade after he joined the faculty. In the early years he bootstrapped his research and writing while still carrying a full teaching load. "These were years when I had no research assistant, no secretary, and no research funds. Finally, in 1956, the University began to give me small grants, and over the years these became more and more generous."[16] The first grant, in the modest amount of $500, came from the University Research Council and provided support for six months on projects relating to "Economic Development in Utah after 1890."[17] Modest though the grant was, it was precedent setting, for the university had never before given monetary support to any research in economics or history.[18]

With continual support from D. Wynne Thorne, Vice President for Research, Leonard received grant money continually through 1971, thereby supporting dozens of students and staff in an enterprise of unprecedented productivity at the university. In a letter Leonard wrote Thorne shortly after leaving USU, he listed 153 publications that the research grants had made possible.[19] As Leonard's productivity increased—and as his interest in teaching waned—older colleagues in the department stepped in to free up more time for him. Doug Alder, then teaching in the History Department, saw it as an arrangement that benefited both him and his colleagues. "Utah State was moving, in those days, into becoming a major university. The old, senior faculty had been college teachers, and were not in the publishing business. . . . Leonard moved into that mold, that part of his load was his research. . . . But old Evan [Murray] and Vernon Israelson just said, 'You keep it up. We'll help. We'll step in for you.' "[20]

Leonard's research and writing were first-rate, although often more because of his intuitive skills than his formal training. Dwight Israelsen, who spent his entire career as a professor of economics at USU, later commented on Leonard's remarkable intuition.

> He was trained in economic theory in North Carolina, and it was his dissertation that moved him in the direction of economic history. . . . What I've done that is different from what he did is to use econometrics.[21] In other words, I've been able to get all of the data that he didn't have, but I had them because of him. And so a lot of the questions that were raised in his work on the economic history of the Church and of the West, I've been able to answer. I do not believe there is a single case in which I analyzed a question that he looked at in which he was wrong. He was right every time, in terms

of his understanding of what happened. And what I've done really is just simply to prove with the data that what he thought was correct. . . . So I guess what I conclude from that is that he was a really good economist.[22]

Leonard's dean, Robert Collier, approved of his innovation in cobbling together a research team primarily because it proved to be remarkably productive. In 1961, in a letter whose primary purpose was to inform Leonard of a salary increase, he wrote: "Without doubt, at present you are our most productive faculty member in the College of Business and Social Sciences in terms of scholarly and professional publications. I sincerely hope that this will continue in the years ahead and that administrative commitments will not lead you astray from your major professional interest of Economics and Economic History."[23]

Dean Collier's wish was more than either a pious hope or a strong hint. He obviously collaborated with Leonard in leveraging scholarly production as much as possible—certainly for the impressive statistics that the department could display for this college aspiring to be a university, but also out of genuine admiration for Leonard's work ethic, creativity in finding and managing important topics, and contributions he was making to his field. And if it was a hint, Leonard certainly seized it. Administrative commitments did not lead him astray, for the simple reason that he avoided them conscientiously. "I let everybody know I was not interested in administration and so no such posts were offered me at any time."[24] While this strategy helped while he was at USU, it returned to haunt him in his next career move, when he suddenly became a director within a large and complex bureaucracy, but with virtually no administrative experience and with few political skills to navigate minefields.

Transition to Mormon History

In the period between 1939, when Leonard began his doctoral studies, and 1952, when he received his degree, the field of economics underwent a dramatic transition. He had been trained in "qualitative and descriptive economics," so he regarded with some anxiety the "preoccup[ation] with quantitative economics—econometrics, statistics, and cliometrics.[25] I had published articles in the *Western Economics Journal, Southern Economics Journal, Journal of Economic History*, and the *Bulletin of the Business Historical Society*. But they became less and less interested in the kind of articles I wrote, and I was not prepared to do the kind of quantitative work that they preferred."[26] One obvious answer would have been to retool, but given his waning passion for economics, he instead moved laterally into a different field: Mormon history.

Three factors reinforced his shift. The first was the small study group that he and George Ellsworth had formed shortly after Ellsworth joined the faculty in 1950. Ellsworth was a historian by trade, and Wendell Rich and Eugene Campbell, the other male members of the group, were deeply immersed in Mormon history as director and associate director of the LDS Institute of Religion in Logan.

The second factor was an invitation in the early 1950s to join the "Mormon Seminar," a larger group being organized at the University of Utah by William Mulder and Sterling McMurrin. These scholars, attached in varying degrees to Mormonism, were applying the tools of their own trade to the field of Mormon studies, and Leonard could see himself fitting comfortably in that circle and adapting his own skill-set to its big questions. In 1984 when he recalled his own beginning interests in the field, he commented, "Although I did not attend all the meetings of this group, I did attend frequently enough to become acquainted with many prominent Mormon educators and scholars, particularly older ones whose primary contributions had been made during the 1920s, '30s, and '40s." While all members of the group welcomed Leonard, who would have been seen as a promising young scholar, and encouraged his research, one man in particular made a deep impression on Leonard:

> Perhaps the most satisfying commendation came from Lowell Bennion, director of the Institute of Religion at the University of Utah and probably the single most respected author and educator in the church. It was he who had started the process of my acquisition of a testimony of the truth of the Restored Gospel with his manual, *What about Religion?*, which I had studied as part of a Mutual assignment while I was still in high school. . . . Bennion wrote to me early in 1952, after having read four or five of my articles: "Leonard, we like your realistic yet constructive tone. We want to encourage you in this, hoping you can avoid the extremes of 'chip on the shoulder' on the one hand and trying to justify our mistakes on the other. Mormonism is hard to write about objectively and sympathetically. You are in a rich field that interests all of us."[27]

And the third factor was the reworking of his doctoral dissertation into *Great Basin Kingdom*. "The more I worked with my dissertation in preparing it for publication the more it became obvious that I must follow a chronological approach."[28] What began as a dissertation on economics became a book that examined Mormon history through the eyes of an economic historian. Although never formally trained in history, Leonard became a *de facto* Mormon historian—indeed, the most influential Mormon historian of his era, even though he always felt faintly uneasy with the title. Robert B. Flanders, then the preeminent and most professional historian in the RLDS Church, whose book *Nauvoo: Kingdom on the Mississippi* set a high bar for other historians, recalled an almost apologetic conversation with Leonard:

> He said to me on [one] occasion, "You know, Bob, I'm really not a historian. I'm an economist, I'm not a historian. I'm embarrassed when people call me a historian. . . ." I said, "Leonard, there's something you don't know about history. Anybody who writes history, particularly if they write history like you write history, is a historian. This slicing and dicing of academic disciplines breaks down when it comes to history. If you write history, you are a historian. And *you* are a historian." He said, "Oh." It was kind of like he didn't know that before. "I anoint thee historian!" Gosh, I remember that occasion as one of those very good things.[29]

While Leonard never referred to this specific incident, it likely was the starting point for his later and remarkable role in "anointing" others of varied walks of life—housewives, doctors, lawyers, English majors, even a dentist—to write history.

Although nearly everyone welcomed Leonard into the field of Mormon history, there were two notable exceptions: George and Maria Ellsworth. The man who had been his friend, mentor, and enabler remained the more precise historian, and Leonard always scrupulously acknowledged his debt to him; but George resented the limelight that shone on his protégé as Leonard's quantity overshadowed George's quality. It was a painful alteration in the relationship for Leonard, especially since part of the consequences hurt Grace as well. "After I returned [from Italy as a Fulbright scholar] in the fall of 1957, [George] became very cool to me. . . . Maria made some fantastic charges to Grace about my failing to recognize George satisfactorily in *Great Basin Kingdom*."[30] When it was Grace's turn to be nominated president of Faculty Women, Maria intervened and prevented it. This hurt Grace who thought she was entitled. "The Ellsworths were not happy with any of the honors that came to me. They thought I was not deserving."[31] Without rancor, Leonard acknowledged this regrettable chill in the relationship, but he made no effort to counter the charges or lend himself to what could have become an academic feud. A colleague who knew both men well later speculated on the possible cause of Ellsworth's animosity towards his former student and friend:

> I remember George was asked to do a high school history of Utah. In his office he had a board on which he had outlined every chapter,

every section, and gave word counts to every section. And this was before he was writing it. That's how detailed he was. What he produced was very good, but it was not voluminous. I think Leonard just blew him away, in terms of his productivity. . . . One of the lessons that Leonard taught me was to get it done and get it out.[32]

Another student who took classes from both men put much of the blame on Maria Ellsworth. "[Leonard] didn't know anything about history and spent a lot of time with George, picking his brain and getting a lot of information from him. . . . Then years later, Leonard becomes the famous one, and George is a very good and very effective history professor, but he really didn't get the attention that she thought he deserved."[33]

For his part, Leonard was always appreciative of George's mentorship and readily acknowledged his substantial talents, while at the same time understanding his limitations. He mused in his diary in March 1972, within his first year as church historian, "It is a characteristic of George that he always knows how to do things better than others and this is true—he does. He is a brilliant, imaginative person and whether it is doing carpentry work or printing or giving lectures or whatever the task, he can always do it better than anyone else, and because of this he gets bogged down in doing things that should not have high priority."[34] Although Leonard was sincere in his appreciation of George's strengths, the very fact that he understood, appreciated, and even complimented those strengths made it possible for George and Maria to feel insulted and diminished by his appraisal.

The two men managed to work together to found the *Western Historical Quarterly* in 1970, with Leonard as the founding editor and George as associate editor. Nonetheless, one outcome of the animosity was that Leonard never taught a class or even a seminar on Mormon or Western history in his twenty-six years at Utah State University. He commented ruefully, "It was strange. At a time when I was recognized as a historian and wanted to cross-list my economics courses that dealt with history, George opposed it. I was not a historian, had no degree in history, and the History Dept. would not dignify my teaching by listing it in their History offering. People often introduced me as a former professor of history at USU. This infuriated George who would never have allowed me to be listed as one of their historians."[35]

GREENER PASTURES

Leonard's daughter Susan recalled a conversation late in his life. "I asked him, not more than a year or two before he died, if he could go back and relive any part of his life, was there any part of his life that was happier than another? And he said, 'My happiest years were at Utah State.' "[36] But the idyllic life was not sustainable in the face of changing university structure and priorities, and by the early 1970s Leonard was capitalizing on his developing interest in Mormon history to make a critical lateral shift. Gary Hansen, who spent his career as a professor of economics at USU, spelled out the shift, including Leonard's strategy of concealing his anxiety behind his trademark optimism. As a result, when Hansen commented to Reed Durtschi, also a professor of economics at USU, that Leonard "left because he didn't feel he was wanted anymore, that there was no longer a place for him," Durtschi was so startled that he denied it by reflex. Hansen checked his perception in one of the short, self-published illustrated family histories Leonard had prepared during his retirement years,[37] which confirmed the accuracy of Hansen's memory. "Leonard was not appreciated when the new administration [of President Glen Taggart, in 1968] came in and wanted to merge the departments [of Economics and Agricultural Economics]. Their justification was that they wanted to have a Ph.D. program, and they needed to get a critical mass. But Leonard clearly saw the handwriting on the wall, that there was no place for him." In Hansen's analysis, that stimulated Leonard's desire to seek greener pastures. When the administration cut his research funding, Leonard got the message.[38]

In other words, Leonard's scholarship simply became obsolete within the framework of an increasingly research-oriented university. The primary fact of life for research universities is that dollars determine priorities. Neither the larger funding from outside sources nor the internal funding that had been the foundation of Leonard's very modestly priced research operation was to be directed towards economic history, the area of his passion and expertise. Research dollars looked forwards more than backwards, and Leonard's impressive track record of publications became largely irrelevant to current funding priorities.

At this point a new opportunity beckoned from Brigham Young University, the school about which Leonard had expressed such strong misgivings a quarter-century earlier. Charles ("Charlie") Redd, a prosperous rancher in southeastern Utah, was remembered by his son Hardy as having "greatly admired Leonard, as he did Juanita Brooks, because he told what my father thought was honest history. The implications of that are that my father thought that, oftentimes, church history was not completely honest. It wasn't that they didn't tell the truth; they didn't tell all the truth. So he admired Leonard." When the university began wooing Redd for a substantial contribution, Charlie and Hardy considered, but rejected, art acquisitions in favor of a history center. "My father said, 'We will do a chair *only* if Leonard Arrington comes down and occupies it.' BYU agreed, and Leonard agreed."[39]

Ernest Wilkinson, BYU's abrasive, ambitious, and ardently conservative attorney-president, likely would have preferred gifts that came without strings attached, but he was not going to turn down an endowed chair when one was offered, even if Redd set it up with a keen eye toward keeping the half-million-dollar endowment's independence. And so, in May 1971, Leonard received a formal offer from Wilkinson to become director of the Charles H. Redd Western Studies Center. Aware that Leonard was looking for opportunities in the Church Historian's Office as well as at BYU, he endorsed the possibility of a joint appointment. "We agree that in the event a dual appointment becomes possible that such appointment would be entirely acceptable to the University. Indeed, we would like to see the closest possible relations between the Church Historian's Office and the Western Studies Center."[40]

With the possibility, but not certainty, of something else emerging from those negotiations, Leonard accepted Wilkinson's offer, and then wrote a letter to his dean describing the new position and severing his ties to Utah State University. "It therefore becomes my responsibility, after 25 years of teaching in the Department of Economics of USU to resign from my teaching responsibilities in the Department, effective June 30, 1972."[41]

10

THE CHURCH
HISTORIAN'S OFFICE

The Mormon Church responds to growth the way organizations of any type tend to respond: conserve the *status quo* until it becomes sufficiently unwieldy that change becomes a necessity. Mormonism's *status quo* from its earliest days had been a bureaucracy that answered directly to the church president—essentially a monarchy wherein the president was both head of state and head of government. The Quorum of the Twelve Apostles served a staff, rather than line function. The church's chief financial officer during the 1970s and early 1980s noted, "I recall a discussion of the church organizational chart, which was overly flat with over 20 departments and agencies reporting directly to the First Presidency."[1]

As church growth accelerated dramatically during the early 1960s, some departments and agencies received diminished attention from the First Presidency. One example was the Deseret Sunday School Union—now known simply as the Sunday School—which functioned almost autonomously. Lynn Richards, who served on its general board for over three decades before joining its presidency, noted, "The Quorum of the Twelve and the First Presidency interfered very seldom with the actions of the General Board and the Presidency of the Deseret Sunday School Union. . . . We were pretty much independent, of course, knowing what was expected of us. . . . We decided who would write the manuals and who would do the traveling."[2]

A similar situation existed in the Church Historian's Office. Joseph Fielding Smith, the senior member of the Quorum of the Twelve, who had succeeded David O. McKay as church president in January 1970, had become church historian in 1921 and remained in that office until McKay's death. After publishing *Essentials in Church History* in 1922, Smith viewed the primary mission of the office as acquisition, with little emphasis on cataloguing and even less on writing new history. Employees consisted largely of family and friends including Smith's brother Alvin, and Earl Olson, grandson of former Assistant Church Historian Andrew

Jenson. According to longtime Historical Department employee and future Utah State archivist Jeffery O. Johnson, Olson "started there when he was in high school, because Andrew Jenson was crabby and no one could work with him."[3] Although completely devoted to Joseph Fielding Smith and to the church, none of these staff members had professional training in the field. Much of the collection had never even been catalogued. Johnson described a subject-only filing system. For example, "There would be a folder for the Kirtland Temple, and it might have a newspaper article from the 1920s, or a letter from Joseph Smith."

Johnson, whose training was in library science and who had been hired in 1969 to catalog manuscripts, recalled the shape of the argument cycle: "Earl [Olson] thought we shouldn't do registers. Of course, I would argue that that is what professional archives do. His argument to me was, 'We are different than other archives. We are the Lord's Church. We don't follow what they are doing.' I remember him opening the Doctrine and Covenants and reading me scriptures. But I would make registers, because we knew that was right." Olson changed when his colleagues convinced him to accompany them on a training trip to the National Archives in Washington, D.C. "When he came back, he wanted us to know that the right thing to do was not what we had been doing, but to create registers!"[4]

Even if a scholar knew what materials to look for, the atmosphere in the archives was often less than supportive. Davis Bitton, who later became assistant church historian with Leonard, noted, "The horror stories about the old days when Alvin Smith and Will Lund reluctantly opened the gates of access, screened notes, and on occasion helped a generation or two of scholars are true enough in general, as many of us can testify."[5] Another scholar, Leo Lyman, concurred: "I had been in the Church Historian's Office when I was working on my master's degree in 1967. Old A. Will Lund was literally looking over my shoulder at my notes." Lund was then approaching his nineties, so Lyman took the long view: "I went home and told my wife, 'I can wait until those old duffers are gone.'"[6]

Suspicious treatment was not restricted to outside scholars, perhaps the most dramatic example being when Dean C. Jessee, employed by the Church Historian's Office in 1964 and unquestionably the leading expert on Joseph Smith documents, was chastised for having written on the sensitive subject of Joseph Smith's "First Vision"—notwithstanding the fact that the article was published in the scholarly journal of the Mormon Church's own university. His supervisor wrote him a panicked and angry rebuke:

> You have had published photographs of manuscripts which I have been instructed not to talk about. I have no record of you being signed up to do such research, thus you have gone contrary to the

policies set up by Pres. Smith and the Asst. Historian's. Who gave you clearance for such a writing? . . . What am I going to answer the First Presidency when they enquire of me as to what has been done? . . . Why was I bypassed in knowing of such a thing being done? I suspicioned that you were doing some writing as other work was being left undone, but not having evidence I could do nothing. Please put in writing your answer so I might present this to the First Presidency for their files and I might be cleared of any responsibility in this matter.[7]

Jessee, duly chastised, provided the necessary documentation and apologized but published a follow-up article, "The Original Book of Mormon Manuscript," in the same journal exactly a year later in the spring of 1970.[8]

Although the supervisor's explosion occurred in early 1969, by the middle of the 1960s N. Eldon Tanner had already begun to effect a quiet but significant change in the Historian's Office. One of his colleagues said of him, "He had more common horse sense than anybody I ever ran across, and he certainly knew how to bring people together."[9] After being called into McKay's First Presidency in 1963, Tanner began to acquaint himself with the Historian's Office and publications in the field of Mormon history. Leonard recalled, "He held several meetings to discuss historical literature, acquaint himself with LDS scholarship, and explore how to encourage research with Dr. Lyman Tyler, a historian who was then director of libraries at Brigham Young University." Tanner held several meetings with Tyler, who on one occasion brought along Leonard. "President Tanner was very friendly, asked me many questions, and seemed interested in my answers. I sensed that he had an understanding of the frustrations historians felt about obtaining access to materials in the Church Historian's Library and Archives and that he sympathized with my arguments about the need for more openness."[10]

Six months later in June 1966, Tanner extended Leonard a dazzling invitation to take a leadership role in Mormon historiography: "We sincerely appreciate your willingness to take the leadership in encouraging Mormon scholars to produce positively written articles and monographic studies of 'Mormon Social and Religious Institutions in the Twentieth Century.' We realize that research is very demanding in time and effort and would suggest that you consider your participation in this program equivalent in importance to other major assignments you have held in the Church. If you feel that I can be of assistance I shall appreciate having you call on me."[11]

However, the offer came without the critical element of support funds—only permission to give this project precedence over a time-consuming ecclesiastical calling such as a bishopric or stake presidency. Furthermore, the timing was bad. Only a few weeks after receiving the letter, Leonard moved his family to Los Angeles where he spent a sabbatical year at UCLA. He had not ignored or brushed off Tanner's offer, however; and he soon received a second invitation that made it possible for him to see how to combine writing a book and simultaneously achieving the goal of a more open policy in the Church Historian's Office. He wrote to Tanner in January 1967, reminding him of the earlier meeting with Lyman Tyler. "During the past few weeks I have been exchanging correspondence with Alfred A. Knopf, of the Knopf Publishing Company, who has been urging me to write a history of Utah and the Mormons. Such a book, he writes, would 'fill the biggest single gap in Western history,' and he is very interested in publishing it." The clincher, as noted in an earlier chapter, was that Leonard needed greater access to the archives than was then possible.[12]

With this relatively concrete proposal, Tanner acted quickly to change, albeit on a small scale, the playing field in the Historian's Office. Leonard recounted that he was in his office at UCLA after hours on Friday afternoon when the phone rang. "The caller identified himself as Nathan Eldon Tanner—President Tanner— and he said, 'We in the First Presidency have been reviewing your letter and you will be getting a letter soon giving you permission to have full access to the material in the Church Archives to do this book.' "[13]

The promised letter followed only a week later, evidencing both Tanner's common sense and diplomacy. "With President Joseph Fielding Smith's approval I am authorized to tell you that it will be quite in order for you to arrange with Earl Olson of the Historian's Office to use material available in that office and library."[14] Tanner did not stop with this single project. "In the years that followed," Leonard continued, "unsolicited invitations were sent from the historian's office to several Latter-day Saint scholars (and a few others) to conduct research in the archives. These included James B. Allen, Davis Bitton, Truman Madsen, Kenneth Godfrey, Richard Anderson, Charles S. Peterson, T. Edgar Lyon, Robert Athearn, and Donald Moorman—the latter two not church members. President Tanner had taken a major step in opening the archives to earnest and established historians."[15]

HOWARD W. HUNTER

Upon the death of David O. McKay in January 1970, Joseph Fielding Smith became the new church president and, with reluctance, gave up the position of church historian which he had held for five decades. Replacing him was Howard W. Hunter, a member of the Quorum of the Twelve who had spent his earlier professional life practicing law in Southern California. Archivist Max Evans, who was hired after Hunter's appointment, explained the change: "Howard Hunter brought an entirely different sense of what the church historian's office should be. . . . He had an interest in making it a much more professional place than it had been. When I went there were no policies about what you let people see and what you didn't. There were absolutely no policies—it was all completely arbitrary. People would come in, and if they liked the looks of you, you'd get in."[16]

One major change was that access to documents, which had begun to ease in selected cases because of Tanner's actions, became even more open. D. Michael Quinn, whose career would intersect archival developments for the next four decades, became Davis Bitton's research assistant after returning from a three-year stint in Germany with U.S. Army Intelligence. He noticed the difference in tone and attributed it to Hunter. "I don't know how soon it happened, but it happened quite soon, within months. Howard Hunter as Church Historian, possibly without consulting in advance with Joseph Fielding Smith, opened the archives completely. They had *never* been completely open. It had always been on a who-you-know basis. One person would come in and Will Lund would dog their notes and review them, all these horror stories that would occur. Howard Hunter changed all that in a stroke. He opened the archives." As an example of the openness, Quinn described an occasion where he was reading the diaries of church president Heber J. Grant, while the non-Mormon scholar from Princeton University sitting next to him was reading First Presidency files from the 1880s. "*This* is how open it was!"[17]

Old habits die hard, however, and on occasion vestiges of the old order emerged. As they did, Hunter intervened to manage the transition. Richard Bennett, who worked as a teaching assistant for Marvin Hill of BYU's History Department, recalled one memorable episode:

> Ninety-two-year-old Will Lund was there when I began. . . . I remember vividly working on a microfilm. We were comparing the Manuscript History of the Church with the published *History of the Church*, word-for-word. Brother Lund came shuffling by and he peered over our shoulders and said, "What are you two doing?" Marvin said, "We're working on the *History of the Church*." He just looked at it for a moment, and then he leaned over and yanked off the reel from the microfilm machine and said, "You cannot do this!" Marvin was very patient. He didn't get upset. Then we went into the office of Brother Hunter, and he very kindly said to Brother Lund, "This is a new day, Brother Lund, a new day." He let us go back and use them, and he gave Brother Lund a big hug and said, "Don't worry too much about this. It will be okay."[18]

Other changes implemented by Hunter involved structure rather than policy. Of particular importance was that new hires were made on the basis of professional expertise rather than relationships. For instance, although Max Evans was hired as "a regular processing archivist," he quickly sensed that Hunter had a different vision for the archives. "He started to bring in people who had advanced degrees. . . . After about a year they brought me to Washington and let me go to the Modern Archive Institute, a two-week class. I came back and said, 'You know, the way we're doing things here is all wrong.' I started telling them what was wrong and what we ought to do to fix it, and they started listening to me. After about a year they made me a supervisor over all the people that were processing historical records."[19]

A NEW CHURCH HISTORIAN

Hunter had already sown the seeds of major administrative change when, on August 24, 1970, he met in his office with five prominent Mormon historians: LaMar Berrett, chair of the Department of Church History at Brigham Young University; James Allen, professor of history at BYU; Reed Durham, director of the LDS Institute of Religion at the University of Utah; Davis Bitton, professor of history at the University of Utah; and Leonard Arrington. The purpose of the meeting was to discuss the organization and function of the Church Historian's Office. The most important recommendation that came out of the meeting was summarized in a follow-up letter to Hunter that Leonard drafted on behalf of the five guests: "As we stated in our meeting together, we wholeheartedly endorse a member of the Quorum of the Twelve as the Church Historian. . . . We feel equally strongly the advantages to the Church of naming as an additional Assistant Church Historian a Latter-day Saint who is a recognized professional historian, and the desirability of granting to him a budget, which would make possible an historical program, which would give intellectual status to the Church and its history, as well as carry out the commandments of the Lord as contained in the revelations."[20]

Unbeknownst to Leonard, Davis Bitton, who was then president of the five-year-old Mormon History Association, put his thumb on the scale: "I took it upon myself . . . to write a letter . . . recommending Leonard Arrington" to be the proposed professional assistant church historian. "Unsolicited," he insisted. "Totally unsolicited. . . . I didn't think there was a chance in the world that [any higher appointment] would even be remotely possible. Certainly, others may have suggested the same thing. I don't want to claim that I was *the* cause of this. But I do mention the fact that I wrote that letter."[21]

The letter was unrestrained in its enthusiasm for Leonard. "The more I have thought about this the more firmly convinced I have become that Leonard Arrington would bring a combination of qualities that no other Latter-day Saint historian can come close to duplicating. He is by all odds the most important historian working on our LDS history." Bitton emphasized that Leonard's stature was not tied merely to *Great Basin Kingdom*. "His productivity as a scholar is without parallel. . . . This man is held in the highest regard by the history profession. . . . He knows personally practically everyone, LDS or non-LDS, who is currently working on any aspect of our history."[22]

Hunter made no direct response to the letter, but by April 1971 a decision had been made to select a professional historian as the new assistant church historian. The remaining questions were who would be chosen and when the announcement would be made. That month, at Hunter's request, Leonard met privately with him for a conversation of "more than an hour about the Historian's Office, about the best persons to direct the research and publications program, etc." Leonard described this meeting to son Carl, then serving a mission in Bolivia, as "very pleasant" but also as somewhat mystifying. "Never once did he ask me anything about myself, my work, or my own interest in the position." Although such general interviews were fairly standard in an ecclesiastical setting where a bishop or stake president would sound out a prospective counselor in general terms but not tip his hand, it was radically different from a standard job application or employment interview. Leonard did not press but reported Hunter's assurance that the First Presidency would announce the appointment in "about two or three weeks."[23]

But "two or three weeks" turned into nine tense months. Leonard's appointment to the endowed chair at the Redd Center for Western Studies at BYU was confirmed in May but remained unannounced. In essence, Leonard held the endowed chair but could not occupy it. Month after month, through the spring, summer, and into the fall, Leonard confided in his weekly letters to Carl that he still considered himself in the running for the job. He was keeping his ear to the ground and was virtually certain that no one else had been offered the position. In late September he wrote to Carl with mingled impatience and hope: "General Conference will be this weekend, and there is back in our minds the possibility that they might want to sustain a new Assistant Church Historian. But so far no word on it."[24]

But conference came and went with no announcement. In November, Leonard received an update from Robert Thomas, a vice president of BYU. "He told me that BYU was all ready for the announcement of the Redd Chair" but that Brother Hunter "asked them to hold up the announcement for a couple of weeks" since "they still hadn't completed their discussions with the First Presidency."[25]

Leonard must have speculated on causes for the delay. Was the increasingly frail Joseph Fielding Smith too feeble to follow through on the discussions to make a decision? Even though Hunter sounded confident that the creation of the new post of assistant church historian was firm, were other apostles balking? Had Leonard himself been found wanting? Or were proponents of different candidates deadlocked?

Two weeks later, just before Thanksgiving, Leonard's hopes brightened. "I have been told [that] Brother Hunter has recommended my name for a dual appointment as occupant of the Redd Chair of BYU and Assistant Historian for the Church."[26] Yet he heard nothing from Hunter or anyone else in the hierarchy. Leonard was in limbo but had no idea why. The reason was an intriguing administrative development that was taking place under the radar. It would result, among other effects, in the creation of the Correlation Department, which had a bruising impact on the pursuit of professional Mormon history, and, ironically, in Leonard's appointment as church historian.

THE CRESAP REPORT

In April 1971, a year after Hunter became church historian, the church engaged Cresap, McCormick & Paget, one of the leading consulting firms in the United States, to examine the structure, policies, and practices of the church headquarters organization and make recommendations to modernize them. Four months later, while Leonard fidgeted during the long summer with no news, Cresap submitted its report. In the first one-volume history of the church to be produced by Leonard Arrington's new team, James B. Allen and Glen M. Leonard summarized, "The Cresap report pointed to the obvious problem that General Authorities had become too heavily burdened with administrative responsibilities, and it recommended that most administrative functions be turned over to full-time managing directors. General Authorities, and especially the First Presidency and Quorum of the Twelve, would thus be freed to attend to their roles as spiritual leaders and policymakers."[27]

Harold B. Lee, the seventy-two-year-old president of the Quorum of the Twelve and a counselor to nonagenarian Joseph Fielding Smith, was the driving force behind the report. According to his son-in-law and biographer, Lee took it with him over Thanksgiving weekend in 1971, just two weeks after Elder Hunter had assured Leonard that he was recommending him for the joint appointment of assistant church historian and the Redd Center's endowed chair. The Lees were observing the holiday at "the country home of relatives," meaning that Lee could be uninterrupted by telephone calls or the work on his desk at the office. By the holiday's end, he had "put together an outline of proposals for strengthening the missions of the Church and for restructuring the work of the Twelve. He defined the staff and administrative roles of the Assistants to the Twelve and the First Council of Seventy, who would be asked to assume the direct administrative load of supervising the departments of the Church." Based on the Cresap report and incorporating some suggestions from other General Authorities, the Lee proposal "was the beginning of major changes in the administrative functions of the General Authorities."[28]

Part of Lee's plan was to release Hunter as church historian—as other apostles would be released as department administrators—and replace him with a professional historian. It was a move unprecedented in the history of the church. Apparently Lee had done whatever lobbying he felt was necessary between August and November with the other General Authorities to gain their approval for the reorganization of the Church Historian's Office. Hunter, who had no idea that the apostolic mantle would be lifted from the Historian's Office, welcomed Lee's proposal and worked with him over the next few weeks in identifying whom to call as the new church historian.

Hunter paid a visit to historian Richard Bushman, then a professor at Boston University and president of the Boston Massachusetts Stake. It was a low-key, half-ecclesiastical/half-tourist visit. According to Bushman, Hunter "just wanted my thoughts about church history. And I remember taking him to Widener Library," Harvard's flagship library with more than three million volumes. The next stop was Harvard's Houghton Library, a specialized library within Harvard's library system designed especially to house rare books and manuscripts. Richard reported that he "extoll[ed] the architecture of Houghton, which I pitched as an endorsement of the scholarly enterprise, that you try to create space that honored the whole practice of history writing. I realize probably he was interviewing me, but I didn't see that at the time. I took him at his word, and I was just telling him about history."[29]

Meanwhile, back in Utah, Harold B. Lee phoned Stanford Cazier, then in Utah State University's History Department but preparing to accept the presidency of Chico State University in January 1972. (Eight years later, he would return to USU as its president.) When Lee "wanted to know what kind of a man Leonard was," Cazier "gave him absolute praise. I said, 'That is a quality person. He is a good member of the Church, and his star is going to rise.' He didn't ask me about the Church Historian's Office, at all. But he asked me what kind of person [Leonard] was, and I said he was a first class kind of human being, intellectually balanced and with incredible energy."[30]

By January 1972, probably in the first meeting that year of the First Presidency and the Quorum of the Twelve, they reached and ratified the decision: Hunter would be released as church historian, and a professional historian would replace him. N. Eldon Tanner, the other counselor in the First Presidency, was asked to extend the calling. "On 5 January 1972," Leonard wrote, "President Tanner telephoned me in Logan, asking me to come see him at my earliest convenience."[31]

11

A Portrait of Leonard

Physical Presence

- "He was short enough to be non-threatening, but not short enough to be comical."[1]

- "We saw you on TV last night for the first time. My Dad says not to worry. You are a lot smarter than you look. Anyway, I want you to know that I'm going to be a historian myself some day. My Dad says I should finish grade school first, because I need an 8th grade education to be as smart as you. In school tomorrow we have a test about polecats. I think of you often. Sincerely, Your Nephew."[2]

- "We could talk about Leonard's sartorial sense. He had that absolutely shapeless tweed jacket that he wore forever."[3]

- "I remember the time that he came in with four big pastry boxes. He put them on his desk and called the office staff. He'd just stand at the door and say, 'Everybody come! I finally tipped the scales at 200 pounds, and we're going to share it!' He had chocolate pies. Unfortunately, he tipped the scales going up, not going down. But it didn't seem to worry him."[4]

- "The thing is he was such a presence, this little round Santa Claus with a big grin. That's the way you always think of him."[5]

- "Leonard surprised me because I didn't even know what he looked like before that. Somebody of his accomplishments I sort of thought would be tall and slim and maybe kind of austere. But he was nothing like that, and he was very much enjoying just being one of the guys there. Not a whiff of pretense, pompousness, or anything of the kind. It was just really a great introduction for me, not only to Leonard but to the world of Mormon history."[6]

- "First meeting. I remember we made a date to meet in the lobby of the Muhlbach Hotel, which is where the convention was. I went there

89

looking for Leonard, and I couldn't find him. I was looking and looking and looking, and I couldn't find him. All of a sudden, a voice from down here [gesturing towards the floor] said, 'Hi. I'm Leonard Arrington.' I realized, as I reflected on it, I was looking for a giant!"[7]

INFECTIOUS OPTIMISM

The single word that best describes Leonard's personality is *optimistic*. "From as early as I can remember I had a positive attitude toward people," he wrote in a letter to his children in 1995. "I had confidence in them, trusted them, felt goodwill toward them. . . . This attitude was bolstered by Mormonism. Man was a potential god. A child of God with good qualities and the capability of extraordinary goodness."[8]

While scores of LDS Church members could share Leonard's theological optimism, he was able to do what few adults are able to do: maintain childlike optimism throughout life. "He just had one of those innocent personalities that you read about," commented a longtime friend, Mary Bradford, a leader in her own right in the Mormon intellectual community and a staunch supporter of the New Mormon History, particularly during the years she was editor of *Dialogue*. "Psychologists talk about the innocents that can go through life, and everything washes off of them, and they inspire people and don't even know it."[9] "He insisted, almost to a fault, in seeing the best in everyone," observed a student secretary who also became his daughter-in-law. "He probably read Machiavelli, and he didn't believe it."[10]

Elbert Peck, longtime editor of *Sunstone*, liberal Mormonism's foremost magazine, was living in Washington, D.C., when he met Leonard. He and a friend drove Leonard "down to Williamsburg on I-95, . . . plying Leonard with all these questions about Mormon history. We couldn't get Leonard to say a bad thing about anyone. He just didn't dish dirt." The closest he came to it was when Peck commented disparagingly about a well-known scholar "who would hold these things [documents] and *never* share them." Leonard couldn't refute it and uttered about that individual "the worst criticism [he] made the whole day": "Well, you couldn't say that he was a collaborative person, could you?"[11]

His optimism was infectious, shaping the environment in which he worked and endearing him to coworkers. Lavina Fielding Anderson, an associate editor at the *Ensign*, which published many of the first articles of the new History Division, commented: "Whatever it was, it always delighted him. He always seemed to have such relish for what he was doing. I think that's why there was such a positive attitude in the division. People weren't afraid of him, even though they probably had reason to be. There was no sense that they were doing anything inappropriate. . . . When you work for the Church you see a lot of stuffed shirts. . . . Leonard was so real. . . . I wanted to be Leonard when I grew up."[12]

Leonard's unstinting affection for an interest in others, combined with his passion for history, was fully reciprocated by his staff. Perhaps the ultimate compliment is that they felt free to tease him, knowing that he would laugh the longest in this parody of a Gilbert and Sullivan ditty:

The Modern Church Historian

(Solo)
I am the very model of a modern Church Historian,
In matters economical, doctrinal, and folklorian.
I know the Mormon leaders and I write their prosopography
With research that enlarges and illumines their biography.

I've studied men and women both quixotic and mercurial,
I tend to favor those like me, somewhat entrepreneurial.
I've drawn my own conclusions about Brigham Young's maturity
And analyzed investments of the Eccles' First Security.

(Chorus)
He's analyzed investments of the Eccles' First Security,
He's analyzed investments of the Eccles' First Security,
He's analyzed investments of the Eccles' First Securi-curity.

(Solo)
I've also dabbled quite a little bit in social history,
The arts and letters of the Saints provide a lot of grist for me.
Since I can chant "Come, Come Ye Saints" just like a true
    gregorian
I am the very model of a modern Church Historian.

(Chorus)
Since he can chant "Come, Come Ye Saints" just like a true
    gregorian
He is the very model of a modern Church Historian.

(Solo)
I'm very good at research and I know historiography
As well as hermaneutics and statistical demography.

I know the folklore: the Three Nephites, and Jim Bridger's ears of
    corn,
The so-called White Horse Prophecy and Porter Rockwell's locks
    unshorn.

I'm awfully well acquainted too with matters economical.
In this Great Basin Kingdom throughout all its chronological
Development, I understand its finances and enterprise.
I've counted ev'ry thing in sight from Sunday eggs to railroad ties.

(Chorus)
He's counted ev'ry thing in sight from Sunday eggs to railroad ties
    (etc.)

(Solo)
I'm very well acquainted too with issues in theology,
I understand statistics, mystics and phenomenology.
Since I can Bible bash with any Institute scriptorian
I am the very model of a modern Church Historian.

(Chorus)
Since he can Bible bash with any Institute scriptorian
He is the very model of a modern Church Historian.

(Solo)
In fact, when I can write a book devoid of all tendentiousness,
Accept awards and accolades without the least pretentiousness,
When I have learned the ins and outs of writing up a grant
    request,
When I explain with utmost tact polygamy post-manifest,

When I can smell a controversy brewing and put up my guards,
When I can spot a phony Salamander at a hundred yards,
When I am granted access to the archives of the DUP,
Then I'll deserve a pardon and an honorary PhD.

(Chorus)
Then he'll deserve a pardon and an honorary PhD. (etc.)

(Solo)
When I learn that I need more than a scholar's normal bag of
    tricks,

Especially a healthy grasp of bureaucratic politics,
In matters economical, political, folklorian,
I'll be the very model of a modern Church Historian.

(Chorus)
In matters economical, political, folklorian,
He'll be the very model of a modern Church Historian.[13]

Assuming the best in everyone put Leonard in a position of being able to see the best parts of opposing arguments—the stuff of which mediation is made. He viewed himself as a natural-born mediator[14] and placed great stock in an unusually vivid dream in November 1984, a painful moment in personal and historical developments. Although parts of it puzzled him, it strongly reinforced his self-image and he recorded it in detail:

> I dreamed that I was with a large number of people. I do not recall who any of them were, but I have the impression that they were all Latter-day Saints. They seemed to be on the verge of splitting. It is not clear to me what the reason for the schism was. Was it ideological? About to form separate organizations? Was it in anticipation of a trip, with one group going one way and another group another?
>
> At any rate, the essence of the dream was my talking to everyone—people in both groups. I was trying to get each group to accommodate to some of the wishes and desires of the other group. I was trying to get the Liberals to trim down their views to accommodate to those of the Conservatives. And similarly trying to get the Conservatives to modify their position to accommodate the Liberals.
>
> In a way, this has been my stand, whether it was at the University of Idaho among Greeks and Independents, whether at Utah State University among agriculture and science faculty and the faculty in the social sciences and humanities, whether at the Church Office Building among the Iron Rodders and the Liahonas.[15]

In addition to allowing him to mediate disputes as a third party, his optimism propped him up when he was a party to a dispute—particularly the dispute that eventually resulted in the disassembly of the History Division. Davis Bitton, one of his two Assistant Church Historians, recalled, "In private with me, he was never depressed, in the sense of, 'What's the use?' . . . During the closing period in the Salt Lake operation here, when there were these negative signs and it looked like we were coming under sharp criticism and might be forced to cut back on our staff, and might have to fold, he would always emphasize the positive. 'We're still here. We've had no announcement.' "[16]

And yet, too much optimism in the face of a strategic threat can leave one vulnerable, in a state of denial. "It cost him," Mary Bradford observed. "It always costs you a lot." She saw denial working against Leonard in his refusal to "have his defenses up" as manifested in his insistence that "he was chosen Church Historian and sustained in General Conference!"[17]

GREGARIOUSNESS

Richard Howard, the Church Historian of the Reorganized Church of Jesus Christ of Latter Day Saints (RLDS), recalled meeting Leonard: "I didn't really know what to expect when I met Leonard. He was such an open and friendly, gregarious kind of person. It was magnificent to be in his presence. He was eager to meet people and connect with them on a level deeper than small talk. I just had a marvelous first impression, and then second, third and fourth. Then, in 1972, he became the historian of the LDS Church."[18]

Even when Leonard became historian of the LDS Church, his demeanor did not change. Maureen Ursenbach Beecher, the first woman he hired for his division, recalled that, when his employees wondered how to address their boss in that protocol-conscious ecclesiastical environment, the answer was always the same: " 'Call me Leonard!' He wasn't even going to be addressed as 'Brother Arrington.' When I was his secretary I said, 'Are you Doctor, Professor, Brother? What are you?' He said, 'I'm Leonard!' I said, 'I know you've told *me* to call you that, but what about on the letters?' 'I'm Leonard!' "[19]

D. Michael Quinn, whose idea of a good time was doing research twelve hours a day, mused, "I had no idea what friendly was until I saw Leonard in action, greeting people and all."[20] And when he greeted people, he drew them in and made them part of his world. "If he read anything we wrote, he would send us a note. I'm sure he did that with everybody; we weren't even his closest friends."[21] Leonard's interest was in learning about other people and what they were doing, thinking, and writing—not in letting them know who he was.

Jill Mulvay Derr, another of his employees whom he enthusiastically mentored, appraised Leonard's rare quality of spiritual stature:

> He was always eager to learn. If there was something new, he wanted
> to know about it. It was a kind of humility and curiosity that is
> rare in a scholar of that kind of stature. . . . He was quick to ac-
> knowledge and praise anything. Whatever you had written that was

published, if it was your birthday, if he happened to think of you out of the blue—he would know, after I left, that I was working on a project, and he would send me money from the Mormon History Trust Fund, along with a letter of encouragement. It was always "Bravo" for the person who got out an article, or won an award, or gave a great presentation. He was always there to show his enthusiasm and support, and give you a big kiss.[22]

Leonard reached out broadly to engage anyone in the field of Mormon studies, regardless of credentials—or lack thereof. The latter group, enthusiastic about Mormon history but lacking formal training in the subject, has always been part of the mix at annual meetings of the Mormon History Association, and Leonard made it a point to reach out to these "history buffs." One example was G. W. Willson, an architect, who reminisced happily about their first meeting. "I was rather unknown, and we were standing in line to get our tickets at one of the conferences. He reached out to me, asking who I was and what my interests were and where I hailed from. . . . There are a lot of people who run around here with their nose in the air. They are not very interested in making contact with new people. You see them everywhere; they are a dime-a-dozen. But it is unique and extraordinary that a man of his stature would reach out to an ordinary person."[23]

Howard Lamar, president of Yale University and a towering figure in Western American history, saw Leonard through the eyes of an Easterner and an "outsider"—a non-Mormon:

I've never known anybody that I thought was so open to ideas and to meeting different people. He was always exploring. . . . Everybody thought he had total integrity, and so he was trusted. Nobody ever said, "That Mormon, Leonard Arrington." They said, "Professor Arrington." They had great respect for him. . . . We would talk, but it wasn't narrowly on Mormon history or Western history. It was on what were the issues of the day, politics and so on. I can't remember him ever expressing a firm anti- or pro- opinion of some big issue; rather, he just analyzed it.[24]

History meetings provided a particularly useful forum for engaging groups interested in Mormon studies, and Leonard took advantage of the opportunity for years. James B. Allen, his other Assistant Church Historian, recalls seeing Leonard at work from the 1950s, prior to the founding of the Mormon History Association. At meetings of the Association of American Historians or the Western History Association, Leonard would inevitably seek anyone from Utah and then announce, "We've got to have a rump session." The format was set: "It started out small, maybe 10, but sometimes there would be 25 or 30 people there. He would want to go around the circle and find out exactly what everybody was doing. He wouldn't rest until he knew what everybody was doing. . . . Unless you understand that part of his personality, you don't understand him."[25]

Of particular significance was his ability to reach out to "the other," regardless of what that meant. As already noted, one important "other" was the RLDS Church which, for over a century, had engaged in low-level theological warfare with the LDS Church that Leonard represented. Missionaries from the two churches perennially attempted to raid each other's flocks, and the few converts in either direction were viewed as prizes. But not so with the historians, and the radically cordial personal and professional relationship they shared was built largely on Leonard's outreach to individuals. Alma Blair, one RLDS historian, explained a typical encounter with Leonard: "I told my wife, 'He is very friendly,' so we went out and ate at his house [in Salt Lake City] one time. Here he came running across the lawn to meeting us—he kind of waddled when he ran—and he grabbed my wife [Kaye] and gave her a big hug. I said, 'I told you he is friendly.'" The initial meetings between the two groups of historians were a bit tense. "We weren't too sure about Mormons, and Mormons weren't too sure about us. But Leonard was open and smoothed the way for us to talk to each other, and to talk to each other in a friendly fashion, and to learn from each other. I think he was the oil that smoothed all of those possible problems out."[26]

Paul L. Anderson, a Princeton-trained architect whom Leonard funded for a summer to start listing historic meetinghouses in the Mormon corridor, attended his first Mormon History Association meeting in 1974. That year, it was held in Nauvoo, Illinois—long contested territory for the two churches—and he remembered it as a watershed event. "There was a sense in that Nauvoo meeting that everyone was happy to see each other. This really was the first group of people who had genuinely friendly relations between the two churches. They were so delighted to find out they could be friends, that they had so much in common." Anderson had a "real sense that the fondness was made especially precious because it was such a surprise that they could get along and like each other."[27]

Because of Leonard's gregarious influence, MHA meetings began to gain the name of the "Third Church"—one that met only once a year, where members of both churches, and of neither church, not only intermingled, but also worshipped together.

Leonard showed a particular sensitivity toward those of either tradition who were viewed by some as pariahs. One such person was Martha Sonntag Bradley, who resigned her faculty position in Brigham Young University's History

Department only weeks before a half-dozen intellectuals—thereafter known as the "September Six"—were excommunicated from the LDS Church. "After I quit BYU, I was sort of a pariah for a while. Leonard would invite me to parties. He would have a party where all the people from the Joseph Fielding Smith Institute would come to his house, and he would invite me. . . . . So he really made a point of being inclusive in a subtle, social way. He brought me along, and it meant so much to me, because there was a time when I wasn't good enough for a lot of people."[28]

Someone who *was* excommunicated as part of the September Six in 1993 was Lavina Fielding Anderson. Leonard and Harriet, his second wife, immediately sent her a living plant, sparkling with silk flowers. "The plant's still alive," says Anderson. "The flowers are still beautiful." But what puts a lump in her throat to this day is the fact that Leonard invited her and her husband to the History Division's Christmas party at his home and asked her to give the opening prayer and blessing on the food: "Since praying in a public Church meeting is one of the things specifically forbidden by excommunication, he could not have said in stronger terms that I had a valued, even a cherished, place in his world."[29]

The RLDS tradition doesn't excommunicate, but it does silence and exclude. For Robert Flanders, the road to pariah status involved his doctoral dissertation, which eventually was published as the groundbreaking *Nauvoo: Kingdom on the Mississippi*. While the book's focus was the entire history of the Mormon city, members of Flanders's church focused on the one issue that had largely defined their tradition: polygamy. "That was the only thing that was of concern or interest. Who knows what they thought, because nobody was telling me. . . . Nobody ever told me. It was as though either people were embarrassed to bring it up, or they hadn't read the book, or they were scared to think about it—or all of the above." Against that backdrop of shunning, Leonard's outreach shone brightly. "I think Leonard invited me to have dinner with him, which was probably a hamburger. And then, we went to his hotel room and talked until four o'clock in the morning. Remembering this is an emotional experience for me. This is the first person that I had really had to talk to. Through all of this, I hadn't had anybody opposing me, but I hadn't had anybody with me, either."[30]

The exclusion was so thorough that Flanders, deeply hurt and sorrowing, joined another church and turned away from Mormon history for decades. It was a healing moment—one Leonard was not alive to see—when Flanders began attending Mormon/Community of Christ history conferences again and delivered a moving address in 2002, "Nauvoo on My Mind."[31]

HUMOR

Optimism and humor are not always coupled, but in Leonard's case, they were close companions. He knew how to tell a good story and relished doing so in small groups or large. Mormon history—particularly Brigham Young—provided ample grist for his humor mill. Elizabeth Dulaney, editor of the University of Illinois Press who handled the Mormon titles for decades, recalled one of Leonard's favorite stories: "It's the one about the Mormons traveling across the plains with Brigham Young, and arriving at the Salt Lake Valley. Brigham sent a scout on to check it out, and the scout came running back saying, 'Brigham! Brigham! We've found the perfect place. There is a beautiful lake, and nothing to do but fish and make love!' Brigham said, 'Salt the lake!' That's just the way Leonard told it."[32]

On occasion, Leonard would use the past not just to tell humor, but to create it. The darkest episode in Mormon history was the Mountain Meadows Massacre in southern Utah, a grisly episode in which Indians attacked a train of Arkansas travelers en route to California. The emigrants held them off with few casualties, but the local militia—Mormons acting under the leadership of ecclesiastical figures who were also militia officers—pretended to rescue the travelers, disarmed them, separated the men from the women and children, and walked them out, each escorted by a Mormon rifleman. At the shouted signal, "Brethren, do your duty," each Mormon killed the traveler he was accompanying, followed by a slaughter of all of the women and children over the age of seven or eight. The Indians were still being officially blamed for the massacre more than a century later, even though historians knew that the actual situation was much more complex and fraught. Amazingly, Leonard used situational humor to defuse this emotionally burdened situation. Alma Blair, who taught history, including denominational history at the RLDS Church's Graceland College for most of his career, still chuckles at Leonard's spry approach:

> We were going to St. George for the Mormon History Association. We had stopped at Parowan and had a lecture there. The fellow was talking about that thing [the massacre], and opening up the problems of what had happened, and there were a lot of people there who were not members of the historical group. They were sitting there with their faces turning white, because they were learning about this thing that they had never really touched before. Juanita Brooks had written about it, but most of them had never read it.[33]
>
> Then from Parowan, we went down to the Mountain Meadows. Well, we had to walk single-file, or two or three together, and got

strung out down through this dry creek bed; and Leonard said, in a loud voice, "Brethren, do your duty!" We just . . . laughed like crazy.[34]

Everyday life—and death—sometimes provided the stuff of humor. To his children he wrote: "Since I want Susan, along with James and Carl, to be among my pall bearers, I just thought of a story I once heard of an aged woman who had never married. She left instructions for her funeral service, insisting that there be no male pallbearers. She gave the reason: 'They wouldn't take me out when I was alive, and I don't want them to take me out when I'm dead!' "[35]

And his wife Grace recalled in her autobiography that Leonard could find humor in his own misadventures. "He came home from work one day with his pants split wide open—and what's more, it showed. When I told him about it he just said, 'No wonder I've felt so cool today; a little ventilation really helps!' "[36]

But the most frequent source of humor was the LDS Church's "Word of Wisdom," a dietary code that, on its surface, is unambiguous in proscribing the use of tobacco; but ambiguous on alcoholic beverages, forbidding "strong drinks" but not defining the term; ambiguous on the definition of "hot drinks"; and silent on what did not exist in 1833: carbonated beverages. The American Temperance Movement, which began in 1826 and provided the environment from which the Word of Wisdom emerged, proscribed "strong drinks," defined as distilled spirits because their high alcoholic content promoted drunkenness, but not wine or beer; and "hot drinks" because of their temperature, and not their chemical content. In early decades, church leaders and members generally interpreted the Word of Wisdom along similar lines, but more restrictive proscriptions including wine, beer, coffee, and tea were defined by the late nineteenth century, albeit inconsistently enforced. Carbonated beverages remained in legal limbo, with some high-profile church leaders condemning caffeinated soft drinks at the same time that even higher-profile church leaders consumed them.[37] Stiffer Word of Wisdom compliance became an issue of boundary maintenance in the 1930s and became even more important as Latter-day Saints scattered across the United States in the 1950s.

Leonard's wartime experiences in North Africa and Italy had included the consumption of wine; and while he always maintained an active "temple recommend" in later years, one element of which was adherence to the Word of Wisdom, he managed on occasion a workaround. Jan Shipps, proclaimed as the Methodist "den-mother of Mormonism," recalled hearing a Word of Wisdom story from a mutual historian-friend, Klaus Hansen: "Leonard came to see them when Klaus's children were little. One of his children went up to Leonard and said, 'What's in that glass?' Leonard said, 'Yesterday it was probably wine, and tomorrow it will probably be wine. But *today*, it is grape juice!' "[38]

Leonard did not drink coffee, on which there was no leeway, but being sensitive to the dietary preferences of occasional non-Mormon houseguests—usually members of the RLDS Church, for whom coffee is not proscribed—he made it available, albeit with unintended humorous results. Paul Edwards, a great-grandson of Joseph Smith III, had his favorite coffee mug emblazoned with the quotation from the revelatory statement: "They shall run and not be weary." He recalled that Leonard "used to keep a jar of instant coffee in his kitchen cupboard. The poor man and his wife didn't realize that after a couple or three years, you might want to get a new jar. I'd show up at their home, and she would go make me a cup of coffee. It was atrocious! But boy, I drank it!"[39]

Coca-Cola, however, was in a different category, and here Leonard led by example, as Maureen Beecher recalled: "We went up to a [staff] retreat in Park City, and took with us our managing director, who was Earl Olsen. We were sitting at two long tables, and all of us were wanting something to revive us. The difference between a lapsing Mormon and a real Mormon is the temperature of their caffeine. So Leonard said, in a big loud voice, 'I'd like a Coke, please. A big one!' Of course, up and down the line, then, the Cokes were ordered."[40]

Well aware of the curiosity that the Word of Wisdom represented to non-Mormons until campaigns against tobacco and alcohol kicked in for health reasons in the 1970s, Leonard employed hyperbole that Bob Flanders recalled with relish. The occasion was a meeting of the Agricultural History Association, at which Leonard had just given the presidential address. "There was a party afterward in his suite. The sugary drinks flowed! I said, 'Leonard, on a celebratory occasion like this, do you ever break over and celebrate?' 'Oh,' he said, 'yes, I do! If it's really special, I'll have a little glass of Coke!' And then he kind of looked around and said, 'And if it's *really* special, I'll put in a drop of lime juice!'"[41]

From the 1970s on, caffeinated soft drinks could not be purchased on church properties,[42] but Leonard winked at the regulations. One of daughter Susan's favorite stories is Leonard's deliberate "naughtiness" in bending this rule when he had to work late in his office. "This secretary was staying there to help him. He came out at a certain time and said, 'Could you go across the street and get me a can of Coke?' So she went across the street, got the Coca Cola, and put it in a brown paper bag and took it into the building. He took it, disappeared into his office, and maybe 45 minutes later came out, put the empty Coke can in this brown paper bag, stapled it shut, and dropped it in the garbage."[43]

As he prepared to move the Historical Department from its old quarters in the Church Administration Building to the newly completed Church Office Building in 1972, he reflected on his new perks—and on the idealized future state that he contemplated. "In the new office building the managing authorities have their own toilet facilities—and their own refrigerator where they can keep their own Coke. The Millennium—where Mormons can drink Cokes in front of each other."[44]

Work Ethic

Leonard's professional passion was writing—not teaching, and not administrative work. His massive bibliography[45] attests to his devotion to writing and reflects the work ethic necessary to produce such a record. Although the personal computer was a standard office fixture many years before his death, he remained steadfastly committed to an earlier form of writing. His son James recalled:

> I believe that his writing style, on that old, manual Olympic typewriter, was a kinesthetic way that he wrote. He couldn't write on a computer. He could write longhand, but that was notes. His way of writing was on that old thing, and he got into a rhythm as he would type. You could hear it, and it had to do with slapping back the carriage. He had this rhythm that he would write in, and I believe that he stayed writing on that old Olympic because he liked to do that. With a computer, you don't ever do that. To him, it was some kinesthetic part of the physicality of writing. Writing was a physical thing for him. When I finally figured all of this out, it was when I was trying to get him to change over to a computer. To me, the computer changed everything. Boy, what a difference it made! I love to write on a computer, but I tried to force him to put his fingers on a computer keyboard, and he wouldn't even put his fingers on it. He just didn't want to change his style. It's like some people who write movie scripts on yellow pads, by longhand. They develop a way to do it, and that's the way they do it. My father had that kinesthetic need of creating that rhythm with that bell and that shifting. Somehow, it was necessary for him to write that way. [But] he put more words and notes and speeches and articles out of that old Olympic than all of those other guys did on their computers, because he never let up.[46]

After becoming church historian, Leonard wrote at night out of necessity, because there simply wasn't the time during working hours. But in his Utah State years, with his children still at home, he wrote at night by choice. His daughter, whose bedroom was next to his, remembered, "Literally every night I went to bed hearing that manual typewriter go, and that little bell at the end that says it's time to return the carriage. Almost any time of night, if I got up for whatever reason, he was in his study." Susan never bothered to ask her father what the typing was all about. "It wasn't until years later that I had any idea what he was doing. In fact, I have a book downstairs, *Mormons and Their Historians*, that he and Davis Bitton did together. When Dad inscribed the book to me he wrote, 'Now you know what all the late night typing was about.' "[47]

A break—of sorts—in this routine came when Leonard was pressing to complete a project, at which time he shifted from all-night to all-day-and-night. Doug Alder in USU's History Department recalls: "When they built this new home [in Logan] he had a study in the basement. He had all these files of articles that he was putting stuff in and thinking about and getting ready. When he got to the point that he was ready to write the article, he would go down into that office and stay there for 72 hours. His wife would bring him food. He would not take telephone calls, he would somehow not be on campus for three days; and he'd come out with a draft."[48]

Grace, while generally supportive, had her limits: "Leonard has strong powers of concentration, and perhaps this helps to explain why he has been able to write as much as he has, both at the office and at home. If he is working on something and I come up and kiss him, he just pats me on the head as if he were reaching out to pat a puppy. Sometimes this preoccupation gets to me and I rebel against his failure to pay proper attention to me."[49] Unfortunately for the reader, Grace chose not to elaborate on the nature of her rebellion.

The Emotional Leonard

"He wasn't sentimental," commented Richard Bushman, who wrote the most definitive biography of Joseph Smith. "He didn't fill the air with sentiments. He filled it with good feeling and cheer, but if you asked him a question he'd come up with some concrete incident, some fact. His mind was just stuffed with all these realities."[50] Leonard possessed a spectrum of emotions, but controlling some and expressing others proved at times to be a challenge. In a rare example of introspection, from a time when the History Division was under assault by ecclesiastical authorities, he wrote candidly about the things that brought out the emotional man. "Grace has wondered why I don't enjoy the 'Waltons' or 'Little House on the Prairie.' These stir up too many emotions. I cry too easily, or get apprehensi[ve] so easily. These touch things which are dearest—family, personal values, religion, integrity, etc. Perhaps one reason I like opera is that, while it stirs fundamental emotions, it does so without maudlin sentiment, and it all wells up toward a climax where one can feel justified in releasing his emotional feelings."[51]

At times Leonard responded to a potentially trying situation orally, but not verbally, drawing on the example of his father Noah, who would spit in response to traumatic situations. "When a horse fell in the mud and broke his leg, when my brother injured his hand when fixing the cultivator, when the tire of our Model T Ford went flat, when our dog was run over by a passing car," Noah's reaction was silence. "He wouldn't say a word; he just spit."

Leonard's adaptation of Noah's nonverbal expression was to start laughing, a habit of such long standing that he tried without success to explain its genesis. "I have done this for so many years that it has become habitual. It comes automatically. When I spilt milk on the rug the other day, I caught myself chuckling, and laughed because I was laughing about a 'disaster.' When I stub my toe against the bathroom door, when I read a stupid letter to the *Deseret News*, when I misplace a book I need or break a glass, I let out an involuntary chuckle. I suppose if I came home and surprised a thief, I'd let out an involuntary chortle that would perplex him just enough to hold off shooting." He supposed that he reverted to laughter because the usual conduit for extreme emotions, swearing, was inaccessible. "Neither of my parents swore, so I didn't. It was also bad form to show anger. So I cloaked my unhappy moments in humor. Humor was my armor against hard emotions. If it was a distortion of truth, it was at least a happy escape, not an angry one. And it was better than striking out against an innocent bystander—a spouse, a child, a friend. It was also, as I tell myself, better than my father's habit of spitting."[52]

His daughter recalled that the response of others to his laughter was not equally jovial. When Grace was "really mad," she might "throw a pan or something across the kitchen." Rather than sympathy or attempts to soothe her, Leonard would say, " 'Well, Momma,' and he'd stand just laughing. It just drove her nuts."[53]

On rare occasions, Leonard allowed tears to sweep him into deep waters of soul-stirring emotion. He recalled two such instances, both of which were major game-changers on the world history scene. On November 10, 1989, he wrote his weekly letter to his children and described seeing on television one of the iconic moments of twentieth-century history, the tearing down of the Berlin Wall. "The whole thing came out like the projection of a beam of light, like the news of an important victory for which we all had prayed. I burst out in tears and went in to tell Harriet and could hardly choke it out. It was the first time I had been affected this way since June 9, 1978, when I learned that the First Presidency had announced the revelation giving the Priesthood 'to all worthy males.' "[54]

While the separate elements of Leonard's personality may be appreciated in isolation, his overall persona was far greater than the sum of its parts. He was a complex, fascinating, engaging man who approached work and life in a manner unique even within his extended family. He was well equipped for success in a university setting, but the next stage of his career was as much ecclesiastical as academic. What he brought to that stage was often in sharp contrast to the buttoned-down, often dour personalities of the ecclesiastical officers to whom he would answer.

12

WALKING A SPIRITUAL PATH

Religion defined Leonard's entire life, both personal and professional. He was born a Latter-day Saint, lived a Latter-day Saint, and died a Latter-day Saint, but his upbringing outside of Utah, his graduate education in the East, and his war experiences all worked to shape a religiosity that was genuine to him but atypical of the Mormons among whom he worked and lived once he began his career. Indeed, not until 1946, at age twenty-nine, did he live among the Great Basin Mormons with whom he spent the remainder of his life.

FORMATIVE YEARS

Although Leonard was born and raised in a Mormon family, his contact with other Mormons was limited by community—few Mormons lived in Twin Falls during his formative years—and by geography—the Arrington farm was several miles from town, and for most of Leonard's childhood the family transportation was a horse-drawn buggy.

Noah Arrington held positions of leadership in the Mormon community, serving for years as a member of the stake (diocese) high council and later as bishop of the Twin Falls Ward; but while he served faithfully in those callings, he did not imbue his family with religious zealotry—indeed, quite the opposite. Leonard described them as being "not a strongly religious family; by that I mean that we didn't bend the natural pattern of our life to religious observance. If it was necessary to water on Sunday, we did so. If it was necessary to thresh on Sunday, we did so. And of course we had to feed the stock and milk the cows on Sunday, and Sunday was the usual day for breeding horses, etc." The church's monthly observance of fasting, which in most Mormon homes meant going without food and drink for a day, was interpreted differently in the Arrington household. "Mom used to give her growing children something to eat Sunday morning. She used to say, 'We fast on bread and butter.' " Because the family lived on a farm a few miles from the city, the children never went to Primary (the church's auxiliary organization for the children) and rarely to the Mutual Improvement Association (the organization for teenagers). Their record of attendance at Sunday meetings was better, but not flawless. "We seldom attended Sacrament meeting in the evening, but always went to Sunday School. Remember that we were 4 miles from town, almost 5 miles from the Tabernacle, and my father usually had the buggy or the car for his high council trips." Leonard remembered his parents as being loyal to the church and living church standards, "but they were not fanatics nor preoccupied with religious principles and practices."[1] They set a standard that Leonard adopted.

Although scripture study was not part of the family routine, Leonard determinedly read the Bible and the Book of Mormon all the way through when he was thirteen—a feat he never repeated again.[2] He was unenthusiastic about the King James Version of the Bible because it "was in a strange and unfamiliar idiom"—and so was the Book of Mormon, which not only quoted hundreds of verses from the King James Version, but whose prose closely resembled Jacobean English. Thus, his early foray into the scriptures did little to shape his religious self-awareness and nothing to cause him to think that his religion, at least within the Twin Falls area, was in the minority. But what the scriptures did not teach him, school did. He recalled a classmate in junior high school who was Roman Catholic. "Just to be clever or witty or something one time I called her 'cat-licker.' A fellow who heard me called me down for it; said how would you like to be called 'Mormonee'? For the first time, I suppose, I realized that I was considered, as she was, as part of a minority group. I was careful never again to make fun of a person's religion. Indeed, I had not recognized that I was doing so then."[3]

At the same time Leonard's awareness of other religions began, he experienced the first of three epiphanies over a period of two decades that defined a personal, extrachurch relationship to God and allowed a nuanced relationship to Mormonism. It occurred in the summer he turned thirteen. "I had gone through a long day of hard work and had gone to bed at twilight. I read for a while in the *Boy Scout Handbook* and *Two Little Savages*. I gazed at the stars and saw blackbirds flying toward their roosting place among the cattails below Shoshone Falls. Suddenly I was overwhelmed by a feeling of ecstasy, of connectedness, of intimate kinship with the world and its human, bird, and animal inhabitants." He felt that God was smiling upon him and encouraging him, and he "had a feeling of acceptance and self-validation in an affectionate environment." And in sharp contrast to the often-dour portrayals of religiosity that he saw in worship services, his was consistent with his own joyous demeanor. "I was having an enhancing experience of the holy, and the holy was not somber; it was happy, festive, even playful. People often weep during such experiences; I was smiling—even chuckling with pleasure. How fortunate to get this feeling of intimacy with the spiritual universe! How fortunate to get this feeling of self-worth!"

Having had this experience, he immediately empathized with the young Joseph Smith. "I now knew for certain that Joseph Smith had had mystical experiences. Not only was it easy for me to understand his experience, but I felt a certain kinship with him. Not only that, I could feel more confidence in myself. God had acknowledged me, had given me self-assurance; I could move confidently ahead to do the many things I wanted to do." When times got tough, which was particularly the case when his History Division was under siege, he would refer to this early experience to remind himself that in addition to "the formally taught belief system, inculcated behavioral standards, and procedural discipline of the church 'here below,'" he could lean on "both the joy and wonder of subjective manifestations 'from above.'"[4]

Not long after having this epiphany, Leonard began an intellectual wrestling match with his religion that continued throughout his life. He accepted that he was "wired" for questioning, and while he was passive in school, "where we were supposed to accept what the teacher said," he considered his religion to be fair game. "I would say that my spirit of questioning arose from my Mormonism. Questions in Sunday School, in MIA, in Priesthood quorums. Far more questioning than in school."

A signal event in his life of questioning came when a neighbor gave him a birthday present, *Joseph Smith, An American Prophet*, by John Henry Evans. "The book portrays Joseph Smith as a person with an open mind, a questioning mind, a person in pursuit of education and knowledge. I accepted this as representing the spirit of Mormonism, and still hold to it."[5]

COMING OF AGE AT THE UNIVERSITY

The process of spiritual maturation that began in Leonard's teens accelerated with his matriculation at the University of Idaho. Earlier he had learned that there were other faith traditions beside his own; now he learned to accept and even embrace the "other," a lesson many of his coreligionists were never able to absorb. The "teaching moment" came quickly. Having been schooled by his mother to despise agnostics, one of whom was an uncle for whom she had no good words, he found that his first college roommate was agnostic. "What a thought! I was to room with one who would go to hell! But when I saw him I found that he was built the same as I: he did not even have horns or a forked tail! I grew to like him—I liked an agnostic! Today I possess the same ideas of God that I possessed when I came to college, but I no longer hate those who disagree. I respect them.

I tolerate them." And he was able to generalize his feelings, accepting through-out life not only those outside his faith tradition, but also those within whose beliefs and actions differed from his own—even the general officers who became his nemeses. "I no longer hate those who disagree; I respect and tolerate those persons. Most of all, I tolerate and respect the ideas and opinions which these people possess. That is what counts."[6]

George Tanner, director of the LDS Institute of Religion, reinforced the lesson. Similar to Leonard and different from most of his coreligionists, Tanner had experienced religion outside the often narrow confines of the Great Basin, earning a graduate degree at the University of Chicago Divinity School. He taught Leonard the lesson he had learned: to be a Christian first, and a Mormon second. "There are so many Mormons who give first emphasis to the unique or distinctive doctrines and practices of Mormonism. And this is wrong, very wrong, if we are in truth restored Christianity."[7]

Leonard's struggle to "own" his religion through intellectual wrestling, which began in his early teens, came of age on the college campus. For him, it was the only legitimate approach. "Those who have asserted that conversion comes only thru the Spirit—it does not come through the mind—are wrong. Or at least my own conversion was not the product of action by the Spirit, unless it can be said that the Spirit works through the mind."[8] At the core of his quest was honest doubt. "I have heard many, many people say that they have always known that the Church is true; at no time have they had any doubt that the Gospel is true. . . . While unquestionably this is the experience of most active Latter-day Saints, it was not mine. I have undergone the experience of deciding whether the Church was true, whether Jesus was a great man or a Son of God, whether Joseph Smith was an inspired religious teacher and prophet or leader who deluded people into following him."[9]

Leonard's road through these questions to a decision by which he could steer his life was intellectual—a legitimate road, but one foreign to many of his coreligionists, who relied (and rely) more on feeling than intellect. Leonard did not denigrate the legitimacy of religious conviction based upon feeling, nor did he rule out feeling as part of his own conviction. Nonetheless, he made it clear that intellect was the key to his own. He reflected on his own spiritual development in a 1983 essay that began with a frank assertion:

> Let me confess at the beginning that I believe the intellect is enormously important—more important than the heart, more important than tradition. If my mind could not confirm the truth of my religion, I would be disturbed, uncertain, and confused. Nevertheless,

as you will see, I feel very comfortable with poetry, music, art, drama, testimony, ritual, ceremony, and other expressions of religious feeling and thought. I am also comfortable with people who contend that religion is a matter of spirit, not mind, and that testimonies can come only through the assurances of the Holy Ghost.[10]

The serenity of that assertion came at what could have been a low point when he was assailed by doubts and resentments—two years after Grace's lingering illness and death, and a year after his History Division had been shut down and its surviving personnel moved to Brigham Young University. Instead, he turned to the foundation of his belief, which was faith that spiritual knowledge was accessible by intellectual means. He gave credit to George Tanner for having helped him initiate that process of intellectual conversion. "He oriented us on 'the Higher Orientation.' This had been around for about 100 years, but was new to me, as it was to most LDS students. This is the literary-historical study of the Bible, seeking to determine such factors as authorship, date, place of origin, circumstances of composition, purpose of author, and historical credibility of each of the writings, together with the meaning intended by their authors." Some of Tanner's professors at the University of Chicago had been pioneers in this approach to biblical study, and Tanner assigned his students some of their books. "It was perhaps the most satisfying intellectual experience of my life—to be able to reconcile my religious beliefs with the very finest scholarship. It was satisfying for me permanently because I have derived enormous pleasure through the years reading the Bible as books, as writings, as spiritual narratives, as history, as poetry."[11]

Leonard read widely, not only the books recommended by George Tanner, but also a broad spectrum of nonfiction and fiction that included works by Mormon intellectuals such as James E. Talmage, John A. Widtsoe, and Lowell Bennion; Christian philosophers, notably John Henry Newman; and religious and philosophical novels such as Samuel Butler's *The Way of All Flesh* (1903), Somerset Maugham's *Of Human Bondage* (1915), and George Santayana's *The Last Puritan* (1935).

But the most important was another of Santayana's books: *The Life of Reason: Reason in Religion* (1905). Raised in a church that took primarily a fundamentalist viewpoint of the scriptures—that the scriptures were inerrant, not self-contradictory, and contained only literal truth—Leonard had already come to realize that such a viewpoint could not withstand the scientific scrutiny of historical-critical methodology. *Reason in Religion* became his Rosetta Stone for deeper understanding. He bought his own copy in 1937, not an insignificant purchase for a student who did his own laundry by hand. "The book was very influential for me; it helped me to see that one might be a sincere believer in Mormonism and at the same time accept the findings of the brightest intellects, whether in philosophy, or science, or the humanities. In particular, *Reason in Religion* helped me to understand that it isn't important whether certain religious or theological affirmations are truths in a literal sense, or whether they are true in a symbolic or poetic sense." The ability to see truth as being both symbolic and literal, and to understand that one kind did not work against the other, set Leonard apart from most of his coreligionists. Indeed, he went the next step by realizing that both kinds of truth are essential to a balanced faith. "While religious doctrines may be right symbolically, they should not be substituted for scientific truth. At the same time, those who accept scientific truth as the only truth, as the final truth, end up substituting inadequate personal symbols which are unsatisfying and unedifying." Santayana introduced Leonard to the ideas of "myth" and "mythical truth," concepts that continue to escape many of his faith tradition. As a result he had "no difficulty in trying to harmonize religious assertions with scientific 'truth.'"[12]

The ability to view scripture either as history (such as the book of Kings I and II and the book of Acts) or as allegory (such as the book of Job and the book of Revelation) allowed Leonard to embrace its layers of truth while at the same time accepting scientific insights, such as an earth billions of years old and evolution as the process driving the development of progressively higher life forms, that others had to brush aside in order to cling to a strictly literalistic view.[13] The tutelage provided by the books he read and his mentor George Tanner equipped him well to deal with a modernistic view of the world, and Leonard praised the "intelligent and sweet reasonableness" of Tanner's approach. He looked forward to the thoughtful openness and well-informed perspective that prevailed in Tanner's Institute of Religion classes. "When we raised questions about the theory of evolution, about mechanistic psychology, about modern criticism, he responded with long, educated answers that reinforced our faith." Almost fifty years later, he still quoted Tanner's maxims: "'Our faith was built on the firm rock of truth. Truth is truth, and the Lord never requires us to believe anything that is not true,' he would say. We thus came away from the University with the truths of secular learning and the truths of the Gospel in perfect harmony."[14]

While this reminiscence, written four decades after the fact, likely portrays accurately the rather smug self-assurance of a college graduate, Leonard found later that, while secular and religious truths may be in perfect harmony, determining what is entitled to the label of "truth" is an extremely difficult, sometimes impossible, and always threatening process. Years after college, as will be described later in this chapter, Leonard found himself unable to reconcile scientific truth regarding the Book of Mormon with what he assumed to be elements of its religious truth. Indeed, the interface between science and religion over the past century is largely the story of religious assertions retreating in the face of scientific discovery, a story that Leonard's black-and-white college worldview was ill-equipped to process.

Later misgivings notwithstanding, Leonard set out to confront three basic questions about his own Mormon tradition and the larger Judeo-Christian tradition from which it emerged: Is there a living God? Was Jesus a teacher worthy of being worshipped? Was Joseph Smith a prophet deserving of allegiance? Significantly, not on his list then when his exposure to Mormonism was limited, or even in his sixties when the kind of exposure he had would have sent many believers into withdrawal, was the key question: Was Mormonism really the "only true and living church upon the face of the whole earth" (Doctrine and Covenants 1:30) as its leaders, missionaries, and members assented to as revelatory?

In an essay that he wrote and published four decades later, he described his collegiate struggle with faith. The first question—is there a living God?—occupied his attention from his freshman year at the University of Idaho until his third year of graduate school, a bracket of time that also included his three years in the army. "I acted as a believer, and was willing to assume there was a loving and powerful Creator. But I was not satisfied until I had studied the matter through and came to a conviction that my intellect could defend." He read extensively, paying particular attention to a church lesson written by Lowell Bennion, *What About Religion?*, that portrayed Mormonism as representing truth and enlightenment, rather than superstition and ignorance. "The manual also quoted with approval Brigham Young's statements that we accept truth no matter where it comes from, that Mormonism comprises all truth including truths that are taught in the various arts and sciences, and that there is an indissoluble relationship between religion and learning. These became articles of my religious faith and continue to remain so." By the third year of his graduate work, he had satisfied himself about the existence of God, and he "never seriously worried about it since."[15]

Two things are significant about Leonard's question concerning God. The first is that his answer came after seven years of study—a marked difference from many of his coreligionists whose conversion stories are often compressed into months, weeks, or even days. The second is that his question dealt only with the existence of God, and not with His attributes. Leonard's focus on the broad outline enabled him to respect and even empathize with variable views of Deity embraced by others.

His second question also was framed in a way distinctive to himself: "Was Jesus a teacher worthy of being worshipped?" And his answer was far more pragmatic than that of more literalistic believers. He had begun thinking about Jesus Christ "when I was still in high school," but his concept remained inchoate and shapeless until, once again, George Tanner refocused him on a search for Jesus as a person, as a historical figure, as a leader. "He introduced me to new translations of the Bible and I read through the New Testament versions of James Moffatt and Edgar Goodspeed, and Richard G. Moulton's *Modern Reader's Bible*. These were very helpful and I still use them. At his suggestion I also read Shirley Jackson Case, *Jesus: A New Biography*; Ernest Renan, *The Life of Jesus*; Albert Schweitzer, *The Quest for the Historical Jesus*; and James E. Talmage, *Jesus the Christ*." As with the first question, his intellectual engagement gave him the answer that he sought—"that Jesus was, indeed, a historical figure; that the values he taught were as good as mankind had ever devised; and that his life provided a model worth imitating in meeting the difficult problems one encounters in this complex world."[16] And also, as with the first question, he plowed around a question that was central to the faith journey of most of his coreligionists and, indeed, most Christians: Was Jesus the divine Son of God whose atoning sacrifice offers salvation to all?

To the third question—"Was Joseph Smith a prophet deserving of allegiance?"—his answer was both affirmative and contextualized. Yes, he concluded, Joseph Smith fit well within the traditional role of a prophet as one who speaks in a voice to call people to God's work and to a higher level of living. However, he saw Smith in an inclusive, rather than exclusive, context, as one of many in the same tradition, and not necessarily standing apart from the others.

While later incidents in Leonard's life, notably the kneeling prayer offered in his office with his colleagues as he began his tenure as church historian, demonstrated his awareness of the power of prayer, his personal record is silent about what role, if any, it played in shaping his religious persona during his formative years. Leonard's conversion came about "as the result of study and thought; it was not the result of sudden intuition, or a vision, or inspiration, or feeling of repentance." In consequence, he reacted strongly to those who attempted to denigrate the intellectual approach: "My own experience as a university student and professor suggests that the emphasis on the spirit, the 'put down' of the intellect, does a disservice to religion in general and to Mormonism in particular, for it suggests that religion—Mormonism—cannot be intellectually supported; its support rests on an emotional basis; one must put one's mind aside to accept its truths. This is palpably false. Or at least this is my own experience."[17]

Decades later during retirement, looking back on his long career, Leonard lamented the ascendancy of anti-intellectualism in the LDS Church, particularly in the ranks of the church's corps of professional religion teachers who, in his estimation, knew better, for they "were brought up, as I was, to believe that there is a close relationship between religion and intellect. . . . Faith, we were taught, was consistent with thought, learning, and the use of the intellect. This is still primary in my belief and in the belief of my friends and associates, but I have seen a retraction from it among various younger educators who give greater emphasis to Scriptural literalism."[18]

Religion in a Foxhole

Although Leonard spent three years in Africa and Italy during World War II, he was never in combat. Nonetheless, he had a front-row seat and his views of religion were shaped not only by his own experiences in combat zones but also by the narratives of fellow soldiers. In 1943, he wrote candidly to Grace, "I have talked to men who were under fire—heavy fire, when large numbers were killed. They confirm Gen. MacArthur's statement, 'There are no atheists in foxholes.' In the foxholes & slit trenches, during the time of waiting, they read Testaments & repeat prayers from prayer books." But he also added a caveat that was consistent with his own feelings about conversion, "for I am not trying to show that a man gets converted at the front. All I'm saying is that when men are under fire, they clutch at their gun & their God. That is all they can rely on."[19]

Leonard did not say whether his own experience a reasonable distance back from the front lines drove him to his knees; but from every indication, he joined the ranks of his fellow soldiers in offering prayers for safety that were likely the most sincere of his life, "for that is all [we] can rely on." He also knew that he was writing to a believer, and that Grace fervently prayed for his own health and safety, just as he prayed for her. Most of the letters from Grace during the war years have not survived, but it seems likely that Leonard accepted with comfort and thanksgiving these prayers on his behalf from a Baptist believer, just as he accepted and drew consolation from the fact that his parents and siblings in Idaho were also calling on the powers of heaven to protect him.

The overall religious effects of Leonard's army experience were to heighten his appreciation of religious pluralism and to broaden his own religious life. Shortly after arriving in North Africa, Leonard had the second of his three epiphanies, which, like the first, strengthened his bond to the Infinite but did not channel itself into a specific affirmation of Mormonism. He recalled this experience in considerable detail in a letter to Grace, the candor of which revealed an intimacy that held nothing back.

The epiphany occurred on the night of September 1, 1944, three weeks after his unit arrived in North Africa. Alone in his tent, he finished reading Dostoevsky's

The Brothers Karamazov, and then began to write a long letter to Grace. "The reading of the novel and the writing of the letter set the stage for what followed, a peak experience not unlike the one I had in the orchard back of our farmhouse in Twin Falls County in 1930." As he finished writing the letter, he exited his tent and then "prayed that all would be well with Grace while I was gone, that we would both be contented in our separation, and that we could resume productive and happy lives after my return"—likely a prayer that he had spoken many times previously and would speak many more times before his return from the war. "Suddenly I felt an exhilaration that transported me to a higher level of consciousness. . . . I felt I was absorbed into the great Eye, the Kingdom of the Heavenly One, the universe of the Holy Spirit. . . . I felt I was lifted out of the ordinary world into the beautiful world of the divine." As he was enveloped in his epiphany, his career plans were redirected. "Erased was the feeling that I wanted to be a Senator.[20] I would be a teacher and writer, and I would prepare talks, articles, and books about religion, about the economy, and about people and their cares as they made their way in life."[21]

Because Leonard wrote regularly to Grace, it is possible to track the evolution of his outlook on religion from 1943 through the end of the war—an evolution from the theoretical to the decidedly practical:[22]

- November 1943: "Religion is not something passive, nor something passively acquired. It is meaningless if it is developed outside the hustle and bustle of everyday life. Religion is the way you work and play. Religion is worshipping God in the field, in the workshop, on a city street, on a baseball diamond, and in a theater."

- March 1944: "There are so many questions that can be answered only by the use of Reason. Even faith contains a large element of Reason. Our faith must not be blind; it must be guided by Reason. That is why God endowed us with a mind as well as a will and a conscience."

- May 1944: "The 2½-minute talks [at a hastily convened LDS worship service] were also pretty orthodox. It is only after attending to that service & listening to them that I discovered just how far I have traveled since I went to high school in Twin Falls. Up to that time I undoubtedly had the same opinions, hopes, & ideals [as other Mormons]. If I were honest with them about how I feel, they wouldn't own me. I just wonder how many of the young LDS would agree with me—would think I had the right approach—would want me to teach their children? Probably not very many. But the LDS desire

for education & learning is so strong that I think they will accept
me & let me teach them in spite of some of my 'radicalism.'"

Leonard was well aware of his heterodoxy. Without defiance or sneering at
those who clung—whether in faith or in fright—to the most rigid orthodoxy,
Leonard stood apart, weighing, measuring, rejoicing in the fruits of his study and
his openness to inspiration from many sources. Grace may have expressed concern, drawn from her own Presbyterian and Baptist background, that Leonard
had not experienced the all-important experience of "being saved"—an identifi-
able event that those who experienced it could identify by time, place, and transcendent contact with a loving God who accepted the open heart by pouring out
grace upon the recipient—and so Leonard hastened to reassure her:

- July 1944: "There is something more to religion than merely good
  conduct. . . . Religion means the addition of love of God to one's experience. That is, before one can be truly religious, he must have
  had one or a series of religious experiences. . . . I do not believe that
  everything can be solved by thought, by reason. There is a legitimate
  and necessary experience called feeling."

- September 1944: "I want to tell you of our discussion last night.
  There were 4 of us sitting around the table in the orderly room. Two
  were on one side of the table, two on the other, and a candle in between. It is a remarkable coincidence that the four were a Catholic,
  a Jew, a Protestant & a Mormon. Each of them was brought up
  strictly in his faith but considers himself, more or less a free thinker,
  liberal & broadminded. . . . The Jew has become a very good friend
  of mine. . . . He does not consider himself an orthodox Jew in belief, but follows Orthodox practices. In other words he's the kind of
  Jew that I am a Mormon."

Leonard would remember and call up this experience as he worked out his
own accommodation with Utah Mormonism: orthodox behavior and loyal support of leaders, an understanding of doctrine deep enough that he could converse
with Mormons across the spectrum from those clinging, in hope and fear, to the
"Iron Rod," but a serene self-confidence in his own relationship with God and
the growing clarity of his mission—which he, with growing confidence, defined of
divine origin—that he could accept divergent views without feeling threatened
or challenged.

- December 1944: "Altho I seem to be drifting farther away from the
  Church in some ways (theology) I agree more than ever with their

fundamental social & economic ideas, and I'm going to plug (support) them for all I'm worth when we move west."

- November 1945: "My experience in the Army has taught me, if anything, that our Church has the best approach: make it a church of young people; make it a practical religion. . . . A church of pious old women, like so many Protestant churches, is a pretty useless thing in this 'brave new world.'"

LOGAN YEARS

Leonard's move to Logan in 1946 when he was twenty-nine was his introduction to a predominately Mormon environment, and he remained in that environment for the rest of his life. If Grace feared entry into a different geographical, social, and religious world, she kept her anxiety to herself and counted on Leonard's happy confidence to smooth the path to a new home and a new life.

Just weeks after they drove into Cache Valley, Leonard and Grace attended their first stake (diocese) conference—his first since college. While this formal, group preaching service did not rise to the level of his prior epiphanies, the experience was still strongly affirming to him. More than a thousand people were in attendance, thanks in part to the presence of Apostle Albert E. Bowen. Halfway through the service the congregation was asked to stand and sing the Mormon standard, "Come, Come, Ye Saints." It was the first time in seven years that he had heard the hymn, and he was overcome with emotion. "I cried all the way through the four verses. There was a soul-stirring feeling of communion with those in the congregation, with the people of Cache Valley, with the pioneers and their struggle to make the desert blossom." He noted, in one of his privately published autobiographical sketches, that the experience did not rise to the level of "the epiphanies in the orchard back of our Twin Falls County home in 1930 and the revelation or insight that came to me under the stars when I was a soldier in North Africa in 1943," but the experience served to strengthen his bond "to 'my' people, to Mormon Country, and to the research I was doing in the Church Archives."[23]

Although he felt at home among "his" people, Leonard initially held back from full involvement in the Mormon community, in large part because he respected Grace's Presbyterian faith and felt no compulsion to try to convert her to Mormonism. Instead, they easily worked out an accommodation that was mutually respectful. Carl, their second child, noted: "When they first came to Logan, they . . . were going to go to all of them [the available churches]; my mom wasn't a Mormon then, so they were going to give it a go."[24]

After Grace's conversion, Leonard's church activity increased; and within a year of their arrival, he began to rise within the local hierarchy of the all-lay Mormon priesthood. "I had been ordained a Seventy in April 30, 1947," he noted, "and very soon thereafter was made a president of Seventies, and very quickly became Senior President.[25] I held this position until 1959 when I was ordained a High Priest and sustained as a High Councilor for the new Utah State University Stake, with Reed Bullen as stake president."[26] Later, he became a counselor to Bullen.

A primary responsibility of high councilors is to rotate among congregations within the stake and preach in sacrament meeting. Not all have speaking ability of equal eloquence, leading to the lament of "Dry Council Sunday." While Leonard never tried to avoid this responsibility, his speeches differed markedly from those of his peers. Theirs were generally sermons, but his were history lectures. Decades later he wrote to his children: "Today, as a by-product of a search for something else, I ran across a box that had the cards I used in my talks on religious themes when I was on the USU High Council and in the Stake Presidency. Perhaps as many as forty or fifty different talks, all delivered in Logan. I realize now that every talk I have given since coming here was on a history topic. Not a single talk with a religious theme."[27] Probably his listeners had no objections, for much of the history, peppered with humorous, inspirational, and personal anecdotes, would have been new to them after a long string of exhortations on such standard topics as the Word of Wisdom, tithing, and home teaching (then called "ward teaching"). Furthermore, in Cache Valley, most of his listeners would have been only three, two, or even one generation away from the Mormon pioneers who settled the area. Leonard was too modest in saying none of these talks had a religious theme: history *was* religion in Cache Valley.

THE THIRD EPIPHANY

While on unpaid leave from Utah State in 1949–1950 to complete work on his doctoral dissertation at the University of North Carolina, Leonard experienced the third and final of his life-affirming epiphanies, this one in the unlikely location of the university library. While containing the same element of the Divine as the prior two experiences, it differed materially in affirming Leonard's specific mission within the LDS tradition. The earlier transcendent experiences had connected him to the Divine in a joyous overflow of love and grace, but Mormonism had played no specific role. When he recorded the third experience, he used devotional language that was seldom part of his intellectual and religious vocabulary.

As he pored over his massive compilation of research notes while sitting in a quiet alcove of the library, "a feeling of ecstasy suddenly came over me—an exhilaration that transported me once again to a higher level of consciousness." Referring to the verse in the Gospel of John that speaks of two baptisms, one of water and one of spirit (John 3:3–5), he wrote, "I was unexpectedly absorbed into the universe of the Holy Spirit, a gift presumably of the Holy Ghost." Then, the message: "In an electrifying moment, the lives and beliefs of nineteenth-century Mormons had a special meaning; they were inspiring—part of the eternal plan— and it was my pleasure to understand and write about their story. Whatever my talents and abilities—and I had never pretended that they were extraordinary— an invisible higher power had now given me a commission and the experience re- mained, and continues to remain, with me. . . . I knew that God expected me to carry out a research program of his people's history and to make available that material to others."

His recounting of the third epiphany took place in a public symposium nearly two decades after the History Division had been dismantled, and only one year prior to his death. As one looks back at the remarkable, almost unbelievable way in which he came to accept, calmly, the tragic disassembly of his dream, the power of this epiphany looms large as his anchor in the storm. He acknowledged the same as he concluded his remarks: "Whatever people might say about this mortal errand, I must persevere, and do so in an attitude of faithfulness. My experience was a holy, never-to-be-forgotten encounter—one that inspired me to live up to the promises held out for those who receive the gift of the Holy Ghost."[28]

CHURCH HISTORIAN YEARS

By the time Leonard became church historian at age fifty-four, the general out- lines of his religious convictions, his pious lifestyle, and his personal values— intellectual, emotional, and spiritual—were strongly intermingled and well defined. As he began his new job, however, it became apparent to him that he needed an additional skill set. Months later he wrote to a non-Mormon colleague of his challenge: "I have never pretended to be an authority on religious experi- ences and theology. If I have any confidence at all, it is in the field of economic history, which in many respects is far removed from the subject assigned me to answer. With my new assignment, however, I shall have to do some intense read- ing in the field of religious psychology and religious history. I hope I will be able to do justice to the totality of The Mormon Experience."[29]

Acquiring the new knowledge was not a great challenge for Leonard, for he had already spent decades expanding his intellectual horizons. *Delivering* it to a different audience with different expectations than past audiences proved more problematic. He turned for help to his son James, an accomplished actor who had mastered the art of connecting with an audience. James recalled:

> When he became Church Historian, he came to me and said, "You're a performer. I'm giving all these talks as the historian of the Church. I don't know exactly how to end my talks. It's like people want to know something, and I don't know what to tell them."
>
> "I know what they want to know, Dad."
>
> "That's the reason I came to ask you! What is it they want to know?"
>
> "They want to know about the deep, dark secrets of the Church."
>
> "What are you talking about, the deep, dark secrets of the Church?"
>
> "Everybody thinks that there are deep, dark secrets about the Church, and that they are hidden in a vault somewhere, and if they could only get into that vault, they could suddenly understand why the Church does what it does, and why the Brethren are this or that or the other, and where the Book of Mormon is right now, and the Sword of Laban, and all that stuff that somehow is hidden away and deep-sixed into the Church. Do you know about that stuff?"

Leonard was bemused. Faithful but ordinary church members were quite aware that the church was a secret-keeping organization. This culture began with Joseph Smith, who created ever-more-inner circles of confidants who alone were privy to some of the prophet's most challenging theological innovations and refinements. It was magnified by Brigham Young's ultimately fruitless attempt to keep secret the practice of plural marriage that Smith had initiated but that was not announced publicly until 1852, and perpetuated by his successors with respect to temple ordinances, which had always been guarded by the seal of sacredness—"Top Sacred" in the words of some—finances, and inner workings of the church hierarchy.

This was the context in which Leonard posed his question to James and, surprised by his ready answer, repeated, "About the Sword of Laban?" James continued his memory of that conversation:

> "Well, all that stuff. Is there such a place?"
>
> "Well, the First Presidency has a vault, and I don't go in there. But I've seen everything else."
>
> "What have you discovered from everything else you've seen?"

"There is no question that this is the True Church. Otherwise, we wouldn't ever have [survived]."

I don't know that those are exactly the words that he used, but he said, "When you look at the records of this church, it is a remarkable rise. It is inspired, and it is beautiful, and there is no question that it has been helped by supernatural powers."

I said, "*That's* what you need to say!"

And so, we practiced. I said, "I want you to give me the last line of your talk."

[Leonard did so.] And then I said, "Okay, here's what you do, Dad. When you get to the part where you start talking about these things, I want you to take off your glasses, and lean over the pulpit and talk to the people."

"What do I want to do that for?"

"Dad, just trust me. You need to bear a testimony that no one thinks you are hiding, or that you have prepared it, or that it is anything but the real, exact truth. You get to decide what you want to say there, but when you get to that point, you whip off your glasses, carefully, gently, and lean on the pulpit, and you talk to those people. You tell them that you've seen the deepest, darkest parts of the Church's history, and that it bears record of the truthfulness of the Gospel."

I went to the first talk he gave after that. Rather mechanically, he took off his glasses and did it. Because I know him so well, I just thought, "He hates this. He sees that this is subterfuge. He's trying as hard as he can to do what I told him to, but with difficulty."

He leaned up and he said, "Brothers and sisters, I have seen the things of the Church. I have seen the deepest parts of the Church, and I can tell you that it is inspired, and there is nothing in there for us to be ashamed of." He bore a very short testimony, with his glasses off and leaning over. And you know what? People went out of there going, "Hallelujah! That's the greatest testimony I've ever heard," because they "got" my dad in a way—after he had read through all of his notes on his cards, and he delivered this wonderful speech that had humor and depth; but then he just left the notes, took off his glasses, leaned over, and said, "Now, I'm going to tell you the truth." And boy, they got it! I went up to him and said, "Dad, that was great!"

"Did I do okay?"

"Yeah."

"Did it look like I was scared?"

"No. You did a good job."

After that first time it became very natural to him to do that. He really got what he was doing. The first time, it felt very directed; but after that, he just did it regularly, and it was great. People just adored him. All I did was just help him say what he was going to say anyway. I just gave him a way to do it that signaled to everybody, "Okay, all the fabrication is gone, the notes are gone, the glasses are gone. I'm telling you the truth."[30]

The testimony that Leonard bore was inclusive, and not exclusive. That is, while he pledged allegiance to the Mormon Church and witnessed that he saw God's presence within it, he was comfortable with the truth claims of believers within other religious traditions—perhaps not surprising given his extensive contact with such believers in Idaho, North Carolina, North Africa, and Italy. Feminist and poet Carol Lynn Pearson later queried him regarding the Mormon Church's exclusivist claims. "I asked Leonard if he could ever foresee a day when the Brethren would ever, *ever* modify the stand of being the only true Church and just say we're a darn good Church. He said—seriously—that he thought maybe in twenty years they might be ready for that. I expressed my surprise, and he said that the young people today are not buying everything they're told."[31]

Leonard's job as church historian was the first in his professional career that carried an ecclesiastical dimension. On a daily basis he conducted or attended meetings whose agendas included vocal prayers. Almost daily, he interacted closely with fulltime ecclesiastical leaders who were accustomed to receiving deferential attention because they were presumed to have special insights into God's will. Correspondingly, they were often unaccustomed to working through a problem that required organized information and persuasive argumentation, since their ecclesiastical position allowed them to preclude discussion. Leonard had to adjust. The public face of his piety became the same as the private face that few had previously seen: simple and unpretentious. His role model was George A. Smith, an apostle and counselor in the First Presidency from the previous century, who was "impatient with ceremony and did not hesitate to end long meetings with the prayer, 'Lord, forgive us and continue to bless us. Amen!' "[32] James recalled, "In his faith, he was very simple, like a child in a lot of ways. His prayers were very simple. He never gave big, long, expansive prayers. They were always very, very childlike. And I mean that sincerely. He'd say, 'Bless the food. Bless us that we can be happy.' They were just really, really simple, childlike prayers."[33]

While never wearing the ecclesiastical dimension of being church historian on his sleeve, Leonard took it seriously for, as he confided to a friend, "I sincerely believe that the Lord called me to this position."[34] Whereas in the past he may have been reluctant to let his spiritual side show through at the expense of the professional, he now became comfortable doing so. One of his closest associates, Assistant Church Historian James Allen, recalled, "I remember he was preparing to give a blessing to a member of his family, and he asked Davis [Bitton] and me to come and be in on it with him. He prepared very thoroughly for the blessing that he was going to give to that member of his family, and Davis and I went to the home with him and stood with him as he gave a blessing. I remember feeling very grateful that I could see this side of Leonard." Allen was also part of a solemn, impromptu event that essentially signaled the beginning of the new History Division. "After we were interviewed, and Elder [Alvin] Dyer issued the call, we went out to Leonard's office, and then he said, 'Now, we need to have prayer.' And so we went into his office—Davis, Leonard, and I, and two or three other people—and knelt, and Leonard led in a very powerful, spiritual prayer about the kinds of things that we were going to accomplish."[35]

Throughout his tenure as church historian Leonard maintained the humble, spiritual tone he had set in the earliest days of his calling. Gene A. Sessions, one of his earliest employees, recalled that the staff meetings, held Monday mornings, "were always spiritual. He would always invoke a blessing on us, as if he were a General Authority. He was often very ecclesiastical in the way he dealt with us." As the meetings concluded, he would dismiss the staff with a warm sentence, typically something like "The Lord bless you and guide you." Sessions "always had the sense that he really believed that he was giving us his spiritual invocation."[36]

The one "badge" of religiosity that Leonard bore, albeit in his wallet rather than on his shirtsleeve, was his temple recommend, a small card signed after interviews with the bishop and stake president and countersigned by the member, which had to be renewed each year. It certified that the bearer was a church member in sufficiently good standing to qualify for entrance into any of the church's temples. George Daines, a former student who became Leonard's personal attorney, was struck by the fact, when he had the chance to see Leonard's multivolume diary at Utah State University, that Leonard "copied his temple recommend every year and stuck it in his diary. So each year, as you go through his diary, you see that Xerox copy of his recommend. With all the warts and mistakes [in the church and its leaders] and everything, he was a believer and he wanted it known that he was a believer and that he could see all of the foibles and misunderstandings, but he wanted to communicate, 'I still believe.'"[37]

By the time he became church historian, Leonard was arguably better versed on the content of the Church Archives than anyone else; yet, the sheer volume of records went far beyond what his previous studies had enabled him to read. Now that his stewardship included the content of all the records, he dug deeper, including the contents of the First Presidency vault that had always been off-limits to scholars. Joseph Fielding Smith, as church historian, had a special safe in which he deposited materials that, for reasons he never articulated, he felt that only he should see. When he became church president, he physically transferred the safe and its contents into the walk-in First Presidency's vault, giving rise—and not without justification—to the church's reputation for secrecy and concealment and, furthermore, providing a sort of confirmation that the church indeed had possession of embarrassing materials. Leonard read and absorbed the material without qualm or shock, and felt a need, as church historian, to communicate that message to others. One of his first confidants was George Daines. When business brought Leonard to Yale, where George was a law student, the two men went out to dinner with a small group of historians. During the casual conversation, Leonard made a point of confiding to Daines, "You and I have often chatted about what's in the First Presidency vault. I have seen *everything*. I think I have actually been able to see it all, and I don't think they've held anything back. I want you to know that I have a strong testimony, that nothing I saw bothered my testimony. I don't have any problems sustaining this prophet or anyone that comes after him. I have seen it all, and I am deepened in my beliefs." Daines was struck by Leonard's earnestness and commented, "You can misinterpret that by saying that he believed that every Church leader was right. Quite the opposite. But Leonard wanted to communicate that to me that there wasn't something there that he felt substantially changed his views."[38]

Indeed, it is clear from reading *Great Basin Kingdom* that Leonard's understanding of the fallibilities of former church leaders was longstanding and well informed by data. And he could extrapolate. "He was able to view the people that he dealt with in the same way that he was able to view Brigham Young or Charles C. Rich or the guys that had lived a hundred years earlier," commented a fellow USU professor, Ross Peterson. He knew "that they were human beings, that they were trying to do a job, they were making some mistakes, they'd step on people. And that's just the way it was. It had nothing to do with the person's relationship to Jesus Christ or to the Church."[39]

Leonard's ability to deal with data that did not square with the polished image of the church served him well, but occasionally he overestimated the ability of other church members to deal with the same data in the same way. One incident involved *A View of the Hebrews*, a book by Ethan Smith (no relation to Joseph Smith) with many of the same themes as the Book of Mormon but published seven years earlier. Michael Quinn recalled that Leonard was flying back from a meeting and using the plane-time to read *A View of the Hebrews*. As luck would have it his seatmate was an acquaintance and "a devout Mormon." Intrigued by Leonard's reading material, this "person was kind of looking over his shoulder—but as Leonard would come across something that he thought was interesting, he would mention it to this person, because Leonard found it interesting. Just interesting." This pattern had been going on for some time through the flight when Leonard suddenly realized, "with a sense of real surprise, . . . that this person was having a faith crisis" over some of the details that Leonard found mildly interesting. This reaction "astounded Leonard. . . . whose statement was, 'It was just a book!' "

Quinn reflected: "But in that experience, maybe for the first time in his life, even though he had run into various kinds of criticism, I don't think he had ever seen somebody begin to crumble in their faith, in front of him. And that's what he saw in this person next to him. It really shocked him. It really, really got to him. I think that's the first time that he really ever got it, that history could really be dangerous. And he was Church Historian before he saw that."[40]

The greatest challenges to Leonard's religious convictions did not come from the data he read, but from the people above him in the church hierarchy. Even when it became apparent that his department would be dismantled, his inner convictions sustained him. He told a non-Mormon colleague "that he knew what his task was, and what he had to go through was nothing compared to knowing what he knew."[41] It was, in Mormon terms, the articulation of his deep, strong testimony. Not long before he was relieved of his office and moved to Provo, he showed his inner strength to his closest associates. Maureen Beecher recalled "one of those beautiful moments" that came at perhaps the nadir of the History Division when the surviving staff members were being moved to an ancient building slated for demolition on the BYU campus. Morale was predictably low. "We were all feeling his patriarchal position, father of us all," she reflected. "We were about to have our summertime retreat, and we said, 'Leonard, we would like you to give us the sermon.' We climbed to the top of Ensign Peak. . . . Leonard had a hard time getting up Ensign Peak, but then he delivered a most wonderful sermon. I can't remember the content, but the feeling was one of, 'As individuals, we do what God expects of us. We don't need to be tied down by this corporation that wants to control everyone's lives. We are individuals trying to serve God the best way we can.' That was just pure Leonard."[42]

THE BOOK OF MORMON

For all of Leonard's success in dealing with history that was problematic for others of his faith, one subject remained problematic for him: the historicity of the Book of Mormon. For many—perhaps most—Latter-day Saints, including Leonard, the personal encounter with the Book of Mormon is foundational to one's religious life, and lacking a "testimony" of its divine origin is a boundary issue that separates believers from nonbelievers. Most church members, including Leonard, linked its status as canon to its claims of being a literal translation of the ancient history of the New World as created and preserved by a multigenerational line of prophets, warriors, and kings, and saw Joseph Smith's role in translating it as cementing his claim to be a prophet. But during his tenure as church historian, Leonard's assumptions were challenged by contradictory documentation.

During Leonard's youth, church manuals for all age groups continually reinforced the message that the book was a literal history of ancient America. As a teenager he defended the historical Book of Mormon in a speech, "Proof of the Book of Mormon," that concluded, "Therefore, I think it no more than reasonable and logical to believe that there is a Bible somewhere with a history of this Western Hemisphere, written by the Ancient American Indian prophets living many centuries [ago]. That the American Indians are descended from the ancient Hebrews and came to America to live and prosper."[43] It was and still is an orthodox position, although it would today be considered incomplete without a missionary-style assertion of personal knowledge based on revelation.

Leonard's exposure to religious philosophers during college broadened his concept of religious truth to include both the literal and the symbolic. As late as 1977, five years after becoming church historian, he declared his openness to either kind of interpretation of the founding narratives of Mormonism. "In the Mormon Epic, one may believe in the First Vision without worrying unduly as to whether God and Jesus literally appeared in person to Joseph Smith, or whether he thought he saw them in a mystical sense. Did the plates of the Book of Mormon exist in a concrete literal sense or did they exist in a symbolic sense? I feel comfortable either way."[44] His refusal to be ruffled ran headlong into the orthodoxy of fundamentalist church leaders such as Bruce McConkie, Joseph Fielding Smith, and Mark E. Petersen, an orthodoxy that refused to see as acceptable anything but a literal interpretation.

Attacks on the claims that the Book of Mormon was an ancient history had begun shortly after the book was first published in 1830 and have continued unabated ever since.[45] The most persistent claim against its historicity—that Joseph Smith plagiarized a manuscript written by Solomon Spalding—was thoroughly

debunked in a 1977 article by Lester E. Bush, who in 1973 had written the landmark history of the development of the policy banning black men from ordination to the priesthood.[46] Bush's dismantling of the Spalding theory included some
archival material that Leonard's division had provided to him.[47]

What had characterized earlier challenges to Book of Mormon historicity was
that they came from without. In 1978 Leonard became aware of a challenge from
within that shook him deeply.

In 1921 William Riter, a young man from Salina, Utah, relayed to LDS apostle James E. Talmage five questions about historical aspects of the Book of Mormon that had been sent to him by a Mr. Couch of Washington, D.C. Talmage
asked B. H. Roberts, a fellow General Authority and one of the brightest intellectuals in the history of the LDS Church, to respond to the questions.

After studying them for nearly two months, Roberts wrote a sobering response
addressed to his fellow General Authorities, including church president Heber J.
Grant: "I very gladly undertook the task of considering the question here pro-
pounded, and hoped to find answers that would be satisfactory," he began. "As I
proceeded with my recent investigations, however, and more especially in the, to
me, new field of language problems, I found the difficulties more serious than I
had thought for; and the more I investigated the more difficult I found the formulation of an answer to Mr. Couch's inquiries to be." It was an astounding confession by Roberts, for he had never been at a loss for words in the frequent and
often heated debates that took place with his fundamentalist counterparts in the
church hierarchy. Instead of writing an impromptu response to Couch, which
would have been based on assumptions but not data, Roberts stepped back and
gave the questions serious study, hoping to be able to draft a response that would
then draw on the collective wisdom of his fellow General Authorities so that "we
might find such a solution of the problems presented in the accompanying correspondence, as will maintain the reasonableness for the faith of all in the Nephite
scriptures."[48]

Appended to Roberts's letter was a lengthy manuscript in which he discussed
Couch's questions but did not purport to provide more than tentative answers
and suggested hypotheses. During several meetings in January 1922, Roberts and
his colleagues discussed the questions and his manuscript, but the meetings "were
so unsatisfactory and disquieting to Roberts," as his later editor put it, "that he
wrote a letter to President Grant . . . expressing his disappointment about the
irrelevancy of the comments expressed but promised to continue his investigations,
fully aware that Couch's questions had been inadequately answered."[49] Grant,
whose interest in the question of historicity—and even about theological questions
in general—was minimal, was relieved to have the whole matter quietly shelved.

Despite his continued studies, Roberts reached no satisfactory conclusions, and never published his manuscript. Few outside of his immediate family even knew of its existence. In the late 1970s, members of his family gave the book-length manuscript to the Marriott Library of the University of Utah, and in 1985 it was published, edited by well-regarded historian Brigham D. Madsen, who squarely faced the difficult questions Roberts raised.

Leonard had become aware of the manuscript shortly before the family donated it to the library. On September 19, 1978, he noted in his diary that Davis Bitton arrived at work with two copies of Roberts's "Book of Mormon Difficulties," one for Leonard and one for himself. Bitton had received the three-hundred-page manuscript from an anonymous source. Leonard candidly admitted his surprise at seeing it. "None of us have heard of the existence of this document until the last few weeks. As far as we are aware, it is not in our vault and we've never heard it mentioned in the vault of the First Presidency or the Joseph Fielding Smith safe." Bitton had had a chance to read it prior to giving a copy to Leonard, and noted that he had been impressed with two things: "1. B.H.'s absolute honesty in pursuing the difficult questions, with courage and determination. 2. That he came to grips with every aspect of it and did not hesitate in coming to conclusions warranted by the evidence despite what they might do to traditional beliefs." One of those conclusions was deeply unsettling to Leonard: "[Roberts] admits quite candidly that the Book of Mormon could have been the production of one mind."[50]

When Leonard learned that the manuscript was going to be published in book form, he lamented, "This is a great mistake, . . . a disservice to Roberts, to the Book of Mormon, and to the Church, as well as to Mormon scholarship generally."[51] Rather than engage the content of the manuscript, which had been his consistent approach to even the most problematic historical issues, he responded with anxiety and distress. But help was on the way.

Only two months after Leonard saw Roberts's manuscript, he obtained a work written by BYU anthropology professor John Sorenson and later published as *An Ancient American Setting for the Book of Mormon*. Sorenson had long been interested in theories and evidences of transoceanic communication and emigration, which he examined with a scholarly rigor unusual to most "defenders" of the Book of Mormon. In *An Ancient American Setting*, he argued what has come to be known as the "limited geography" thesis, which located the Book of Mormon peoples in Central America surrounded by a vigorous indigenous population that, over time, absorbed the warring tribes of Nephites and Lamanites. Leonard read this manuscript eagerly and was impressed by Sorenson's argument, especially by his careful teasing out of cultural and geographical clues from the scriptural narrative. He wrote triumphantly to his children, "I spent the long Veterans Day weekend reading [Sorenson's manuscript]. It was a great intellectual experience. All of the intellectual problems I have had with the Book of Mormon have now been put to rest as the result of reading that book. My understanding of New World history and archeology is now perfectly reconciled to the Book of Mormon accounts. I am so grateful to him for this work of scholarship."[52]

Leonard wrote to Sorenson on the same day, "This is a confession and an expression of profound gratitude. Until I read the manuscript of your volume on the Book of Mormon, I had accepted that standard work strictly on faith. I had been unable to reconcile or harmonize my understanding of history and archeology with the Book of Mormon accounts. Your book has opened up a whole new intellectual world, wholly consistent with my faith. Thank you, Thank you."[53]

Although he did not say so, Leonard apparently found in Sorenson's work sufficient answers to ease his mind about the Book of Mormon conundrums that appeared in Roberts's manuscript. Sorenson's main arguments were first published in a series of *Ensign* articles before his book was published by Deseret Book—as close to an official imprimatur as Mormonism allowed.

In reality, however, the matter was far from settled, and Leonard's relief was short-lived. A stream of publications employing increasingly sophisticated tools continued to challenge traditional beliefs regarding Book of Mormon historicity. A decade after Leonard declared victory after reading Sorenson's manuscript—a decade during which he encountered but did not engage the new challenges—he again wrote triumphantly in response to an article published in *Dialogue: A Journal of Mormon Thought*.

The author, Blake Ostler, sidestepped Sorenson's literalistic interpretation and offered a hybrid, "a theory of the Book of Mormon as Joseph Smith's expansion of an ancient work by building on the work of ancient prophets to answer nagging problems of his day. The result is a modern world view and theological understanding superimposed on the Book of Mormon text from the plates." By allowing for both ancient and modern components, Ostler's construct allowed Leonard "to believe in the gold plates, as I have done (the evidence is overwhelming that they existed), and in the evidences of ancientness in the text (there are lots of those), and at the same time have a suitable explanation of the modernisms (and there are certainly some of those)." Ostler's "creative co-participation theory of revelation," in which Smith was an active, rather than passive instrument in producing the Book of Mormon, fit nicely "a view of revelation which the historian is almost forced to accept."

Having moved beyond Sorenson's paradigm, Leonard again declared personal victory—"[It] takes care of nearly all of the problems that have arisen, and helps believers like myself reconcile with scholarly problems"[54]—and went home. The Ostler paradigm was sufficient to carry him through the remainder of his life, although he continued to hold his cards close, even in private. A friend noted, "I have pushed him before on certain things and got something of the same answer. I said, 'Okay, Leonard, were there really Nephites and Lamanites?' He laughed and eventually said, 'Well, let's put it like this. That is part of the great Mormon myth that we all hold to and all benefit from.' "[55]

POST–CHURCH HISTORIAN YEARS

The early months of 1982 were the most difficult of Leonard's life. On February 2, G. Homer Durham was set apart as church historian, thus ending officially Leonard's decade-long tenure in that position. One month later, after a lengthy illness, Grace died. Durham, a former university president, had been welcomed as someone who would understand and defend the production of serious and professional Mormon history; but his actual behavior was a shattering disappointment. He had been instructed to dismantle the department and did so with enthusiasm, acting directly on instructions from his mentor, Gordon B. Hinckley. Between those two painful events, intensified by the sadness and distress of his division members who clearly understood that their efforts were not only unappreciated but seen as dangerous, Leonard's usual ebullient optimism was harder to sustain. Writing to his children, he expressed with unusual candor some of his thoughts about religion.

Always the optimist, he began with a positive spin on the downward spiral of events. "Having doubts, having fears, having reservations about counsel is not necessarily an opening wedge toward the loss of faith. Indeed, it might be the avenue to renewed faith, deeper faith, greater understanding. 'No one truly believes who has not first served an apprenticeship of doubt.' "

But then he lashed out at actions by church leaders that he saw as ultimately destructive to the institutional church: "The attempt to suppress problems and difficulties, the attempt to intimidate people who raise problems or express doubts or seek to reconcile difficult facts, is both ineffective and futile. It leads to suspicion, mistrust, the condescending slanting of data. The more we deny or appear to deny certain demonstrable 'facts,' the more we must ourselves harbor serious doubts and have something to hide."

Having vented, he immediately stepped back into character. "However, your optimistic, buoyant father believes it is important, after recognizing that doubts and problems should not be kept back, to not forget the sun for the sunspots. We must also reaffirm the good, that with which we have no problem."[56]

Six weeks later, only days after Grace's death, an uncharacteristically sober Leonard reached deep in another letter to his children. "I am going to try to live worthy to receive special blessings from the Lord. I do believe He will bless me if I live for it. I am a believer; I do have faith and hope."[57] He was clearly talking as much to himself as to his children, who were also dealing in their own ways with their mother's death.

During his years of church employment, Leonard had acted judiciously with respect to participating in public meetings and publishing, fully aware that he was representing the church as church historian. Once relieved of his title, he began to speak and write more freely. In 1983 he wrote an essay, "Why I Am a Believer," the first of a series called "Pillars of My Faith," delivered in a plenary session of the Sunstone Symposium and later printed in *Sunstone* magazine. Although it was a restatement of earlier writings and speeches, it achieved new—and dubious—status not only for being in print, but for having been published in a magazine disdained by many orthodox Mormons.[58]

He began by reaching back to the philosophy that had driven his college-age wrestling match with his faith tradition—indeed, his *credo*: "I believe the intellect is enormously important—more important than the heart, more important than tradition." While willing to begin with the assumption that there was a God, "I was not satisfied until I had studied the matter through and came to a conviction that my intellect could defend." As he had noted on prior occasions, by the third year of his graduate studies he had satisfied himself, through intellectual inquiry, that God existed. "My religious experiences in my more mature years have merely served to corroborate what I had then come to believe." In other words, his understanding sought faith, whereas most of his coreligionists gained faith first and then sought understanding—or closed their minds to the possibility of understanding.

He then reached back to Santayana's observations about literal versus symbolic truth. "Because of my introduction to the concept of symbolism as a means of expressing religious truth, I was never overly concerned with the question of the historicity of the First Vision or of the many reported epiphanies in Mormon, Christian, and Hebrew history." Tellingly, he did not include the Book of Mormon in his declaration.

And also tellingly, he ended his sermonette with an emphasis on the practical aspects of Mormonism, rather than the spiritual:

> This was a great church, I came to believe. It perpetuated fine ideals
> of home, school, and community life; its approach and philosophy
> enabled its members to reconcile religion with science and higher

learning; its emphasis on free agency encouraged individual freedom and responsibility; its strong social tradition taught its members to be caring and compassionate; and its strong organizational capability empowered its people to build better communities.[59]

By almost any measure, Leonard's statement was strongly affirmative of loyalty and support of the church; but his few candid statements of heterodoxy did not sit well in some circles. Within days of the article's publication, Leonard wrote a diary entry suggesting that feathers had been ruffled in very high circles—specifically, the office of Ezra Taft Benson, who later that year became president of the LDS Church. He reported the rumors that had quickly reached him: "I was also informed that various people in the Religious Instruction college at BYU were fluttering around about my testimony as it appeared in *Sunstone*; it was not an orthodox testimony, and they didn't know what to think of this kind of a testimony. Apparently Bill Nelson, Elder Benson's secretary, telephoned the head of church curriculum to tell him to 'look into this Arrington piece.' Whatever that means."[60]

Five months later, Leonard became aware that he had been targeted by a particularly energetic and zealous defender of the faith at Brigham Young University, Louis Midgley. Midgley's degree was in political science, but he had devoted most of his career to attacking coreligionists whom he found to be insufficiently orthodox. In a private diary notation, Leonard responded to Midgley's diatribe with characteristic grace. First, he suggested that a person's religious convictions should be above reproach. "One's testimony of the Gospel is an intensely personal thing. Arguing with it is like arguing with his or her choice of a spouse, his or her taste in art, his or her preference for Verdi over Wagner. It is a product of one's feeling at a particular moment—feeling about God, feeling about the Church, feeling about one's fellowmen."

Next, he privately defended his decision to go public with his beliefs, heterodox though some of them might be. "I have had assurances from several dozen persons that the publication of my testimony, brief and incomplete as it was, was helpful. For that I am grateful. If it has been a stumbling block to anyone, I apologize."

And finally, he held out a symbolic olive branch to Midgley—symbolic because there is no indication that the two men ever communicated directly to each other. "If Brother Midgley will visit our Parley's First Ward testimony meetings over a series of years, he will hear many testimonies given by me, all different, but all expressing my love for God, for Gospel principles, for the Prophet, for our bishop, and for my wife and children. Hopefully, he will then accept me as a fellow

Communicant—one who is committed, willing to share, and anxious to improve."[61]

Though occasionally assailed by fellow Mormons for his heterodoxy, Leonard consistently defended his church. Several months after Midgley's attack, he wrote to a correspondent, "Let me say that those of us who have worked long and thoroughly in the Church Archives have had our testimonies strengthened, and deepened. All of us know for a surety (having examined the most intimate documents) that the Church is of divine origin, and that the Prophets speak with, or have spoken with, God. . . . No conflict there."[62]

With the passage of time Leonard's participation in one foundational element of Mormon group life waned, apparently in reaction to increased restrictions on access to the archives. To his children he wrote, "I have not yet come to feel the necessity of frequent attendance at the temple. I think I get as much inspiration watching birds, or looking at the mountains and the wilderness, as participating in the rituals there. The one regret I have is the failure of the Church authorities to recognize that by restricting the use of the archives they are concealing vast riches of inspiration and revelation."[63]

While Leonard continued for the rest of his life to see God within the Mormon tradition and to participate in weekly worship services, he grew increasingly frustrated—albeit in private—about the institutional embodiment of that tradition. In a diary entry entitled "Things I don't like about the church," he vented, with disarming candor, in laying out an agenda for change that has remarkably relevance to the contemporary Mormon scene over two decades later:

1. The imposition of one pattern for everybody rather than suggesting two or three patterns and letting local wards or stakes or districts follow the one most convenient for them. Examples, the three-hour meeting schedule on Sunday.

2. Appointing the highest tithe payers to positions of leadership rather than the most capable or worthy. In choosing stake leaders, the General Authority comes with a list of the 15 or 20 highest tithe payers and starts down the list to choose a stake president and high council.

3. The maintenance of a disloyalty file on liberals, including articles they've written with questionable statements, newspaper clippings. These are used against the person without him or her knowing what is in the file and having a chance to deny it or explain it. The supposition is that liberals are out to destroy or embarrass the church, a supposition entirely false.

4. The insistence on unanimity among the Twelve, which means that the most obstinate member, the one holding out against the rest, wins.

5. The insistence on choosing a new president from the senior member of the Twelve. This means we'll always have a president far beyond his energetic, creative period of life. We should retire persons from the Twelve at age 75 and never choose anyone over that age to be president of the Church.

6. The First Presidency and Twelve should call a person in to talk with him/her before putting the person on the blacklist, not to be cited, his/her books not to be sold in Church bookstores, not to be allowed to speak in Church, etc.

7. The church should allow historians to present "human" material in biographies of presidents and General Authorities.

8. We should allow women to be associates to the Twelve and sit in on their meetings. The Relief Society president should sit in on bishopric meetings. Mothers should be allowed to stand in the circle to bless babies, confirm newly baptized persons as members of the Church, just as they now can open and close meetings with prayer.

9. The manuals used in adult Sunday School, Priesthood, and Relief Society classes are absolutely hopeless. Using the same gospel doctrine manual every fourth year; the same with Priesthood manuals. Hopeless. Why can't they assign a skilled and experienced writer to do a new manual every year?[64]

Months before his death, Leonard bore final testimony to his children of his loyalty to the tradition, but he coupled with it an injunction that however noble the organization and its aspirations may be, the encounter with the Infinite is ultimately the responsibility of the individual and not the organization:

> There are LDS families in which loyalty to Mormon doctrines, practices, and leaders is so strong that the children feel they have to conform in order to assure the love of their parents. The parents love the church more than their children. Children sense that the parents would choose the church over their children if there was that choice. Young people are sometimes brought up to idealize church leaders, both past and present. But no human being is perfectly benevolent and wise. Leaders have their own life stories, complete with biases, fears, and needs as well as unique strengths and gifts. They can seek for the Spirit—for the Light—but they are still human

beings. The idolization of our leaders can be unhealthy—can keep us from realizing that *we* must search for the Spirit and the Light.[65]

While Leonard chose not to engage every troubling historical or theological issue that came his way—the Book of Mormon being a prime example—he engaged enough to "own" his religion, as contrasted to the "borrowing" done by so many of his coreligionists, who accepted uncritically whatever was presented to them by the church hierarchy. He paid a price, both professionally and personally, for the authentic religiosity that was a good fit for him, but that sometimes drove a wedge between himself and the church he loved. And yet, he did so willingly and even jubilantly, knowing that he was reaching higher.

13

PROMOTING MORMON HISTORY
THE PRE-CHURCH HISTORIAN YEARS

In a late-night conversation in Philadelphia after a day of sessions at a history meeting in 1969, Leonard discussed with two other scholars the existence of two Mormon churches, "the formal church of Sacrament meeting, Sunday School, MIA, etc., and the Underground church. The latter is the church of study groups, circles, discussions groups, family get-togethers, etc. where there is Christian fellowship with ideological similar[ity], both within and without the Church." Though not described in any church manual, the underground church, according to Leonard, has existed since the church was founded in the 1830s. "The Church has survived despite its formal church life. There has always been an underground. The church could eliminate much of the organized life—SS, MIA, Priesthood groups, etc., and there will still be a church because the essence of the church is in the underground group life."[1]

"Underground" was an intentional misnomer, for Leonard was well aware that such groups were common, visible, and implicitly sanctioned by church leaders. Indeed, he was invited to speak at and join the most prestigious of all, the Cannon-Hinckley Church History Club, shortly after becoming church historian in 1972, and he remained active in it for well over a decade. When he addressed it in 1972, he spoke to a group of over a hundred people—"the largest group ever to meet and they filled the large banquet room of the Lion House." Significantly, it included all three members of the First Presidency: Harold B. Lee, N. Eldon Tanner, and Marion G. Romney.[2]

Leonard considered the underground church to be a sign of institutional health, for it was (and generally is) composed of church members who feel deeply about the gospel, but who have no outlet within the formal church structure for discussing many of the issues that are of greatest importance to them. "One can't raise meaningful questions or discuss them honestly and fully in SS, seminary, Institute, MIA, Sacrament meeting, etc. So congenial and kindred souls meet in dinner parties at homes, fireside groups, study groups, vacation groups, and at professional and trade conventions. I have met with such groups in Utah, California, the Midwest, the Upper South, and the Northeast."[3]

Another "cell" of the underground church to which Leonard had belonged was organized in Logan in 1951 and consisted of four couples: George and Maria Ellsworth, Eugene and Beth Campbell, Wendell and Pearl Rich, and Leonard and Grace Arrington (see chapter 9). Meeting once a month, they would read each other drafts of papers that they were writing, and elicit criticisms and suggestions. "As time went on, we broadened our associations to include persons interested in Mormon history and culture at other universities. Some of these belonged to study groups of their own and invited some of us to make presentations. Similarly we invited some of them to make presentations in our homes in Logan."[4]

Publishing papers, particularly in Mormon history, was far more difficult than writing them, for at the time no scholarly journal regularly published articles relating to Mormonism. Even the *Utah Historical Quarterly*, the state-subsidized quarterly of the Utah State Historical Society, only occasionally published articles on Mormon history, and it steered clear of those with religious content. "Some of us in the field of Mormon studies discussed the founding of a journal of Mormon history, even toying with possible names for the journal such as *Latter-day Saint Quarterly*, *LDS Historical Review*, or *Journal of Mormon History*," Leonard recalled in his memoirs. "These discussions were temporarily ended by the creation of *BYU Studies* in 1959."[5]

The catalyst for *Brigham Young University Studies* was a young professor, Robert Kent Fielding. "I was assigned to be on a committee on intellectual climate at Brigham Young University," he recalled in a later interview. "My assignment led me to do certain things that had certain results, one of which was to establish the *Brigham Young University Studies* magazine,"[6] which was actually a repackaging and rebranding of the *Brigham Young University Bulletin* which previously had published fifty-five volumes.

A member of its executive committee and editorial board, Fielding invited Leonard to contribute an article to its first issue. "An Economic Interpretation of 'The Word of Wisdom'"[7] was the only article in the issue that dealt with Mormon history—and also the only one that ignited a firestorm. Heavily documented, the article argued persuasively that Brigham Young's enforcement of the Word of Wisdom as a binding commandment, rather than as the "good advice" that it had been for decades, was driven by the need to keep scarce cash in Utah Territory; and a proscription on the purchase and use of "luxury goods" such as tobacco, tea, coffee, and alcoholic beverages, which were imported from the States, was a good way to do so.

To those who had been taught that such things in the church happened by divine intervention—"Thus saith the Lord"—the article was jolting, and particularly to one apostle. The invitation had come to Leonard because "the first editors of *BYU Studies* were anxious to print sound historical essays," so they—and Leonard—"were startled" when his first article in that first issue "created such opposition from Elder Mark Petersen of the Twelve that the journal was suspended for a year."[8] Since Leonard learned this fact from BYU's heavy-handed president, Ernest L. Wilkinson, in person, he and the periodical's editors had every reason to see warning flags where any topic suggesting revisionist Mormon history came up.

The Mormon History Association

As a result, for years after publication resumed in 1960 *BYU Studies* shied away from the interpretive, cutting-edge articles that scholars were increasingly eager to publish, and the demand for an alternative journal grew. "We made it a point at professional historical conventions to 'look up' other Latter-day Saint persons and inform ourselves as to what they were writing and thinking," Leonard commented in 1976, his fourth year as church historian.[9] He had done much of the "looking up" and networking himself. And through the early 1960s, he gradually formulated a plan that he bounced off professional colleagues, not only between sessions at professional meetings but more formally in notes and letters. The recipient of one of these written proposals, Alfred Bush, curator of Western Americana at Princeton University Library, responded, "Your letter suggesting an association of Mormon scholars with a journal and meetings especially needs the leisure of conversation."[10]

Leonard was already conducting such a conversation, some of it markedly one-sided. In the summer of 1965, prior to formalizing plans for the meeting that would launch the Mormon History Association just after Christmas, Leonard wrote a detailed and remarkably candid letter to Hugh B. Brown, first counselor in the First Presidency. There is no indication that the two men were friends or even acquaintances, but Leonard no doubt selected Brown as the recipient of this information because he was considered the most liberal General Authority in the church.

The letter informed Brown not only of the need for an independent journal to give voice to LDS intellectuals, but of several plans for such a journal and the extent of enthusiasm among the postwar boom of professionals educated under the G.I. Bill. Leonard's description, while factually accurate, maintained a discreet silence on *BYU Studies*' rocky beginning and the role his own article had played in the scandal. If Brown knew about it, he could fill in the blanks himself. If not, there was no point in muddying the waters.

The letter began by acknowledging the pioneering role of *BYU Studies*, but suggested that "the purpose of 'Mormon scholarship'" had only been partly accomplished by it. One dilemma was the obvious affiliation of the journal with the church-owned university, which implicitly suggested church approval of its contents. The institutional affiliation had already resulted in self-censorship on the part of the editors. "Only articles which were thought to be non-controversial were accepted and published." Furthermore, not all authors would want such endorsement, even if only implied. Instead, they preferred a Mormon equivalent to "the Jewish *Commentary*, the Catholic *America*, and the Protestant *Christian Century*."

Leonard then informed Brown that he knew of three efforts to establish such a journal, independent of actual or implied institutional affiliation, all of which were being directed by active church members, and none of which showed "any inclination to establish a magazine of destructive criticism."

Next, he moved from journals to a broader issue. "The Church has made little or no provision for the use of its intellectuals. They may teach at BYU, of course, or within the Church Educational System, or at such 'Mormon' schools as Utah State University, but their training and scholarship have not been utilized to any significant degree in the councils of the Church. They are seldom given high positions of authority; they are seldom consulted on policies in which they are regarded as experts and specialists." Those who chose employment within the Church Educational System faced likely degradation of their intellectual curiosity, for "the Institute system tends to stress testimony-bearing rather than reason and scholarship, and Institute instructors are encouraged to use only 'testimony building' books for texts and reading assignments. Many of us think we detect an 'anti-intellectual' trend in the Seminary system, and it is often from the ranks of this group that Institute teachers are selected."

Finally, the "ask": "I suppose that what I am suggesting in this letter is that the Church form a Committee to encourage and facilitate the publication of scholarly studies, with a budget realistic enough to do some badly needed things." He suggested two possibilities for a new publication. One would be tacit encouragement for the creation of a fully independent journal, while the other would be the establishment of "a semi-official outlet for scholarly and intellectual discussion which would in a sense, forestall the scattered attempts of private groups."[11]

There is no record of a response or of a later comment on this topic from Brown. But despite the silence, Leonard took the next step two months later. In September 1965 his plan coalesced at an otherwise uneventful Utah Conference on Higher Education, held in Logan. Douglas Alder, then a professor of history at Utah State University, recalled: "One day I got a phone call, and [Leonard] asked me to meet with him and George [Ellsworth] over in the Rare Books Room in the library. I think Blythe Ahlstrom and Stan Cazier were also there, and we began to draft the plans to form the Mormon History Association."[12] Leonard documented his own memories of the hatching of his brainchild in a 1988 interview: "We had a little rump session in the Hatch Room of the USU library to discuss the formation of an organization. There were fourteen of us present, some from BYU, some from the University of Utah, and some from USU. And we decided that we would formally organize at the time the American and Pacific Historical Associations were meeting in San Francisco in December right after Christmas."[13]

Eager to cast as wide a net as possible, Leonard encouraged his colleagues to invite anyone they thought might be interested. He even extended an optimistic invitation to Church Historian (and president of the Quorum of Twelve Apostles) Joseph Fielding Smith, then age ninety, hoping thereby to have representation from the church. "While the main objective is to provide an opportunity for the Latter-day Saints to get together for discussions of mutual interest at the annual conventions of these great history associations," his carefully phrased letter read, "we might also be able to make some worthwhile contributions toward our Church history."[14]

When Smith surprisingly accepted the invitation and asked Earl Olson, assistant church historian, to attend as his representative, Leonard promptly provided more details to Brown. He was careful to give descriptions and explanations, but wisely did not frame it as a request for permission or validation, either step being one that would have put both Brown and himself in a difficult position. "Although we are forming this organization independently of the Church, we certainly have no intention of embarrassing the Church in any way. . . . I wanted to mention this to you directly so that if the matter is ever reported to you, you will know of it, our aims, and intentions."[15] It was an optimistic but also prudent move.

As the time of the inaugural meeting approached, spirits were high among most, but not all historians. "These are exciting times for a Mormon Intellectual, with the expected formation of the Mormon History Association," Leonard confided to John Sorenson, whose "limited geography" hypothesis twenty years later temporarily resolved Leonard's most pressing concerns about the historicity of the Book of Mormon. "I continue to get letters from a few pessimistic friends who volunteer to testify at my trial, which they think is inevitable, but I feel sure that the time is ripe."[16]

About fifty people attended the inaugural meeting of MHA held on December 28, 1965, in San Francisco, as an adjunct session to the annual meeting of the American Historical Association. Present were "not only professional historians and persons of some other disciplines interested in Mormon history but also institute teachers, seminary teachers, and 'buffs.'"[17] Among those buffs was a young sociologist, Armand Mauss, who would become MHA president in 1997–1998. "I remember how welcoming and gracious he was to all of us who showed up," Mauss commented, "especially those of us who, compared to him and some of the folks that had come to that gathering, felt like we were unknowns and out of our league. I was at the time teaching at a community college and hadn't done any scholarly work."[18]

Welcome inclusion of amateurs was almost unheard of at professional meetings, which tend to be clannish and exclusive, but MHA set the tone at the first meeting and has retained it ever since then. Robert Flanders, who had not attended the inaugural meeting, was at the MHA meeting in Casper, Wyoming, forty-one years later, and provided a snapshot that captured the openness of the MHA spirit, a remarkable reflection of Leonard's own hospitable approach:

> After lunch, waiting for afternoon sessions to begin, people coursing up and down the corridors, there was a lady sitting on a bench in the corridor, a late-middle-aged lady, probably 65 or 70. So I sat down by her and introduced myself by name.
>
> I said, "Are you a historian?"
>
> "Oh, no," she said.
>
> "Where are you from?" She was from somewhere in Utah, not Salt Lake.
>
> "What brings you to the MHA?"
>
> She said, "Oh—well this is where it's happening."
>
> I encouraged her to go on with that thought.
>
> She said, "Well, these people here are really interesting. They've got new ideas." I remember that term, "new ideas." She went on to say, without any hint of derogation at all, that "Nothing else new is happening, so here I am."

Intrigued, Flanders asked if she always attended the annual conference, which traditionally met at some site that had some connection to Mormonism's many pasts. She eagerly responded: "Every time I can. If it's in London [the 1987 conference had been in England] or Timbuktu, I can't do it, but if it is within reach, I come."

"I thought that was very interesting," reflected Flanders. "There are a lot of people at MHA like that. They have no professional involvement; they just find it interesting. That's where 'it's happening.' I know of no analogy for that anywhere else."[19]

Leonard had invited one of the speakers at that inaugural meeting, Wesley Johnson, then a graduate student at Columbia University, to describe a proposed new journal of Mormon studies, one whose genesis had taken an entirely different track than that initially envisioned within the Mormon History Association. By a unanimous vote, the new association tabled plans for its own journal in favor of Johnson's.[20]

DIALOGUE: A JOURNAL OF MORMON THOUGHT

The desire for an independent journal of Mormon scholarship had been in existence for decades, but there had never been a critical mass of scholars able to bring it to fruition. Leonard had had his own dreams for such a journal. "During the years I was a graduate student in North Carolina, and, because of the war, in North Africa and Italy, I kept wishing there was a Latter-day Saint scholarly journal—an outlet for thoughtful articles by Latter-day Saint chemists, physicists, economists, sociologists, historians, lovers of literature, and lovers of art. I had no doubt that Mormonism—the Gospel of Jesus Christ—was exalting and that Mormon professionals could demonstrate the superiority of our doctrine and way of life in every aspect of thought." Upon moving to Utah after the war, he repeatedly brought the subject up in conversations with other scholars, including G. Homer Durham, who eventually became his nemesis. He also discussed it with members of general boards of two LDS Church auxiliary organizations, the Mutual Improvement Association and the Sunday School. From both the response was enthusiastic—"We'll see what we can do!"—but empty.[21]

Some of the scholars knew of the dark cloud of suspicion that only then was dissipating over *BYU Studies*, largely because it had retreated to publishing only unexceptional, noncontroversial articles for the past five years; so this level of enthusiasm was heartening.

One of the three efforts to establish an independent journal that Leonard had mentioned in his letter to Brown involved Eugene England who, like Wes Johnson, was a graduate student at Stanford University. He wrote in his diary of their first discussion about the proposed journal. "About 1964 or 1965 I sat next to Eugene England on a plane and he talked about the plan of a small group at Stanford to start a new journal, to be called *Dialogue*. We discussed it at some length. Gene England promised that if our historians would submit articles to *Dialogue* instead of starting our own journal, he would promise to run the articles often and provide a good outlet."[22]

The seeds from which *Dialogue* sprouted had earlier been sown a continent apart by two young scholars who had never met each other. Once sown, Leonard then energetically watered and cultivated them. Wes Johnson had begun discussing with fellow graduate students at Columbia the idea of an independent journal since the 1950s, while Eugene England, then an undergraduate at the University of Utah, told friends that his own uneasiness with the church's indifference toward intellectuals moved his thinking in a similar direction.[23] Their paths intersected in the early 1960s at Stanford, where Johnson was a junior faculty member in history and England a graduate student in English. Introduced by a mutual friend, they then enlisted a trio of other friends—Frances Lee Menlove, Joseph Jeppson, and Paul G. Salisbury—and formulated a plan for launching the journal.

Jeppson reached out to Leonard for advice and support, both of which he gave in abundance. Leonard's enthusiasm for the enterprise was tempered only slightly by the realization that a scholarly journal out of the immediate control of the church posed a potential threat to those who assumed leadership, and he urged Jeppson to remain aware of the danger: "I am reasonably sure the Church authorities will not fight you if the journal is reasonably favorable to the Church. Some of the more liberal authorities have long wished there was a journal to provide an outlet for the expression of Church intellectuals who do not have such an outlet through the Church Educational System. Many of them will welcome this journal—again, so long as it is reasonably favorable to the Church."[24]

Jeppson took the counsel to heart: "We hear, from all over, and continuously, that you are exercising great effort to help us. We would like you to know that we are grateful to you, and that we will endeavor to make *Dialogue* the kind of journal you hope it will be."[25] The aim of the journal, England told Leonard, "was to reinforce the sense of community among thinking Mormons, to help Mormon students as they meet the challenges of university life, and to demonstrate that one need not relinquish faith in order to be intellectually respectable nor relinquish their intelligence to be faithful."[26] He invited Leonard to be an advisory editor.

At this time, Leonard was the second counselor in the presidency of the Utah State University Stake. As a courtesy he discussed the invitation with the stake president, Reed Bullen, a state senator and businessman who owned a radio station in Logan. Bullen "had no objection." Neither did the first counselor, Wendell Rich. "Both recommended, however, that I consult with the First Presidency." Leonard's request for an appointment was answered by a disappointing response from Brown, who said that he "was very busy, and probably could not spare the time necessary to discuss this in detail, but that he would contact President Harvey Taylor of BYU and ask him to discuss it with me. President Brown said he had great confidence in President Taylor, and that whatever advice I received from President Taylor should be regarded by me as equivalent to advice from the First Presidency." It is not clear whether Leonard was already acquainted with Taylor, BYU vice president. Brown likely referred the matter to Taylor, rather than Ernest Wilkinson, in anticipation that Taylor would give it a more favorable response. Taylor responded to Leonard's request with an appointment, and Leonard made the trip from Logan to Provo—a three-hour journey in pre-freeway days. "We spent about an hour talking. Basically, President Taylor's advice was to accept the appointment. They will benefit from your advice, he said; and if people like you don't counsel with them, they may depend on persons who are less committed to the Church. Upon my return, I replied favorably to *Dialogue*."[27]

The editorial staff also reached out cautiously in an attempt to buffer possible negative reactions from the church hierarchy. They had good reason to be cautious. In November 1965 Richard Bushman, a member of *Dialogue*'s charter editorial staff, alerted Wes Johnson: "*Dialogue* was brought up in the meeting of the Board of Trustees of the BYU"—most of whom were members of the Quorum of the Twelve—"where quite a number of the Brethren were present. . . . The attitude was simply, let's wait and see."[28] Two weeks later Bushman and Eugene England, the managing editor, took their case directly to the First Presidency by means of a thoughtful, nuanced letter:

> Our combined experience in many universities has made us keenly aware of the intellectual pressures on our youth. We believe that to hold them we must speak with many voices. A straightforward testimony by a man of spiritual power is most effective; Institute classes and the church schools help a large number. Unfortunately, these methods do not reach certain ones, including some of the finest students. Often these are overawed by the brilliance of secular culture. By comparison their own beliefs, as they perceive them, seem embarrassingly unsophisticated. They ascribe intellectual superficiality to Latter-day Saints and the Gospel itself and feel compelled to choose reason over faith.
>
> We believe that *Dialogue* can help reach these young people. Its contributors have the training and the qualities of mind respected in the universities, and its manner will be suitably candid and objective. At the same time it will display the rich intellectual and spiritual resources of the Gospel as mature men have discovered them and how relevant our faith is to contemporary life. The content of the magazine will be proof that a Latter-day Saint need not abandon thought to be a faithful Church member nor his faith to be thoughtful. All of our young people, however firm, should benefit from that kind of testimony.[29]

The First Presidency, in one of its daily morning meetings, discussed the letter in early December, shortly after receiving it. Minutes of the meeting, not normally accessible to scholars, became part of the David O. McKay diaries.

These brethren explain that they are making plans for a quarterly journal to be called *"Dialogue"* in the hope that this magazine will reach people who do not respond to the usual appeals of the Church. They indicate that various Church leaders with whom they have spoken have expressed interest in the project. They are sending out announcements describing their policies and their hopes for the magazine, and express the hope that the magazine will appeal particularly to students who seem to lose interest in the Gospel while under the influence of secular learning. They say that they will indicate explicitly in each issue that the magazine does not presume to speak for the Church. They state, however, that they would be pleased to have individual General Authorities submit articles appropriate for the magazine.[30]

The minutes of that meeting do not record any comments by Hugh B. Brown, even though by that point he had received relevant first-hand information in two communications from Leonard. Rather, it was President N. Eldon Tanner, second counselor in the First Presidency, who spoke up, reminding them that in a prior First Presidency meeting when the subject had been discussed, the consensus was that they would neither endorse anyone becoming a member of the *Dialogue* staff, nor prohibit BYU faculty from joining it. "It was the sentiment at that time that we do not think it wise to oppose it nor to support it. . . . It was the general sentiment of the Brethren that we would not wish to become involved in the matter in any way."[31] Having decided not to take any position, they reasoned "it is not necessary to answer the letter."

Four days after the First Presidency meeting, an article in the *New York Times* announced the launch of *Dialogue*, but in words that were problematic for the editors. The source for the story was Paul Salisbury who, although one of the founding group, was mistakenly identified as the editor, and thus the presumed spokesman. While the article quoted Salisbury as saying that the members of the editorial staff were "active members of the church," the remainder of the article had a decidedly less positive tone. The goal of the journal, "to open the door to a variety of viewpoints impossible to express in existing Mormon Church journals," while it might have been interpreted in two ways, was then fleshed out with examples that were certain to raise red flags among the church hierarchy.

> Mr. Salisbury said: "We will of course be concerned with the church stand against the repeal of 14(b) [a section of the Taft-Hartley Law permitting state "right-to-work" laws], the stand of the church against pacifism in the Vietnam war and the position taken by Mormon leaders in relationship to Negroes."

Members of the National Association for the Advancement of Colored People recently charged Latter-Day Saints leaders with "lack of concern" regarding efforts of Negroes to gain full equality.

Mr. Salisbury, asserting that "the church gives too much an appearance of being monolithic," said the new journal would "welcome an exchange of opinion through editorials and letters to the editor."[32]

A follow-up article two weeks later by Wallace Turner kept the subject alive and this time named Leonard as a key player. With a provocative lead sentence, "Within the Church of Jesus Christ of Latter-day Saints—more commonly known as the Mormon Church—the liberal intellectuals are hungry as never before for avenues of discussion," it went on to assert that while the journal would seek to be independent of church control, "it will not be antichurch, nor rebellious." The article quoted England, the actual editor, in contrast to the *New York Times*'s reliance on Salisbury. "One of the things we want is a place where outside theologians can enter into a discussion with those in our church."[33]

England's statement was reflected in *Dialogue*'s mission statement, which from that first issue to the present, includes the expressed desire of the editors "to bring their faith into dialogue with the larger stream of world religious thought and with human experience as a whole."[34] That first issue, mailed in March, contained 166 pages. Leonard authored the lead article, "Scholarly Studies of Mormonism in the Twentieth Century." The remaining five feature articles covered such topics as "The Autobiography of Parley P. Pratt: Some Literary, Historical, and Critical Reflections" (R. A. Christmas); "The Challenge of Honesty" (Frances Lee Menlove); "The Faith of a Psychologist: A Personal Document" (Victor B. Cline); "The Quest for Religious Authority and the Rise of Mormonism" (Mario S. De Pillis); and "The Student: His University and His Church" (Claude J. Burtenshaw). In keeping with the journal's title, it also included a three-person roundtable dialogue, "The Theological Foundations of the Mormon Religion."

Reaction to the articles in the first issue was mixed among members of the church hierarchy. N. Eldon Tanner of the First Presidency was remarkably supportive of the mission of *Dialogue* when he discussed the matter with Leonard in a personal meeting in late January 1966. Leonard reconstructed that meeting in a detailed letter to Wes Johnson. The primary purpose of the meeting was to discuss the Mormon History Association and its objectives and activities at some length; but *Dialogue* was also brought into the discussion. Leonard interpreted Tanner's attitude toward the journal as benign, with the caveat that he hoped there would be a mechanism "for an immediate or early refutation" in the event that an anti-Mormon article or point of view was published.

On the issue of General Authorities writing articles for *Dialogue*, Tanner's answer was in the negative, but out of well-thought-out reasons rather than hostility to the journal. First was that General Authorities were not scholars in the sense that other literary contributors were, "so any contribution they might make would not fit into the tone of the magazine." Second, because of the deferential treatment traditionally afforded General Authorities by church members, the kind of dialogue that the journal envisioned would not likely occur. "Every reader would know that what he writes, he must write the way he writes it; and anyone criticizing this would seem to be criticizing the Church, in a formal sense. Whereas what the rest of us write can be criticized and kicked about because it is in the arena of public discussion." Finally, having articles written by General Authorities would give the impression that *Dialogue* was church-sponsored, "which, from the point of view of both the Church and *Dialogue*, would be unfortunate."

Tanner reiterated that he had no objection to the publication of articles critical of the church, provided there were counterbalanced articles. "Knowing that it is an independent journal, the reader could expect criticism from time to time. If there were no criticisms he would assume that it was very strictly a Church periodical. The independence of the journal can be demonstrated by occasional critical articles or remarks."

Leonard's takeaway from the meeting was that "President Tanner's attitude was completely wholesome, open minded, and fair; and when I mentioned my own connection, he seemed to think this was a good thing for me and for the Church."[35]

But on the other side of the issue was Gordon B. Hinckley, a member of the Quorum of the Twelve who had, for the past twenty years, been almost single-handedly in charge of public relations for the church. According to Devery S. Anderson's history of *Dialogue*'s early years, Hinckley, "sensitive to church coverage in the press" that had focused on the church's increasingly controversial refusal to ordain black men to the priesthood, combined a stake conference in San Mateo, California, with a private meeting on the preceding Saturday evening with Gene England. Hinckley had read the two *New York Times* articles, concluding "that *Dialogue*'s aim was to attempt to speak with finality on Mormon issues. England responded to their conversation in a follow-up letter: 'I can't emphasize too strongly that *Dialogue* is not a theological journal or anything remotely like one; when we talk about a journal of Mormon thought, we are not talking about the Mormon position on any doctrine.'"

England went on to do damage control on behalf of Paul Salisbury, saying that he was not the editor, that he did not speak for England, and that he "was entirely misrepresented and misquoted from the very first paragraph, which erroneously called him the editor. He is a devoted and orthodox member of the church whose association with *Dialogue* can only be to our benefit."

England's assurances seemed to relieve Hinckley's misgivings, and two days later the apostle wrote to him, "The explanation helps," although he expressed concern that *Dialogue* not become known as a journal of dissent.[36]

Public response to the first issue was positive and almost overwhelmingly enthusiastic. In the preface to the second issue the editors wrote jubilantly that the fifteen hundred prepublication subscriptions were expanded by another one thousand in the immediate aftermath of the first issue, and suggested "that *Dialogue* is beginning to satisfy that need. With what seemed to be foolhardy confidence, we printed twice as many copies of the first issue as we had orders for. But our faith proved to be too little; the supply was exhausted in a few weeks, and many who specifically requested the first issue have had to be turned down until a possible reprinting."[37]

Leonard was delighted with the rollout. "I will never forget the day when the first *Dialogue* came to our home in Logan," he noted in his diary. "It was beautiful—more beautiful than any professional magazine I knew about."[38] He was particularly pleased with what it offered to his primary constituency—college students—and he optimistically saw change on the horizon. He wrote happily to John R. T. Hughes, a former student of his at Utah State University and subsequently a Rhodes Scholar, of the symbiotic relationship he saw between college students and *Dialogue*. "The college students are forcing a liberating of Church programs and policies. This is stimulating and healthy. The Church has a real place in the lives of the vast majority of these students, and thus, because of the creativity and wholesome activity and re-thinking, the Church has a role among these people that resembles that in pioneer days. . . . It is these changes which have made possible *Dialogue*, for instance."[39]

A month later, Leonard wrote an even more upbeat assessment to Rodman Paul, a colleague and historian teaching at the California Institute of Technology, assuring him that the church and its membership were now sufficiently "mature" to deal with *Dialogue*'s content, "even when adverse, as part of the process of obtaining understanding and truth."[40]

More national publicity followed when *Time* magazine published a brief article five months later, in August 1966, that began with a solid endorsement of *Dialogue*'s vision: "Unquestioning belief rather than critical self-examination has always been the Mormon style. Breaking with this tradition, a group of young Mormon intellectuals, all of whom went to either Harvard or Stanford, have brought out *Dialogue*, a learned quarterly dedicated to the proposition that the faith of the Latter-day Saints is compatible with reasoned inquiry." Although the journal's tone "contrasts sharply with that of the vast array of official Mormon publications—ranging from Salt Lake City's daily *Deseret News* to the *Relief Society Magazine*," its stated purpose was above reproach: "[It] is designed to keep intelligent, educated Mormons who might otherwise fall by the wayside within the community of Saints."

Despite the warning of an unnamed church leader who ominously predicted, "*Dialogue* can't help but hurt the church," the subscription list of three thousand—double the prepublication number—suggested that it was benevolently fulfilling a previously unmet need. The article concluded by quoting Eugene England: "A man need not relinquish his faith to be intellectually respectable, nor his intellect to be faithful."[41]

In spite of the upbeat assessment from the national press, an article from the issue cited by *Time* became problematic for Leonard. Written by political science professor J. D. Williams of the University of Utah, the twenty-five-page article mentioned the John Birch Society in only one paragraph, and that paragraph contained a single sentence mentioning Apostle Ezra Taft Benson: "The rental of the Assembly Hall in February to a Birch Society front group for five lectures (with paid admissions); Elder Benson's keynote speech in that series, defend[ed] the Birch Society in its fight against Communism."[42]

But that was sufficient to elicit the ire of Benson and deprive Leonard of what would have been a life-defining church calling. He wrote, without bitterness but with palpable regret: "I learned from a friend among the general authorities that I had been approved as president of the Italian mission when it was opened in 1967, but just prior to my call an article written by J. D. Williams that was regarded as critical of Ezra Taft Benson had appeared in *Dialogue*. Because of my connection with *Dialogue*, my name was withdrawn. Although I had nothing to do with the approval of the article, I lost this opportunity of preaching the gospel in Italy in Italian."[43]

Benson's animus toward *Dialogue* did not end with the Williams article. In December 1967 he told Alvin R. Dyer, then a counselor in the First Presidency, "that the continued publication of the magazine, and of its liberal content, was a matter of discussion in the Quorum of the Twelve meeting on Thursday, November 30."[44] On another occasion, in a meeting of the Church Board of Education that was chaired by church president David O. McKay, Benson pushed for a drastic response to its continuing publication. In 1972, Leonard recorded the details as he learned them later from a General Authority who was in the meeting:

> Brother Benson raised the question of BYU staff members publishing in *Dialogue*. He thought that they should not do so—that they

should be prohibited from doing so. It was clear from the discussion that about half of the brethren were in favor of supporting publishing in *Dialogue* and the others were opposed to it. Brother Benson saw this cleavage, this division and brought his hand down firmly on the table and said that he thought this kind of thing should be done: he thought that *Dialogue* should be burned. President McKay, who had said nothing during the discussion suddenly stood up and said, "Let me say this[,] brethren, that this Church is not about to burn any publication. We have no business burning books and if we should burn a publication of this nature then to be consistent we ought to burn some of the books of brethren in this room who have published books." So that ended the discussion.[45]

The official position of the church toward *Dialogue*, both then and now, has been one of acknowledging its existence without either approving or disapproving it. In 1967 the *Priesthood Bulletin*, which was sent to local ecclesiastical leaders throughout the church, contained the following statement, the only official statement to this day concerning *Dialogue*: "In answer to questions from stake and ward leaders and from individual members of the Church, the magazine *Dialogue* is an independent magazine, privately owned, operated and edited. It has no connection with The Church of Jesus Christ of Latter-day Saints either officially or unofficially. Articles appearing in this publication are never submitted to Church Authorities for approval and therefore are the sole responsibility of the editors."[46]

On two other occasions prior to Leonard's calling as church historian in 1972, *Dialogue* was the subject of discussion among members of the First Presidency. Both concerned the church's policy of denying priesthood ordination to blacks of African descent, and in both instances President McKay and at least one of his counselors were displeased. In the first instance the journal published a letter by Stewart L. Udall, then U.S. Secretary of the Interior, an inactive Mormon, and the descendant of a prominent, pioneer Mormon family, calling on church leaders to drop the policy: "It must be resolved because we are wrong and it is past the time when we should have seen the right."[47]

The *New York Times* ran an article on the letter entitled, "Udall Entreats Mormons on Race," which noted, "A demand that the Mormon church immediately remove all restrictions on Negro members has been made by Stewart L. Udall, Secretary of the Interior. . . . 'This issue must be resolved—and resolved not by pious moralistic platitudes but by clear and explicit pronouncements and decisions that come to grips with the imperious truths of the contemporary world,' Mr. Udall said."

The *Times* article was troublesome for the church on two levels. One was that it focused an international spotlight on a church policy that was increasingly problematic. The other was that observers of the political scene saw the article "as creating new problems for Gov. George Romney's campaign for the Republican Presidential nomination."[48]

Three members of the First Presidency were contacted by the press for reactions to the letter—Hugh B. Brown, N. Eldon Tanner, and Joseph Fielding Smith. All declined public comment,[49] but David O. McKay's diary summarized the First Presidency's private discussion of the matter. Brown reported that the prior day he had had visits from two prominent church members, Rex Campbell, a broadcaster for church-owned radio station KSL; and Lowell Bennion, former director of the LDS Institute of Religion at the University of Utah. Both felt strongly that the First Presidency needed to clarify the policy with regard to the priesthood ban, pointing out "that means all the rights and authority that go with the Priesthood. More than that, we have nothing to say." But the suggestion was problematic, for nothing had changed with respect to McKay's feelings on the subject, even though, unbeknownst to his counselors, he had sought unsuccessfully the revelation he believed would be necessary to change it. Merely to restate a policy that was already widely criticized in the public square would invite even more criticism, and thus, "It was our sentiment that no official statement on the matter should be published at this time."[50]

The second occasion, which focused on the same issue, proved more vexing.[51] Stephen Taggart, an undergraduate at the University of Utah, wrote and submitted to *Dialogue* a manuscript that challenged the church policy on historical grounds and made public a recent letter written by Sterling McMurrin to Llewelyn McKay, President McKay's second-oldest son. McMurrin described a 1954 meeting in which President McKay said that the policy was a practice and not a doctrine. A "practice," in the minds of some, including First Counselor Hugh B. Brown, who had been given a copy of Taggart's manuscript, suggested the possibility of change, whereas a "doctrine" did not. Indeed, in a meeting with his father on September 10, 1969, that included Llewelyn's older brother Lawrence, First Presidency counselor Alvin R. Dyer, and Roy Cheville, presiding patriarch of the Reorganized Church of Jesus Christ of Latter Day Saints, Llewelyn "asked his father if this was not perhaps the time to announce that the Negro could be given the Priesthood, which he alone could announce, and to do so now voluntarily rather than to be pressured into it later."[52] Dyer, who was adamantly opposed to any change in the policy, said to the other members of the presidency that he "considered it one of the most vicious, untrue articles that has ever been written about the Church."[53]

Taggart's essay won *Dialogue*'s best article prize for the year and was scheduled to appear in a forthcoming issue, but later in the year Taggart died of cancer and his family decided to withdraw the article from *Dialogue* and have it published as a booklet.[54] Prior to the family's decision, however, Lester Bush wrote a lengthy critique of the manuscript that was published in *Dialogue* and that set the stage for his own game-changing article on the subject several years later.[55]

These incidents notwithstanding, Leonard remained one of *Dialogue*'s greatest cheerleaders. While on sabbatical at UCLA in 1967, he wrote to a member of the editorial staff that he had met a "considerable number" of Southern Californians who not only read *Dialogue*, but who credited it with keeping them in the church. "There are many who have found this proof of intellectual respectability of Mormonism and the intellectual excitement that comes from reading and discussing such practical and theological issues as are discussed in it. In other words, I continue to cast my vote for *Dialogue* as the finest thing that has happened in the Church since the creation of the university stakes."[56]

The following year he went a step further by asserting to a friend with ambivalent feelings about the journal that *Dialogue* was doing something that no other factor in the church had been able to do in reaching students and keeping them in the fold. Notwithstanding the fact that he did not expect to agree with everything published in it, nor did he even agree that everything thus far published should have been published, "I have found it personally to be a wonderful missionary for the Church. I personally know more than fifty persons who have been brought into activity as the result of 'exposure' to *Dialogue*. . . . There are certain students—and former students—who can be reached through *Dialogue* that can't be reached by the conventional means."[57]

One ironic—and unforeseen—effect of *Dialogue* was to reinvigorate with new funds, a new editor, and greater autonomy the journal whose retreat had been a major factor in promoting the birth of *Dialogue* in the first place: *BYU Studies*. In 1967 its new editor, Charles Tate, acknowledged to Gene England, "I will freely admit that if I am able to bring [*BYU*] *Studies* 'of age,' it will be because of the impact of *Dialogue*, which has given the Church a challenge and in that way aided it."[58]

Leonard's calling as church historian in 1972 obliged him to pull back in his public support of *Dialogue*—he published no articles in it as long as he held the position—but he continued, largely behind the scenes, to promote the publication of Mormon studies.

14

CHURCH HISTORIAN
THE "CAMELOT" YEARS

In a nostalgic narrative of the decade that Leonard served as church historian, Davis Bitton, one of the two assistant church historians during that time, borrowed from Jacqueline Kennedy by invoking the name of King Arthur's mythical kingdom of Camelot and applying it to those years.[1] In both instances, the name was applied retroactively, and in both it was less than a perfect fit. Nonetheless, a new era in Mormon history began on a very bright note.

THE CALLING

Leonard documented the first official steps, in 1972, with meticulous detail:

> On the afternoon of Wednesday, January 5, while in my office at the University I received a telephone call from President Eldon Tanner of the LDS Church. President Tanner asked when I would next be in Salt Lake City. I replied that I would come whenever he wished it. He replied with a chuckle, "How about yesterday?" He said that he had a serious matter to discuss with me and would appreciate my coming down as soon as possible. . . .

Leonard and Grace the next day drove to Salt Lake City, where he met with President Tanner at about 11:15 a.m.

> I was ushered into his office immediately, and he sat me in the big leather easy chair next to his own. He said, "Brother Arrington, I'll come straight to the point and not waste our time. You have been asked to occupy an Endowed Chair in Western Studies at BYU, have you not?"
> "Yes."

"In my office yesterday were Brother Neal Maxwell, Commissioner of Education, and President Dallin Oaks of BYU. They told me about your fitness for the Chair, and of their desire to have you at BYU. Now, Brother Arrington, we need a Church Historian. You know that Brother [A. William] Lund died last February, and we have not replaced him.[2] We would like to initiate a reorganization of the Church Historian's Office. This is the first in a series of reorganizations in which members of the Quorum of the Twelve will cease to occupy staff positions in the various organizations and programs of the church. Such positions will be occupied either by designated officers or by assistants to the Quorum of the Twelve. We would like to organize the Church Historian's Office along those lines. We would like Brother Alvin Dyer to be managing director of the office; you, Brother Arrington, to be Church Historian; and Brother Earl Olson, to be Church Archivist. Will you accept the position of Church Historian under such an arrangement?"

"Well, I suppose so. To whom would I be responsible? To what extent would I be free to function under my own initiative and inspiration?"

"Well, Brother Arrington, you would normally go through the channel of Brother Dyer to obtain budgets, personnel, and approval for policies and programs. Brother Dyer would in turn be responsible to one of the Apostles—possibly Brother Hunter, who as you know, is the present Church Historian. Will you accept?"

"President Tanner, if you think I am capable, and if you think the arrangement is practical, then I am willing to do my best."

"Now, of course, this doesn't change your appointment to the Endowed Chair at BYU. It simply means that you will have to divide your time in a way you think best between BYU and the Church Historian's Office. President Oaks is willing to support you in both positions, and I am also. You will have the opportunity of working with graduate students and faculty and the administration there in a purely professional way; and you will have the opportunity of writing and publishing the history of the Church. As you know, Brother Arrington, we have done very little writing of Church history in the last 40 years. We are under obligations to write our history for the benefit of the generations to come, and we want it to be done in a thoroughly professional way, and we have confidence that you can do it. You ought to know, Brother Arrington, that we have consulted historians in the church and the overwhelming desire of them is to have you as the Chief Historian of the Church."

"President Tanner[,] that's a pretty big order for a farm boy from Idaho, but, as I said, I will do my best."[3]

As the meeting concluded, Tanner made a generous gesture to Leonard, highly unusual for a member of the First Presidency to extend to a church employee not in the ecclesiastical line, saying that his door would "always be open for any matter, which I would like to bring in directly to him, if I have any difficulties with Brother Dyer."

The following day Leonard wrote to his son Carl, then serving an LDS mission in Bolivia, alerting him to the probability of a family move to Salt Lake City rather than Provo and noting that "Mamma frankly is not charmed by SLC." Though she much preferred Provo, she accepted the likely necessity of a move to the bigger city.[4]

DRAMATIS PERSONAE

N. Eldon Tanner, a Canadian citizen, served as Minister of Lands and Mines in the province of Alberta for many years, and then moved into the private sector as the president of Trans-Canada Pipelines prior to being called to fulltime church service in October 1960. His career success was largely due to extraordinary people skills. A non-Mormon executive on whose board of directors he served recalled, "Tanner had probably the greatest touch of anybody I've ever met, with respect to bringing people together and managing tough situations. He did it differently than anybody I've ever known."[5] Initially called as an assistant to the Twelve, Tanner rose within the hierarchy at an astonishing pace, joining the Quorum of the Twelve in 1962, and the First Presidency one year later. So rapid was his ascent that, at the time of his calling into the First Presidency, he was the most junior of the Twelve, and yet occupied a position in the hierarchy over his eleven senior colleagues. One apostle remarked in a general conference address, "Seniority is honored among ordained Apostles, even when entering or leaving a room."[6] In such a system where seniority was paramount, Tanner's junior status likely factored in his later silence when apostles senior to him acted adversely toward Leonard.

Joseph Fielding Smith was church president at the time of Leonard's calling. Born while Brigham Young was still alive, Smith had intimate knowledge of conflicts with the nation that had informed the largely polemical histories of Mormonism written by church members during the first century of the church's existence. Although lacking any formal training in history, he became church historian in 1921 and served in that capacity until becoming church president in

1970. His only historical work, *Essentials in Church History*, published a year after he became church historian, was thoroughly apologetic, and thus a sharp contrast to the more objective, balanced histories produced during Leonard's tenure in that office. He died only six months after Leonard's calling, and although his style of historiography clashed markedly with Leonard's, he was never a major player in the workings of the new Church Historical Department, and he made no effort to shape the history that Leonard proposed to write. *Essentials* was reprinted as late as 1979 and is still available as an e-book to this day.[7]

Howard W. Hunter succeeded Smith as church historian and served for two years until Leonard was called to a position with the same name but with a far different job description. Hunter was a strong supporter of the kind of history that Leonard and his colleagues produced but was not a significant voice when, after the death of Harold B. Lee, two apostles who were senior to him moved to clip the wings of the History Division.

Alvin R. Dyer was Leonard's first General Authority supervisor. Dyer came to the attention of the hierarchy when, as president of the Central States Mission in the mid-1950s, he revolutionized proselytizing by taking an emotional, rather than didactic approach, with missionaries bearing fervent testimony and pressing investigators to commit to baptisms, often within a few days of the initial contact, rather than the prior approach that involved careful and thorough doctrinal discussions, emphasis on studying the scriptures, and attending church meetings to be more thoroughly integrated into the congregation by the time they committed to baptism. Called to be an assistant to the Twelve in 1958, he directed the unprecedented—and sometimes scandalous—surge of convert baptisms in the British Isles in the late 1950s and early 1960s.[8] President David O. McKay ordained him to the office of apostle in 1967, even though there were no vacancies in the Quorum of the Twelve, and, six months later, called him as an "additional counselor" in the First Presidency, a status also conferred upon Thorpe B. Isaacson and Joseph Fielding Smith. This situation produced a fluidity in the arrangement of the First Presidency that had rarely existed since the days of Joseph Smith himself;[9] and upon McKay's death, the new First Presidency and Quorum of the Twelve took swift measures to revert to the more typical pattern. Dyer was released from the First Presidency and spent the rest of his life as an assistant to the Twelve (1970–1976) and a member of the First Quorum of the Seventy (1976–1977), but never served in the Quorum of the Twelve. An amateur historian, he wrote *The Refiner's Fire: Historical Highlights of Missouri*.[10] He was a strong supporter of Leonard and his vision of what the History Division could and should be doing. However, he suffered a debilitating stroke only five months after Leonard's calling as church historian. Although he partially recovered and retained his ecclesiastical position until his death, his involvement with the History Division was limited to occasional meetings in his car in the underground parking lot of the Church Office Building. Thus, Leonard lost both a strong advocate for History Division projects and also a mentor who understood the difficulties of being an outsider imposed on an entrenched and protective bureaucracy. Dyer was released as managing director in December 1972 and replaced by Joseph Anderson (see below).

Harold B. Lee came to the attention of the church hierarchy when, as a stake president in Salt Lake City during the Great Depression, he initiated a program of self-help that was soon expanded to the entire church, first as the Church Security Program and then as the Church Welfare Program. Called into the Quorum of the Twelve in 1941 at age forty-two, he began to envision a modernized church organization. "He had his charts for correlation all prepared," according to his son-in-law and biographer, Brent Goates. "But he rolled them up and put them in his roll-top desk, and there they sat gathering dust for 15, 20 years."[11] In 1960, church president David O. McKay appointed Lee to head what became known simply as Correlation, a major and continuing initiative that largely defines both the structure and function of church components. As noted in chapter 10, Lee played a major role in the restructuring of church departments. Part of that reorganization transformed the Church Historian's Office into the Church Historical Department, replacing, in an unconventional calling, the apostolic church historian with a trained professional, Leonard Arrington. Lee was perhaps Leonard's strongest champion in the hierarchy; and only six months after Leonard's interview with Tanner, Lee became the eleventh church president at the relatively young age of seventy-three. His unexpected death only eighteen months later shifted the internal balance of power, leaving Leonard without a strong and/or knowledgeable advocate.

Spencer W. Kimball became the church president at Lee's death. Few had expected that Kimball, a cancer survivor four years older than Lee, would become president, but he served in that position for twelve years. Although the last four or five of those years were a time of diminished capacity (he delivered his last conference talk in person in April 1981, four and a half years prior to his death), he effected the most dramatic change in the LDS Church in the twentieth century: extending priesthood ordination to worthy men of African descent. He thus reversed more than a century of exclusion based upon shaky theology and historical tradition and, what is more, did it in a way that brought the Quorum of the Twelve to a unified decision instead of creating division and abrasive internal relationship. Even the charismatic David O. McKay had failed to achieve this goal, despite his personal conviction that black exclusion was a policy, not a doctrine.

Noah and Edna Arrington, Leonard's parents, Twin Falls, Idaho, 1913, shortly after their wedding.

Leonard, age three, 1920.

Noah and Edna Arrington, Twin Falls, Idaho, 1927, shortly after Noah's return from his proselytizing mission.

The first page of Leonard Arrington's first diary, 1927. He wrote, "When I was ten years old, my mother gave me for Christmas a tablet and suggested I write my personal history. I did write, perhaps ten or twenty pages, and then continued to add things that happened when I was eleven, twelve, and thirteen. I still have the tablet, in which I wrote with a pencil."

Leonard Arrington, age fifteen, and his prize Rhode Island Red roosters in front of his first chicken house, 1932.

LDS Institute of Religion, University of Idaho, where Arrington lived from 1935 until 1939 while an undergraduate student. Years later the building was demolished after a fire.

Leonard Arrington at the commencement of his senior year at the University of Idaho, age twenty-one, ca. November 1938.

The Arrington family, 1943, shortly before Wayne (navy) and Leonard (army), both in uniform, were deployed to Europe. Front row: Noah, Ross, Edna, Doris. Middle row: Donald, Ralph. Back row: LeRoy, Wayne, Kenneth, Leonard, Marie.

Leonard Arrington and Grace Fort on their wedding day, Raleigh, North Carolina, 1943.

Private Leonard Arrington prior to overseas deployment, 1943.

Leonard Arrington and his brother Wayne, reunited briefly in Oran, North Africa, July 26, 1944.

Corporal Leonard Arrington's office at the Instituto Centrale di Statistica in Rome, 1945.

Leonard Arrington as a junior faculty member at Utah State Agricultural College, 1954.

The Arrington family aboard RMS *Queen Elizabeth*, returning from Leonard's sabbatical year in Italy, 1959. From left: Carl, Grace, Susan, Leonard, James.

Kimball was personally supportive of Leonard, on one occasion telling him, "I want you to know that I love you very much, and that the Lord is pleased that you are the historian of His Church."[12] Leonard cherished this warm expression, but Kimball's priorities lay elsewhere and he was not an advocate for the advancement of a historical agenda. Leonard's son Carl observed, "President Kimball really loved my dad. But he wasn't very interested in history; he was a missionary guy. . . . So Dad lost his protective covering, and after that the bureaucracy—he couldn't fight it."[13]

Ezra Taft Benson was ordained an apostle on the same day, October 7, 1943, as Spencer W. Kimball; but, four years younger than Kimball, Benson was the junior of the two in terms of the all-important quorum seniority. A decade after becoming an apostle, Benson became the first Mormon to serve as a U.S. cabinet secretary—of the Department of Agriculture—and was one of only two cabinet members to remain in office during all eight years of the Eisenhower administration. Leonard learned late in the game, in 1979, that Benson's attitude toward research and writing in Mormonism was consistent with his attitude toward research in agriculture:

> Glen Taggart . . . had been an employee of the Department of Agriculture during all of the years that Elder Benson was Secretary of Agriculture. . . . When I reported to him that Elder Benson took a dim view of our analytical history, believing history ought to help sell the cause of Mormonism, President Taggart said that that was consistent with his management of the Department of Agriculture. Under his administration they cut down on the research in the Department of Agriculture quite drastically . . . [and] also cut down the appropriations for research for the agricultural experiment stations around the country. . . . Elder Benson wanted the research activities of the Department to concentrate on "selling agriculture" and "selling agricultural products," both in this country but especially overseas.[14]

Benson thus lined up with Joseph Fielding Smith in being wary of innovation and protective of the oversimplified and iconic triumphalist history in which "the hand of the Lord" was conspicuously and constantly visible.

Mark E. Petersen was ordained an apostle six months after Kimball and Benson. A lifelong journalist, even after becoming an apostle he held the strongly influential positions of president and chairman of the board of the church-owned *Deseret News*. While never a supervisor of the Historical Department, he, along with Benson, exercised close surveillance of publications by Leonard and his associates, primarily through church employees who zealously highlighted and forwarded to him, generally out of context, passages that were at odds with apologetic histories.

Boyd K. Packer was a career educator in the LDS Church Educational System prior to being called as an assistant to the Twelve in 1961. He became an apostle in 1970 following the death of David O. McKay. Although only one other apostle (Bruce R. McConkie) was junior to him at the time of Leonard's call, Packer moved continually and forcefully to impose his views of apologetic and defensive church history, making himself a significant voice within the Quorum of the Twelve on the topic. Late in 1974 he breached protocol by sending a lengthy letter directly to the First Presidency. This action was an end run around the two senior members of his quorum who were the advisors to the Historical Department, and it might have resulted in a disciplinary rebuke. However, it instead made him something of a self-appointed and unchallenged spokesperson on historical issues. The letter, which was highly critical of the History Division and focused on its first published book, Dean C. Jessee's landmark compilation of Brigham Young's letters to his sons, took advantage of latent uneasiness among some of his senior colleagues who saw him as their ally and aide in changing the direction of the History Division. He thus accrued power out of proportion to his position and showed himself adept at retaining and expanding it.

Joseph Anderson, born in 1889, was the oldest of the church officials with whom Leonard worked. After serving for forty-eight years as a secretary to the First Presidency, Anderson's faithful service was rewarded with the calling to be an assistant to the Twelve in 1970. When it became clear that Alvin Dyer would not recover sufficiently from his stroke to resume his church duties, Anderson replaced him in December 1972. Leonard's initial response to the change was negative: "I fear for our programs. Brother Anderson is far more conservative and, of course, was brought up in the old school of Joseph Fielding Smith and A. William Lund. The image he would project of the Historical Department would not be a good one, and I am fearful that his decisions will be restrictive and unprogressive."[15] But Anderson turned out to be just the opposite where his personality was concerned: "Elder Anderson was genial, helpful, and kept himself fully informed of our work. He fully approved our projects and programs."[16] This description is not completely accurate, as events would show. Anderson manifested dismay at some innovations and, well trained as a secretary but not an executive, was remarkably reluctant to make decisions. As a result, although he was a cordial and pleasant presence, he failed to provide the energetic leadership and advocacy that were crucial as key issues emerged. Anderson remained the General Authority supervisor over the Historical Department until 1977, when he was replaced by G. Homer Durham.

G. Homer Durham was an educator with a degree in political science, whose academic career was capped by nine years as president of Arizona State University (1960–1969) and seven years as the first commissioner of the Utah System of Higher Education (1969–1976). Shortly after being called to the First Quorum of Seventy in 1977, he became the supervisor of the Historical Department. Leonard's first impression was the opposite of what it had been with Joseph Anderson: "Homer Durham, our new managing director, took over and we are thrilled to have him. He will be professional help as well as providing good ecclesiastical interference and administration. We are grateful for him."[17] And as with Anderson, Leonard's first impression proved misleading, for Durham's assignment came with a mandate to change the direction of the department. Durham undertook the task with an enthusiasm bordering on ruthlessness, contemplating firing or transferring most of the staff and curtailing authorized projects without hesitation. Such a plan would have consigned Leonard to his academic position as incumbent of the Redd Chair only. Ultimately, however, a less destructive plan was enacted. Some, but not all, of the History Division employees survived its dismantling and were transferred to a newly created institute at Brigham Young University. In a fuzzy, awkwardly dated, and never publicly announced move, Durham replaced Leonard as church historian without the traditional formality of releasing Leonard publicly and sustaining Durham. From that point, the church historian has always been a General Authority, although rapid rotations of assignments, often only three years, has meant that the degree of leadership provided varied markedly from man to man.

Earl Olson was a grandson of Andrew Jenson, who had served as assistant church historian for much of the early twentieth century. Lacking formal training in history, Olson nonetheless spent his entire career, beginning in 1934, working in the Church Historian's Office, which later became the Church Historical Department.[18] Initially a peer of Leonard on the organizational chart as church archivist, he became Leonard's immediate supervisor. Fiercely loyal to the tradition of apologetic history after more than three decades of working under the direction of Joseph Fielding Smith, he disagreed with Leonard's vision. Interviewed in 2006, he asserted: "[Leonard] wanted to start a completely new history. I object to that. I told him we ought to continue what had already been going on for years."[19] Olson remained in the Historical Department until his retirement in 1986.

A New Beginning

A week after Leonard met with Eldon Tanner, all employees of the Church Historian's Office gathered in the third-floor auditorium of the historic Church

Administration Building at 47 East South Temple Street. Seated on the platform were Tanner, Howard Hunter, Alvin Dyer, Earl Olson, and Leonard. Tanner announced the reorganization of the office, released Hunter as church historian, and asked for a sustaining vote for Dyer as the new managing director of the office, Leonard as church historian, and Olson as church archivist. The sustaining vote, carried over straight from ecclesiastical reorganizations in wards and stakes, was—to no one's surprise—unanimous. Tanner said the changes would take effect immediately. Hunter would continue to have a relationship with the office, albeit as advisor rather than manager.

Reaction to Leonard's appointment was immediate and overwhelmingly positive. Leonard recalled to his son in Bolivia, a diary entry Carl had written while at the Language Training Mission that recounted "positive assurance" in response to fasting and prayer.[20] Leonard wrote exuberantly that many people were excited by his appointment,

> mostly because it represents such a departure from tradition: a professionally trained person, a non-General Authority, a person outside the family of a General Authority, and so on. Also a person with a reputation already established of "telling it like it is." Also a person who has felt free to publish in church magazines, *Dialogue* and professional historical magazines. . . .
>
> In my heart, I suppose I have known all along this would happen, although my logic and experience told me that it was only an outside possibility. I am reconciled, partly as the result of your diary, that it is the Lord's will, and I shall do my best.

Leonard concluded this letter with a sentence that proved to be quite true, but in a way that ultimately worked against him: "I cannot see that I can handle things significantly different than I have done previously as a professional here at the University."[21]

A week later he reiterated to his son the novelty of his appointment, the first of an academic to the post, perhaps an early realization that the degree of surprise was also a measure of how much disapproval might be building among those who had not sought him out with congratulations: "I suppose a lot of 'intellectuals' might have been pleased that an academic person who was a 'liberal' received the appointment. Not since 1843 had a person been appointed Church Historian who was not a General Authority."[22]

A week after the transitional meeting, a relaxed and friendly Hunter invited Leonard into his office for a private and extraordinary conversation, passing on explanations of the office he had held and suggestions he had received. He told

Leonard that his appointment was due to Hunter's strong feeling that the church needed a professional historian and also to the recommendations of Arrington's professionally trained peers. Hunter reported that "it had seemed impossible to arrange the matter financially until the possibility arose of a joint appointment in which the Redd Endowment at BYU would pay half of my salary and the Church would pay the other half." The reorganization of church authority "liberating the Twelve from administrative responsibilities," which had begun even before William Lund's death, had delayed the appointment for months. Based on a study initiated by Lee Bickmore, CEO of the National Biscuit Company, the Twelve were seeking relief "from administration to do constructive planning. The various departments of the Church would then be administrated by competent professionally trained people."[23] The Historical Department was one of the first to change.

> Elder Hunter said that he felt that the Church was mature enough that our history should be honest. He did not believe in suppressing information, nor hiding documents, nor concealing or withholding minutes for possible scrutiny. He excluded from this, however, people who were setting out diligently to discredit the Church. The only name he mentioned under that heading was Gerald [Jerald] and Sandra Tanner.[24] He thought the best way to answer anti-Mormonism is to print the truth. He thought we should publish the documents of our history. He did not see any reason to conceal the minutes of the Council of 50.[25] "Why not disclose them?" he asked. "They are a part of our history, why should we withhold things that are a part of our history?" He thought it in our best interest to encourage scholars— to help and cooperate with them in doing honest research.[26]

This was music to Leonard's ears. Also buoying Leonard's spirits was the imminent move of the entire department. The Church Office Building, at twenty-six stories the tallest building in the State of Utah at the time, had been mothballed for several years because of budget constraints; but it was nearly complete, and the prospect of new quarters for the historians was most encouraging. They would occupy four floors of the east wing of the building instead of a single floor in the Church Administration Building, and thus would enjoy both ample working space and plenty of shelving room for their library and manuscripts.[27]

Then there was the heady issue of archival access. Having been one of the few outsiders ever to navigate the inner corridors of the archives, Leonard saw limitless potential coming from his new mandate. Two decades later he reflected that "in more than one hundred fifty years only a handful of trusted church leaders had had unrestricted access to . . . one of the most important depositories of America in the Mountain West."[28] The euphoria of access was buffered by the sobriety of balance. He reflected in an August 1972 diary entry, after the physical move to the Church Office Building and Alvin Dyer's crippling stroke but also after he had been formally sustained in general conference with the other general church officers: "On the one hand, I am the *Church* Historian and must seek to build testimonies, spread the Word, build the Kingdom. On the other hand, I am called to be a *historian*, which means that I must earn the respect of professional historians—what I write must be craftsman like, credible, and of good quality. This means that I stand on two legs—the leg of faith and the leg of reason."

He had been assured from the first that he "should *both* work to improve the quality of history writing within the church *and* continue to do work of such professional quality that it will win and deserve the respect of professional historians." Yet he recognized the difficulty of a task that involved building religious conviction and thereby achieving recognition from members of the LDS Church who expected no less from him but would not recognize or appreciate his efforts to "build the reputation of the Church in the professional field of history."[29]

Leonard and Earl Olson moved quickly to reorganize the office. They agreed on the utility of renaming it from the "Church Historian's Office" to the "Church Historical Department," a proposal that was approved. Leonard's own responsibility as a church historian charged with writing history rather than overseeing the entire operations of the department—including the archival, acquisitions, and library—was new: "there have been no persons employed to do this task, and so my division—the Church Historian's Division—is having to be created from nothing."[30] (Leonard's division rapidly adopted the name of "History Division," rather than retaining the earlier allusion to the older Church Historian's Office.)

When told that he could hire an assistant church historian, he asked instead that two be hired, each on a half-time basis: James Allen was a professor of history at Brigham Young University and one of only a handful of historians whose work focused on twentieth-century Mormonism—the others still concentrating on the nineteenth century. Davis Bitton, a professor of history at the University of Utah, had trained in Renaissance and Reformation history. With Leonard's connection to Utah State University, all three universities in the State of Utah were thus represented in the inner circle. The three men sometimes referred to themselves as the "stake presidency," an unofficial title that easily communicated the close way in which they worked together and shared a sense of mission.

Leonard's official title of church historian, however, was problematic. While it was the same title as that of his predecessors Joseph Fielding Smith and Howard W. Hunter, his job description was radically different. Smith and Hunter presided over all functions of the Church Historian's Office but wrote no histories, with the exception of Smith's 1922 *Essentials in Church History* and occasional articles. Leonard, by contrast, was one of two (later four, with the addition of Donald Schmidt as director of the library, and Florence Jacobsen as director of arts and sites) division directors who answered to Alvin Dyer as managing director of the Church Historical Department, and then to Hunter as apostolic advisor to the department. Leonard's primary mandate was to do what the other church historians had not done since 1922: write books on church history. Earl Olson, who began as his peer but became his supervisor, commented that Leonard's title and position as one among equals "created real problems, because they called him Church Historian and everybody thought, from the title, that he was in charge of the Historical Department."[31]

Yet another issue was the ambiguous nature of the position, alluded to by Leonard above. A colleague explained, "He told me that he asked them, 'Is this a calling, or are you offering me a job?' And the answer was, 'We'll just have to see.'"[32] The ambiguity was never resolved, for he was paid as a salaried professional (ecclesiastical officers are paid a "living allowance" instead of a salary to allow the church to state that it has no paid ministry), but "released" as church historian (as is the case when ecclesiastical officers conclude the service to which they were "called") when he was transferred to BYU in 1982.

The explosion of activity combined with the multitudinous ambiguities and potential opportunities tapped a wellspring of feeling that surprised even Leonard. With the "stake presidency" fully constituted, Leonard, the two assistant church historians, and Dean Jessee, the most senior researcher in the department, gathered in his office, where they began their journey by kneeling in prayer, offered by Leonard. He was surprised by his emotional and spiritual reaction at the conclusion of the prayer: "I just cried and cried," he wrote to his son, "the first time I had broken down in this fashion in a long time."[33]

THE GRAND PLAN

Although Leonard was surprised to be chosen church historian, he did not go into the job unprepared. Indeed, he had expected for several months to be assistant church historian, and he had spent many years reading hundreds of books written about Mormonism. He fully appreciated that they lacked balance. The very first book produced by the new religion, in 1830, was the Book of Mormon, which by its very existence made demanding truth claims and was an exposition of two main propositions: that it was an ancient scripture and that Joseph Smith was God's prophet. The very first book written about Mormonism by a non-Mormon, Eber D.

Howe's *Mormonism Unvailed* (1834), was a cover-to-cover attack on those truth claims. As has been noted, nearly all books on Mormonism written for more than a century thereafter fell into one or the other of these two camps. Leonard viewed his primary responsibility as church historian of writing books on Mormon history as requiring that he occupy the nearly vacant middle ground between apologetics and attack.

The few who had ventured away from polemical history were contemporaries of Leonard and included Wallace Stegner (*Mormon Country*, 1942); Bernard De-Voto (*The Year of Decision: 1846*, 1943); Fawn Brodie (*No Man Knows My History: The Life of Joseph Smith the Mormon Prophet*, 1945); Dale Morgan (*The Great Salt Lake*, 1947); and Juanita Brooks (*The Mountain Meadows Massacre*, 1950). While Brodie's book displays a clear bias against Joseph Smith, it represented a new level of scholarly research and writing. Continuously in print since 1945, it remains the most influential of the group.

Beginning in 1956, two years before *Great Basin Kingdom* was published, Leonard gradually mapped the terrain that he would later navigate as church historian. He first commented on the inadequacies of what had been written and on the opportunities for future writing. In that year he wrote to George Ellsworth and pointed out how few authors had taken advantage of the vast collection of Mormon pamphlets and documents, putting some of the blame on the church itself:

> I have the impression that with regard to the early pamphlets, [Bro-die] pretty well relied upon the apostate and anti-Mormon. This may have been either due to the fact that most libraries have only the scalawag literature on early Mormonism (and the church's collection was not of easy access), or she may have early formed her opinion of the prophet and simply selected these materials that seemed most likely to fit in with that interpretation. In some respects the church is at fault for the widespread use of Brodie, Linn, etc., because it has done nothing to encourage (and has done much to discourage) the use of the Mormon pamphlets and documents.[34] We seem to have rested on the Pratt-Smith collection in the so-called documentary history and done nothing to add to our side of the case since. And I did find things that help to explain some of the more questionable early activities.[35]

Four years later and still a decade before his appointment as church historian, Leonard bemoaned the sorry state of Mormon biography in an address to the Timpanogos Club by noting that the only important Utah diary published with scholarly apparatus was Robert Cleland and Juanita Brooks's edition of John D. Lee's diaries.[36] "What about Wilford Woodruff, George Q. Cannon, George A. Smith, Brigham Young, Charles C. Rich, and others?" Noting eastern foundations' support of publications on prominent early Americans, he asserted, "As a Utahan, I am ashamed [to] find no effort being made to publish even a small part of the documents pertaining to Brigham Young. And yet here is American's greatest colonizer in a nation of colonizers!"[37]

A year later, in an address to history majors at Brigham Young University, he noted the general absence of Mormons from histories of the American West and again put some of the blame at home. That Arnold Toynbee, in his ten-volume history of civilizations, mentioned Mormons briefly only three times—"Once in connection with plural marriage; once in connection with the trek West, and once by mentioning the Book of Mormon"—was primarily due to a lack of scholarly literature for him and other generalists to draw on. It did not reflect a low opinion of Mormon's historical role or contributions. "Things don't get into the textbooks until there is a significant body of scholarly writing about the subject that one cannot ignore. And who is to blame for this? No one but ourselves for not doing our homework adequately and effectively."[38]

Five years later, Leonard criticized, in correspondence with prominent western historian Rodman Paul, the prevailing philosophy of the Church Historian's Office regarding access to manuscript material and suggested that the time had arrived for a change. The office had for forty years been under an "ecclesiastical authority [Joseph Fielding Smith] who is not a trained historian. His specialty is scripture. He has written a good deal about Mormon Church History, but it is basically a theological approach. History is the story of the revelation of God's word to man and of the never-ending conflict between God and Satan."

The office had become "a repository for documents pertaining to God's dealings with man . . . not a place where one seeks a creative understanding." The documents were in a suspended state, preserved for eternity without any "excision, no burning, no expulsion from the record, and no selectivity as to pro or con" nor any concept of their value to historiography.

They needed to be employed in the service of history, and those, like Arrington, who were "sponsoring *Dialogue*, the Mormon History Association, and other similar professional activities," were confident "that the Church and its membership are now sufficiently 'mature' to accept our findings, even when adverse, as part of the process of obtaining understanding and truth."[39]

Leonard's criticism consistently expressed such optimism, driven by his total conviction that telling the truth about Mormonism's history would ultimately help the church. To Richard Bushman, writing five years before his appointment, he described how his own research efforts in the Church Archives had met his expectation that most of what he found would "serve to support or bolster the Church's position. To put it another way, the Church has a lot of ammunition on its side that it has never made generally available." Leonard saw no reason why it should not provide access. "This old bugaboo about the Church having secrets to hide . . . is largely a matter of certain secrets of certain family members—that so and so was divorced, or at one stage excommunicated, or had trouble with such and such wife, and so on. The skeletons are not *church* skeletons but family skeletons." A better solution for the church would be the employment of professional historians to edit documents and reveal them "for the good of the Church."[40]

Fortified by years of contemplating the subject, Leonard had a well-thought-out plan when, just six weeks after becoming church historian, he was invited to address the First Presidency and Quorum of the Twelve in the Salt Lake Temple and lay before them his vision of the future. He had a solid list of important, paradigm-changing projects, coupled with what he hoped would confirm his eagerness to prove his division useful to the larger organization:

1.   Carry out historical research desired by the General Authorities.

2.   Assist and counsel scholars doing research in topics related to Church History. Read manuscripts[,] consult Prest. [Ernest] Wilkinson on BYU history.

3.   Prepare articles on Church History for Church Publications.

4.   Publish, with appropriate introductions and comments, important documents, diaries, letters, and sermons important to our history, but previously unpublished.

5.   Prepare biographies of leaders and books on important topics related to our history.

6.   Prepare a multi-volume history of the Church for the sesquicentennial anniversary of the Church in 1980.[41]

The discussion that followed his formal presentation demonstrated to him, perhaps for the first time, a substantial division of opinion in his audience of church leaders. "For example, Brother [Boyd] Packer was concerned about two or three people listed for our historical advisory committee. Brother [Mark] Petersen, was concerned about policies with respect to giving access to sacred materials in the archives to unfriendly persons. Brother [Ezra Taft] Benson was concerned about the multiplication of staff positions and bureaus." Petersen and Benson wanted to carefully screen access to the archives for the sake of protecting the church's image. Meanwhile, Alvin Dyer and Eldon Tanner advocated free scholarly access, and Tanner noted how restrictions damaged the church's image. Thomas Monson "expressed his delight that after many years we were finally going to get down to the task of writing our history."[42]

Tacit approval of the basic outline of Leonard's plan emerged from the meeting, although final approval of specifics lay several months in the future. Leonard gave no indication that he understood the strategic significance of the objections from Benson, Petersen, and Packer, which meant that he had no plan for countering their objections and finding ways to make them allies. As a result, among the Twelve, they became the adversaries of the History Division over which he presided.

Over the next several months, Leonard, Davis Bitton, and Jim Allen fleshed out the beginning roster of the History Division, prepared for the move to the new Church Office Building, and refined their proposals for the mission of the division. Allen recognized Leonard's "grand vision," and Bitton his responsibility to help work out the details. The meetings of the three led to a plan for "two good histories of the Church, one that would be published by Deseret Book and would be mainly for church members, and one that would be published by a major publisher." That second volume would end up with publisher Alfred Knopf. Written by Leonard Arrington and Davis Bitton and intended for a broad audience, they would entitle it *The Mormon Experience: A History of the Latter-day Saints.* The volume designed for members was ultimately authored by James Allen and Glen Leonard and entitled *The Story of the Latter-day Saints.*[43]

In early August 1972, Leonard and Howard Hunter met with Harold B. Lee, who had become church president only a month earlier, and Marion G. Romney, one of the two counselors in the new First Presidency. Eldon Tanner, the other, was out of town. Leonard presented for their approval an ambitious program that focused on publications:

1. The preparation of a series of articles for the *Ensign* and *New Era* [church periodicals for the membership].

2. The commencement of books for a "Heritage Series" to be published by Deseret Book. These would be edited documents like the diaries of Joseph Smith, letters of Brigham Young to his sons, letters of Brigham Young to Indian chiefs, selections from the letters and diaries of women, and so on.

3. The preparation of a sixteen-volume sesquicentennial history of the Church. . . .

4. The preparation of two one-volume histories of the Church, one to be published by Deseret Book, intended primarily for members of

the Church, the other, to be published by Alfred Knopf, intended
to reach nonmembers. . . .[44]

5. The preparation of biographies of Brigham Young, Eliza R. Snow,
    and other Church leaders.

6. The inauguration of a program of oral history.[45]

When Leonard finished his presentation, Lee responded that the plan
sounded fine to him. While he saw no problems with it, before taking formal action he wanted to wait a week until the First Presidency could assemble, to be
certain they were united in their approval. He especially wanted Eldon Tanner to
go over the plan.[46] A month later, Leonard got the green light: "This morning we
received the most important communication from the First Presidency dated
September 13, 1972 and signed by Presidents Tanner and Romney, giving approval
to the program, which I presented to them on August 8. This seems to be blanket
approval to go ahead with everything we listed." He shared the letter with his
staff and Earl Olson. Some programs were already underway, but they could now
implement others awaiting approval. The highest priority was the sesquicentennial history of the church.[47]

THE SESQUICENTENNIAL HISTORY

In 1964 while at Brown University, Richard Bushman had proposed to Leonard a
comprehensive history of the church, with a target date of 1980, the church's sesquicentennial anniversary. Leonard responded with enthusiasm and agreed Bushman should submit the proposal to Presidents Hugh B. Brown and Earl Crockett
first.[48] "I know lots of 'Mormon scholars,' including some in substantial positions
in the Church, who will give all the support they dare to a proposal of this nature. This is the sort of thing I'll be willing to stick my neck out on and go to bat
for—to use all the clichés I can think of!"[49]

With input from Leonard, Bushman sent a formal proposal to Hugh Brown
in July 1964:

> By 1980 the Church will be ready for a new comprehensive history.
> New sources and research, and the continued growth and extension
> of the Church, have already made our standard histories obsolete in
> some respects. Another fifteen years and these works will be quite
> inadequate for serious students.
>
> Moreover, the Church will have had such an impact on the world
> by then that scholars will be more interested than ever in our ori-
> gins and growth. If we do not write our own history, others will,
> and perhaps not so sympathetically as we would like.

While the proposal was sound, thorough, and upbeat, it contained one idea that, while totally reasonable given the anticipated impact of the series, was likely a red flag. It recommended the involvement in the project of "the heterodox and hostile." As Bushman noted, "Some of them are acute students of our history and can make useful suggestions." He further reasoned that "though the finished product will be the work of friendly historians, we will defeat one of the purposes of the project if we do not thoroughly investigate areas our critics think discredit the Church."[50]

Brown passed the letter to Harold B. Lee, then a senior apostle who headed the increasingly powerful Correlation Committee; and Lee referred it to Antone Romney, chairman of the Correlation Committee secretaries. Romney's written response to Lee was unenthusiastic: "It is generally assumed that scholars have the responsibility and opportunity to develop scholarly papers in fields of their specialty, but it seems unwise for the Church to authorize and endorse such endeavors unless the presiding authorities of the Church desire the results of such studies in the carrying forth of their responsibilities."[51]

In other words, Romney viewed history as a tool to be used by church leaders to carry out their agenda, rather than a stand-alone discipline whose primary driving force is data, rather than dogma. Sanctioning a rewriting of history by professional historians would shift control away from the ecclesiastical arm of the church, where it had always resided—a dangerous move. Boyd Packer later summarized this viewpoint with remarkable candor when he said, "Some things that are true are not very useful."[52]

Romney's letter continued, "If such studies as those proposed in this letter are to be endorsed by the Church it would seem they should be done at the suggestion of and under the direction of the Church Historian's Office or some other priesthood authority within the Church."[53] Lee wrote to Bushman and effectively killed the proposal: "The recommendation of our Correlation Committee secretaries accords with our feelings and we trust that you will be guided by these suggestions."[54]

Discouraged, Bushman reported back to Arrington, "What do we do now? It seems to me we have to win the personal support of someone."[55] Lacking such support, the two men put the proposal on the shelf. Eight years later, though, three months after he became church historian, Leonard resuscitated the proposal; and in early April 1972, he sent a memorandum to Alvin Dyer asserting that "the single most important task of our division, as we understand it, is to write church history for the information and edification of the members of the Church."[56] He proposed a "History of the Latter-day Saints, 1830–1980" comprising ten to fifteen separately authored volumes "covering each significant phase of the history of the Church, each done by a recognized authority." He would be the general editor of a series that "would be thoroughly researched and well written, and . . . authenticated by bibliographic citations." And he anticipated that sales would ultimately cover the costs of creating the volumes.[57]

The following day, Leonard noted in his diary: "Elder Dyer stated that the First Presidency was very pleased with this Sesqui-Centennial History of the Church. It was noted that all writings that are produced should be submitted to the Correlation Committee for their approval."[58] This multivolume work was part of the September submittal that the First Presidency approved. Leonard and his group moved quickly. Only a month later, they had sixteen subjects and sixteen authors committed to the project. Furthermore, the church's Deseret Book Company agreed to publish the series.

Although Leonard and his colleagues failed to grasp the existential threat that the series represented to the religious worldview of several apostles, and thus were genuinely shocked when the series was ultimately canceled in spite of the First Presidency's initial approval, they understood well its historical significance. The only prior attempt at comprehensive, interpretive LDS history, *A Comprehensive History of The Church of Jesus Christ of Latter-day Saints, Century I*, had been written more than a half-century earlier by General Authority Brigham H. Roberts, and while Roberts is still regarded as one of Mormonism's brightest intellectuals, he had no professional training in historiography. Furthermore, the dramatic advances in the discipline of historiography in the succeeding decades, coupled with the explosive growth of archival source material, cried out for a new interpretive history.

Harold B. Lee's death in December 1973 resulted in a review of major church programs and initiatives by Spencer W. Kimball, his successor. It was not until April 1974, however, that Leonard, in the company of Howard Hunter, the apostolic advisor to the department, had his first meeting with Kimball and his counselors, Eldon Tanner and Marion G. Romney, both of whom had also served in the Lee First Presidency. The agenda was an anxiously anticipated, detailed discussion of the history project, which Leonard described in detail in his diary. "President Kimball asked a series of questions about the sesquicentennial history. He asked me to list the names of each of the sixteen authors and what their connection was."[59] The list was essentially a Who's Who of scholars of Mormonism:

    I.   Introduction and Background to 1830—Richard Bushman

    II.   The Ohio Experience to 1838—Milton V. Backman Jr.

    III.   The Missouri Experience to 1839—Max Parkin

After Leonard presented the list, Kimball said, "That is a fine group of writers. I need to raise a question about one of the persons you mentioned—Brother Eugene Campbell. I do not know him personally and have not read much of his writing, but I have heard people say that he was not completely orthodox." Leonard vouched for Campbell, saying that he knew him personally and that he had been an active member of the church who had served in several important ecclesiastical callings as well as director of two LDS Institutes of Religion. Then, to reassure Kimball that Campbell's book—and, by inference, the whole series—would be acceptable even to the orthodox Mormon, he offered, "If there is any problem with his writing, I will expect to go over it and change it as necessary." This seemed to reassure Kimball, who did not raise any questions about any other writer.

Eldon Tanner, who had given enthusiastic support for Leonard's franchise from the beginning, then offered advice in a gentle manner: "You will obviously have gray areas where there will be things in our history where you will be in doubt as to whether they should be included—whether it would be good policy to mention these items. Should you not seek the advice of some of the General Authorities of the Church on these matters?" Leonard's response suggested that he hadn't really taken the hint, for he sidestepped the issue of seeking advice from ecclesiastical officials: "My associates and I will have the opportunity to discuss these matters in great detail on what should be included, how much treatment is required, how it should be worded, and so on. This is true on matters like polygamy and politics." Romney interrupted to say, "Yes, things like the Danites and the Mountain Meadows Massacre," and Kimball added, "And, of course, the Negro question. We are faced with that every day. We cannot avoid mentioning it. You will have to say something about it, but we try to be very careful about the way we bring these matters up."

Howard Hunter, who until then had been a passive observer, nudged the First Presidency members for a decision. "Do we have your approval on this matter?" Tanner and Romney raised their hands as if to vote yes. Kimball, despite his expressed concern over Eugene Campbell's alleged heterodoxy, weighed in with consent coupled with an unexpectedly progressive directive:

> "Yes, I think this is fine, but I think we should counsel Brother Arrington on the other side of the matter. I think Brother Arrington should get a person who is not within the inside—a person who is on the outside of the office to read each of these manuscripts and give a critique which will enable us to know what outsiders will say about the books after they are published. We want to know in advance what reviewers are going to say about these works so we can have a chance to alter them or improve them before publication if possible. . . . You might consider having as a member of the initial screening committee someone from the outside, someone who can be objective and will be honest—perhaps someone from the *Dialogue* group—so that we would be able to take into account these criticisms before the work is published."

Leonard, not surprisingly, said, "I would be delighted to do this and it would be no problem at all in getting a suitable person to do it." Hunter, wanting to make sure that approval was explicit and unanimous within the group, said, "Do you then approve this recommendation of ours?" Kimball looked at each of his two councilors and each nodded affirmatively to him. He then said, "Yes, I think this is one of the most important projects we have inaugurated in the Church in many years. Our history needs to be written responsibly and I am very glad that we had this discussion. I am very glad you are going ahead with this, Brother Arrington, and we offer you our support."[61]

Given the earlier negative reactions to *Dialogue* by senior apostles, Kimball's earnest suggestion that Leonard recruit someone from the journal as an outside reviewer could not have been a more welcome endorsement of the project. The conundrum that is readily apparent in hindsight, of an almost impossible balancing act that preserved orthodoxy on the one hand, while gaining an independent endorsement from heterodox scholars, passed by without comment. With wind in his sails, Leonard moved forward quickly, giving active support to the authors. Richard Bushman, who would author the volume on Joseph Smith's early years, recalled, "He was extremely helpful, as you could imagine. All the source materials I'd want he'd photocopy and mail them to me so I really didn't have to do a lot of scrounging around in the archives."[62]

Oral History

With the development of reliable and increasingly portable voice-recording devices throughout the middle of the twentieth century, by the 1970s interviews could be recorded in their entirety with ease—a sharp contrast to earlier years when interviewers either took notes of what their interviewees were saying or employed secretaries to record the interviews in shorthand. In 1948, Allan Nevins, one of the premier American historians of the twentieth century, created the first university-based oral history program at Columbia University. Interest in the new genre grew steadily, and by 1966 there was sufficient activity nationally that American historians founded the Oral History Association.

Having conducted interviews the old-fashioned way, Leonard appreciated the potential of a format that preserves the voice of the interviewee while at the same time yields a transcript that is easily accessible to historians. Within weeks of becoming church historian, he began to establish an "absolutely indispensable" oral history program within the Church Historical Department by securing funding for a historian to train the department's staff and get the program going. Relying on recommendations from professional associates, including those at the state's universities and history society, he chose Gary Shumway of California State–Fullerton to work with Davis Bitton setting up the program. "As a professor at Fullerton, Gary had established a model program there and thus had the experience to guide us along the right lines. Much of the credit for our excellent program goes to Gary."[63]

Initiated in the summer of 1972, the program had already accumulated fifty-four interviews by the end of the year, focusing on "general authorities, mission presidents, and other prominent people who have played significant roles in various phases of Church history."[64] At the end of 1975, Leonard showcased the growing collection in a presentation to the General Authorities, reporting that the collection had grown to interviews with seven hundred persons, then "in the process of being typed, checked, rechecked, retyped and bound."[65]

The following year, the program moved to a new level when the James H. Moyle family donated $100,000. Renamed the James Moyle Oral History Program, it took on a broader mission "related to almost all aspects of contemporary Church history." LDS leaders at all levels from General Authorities through stake and mission leaders were interviewed, and special projects included "the history of the Genealogical Society, Relief Society, LDS Social Services, Welfare Services, including Welfare Services missionaries; the LDS response to the 1976 Teton Flood, the Young Women, and numerous other aspects of the Church."[66]

The program continues today, with a current database of over 6,500 oral histories that includes interviews from across the globe.[67] Its value to historians of Mormonism's twentieth and twenty-first centuries is incalculable, for two reasons. The first is that much of the history contained in the oral histories would otherwise have gone unrecorded, for the paradoxical reason that, in spite of the ease with which written records can now be made—there are even software programs that translate speech into text in real time—people make far fewer written records than their ancestors, who regularly wrote letters and diaries. The second reason is that oral histories capture reflection, nuance, and context that are usually missing from contemporaneous written records.

Within weeks of beginning the program, Leonard encountered a problem that remains at the core of any initiative to create *new* history, as contrasted to gathering *existing* history: interviewees or documents that presented "unfriendly or unfavorable stories and facts and information." The researchers expressed their hesitancy to conduct such interviews or gather such information, "as if they expected our office to approve only the acquisition of information that was favorable to the Church." Leonard saw this as evidence of a long-standing policy in the Historian's Office to avoid collecting "information which might be regarded as deleterious to the Church and its interests and image." His response was consistent with his background as a professional historian, but it was also at odds with the philosophy of history espoused by some of the General Authorities with whom he had to deal:

> On each occasion I have assured these persons that we must be interested in obtaining all the information possible about personalities and episodes, even if in the opinion of a current researcher it might be harmful to the Church's interests. If we are anything, we are an organization dedicated to finding the truth about the Church and its history and we have complete faith that the Church will in the long run not suffer as the result of this activity. . . . I do not see how we can successfully counteract anti-Mormon articles and books

without knowing the extent to which they are based on correct information, nor can I conceive of persons having confidence in our own publications unless they know that we are pursuing all avenues in the attempt to find out what really happened.

He was confident that taping unfriendly oral interviews would not threaten with excommunication the interviewees who gave information that was "not consistent with the 'official' account of what happened." "In our publications, of course, we shall have to use good judgment in the manner in which we present our findings, but at least we must be honest, we must recognize the existence of contrary facts and ideas."[68]

The problematic aspect of oral histories came to the forefront only four years after the program began, when Leonard deployed oral historians to capture the fresh recollections of victims of the collapse of the Grand Teton Dam. Construction on the dam in southeastern Idaho, upstream from cities such as Rexburg that had large concentrations of Latter-day Saint populations, began in 1972. In June 1976, before the new lake was completely filled, the dam ruptured catastrophically. The water, which poured through the break at a rate of 2 million cubic feet per second, flooded hundreds of square miles of land, killed eleven people, and damaged or destroyed thousands of structures.

While the oral histories documented many heroic deeds of local citizens—including LDS Church members—in the aftermath of the disaster, they also captured a less heroic story. Historian Ross Peterson recalled that as he undertook in 1977 a Teton Dam oral history project, he had discussions with Arrington about the interviews his staff had already done and how some of what they had heard had surprised him.

> There is a great story about how people helped each other, but the Church ignored one area out by Roberts, because it was in Jefferson County, and a lot of the relief never got there. And then there was the thing about how the individuals responded to the claims. Some people weren't as honest as they might have been. The oral histories reveal a lot of tension. What is now FEMA [Federal Emergency Management Agency] took the advice of the local county commissioners. "When you put people in trailers, put them in by the neighbors they live with now." So then you have your ward together. It was viewed as a real positive thing. But then, when they started to go back into their homes, they saw that So-and-so had a new fence, or new snowmobiles or a new tractor, and that wasn't what he had before.

Meanwhile many of those coming back to their homes had reported more honestly exactly what they had lost. The contrast between neighbors created tension. Peterson remembered that when Leonard and he talked about those tensions, Leonard "said he wasn't sure how many people he wanted to read this, because it wasn't always the story upon which General Conference talks are made. There were underlying difficulties that emerged."[69]

WRITING CANDID HISTORY

In wrestling with the dilemma of producing candid history, be it oral or written, Leonard reached back to the goal expressed by George Tanner, his college Institute of Religion advisor, to help "my students to see life's real problems instead of having to butter everything up for them. The Church does Institute students a disservice by not teaching things realistically. When they get out in life they will have to face up to reality; we should prepare them for it." Good intent notwithstanding, Tanner's philosophy carried a substantial risk—one that was underscored by Apostle Mark Petersen in Tanner's presence: "We don't need or want the learning of the world." Tanner paid a price for his liberal views by being released from his position in the Church Educational System only two and a half years prior to retirement.[70]

The examples of Tanner and others of similar philosophy caused those within the church bureaucracy to yield quietly to censorship or to self-censor, thereby avoiding a similar fate. Shortly after Leonard became church historian, he had lunch with the editor and associate editor of the *New Era*, the church's publication for teenagers, who tutored him on some facts of bureaucratic life. With some amazement, Leonard recorded that the editors first used their own judgment regarding what to publish, but then submitted it to managing director Doyle Green to check. He, in turn, worked through Correlation Committee review. If a disagreement then emerged, the proposed publication went to the Quorum of the Twelve, where Thomas Monson, Gordon Hinckley, and Boyd Packer made the ultimate decision. There were subjects the editors were not allowed to broach:

> They cannot have a Latter-day Saint doing something he shouldn't do in any fictional account, whether it be smoking, lying, being disobedient, etc. If we were to send him an article on Brigham Young's letters to Indian chiefs, they would cut out Brigham Young's references to the sending of tobacco to the chiefs to smoke. They also avoid references to polygamy.

The most common question submitted to the magazine by its young readers, in dozens of letters every week, was whether it was all right to pierce their ears.

The *New Era* editors noted, though, that "they cannot run a question and answer column on this because the brethren are divided on it. They cannot even run an article saying the brethren are divided."[71]

Several months later, the same editors provided Leonard with concrete evidence of their dilemma, rewording one of his submissions to the *New Era*: "In my article on Arizona women they had to change the word coffee grinder to small mill. They also had to change the word adultery to infidelity." While these changes related to doctrinal matters, the editors also felt compelled to censor terms that might arouse entirely different member sensitivities: "a splendid article on missionaries' experiences in the Philippines . . . had started out by [one missionary] saying he hadn't been prepared for the cockroaches. They had to eliminate that because nobody wanted the mothers to know that their missionary sons would be sent out where there were cockroaches."[72] These examples would have been amusing except for their implications for Leonard and his colleagues' underlying struggle with LDS leadership over what constituted "appropriate" and "professional" history. Leonard regarded such pettiness as both annoying and counterproductive, and his feelings on the subject reached back to his days of teaching at Utah State University. One former undergraduate recalled how Leonard, who was both his advisor and a member of his ward, gave a homily to the Sunday School faculty at a prayer meeting: "It was something to the effect that we needed to inoculate people—and I think he was thinking about young people, as well as anybody else—by giving them exposure to facets of the history of the Church that might be uncomfortable. In becoming able to accommodate this . . . they would be in a better position to deal with the tougher stuff as that came along.[73]

Leonard's basic framework for Mormon history was that the current church was a success story and the better the understanding of the past that brought it to this stage, the better equipped the institutional church and its members would be to perpetuate the success. One colleague put it succinctly: "Determining what actually happened is of value, and it hasn't been in the past."[74] On one occasion Leonard put it even more succinctly: "God does not need our lies."[75] To the editor of *Brigham Young University Studies* he explained:

> Is there any area of the history of the Church and its leaders which deserves being cloaked in half-truth or consigned to chilly silence? Our office has the conviction that any aspect of the history of the Church can be discussed frankly and analyzed in depth at least among mature scholars. . . . As long as the narration and analysis is kept within perspective it ultimately will be a contribution toward spiritual uplift and understanding. Inevitably, interpretations on

some points will differ among those committed to the same standards of research, religion, rationality, and revelation, but the differences should be occasions for reflection and reassessment rather than retrenchment or fear.[76]

Following a discussion of the topic in an academic setting, Leonard responded to one of the participating professors after further considering the latter's question, "Do we really want to publish the truth about Church history?" He replied, "Of course we want the truth in Church history, and those of us who have worked intimately with the documents . . . are confident that the truth is palatable and basically, if not completely, faith promoting; and that is the way it should be, shouldn't it, if this really is the Lord's Church?" He assured his correspondent that he saw "no conflict between my integrity as a scholar and my faith as a Latter-day Saint."[77]

Candid history would not only help church members but also oblige non-Mormon historians to rethink their treatment of the Mormons' story. Recall the scant treatment of Mormons with only three sentences in Toynbee's ten-volume history. Howard Lamar, an eminent historian of the American West and later president of Yale University, recounted how Michael Quinn, an Arrington protégé, had completed a dissertation that the Yale history department thought "was one of the most important dissertations ever written. My old mentor, Ralph Henry Gabriel, said, 'This is just superb.' This particular historian had grown up in a Mormon area in New York State, and didn't have very favorable opinions of Mormons, and Mike's dissertation just re-informed [him] about everything."[78]

Reorienting an entire church to a new way of viewing its own history was a daunting challenge, and Leonard had at least some awareness of how difficult the task would be. But he also saw his role and that of his colleagues as responding to a divine mandate. Although he never talked publicly about his personal spiritual experience confirming that mission, that experience fueled his missionary zeal as he plunged forward. According to Ron Esplin, who would have to negotiate the difficult task of directing the History Division when it was later transformed into the Joseph Fielding Smith Institute for Latter-day Saint History, Leonard saw himself as racing against time in a narrowing window for his "grand experiment," but "if he could produce enough, quickly enough, the body of evidence, the weight of that evidence would be sufficient to prove the experiment and give some additional time and space for protection." He was convinced that "doing credible scholarship for the Church" was both viable and worth the "hard sell" to both his church and his fellow scholars.[79]

Leonard's sense of mission was not totally naïve, for it was buttressed by the explicit support of the most powerful man in the Mormon Church: Harold B. Lee. As long as Lee remained church president—and the lifespan of his predecessors in that office predicted a tenure of up to two decades—Leonard's back would be covered.

While Lee was the most important patron, he was not Leonard's sole supporter among the hierarchy. Cheryll Lynn May, whose husband, Dean, was one of the early employees of the History Division, recalled that there was a faction of the General Authorities that aligned with the professional Mormon historians and "had an eagerness to really dive into Mormon history and treat it as more than 'holy writ.' " They, like Leonard, "had enough faith to believe that trying to tell a fuller story, and not just the mythic tale, would in the long run be healthy for the Church." Moreover, they perceived "that this was coming in any case, and it was probably better to have some faithful church members involved in doing it."[80]

Even with protection, Leonard had to proceed cautiously in writing about the inconvenient truths of the church's past, for the transition to objective history would be harrowing for church members raised for decades on a steady diet of sanitized accounts. The texts that he and his coworkers produced, rather than any statement from church leadership, would have to lead those members through a potentially hazardous minefield.

The key to success could be summarized in one word, context, for everything: "what they knew, what their lives were like, how they were trying to accomplish things or just get by. That's a good lesson. . . . You can't take a standard today and put it on the people who were around 150 years ago."[81] Most previous writers of Mormon history, whether sympathetic or nonsympathetic, had retreated to opposite poles instead of seeking explanatory context. While Leonard was not pleased with the sympathetic literature, asserting that "our own works do not carry conviction as being the real story," he reserved his harshest criticism for the nonsympathetic writers.[82] His son James recalled asking him, "Dad, why doesn't the Church let this stuff out? Why doesn't the Church just tell the truth? The stuff I read, even if it is negative about the Church, doesn't do anything but prove to me that the Church is true. I see God's hand everywhere. Every time I read these original things, I see it. Why does the Church sweep it under the rug?"

Leonard's reply revealed his confidence in the Mormon perspective. He said, "James, there is nothing under the rug. The anti-Mormons have swept all the stuff out from under the rug long ago. They are so careful about stuff under the rug. The fact is that the truth will make us free. That's what I believe. That's how I write what I write. The truth is what is right to write. The problem is that they don't have anything under the rug to talk about, and so they have to cut the truth into pieces, and then they tell this part of the truth, and not that part."

The facts of the church's history were not the problem in his mind. It was understanding that church members lacked and confidence in the strength of those members' faith that those seeking to restrict information needed:

> "The thing that is missing from history, for the most part, is just for people to understand it. When you get in there and read it, like you have, you get it and you suddenly go, 'Wow! This is amazing stuff! This is great stuff!' That is what I am trying to do. . . . just get the information out there. But there are those people who just think that the Saints are too weak for this. And maybe there are [such Saints]. I don't know those people. Maybe the people in South Africa or South America, or Brazil, where you went on your mission, are too weak to handle this kind of stuff. But the fact is that the truth is the truth, and there is no reason to hide it. The more truth we know, the more we understand things. For my whole history, I have tried the best I can to keep things out from under the rug, because that is where it functions. It's the anti-Mormons, now, who are putting things under the rug. They tell half-truths."[83]

Arrington's enthusiasm for the power of truth carrying the day is still palpable. Indeed, he comes across as a cheerleader for objective history, never doubting that its effect would be benign, and never fully comprehending the threat that such an attitude represented to senior church leadership. The irony of their reaction to him was on two levels. First, they failed to appreciate fully that he was as devoted as they to the task of "building testimonies"—of keeping church members in the fold. Although his approach to the task was different than theirs, their goals were the same. Nonetheless, they perceived him as a threat of sufficient magnitude to require removal. And second, as threatening as he was to their *status quo*, he operated under self-imposed constraints of which they knew nothing. Other sections of this book detail his "this far, but no farther" stance towards the most challenging aspects of LDS church history and doctrine—aspects that the Internet age has made even more challenging to current church members.[84]

Although the historian will always have a bias, both in the source material chosen to inform the narrative and in the interpretation of that source material, Leonard sought openness and honesty, believing that it would ultimately be beneficial to the reader even when that balance involved acknowledging the flaws of church leaders of the past. Dwight Israelsen, a colleague at Utah State University recalled conversations where Leonard said, "Our history is the history of not just the Church, but of human beings and of men and women. Men and women are imperfect, but that doesn't mean the Church isn't true." Israelsen felt that much of the criticism that came to Arrington from inside the church came because his idea of the "faithful history" that President Lee had tasked him to write was history that was "faithful to the facts. The facts didn't have to be covered up in his mind." While some critics thought his work was not sufficiently faith promoting, "His attitude toward that was always the same, which was it was faith promoting to know that people who have faults still do what is right in the end and still can carry out their assignments. People aren't perfect. Nobody's perfect, and yet the Church goes on and prospers."[85]

Writing honest history is contingent upon having access to as much of the data relating to that history as possible, and one deficit that Leonard never resolved was the limited access he had to the inner workings of the church hierarchy. Earl Olson, initially Leonard's peer but later his supervisor, recalled, "Leonard wanted eventually to write a more detailed history by having access to all the minutes of the Brethren, the Twelve and the First Presidency. Of course, that was never permitted."[86] That "of course" was a fact of life to Earl Olson, and it is true that many churches and businesses maintain tight control on their proprietary documents. But some take a different approach.

The next largest movement that sprang from Joseph Smith's Mormonism, the RLDS Church (now Community of Christ) has a policy that even the minutes of its leading quorums are available after fifty years. Also, in marked contrast to the LDS Church, the Community of Christ publishes its annual budget and accounts in its official magazine.

Writing more than a decade after being released as church historian and several years after the death of one of the two apostles who had clearly opposed his history initiative—Mark Petersen—Leonard doubted that the points of view of them, the First Presidency, and the managers to whom he reported would ever be revealed. It seemed likely that only the perspectives of the staff members of "the faithful but beleaguered" history offices would be published, since the official records of the LDS Church did not as a rule "divulge inner conflict," and it was unlikely the minutes of the Quorum of the Twelve would ever be open to examination: "One can only guess at the fears, misinformation, and wider policy implications that inspired their reactions to our books, articles, and public speeches, however carefully prepared and however well intended." He hoped his own "insider" comments had been "fair-minded and honorable. My study of early church diaries, letters, and other documents has persuaded me that our leaders have honestly and sincerely tried to direct the Church along a godly path. I respect and admire them. But I insist that they are human beings and are not above misunderstanding, misinterpretation, and error."[87]

THE MORMON EXPERIENCE

Leonard's broad agenda went beyond the sesquicentennial history and the oral history program. A major project that predated his calling as church historian but that Davis Bitton and he did not complete until several years thereafter was a one-volume history of Mormonism written especially for the non-Mormon audience. Alfred A. Knopf, who had published Fawn Brodie's *No Man Knows My History*, asked Leonard, when he was teaching western history at the University of California at Los Angeles (UCLA) as a visiting professor, to write such a history. Leonard recalled, "I had the feeling that he wanted to publish something about the Church, which was more friendly—and also something which treated the history of the Mormons in the West." Knowing he could not write such a book without access to the LDS Archives, Leonard wrote the First Presidency.[88] "I have not made application to do this, but he [Alfred Knopf] has urged me to do so on the basis of work that I have already done." He noted that he was unaware of any other instance "that a major national publisher has asked an active Mormon to write a major work on the history of his people."[89] He then made his unprecedented request for access to church records, asserting that such a history could not "be written from newspaper accounts, published speeches of the General Authorities, and so on." He would need access to a wide variety of documents—correspondence diaries, minutes, financial records, and other—that were housed in either the church historian's library or the First Presidency's office. Seeking to reassure the leadership, he wrote,

> I think that those who know me can testify that I would handle such materials responsibly. I have devoted most of the past 20 years to writing about the Church, and what I have written furnishes a pattern. . . . I regard this opportunity as a splendid chance to demonstrate that Mormon scholars can write responsibly and professionally about their faith, their Church, and their people. It would also offer opportunity for an antidote for the works by hostile writers, such as Whalen, Turner, and others.[90]

Within the week, Tanner read Leonard's letter in a meeting of the First Presidency. Both he and Hugh B. Brown saw this as "an opportunity for us to have a professional writer who is a devoted Church member" write a history of the church. They agreed that Leonard could be authorized to use the Historian's Office archives, "with the understanding that he could not take any of these materials out of the office, and that if he wanted anything from the First Presidency's Office, it would have to be cleared first by the First Presidency."[91]

Tanner telephoned Leonard to give him the good news, and then followed up with a letter reporting the he had discussed the matter with the church historian, Joseph Fielding Smith, as well as the First Presidency, and with their approval "I am authorized to tell you that it will be quite in order for you to arrange with Earl Olson of the Historian's Office to use material available in that office and library."[92] Tanner's letter was followed by written permission from Olson, assistant church historian, for access as outlined by the First Presidency decision but only for a period of two years, with the possibility of a one-year extension.

Leonard's papers do not contain his immediate reaction to this approval-with-a-deadline. As he prepared to return to Utah State University following his sabbatical year at UCLA, he described to his dean the project, noting that he had "a letter from the First Presidency" but overstating the nature of his access as "unrestricted": "This is the first time I or anyone else has had unrestricted access, so I may run into some rich things. I made no commitment to them except to tell the truth and let the chips fall where they may."[93]

Leonard signed the contract with Knopf, which called for completion of the manuscript by January 1970.[94] Having resumed fulltime teaching at Utah State, he was limited in how much time he could spend on the project. The restriction against taking any materials out of the archives meant that he had to drive eighty-two miles from his home and office to reach the Church Archives. As he worked, he was unaware of opposition coming from an unlikely source: Alvin R. Dyer, who later became a staunch ally of Leonard as church historian.

Dyer joined the First Presidency more than a year following the First Presidency decision that approved Leonard's project and granted him archival access. Upon learning of it, he reacted adversely, asking "why we are writing another history prior to 1930, since this has been written in comprehensive form by B. H. Roberts."[95] Joseph Fielding Smith agreed that the church "had a good written history to that year and no need for another." Dyer asserted "that contemporary histories could only prove confusing to members and non-members alike." Hugh Brown suggested that a history that only summarized events up to 1930 but gave comprehensive coverage to later years "would not be detrimental." Dyer remained opposed, replying that they needed to avoid "variant historical records" so a summary "would have to be stated in the virtual words of the Comprehensive compiler of the 1930 and prior history." Following the meeting, Dyer approached Church Historian Joseph Fielding Smith, who denied that he knew anything about the Arrington project or about Tanner's authorization of Leonard to work with

Earl Olson on research. Smith stated further "that Arrington, anyway, should not be writing it." Dyer and he agreed that the former should look into it further and report to him, taking "the matter to President McKay if need be."[96]

Smith was eighty-eight years old at the time of the First Presidency decision and Tanner's conversation with him in which he gave his own approval. He appears merely to have forgotten the entire episode. His and Dyer's sudden objection to the project dissolved without effect. In their later professional relationship, Dyer never informed Leonard of his earlier antagonism, nor did he leave a record explaining his conversion to a prohistory stance.

Inertia accomplished what Smith and Dyer had not. The January 1970 deadline passed, and there was no manuscript. Early in 1973 Leonard received an embarrassing letter from Alfred Knopf. Now age ninety-two, the venerable publisher asked if Leonard would be able to complete the book. Since Leonard had by then become a church employee, and since the term of his access, granted by the First Presidency in 1967, had long since expired, he appealed to Joseph Anderson for renewed approval of the project and use of the Historical Department's facilities in completing it. He described how Knopf and he had planned a book "primarily for non-Mormons—for secular historians, university students, and the general reading public who desire an 'objective' history of Mormonism." They hoped it would be stocked by libraries and become a standard reference on Mormonism.

> Unfortunately, a large number of libraries in the United States carry just four books on the Church: W. A. Linn, *Story of the Mormons* [1902], a viciously anti Mormon work; Thomas F. O'Dea, *The Mormons* [1957], by a Roman Catholic sociologist; *The Year of Decision* [1943], by Bernard DeVoto, which is basically sympathetic with Mormon achievements but not its doctrine; and *No Man Knows My History* [1945], by Fawn Brodie. I am sure the Church is not happy to be represented exclusively by such works.[97]

Anderson, predictably, referred the request to the First Presidency, which quickly approved it.[98] With renewed access and hitherto unavailable assets—staff within the History Division including Assistant Church Historian Davis Bitton, who became coauthor—Leonard plunged back into the project.

DOCUMENTARY WORKS

Since the publication in the early twentieth century of *History of the Church*,[99] a quasidocumentary work, the Church Historian's Office had published none of the countless pages of original source material in its archives. Leonard's initial plans for the Church History Division were to begin publishing the papers of Brigham Young, a massive collection whose bounds he could not even measure at the time, as well as a Heritage Series that would include "some of the historically important selections from diaries, letters, sermons, and papers of the Prophets and other Church leaders."[100]

The idea for the Brigham Young Papers was not original to Leonard, as three years earlier it had been proposed to the First Presidency by Oliver Holmes, executive director of the National Historical Publications Commission, which had for several years been initiating "the publication of papers of outstanding Americans" through grants to universities and scholars. The projects had included the papers of George Washington, Alexander Hamilton, and Thomas Jefferson, among others. Holmes felt the papers of Brigham Young should now receive first priority and was proposing that Leonard Arrington and George Ellsworth be the principal editors of these documentary editions, which "undertaken in the most scholarly manner . . . would be well received by the scholars of the nation and would be published at no cost to the Church."[101]

The First Presidency "decided to give the matter further thought." Leonard, in resuscitating the proposal, noted that the National Historical Publications Commission had committed $40,000 to the project. But although he eventually wrote a one-volume biography of Young, the papers project went nowhere.

The Heritage Series, by contrast, elicited quick approval. The first volume in the series, *Letters of Brigham Young to His Sons*,[102] received critical acclaim in some quarters, but criticism in others—notably from an apostle, Boyd K. Packer. It was the only book ever published in the series.

THE STORY OF THE LATTER-DAY SAINTS

While Leonard's initial strategic plan included a one-volume history of Mormonism for the non-Mormon audience, it did not suggest replacing Joseph Fielding Smith's *Essentials in Church History*, originally published in 1922 and updated and maintained in print ever since in more than twenty editions. Five months later, on the same day he received formal, written approval from the First Presidency for his strategic plan, Leonard met with James Mortimer, a manager at Deseret Book Company, who asked him "what to do about the Joseph Fielding Smith *Essentials in Church History*," noting that he sold about ten thousand copies a year and only had four thousand in stock. Leonard suggested several options to him, including a new history "written by the new Church Historian." Another possibility might be a yearbook of church history published annually and containing "a core of pertinent facts" along with essays prepared by the church history staff.

Or they could reprint Joseph Fielding Smith's *Essentials in Church History* and "bring it up to date by adding a brief essay on President Lee."

Asked which he would prefer, Mortimer referred the question to James Allen for an assessment of what the faculty at BYU and in LDS seminaries and institutes might prefer. Allen replied that there was no question they would prefer the new one-volume history. Mortimer agreed and offered to discuss the idea with Thomas Monson, but because of the delay such a project entailed, he asked for a straight reprint, without updates, of *Essentials in Church History* as an interim solution to his shortage.[103]

In fact, all three possibilities occurred. *Essentials* was published in its final print edition in 1973; a yearbook of church history was published the same year, beginning a tradition that eventually became the annual *Church Almanac*;[104] and Jim Allen, with Glen Leonard as coauthor, wrote *The Story of the Latter-day Saints*, the replacement volume for *Essentials*.

EUPHORIA

While the planets had aligned in his favor, it was the persona of Leonard, more than anything else, that led church history in a new direction. What he lacked in administrative skills, detailed in other sections of this book, he more than made up for in enthusiasm, even charisma. A non-Mormon scholar at the University of Utah, not disposed to gushing accolades, said of Leonard, "I admired something in Arrington that none of the other historians within the state had. That was a remarkable enthusiasm—it was more than that; he was jocular. He was very interested that people feel good, not just about him, but about everything. There was a time or two when I thought that he might be just a hopeless Pollyanna, but he wasn't. He was more than that. It was deeper. It was more sincere."[105]

It was sincere because Leonard projected what he, himself, experienced. Writing to a colleague within the first few months on the job, he displayed his sense that all was going well with church history. He and his staff had good support from church authorities and members alike who were counseling them "to tell it like it is" and felt they were "rendering a real service." Moreover, the documents they were studying continued to "reflect favorably on the Church and its mission." His response to the unfavorable impression of the department that had hitherto existed was to encourage scholars to make greater use of the archival material, the assumption being that access to data would solve all problems."[106]

The staff's move to the new Church Office Building, which occurred two weeks later in November 1972, pumped up the level of enthusiasm, as did a subsequent pat on the back from Harold B. Lee. At a meeting in the First Presidency office that included Leonard's fellow administrators Anderson, Olson, and Schmidt, "President Lee reasserted to me what he had said last August—how important it was to write the history of the Church today."[107]

As Leonard brought others into the division, either as employees or guest workers, enthusiasm multiplied. For the first time ever, young professional historians were made welcome and encouraged to research and write where others had not gone. Thomas Alexander, one of the sixteen authors assigned a volume in the sesquicentennial series,[108] was elated at the access he was given to records that had not previously been opened to scholars—virtually everything except tithing records and the journals of George Q. Cannon, which were in the First Presidency's vault and which Alexander felt he did not need since Cannon had died in 1901. What he saw included "minutes of the Council of the Twelve, the diaries of everybody who was active during that period . . . minutes of the First Presidency and records of the Presiding Bishop's Office."[109]

Leonard did not really "open" the archives, for the simple reason that they had not been closed, although access had been strictly controlled. But he instituted a totally new policy of openness whereby qualified scholars, particularly those working in the division, were often allowed to peruse the shelves of the archives—essentially an open-stacks policy. An employee recalled, "There was nothing to fear. These were the days when we could go up to the stacks and pull things off the shelf and look at them, just nose around and read everybody's mail in the archives, the correspondence that was there. There was no fear."[110] A university student was astounded at the openness and the spirit of cooperation: "I could Xerox anything, I could read anything. I could ask them to Xerox things for me for free. Everything was just given to me. . . . The main document I worked with was the Relief Society minutes from the Salt Lake 13th Ward, where Rachel Grant was the Relief Society president for about 40 years. This old secretary took notes of their meetings for 40 years. 'Sister Grant said this, and So-and-so said this.' It was just a gem of a document."[111]

And access, as Leonard had predicted, led to discovery:

> [Leonard] knew that the archives were full of the stories of the Church, and he wanted to plumb that. . . . It hadn't been brought out before, to let the little people, the average Joe and Jane in the Church, have a voice in the history of the Church. . . . The excitement of discovery into the sources was what was so wonderful about working with Leonard. . . .
>
> Along the way you would discover all kinds of things. . . . It was just an academic revelation working with Leonard Arrington. In that

sense it was similar to what was going on in American history, a discovery of the little person. We were able to speak to a lot of people
that way. It wasn't an institutional history; it was more the story of
the persons. Leonard had a great testimony of this Church and the
gospel, but he was trying to tell it from the bottom up, rather than
from the top down.[112]

On one occasion six months after Leonard's tenure began, the discovery was
of mind-blowing proportions: dozens of boxes containing manuscript material
that had been moved south of Salt Lake City during the Utah War in 1858, and
never reopened. Leonard had asked Michael Quinn to write an article for the
Utah Historical Quarterly dealing with the history of early educational institutions in Utah. "In the course of hunting for the minute books of the Board of
Education . . . Mike found in our basement archives two large stacks of uncata-
logued material, mostly in cardboard boxes, some in wooden boxes. The stacks
were about seven feet high and there were perhaps as many as 300 books among
this material and several boxes of loose papers." An earlier archivist had been
aware of the existence of the documents. "He said that Brother A. William Lund
had instructed him that no one was to look at that material but himself, . . . and
that Brother Lund occasionally took one or two items from the pile to look at
and then catalogue. Obviously he had not done very much in 20 years!" Leonard
found it "unbelievable and inexcusable" that Lund had left these documents hidden and uncared for in the basement where scholars knew nothing of their
existence.

We found a great profusion of valuable documents including land
books from Nauvoo, account books and other records pertaining to
the Nauvoo House Association, correspondence with Governor
Cumming, documents signed by Joseph Smith, Sidney Rigdon, and
others, high council minutes—all kinds of extremely valuable material. I stated that if any archive in Utah had any single box of this
mass of material it would be regarded as a rich archive. . . .

This illustrates the psychological fear, which haunted Brother
Lund that someday somebody might find something that was detrimental to the Church and its interests and his lack of confidence in
other persons who might have access to the materials.[113]

In this atmosphere of access, trust, and discovery, enthusiasm among the historians soared. Paul Anderson, a Princeton-trained architect, almost accidentally
bumped into a summer fellowship in 1974 to catalogue historic Mormon meetinghouses in Utah, and was, almost at once, drawn deep into the enterprise—deeper

still when Florence Jacobsen, curator of the newly created Arts and Sites Division, hired him as her assistant in 1976.

> There was a wonderful sense of *esprit de corps* among the historians in those early days. Davis Bitton referred to it as Camelot. There was lots of excitement; it was really kind of an electric time. Everyone was really excited about what they were doing. I think everyone felt that they were doing a tremendous service to the Church. There was no sense of people being sneaky or that they were going to prove anything to people or make trouble. It was a very positive culture that [Leonard] had developed there, and that grew. I always thought afterwards, when people sort of criticized the Historical Department as though it was a hotbed of radical troublemakers— these people were all bishops, they were active. It was really, really positive, and the loyalty to the Church was just sort of unquestionable. These were people who thought they were doing a great service to the Church. . . .
>
> It was fun to have lunch, because every day at lunch a bunch of the historians would sit around a table and gossip about things that happened a hundred years ago, and what they had just learned. Everybody was just very, very excited about it.[114]

Although Carl Arrington was never a researcher, he picked up on the enthusiasm and energy of his father's colleague-employees, recalling how lively and industrious they were. They were all writing and producing articles or books and collaborating. They socialized and went on retreats together. "It was very much like a campaign group, highly bonded in a social way. Each one had their own gift that they brought to it."[115]

The enthusiasm was not limited to the insiders. Outsiders were welcomed both to the archives and to the lively discussions. Richard Bennett's wife, Patricia, had a similar take on the mood in the archives. Though not a scholar, when she helped with research she was "having a ball. It was not work. I don't think history was work to Leonard. I think it was a passion, it was who he was . . . It was fun, it was exciting, it was inspiring." She was learning new things and wishing she could work there forever, and gaining a passion for church history that subsequently never left. "It even came out in the borscht at lunch. We weren't discussing the weather; we were discussing history." In retrospect, she noted, "I think that's what Leonard's legacy is. His writings were great, but it was what he inspired in other people to tell the story. . . . It wasn't *what* we were studying; it was the *excitement* of it and the humanity of it that I felt from Leonard."[116]

One outsider who was particularly grateful for the new atmosphere was Maurine Whipple. A lifelong Mormon and a native of St. George, Utah, Whipple won the Houghton Mifflin Literary Prize in 1938, which assisted her in writing *The Giant Joshua*, a novel portraying pioneer and polygamous life in southern Utah. While critically acclaimed—at one time it was a bestseller ranked second only to Ernest Hemingway's *For Whom the Bell Tolls*[117]—the novel was problematic for fellow Mormons who were attempting to distance themselves from the legacy of polygamy. The reception she received from Leonard and his colleagues stood in stark and welcome contrast to treatment she had received from coreligionists. After a visit, she wrote, in a combination of amazement and gratitude:

> I can't wait any longer to thank you for being so wonderful to me. I haven't always been given the red-carpet treatment by the Church, as you know. But I'll never get over the welcome you and those marvelous folks in that office gave me! It was like a breath of fresh air blowing through long closed up corridors. There was a feeling of helpfulness and (yes, I'll say it!) love that warms me just remembering it. *You* must have been responsible! No more suspicion and cold shoulders, not to mention acrimonious words. I honestly believe that appointing you has brought brotherhood within tangible distance again. I'm *still* happy.[118]

At the end of 1974, Assistant Church Historian James Allen summarized what he felt to be the most important achievements of the History Division to date. First, he thought they were helping "change for good the image and understanding many Latter-day Saints have of their history. If their historical perception is clouded by myth and misunderstanding, and if their faith in the Church is such that any little bit of surprising information about Church history would shake it," the historians sought to help them understand "so well that historical problems no longer bother them." While that high ideal might be out of reach, Allen thought "there were some welcome indicators that at least we were beginning to make that impact."

In addition, Allen could see the new department was "beginning to have a clear and unmistakable influence on the image of Mormonism and Mormon history in the scholarly world." The particular things that were helping to promote a new Mormon image included "the quality of the publications emanating from the Historical Department, and from those people who have done work under its auspices."

Next was the fact "that any scholar, be he Mormon or non-Mormon, who wishes to do serious research in Mormon history must now visit the Historical

Department of the Church." There, scholars now knew, they would find the library and archives "open to responsible researchers" seeking those materials that were "so important that they cannot be ignored."

Finally, "fellowships to Mormons and non-Mormons alike" had "increased the friendliness of the scholarly world toward the Church Historical Department." Allen held back from claiming that "a golden era" had arrived "where everyone in the Church or in the academic world knows, or even cares, what we are doing," but noted that while only small minorities in either world might be aware, the first year had shown "that the impact is becoming real."[119]

The following year, Leonard's enthusiasm reached a high-water mark. He confided to his diary: "I do believe very strongly in what I am doing. I regard my work as the most desirable in the field of American history and the most desirable activity in the Church. . . . To put it in terms of orthodox Mormon language, 'I believe the Lord wants me where I am and that He approves of my labors.' "[120]

15

THE BUREAUCRACY

Leonard, having spent over two decades in a university, understood that every large organization requires a bureaucracy. What he failed to appreciate were the dramatic and often discomfiting differences between the bureaucracy of a university and that of a church. In a midtenure summary he wrote, "All of us have enjoyed or become used to academic life, where a minimum of bureaucratic regulations interfered with our work. Here there are many. They are frustrating, irritating, and mostly unnecessary. Bureaucratic officiousness is an ever-present bother."[1]

Leonard admitted that he entered church employment starry-eyed: "I thought it would be wonderful to go to a place where there would be no smoking, where everyone would be a Latter-day Saint, where there would be no conflict."[2] Diary entries during his first year, however, document a very brief honeymoon followed by a strained marriage—and this during the best of the "Camelot" years.

Writing two months after being sustained in general conference as the new church historian, he noted that many of the policies and procedures of the church bureaucracy were established "when the Church office staff was small and the budget was miserly." His initial response was to try to circumvent a system that was "far more inflexible than that of a university or large corporation." General Authorities, who usually came to their callings from professional lives outside the church bureaucracy, found it easy to "react in terms of what has been the way this was always done and what is the cheapest alternative," rather than give serious deliberation to a question and frame it in the context of that bureaucracy. Whenever he could, Leonard plowed around some issues, tackled others through back-channel communications, and generally found "a certain amount of joy in the little intrigues, which are intended to overcome the stupidities of bureaucratic inefficiency."[3] But those were small skirmishes in a large, never-ending battle.

Particularly annoying to him were the status symbols at church headquarters, which he found to be a troubling contrast to the egalitarian spirit that he had enjoyed in Mormonism's all-lay ministry at the local level. "General Authorities, but no others by and large, are entitled to bathrooms adjoining their offices. There are four sizes of desks depending on rank—large desks for General Authorities, not quite as large for persons of my rank, still smaller for Assistant Church Historians and the Historical Associates, still smaller for Historical Assistants and other staff." Chairs were also assigned by rank; credenzas and filing cabinets were available only to those of a certain administrative level. Secretaries carried status on the basis of the person for whom they worked, rather than seniority or merit. "I suppose if there were a Mormon tea, the secretaries of persons of lower rank would have to stand when the secretaries of General Authorities entered the room. All of this sounds so strange in the Gospel setting where we are all brothers—where a janitor may be the bishop of a corporation president—where this is not at all rare."[4]

He bristled at the delays that he regularly encountered as a result of the decision-making process above his rank, likening the church to an iceberg in the velocity at which it moved. "No decision is made unless it has to be made. They will not answer questions unless they must do so immediately." He saw as an underlying problem the fact that "only three or four people," including the First Presidency and some senior apostles, made the binding decisions. Since few of Leonard's questions rose to the level of the First Presidency, he was frustrated that the decision makers to whom he reported often declined to make definitive decisions because they were constantly looking over their shoulders. "I don't seem to be getting very rapid approval on any of my projects and those that are approved are hedged with a number of restrictions that will make it difficult for us to do a proper professional job."[5]

Having enjoyed an atmosphere of academic freedom for twenty-six years, he found it difficult to adapt to a culture that stifled such freedom. He complained in a diary entry that the church "will not allow a direct vote on officers, either local or general; will not allow a free press; strives to suppress a free press; and so a little criticism that comes has a magnified effect; therefore it is super cautious."[6]

As Leonard settled into the job, he realized that he had to deal with two categories of bureaucratic challenge: strategic (related to organizational structure and flowcharts) and tactical. Some strategic issues were longstanding, but others were of recent vintage and due to the bureaucracy-wide reorganization of which the Historical Department was but one component. In response to the recommendations of the Cresap Report, church leaders had created twelve divisions of church administration, each with a managing director. While in the past General Authorities had managed various departments, the new structure created entities requiring expertise not present among the General Authorities. The obvious solution was to hire professionals in those areas, but that created yet another problem. "It does not work well to have some General Authorities as managing directors and other departments managed by persons who are not General Authorities. They cannot deal with each other on an equal basis."

The solution was to place non–General Authorities as managing directors over all departments, with these directors answering to an advisory committee consisting of Assistants to the Twelve (who were General Authorities). Solving one problem created another, for there was no mechanism by which the advisory committees could reach directly into the Quorum of the Twelve. Ultimately, a member of the Quorum of the Twelve was appointed as liaison to each advisory committee; but since that person had a reporting function but no line authority over the department, one solution continued to create yet another problem.[7]

A second strategic issue was "turf," with policies that required buy-in from "everyone before anything is done. If one mentions education or the history of education, he should be certain that the people in the education department approve of everything being written or said. If one mentions Aaronic Priesthood, it should be something approved by the PBO [Presiding Bishop's Office] and the relevant officials." Getting buy-in at that level was difficult enough; but everything of consequence then had to go to the Quorum of the Twelve for final approval, where "any single objection, or hint of objection by any of them"—whether in their field of expertise or supervision or not—"is sufficient to throw an idea or thought or suggestion overboard."[8]

Concerns over turf were coupled with a not-invented-here mentality that looked for all initiatives to begin at the top,[9] rather than harness the creative energy at the bottom. "Nothing could put more strains on imaginative programming than the feeling that if it did not come from a General Authority, it should not have been thought of. It is suspect immediately if it comes from any other source."[10]

The net effect of these factors was a culture of indecisiveness at the level at which Leonard worked. That culture favored the *status quo* even if it was outmoded and worked against innovation. The problem wasn't consequential in the early months, thanks to the proactive stance of Alvin Dyer. "Brother Dyer was so great a support and help that I guess we were spoiled," admitted Leonard.[11] But after Dyer suffered a debilitating stroke that removed him from supervising the Historical Department, it became a major impediment to Leonard's progressive agenda. He described in almost comic language his frustration following Dyer's tenure:

We want to determine a matter of policy. We take it to Elder [Joseph] Anderson [who was then eighty-seven and had only recently been replaced as secretary to the First Presidency where he had served for decades]. Elder Anderson does not make a decision—almost never does he make a decision. He recommends we take that question to the Advisors to the Twelve. The Advisors almost never make a decision; they recommend we take it to the First Presidency. We do not receive answers on many of the questions we take to the First Presidency: The First Presidency wants to discuss it with the Twelve. It never gets on the agenda of the Twelve, or if it does make the agenda, they don't get to it. Or if they get to it someone asks a question about it which our Advisors can't answer, so it is referred to them to get the answer. They subsequently ask us the question, we provide an answer, they go back with it to the Twelve. By that time, the Twelve have another question. We have had several of our proposals follow precisely this route, with no decision in a year or even two.[12]

Tactical problems related more to human nature than organizational structure, but they were no less troublesome. Four were particularly vexing for Leonard: access to the First Presidency, self-protective reflexes, end runs, and disparities in credentials and salaries within his department.

ACCESS TO THE FIRST PRESIDENCY

Although N. Eldon Tanner rather than Harold B. Lee called Leonard to be church historian, Lee was perhaps even more supportive than Tanner of the new franchise. He was consistently complimentary of what Leonard and his coworkers were doing and met frequently with Leonard and other executives within the Historical Department.[13] With Lee's untimely and unexpected death the day after Christmas in 1973, access effectively terminated. Spencer W. Kimball, the new church president, was sympathetic toward Leonard's new direction in church history, but his priorities were elsewhere.

After Kimball became church president, Leonard was never called into consultation with the First President or Quorum of the Twelve on historical matters, despite having unmatched breadth and depth of knowledge on such matters. "One would think that the church historian, duly sustained in annual and semiannual conferences of the Church, would be consulted on policies and programs relating to history. And if there were complaints, they would have been brought to me; if we were derelict, we could be informed; if the Church was about to dedicate an historic spot, we could verify the history." But instead of turning to Leonard, Kim-ball deferred to the two senior apostles who had antipathy towards the History Division.

On several occasions, Leonard attempted to gain an audience with the First Presidency, but always without success. While Kimball "told us the Lord was happy with our presence and work, . . . it would have been helpful if we could have con-ducted a periodic morning or afternoon seminar with the relevant authorities to inform them of our work and of the 'facts' of church history."[14]

SELF-PROTECTIVE REFLEXES

An unusual, almost unique feature of the Mormon Church is the enormously deep body of documentary history that goes back to the founding days of the church in 1830. Although the church carefully collected and preserved those documents, for many decades they were ignored as deference was given to outdated, apolo-getic published histories. Leonard and his colleagues, nearly all of whom had graduate degrees in history and related fields, came into their new jobs already well versed in Mormon history; and they quickly became expert in new areas as they plowed through thousands of pages of documentary materials that had laid unexamined. People in the church hierarchy who were not well read in the manu-script history were at a disadvantage, and their response to the new versions of history was often one of self-protective (or turf-protective) reflex that invariably was counterproductive to Leonard's plans.

Leonard commented with rare indignation on this pattern in December 1976: "We have observed instances in which a member of the Twelve 'sounded off' about our work without really knowing what we were trying to do or why, and without consulting us, our advisors, or our managing director, and without giving them or us a chance to 'answer' the charges." In sharp contrast was the fact that only on one occasion had they received praise from a General Authority for any of their books or articles, and that was from S. Dilworth Young, who was not in the First Presidency or the Quorum of the Twelve. "With all the books we have published, and articles, we have never had written or oral communications from Elder Anderson, our Advisors, members of the Quorum of the Twelve, or the First Presidency about them. As if each is fearful of putting something in writing which would later embarrass him."

Particularly annoying to Leonard were the opportunities lost when General Authorities failed to grasp how powerful the history would have been in the con-duct of their business. "Instead," he lamented, "[they] rely on legalistic pronounce-ments and coercive administrative power. I have never seen a group of people so afraid to do something, so fearful of doing wrong, terrorized by the possibility of vindictiveness. And this is a Church!"[15]

End Runs

The Doctrine and Covenants, one of Mormonism's four books of scripture, contains the canon law that is supposed to guide both the governance of the church and the behavior of its members. Where there are disputes between two church members, the scriptural mandate from the Doctrine and Covenants is unambiguous about the process to be followed: "If thy brother or sister offend thee, thou shalt take him or her between him or her and thee alone; and if he or she confess thou shalt be reconciled."[16] Only if direct communication between the offended and offending parties fails to resolve the situation is the circle of communication to extend outwards, and then only along canonically prescribed lines. Although Leonard certainly knew this scripture, curiously, he never cited it in his papers, and there is no record that he ever used it in conversation with his superiors in an attempt to reset the discussion.

He was particularly irritated by two kinds of breach of the scriptural mandate. One was when parents of BYU students bypassed professors and even university administrators, and complained directly to a General Authority about what a professor may have said in the classroom, often without merit and always giving the professor no opportunity to defend or correct the record. The other was when a church member complained directly to a General Authority about what a scholar had published, rather than taking the matter up with the scholar as the scripture mandates. He had been the victim of the second action, as he noted with exasperation in a diary entry in 1976: "I write an article on the Word of Wisdom. Someone complains to a General Authority. The General Authority writes to the president of BYU. The president of BYU calls the dean. The dean calls me in. The dean tells me it looks O.K. to him, but since the general authority complained, I must write him a letter of apology. This is the way to be creative? This is the way of academic freedom? This is the way of history?"[17]

Disparities in Credentials and Salaries

From the time the church began to have a salaried bureaucracy in the nineteenth century, it paid salaries that were not competitive with the private sector. "The result," wrote Leonard, "was that most of the old-line employees were not university-trained people. Moreover, they were suspicious of highly trained people. A few set out to undermine the university people by spying on them and reporting back to general authorities they knew, the secretaries of general authorities, etc."[18]

Clashes between the Young Turks and the Old Guard, who though lacking in professional training were well versed in the workings of the bureaucracy and had long-standing alliances with ecclesiastical officers, were inevitable. The idyllic work environment that Leonard had originally envisioned was illusory. He reflected ruefully in his diary: "I was not prepared for the lack of historical training, the lack of appreciation of those who did have professional training, the lack of tolerance for new suggestions, new approaches, new contributions, new publications. I began to wonder. Better to put up with a few smokers and anti-Mormons than the spies and anti-intellectuals in the Church Office Building."[19]

Another division between the old and the new was attitude concerning salaries. Whereas the long-time employees had accepted lower salaries in return for a feeling that they were privileged to be working for the Lord, the new professionals began to compare current pay scales with what their credentials would bring them in a university setting. Ronald K. Esplin, one of Leonard's original hires, later reflected on the unexpectedly bitter turf battle that erupted over salaries, triggered by one historian being told by the personnel office that he would "never in my lifetime earn more than $8,000 a year if I stay here."

Esplin explained that department employees responded to the news by gathering comparative wage data that they could present to their supervisors in an effort to improve income. "That's subversive, of course. Pay was supposed to be totally confidential in the church system, and 'You should feel it is a blessing to work here.' We had just emerged, in the Historical Department, from a period when it was a welfare program for people who needed jobs a generation before." While Leonard was not part of the drama—"we weren't asking him to bless it or to be responsible for it"—the move placed his department at some risk. But ultimately it worked to the department's benefit. "A month later, when they came back to us, they said, 'This has made no difference, but if you ever do it again, you will be fired.' But within the next year, we got substantial raises. So it did make a difference."[20]

LEONARD AS PART OF THE PROBLEM

The most famous line from *Pogo*, the long-running daily comic strip, was a parody on the message from Commodore Oliver Hazard Perry to General (and future U.S. President) William Henry Harrison after Perry's victory in the Battle of Lake Erie in 1813: "We have met the enemy, and they are ours." Pogo's version encapsulated one of the dilemmas of Leonard's History Division: "We have met the enemy and he is us."

As noted in an earlier chapter, Leonard as an economics professor "was not interested in administration and so no posts were offered me at any time."[21] While that strategy bought him more time for research and writing, it worked against him when he joined a church bureaucracy that was quite a bit more perplexing than the one that had surrounded him in the university, and when he had to create a new bureaucracy within the larger one as he built the History Division. His lack of bureaucratic skills worked against him and the division.

Rather than working in a conciliatory way with bureaucrats above his pay grade, he adopted a confrontational posture that worked against him—and although he realized that it would do so, he pursued such a course anyway, imbued with a sense of mission that likely blinded him to the dangers of such an approach: "The Church of the future will be grateful for what we do, we must do it even by fighting the bureaucracy, and we must expect to lose many of our fights with officialdom, and expect heavy criticism. But in the interest of the Church, in the interest of the Lord, we should persevere."[22]

With the best of intentions toward those within his division, Leonard was nonetheless tone-deaf to some of the problems that he created for them. A central question in their minds was, "Are we colleagues or hired help?" The "stake presidency" of Leonard, Davis Bitton, and Jim Allen "routinely trooped off to have lunch together," leaving the rest of the staff to wonder how much collegiality resided in the History Division. An *ad hoc* committee of junior staffers solicited suggestions, proposals, or areas of conflict from other staffers, consolidated the input into what they called the "Rage Gauge," and presented to Leonard a list of grievances that included "a general breakdown in communications"; disagreement about how contributions of staff should be acknowledged in published materials ("should Leonard receive 'credit' when most of the research and some of the writing was done by someone else who merited only a footnote?"); exclusion of junior staff from the decision-making process; and lack of office time to pursue their own research interests.

Confronted with a consensus of discontent, Leonard and the two assistant church historians began to respond with substantive changes. One staff historian recalled, "It was an exercise that was not welcomed by Leonard, but at the end, I think he responded and it did get better."[23]

What Leonard failed to realize, and what likely would have reshaped the outcome of the History Division had he realized it from the start, was that the church—or *any* church—is an organization, and the larger the organization, the more predictably its bureaucracy will act. One of Leonard's colleagues, a professor at the University of Utah, stated the matter succinctly: "I talked with Bob Hales when he came from a corporation in the East and was appointed an apostle.[24] He was on the board of regents, and I met him there. I said to him, 'What is the difference between being a corporate executive, at a high level, and being an apostle in the Church?' He said, 'None.' I think that goes to part of the matter."[25]

16

Promoting Mormon History

The Church Historian Years

Friends of Church History

As Leonard focused on building the History Division, he did not lose sight of the larger picture that had animated him for years: promoting Mormon history. One way of expanding the franchise was to engage the support of *consumers* of the history so that they became *patrons* and, ideally, *producers.* It was a tried-and-tested process that had proved its worth in building loyal clients and expanding interest in every arena from sports to scientific research. But it backfired in a spectacular and irreversible example of the protectiveness, even fearfulness, of church hierarchs who were wary of innovation, particularly of innovation involving church history.

In March 1972, just weeks after becoming church historian, Leonard met with Earl Olson and Alvin Dyer to propose the organization of Friends of Church History. "Elder Dyer approved of the idea but said we should do it in anticipation of the move to the new building."[1]

In meeting with the First Presidency and Howard Hunter on August 8, Leonard proposed orally the creation of the organization and included it in the written outline that he distributed at the meeting. In response, the First Presidency sent a brief letter in mid-September: "This is to inform you that the proposed program of the Historical Department, which was presented to us at a meeting, held on August 8, 1972 has been approved."[2] Leonard interpreted this generalization as specific approval of Friends of Church History, in addition to the other items in his proposal, and announced at a departmental meeting a week later: "We have been given approval to organize 'Friends of Church History.'"[3]

Following the move to new quarters in the fall of 1972, Leonard sent a letter to potential members of the new organization, as well as to Hunter and church president Harold B. Lee, announcing the first meeting on November 30 and offering a summary of its purposes. While not a fundraising organization, it would levy dues "at a level necessary to carry out the organization's own program." Dues-paying members would be invited to monthly meetings that would include papers and discussions on church history, and would be invited both to volunteer in the division and to pursue their own research using archival materials. The informal mission of the Friends was stated in the conclusion of the letter: "History buffs meeting and knowing each other can encourage study and stimulate thought among themselves. By meeting regularly to hear from established scholars, they can keep current on new findings and interpretations in the field."[4]

Given the careful groundwork that he had done, Leonard was stunned to receive a call from Hunter on the very day of the inaugural meeting, particularly in light of the consistent support that otherwise informed his relationship with Harold B. Lee. A lengthy diary entry recorded Leonard's frantic activities during the afternoon, beginning with a phone call from Hunter in which the apostle reported on the adverse response to the Friends in the morning meeting of the First Presidency and Quorum of the Twelve in the Salt Lake Temple. Lee, who had received a copy of the invitation letter, failed to link it to the blanket approval the First Presidency had earlier given to Leonard's proposed program. He read it aloud in the meeting and raised serious questions about it. Leonard's account, "apparently some members of the Twelve raised serious questions about it," was an understatement, because Lee had been an unquestioned leader for years, even before becoming church president. (One fellow General Authority remarked to him, "Haven't you ever noticed that when items are being discussed, more often than not they'll wait to see what your position is before they'll declare their feelings?")[5] So with Lee opening the gate of questioning Friends, others walked through. "Would it be a forum for discussing Church history? Would it be a forum for *Dialogue*-type people? And so on."

Hunter, although generally an advocate for the History Division, took the hint from Lee and hedged his bets. "Brother Hunter, although he had received a copy of the letter and had been with me when I presented it to the First Presidency, seemed to be very vague about it and seemed to feel that we had gone too far without clearing with the First Presidency." Hunter relayed to Leonard many of the questions asked in the temple earlier in the day, which Leonard attempted to answer impromptu.

Given the lateness of the hour and the fact that the charter meeting of Friends was already scheduled for that evening, Hunter asked "if we could prevent them from organizing tonight. I told him I didn't think we could. He seemed to be very concerned and very upset—very fearful. He said he would try to get an appointment with the First Presidency for me and him sometime before our meeting occurred at 7:30. I told him I would remain here and await his call."

Hunter called back "just before 5:00" and said that it would not be possible for them to meet with the First Presidency prior to the scheduled meeting of Friends. "He suggested that we go ahead with the meeting, that we accomplish as little as possible in the meeting, that we not take any money and that we not elect officers, that we talk about the whole thing and propose that we would get in touch with people later." Although Hunter had been invited to attend and, before the temple meeting that day apparently planned to do so, he pulled back, saying "he should not be present because it would give the official sponsorship of the Church, which apparently President Lee was a little concerned about."[6]

Leonard put on a game face for the meeting, which turned out to be successful beyond all expectations. He dictated a diary entry from his office as some attendees still lingered in the building: "Upward of 400 people were in attendance according to the best estimates—there may have been as many as 500 that came. Every chair in the entire department was placed in the general reading room and filled, and in addition there must have been 100 people on the ledge and perhaps another 50 or 100 standing, so we estimate between 400 and 500."

Contrary to the fears of Lee and his colleagues, Leonard "did not see a tendency for anybody to regard it other than as a fine well-motivated Church group. The size of the crowd and their enthusiasm suggests the support for the Historical Department. . . . Virtually all of them remained afterwards to circulate among the facilities on the four floors and at this time—9:30—there still must be a couple of hundred wandering around seeing the facilities."[7]

Having received approval to organize Friends well in advance of the first meeting, Leonard was devastated at the reversal at the highest level of the bureaucracy. His diary entry the following day made no attempt to buffer his feelings, even his thoughts that his tenure as church historian might be very brief:

> I will not deny that I have been shaken by the telephone calls of Elder Hunter yesterday. They took away some of my self-confidence, my enthusiasm, my ebullience. I now question my ability to survive in the uncertainties of church policy and practice. Why is every experienced bureaucrat so afraid of President Lee? It was such an unlikely action for the Twelve to criticize the formation of a Friends of Church History group. What does that portend with respect to more sensitive matters—the publication of diaries, of objective history, of realistic biography? I wonder how long it will be before I am sent off to be a mission president or some other assignment that will take me away from this sensitive position? And who would they place in charge of it?[8]

Leonard wrote to Hunter the same day. With obvious frustration, he enumerated the steps he had taken to get proper approval for the Friends meeting, only to have it blow up in his face: "I did mention it orally and had it on the outline I presented to the First Presidency in the August 8 meeting. Subsequently on September 13, I had the letter from Presidents Tanner and Romney which said the program I presented was approved. I then mentioned the forthcoming organization in the meeting of the Cannon-Hinckley History Club at which Presidents [Eldon] Tanner, [Marion] Romney, and [Spencer] Kimball were present."[9] He received no reply from Hunter, but in the course of the following week he pieced together, from two back-channel sources, the details of the painful story.

Leonard spoke to the first source, History Division employee Ron Esplin, four days after the Friends meeting. Esplin relayed the essence of a lunch conversation that involved two apostles, Bruce McConkie and Boyd Packer, and F. Briton ("Brit") McConkie. Brit told Esplin that he had brought up the matter of the Friends of Church History, and that the two apostles had differed markedly in their comments. McConkie "said that he would have come to the meeting if they hadn't had the discussion in the [Quorum of the] Twelve about it. He seemed to think it might be worthwhile." Packer, on the other hand, "thought it would be a *Dialogue*-type program that would rake over old controversial subjects and stir up trouble and mistrust."

Then, the conversation took a turn that might have sent a strong signal to Leonard, but apparently did not. "Brit said very freely that he believed that it was a good thing and Bruce seemed to want to agree with him, but Brother Packer sort of cringed." Seniority. McConkie became an apostle two years after Packer, and the same kind of deference that all of the apostles had shown Harold Lee in the temple meeting weighed in on the luncheon conversation. Indeed, Esplin concluded the conversation by emphasizing the point: "When you want something accomplished you have to go to the First Presidency because the Twelve will not universally approve anything unless the First Presidency are willing to give their sanction."[10] If the First Presidency has not taken a strong stand on something, then the matter is likely to be addressed and resolved by senior apostles, which is exactly what happened after Lee's death. Because Spencer Kimball took a hands-off approach to the History Division, the next two senior apostles, Ezra Taft Benson and Mark Petersen, took control of the agenda. The message was already there in 1972, albeit between the lines, but Leonard didn't see it.

Compounding Leonard's frustration was the fact that the First Presidency *had* approved the meeting, only to reverse field when the matter was discussed, at the eleventh hour, with the Quorum of the Twelve. Four days later William

Smart, then editor of the *Deseret News*, who had chaired the Friends meeting at Leonard's request, reported to him a conversation he had had that day with Eldon Tanner, wherein Tanner suggested that the hang-up was with archival access. Lee felt strongly that "this was not a public library, but a private archive," and that the church had every right to grant archival access at its own discretion. Leonard's diary account of the conversation with Smart noted, "Somehow, apparently, President Lee and perhaps others had interpreted that sentence in Bill Smart's letter about Friends of Church History using our archives to mean that they would be pressuring us to open up everything to everybody." Tanner told Smart that he did not consider this to be an insurmountable problem. "He thought we could be depended upon to make rules that were reasonable and protective." Leonard put the best face on the comment, and assumed that a quick rewriting of archival policy was all that was necessary to get back on track with Friends. "I suppose that means we'll get the go ahead in forming the organization eventually."[11]

His optimism was short-lived. At a meeting of the executives of the Historical Department the following month, the decision was made to cancel the second meeting of Friends, which had been scheduled for January 25, and not to reschedule it.[12] Joseph Anderson, on Leonard's behalf, spoke to the First Presidency in an attempt to clarify the issue. Anderson was told that membership in Friends would not give preferential access to the archives, and that "an individual who is a member of Friends of Church History could not write an article without having the article screened before publication." In other words, the creation of Friends of Church History paradoxically would take academic freedom backwards a step. Rather than seeing Friends as a threat, the First Presidency apparently had come to view it as an opportunity to control the message. "We would have much better control if the Friends of Church History organization were affiliated with the Church so that approval could be given to anything published by the organization; otherwise, on an individual basis, we would have no control over what they want to publish."[13]

In a meeting with the First Presidency at the end of January 1973, Leonard once again received a nod of approval from Eldon Tanner, who "said that it was a fine idea—that it would be a fine organization and would serve a number of useful purposes provided we establish sufficient safeguards and controls."[14] But a First Presidency decision on the future of Friends was delayed indefinitely.

Five months later Leonard again petitioned the First Presidency for a decision, explaining that "many research libraries have similar groups as a means of obtaining volunteer aid in research and in the collection of historical materials. . . . President Tanner spoke up to say that he thought one of the principal benefits of the organization was helping us to collect materials, diaries, correspondence, and other materials that ought to be in the Church Archives. I pointed out some of the advantages of having the organization. They seemed to agree."[15] Perhaps they agreed, but they declined to decide, and Friends of Church History died a quiet death.

Looking back five years later, Leonard retraced all of the steps he had taken to ensure a successful birth of the organization, only to see all of them come to naught, and then he lamented:

> So the whole "brilliant idea" was dropped and the momentum of enthusiasm that had been built up fell like a ton of lead. We were embarrassed, humiliated, and set back in our public relations and good will and simply not able to get the idea back to the First Presidency for their stamp of approval because of the misgivings and cautions of our advisers and our managing directors. This would have been a great help to the cause of Church history and in my judgment would have helped in building the kingdom and would have built good will for the Church. I very much regret we were not able to carry it through.[16]

Writing his autobiography two decades later, he expressed his feelings even more strongly: "We were embarrassed and humiliated and we lost public good will."[17]

Many years thereafter, several of Leonard's colleagues reflected independently on the failed initiative. Everett Cooley, former director of the Utah State Historical Society, attended the first and only meeting of Friends. Well versed in the prevailing antischolarship culture at church headquarters, he recalled his reservations, even cynicism, upon hearing of the meeting. "I remember that night that they were talking about these great publications that would come out—not the usual Deseret Book. Bill Smart was one of those who worked hard on this, but Leonard's reputation drew a lot of us in. I know I wasn't too enthused when I heard rumors of it."[18]

James Allen, assistant church historian, recalled, "There wasn't much enthusiasm from the Brethren, even from the advisors to the Historical Department. I don't know why, except there may have been a feeling that, 'This thing could get out of hand. We could have the tail wagging the dog.'"[19]

And Sandra Tanner, who, with her husband, Jerald, had for years scratched out a living by selling photocopies of scarce church publications and manuscripts along with their own narrative—albeit sensationalized—histories, spoke wistfully of what briefly appeared to be a new era of scholarship and camaraderie:

We thought it was great when Arrington went in to be Church Historian. We hoped that was going to signal more openness, and obviously, Arrington hoped it was going to signal more openness. We went to the infamous first meeting of Friends of Church History that lasted one night. All these things sounded so exciting. "Wow! They are going to open the archives. They are going to bring out this stuff, and we are going to have some responsible scholarship." And then we heard about the sesquicentennial history. "Wow! That's a neat idea." But then you started to get all the rumors, "Well, it's kind of hitting the skids. The Brethren are getting a little nervous, now that they are seeing some of the manuscripts. They don't feel comfortable about where this is all going."[20]

DIALOGUE AND OTHER INDEPENDENT JOURNALS

Dialogue: A Journal of Mormon Thought was the first independent journal in the field of Mormon studies, and it remains the most prominent to this day. Its birth in 1966 elicited mixed reactions among the LDS Church hierarchy (see chapter 13). Some, with the LDS scriptural dictum of "the glory of God is intelligence"[21] in mind, welcomed without reservation new and serious scholarship from editors and writers who clearly were faithful church members or church friends, including a future apostle.[22] Others were wary of a publication over which the church exercised no direct control, while still others opposed the idea of the journal because of fears that its scholarship would confront the church with inconvenient truths.[23] The early mixed reactions from the McKay First Presidency led to no official church policy—either of endorsement or condemnation of *Dialogue*—and so its *de facto* status remained ambiguous. As a result, and to the frustration of the editors, it was often misrepresented in either direction.

Several months after Leonard became church historian, he visited the Church College of Hawaii.[24] At a question-and-answer session at a reception in his honor, the subject of *Dialogue* was raised. He knew the cross-currents he was stepping into, and he spoke judiciously. "I said I was well acquainted with those who launched and edited *Dialogue*, and they were all fine[,] loyal, active members of the Church. That the journal contained many fine articles that were important for the historian to read." While noting that his current position as church historian made it improper for him to declare either support or nonsupport for *Dialogue*, he leaned in the direction of support by saying, "I thought it an important source of items about church history, both contemporary and for earlier periods," even though he did not agree with everything that it published. "Many persons afterward commented on this response and said it was just right. And this seemed to come both from regular readers of *Dialogue* and from others that had been suspicious of it."[25]

Later in the year, Leonard wrote of the most recent issue of the journal, to which he had contributed an article in tribute to Joseph Fielding Smith, the church president who had died earlier that year. While he approved of most of the content, he was troubled by one article and felt it was "in bad taste to attack some BYU brethren with conservative political philosophies. If I would have known about it, I would have counseled very strongly against the inclusion of those paragraphs. It is far better to make a point subtly than to editorialize as this one does. . . . I am sure the publication of this will cause us trouble."[26]

Leonard's fears were unfounded, at least in the short term, for three months later church president Harold B. Lee—apparently a *Dialogue* reader—spoke favorably to him about the journal. "He said that there is a philosophy that we ought to be critical in our writings so as to make accommodation to the Jack Mormons and non-Mormons and dissenters. This had been the policy of the editors of *Dialogue*. President Lee said that he discerned a more conservative turn of *Dialogue* in recent issues and he thought that this was praiseworthy."[27]

Lee's private endorsement notwithstanding, an April 1973 department meeting underscored the ambiguous and sometimes misstated position that *Dialogue* held in the minds of many within the church bureaucracy. When Leonard mentioned the journal, Joseph Anderson rebuked him mildly: "You surely wouldn't be having anything to do with *Dialogue*, which you know is under a ban." Leonard challenged the statement, saying that he was unaware of any ban and adding, "I certainly would feel more friendly disposed toward *Dialogue* than toward all the magazines published by non-Mormons."

At that, Anderson drew back a bit "and said that he had understood that some people had their fingers crossed about *Dialogue*." Leonard responded by pointing out that prior to embarking on the venture, the founding editors of the journal had "consulted with at least one member of the First Presidency and got the okay. I also told him that when I was asked by *Dialogue* to be an advisory editor, I consulted individually with two members of the First Presidency, both of whom advised me to accept the appointment."

At that, Anderson stood down and allowed that at least the church did not want to give the impression that it was supporting *Dialogue*. Leonard had the final word in the meeting, saying, "Of course not, nor does *Dialogue* want the Church to give the impression that the Church is supporting them. It is an independent magazine and wants to remain such, but we must not neglect the fact that it is a magazine by and for Mormons and we ought not to be hesitant about making use of it as all of the other magazines which made no pretense of being a Mormon magazine."[28]

Diary entries over the following two weeks underscored the ambivalence with which *Dialogue* was greeted by church officials. The first entry described a meeting with the journal's new editor, Robert Rees. "He said he had sent copies of the last three issues to all of the General Authorities and had received replies from eight. Favorable replies were received from President Tanner and Theodore Burton and Hartman Rector. He received no negative replies."[29]

But the second diary entry, just four days later, described a different perspective. Joseph Anderson again brought up what he called "the meetings of *Dialogue*," a confusing description since *Dialogue* did not sponsor scholarly meetings, informal study groups, or even periodic firesides. Anderson gave no reason for his concern, which left Leonard wondering if the rumor mill had ground out a new scandal, or if the formerly expressed concerns were only now working their way to Anderson's level. The latter seemed more likely, since Anderson's message was the far-from-fresh one that the church needed to avoid giving the impression that it, or even the Historical Department, sponsored or supported the journal.

At this point in the meeting Leonard pointed out what probably had escaped Anderson's notice, that Assistant Church Historian Davis Bitton had been the book review editor of *Dialogue* for several years. Earl Olson, who probably had been unaware of Bitton's role, asked Anderson if he thought Bitton should resign from the position. Anderson then reversed field and said, "No. . . . *Dialogue* seems to be having enough trouble"—referring to ongoing financial struggles—"without us creating additional troubles for them."

Leonard ended the discussion by noting that since he was a contributing editor for the *Ensign*, the church's magazine for adults, James Allen was a contributing editor for *BYU Studies*, and Bitton was book review editor for *Dialogue*, "this made it possible for us to be aware of everything that was being published in the field of Church history."[30]

Later the same year, *Dialogue* published a landmark article on blacks and priesthood—detailed in chapter 21—that appeared to move some church leaders to a position of overt opposition—if not to the journal as an entity, then at least to the participation of employees of the Historical Department. On June 24, 1974, Leonard recorded without commentary the outcome of a ninety-minute meeting with Anderson and the heads of the archives and library (Earl Olson and Don Schmidt, respectively). Leonard "asked them for permission to publish the humor article in *Dialogue*. They replied with a flat no. The reason they gave was that they did not want a Church official dignifying *Dialogue* with articles they have prepared. They told me members of the Church would reach the conclusion that if articles by official Church appointees were published in *Dialogue* this gives a semi-official approval of the publication and of other articles in it."[31]

History Division's involvement in *Dialogue* was further curtailed six months later in a meeting with the department's two advisors, Howard Hunter and Bruce McConkie. Leonard recorded gloomily, "There was a general feeling that we should be less involved in *Dialogue*, to avoid any impression that the Historical Department was placing a stamp of approval on *Dialogue*, and to avoid a tendency for us to dignify the magazine by contributing regularly toward it."[32]

Three weeks later one of Leonard's coworkers, Maureen Ursenbach, received a letter of appointment as a writer for the instructional development group in the church. This correlation-sponsored group replaced the lesson-writing committees that each auxiliary had previously organized, and wrote lessons according to a topic schedule that assured that key principles (e.g., baptism, prayer, missionary work, etc.) would be covered at regular intervals. Because it was a general church committee, Maureen would be released from any ward or stake positions she held. The calling itself was a well-merited endorsement of her writing and editing skills, but it came with a string attached: "This condition was that she not publish any articles in *Dialogue* or *Woman's Exponent II* or be involved or associated with them in any official capacity during the period of her appointment which is 'indefinite.' "[33]

While there was still no official church position on *Dialogue* (nor is there to this day), Leonard sent a letter to Bob Rees suggesting a more guarded profile. "Just a personal, confidential note to you. In my judgment it would be preferable if you did not send complimentary copies of each issue of *Dialogue* to the General Authorities of the Church. In my judgment it would be preferable if you sent copies only to those who subscribed. I see almost no advantages in sending the free copies, and on the basis of personal experiences we have had, we can cite a number of cases that it has been disadvantageous for *Dialogue*."[34]

While Leonard urged more caution on the part of the editors, he did so with the intent of maximizing its chances for long-term success, rather than reducing its impact. Writing retrospectively late in 1976, he lamented the fate of pre-*Dialogue* generations who, lacking its intellectual content and the wider intellectual community that had coalesced around its publication, had withdrawn from the church. "I have the feeling that many LDS university students of my generation and a generation earlier who left the Church, really left, not just Mormonism, but religion. And may one reason have been the failure of our faith to preach and teach religion, along with theology and the unique elements of our faith[?]" He saw *Dialogue*, *Sunstone*, *Exponent II*, and even *BYU Studies* as providing LDS young people, in particular, "the opportunity to have intellectual discussion of history, doctrine, practices, and activity."[35]

As the fortunes of the History Division waned in the late 1970s, Leonard mourned the adverse role that *Dialogue* had played inadvertently, even as he remained a steady supporter of the journal. "*Dialogue* was (is) an anathema to Elder [Ezra Taft] Benson and Elder [Mark] Petersen, and they can never forgive us for our associations with them before our appointments. If they saw evidence of our association with them today, they would press for our release."[36]

The June 1978 revelation that ended the ban on ordination of black men to the LDS priesthood should have been a time of unqualified joy for those associated with *Dialogue*, given the pivotal role of its 1973 article on the subject, but a letter the same month from Mary Bradford, its editor, to Leonard mingled qualified joy with lamentation. "Today when I opened the *Church News* and saw it practically full of black faces, I cried in joy, and what a time to be Editor of *Dialogue*. I think of the suffering [of] former editors and I feel grateful."

But that joy was coupled with the realization that, in spite of the role the journal had played in moving the needle for the entire church, those associated with it still had "second-class status" in the church. She appealed to Leonard for help: "It is not right that writers should be forbidden to write for us. How can this ban be lifted? Can President Kimball be reached on this subject somehow? I am asking this confidentially—I don't want you to say anything to anyone—just tell me truthfully what can be done."

Then, Bradford aired a specific grievance. "You know it isn't right that the *Church News* would run a whole article on Dick Motta, just because he is the Bullet Coach,[37] when he is NOT active in the Church at all, and then blanch at the suggestion of a special interest article on *Dialogue*. It is not right that people are told they cannot serve on our Board. . . . It is not Christian and it is not Mormon—and it is crippling to us, Leonard."[38]

Leonard did not intervene with Kimball, if for no other reason than the fact that he had no direct entrée with the First Presidency after the death of Harold Lee. That he continued to support *Dialogue*, in spite of his inaction in Bradford's behalf, is plainly stated by a diary entry just a few weeks later under the heading, "This I Most Regret about My Service As Church Historian, 1972–1978": "I regret the ukase which prevents us from making the contributions we should to *Dialogue* magazine. *Dialogue* is making an important contribution to LDS culture and we should be represented in it more than we are."[39]

While *Dialogue* held a special place in Leonard's universe, he also was strongly supportive of the other journals focusing on the Latter-day Saint tradition that emerged in its wake: *Courage: A Journal of History, Thought and*

Action (published by members of the Reorganized Church of Jesus Christ of Latter Day Saints, 1970–1973), the *Journal of Mormon History* (1974–present), *Exponent II* (1974–present), Sunstone (1975–present), *John Whitmer Historical Association Journal* (1981–present), and *Seventh East Press* (1981–1983). The founding editor of *Sunstone* recalled what "strongly supportive" meant in the context of the new magazine: "During that time—it must have been in 1974—I told Leonard about a project that a few of us were trying to start, and that would be *Sunstone*. He said, 'How much will that subscription be?' I said, '$10.' He wrote me out a check for $20 and said, 'I want to be your first subscriber,' and I think he was."[40]

MENTORSHIP

Leonard's most significant and lasting contribution to the promotion of Mormon history was his mentorship at all levels: peers, younger historians with advanced degrees, graduate and undergraduate students, and "history buffs" of all flavors. It was the epitaph his family chose to engrave on his tombstone. Leonard had chosen "Blessed Damsel" as the inscription on Grace's headstone; when his daughter Susan said, "Well, Dad, what do you want us to put on yours?" he said, "Oh, you guys decide. Whatever you decide is fine." The three siblings discussed the matter and decided on "Beloved Mentor"—a good choice, as Susan recalled. "There were so many people that came through at the viewing and the funeral who said, 'Your father was my mentor. I wouldn't have done this if it hadn't been for him.'"[41]

His son Carl reflected similarly on Leonard's legacy of mentoring: "That ability to bring people in from the outside, integrate them, train them, and send them out into the world—I think that was one of the things that stunned me at his death. When they had the wake of the historians afterwards, there was story after story. 'He wrote a letter for me.' 'He intervened to get me this job.' 'I was in trouble here.' It was just a whole string of his wise and compassionate intervention for good, in so many different ways."[42]

His impulse to combine mentorship with his new position of church historian became apparent in one of his first meetings with the other executives of the Historical Department, only one month after Eldon Tanner asked him to be church historian. Leonard made a pitch for a new summer program to bring outside scholars into the archives. "It was suggested by Leonard Arrington that some summer research fellowships be given to scholars to work here in the library using the materials, which we have with a grant of $1,000 each. It is proposed that this announcement be made, applications considered submitted up to April 1, and then decide just who would qualify."[43]

Alvin Dyer, the department's managing director, approved the proposal, and three fellowships were awarded for the summer of 1972. The following spring, however, the new director, Joseph Anderson, openly questioned the nascent program. Leonard summarized the conversation: "He raised many questions about it, and in a tone which suggested that he didn't approve of it. He couldn't see any advantage to us in giving research fellowships. I explained, defended, justified the program, and of course Brother Anderson learned how keenly I felt about it because I suppose my voice raised to some extent, and I may have seemed a little impatient with some of his objections. Brother Anderson couldn't see us spending money to help people make money by writing books."

Leonard pointed out that these people weren't writing books for money; indeed, that works of scholarship are not money making in nature. This was news to Anderson, who couldn't see any other motivation than money. Leonard responded, "They do it for the same reason people do genealogical work—because they believe in it," but to deaf ears.

Notwithstanding his puzzlement, Anderson "didn't tell me to stop it, and we ended it on a perfectly friendly and cordial basis, so I assume that it is okay for another year, but it shows the problems of getting programs approved and then new administrators, which may not approve of programs which have been approved by their predecessors."[44]

The fellowship program became one of the most important initiatives of Leonard's tenure, enhancing the careers of established scholars and launching the careers of others. Assistant Church Historian James Allen remarked, "People don't realize how many young scholars got their start as a result of having had a fellowship from Leonard Arrington. . . . Marv Hill, Richard Bushman, Dave Whittaker, and Jill Mulvay Derr. . . . Jessie Embry came in as a research fellow and as a research assistant. And Dean May. Leonard would bring both young scholars and established scholars in as fellows to work on projects, and those projects got published."[45]

Leonard's own academic peers, particularly George Ellsworth, had reached out to him and helped him to reorient his own career, and he subsequently returned the favor to other peers. Doug Alder, who did a landmark study of Mormon bishops, was keenly aware of Leonard's downstream influence. "Leonard promoted a generation of at least a hundred scholars. He took it on as his role to encourage young scholars, and he did it at every level of his life. A couple of those young scholars were unknown guys like Tom Alexander and Jim Allen, who were students at Utah State." But Leonard's encouragement went far beyond that of most people in his field. "It was not unusual when a young scholar would come to Leonard, that Leonard could see this young scholar was doing something that

Leonard had in his distant mind to do himself. Leonard would go downstairs into the basement, get his file, take it up, and give it to that young scholar and say, 'Go do it.' He must have done it twenty-five times, asking nothing in return."[46]

Tom Alexander was one of scores who acknowledged that assistance: "Leonard helped me with my writing and publication more than anybody else that I ever worked with. He provided opportunities for me to do research and opportunities to publish early in my career, in ways that I probably would never have been able to otherwise."[47] Although those two men collaborated on publications, Leonard's largesse extended to colleagues with no expectation of coauthorship. Stanford Cazier, a professor at Utah State University who later returned as president, used religious language to describe Leonard's actions: "What Leonard did for me, and for so many of my colleagues, was to stimulate our scholarship. He was on a *mission* to help us get airborne. . . . Leonard was so good that way, better than anyone, in encouraging the younger faculty to not just be parasites and draw upon the scholarship of others, but to make our mark, our contribution."[48]

Part of the way Leonard encouraged his peers was to read what they were publishing and then write appreciative letters to them. "Leonard was good at reading every journal that came, the day it came," recalled Glen Leonard, one of the History Division's employees and later director of the LDS History Museum. Then, also often the same day, Leonard would write "letters to each author to congratulate him for what he did."[49]

In monitoring the literature, Leonard read widely. Folklorist Bert Wilson commented:

> I published a little piece in a journal with a very limited circulation. It was a piece on farming customs in Idaho, in which I had simply described the farming customs that my family came from. I didn't think anybody would ever see it. A couple of days after that appeared, here came a nice letter from Leonard, thanking me for that and telling me how what I had experienced was very similar to what he had known in Idaho. I think the number of people who received letters like that are probably legion. Leonard supported everybody.[50]

At times he would go a step further and assist a peer in finding a job. Ross Peterson, who attended Utah State University as an undergraduate, recalled the process whereby he returned as a faculty member: "I was teaching down in Texas, and in March of 1971 Leonard and George Ellsworth called me on a Saturday morning and said that Stan Cazier had just been named president of Chico State, and was taking Blythe Ahlstrom with him. That was two openings in the History

Department. 'Do you want to come back?' That was the advertisement, the interview, the search and the decision."[51]

On one notable occasion, Leonard extended himself in a risky and successful initiative to secure employment for a colleague who had been blackballed as a result of earlier employment at a Utah college. Charles ("Chas") Peterson, who served as director of the Utah State Historical Society from 1969 to 1981, saw the emerging field of oral history as essential to the society's mission. He obtained a budget for a new position to run the program, "and the only person I could find that looked to me like he had the vita for it and the ability to do it, was *persona non grata* because he had had a battle with Ferron Losee.[52] [This individual was] Mel Smith. . . . Every junior college, every university that had an opening in the West, Losee had letters out to them, warning them of this troublemaker. Mel had nine kids. Everybody was telling me, 'Don't touch him! Don't touch him!' But one man wasn't: Leonard Arrington." Leonard went to bat for Peterson and Smith, "in a way that talks of courage and guts," leading Peterson to conclude, "I *knew* I could depend on Leonard Arrington."[53]

For young professionals on the front end of careers, Leonard often stepped back to create space that allowed them to step forward. Jill Mulvay Derr, hired from a background in education, recalls, "He wasn't afraid to give young people assignments. I can remember helping him out with some work on an update of the presidents of the Church volume, trying to write an essay on that. I was a kid who knew nothing about Mormon history, and he took a chance on me." Having left a job as schoolteacher to move laterally, Derr was stunned when Leonard told her, shortly after her arrival in the History Division, "You are going to go to the [American] Association for State and Local History. We will send you there, and this is what we expect you to learn. These are the kinds of people we expect you to talk to." While he tutored her on the manner in which she needed to interact with those at the meeting, he had no hesitancy in playing a rookie into the fray. "There was none of that sense of 'I will do all the travel.' "[54]

The young scholars who began to produce under his mentorship often found themselves showcasing their scholarship because of Leonard's behind-the-scenes work. Leo Lyman remembers what was, in retrospect, a daring assignment: "He did make me go speak to the Cannon-Hinckley Study Group, which no rookie scholar should ever have done. That was probably fifteen General Authorities, and most of the cream of Salt Lake City society, but I was too naïve to know how scared I should have been. He did that to others, too, but he was proud of us! He wanted us to show what we had done."[55]

The primary currency for scholars is publications—"publish-or-perish" (and sometimes, in Mormon history circles, "publish *and* perish")—but young scholars are at a disadvantage when competing with veterans for publishing space. A good mentor helps to even the playing field. James Allen noted, "I don't know how many young people he encouraged and worked with. Look at all the people he co-authored things with, including Tom Alexander and others. A lot of those are people he kind of took under his wing, had them do some research, and then he'd work with them, and they'd put their names on an article and they'd have a publication, even before they were out of school, because Leonard took them under his wing."[56]

Sometimes Leonard would simply do a hand-off, setting up a young colleague with a topic and references and then letting that person go the rest of the way. That was how Michael Quinn wrote a foundational article on a turn-of-the-century weekday program in LDS religious education for school-age children. "He would come in and say, 'There is a subject I would like you to write about, and I don't want to be credited.' . . . And in some cases, I knew *nothing* about the topic. The one, in particular, that I remember was the religion class program. I had never heard of it." Nonetheless, Leonard gave Quinn resources, a nudge, and a promise: "I'll make sure that I put in a good word for you with the *Utah Historical Quarterly*."[57] And he was good for his word, even foregoing having his own name on the paper as coauthor.

More often, articles would bear coauthorship. The quality was varied, but the intent was constant: "He gave his name to a lot of students who would write papers, and sometimes you weren't sure how much of the student paper was his," recalled RLDS historian Alma Blair. "But I think his intent was okay. 'Here is a beginning student who needs some support, so I will help him a little bit, and then we will put both names on it, and that will give him the shove that he needs to get out there.' His name was already made; he didn't need to make a name for himself."[58]

Not everyone agreed with the division of labor, with some feeling that Leonard's name appeared at times when his contribution wasn't sufficient to merit coauthorship. Ronald Esplin recalled, "Very often, especially on the books, if you read his acknowledgements on who did what, you have to say, 'So Leonard, what did you do?' Very little."[59] Others put the matter in a different light: "There was the classic argument that said that he was publishing things, but his staff was actually doing the writing. Of course, that wasn't unusual for people who were the head of that kind of thing," commented Lester Bush, a physician who also understood the parallel with the "senior researcher" on scientific papers. "My understanding was that he thought it was in the best interest of the thing getting out and having readership, to be associated himself directly with the stuff, rather than a nobody being published."[60]

There was another reason for his name being almost omnipresent, observed Jan Shipps, one of the best known non-LDS scholars of Mormonism. "I know that the Brethren—Leonard told me this in conversation—that the Brethren wanted him to put his name on everything that came out of the Historical Department."[61] Indeed, in so strict a hierarchy, Leonard was constantly held responsible for the production of his employees, as he was for even more distant associations such as his link to *Dialogue*. As director of the History Division and as incumbent of the Redd Chair at BYU, Leonard was fully aware of his changed role. Administrative responsibilities simply did not allow the kind of discretionary time for researching and writing that he had enjoyed at USU, and so he morphed from historian into a new role—that of "historian-as-entrepreneur,"[62] commented David Whittaker, but with varying reactions from colleagues.

> He saw himself as a team leader, getting resources and funding, and then channeling things through. Often his name had to appear on it, because he was the one who was given the money. I think he might have felt a little bad about some of that. I know there were tensions early on. I think Gene Sessions left the Historical Department over that. He was tired of having all of his work appear under somebody else's name. All of us did that as we earned our historical wings, so to speak, and were mentored. I went into it with my eyes open. Leonard was very plain and open to me that if I did writing for him, it would not appear under my name. I would get thanks for it. I guess that was okay, but I think there were some who didn't feel good about that.[63]

But on one point, all could agree with Everett Cooley's assessment: "He didn't need those publications. He was already recognized."[64]

Leonard did not hold himself aloof by virtue of his position as church historian. Often he offered close-up, hands-on assistance to students—not just in their research, but also in the basic skill of writing. George Daines, who worked for Leonard prior to pursuing a career in law, recalled being "just an uneducated and relatively unskillful college sophomore" when Leonard tutored him in writing. Leonard would have him write a first draft, edit it, return it to George, have him rewrite it, edit it again, put his name on it, and out it went. "But the point was that he took twice as long to do it, because he wanted me to have that process with him. He talked with me, told me things I should go read to learn how to write better. He said, 'You need to go read this fiction.' . . . Leonard was extremely busy, but he was spending time with me to teach me how to write."[65]

Leonard was particularly supportive of scholars who wished to reach for graduate degrees. Charles Peterson had earned a master's degree but was taking a four-year hiatus in his graduate studies, not sure if he wanted to pursue a doctorate degree, when he had a chance encounter with Leonard at a meeting of the Western History Association in Salt Lake City in 1962. "The guy who stood behind me in the line for registering was Leonard Arrington. . . . We were in that line for at least thirty minutes, and it may have been an hour. He opened up and talked to me about every question I wanted to put to him. . . . But by the time we got through, I loved Leonard Arrington. He was the only person there I really knew. So that was maybe the first step toward what the rest of my life has been."[66]

The rest of Peterson's life turned out to be a distinguished career in Western American history: director of the Utah State Historical Society from 1969 to 1981, professor of history at Utah State University from 1971 until his retirement in 1989, and author of many books and articles on Mormon history, most notably *Take Up Your Mission: Mormon Colonizing along the Little Colorado River, 1879–1900* (Tucson: University of Arizona Press, 1973), which won the Mormon History Association's Best Book Award in 1974.

Leonard was even more proactive when his own employees decided to go for advanced degrees. When Michael Quinn, one of the earliest hires in the History Division, decided to apply for a doctorate program at Yale University, Leonard played a crucial role: "Leonard is the one who got me into Yale when Yale turned me down as a Ph.D. candidate. Leonard wrote a letter of inquiry and got a phone call from the dean of the graduate school at Yale on a Saturday. They spoke for two hours and the final result was that Yale offered me a half-tuition fellowship."[67]

Leonard's largess was not provincial—that is, he was as willing to boost the career of someone outside the field of history as to help fledgling historians. When George Daines applied for law school, also to Yale, Leonard again took a proactive role. Daines recalls unalloyed enthusiasm when he told Leonard his plans. Leonard's response was: " 'Fine. Great! How can I help you?' I'm sure he wrote me a wonderful letter of recommendation. I don't even know but what he had a friend or two at Yale in Western History. He may have had him go over and talk to the law school. He may have called him on the phone. I don't know just what he did. But getting into the Yale Law School from Utah State was a real stretch, and Leonard helped me do that,"[68] and, as usual, with no strings attached.

But Leonard's most unusual—and in a way most impressive—mentorship occurred when he took an active role in assisting interested amateurs with no relevant degree—"history buffs," as he called them—in researching and writing history. The only prerequisite was genuine interest, which in one case began in a most improbable fashion and went on to succeed beyond his wildest expectations. Linda

King Newell was coauthor of a prize-winning biography of Emma Hale Smith—a real "hands-off" topic for LDS historians because she had refused to follow Brigham Young west. Indeed, Young blamed her for the creation of the Reorganized Church of Jesus Christ of Latter Day Saints under the presidency of her oldest son, Joseph III. Newell and Valeen Tippetts Avery, her eventual coauthor, were "a couple of housewives out of the kitchen. Neither of us had written anything more than a term paper."

But during Christmas holidays in 1975, one of Val Avery's friends "knew somebody in the Church Archives and took me in and introduced me to her friend." It was a life-changing meeting where she met Leonard, Davis Bitton, Dean Jessee, and Maureen Ursenbach Beecher. "Leonard was just cordial and enthusiastic. I said—and I will be forever grateful that none of them laughed when I said it—that I wanted to do a biography of Emma Smith. That was the *first* day. That was my first step, going to the Church Archives. . . . There was nothing written about Emma. I wanted to know about her, and there was no way to do it except to find out myself."[69]

Leonard encouraged the two women and gave them guidance as they began to peruse the collections at the LDS Archives. When he saw that they were both dedicated and gifted, he wrote a glowing letter of recommendation to the director of research grants of the National Endowment for the Humanities, to whom they had submitted a grant application. Calling their research project one "of unusual promise," he noted that in discussing the proposed biography with colleagues from across the country there was "a keen interest in the subject and a particular readiness for this work." He then gave them a resounding, personal endorsement: "Linda Newell and Valeen Avery are both unusually versatile women with broad backgrounds. I have observed them for about two years as they have sought and sifted evidence in various locations and moved among professional historians. They have earned my confidence and enjoy the respect of those whose research is tangential to their own. In my opinion, they have the commitment and ability to see their project through to a work of merit."[70]

Leonard's trust in the two women was well placed. Nine years after Newell self-consciously walked into the Historical Department for the first time, after thousands of hours of research, writing, rewriting, delivering papers, and more research in both the LDS, RLDS, and other archives, she and Avery published an award-winning biography of Emma Smith through a national publishing house, Doubleday & Company.[71] Newell completed the story: "I told Leonard later, 'I'll always be grateful that none of you laughed that day.' He said, 'Well, we just said, "Let's see what they can do."' And then he, I think, was the one who introduced us to Jan Shipps, at the Mormon History Association meeting that spring in St. George. He said, 'You don't have to have a professional degree to write history.' "[72]

How Leonard mentored was as important—and impressive—as *who* he mentored. Even in his pre–church historian days, he was laying the groundwork for his role as networker-in-chief. Richard Bushman, author of the most definitive biography of Joseph Smith, senior statesman of Mormonism, and quite possibly Leonard's successor as networker, remembers his first encounter, which occurred in 1960 at BYU where he took his first job after graduate school. "I realized by what happened that Leonard Arrington, even at that time, had become the dean of Mormon history, as exemplified by the fact that soon after I arrived in Provo, I received a letter from him in Logan, welcoming me to Utah and sort of inviting me to join the fraternity of Latter-day Saint historians. So from that early stage he already had taken responsibility for the whole historical enterprise."[73] Bushman left BYU and took a hiatus from Mormon history while he developed a superb reputation in colonial history, but maintained contact in the Mormon history field and then returned to it full-time.

Leonard "was the one who built the tent," commented Richard Bennett, who like many of his protégés was a future president of the Mormon History Association,[74] and it was an impressive tent. "He would reach out all over the place to these people. He was just incredible that way. His Christmas card list got up to about 5,000. It was huge! He taught me something about networking. He just collected friends, everywhere he went."[75] Leonard's memory for detail was prodigious, for he remembered not only names and faces, but specifics about the research they were doing. Stan Cazier, himself no mean networker as president of two universities, stood in awe of Leonard's network:

> "We'd go to conferences together . . . and I thought Leonard might know one or two people. He knew dozens, literally dozens of people! He knew exactly what they had done, and what they were working on. I just stood with my mouth open, that's all. I thought, "Yes, sure, he's got friends. But how does he keep abreast of what they are doing?" He knew exactly what they had done before, and where they were, what projects they had under way, and he wanted to know how close they were to completion. We were in the lobby for an hour, while people were coming in to register. I don't want to exaggerate this thing, but it's hard to exaggerate. Almost everyone who walked through that door—most of them were from the West—knew him. New Mexico, Arizona, Colorado—he knew them. I thought, "Good heavens, Leonard!" That was just remarkable. In my judgment, nobody else in that room could have done that. I didn't see anybody

else doing it, and I was just in awe at his breadth and sensitivity and awareness. It was like he just drank it all in. I was aware of what one or two were doing, but not the whole crowd![76]

Part of Leonard's "secret," if one could call it such, was to gather people together in his hotel room in the evening for his famed "rump sessions." Robert Flanders described one such session that occurred at a meeting in Montana, just as his landmark and controversial book, *Nauvoo: Kingdom on the Mississippi*, was going to press. "That was my first late-night meeting with Leonard and his protégés. I was invited. Leonard was the only one, of course, who knew about *Kingdom on the Mississippi*, because he had read it in manuscript. But that's not what the meeting was about. The meeting was about *meeting*. Here were all these young guys. I don't remember who all they were. The important thing was that I saw Leonard as the leader of this little group."[77]

The gatherings always took the same format, as described by RLDS historian Paul Edwards. "After the sessions he would bring a bunch of people into his hotel room and they would sit around and talk. He'd point to you and say, 'What are you doing now?' Before long, everybody was offering everybody suggestions."[78] If you were in the room, you were an insider—even if you didn't self-identify as such. For sociologist Armand Mauss, another future MHA president, the experience was both exhilarating and intimidating:

> Leonard's way was to have us each get up and say something about ourselves. I was one of the last to get up. I'd heard all these other people get up and talk about their PhD's and their dissertation topics and what they were doing now and where they were working, and I was thinking, 'Oh, gee, will I ever get there?' And so when it came my turn to stand up, I was sort of feeling like I didn't have much to say about myself. But I said what I could, and with some embarrassment acknowledged that I was working at a community college and not at one of the universities. I remember when the introductions like that were over, Leonard spoke up and said something about my comment. I had made a comment about myself that he had picked up on at the end and turned it around. He made it seem like a thing to be proud of instead of feeling a little sheepish about it. And that was his way. He sensed somehow that I was feeling a little out of my element in that group, and he just went out of his way to make me feel that I belonged there.[79]

What Leonard did in the rump sessions was far removed from what had happened in the past, when the few researchers in Mormon history worked largely in isolation. Leo Lyman remembers one such gathering that struck him almost as a literal passing of the baton, and the first time he had been invited to one. It included perhaps a dozen people, including LDS and RLDS scholars. "What I really remember is Richard Poll, who had been a vice president of Western Illinois University, and Gene Campbell. Leonard had each of us speak about what we were doing research on. These two old Mormon scholars had tears in their eyes, that these young, enthusiastic, well-trained people were into those subjects that they had wanted to do all their lives, but couldn't."[80]

In addition to his rump sessions, Leonard broke new ground in Mormon studies through his generosity in sharing information. "Your files are your stock-in-trade," said one of his colleagues in the History Division. "One of the most beautiful things about Leonard was that he believed everything in his file belonged to everybody who could use it."[81] Another described the details:

> In the Church Office Building, access was power and information was power, which was why rumors just swirled constantly, because you could never find out anything for sure. Leonard would share everything. You could walk in off the street and he would pull out a file and say, "Oh, you're interested in this," pull a file out of his filing cabinet and hand it to you. He empowered people. People didn't use that language at the time, but that's what he did, almost instinctively. He called himself an entrepreneur. He created Mormon historians by sharing his information with them, by pushing them into projects that they didn't know they were interested in, by facilitating the research. He had his secretaries type up journals that somebody thought someday they might want to look at, and made them available to people. He volunteered to coauthor things with young scholars so that they would get themselves published. I don't know if he sat down and ever worked out a master plan for how to do it. I think it was instinctive to him because he was that kind of person. How could you not want to be around that, and how could you not want to be that kind of person?[82]

Several years after Leonard left the Historical Department, colleague Ross Peterson asked him about the file sharing. Leonard replied, "This business of sharing materials is a very important thing in Mormon history because the materials aren't always available to everybody. It's more important in Mormon history perhaps than in some other fields where you have open access without any problems. Maybe people that use the National Archives don't feel any obligation to share material with other people, but people that use LDS material, you have to share because it may not pass again that way."[83]

Leonard's comment was both reflective and predictive. It was reflective in that it drew upon his own experience, beginning decades prior to his calling as church historian, with the difficulty of gaining access to primary source documents in the LDS Archives. It was predictive in using the phrase "materials aren't always available to everybody." Even before his tenure as church historian ended, availability of documents began to be restricted for History Division employees as well as public researchers. While the quoted interview was recorded nearly a decade after Leonard's term as church historian ended, and thus has the advantage of hindsight, it is likely that he sensed even in the early years of his tenure that restricted access might recur, and thus felt a professional obligation to make as much information available to a wide circle of scholars as quickly as possible.

The net result of Leonard's efforts was the blossoming of an entire discipline. "I didn't recognize it at the time," commented Ronald Barney, who made his career in the LDS Historical Department Archives, "but how I got interested in this was because of this aura that he had created. I think we were all riding along on it, unbeknownst to us."[84]

17

BLESSED DAMOZELS

To say that women held a special place in Leonard's life would be trite were it not for two factors: his view of Mormon women, both past and present, was dramatically different than that of most of his male coreligionists; and he never diminished the role of two women—one being his mother—who took an action different from what most Mormon women of the time would have done, and thus saved his life when he was an infant.

The 1918–1919 "Spanish Influenza" struck down Noah and Edna Arrington, along with several of their children. Leonard was the sickest. As noted in chapter 2, Edna and Hannah Bowen, an LDS midwife, anointed and blessed Leonard. Leonard's sister Marie commented on the blessing: "My mother poured oil on his head and gave him a blessing, consecrated oil. He claimed that that kept him alive. Now that was a story between Mother and him, but Leonard had told me about it many times. Now they frown on those kinds of things; but at that time they didn't. . . . He felt very strongly about that: that Mother's faith was equal to the Priesthood."[1]

Leonard's attitudes toward women, which were enlightened beyond those of his male peers, were a contrast to the female stereotypes with which he was raised. His sister described the assigned roles on the family farm: "I was a girl, and girls were not allowed to farm at our house. Mother was not raised on a farm. My father was a real stickler on that. Women belonged in the house and anything that was of the house was women's work, and everything out there was men's work."[2]

As a teenage member of the Future Farmers of America, Leonard wrote an essay that supported the same traditional roles. Beginning by pointing out that girls had their own national organization, the Future Homemakers of America, he chided girls for even wanting to look at farming, for "if they would devote their time & talent to strengthening & supporting their own organization, they would have no time to desire to enter our organization." Then, he parroted the traditional argument against women moving into any occupation traditionally held by men, ending with a borrowed vocabulary normally unseen in a teenage boy in the 1930s: "When one thinks of a farmer he thinks of a man, laboring hard under a burning sun, following the plow, harrowing, cultivating, hoeing, threshing, etc.—earning his living by the sweat of his brow. Girls should not & fundamentally are not made to do such work. They always have & shall always be the mistress of the household, ruler of the cradle & mother of civilization."[3] Not a likely starting point for his later, progressive attitude.

Leonard left no record describing the transformation of his views of the roles of women—whether an event, or a process over time—but it was an incomplete transformation. Whereas in his capacity as church historian he encouraged women to write the story of Mormon women's history, as well as to take on nontraditional professional roles even as mothers, he was content to have Grace remain a stay-at-home mother—as was Grace. Having dropped out of high school and spent years as a beautician in order to help support her single mother, she looked forward to Leonard's return from the war as her opportunity to become a full-time mother. "She was thrilled to be home," her daughter recalled.[4]

WRITING THE HISTORY OF MORMON WOMEN

Leonard's dissertation research, which focused on economic life at the grass-roots level, gave him an appreciation for the underreported role that Mormon women had played in colonizing the Great Basin. In 1955, three years before *Great Basin Kingdom* appeared in print, he published an article in the *Western Humanities Review*. Titled "The Economic Role of Pioneer Mormon Women,"[5] it began with a statement that was audacious for its day—a day when the Mormon story was almost universally written in the genre of Great Events and Great *Men*: "Mormon women played a major role in building the Latter-day Saint commonwealth in the Great Basin." Focusing in part on the group contributions of women through the Relief Society after it was reinstated in 1867,[6] the article concluded: "The Relief Society was indispensable in implementing Mormon economic policy during the last third of the nineteenth century. Its contributions to Mormon economic growth and territorial development have not been negligible."

The article had staying power, eventually becoming a touchstone for Mormon women interested in their own history. Carol Cornwall Madsen, a productive historian in the History Division who got her degrees after raising six children, recalls: "Those of us engaged in reconstructing Mormon women's lives look to him and his path-breaking article, 'The Economic Role of [Pioneer] Mormon Women,' as the door that opened to us Mormon women's history. He not only showed that LDS women *have* a history but gave us a model of how to write their history. His continued interest and contributions have helped to solidify this aspect of the Mormon past as a legitimate field of historical inquiry."[7]

Leonard's interest in the history of Mormon women returned to the forefront in the mid-1960s when he accepted Alfred Knopf's invitation to write a narrative history of Mormonism. To a colleague he wrote, "I have been working for the last two or three years on history of the Mormon people. A part of this will, of course, deal with the lives of various individuals in the L.D.S. movement. Among other things, I hope to give more attention than previous writers to the role of women in Mormon History."[8] Three months after writing the letter, he delivered the presidential address at the annual meeting of the Western History Association: "Blessed Damozels: Women in Mormon History." A colleague who attended the meeting recalled the impression it left with him even after the passage of forty years: "Just stunning! What he said was, 'This mythology about beat-up women in Mormonism, who had to endure the Hell of polygamy, is a bunch of hogwash.' Of course, he said it very beautifully and elegantly, but he said, 'The women of Mormonism are strong, powerful women.' He explained how the economics of polygamy made for strong women. Demanded it. It was essential." One particularly vivid example he used was Martha Hughes Cannon. Her husband Angus was running for political office on the Republican ticket, and no Democrat would oppose him. Martha said, "That is wrong. If nobody else will run against him, I'll run against him." She ran against him on the Democratic ticket, and she won. "There were a lot of stories about that. But in generalities, that was his presidential address. . . . It was path breaking!"[9]

An adapted version of the speech, published in the famous "Pink Issue" of *Dialogue*,[10] "encouraged a whole generation of LDS women to write about their foremothers and themselves."[11]

In the Knopf book, *The Mormon Experience*, which was published a decade later than originally contemplated, Leonard devoted a chapter to the history of Mormon women.[12] Writing in his diary after completing the manuscript but before its publication, he highlighted two of its contributions that dealt with women. One was an extended description of the Mormon concept of the eternal family "and its implications for the roles of men and women. Discussions of sex role stereotyping of LDS women, which goes on in much non-Mormon literature, will hereafter be more balanced." The other was "the best chapter-length study of the role of women in Mormon history. Low-key in tone, this chapter makes it clear that Mormon women have had many opportunities for expression and growth and leadership."[13]

Written in the midst of the battle over the Equal Rights Amendment, which ultimately fell short of the required number of states for ratification, the book broke new ground in describing candidly the debate within the Mormon Church over the place of women, including Mormon women, in society. General church officers who were in their eighth and ninth decades of life clung nostalgically to the idea, as expressed by Eldon Tanner, that "a woman will find greater satisfaction and joy and make a greater contribution by being a wise and worthy mother raising good children than she could make in any other vocation," even though one-third of Mormon mothers at the time (1977) found it necessary to work outside the home. "Church leaders have made no concessions to the rising numbers of income-earning women."

Remarkably, Leonard placed a female counterbalancing voice in juxtaposition to Tanner's when he quoted Camilla Kimball, wife of church president Spencer Kimball, as urging Mormon women to pursue educations and learn marketable skills. "I would hope that every girl and woman here has the desire and ambition to qualify in two vocations—that of homemaking, and that of preparing to earn a living outside the home, if and when the occasion requires." While Camilla's words carried the sentiment of an older generation of women whose views differed markedly from their younger sisters, they nonetheless were a contrast to those of Tanner.

Having displayed impressive audacity in placing Tanner's words in tension with Camilla Kimball's, Leonard and coauthor Davis Bitton concluded the section on an equally audacious note: "The rhetoric emphasizing the importance of the home should not hide the fact that Mormon women, like women everywhere, are expanding their role far beyond what it was a generation ago."[14]

While the book was progressive in discussing Mormon women, its authors pulled some punches—not surprising when considered within the context of the increasing heat that the History Division was receiving from ecclesiastical leaders. Jill Derr, who helped write the chapter, recalled a particularly painful example: "We had included in that chapter a little snippet from Martha Spence Heywood's journal, where she talks about Brigham Young saying that 'a woman, be she ever so smart, will never know more than a man who holds the priesthood.' Maureen [Beecher] and I had included that in the chapter to reflect the tensions that some of the rhetoric caused for very intelligent women as they tried to operate within a system where they needed to obey priesthood leaders, but they sometimes disagreed."

Benign and even humorous though the quote was, it raised the ire of Homer Durham, who by then had been placed over the History Division. He wrote back, "Of course, she was mistaken. . . . Brigham Young would never have intended to say such a thing," despite having evidence to sustain his point, and he pressed successfully for Leonard to remove it. Derr recalled "how hard that was for me, because it didn't ring just right. So a straw in the wind, perhaps."[15]

FACILITATING THE HISTORIOGRAPHY
OF MORMON WOMEN

In a *Dialogue* article published in 1968, four years before Leonard became church historian, he lamented built-in biases among historiographers that had limited Mormons' understanding of their own history, one of them being "the male bias," which he described as "the notion that men hold all the important policy-making positions, therefore they are the ones who determine the course of events. The priesthood holds the key leadership offices, we reason, so the priesthood is responsible for everything that happens. We are inclined toward a male interpretation of Mormon history." As evidence of the bias, he cited *The Gospel in Action*, a 1949 lesson manual for the adult Sunday School class. "Forty-five biographies were given in the manual; and while half of the people attending Gospel Doctrine classes were presumably women, forty-two of the biographies were of men, and only three were of women."

The Sunday School manual was a twentieth-century example of the bias, and Leonard added two from the nineteenth century: Edward Tullidge's *Life of Brigham Young*, which contained biographical sketches of thirty people, all of whom were men; and Orson F. Whitney's *History of Utah*, containing 351 biographies, only twenty-nine of which were of women. But anyone who goes to the archival record, he concluded, "must gain a new appreciation of the important and indispensable role of women in the history of the LDS church—not to mention new insights into church history resulting from viewing it through the eyes of women."[16]

What Leonard did not underscore, but what is immediately apparent to the reader, is that all of the authors whose works he cited were men—men who were tone-deaf to women's contributions to history. Although some of those authors wrote in the nineteenth century, the problem persisted in contemporary histories. Milton Backman, author of one of the volumes of the proposed sesquicentennial series, belonged to the generation for which such tone-deafness was taken for granted. Leonard chided him gently: "You give the facts on the men in Zion's Camp, but there were women, ten or eleven of them. How about saying something about them as you conclude that paragraph on the top of 328? You must acknowledge that there were women and indicate whether they were wives of participants or whether some were single, and what ages they were. And if you know, what did they do?—the laundry? cooking?"[17]

The telling of women's history by men sometimes resulted in absurd outcomes. Leonard noted in a 1974 diary entry the receipt of a manuscript by Kenneth and Audrey Godfrey entitled *Mormon History: A Woman's Perspective*. "We were amused by the title page which lists that title by Ken Godfrey [as first author] . . . Davis Bitton said that reminded him of the phrase on the dust jacket or introduction of Rodney Turner's book *Woman and the Priesthood* which says, 'This is a history of woman from the time of Adam to the present.' Jill [Derr] said it reminded her of a letter from Jedediah M. Grant which said with respect to a certain piece of anti-Mormon legislation . . . 'The women of Utah are opposed to this bill down to the last man.' "[18]

Because of the errors of omission by male writers, the role of Mormon women throughout the church's history was misunderstood by Mormons and non-Mormons alike—but particularly the latter. To a colleague in 1973, Leonard wrote, "Most professional historians tend to regard Mormon women as ignorant, depraved, submissive, nameless creatures, and the purpose of my talk will be to demonstrate that that image is completely false."[19] If anything, he argued, Mormon women had outperformed Mormon men: "Two sisters were among those who saw the Gold Plates from which our founding Prophet Joseph Smith translated the Book of Mormon. The sisters assisted materially in the construction of the Kirtland and Nauvoo Temples. The sisters demonstrated the same resourcefulness and intrepidity in crossing the Plains to Utah as did the brethren. As one of the sisters wrote, 'We had to endure all that the brethren endured, and we had to endure the brethren as well.' "[20]

One way to address the problem was to alter the way in which his group viewed women's history. Less than five months after being sustained in general conference as church historian, Leonard wrote of the changes he had already effected: "We have switched from writing elitist history to writing the history of ordinary members of the Church and their concerns—their housing, their food, their clothing, their recreation, their associations, etc. In all of this, the role of women is clear, definite, and undeniable. We are more interested in women than before and, therefore, are studying women's letters, women's diaries, and the lives of women."[21]

Another way to address the problem was to engage women to become the writers of women's history. He began this initiative within the History Division, where one of his first hires was Maureen Ursenbach. With a PhD in comparative literature from the University of Utah, Maureen had served as managing editor of the *Western Humanities Review* and taught at the University of Utah prior to joining Leonard's staff. In addition to being the division's editor, she moved into writing women's history at the urging of Leonard, despite having been trained in comparative literature. And his support was more than verbal. "Any time there was any opportunity to speak on the subject of Mormon women, Leonard would find the money to do it. I was invited to go to Germany, because there was a

Mormon history study group at the University of Munich, but they couldn't pay my way. Leonard just paid for it."[22]

By 1979 Ursenbach's interest in Mormon women had been piqued to the point of motivating her to propose to Leonard a comprehensive history of the Relief Society, arguing that "the history of the women of The Church of Jesus Christ of Latter-day Saints is inextricably connected with the history of the Relief Society."[23] Contemporary LDS women were looking for role models, and while the women of early Mormonism provided those models, "so little is available in print, and so much of what is available is misleading." Therefore, she proposed "to produce a thorough, well researched, well written history of the Relief Society from its inception to the present day. . . . Included should be consideration of such vital issues as women's contributions to the family, to education and to the economy; women's roles in the body politic, and opportunities for advancement in the Church and in the society; and the Church's role in the promotion of women's rights—all considered in the context of both LDS history and the national developments."

She proposed that two other women be assigned to work with her on the history—Jill Mulvay and Carol Cornwall Madsen—both of whom Leonard had hired to work in the History Division. Ursenbach had unwittingly recruited Mulvay from a budding career as a Boston schoolteacher. Mulvay recalled that a group of local LDS women had invited Ursenbach to address their group, which they expanded for the occasion to include single women. "So I went, and heard Maureen talk about the Historical Department and her work on Eliza R. Snow. I was just absolutely fascinated. My response was how women still respond: 'How did you find out about this woman? How do you do this kind of work?' I had already made up my mind to leave Boston, although I was planning to come to Salt Lake and teach school."[24]

Mulvay came to work in the History Division in 1974 on a temporary fellowship that turned into a career. "I think I stayed for six months on that fellowship. Then, the question was: Could I continue on? I remember going to lunch in the church cafeteria with Leonard and Davis [Bitton], and them talking to me about working with the Moyle Oral History Program. They had just received some funds, so I signed up to do that."

The timing was fortuitous for Mulvay, because it came at a moment of transition—1974—when Belle Spafford and LaVern Parmley were released as general presidents of the Relief Society and Primary. The two women were institutions themselves, having served for twenty-nine and twenty-three years, respectively. The oral histories that Mulvay recorded of them "will probably be among my greatest contributions to Mormon history."[25]

While Maureen and Jill both joined Leonard's group before marrying— Maureen to Dale Beecher, Jill to Brook Derr—Carol Cornwall Madsen raised a family prior to enrolling in graduate studies. Ursenbach played a role in her join- ing Leonard's team, as she had done with Mulvay, inviting her to speak on the subject of Emmeline Wells to the History Division's weekly luncheon.

"After I was through, Leonard said, 'Could you come up to my office?' . . . So here I am invited to see Leonard, and he offers me a job. I had not thought about what I was going to do when I finished school. I was not training, at that point in my life, for a job, necessarily; I was in school because I loved school and this was a goal of mine." The job was available because Mulvay, who had been working full-time, was about to get married and wished to transition to a half-time appointment. Leonard proposed that Madsen fill the other half of the appoint- ment. "That was not in the plan at the time, and I really did have to think about it. . . . I got back to him and said, 'Yes, I'd like to do this.' "[26]

Independent of the three women in the History Division, but coincident in time, was a nascent gathering of Mormon women in Massachusetts whose eventual impact on the entire LDS Church was even higher profile. While many of the women had already known each other socially, a group coalesced around the subject of Mormon women's history in response to a catalytic event: the "dis- covery" in Harvard University's Widener Library by one of the women of a com- plete run of the *Woman's Exponent*, an independent periodical published in Salt Lake City by Emmeline B. Wells, plural wife of Daniel H. Wells and future Relief Society general president. The newspaper began in 1872 and was supplanted in 1914 by the official church *Relief Society Magazine*. Ursenbach recalled interacting with the group: "They were having a wonderful time discovering their Mormon female roots, and invited me to come to Boston to present a paper on the first Exponent Day. It was held at Grethe Peterson's place in Boston. Leonard ap- proved of that so heartily that when they thought that they weren't going to be able to come up with enough money, he said, 'I'll pay [for] your ticket.' "[27]

Leonard's support of what the women in Boston were doing went beyond pay- ing for a plane ticket. He also paid for the launch of a new periodical that was named and patterned after the *Woman's Exponent*. Claudia L. Bushman, who pro- vided crucial leadership and was the first editor of *Exponent II*, recalled those glory days:

> We, a bunch of housewives doing research in libraries and so on, felt
> very poor. We didn't have money that we could use for one purpose
> or another. At one point he offered us money. I think he sent us $275
> to be used for our projects. And of course, by then we had done

things for free and on the cheap so long, we couldn't think what was worthy to spend that money on. So we banked it and waited for some significant thing. Well, when the time came that we decided to start *Exponent II*, we used that money. We published the first edition of *Exponent II*.[28] We didn't make much of that at the time, because we thought it might reflect badly on him, seeing as we were involved in such "questionable" activities [as feminism]. But I always thought it was nice that the Church Historical Department paid for that first issue.[29]

In addition to launching *Exponent II*, the Boston women's group began work on an anthology of essays on Mormon women in early Utah. Once again, Leonard supported the initiative enthusiastically. "He was writing back and forth to us, encouraging us, having people copy documents for us when we were doing the women's issue of *Dialogue* and, later on, *Mormon Sisters: Women in Early Utah*.[30] He was just incredibly helpful, so that when we finally did publish *Mormon Sisters* we dedicated it to him: 'For Leonard Arrington. He takes us seriously.' Which was very true."[31]

Upon learning that Bushman had embarked on a graduate degree, Leonard continued his serious support. "I was thinking that I would do female studies, which was something none of us had ever heard about at that point. It didn't exist, but I thought I would study the lives of women of the past, using myself as a marker, a comparison." Her husband, Richard, happened to mention this in conversation with Leonard at a history meeting. "A couple of days later I [got] from Leonard, whom I had never met, a long letter, a very long letter, very personal, very warm, all kinds of suggestions of possible things that I could do, all kinds of sources that I might look at, all kinds of people I should get in touch with, sending me documents."

Thus began a lifelong friendship between Leonard and a woman he considered a professional peer. "He never condescended to me, never mistreated me the way most people did. No one took returning housewives going to graduate school seriously in those days. But Leonard did from the beginning."[32]

Leonard's overall effect on Mormon women's history was summarized by one of the members of the Boston group: "[He] really did open the door that has never closed."[33]

CHURCH POLICIES AND ATTITUDES TOWARD WOMEN

Although the Relief Society is described as "the oldest and largest women's organization in the world,"[34] its sponsoring church has an uneven history of dealing with its own women. When Leonard became church historian in 1972, the role of the Relief Society and of women within the church was in a state of flux that continued throughout his tenure—and often in a direction of disfranchisement and restriction.

The Relief Society dates from 1842 and, with some exaggeration, asserts continued existence from that point, making it the oldest of the church's "auxiliary organizations." During most of its history, it operated semiautonomously. While the president of the organization was selected by the church president, she, in turn, chose her own counselors and board. Those women, for their part, selected lesson topics, commissioned manuals for the church-wide curriculum, visited local societies, and published the *Relief Society Magazine* from 1914 through 1970. Local Relief Societies held fund-raising activities including annual congregation-based bazaars and controlled money in their own bank accounts. Marion Isabelle Sims Smith Spafford—"Belle"—was an institution when Leonard became church historian, having served as Relief Society general president since 1945.

With the death of church president David O. McKay in 1970, the fortunes of the Relief Society began to change. Within months of McKay's death in January of that year, male church leaders discontinued the *Relief Society Magazine*, cancelled independent Relief Society fund-raising events including bazaars, and directed that Relief Society bank accounts be closed and the monies turned over to male-controlled general and local accounts.

It is true that the Correlation Movement affected all of the auxiliaries. The Sunday School lost its magazine, *The Instructor*, and its "dime Sundays." The Primary lost its *Children's Friend*. The Young Woman's Mutual Improvement Association had published the *Young Woman's Journal* since the nineteenth century, and it had already been enfolded into the Young Men's Mutual Improvement Association's periodical, the *Improvement Era*. The *Millennial Star*, published in England since the 1840s and hence the church's oldest continuous publication, was also shut down, as were the international mission magazines. All were replaced by the age-based *Friend* (for children), *New Era* (for teens), and *Ensign* (for adults).

Despite these across-the-board changes, the women were arguably far more devastated by what the brethren did to the Relief Society than were the constituencies of the other organizations. The year 1974 was the end of an era, for Belle Spafford was released from her record-setting tenure of twenty-nine years. Her successors served an average of less than six years each and, during Gordon Hinckley's administration, the presidencies of the women's three auxiliaries were standardized to five years, unlike the "until death" service of the Quorum of the Twelve Apostles.

In his first press conference after becoming the twelfth church president in December 1973, Spencer W. Kimball responded to a reporter's question in a manner that sent a clear message to those women who had not already heard it through the church's earlier initiatives. The question: "Will there be a change in attitude toward women?" The answer: "Not too abruptly. We believe that the ideal place for women is in the home."[35]

Maureen Ursenbach reacted to the message—which was vocalized consistently throughout the 1970s—in a manner similar to that of many other women, particularly those who were in the workforce. Leonard was so moved by the words in her diary that, with her permission, he included them in his own:

> President Kimball had some things to say about women, among them the point that our women are free to fulfill themselves—as wives and mothers. That was no surprise to me, though. I do wonder how long it will be before someone points out that no one has reminded men that they, too, should (could?) find fulfillment as fathers and husbands. Maybe some do. Though I doubt that many careers would get off the ground if men were in it only as the fund-raising adjunct to the raising of a family! Anyway—I have heard President Kimball on women, and was not surprised.[36]

The second message coming from church headquarters was a natural corollary to the first: the men are in charge. Since the death of McKay, Harold B. Lee had used the Correlation movement to bring church departments under the direct supervision of the Quorum of the Twelve—the Relief Society being no exception. "The Priesthood" thus controlled everything—even the telling of church history. Two incidents illustrate the lengths to which the control over history extended. The first involved the BYU Movie Studio. In May 1976, Leonard recorded details confided to him during a visit from Carol Lynn Pearson, a best-selling, self-published poet, whose minimalist, narrative poems, illustrated by brilliant Rhodesian sculptor and painter Trevor Southey, swept the Mormon literati by storm. She was accompanied by her husband, Gerald, and Kathryn Sirrine, another friend.

She told Leonard that she had been commissioned by the church to write the script for a short movie depicting Joseph Smith's "First Vision." After they had completed the movie they screened it to a group of people among whom were three apostles, one of whom said, "I think it was wrong to give equal attention in the movie to Joseph Sr. and Lucy Mack Smith—to give as much attention as you do to Lucy Mack. After all, Joseph Sr. was the father, the patriarch, the head of the family, and you should concentrate on him. He was the priesthood holder in the family. You shouldn't give so much attention to women since they do not hold the priesthood."[37] It seems to have been irrelevant that, during Joseph Jr.'s childhood and youth, Joseph Sr. was a Universalist who refused to participate in organized religion, held no priesthood at all, and, in fact, pressured Lucy to stop attending meetings to avoid annoying his older brother, the unpleasant Jesse.

The second incident struck closer to home, for it involved a book on the history of the Primary Association, one of the History Division's first institutional histories. In August 1978, when the history of the Primary, written by Carol Cornwall Madsen and Susan Staker Oman,[38] was being reviewed before publication, Earl Olson telephoned Leonard to pass on a concern of Boyd Packer. "He had read the Primary manuscript, thought it was fine, but did have one principal concern, which was that we need to suggest or to say throughout that the Primary operated under the guidance and direction of the priesthood. I told Earl I would take care of it, and I told Carol [Madsen] to put at least one phrase to that effect in every chapter in the book." Leonard confided to his diary that such an action, which brushed against overt historical inaccuracy, "would suggest a certain insecurity. Maybe the priesthood [holders] do feel insecure about innovations being made and policies being determined without explicit recognition of the role of the priesthood in doing so."[39]

Three decades later, Madsen looked back on the incident and fleshed out some of the details—and her reaction to it all. "It went all the way up to our advisor in the Quorum of the Twelve, and it came back to Susan and me that we did not have enough priesthood in that book. We had to show that the women were working under the direction of priesthood. Whether we found that in the minutes or not, we had to remind our readers that the Primary was not an independent entity—although it was very much."

Knowing that they had no choice but to accede to the wishes of Packer, the two authors met with Leonard to work out an accommodation. Leonard told them, "Well, go back through the minutes and see maybe if you can just add phrases like 'with the approval of the Brethren,' or 'with the approval of the advisors.' Give a little more emphasis to the Primary General Conferences and what the General Authorities had to say when they spoke at those conferences, whoever the advisors were, and quote them a little bit more than you have. Just kind of fill in."[40]

While Leonard saw as a hindrance the effect that changing policies and attitudes had on writing women's history, he also saw their increasingly heavy consequences for women throughout the church. He saw the College of Religious Instruction at BYU as a painful example of gender inequity. "How come there is not a single female instructor in the College of Religion at BYU—all the professors are male. Of course, there are lots of women who teach religion at BYU—nearly all the faculty teach religion courses, off and on. But in the College of Religious Instruction, proper, no women faculty."[41]

But even more painful than "a gift not given" was a gift that, once given, was taken away. Leonard recorded that Dennis Lythgoe, a bishop in a Boston suburb, wanted to appoint a woman as president of the ward Sunday School. "He looked through all the manuals of instruction and couldn't see anything that specifically prohibited it. Upon inquiry with his high council representative and stake president, he learned that they also, could see no reason this should not be done, particularly in view of the fact that one of the other wards in the stake had a black as president of the Sunday School who held no priesthood, and another ward had a person who held only the Aaronic Priesthood as president."

With the green light from his stake president, Lythgoe called a woman to the position of Sunday School president. She, in turn, chose as counselors one woman and one man. "The Sunday School functioned very well"—so well, in fact, that another bishop in the same stake wanted to do the same thing. A person in that ward, however, apparently troubled by the unprecedented arrangement of a woman "presiding" over a man, complained to the area supervisor, Rex Pinegar, who referred the matter to the Quorum of the Twelve.

"The Quorum of Twelve then discussed the matter and informed Elder Pinegar to inform the stake president to inform the bishop that this was not a proper procedure and that he would have to release the sister." Lythgoe appealed to his former stake president, L. Tom Perry, who was by then a member of the Quorum of the Twelve. "Elder Perry wrote back a rather curt letter saying that he had not been present when the Quorum of Twelve discussed it but he verified that it had been discussed and that the minutes indicated the decision that Elder Pinegar had conveyed to them. . . . So Bishop Lythgoe will be releasing the sister, and, as he expressed, 'We have taken a step backwards.' "[42]

One incident carried inescapable irony. Alice Louise Reynolds was the first woman at BYU—and the second in the state of Utah—to become a full professor. Voted one of the top ten BYU professors of all time[43] and one of only two women to make that list, she taught an estimated five thousand students in twenty different English courses over a career spanning forty-four years. In 1933, five years before her death, her peers honored her by forming the Alice Louise Reynolds Club, which grew to sixteen chapters, to promote literature and culture among women.

In honor of her longstanding contributions to the BYU library, colleagues funded and furnished the Alice Louise Reynolds Room in the newly constructed library, one of whose functions was to host the meetings of the local chapter of the Alice Louise Reynolds Club—until the 1970s. Maureen Ursenbach Beecher underscored the irony that these women, who had created the room in honor of a role model, were now "banned from having their meetings there," a punishment for taking a liberal view on women's rights as "closet feminists."[44]

Other changes in policies and attitudes towards women had farther-reaching—and often devastating—effects. Leonard was particularly moved by lengthy conversations with Alice Colton Smith, a close friend from Logan who was a member of the Relief Society General Board for two decades. In three conversations over a two-month period in 1978, she outlined for him the generally pessimistic lot of women in the church—a view shared by many women, and some men, at that time.

The first meeting occurred just after Smith returned from regional meetings in Virginia. "Things she has heard the Brethren say and things she has read give her great anxiety. She is very discouraged and doesn't see any reason for hope about the future role of women in the Church. She is surely not a feminist; she is very much a traditionalist." Her travels as a general board member gave her the realization "that we are gradually losing our women. She says this was clear in Virginia, where the attendance of women at Relief Society meeting and at Sacrament meeting is dropping substantially. She has obtained statistics for the whole church which show the same thing happening."

When Leonard pressed her for specifics, she gave several poignant examples:

- Women are not now permitted to pray in Sacrament meeting. Ten years ago women were permitted to close Sacrament meeting while a man was supposed to open it.[45]

- Women used to be permitted to bless other women. This was particularly true of midwives who were permitted—indeed, encouraged—to administer to women who were about to undergo childbirth or who had other illnesses. This had not been true for thirty or forty years.

- Few if any bishops or stake presidents would permit a woman to join or to stand as observer at the blessing of her baby. This was once permitted where the woman requested it.[46]

- The women once had their own magazine and therefore an avenue of communicating with each other.

- The women once had their own money and therefore had a certain autonomy in what they did. They had not had this privilege in the last ten years.

- Once upon a time women were invited to speak in General Conference. No woman has been invited in recent years to speak in the open sessions.

Smith summed up the current predicament as she saw it: "If we are denigrating women and their position we will soon lose the youth, and when we lose the youth our future is dim." She then challenged Leonard to give her "just one example of some action in recent years which has raised the position of women in the Church." He had none.

She continued by noting that neither the Relief Society general presidency nor general board members had direct access to the First Presidency, or even to the Quorum of the Twelve. "The result is that the First Presidency are asked to approve policies for the Relief Society on the assumption that they are approved by the Relief Society presidency when as a matter of fact they have been watered down and are not at all what the Relief Society presidency want."

Wanting to help if possible, Leonard asked if there was anything he or his colleagues could do. "She said that it would be helpful if we continue to stress in our historical writing the broader and more influential role of women in early Church history and the views of the Prophet Joseph Smith. But she is impatient and does not think that influence will be very strong or very immediate." Hoping to inject even a spark of optimism into the conversation, Leonard spoke of the positive effect of *Exponent II*, but was gently rebuffed when "she said that it has so few readers. She said the Relief Society board members were not permitted to subscribe to *Exponent II* and so she and a few others who want to subscribe do so under the names of their husbands."

In a foreshadowing of the situation in the contemporary LDS Church, wherein only a small minority of women desire ordination to the priesthood,[47] "she has never thought that women ought to hold the priesthood, and thinks that that is an extraneous issue. . . . It is just that they be regarded as equals—as not inferior. It is just that women ought to participate in the decision-making process that affects them. They ought to have some say in the decisions of the ward, the stake, and the Church generally."[48]

The second conversation with Smith occurred a month later, this time by telephone, and her tone was even more disheartened. "She called to tell me she did not think the time was ripe to publish a history of the Relief Society. She thought this would be too damaging to the testimonies of LDS women who would read it because, if it tells the truth, it will relate the deterioration of the power and position of women in the Church and will be very depressing to women who care."

Returning to the theme of her recent visit to Virginia, she lamented the manner in which the local women had effectively been cut off from direct communication with the general Relief Society officers, this in spite of the fact that she "assured the women that they might phone up Barbara Smith and invite her to meet with them, but as they were about to do so, they received a letter which informed them that they were not to invite any member of the board or any member of the presidency without clearing it with the stake president." The stake president, in turn, had to clear it with the regional representative, who had to clear it with the area supervisor, who had to clear it with the Quorum of the Twelve. She did not attempt to hide her frustration: "It will be impossible now for any stake to be directly in touch with the central organization of the Relief Society."

In concluding the phone conversation, Smith pointed a finger: "Alice said the deterioration of the Relief Society began under President Lee, under his Correlation program, and that many of his appointees are still functioning and still operating under his philosophy. Dean Larsen, for example, was a Lee protégée, and is now the advisor to the Relief Society. He and those with him are continuing to trim and trim power and authority from the Relief Society."[49]

The third conversation, one day later, lamented the lack of autonomy that Smith had seen within the Relief Society presidency and general board in the years since Barbara Smith had become president in October 1974, particularly with men systematically reconstituting and limiting a general board whose women had, in prior decades, served at the calling and pleasure of the Relief Society general president. "The most important lesson indicated by this experience is that the Relief Society are not very autonomous, even within their own organization. The Brethren are not only directing Relief Society policy but also getting into the actual administration of the organization."[50]

While Leonard could do little more than listen and commiserate, he later vented to his children in his weekly letter to them. "Everything in the scriptures suggests that both men and women are bound to Christ, that they consecrate their lives to Him and His purposes. It is the Lord's plan to exalt each of us—men and women, the married and the unmarried, the educated and the uneducated. Any attempt to degrade any individual must emanate from a source other than the Lord. It is the meaning of the Restoration to exalt all of God's children. And surely that means men *and* women."[51]

The question of how—or if—the status of women in the LDS Church might be improved was a frequent topic of water-cooler conversation during the 1970s. While the problems were obvious, implementation of solutions was generally elusive—although on occasion there was a glimmer of hope. Six months after Alice Smith unloaded her woes on Leonard, she called to tell him that, after three or four years of steady erosion of Relief Society autonomy and responsibility, she now "thinks the pendulum has swung the other way. She had received some confidential information which she cannot reveal to me yet but will later, which suggests that things are on the up in women's affairs. Some of this will be made clear in the weeks to come—I gather not at conference but over the next few months."[52]

The following week, Maureen Beecher brought news to Leonard that appeared consistent with Smith's upbeat tone. "[She] came in to say that she had received a telephone call from John Madsen. John said that the First Presidency and 'the Brethren' had decided that the Relief Society needed more visibility and that he had been assigned to provide additional input into the Church given to the Relief Society by the Brethren in past periods." Beecher told Leonard that Madsen had emphasized several times during their conversation "that the biggest single problem in the Church is the problem of women and the image of women and that the Church is determined to do everything they can to help everyone understand more fully the importance we attach to women and their work."[53]

However encouraging Madsen's phone call had seemed, Leonard observed no substantive changes for women. Indeed, the ongoing battle over ratification of the Equal Rights Amendment and the related excommunication of Sonia Johnson in December 1979 put Mormon women—and particularly progressive Mormon women—in an even more uncomfortable position.

EMPLOYMENT POLICY

Against a backdrop of the deteriorating status of women in the LDS Church, in response to which Leonard could do little but commiserate in public and fume in private, he was the principal actor in a dramatic sequence of events that changed forever an important church policy—and from which women employed by the church have benefited ever since.

At the History Division's annual Christmas party in 1973, Maureen Ursenbach brought a guest, Dale Beecher, and announced to the group that earlier that week they had become engaged to be married. In an era not many years previous, only single women worked at church headquarters. If a female employee got married, it was understood that her employment was at an end.[54] While that policy gradually was phased out, Ursenbach was nervous as to whether it still might be applied to her. Leonard wrote in his diary, "She told me afterwards she had planned to tell me first but she hadn't worked up courage enough. I think she was a little concerned about her position here if she should marry. I told her that I thought there would be no problem whatsoever. I told her that it was my impression that Church personnel would raise the question and if we told them that we insisted she remain they would not try to cause problems. And we do insist that she remain!"[55]

There was no problem with her being married and retaining her job, but a year after her marriage she encountered a far more vexing problem. There was a firm policy in place, covering all women who worked within the church bureaucracy or the Church Education System, that terminated a woman's employment upon the birth of her first child. "When I came on board, a lot of married women were working for the Church," recalls Beecher, "but the policy was that you were asked by your supervisor, on a regular basis, if the policy about children was keeping you from having a family. In order to stay working there, you had to assure the supervisor that you were not preventing having a family just so that you could keep your job."[56]

She brought the issue to Leonard's attention in the spring of 1975 (their child's delivery date was in August), and a short time later he discussed it with executives of the Historical Department. The minutes of the meeting note: "Brother Arrington read a letter addressed to Elder Anderson signed by Brother Arrington, Brother Bitton and Brother Allen, explaining her importance to the History Division and urging that her services be retained before and after her baby is born. This is a matter that will be taken to the advisers for their consideration and decision."[57]

Leonard brought up the matter the following week in a meeting with Delbert Stapley and Howard Hunter, the department's advisors from the Quorum of the Twelve Apostles, hoping that intervention at that level would enable her retention as a full-time employee. The two apostles directed: "I am to write a letter of justification hopefully pointing out unique elements in her case, since the general policy of the Personnel Committee is to fire people after they have babies."[58]

Two weeks later, "Elder Stapley reported that the Personnel Committee have given special consideration to the continuation of employment for Maureen Beecher after her baby is born, and indicated they are making a special exception in her instance to approve her continued employment."[59] The minutes of the meeting give no indication of the flurry of activity on Leonard's part that led to the favorable outcome—or of the fact that Leonard would not be content with just a special exception. He intended her case to be precedent setting.

A final decision about whether the church-wide policy would be changed in response to Beecher's petition was still a couple of months away and required First Presidency action. In the meantime, Leonard recorded in his diary some of the behind-the-scenes details. He referred to his earlier conversation with Beecher just prior to her marriage. "I told her that while I thought she should marry Dale if she loved him and without any regard to the future consequences with respect to her professional work, her capabilities were very much needed by the Historical Department and if she should become pregnant, I would do my best to make it possible for her to remain a member of our staff."

Leonard's first inclination was to take a passive approach, letting the Personnel Department make the first move and then reacting to it. However, "in preparing the lessons for the Relief Society, she had a number of contacts with Roger Merrill of the Personnel Department. In May, noticing her obvious pregnancy, he told her that the Personnel Department would have to terminate her services upon the birth of her baby unless a special exception was made by the Personnel Committee." Sticking his neck out, Merrill "suggested a number of rationalizations which might induce the Personnel Committee to make an exception."

Beecher related the essence of the conversation to Leonard, who wrote a letter to Joseph Anderson requesting an exception to the policy. Anderson, predictably, told Leonard that he would have to take it up with the department's apostle-advisors. "In our regular meeting with the advisors, I explained the matter orally. Brother Stapley, who is a member of the Personnel Committee, suggested that I write a letter to the Personnel Committee asking that an exception be made. I did so."

Stapley later reported to Leonard that the Personnel Committee "had decided to make an exception in the case of Sister Beecher and that no action would be taken to terminate her services. He said a letter would be forthcoming from Russell Williams, head of the Personnel Department, stating this decision." But the letter was not forthcoming, and after several days Leonard mentioned the fact to Stapley. "He said he would phone up Brother Williams to see why he hasn't sent the letter. Elder Stapley later phoned me to tell me that Brother Williams had decided to ask the Legal Department of the Church to render an opinion as to whether making this exception would set a precedent which would force the Church to retain without termination all women employees who gave birth to children."

The matter was taken to the Legal Department, which felt "that the Church would be in clear violation if it fired a woman simply because she had a baby." The department's recommendation was that the church change its overall policy, and not just make an exception for Beecher. Williams, however, dug in and said, "I am not going to accept just your opinion. I'll take it to a national firm which studied the matter for BYU"—the firm of Wilkinson, Barker and Cragon in Washington, D.C., of which former BYU president Ernest Wilkinson had been a founding partner.

The message to BYU from the law firm was unambiguous: continuation of its policy of firing pregnant women would put it in nonconformity with the Civil

Rights Act of 1972, and thus leave it liable to legal redress. While not making public announcement of a change in policy, BYU administrators quietly dropped the policy, and "have not disemployed any of their staff because of pregnancy or giving birth." Back-channel awareness of these developments gave Leonard the sense that Beecher would be allowed to remain an employee of the History Division after her baby was born, "but if so, we shall probably be counseled to keep this quiet."[60]

Though Leonard's diary account was detailed, it omitted one crucial aspect of the case that Beecher later supplied. When told by a member of the Personnel Department that she would be fired when her baby was born, she sought legal advice from a friend and attorney who would eventually become a justice on the Utah State Supreme Court. "I went to Christine Durham and said, 'Do me a memo on what you think my chances are.' At that time she was practicing law. She wasn't even a judge yet.[61] So she did a memo, and she let me pay her $150 for it. It went immediately into Leonard's file." The memo was unambiguous in stating that the church had no justification in firing, or even inquiring about the family life of, any employee. "In other words, whether I planned to have children, whether I had children, or whether I did not have children was not a question that could be asked in an interview."

Beecher recalled that Leonard, having the Durham memo in his possession, made bold in his letter to higher-ups, stating, "It would not enter Sister Beecher's mind so to do, but were she to take us to court, I have every assurance that she would win."

Still, it turned out that the identical advice from the church's own legal counsel and from Wilkinson, Barker was insufficient to carry the day. "I found out from one of my friends who was also working with Kirton & McConkie, which did a lot of the Church's law work, that they had gone to three separate firms to get that affirmed." So there were three legal opinions, and all said the same thing: the policy must be changed. "So on the very day that the baby was supposed to have been born, they finally got around to telling me that I was not going to be fired."

The First Presidency decision was not a special exception, but rather a change in policy that affected the entire professional staff of the church. Beecher recalled the relief—and gratitude—that spread among female colleagues throughout the Church Office Building. "There were colleagues downstairs in the library part who were so grateful, because they wanted to have children, and they had husbands who were not employed. It was either, 'I work and don't have a baby, or I have a baby and don't work.' . . . My case changed the whole regulations *and* the insurance, and the ramifications of this change in policy went down through all the whole Personnel Department positions."[62]

Leonard did not stop with the one policy. He persuaded the Personnel Department to allow women several weeks of maternity leave, after which they could resume their employment.[63]

Decades later, Beecher put the whole issue in perspective: "It's rather flattering to think that someone whom I admire so much thought highly enough of me to go to bat. But he did [for] all of us. If you were one of his people, he would move heaven and earth for you."[64]

THE EQUAL RIGHTS AMENDMENT

On its face, the proposed Equal Rights Amendment seemed simple and non-controversial:

> Equality of rights under the law shall not be denied or abridged by the United States or by any State on account of sex.
>
> The Congress shall have the power to enforce, by appropriate legislation, the provisions of this article.
>
> This amendment shall take effect two years after the date of ratification.[65]

But in fact, the Equal Rights Amendment had been as controversial as the Nineteenth Amendment that finally granted woman suffrage in 1920. First submitted to Congress in 1923, the ERA did not pass, despite almost yearly proposal, until 1972. Then, it gained traction quickly. But as the number of states approving it approached the thirty-eight that would be required for ratification, it became one of the most divisive issues facing the country—and one in which the Mormon Church played a decisive role. Initially it took no stand, and Mormon legislators at the national and state levels helped to pass it in the Congress and in the state legislatures of Hawaii, Idaho, Colorado, and California. According to Neil Young, a historian at Princeton University, "As [Utah's] state legislature's 1975 session opened, thirty-four of the seventy-five members, 70 percent of whom were church members, indicated their intent to vote for the amendment. With just a few more votes, Utah could be the thirty-fifth state to ratify the amendment. Yet only a month later, the Utah legislature, with solid public approval, voted the amendment down fifty-four to twenty-one on February 18, 1975."[66]

The turning point for the Utah legislators was an editorial in the *Church News*, published just before the legislative session began, declaring the amendment "not only imperfect, but dangerous." Masking its denunciation in protectiveness, it asserted, "Over a period of many decades, women have been accorded special protection and the status properly due them." A "unisex" legal climate loomed, and "if five more states ratify the pending amendment, that is what the people will get."[67]

The United Nations designated 1975 as International Women's Year and sponsored a convention in Mexico City. During 1977, follow-up IWY conferences were scheduled in each state throughout the United States to discuss issues relating to women—including the ERA—and to elect delegates to a national convention in Houston, Texas, later in the year. Leonard was invited to give an address at the Women's History section of the Utah convention, held in Salt Lake City in late June. Of his Friday session he wrote, "Everything went very smoothly, harmoniously, and friendly. No controversies, no politicization, no harsh words, no paranoia." But what he saw the following day was ugly, and he was still upset as he wrote his weekly letter to his children.

The planning committee for the convention had expected about three thousand women to attend, but a few days prior to its beginning Barbara Smith, general Relief Society president, urged local LDS women to attend, suggesting ten per ward. Leonard wrote, "Then we understand another person (name purposefully omitted)[68] sent a letter to the Regional Representatives in Utah saying there was a conspiracy on the part of liberal women to get out recommendations and delegates who represented liberal positions on women's matters—ERA, abortion, birth control, etc—and asked the Regional Rep[resentative]s to be sure that the women were forearmed to prevent this conspiracy from accomplishing its purposes."

As a result, thirteen thousand women showed up, the vast majority of them being conservative LDS women who, having been stoked up with a conspiratorial spirit, "pushed through all of their recommendations and most of their candidates. No non-Mormon was chosen as delegate, and no minority person." Furthermore, their position on the issues presented at the convention "was in absolutes, not reason. And there was lots of hostility, discourtesy, name-calling, shouting-down, booing, and so on. It makes you wonder whether the LDS women couldn't use a good lesson in political courtesy. The moderate LDS women felt they had lost all the good will they had taken thirty years to build up."

Leonard concluded his letter by calling the whole affair "pretty devastating. Women are still crying over the Bircher [John Birch Society] takeover. Now don't write or phone to ask me more. It's an unpleasant subject and I don't like to think about it. We're going to have to start right now to rebuild."[69]

Declaring the ERA a "moral issue," which allowed the church to sidestep charges of political interference, church leaders deployed officers, members, and resources in a controversial and successful campaign to defeat the measure, particularly in the two crucial battleground states of Virginia and Florida. In no small part because of the Mormon offensive, even when the window for ratification was extended to 1982, the ERA never took effect. In retrospect, it is apparent that the "morality" of the ERA, in the eyes of church leaders, was linked to a fear that it would lead to general empowerment of women—including Mormon women.

THE EXCOMMUNICATION OF SONIA JOHNSON

In January 1978, shortly after the Houston IWY convention, a small group of Mormon women in northern Virginia organized Mormons for ERA. Later in the same year, MERA had the opportunity to testify at a largely unheralded meeting of the U.S. Senate Judiciary Subcommittee on the Constitution. When other members of the group were unable to attend, Sonia Johnson, a Logan, Utah, native and the mother of four, volunteered. Her unanticipated face-off against Utah senator (and Mormon) Orrin Hatch catapulted her into the national spotlight, and she quickly became both the face of MERA and a pariah among many of her conservative coreligionists. Nearly two years after her Senate testimony, Johnson, who steadfastly campaigned *for* passage of the ERA and *against* her church's position, was brought before an ecclesiastical court and tried for her church membership.

On December 1, 1979, Leonard wrote to his children, "We are all eagerly awaiting word of the trial of Sonia Johnson. By the time this is mailed off, I suppose we'll have word. . . . We await the court's decision with apprehension."[70] At the conclusion of the ecclesiastical trial, Johnson's bishop, who presided, announced that he would convey the verdict to Johnson by mail within two or three days, thus avoiding the large gathering of supporters who clustered outside her LDS meetinghouse in Virginia.

Two days later, before the verdict had been made public, Leonard wrote one of the lengthiest entries ever in his diary, which began, "I thought it might be helpful to some future historian for me to record some personal impressions. It is my understanding that Elder Gordon Hinckley is chairman of a Church political action committee which has been interested in several projects [among which are] a series of movements designed to prevent the ratification of the Equal Rights Amendment."

He went on to detail the activities of this committee, which, according to his understanding, "assists with literature, pins, buttons, etc., state groups attempting to influence the legislature against ratification or in favor of rescinding the ERA." Then, in advance of ERA ratification votes in individual states, the committee organized groups of LDS women and instructed them "specifically not to reveal that they are LDS women but simply that they are residents of the state opposed to ERA."

Knowing of this plan, Sonia Johnson followed the LDS women into the state and counteracted their presence by appearing on television and radio and issuing press releases. "When LDS people have questioned her she has insisted that ERA is a political matter, not a religious matter, and that she has a right to disagree with the Church and its officials on this political matter, also that she has a right to actively campaign against it." Because she was LDS but was campaigning against the stand of her church, she became "a sort of heroine for her courage and determination."

Eventually Johnson's bishop informed her that she would be tried for her church membership. Leonard opined, "Any bishop would be stupid to initiate a trial like this. This had to be something which was suggested to the bishop by his stake president, area administrator, or General Authority."

Now that she had been put on trial, Leonard asked rhetorically what the real issue of contention was. "Does she have the right to argue for ERA in Sunday School class, in testimony meeting, in firesides, in public meetings to which Latter-day Saints are invited? Does she have the right to conduct a public campaign against the Church's position when the First Presidency declared that this is a moral and religious matter? That, it seems to me, is the basic question." He was particularly agitated about the possibility of her being excommunicated when "she is quite vocal in saying that she supports the prophet in all matters which are religious—in all matters which involve revelation."

Still writing prior to hearing the verdict, he concluded, "The Church cannot gain from this entire incident. If the bishop should excommunicate or discipline her, she will become a martyr among pro-ERA women, both Mormon and non-Mormon. Many women who favor ERA will very likely become more inactive, less respectful. . . . On the other hand, if the bishop should not excommunicate her or discipline her, Sonia herself will be the first to say that she has been justified all along in her activities. And this surely will mean a mounting dissidence. People will say that the Church does not hold firmly to its position, that it is not strict enough, that it has not stuck by its beliefs and principles." In summary, "One feels that it might have been wiser from a public relations standpoint to have let the thing die down without having the trial."[71]

Johnson was excommunicated, and the immediate aftermath of the trial was a public relations debacle for the church. Leonard wrote, "I learned that Esther Peterson had complained afterwards about the treatment the witnesses received from the bishop in Sonia Johnson's trial.[72] . . . They refused to let the witnesses sit together, so that they could talk to each other. No witness could talk to another witness. Esther Peterson, an older woman, needed to go to the bathroom, and they told her she'd have to find it by herself. Since it was dark—no lights—she asked if someone could accompany her. They refused."

After they'd been waiting for an hour or so, the pastor of the Unitarian Church across the street saw what was taking place and invited them over to his warm church—the LDS chapel had been left unheated—while they waited. Leonard, who knew that Johnson's bishop was an employee of the Central Intelligence Agency, couldn't resist twisting the blade: "Sounds as though the bishop felt he was running a CIA interrogation."[73]

Despite Leonard's distaste of the manner in which the trial was conducted, he maintained ambivalence about the verdict. Although he did not know Johnson, he had spoken with some of her close friends, who "emphasize that she is not really speaking as herself in the extreme statements she has made but has gotten carried away by 'the movement.'" He also had heard that her bishop had counseled her for eighteen months, emphasizing more her commitment to her family than her ERA position. "In other words, according to what I have been told, it was not so much her belief that the Church was wrong that induced the bishop to 'take up a labor of love' but more her abandonment of her family—her full commitment. . . . There are at least some friends of Sonia who believe that she sought martyrdom in the interest of the Cause."[74]

Johnson had sent her children to Cache Valley to her parents. Was she "sparing" them the turmoil and unpleasant publicity surrounding this episode, or was she "abandoning" them so that she could devote all her time to her political activities? Furthermore, although her husband, Richard, had been supportive, he began distancing himself from her activities, and their marriage ended in divorce after the excommunication. Did the pressure merely "reveal" rifts that had been developing in the relationship, or did Johnson's feminism "cause" the end of the marriage? Supporters and opponents argued both sides.

All of Leonard's comments and opinions up to this point had been based on what he heard and read from others. However, a month after Johnson's excommunication she appeared on the *Phil Donahue Show* on national television and Leonard watched with keen attention. "I was not favorably impressed with Sonia and her presentation. Her statements critical of the Church were pretty strong, and she seemed to be playing to the audience, most of whom were obviously militant feminists, and applauded her frequently. Sonia seemed to be enjoying holding the church and its officials up to ridicule. It is difficult for me to believe, on the basis of her performance, that she regrets for one minute her excommunication from the Church. . . . I can understand now why the bishop finally gave up laboring with her and decided to go through with it."[75]

A week later he wrote to his children with his final appraisal of Sonia Johnson—an appraisal quite different than his impressions when he first heard of her case. In writing, he signaled to them that his ultimate loyalty resided—and always had resided—with the church. Feminist though he was, he was not sympathetic to other feminists whose approach was to attack the church rather than work within it for change.

He wrote, "I must say that I was turned off by Sonia's hour. She stretched and exaggerated criticisms against the Church, she was enjoying making her criticisms against the Church and its leaders, she seemed very pleased that she was excommunicated so she could be the big hero. I did not like the tone; she was obviously using the Church and those who were inclined to go along with her to support her and her cause—and I find it difficult to be sympathetic with those who use others."

While Leonard never gave up his advocacy for women, Sonia Johnson's excommunication caused him to qualify it to his children. "It's one thing to work for the cause of women, as I hope all of us of are doing; it's another to exaggerate and stretch points and get so carried away that you bring disrespect upon the cause."[76]

18

FIRST FRUITS

The measure of historians is not only their productivity but also the persuasiveness of their interpretations. On the one-year anniversary of his interview with Eldon Tanner, Leonard wrote a brief self-assessment that included progress reports on publications by members and surrogates of his division. It began with the launch of the sesquicentennial history series, whose sixteen authors were under contract and had been given advance royalties; continued with notice that the Mormon Heritage Series had been approved and several volumes had been commenced; and concluded with enumeration of "a number of fine articles for the *Ensign, New Era, BYU Studies, Dialogue, Utah Historical Quarterly, Missouri Historical Quarterly*, and other publications."[1]

The following year, 1974, which Davis Bitton called "a year of publication," also saw the first books from the History Division. With satisfaction, Leonard enumerated these first fruits of what he anticipated would be a bountiful and ongoing harvest. "The publication of *Manchester Mormons*,[2] while not specifically sponsored by the History Division, provided evidence of our desire to make primary sources available in responsible scholarly editions. Even more impressive in this regard was *Brigham Young's Letters to His Sons*."[3] A third book, which was not sponsored by the History Division but which had Leonard as author, was a biography of Charles C. Rich.[4] In addition were several magazine and journal articles written by History Division staffers.[5]

At the end of 1974, in a self-assessment, Leonard expressed gratification with what had been published, while at the same time acknowledging disappointment that some members of his division were lagging in their productivity. "One of our primary responsibilities is to develop the implications of new findings in Church History, and to advance new interpretations of our history. We have done this to some extent, but we should do more."

Then, in an explicit acknowledgment that there was a political game to be played, he wrote a note of self-directed caution that nonetheless ended on an upbeat tone: "We must be careful to do some exciting new sources and inter-pretations which are unquestionably positive in their impact on the ordinary church member. . . . We have had experience bridging the gap between pietistic history and professional history; we have had the experience in dealing with the political problems involved. We represent different approaches to Church History. We have the respect of the professionals—and of the ecclesiastics."[6]

The only cautionary note respecting their early publications was almost an afterthought by Davis Bitton: "Criticism of our activities has been virtually non-existent with one important exception—a letter from a General Authority."[7] While the letter, which was written during 1974, was clearly a caution sign, other straws in the wind had preceded it; but they had either been ignored or not appreciated for what they portended.

STRAWS IN THE WIND

The author of the letter was Boyd Packer, who was consistently proactive in mon-itoring and shaping the activities of the Historical Department. He assumed this role despite being the next-to-junior member of the Quorum of the Twelve Apos-tles at the time Leonard became church historian, and even though church his-tory lay outside his assigned portfolio. Leonard wrote in his autobiography, "In noticing the research and writing done in the archives of the church, Packer be-lieved that he and his colleagues were [in Packer's words] 'watching over the Church, defending the Lord's anointed, and protecting a sacred stewardship.'"[8] The subtitle of Packer's authorized biography, *A Watchman on the Tower*, rein-forces that image.[9] Ronald Esplin, who succeeded Leonard as director of the Joseph Fielding Smith Institute for Church History at BYU in 1986, gave some perspective on Packer's concerns, which matured when he was working in the Church Educational System. "Elder Packer and Ted Tuttle [also a CES employee] had a moment in which Frank West, trying to get them oriented to the task ahead and how challenging it would be, said, 'Your job is to stand between the Men and the Brethren, and protect the Men from the Brethren.' That turned into an introspective quest for Boyd Packer to figure out where he stood."

In the course of doing extensive introspection, Packer had a conversation with future church president Harold B. Lee, who said, "Boyd, you have to figure out where you stand. Are you with the Brethren or not?" Packer made a definitive and permanent decision that he was "with the Brethren." Esplin explained, "So from that beginning, from that day, he has seen himself as the guy in the watch-tower. He has had concerns that people that put scholarship first may not stay the course. Even though there are lots of cases where they did, he has had these few cases where they didn't that are indelible to him. It has really impacted the way he looked at Leonard and the way he looked at scholars generally. He didn't think historians had integrity." Where historians saw adventure, Packer saw danger. If he had to take a risk, "it was going to be on the side of safety, and not of experimentation."[10]

After becoming a General Authority (an assistant to the Twelve, called in 1961 by David O. McKay), Packer maintained close ties to his former coworkers in the Church Educational System—ties that likely included back-channel communications. Jeff Johnson, one of the church archive's early employees, saw CES teachers as a major source of complaints about the workings of the History Division. "I know that there were Church Education people who were really upset with Leonard, who probably had the ears of a General Authority. They felt that he wasn't writing faithful history. The CES office back then was writing the lesson plans, and it was important for them to make sure that no negative thing was said. The students would come in with an article they had read of Leonard's, and the teachers would contact the head office and say, 'How do I answer this?' That made them mad at Leonard and what was happening."[11]

Leonard's first substantive conversation with Packer took place in April 1972, two months after the meeting in the Salt Lake Temple at which he had proposed his grand plan to the First Presidency and Quorum of the Twelve, at which Packer had been present. After that meeting Packer had raised questions about Leonard's proposal for an advisory council to the church historian, and invited Leonard to come to his office so that he could tell him "a story or two." In the meeting in his office, Packer laid out for Leonard his philosophy of history. "He said that some historians would say things to their seminary students just because they were true, whether or not it was wise."

Packer then told of an image that had flashed in his mind as he listened to a lecture by a CES employee that poked fun at aspect of the church's history—a photo he had seen in a book used in the fourth or fifth grade of a magnificent, ancient sculpture without head or arms: the "Winged Victory of Samothrace." He likened the statue to the church, "pointing out that despite the weaknesses and shortcomings, the defects, the headless and armless condition, the church was still a great, divine institution, created through divine auspices." Packer had a small replica of the statue in his office, and he pointed to it as he lectured to Leonard.

Although Packer's explanation for the meeting was to tell Leonard "a story or two," in retrospect it is clear that he was giving Leonard a warning. Writing things "just because they were true" was not a wise course to take.

Communicating his meaning in a story that left the listener with the responsibility of deducing the correct meaning was a method that Packer used on other occasions. Two decades later he spelled out the importance of "anticipating counsel," and being able to deduce the "unwritten rules" that governed "priesthood protocol."[12]

Leonard gave no indication that he grasped, at the time, the weightiness of Packer's warning. Indeed, he expressed his ambivalence several weeks later when he was invited to speak to a private study group. After his presentation, "we spent a little while at the end of the discussion talking about the responsibility of Church historians. To what extent are we obligated to tell all of the truth?" One person argued that, while it is permissible to acknowledge that church leaders "have human failings," it is inappropriate to describe such failings. "Another person in the group felt exactly the opposite—that we must point out human failings and weaknesses in order for young people to be able to identify with them and also to prepare them for all of the nasty things they will hear from non-Mormons and anti-Mormons. We must make them credible."[13] Leonard's silence regarding his response suggests that he chose not to take sides—and perhaps that he had not made up his own mind on the question.

The first official caution sign came in the form of a 1973 letter from the Melchizedek Priesthood Committee—one of the signatories being Boyd Packer—that "expressed concern" over a groundbreaking article in *BYU Studies* by William Hartley, a member of the History Division. Titled "The Priesthood Reform Movement, 1908–1922," it described the earliest effort to reshape the largely dysfunctional priesthood quorums into coherent organizations—the actual beginnings of what later became known as the Correlation Movement.[14] The concern was "not what was written, apparently, but the fact that it quoted from restricted sources—minutes of the general priesthood committee and policy directives of the Presiding Bishopric. They expressed concern that such matters be properly cleared before publication."[15] Joseph Anderson brought the letter to Leonard, whose response was that "the article had been properly cleared according to the understanding we had." The explanation satisfied Anderson, who relayed it to Apostles Howard Hunter and Bruce McConkie, the department's advisors, noting, "I trust that this takes care of the request of the Brethren that articles using restricted materials will be properly cleared."[16]

But the incident contained a signal that Leonard misread. He saw the issue as one of misunderstanding, when in fact it was one of control: documents that in the past had been under the strict control of ecclesiastical officials who were wary of historians, were now under the control of the historians—and as a result were in the light of day for the first time. There were some of those ecclesiastical officials who were not willing to accept the new *status quo.*

At the end of 1973, Leonard wrote philosophically of what he viewed to be the primary challenge ahead: *how* to write the history, not yet understanding that the history *itself* was the real problem in the minds of his adversaries. "To this date we have published in professional journals (which are not widely read by church officials and members) and in Church magazines, where the determination of treatment and subject matter is left to the magazine editors and their correlation committee. What happens when we publish books including material which they have studiously avoided including in church magazines? What happens when we revise standard accounts of church history? What happens when we have treatments of polygamy?" While he was confident that he and his colleagues could write acceptable history, even on sensitive issues, he ended his diary entry with a statement that proved to be prophetic, but whose irony he did not then appreciate: "If history is going to be an aspect of doctrine and missionary work, then our department should not exist."[17]

Leonard's next challenge was already in the works when he wrote the diary entry. It came in the form of an article in the December 1973 issue of the *Ensign,* the church's magazine for adults. The problem was not one of access to restricted documents, as had been the case with William Hartley's article, nor with accuracy. In fact, the article was so accurate that it led both the writer and the reader to a single conclusion—but it was a conclusion that differed from the traditional narrative, and thus became problematic.

One of several items in the "I Have a Question" section of the *Ensign* responded to the question, "After Edward Partridge was called to be a bishop there were others who were called to be bishops. Did the Lord call Bishop Partridge to be a presiding bishop?" The author, D. Michael Quinn, who was one of Leonard's associates in the History Division, laid out a convincing case that although Partridge was the *first* bishop in the LDS Church, he "presided" only over the church in Missouri.[18] Eleven months after Partridge was ordained to the office by Sidney Rigdon, Newel K. Whitney was ordained to the same office but presided over the church in Ohio. The two men thus had the same ecclesiastical rank, with neither having authority over the other. Not until 1847—and Partridge died in 1840—was there a single bishop who presided over the temporal affairs of the *entire* church.

The problem for Leonard's group was that the traditional history assumed that Partridge, by being the first ordained bishop, presided over all others, when in fact there was no functional presiding bishop until 1847. At the next meeting of the department executives, "Brother [Joseph] Anderson thought it was questionable wisdom for such a statement to be made as it tends to cause confusion among the members of the Church."[19] Seeing the issue in much broader terms, Leonard jumped to Quinn's defense. "I said that Mike had submitted a fully documented article to me and that I had suggested to him that he submit it to the *Ensign* for publication. The *Ensign*, without consulting with us, had eliminated much of the explanatory and documentary material and published it as simply the answer to a question. In a way, the *Ensign* abridgement had made it appear to be a statement that Edward Partridge was not the first presiding bishop, without giving adequately the reasons why he believed this to be true."

Earl Olson chimed in with a suggestion that, in the future, the First Presidency be consulted prior to publishing anything "on such important matters." Leonard exploded in frustration, noting that such a tactic "placed us in an impossible position"—to say nothing of the extreme unlikelihood that the First Presidency would even have the time and inclination to consider such issues. "I said that we are coming out with dozens of new facts and interpretations in all that we write and will have thousands of them perhaps in the new 16-volume history. I said that it would be impossible for us to clear all of these changes in our history and that I did not think we could determine the truth of what had happened in history by having somebody like the Quorum of Twelve vote on it." Then, he threw down the gauntlet: "You do not determine historical truth by counting noses."[20]

Despite his impassioned defense of full historical disclosure, the following day Leonard wrote to Quinn, asking him to pull back on another article that was in the works, one on the early history of the First Presidency as a council. "There has been a little flak from the presiding bishop question article. To be specific, Bishop Partridge's descendants have been yelling like mad at his dethronement as presiding bishop. They have gone to various Church officials and want to know whether your statement represents the official view of the Church." The message was clear: if they didn't stoke the fire now, then later "we ought not have to clear things of this nature before they are published."[21]

"Stuff happens," and the next challenge to Leonard's enterprise came from a source that he could neither anticipate nor control. Indeed, it had nothing at all to do with his department, and yet he and it took heat as a result.

A highlight of the annual meeting of the Mormon History Association is the presidential address, the topic of which is at the total discretion of the outgoing president. The MHA president in 1974 was Reed Durham, director of the LDS Institute of Religion at the University of Utah, and the location of the meeting was Nauvoo, Illinois. Without prior announcement, Durham gave an address on the relationship between Freemasonry and Mormonism. It was a logical topic inasmuch as Joseph Smith's initiation into Freemasonry occurred in Nauvoo in

March 1842, and two months later he appropriated much of the Masonic ceremony and symbolism as he transformed the Kirtland "endowment," which had been congregational and Pentecostal in nature, into a more narrative format. But it was also one of the most sensitive—and forbidden—topics in the viewpoint of the church hierarchy, as Leonard well knew.

Durham began his speech on a flippant note that, given the nature of his topic, would have the effect of exacerbating any negative reactions from the church hierarchy: "Regardless of the possible incriminations and stigma that might ensue, I should like, in this paper, to interpose some unorthodox findings and fancies upon the more traditional and canonical propaganda of the faith."[22] He proceeded to document many levels of connection between Freemasonry and the Joseph Smith period of Mormonism, including this sweeping statement: "There is absolutely no question in my mind that the Mormon ceremony which came to be known as the Endowment, introduced by Joseph Smith to Mormon Masons initially, just a little over one month after he became a Mason, had an immediate inspiration from Masonry. . . . They are so similar, in fact, that one writer was led to refer to the Endowment as Celestial Masonry."[23]

Durham correctly stated that the first inductees into the Nauvoo endowment were all Masons. Although he stopped short of describing specific elements of the endowment and their relationship to the Masonic ceremony,[24] even the parallels that he described put him at odds with the church that was his employer. As the twentieth century dawned, the church formally proscribed Masonic affiliation for church members, and three decades later Anthony W. Ivins, a member of the First Presidency, published an entire book whose thesis was that the church "was not influenced by Masonry, either in its doctrines, organization, or the bringing forth of the Book of Mormon."[25]

To historians of early Mormonism, Durham's paper broke no new ground. Barbara Higdon, a member of the RLDS Church who attended the meeting and who became president of that church's Graceland College, recalled the immediate aftermath of the speech. "I wasn't disturbed; I was just interested, just fascinated. I said to Reed afterwards, 'Will we get a copy of this paper, with footnotes?' He said, 'Oh, yes.' Well, we never did. I just happened to walk out with Leonard, and I said, 'Is this new to you folks?' He said, 'No, we've known about this.' And that was it."[26]

But to those attendees who had not previously heard of the parallels between Mormonism and Freemasonry, it was most unsettling—so much so that shortly after Durham returned from the conference, his superiors in the Church Education System required him to send a letter of apology to all who had attended the meeting, whether LDS or not. Given his introductory remark in the paper itself, the very different tone of the letter suggests a literary contribution from others:

To Whom It May Concern

On Saturday, April 20, 1974, at the Mormon History Association Annual Meeting held at Nauvoo, Illinois, I delivered the Presidential Address entitled, "Is There No Help for the Widow's Son?" At that time I was gravely concerned that the presentation of my findings and conclusions, as a result of long months of research, would not be properly interpreted; and that regardless of what I attempted to say, misunderstandings would occur. My concerns were justified. I have been informed of instances where even my own colleagues in the Mormon History Association, and also some close friends within the Church misinterpreted what I said, and more important to me, in some cases even questioned my faith in Joseph Smith and the Church.

Of course, I assume the full responsibility for creating those questions, concerns, and misunderstandings. It was because I was not skillful enough, erudite enough, nor perhaps prayerful enough to make my personal position and feelings clearly known.

Therefore, regardless of what I said, or what interpretations were placed upon what I said, let it be known at this time, that:

1. I know that Joseph Smith was/is indeed a true prophet of God—the one called under direction of Jesus Christ to usher in this dispensation of the fullness of time.

2. I know further that Temple Work, with all its ramifications, including Eternal Marriage and the Endowment ceremony, is divinely inspired.

3. Because of the personal witness I have received by the Spirit (which has been complemented and supported by continual study and experience), the prime criterion or standard of judgement I am committed to employ as an explanation of any aspect of the Church—either of Joseph Smith and/or the Temple ceremonies—is that of divine revelation.

Had I delivered my address in Nauvoo, making sure that my knowledge and conviction of the above three statements was clearly reflected in the subject matter of my address, I am confident that fewer misunderstandings would have been occasioned; and my address would have more clearly approximated my honest feelings. I am deeply sorry that such was not the case.

Sincerely,

Reed C. Durham, Jr.[27]

Durham's apology was not the end of his story. He never again attended an MHA conference, and even though he had been designated as one of the authors of the sixteen-volume sesquicentennial history, his authoritative book on succession in the presidency of the LDS Church,[28] published four years prior to his speech in Nauvoo, turned out to be his last.

Several months later Joe Christensen, associate commissioner of the Church Educational System—and Durham's superior—asked to speak with Leonard about Durham's address. Saying that he had received a good deal of criticism regarding Durham's speech, Christensen asked for Leonard's appraisal of it. Leonard recorded in his diary, "I think he was trying to find out if we had read the talk in advance and approved it—I assured him we had not—and whether I thought it was sound historically. I told him we had serious reservations."

The explanation seemed to satisfy Christensen, but he then spoke pessimistically about Durham's future in church employment. "It would 'put a millstone around his neck the rest of his life' because certain of the younger General Authorities will never be able to forget it."

Leonard then attempted to use the episode as an object lesson on the need for the History Division to continue writing scholarly history. "It will take us another year or two to work up books and articles on things in our archives which are enriching and inspiring. Until we get this out people will still work over the same subjects like Mormonism and Masonry, polygamy, and so on."[29]

Several years later Leonard, responding to a question from a colleague regarding Durham's speech, gave the following reply:

> We found it impossible to defend him very strongly because we could not defend what he said. It simply was incomplete and misleading. He was required by his superior to write a letter of apology to those attending MHA bearing his testimony that Joseph Smith was a prophet. He did write such a letter. All of us regarded it as unnecessary and rather silly. In fact, he bore his testimony at the MHA meeting in Nauvoo the very next morning and in my judgment that took care of it. Reed has never been an effective Church history researcher since that date.[30]

The Durham episode, although uncomfortable for Leonard, ultimately had less impact on the History Division than on the Church Educational System. Because "one of their own" had been involved, employees of the CES pulled back in their interaction with others—including Jerald and Sandra Tanner. Sandra Tanner recalled the earlier, more collegial period. "Reed Durham got in trouble in 1974, but up until 1974 many of the institute and seminary guys would come by the bookstore and we would talk. They would buy the reprints they couldn't get anywhere else, and we could talk and exchange ideas and research. It was all congenial. But after Durham's demotion, there started to come in a little more of a hesitancy for fear of guilt-by-association. 'I don't want the Brethren to pull my act up because I talked to the Tanners.'"[31]

While the effect on Leonard of the Durham episode was indirect and mostly an irritant, Leonard's next challenge was direct and substantive. Indeed, it took the issue of historical accuracy all the way to the First Presidency. While earlier challenges to Leonard's franchise had involved narrative history that included authors' interpretations, this one involved documentary history in the form of a published collection of letters, *Letters of Brigham Young to His Sons*.[32] The first— and, as it turned out, last—volume of the Mormon Heritage Series that had been approved by the First Presidency, it caused an immediate firestorm at a high level. Only three days after the book was released, Boyd Packer typed a four-page, single-spaced letter to the First Presidency condemning it, in spite of the fact that in doing so he breached protocol by bypassing the two apostles—Howard Hunter and Bruce McConkie—who were advisors to the Historical Department. Leonard summarized Packer's red-flagging of three specific passages in the book:

> One, it mentioned that one of Brigham Young's sons had had a very serious illness for which the doctors had prescribed morphine and he had become addicted to it, and we acknowledged that in the book. Secondly, Brigham Young had written a letter to one of his sons who was a missionary in England, suggesting that during the period of his mission he ought to not use tobacco. Brigham Young did chew tobacco at one time in his life and he acknowledged in the letter that he had, and said that he'd given it up, so he knew his son could give it up. And the third thing was that the book acknowledged the difficulty with some of the heirs over the settlement of the Brigham Young estate.[33]

But the real essence of the letter was a theme to which Packer often returned: the ecclesiastical always trumps the scholarly. "I have come to believe that it is the tendency for most members of the Church who spend a great deal of time in academic research, to begin to judge the Church, its doctrine, organization, and history, by the principles of their own profession. . . . It is an easy thing for a man with extensive academic training to consider the Church with the principles he has been taught in his professional training as his measuring standard. In my mind it ought to be the other way around." Put simplistically, Packer advocated that dogma would always trump data.

He then focused directly on the History Division. "What concerns me about the Historian's Office is that, unless I am mistaken, the direction they are taking is to judge what should be good for the Church and for the operation of the Historical Department against the rules set down for historians. . . . I have lived in academic circles, have observed the tendencies of highly 'schooled' Church members; have seen how perversely such information as this is often used, and wonder if these projects ought to be carefully reviewed before they continue."[34]

Packer's argument, although inimical to historians generally and to the History Division specifically, had great merit from the ecclesiastical side of the table. The primary missions of the church had for decades been to "proclaim the gospel, perfect the Saints, and redeem the dead"[35]—and not to write history. Since the ecclesiastical arm of the church was mandated to focus on those three missions, all other matters were either inconsequential or were viewed in the context of how they might assist in carrying out the missions. Thus Packer's later statement, "Some things that are true are not very useful,"[36] makes sense if one's viewpoint is to use history selectively as a means to an end. While he and his colleagues in the hierarchy had little control over history written by others, they held the purse strings of the History Division and ultimately pulled those strings, first to control, and then to dissolve the division once it became apparent to them that it was not the tool they demanded it to be.

In meeting with Leonard to discuss Packer's letter to the First Presidency, Joseph Anderson was wholly supportive of the historians. With considerable relief, Leonard recorded Anderson's response to Brigham's use of tobacco, which laid out a remarkably progressive and nuanced commentary on the Word of Wisdom:

> Brother Anderson said he didn't see anything wrong with people knowing that and with Brigham Young, Jr.'s posterity knowing about that. People should understand that our emphasis on the Word of Wisdom today has not always applied. It is true that the Prophet Joseph Smith drank wine after he received the Word of Wisdom revelation. It is also true that Brigham Young used wine, even fermented wine, both at his table and in the Sacrament. I added that was true as late as Lorenzo Snow, who administered the Sacrament in the Salt Lake Temple with wine—and Brother Anderson added not just with a little glass cup but with large goblets so that the authorities drank more than just a swallow.
>
> Brother Anderson in regard to this pointed out a number of General Authorities who as late as his day were not as strict on the Word of Wisdom as we are today. He mentioned President [Charles] Penrose, one of the most beloved persons in Church history, who

being English loved his ale and continued to use it more or less regularly to the end of his life and as I recall he died about 1923 or '24 [actually 1925]. He mentioned Patriarch John Smith, who continued to use tobacco and liquor and had certain problems with both to the end of his days, and yet he was patriarch to the Church. Brother Anderson mentioned President [Anthony] Ivins who used wine, having grown up with its use in Mexico and continued to use it at least many of the years in the 1920s.[37]

Howard Hunter, also present in the meeting, "suggested that we not make any immediate response to this, that we think the problem through, and at a suitable time in the future make appropriate recommendations."[38] The impression with which Leonard left the meeting was favorable to the historians. "Based upon some of their comments, I gather that perhaps Brother Packer has been rather free with his opinion on the work of various committees and departments and that we should take these into consideration, of course, but only as those of one interested and concerned individual. We are in no sense to regard his suggestions as binding or as causing us to change our policies duly arrived at in the past. This is comforting." Leonard felt he had the full confidence of Hunter and Bruce McConkie, their other advisor, and "as long as we keep Brother Hunter and Brother McConkie reasonably well informed on what we are doing, we will be able to carry out the policies which we have desired and wish continued."[39]

Nonetheless, Packer's intrusion into his work annoyed Leonard. Two weeks after the meeting with the advisors, he and Grace went to some friends' home for dinner and an impromptu slide show by one of the architects of the Washington, D.C., temple caused him to chafe openly at the intrusion. "The most interesting thing [the architect] said was that after they had presented their basic plan for the temple, they were left completely free to work out everything with respect to design symbols, construction materials, and so on by the First Presidency and Council of Twelve. This is a case where the professionals are left completely on their own to work out what seems to be best. I said it would be nice if they would treat the historians the same way."[40]

In spite of the supportive words that Leonard received from the advisors, Packer had, in fact, drawn a line in the sand and was determined to defend it. In December 1974, the same month that the advisors had met with the Historical Department executives, Earl Olson attended a wedding reception and brought back to Leonard an ominous report:

While there he happened to sit at the same table with Boyd Packer. Boyd Packer asked Earl if he had seen the letter which Elder Packer had written to the First Presidency about our Brigham Young book and other projects. Earl said he had seen it and we all had seen it. Earl added that we appreciated seeing a copy of it and appreciated his concern.

Boyd Packer repeated very strongly his concerns to Earl and said that we must find some way of preventing the printing of these things from occurring in the future and said that unless we can come to some agreement on it we would have to change the management. I asked Earl what that meant—whether it meant getting a new Church Historian or getting a new Assistant Managing Director or just what. Earl said he was not sure, but he thought he meant that he would seek to have another advisor rather than Brother Hunter or perhaps another Acting Managing Director rather than Brother Anderson. I said to Earl, "Does that mean that Brother Packer himself wants to be our advisor?" Earl said he thought that was the case.

Earl said something about clearing things through correlation. I said that would be the worst thing that could happen. How can they possibly judge us on what is good history and what is bad history? Earl said that we may be forced to it. I said I thought the Twelve would outvote Brother Packer if he made such a suggestion.

At any rate, it seems clear that Brother Packer is making some kind of crusade out of it and will not be satisfied to leave it in the hands of Elder Hunter and Elder McConkie. Earl said as a minimum we ought to bring it up with our advisors at our next meeting and get their counsel of what if anything we should do. Earl says Brother Packer expects some kind of an answer and we need to raise this with the advisors.[41]

A month later, Hunter and McConkie again brought up the Packer letter and asked that Leonard reiterate the policies of his division with respect to *Letters of Brigham Young* and other recent publications. "Brother Arrington made a statement at some length," the minutes report blandly, "and the advisers expressed their approval of what had been done."[42]

That put the matter to rest—but not permanently. At the end of 1975 Leonard wrote another self-assessment in his diary, and this time Boyd Packer loomed large. Leonard's usually exuberant tone was gone. The entry began with frustration: "Within a few weeks, I shall have been Church Historian for four years. I cannot believe it has been so long. Nor can I believe I have accomplished so little in that period of time." Then, he put his finger on the chief problem that faced the History Division, "our uncertainty as to what the Church will accept by way of publishing materials, interpretation, tone and so on."

He then correctly described the balancing act that the division personnel were attempting. On the one hand, "we are trained to publish for our professional colleagues—being honest, straightforward, fearless, analytical, raising questions," while on the other hand, "we know that Church authorities and Church audience want and have a right to expect faith-promoting history. Drawing a balance between professional and faith-promoting goals is our toughest problem."

Defining the problem was one thing, but resolving it in the midst of a complex and often hostile bureaucracy was quite another. "One cannot raise questions with ecclesiastical superiors. If one goes to them with a question, they will inevitably answer no, on the theory that if it is questionable, it ought not to be done. None of *them* will accept responsibility. They push it off by saying no. And so I have to make decisions without consulting with them on the ground that I do not want 'no' answers." His frustration was palpable as he lamented that there was not one General Authority who was both accessible and "who would understand my concerns[,] who would listen, give reactions, and withhold judgment."

Finally, he wrote rhetorically, "Who is everybody afraid of? Once upon a time, it was Harold B. Lee. Now it seems to be Boyd Packer who is free to give advice and to make threats, and who cannot be trusted to keep confidences of this nature."[43]

GRACE IN SALT LAKE CITY

Leonard's four-year self-assessment left out one major aspect of his life, as did most of his diary entries during this time: Grace. When they first moved to Logan in 1946, they had immediately purchased a small home at 754 North 500 East, two lots south of the Logan Tenth Ward meetinghouse and just below College Hill. Leonard had been thrifty with his army pay and teacher's salary; but Grace had saved nearly all of her earnings as a hairdresser in North Carolina. This sum allowed them to purchase their first home and, soon, a lot just one block away on the corner of 800 North and 400 East where they planned to build. Grace's heart was set on a "dream home," and Leonard, though investing much less emotional energy in buildings, wanted her to have her heart's desire. Daughter Susan remembers that Grace spent hundreds of hours thinking through the design of a home that would fit both her practical needs and her aesthetic tastes. "She sat at her desk in the bedroom for hours, designing the floor plan, thinking through the outdoor design, and poring over articles from magazines like *Home Beautiful* and *Good Housekeeping*, searching for even the tiniest details that would add to the comfort and convenience of the home." Susan still remembered her mother's exultant cry when she discovered a new idea: " 'Eureka!', or—more accurately in her Southern accent—'Eu-reee-ker!' "[44]

This dream house was constructed to her specifications, and the family settled in happily in 1963. Grace had no idea, at the time, that she would be leaving it less than a decade later.

Life in Logan was idyllic for Grace. Warm and gregarious, she was a contented contributor to their ward, their neighborhood, and the university's faculty wives. Logan had been an ideal place to raise their three children, and their home was daily filled with the sounds of the laughter of the children and their friends. It was bursting with pleasure and energy during the children's teen years, since all three had many friends who frequently gathered there. The home included a separate basement apartment for Grace's mother, "Nana," who joined Grace and Leonard in 1963. "She was close, but not too close," Susan recalled. "Safe, but not intrusive. Nearby but not suffocatingly nosey."[45]

That changed in 1972 with Leonard's new position. Technically, he and Grace were "empty nesters." James, age twenty-two, had completed an LDS mission to Brazil, earned a Master of Fine Arts degree from BYU, and was working in San Francisco in the Actors Conservatory Theater. Carl, age twenty, was assistant to the president of the LDS mission in Bolivia; and seventeen-year-old Susan was beginning her freshman year at Utah State University, living in an on-campus dormitory.[46] The children were launched in their respective directions, but there was no question that Nana would accompany them to Salt Lake City.

The move was emotionally threatening for Grace's aging, ailing mother, who became steadily more insecure, needy, and anxious. First, "they installed her in a basement bedroom in their newly purchased home," recalled Susan, "but she didn't like being downstairs. They moved her upstairs but she objected to having to close her bedroom door at night. Then, she objected to my parents closing their own bedroom door at night. She hating having my parents go somewhere in the evening. She often complained of feeling ill, dizzy, nauseated, until finally my mother agreed to stay home with her. My grandmother quickly recovered about five minutes after my father left, leaving my mother with our grandmother."[47]

Grace willingly and generously cared for her mother until Nana's death in 1980, but she was also dealing with her own displacement and disorientation. She wholeheartedly supported Leonard in taking the church historian's position, graciously hosted holiday parties for the staff, and even made small, personalized Christmas gifts for staff members. (One was a tube in blue velvet filled with heavy grains of rice or some other substance that was ideal for holding a book open on a desk.) Still, the move was a far greater sacrifice for her than for him, and in her privately printed biography she portrayed candidly her feelings. "We left Logan about 6:00 in the evening on June 7. I didn't cry much; by then I was beyond tears. . . . I had resisted the move to Salt Lake City, and found no happiness here except that Leonard was doing what he wanted to do and enjoyed the esteem and admiration of others. We had enjoyed so much the friendly people with whom we had exchanged news and ideas in the various social, church, and study groups to which we belonged in Logan. We really missed the good times we had with them. Now all this was wiped out."

Grace lamented that in Salt Lake City she had no "let's do so and so" kinds of friends. She truly rejoiced in Leonard's calling and in the special experiences that it brought to "a little country girl from North Carolina," but she also noted that despite the joys and compensations "there have been intervening periods of loneliness and heartbreak."[48]

Carl, who was learning the family news from weekly letters and perhaps from retrospective conversations with Grace after his return, appraised her difficult situation in Salt Lake City:

> They had a million friends [in Logan], and then all of a sudden the Church Historian thing comes up, all the children leave, they go down to Salt Lake, he buys a house that she doesn't really like, and she goes into ten years of depression, clinical depression. She was barely able to keep a diary during this time, but it is just devastating to read what is going on. . . .
>
> What happened with the house was that they went out to look for houses a couple of times, but he was busy with something else, and just wanted to get a house. They went out and looked at a bunch of houses, and after they had looked at about ten, there were three or four of them that they were interested in. After going to see one of them, all of a sudden he just whipped out his checkbook, without really any discussion with my mom about this thing. It was a bad, bad thing. That should have been her decision, completely. His attitude was just, "I've got to get back to the office, so let's just buy a house and get on to the next thing." It was a bad, bad mistake that he made. He was not thinking, and didn't grasp what he had done.[49]

Susan corroborated a similar narrative of sacrifice—a sacrifice that Leonard never fully appreciated:

> I need to tell you that this was a really, really hard experience for my mom. . . . [In Logan] Mom had friends who got together to snip beans and shell peas; they helped each other do tomatoes and they watched each other's kids occasionally. She loved Relief Society—she

was converted through Relief Society; she wasn't converted by means of Dad's telling her and testifying. Dad was very, very laid back about her joining the Church. He just left that alone. They got married in a Baptist Church in Raleigh. She really was immersed in this society here in Logan. She was involved in the Faculty Women's League and all kinds of women's clubs.

With Dad receiving this call in January of 1972, we were all thrilled. The phone rang off the wall for days, with people calling and rejoicing in this great event. But it was very difficult for Mom. I think she really sacrificed as much as anybody for Dad to have the career that he did. . . .

She had a friend across the street who was wonderful, and the two hit it off and she had a confidante in her. But that woman died, and then there was another one down the street who became a really close friend. That's what she clung to, a couple of friendships. That was about it.[50]

19

RLDS

Civil disputes are nasty affairs, whether between individuals or institutions. Because Joseph Smith gave no clear, single mandate as to who should succeed him, several rival factions of the Restoration coalesced following his death, each claiming to be the "true church" while denying the truth claims of the others. The most prolonged and vitriolic verbal sparring, which lasted well over a century, arose between the Church of Jesus Christ of Latter-day Saints (LDS), led by Brigham Young and headquartered in Utah; and the Reorganized Church of Jesus Christ of Latter Day Saints (RLDS), led by Smith's oldest son, Joseph III, which remained in the Midwest, moving from Nauvoo, Illinois, to Lamoni, Iowa, and ultimately to Independence, Missouri, its world headquarters.

Young, who led his group out of Nauvoo in 1846, was irritated that Emma Smith, Joseph's widow, refused to accept him as Joseph's successor. She remained in Illinois with her children and her mother-in-law, Lucy Mack Smith, while Joseph's three sisters also stayed nearby. William Smith, the last surviving Smith son, was dropped from the Quorum of the Twelve, his title as church patriarch was denied, and by October 1845 he was excommunicated by the LDS Church. He raged through the Midwest for a decade, joining and leaving—or being expelled from—one expression of Mormonism after another.[1]

There is no evidence that Brigham found William more than an irritant, but Joseph Smith's sons were a different matter, for which he blamed Emma. Brigham's irritation erupted into verbal warfare several years later when RLDS missionaries, hoping to woo Utah Mormons back into their flock, called on him in Salt Lake City. He told them: "Emma [Smith] Bidamon is a wicked, wicked, wicked woman and always was."[2] Three years later, when two of Joseph's sons called upon him, Young called Emma "a liar, yes, the damnedest liar that lives."[3]

Theological warfare between the two churches centered on two questions: Did polygamy originate with Joseph Smith or with Brigham Young? And who was the true successor to Joseph Smith: Brigham Young or Joseph Smith III? The first question was ultimately answered by historians; the second, by its very nature, will never have a consensus answer.

But other issues added fuel to the fire. Paul M. Edwards, a great-grandson of Joseph III, commented: "My mother had cousins out there, and I had heard about the Mormons. Remember, I was raised on the David Smith story—that he went out there and you guys poisoned him. It was not unheard of in the Church, in those days, to make references to, 'Be careful if you go to Utah. Don't tell them you're RLDS.' This was back in the '40s. So there wasn't a lot of connection."[4]

The path to cease-fire and eventual peace appears to have begun with an arm's length exchange between Israel Smith and David O. McKay, initiated by Smith two years before McKay became president of the LDS Church. In June 1949 McKay wrote in his diary, "Just before leaving the office, I autographed one of my photographs for President Israel A. Smith of the Reorganized Church to be delivered in person to Pres. Smith by Wilford C. Wood on his way east. Last week President Israel A. Smith presented me with one of his autographed photographs, delivered in person by Mr. and Mrs. Harry Clark of Salt Lake City."[5]

In January 1956, when the Los Angeles Temple had been completed but not dedicated, McKay arranged a VIP tour of the temple for Israel Smith.[6] The following year, F. Henry Edwards, a member of the RLDS First Presidency, attended the April General Conference in Salt Lake City, thereafter writing to McKay, "I very much enjoyed the two days that I was able to spend in attendance at your conference, and would like to thank you very much for the courtesies extended me. . . . I thought that you presided over the conference with great dignity and that it is quite evident that you have a very warm place in the hearts of your people."[7]

While McKay left no record of a personal visit with Israel Smith, they occasionally exchanged letters, and there was an authentic friendship between the two men. When Smith died in an automobile accident in 1958, McKay telegrammed to Smith's colleagues, "Please express in person to the family of President Smith and official associates our sincere condolence in the tragic death of President Smith with whom I was only recently in friendly correspondence. I esteemed him highly."[8]

The era of good feelings was advanced by Roy Cheville, presiding patriarch of the RLDS Church, who paid a visit to McKay in 1960. McKay recorded the visit in his diary:

In course of conversation [Mr. Cheville] said, "We may not agree theologically and ecclesiastically, but there is no reason why we cannot be Christian brothers." I told him that I appreciated his call, and invited him to call at any time when he is passing through Salt Lake City so that I might become better acquainted with him. I also told him that I had appreciated my acquaintance with President Israel Smith, and that I valued my friendship with him, and was saddened at his death. . . .

After a pleasant interview Mr. Cheville departed saying that he would call again when next he visited Salt Lake.[9]

Cheville called upon McKay several times over the following decade. Of one visit McKay wrote, "After a very pleasant interview, Patriarch Cheville asked if he could say a word of prayer while he was there with us, and I said yes, and for him to proceed. Mr. Cheville then offered a very lovely prayer, in which he asked the Lord's blessings upon us."[10] Their final meeting was just four months before McKay's death. McKay was sleeping in his chair as Cheville entered the apartment. Alvin Dyer, who accompanied Cheville, recorded, "As he sat in the chair, Patriarch Cheville took hold of his hand and this seemed to rouse the President almost immediately."[11]

Undoubtedly, Cheville's diplomacy had a positive influence on an initiative of Richard Howard, who became RLDS church historian in 1966. Visiting Salt Lake City a year afterward, Howard met with Earl Olson and Don Schmidt of the Church Historian's Office. Howard recalled: "They took the whole day and took me through the archives and the library. It was quite a hospitable time together. Out of that meeting came a determination that we wanted to share some things on microfilm between the two churches. They had a lot of things on microfilm that we wanted, and we had some things on our end that they wanted, for example our copy of the Book of Mormon manuscript and the Inspired Version manuscript. . . . So we worked up a want list of things."[12]

The issue of the proposed exchange came before the LDS First Presidency late in 1967. The matter advanced slowly. In late 1968, when specific documents from each church were listed, Alvin Dyer, a counselor to McKay, commented, "This is really a sort of break-through in our relationship with the Reorganized Church" and expressed his approval of the proposal.[13] Three months later, at a First Presidency meeting held in the absence of the ailing McKay, Joseph Fielding Smith, who was simultaneously a counselor in the LDS First Presidency, president of the Quorum of the Twelve Apostles, church historian, a blood relative of Joseph Smith, and author of two polemical pamphlets concerning the RLDS Church,[14] "said he was opposed to making any exchange of documents with these people. It was decided to leave this matter to President Smith and President Dyer to work out."[15]

Less than a year later, Smith became church president, Dyer was released from the First Presidency, and the document exchange was pigeonholed. Earl Olson and Don Schmidt told Richard Howard, "We can't seem to get ratification on this from some of the Brethren, and so we just have to wait until they find themselves ready to do that."[16]

Leonard and the RLDS

Leonard's association with the RLDS Church began when he met Robert Flanders, an RLDS historian whose 1965 book, *Nauvoo: Kingdom on the Mississippi*, was critically acclaimed among historians but panned by many within Flanders's church because of its candid discussion of polygamy during the lifetime of Joseph Smith. In typical fashion, Leonard began to make connections. To Wesley Johnson, coeditor of the soon-to-be-published quarterly *Dialogue: A Journal of Mormon Thought*, Leonard wrote of Flanders, "He partakes of the spirit of ecumenism in wanting intellectuals in the [LDS] Church and the Reorganized Church to erect a bridge of understanding between the two leading branches of Mormonism. I say all of this by way of making this suggestion—that you appoint Dr. Flanders to your Board of Editors."

Then, Leonard suggested that *Dialogue* broaden its reach by reaching out specifically to RLDS scholars. "I feel sure that there are many intellectuals in the Reorganized Church who will want to subscribe and, if invited, participate. . . . If *Dialogue* is a journal of Mormon thought, what is wrong with allowing it to be just that and incorporating the Reorganized Mormons to some limited extent? There is more in common between the two faiths than many of us were once led to believe."[17]

While *Dialogue* did become the "virtual" meeting ground of LDS and RLDS scholars, the Mormon History Association, founded the same year as *Dialogue*, became their literal meeting ground. Alma Blair, an RLDS historian, recalled the tentative first steps to rapprochement:

> We weren't too sure about Mormons, and Mormons weren't too sure about us. But Leonard was open, and smoothed the way for us to talk to each other, and to talk to each other in a friendly fashion, and to learn from each other. I think he was the oil that smoothed all of those possible problems out. . . .
>
> Bob Flanders was one of the first of the RLDS that went to the Mormon History Association. I didn't go the first few times. I'm not

sure quite why. It wasn't that I was worried about it. But Bob went, and then we started going. . . .

We found that the history was our common interest, and good history was common. And then, Leonard helped us work through that, and he encouraged it at the meetings. We'd not only have the big meetings, but then we'd meet afterwards in the smoke-filled hotel rooms, which didn't have any smoke.[18]

Gradually, MHA meetings pulled in more RLDS scholars. Bill Russell, another RLDS historian, recalled his first trip to the annual meeting. "In 1971 Paul Edwards, my next-door office neighbor at Graceland [College] said, 'Lyman [Edwards, Paul's brother], Dick Howard and I are going to drive out to Provo for something called the Mormon History Association. Do you want to ride along?' I said yes. I didn't think much about the Mormon History Association; I just thought it would be cool to ride with Paul, Dick, and Lyman, all three cool guys."

Aware of their minority status, the RLDS historians sat inconspicuously on the back row of the meeting room—inconspicuous, at least, until Leonard came into the room. "I suspect he recognized Dick Howard. He sees us, and he comes down the aisle all excited. He comes in the row in front of us and meets us all, and then he says, 'Move over and make space.' So he climbs over the theater seats and sits in the middle of us and starts rattling off questions. He was just so excited to meet us."[19]

THE DOCUMENT EXCHANGE

Months after the 1971 MHA meeting, Leonard became LDS church historian. In one of the first executive meetings of the new department, Alvin Dyer resuscitated the dormant idea of a document exchange between the two churches. "Elder Dyer expressed hope that something might be worked out in this regard before too long," the minutes read. "A review of the holdings of the Reorganized Church in original manuscripts was discussed as was the holdings of our Church."[20] Not surprisingly, since Joseph Fielding Smith was now church president, the proposal went nowhere.

In 1973, the year following Smith's death, Richard Howard sent a letter to Leonard that put the issue back on the agenda.[21] Leonard had good reason to believe that the proposal might now go through, for the new church president, Harold B. Lee, had told him earlier in the year, "We are now beginning to enjoy good relations with the RLDS officials."[22] An important aspect of the good relations was an invitation from RLDS Church president W. Wallace Smith to Lee, inviting him to Missouri to discuss matters relating to Missouri lands. The meeting did not take place, for Lee died unexpectedly in December.

Shortly after the New Year in 1974, the executives of the Historical Department once again raised the issue hoping that Lee's successor, Spencer W. Kimball, would act upon it favorably. In April, with the explicit endorsement of General Authority and managing director Joseph Anderson, they recommended to the two apostles overseeing the department that the document exchange move to completion.[23]

Buoyed with optimism that the exchange was imminent, Leonard traveled to Nauvoo for the annual meeting of the Mormon History Association. The meeting was a watershed of friendship and cooperation between two groups that, for over a century, had engaged in a continuous war of words. Paul Anderson, who attended that signal MHA conference, recalled, "I think there was a sense in that Nauvoo meeting that everyone was happy to see each other. This really was the first group of people who had really genuinely friendly relations between the two churches. They were so delighted to find out they could be friends, that they had so much in common. I think that was that real sense that the fondness was made especially precious because it was such a surprise that they could get along and like each other."[24]

Leonard and Richard Howard, each the official historian of his own church, made a symbolic gesture that reset the relationship of the two groups. Maureen Ursenbach Beecher recalled that conference as "one of the most beautiful moments," made especially poignant because Nauvoo had been a "battleground" of historical interpretation between the two denominations. The guides from each church for the various historic sites in Nauvoo that each claimed reacted with some consternation, she recalled. "It blew them apart to see Richard Howard and Leonard Arrington arm-in-arm, walking down the streets of Nauvoo. They couldn't tell which of us was of which ilk as we went into the visitors' centers on either side. It was very confusing to them, because it kind of broke down the barriers."[25]

A month after returning from Nauvoo, Leonard and the other executives of the Historical Department met with the entire First Presidency regarding the proposed document exchange, with Howard Hunter conducting the meeting. Hunter began by raising the question as to whether they were authorized to arrange the exchange with the RLDS Church Historian's Office. The First Presidency turned to Bruce McConkie for a reality check, asking if he had gone over the material to determine whether there was anything that might cause later embarrassment to the Church. "He said he had gone over all the revelations which had not previously been published or published previously in the form which we had them. He said there was nothing he could see that would embarrass us."

Satisfied that there was no downside to the exchange, Kimball asked what were the advantages. McConkie said there were many advantages. "We would acquire copies of material that we had been needing for a long time such as the manuscript of the Book of Mormon, the Bible which had provided the basis for the Inspired Version, and letters of Joseph Smith, and so on." Also he thought it would be in the interest of the LDS Church to let the RLDS have copies of materials that it had "so they will understand why we took the position we did on many things. He pointed out the 1831 revelation which first alludes to polygamy and he thought that would be desirable for them to know of it."[26]

After further discussion the First Presidency then agreed to authorize Earl Olson, representing the Historical Department, to conduct negotiations for such an exchange with Richard Howard and to conclude the exchange.[27]

A short time later, Olson and Don Schmidt, LDS Church Archivist, traveled to Independence, Missouri, for the formal exchange. Grant McMurray recalls the moment with exhilaration: "We actually met in the Joint Council room of the Auditorium—this was long before the [RLDS] Temple was built—and literally pushed our microfilm stuff. 'Here's yours.' 'Here's yours.' We had a passing of the stuff. It was like meeting at the halfway point of the bridge. But, it was a very important time. That was the first time that had ever been done."[28]

Permanent Friendship with the RLDS

Courtesy is easy and asks little; lasting friendship requires continual work, but rewards from the work move in both directions. For his part, Leonard gave unambiguous and continual encouragement to RLDS scholars and, in the process, opened new vistas for their research and publication. Richard Howard noted, "He was such an encouragement to the few people in my church that were seriously involved in [doing church history], and to a person every one of us felt buoyed up by his example and his encouragement. . . . He was just such the genuine article. The integrity of this man was remarkable—to watch him in action at the meetings where we would have both of us, we would have these great conversation sessions. He was just so supportive of everybody in the circle, whoever happened to be there."[29]

The conversation sessions were a regular, after-hours part of Mormon History Association meetings. Topics of discussion ranged widely; but in the early 1970s, Leonard's inquiries focused on a new, independent journal, *Courage: A Journal of History, Thought, and Action*, published by RLDS scholars and patterned somewhat after *Dialogue*.[30] Here he received at least as much as he gave. Bill Russell, the founding editor (and the only editor for the unfortunately short-lived periodical) recalled Leonard's candor and appreciation: "He said, 'It seems like I'm taking half my time reading *Courage* and thinking about these mind-bending ideas you guys have.' . . . The fact that he was reading *Courage* in 1971 and 1972, there were some powerful articles in there, from my perspective, such as Dick Howard's on the Doctrine and Covenants and the Book of Abraham."

The Book of Abraham, while part of LDS canon since 1880, had never been canonized by the RLDS Church, and Howard's treatment of it took Leonard in a direction he had not previously considered. Russell continued, "The fact that Leonard was spending a lot of time reading and thinking about those, always suggested to me that he had his own doubts about the received sacred story. The way I would characterize what he said is, 'These are really interesting and thought provoking. They are causing me to think a lot about my faith. Is the received story adequate?' I'm only guessing, but his comments about *Courage* told me a whole lot."[31]

As close as their friendships were, however, one aspect of Leonard's relationship to the RLDS remained enigmatic. Paul Edwards, in praising Leonard as a "real mentor," recalls one of the famous post-conference report-and-share sessions.

> Leonard was as enthusiastic as ever, but during this particular session he was sitting there on the bed, and he kept twitching and moving and picking at himself. Finally I said to him, "Leonard, are you OK?" "Oh," he said, "it's this confounded underwear! It's driving me crazy!" [The "confounded underwear," also known as the temple garment, is worn by members who have participated in the endowment ritual in an LDS Temple.] This was an epiphany! I had read his books. I had admired him from afar. I had got there and I admired him as a person. I loved the way he acted. But I could not believe this intelligent man was wearing mystical underwear! It must have showed, because he said, "Yeah, yeah, I've got 'em on." That memory is so profound! He was such a remarkable man to me, and it just blew my mind. I had heard about Mormons and temple underwear and temple rituals all of my life. I mean, literally all of my life. I did not believe it. It's one of those things you know, but you do not believe. To this day, I find it hard to believe.[32]

There are two ironies in the relationship of Leonard Arrington and the RLDS Church. The first is that the historians, led on the LDS side by Leonard, rather than the ecclesiastical leaders who had initiated theological warfare between the two traditions, took the first steps toward resolving the squabbles that had put them at odds for well over a century. The second is that the RLDS Church treated Leonard with more respect than he received from his own church. Whereas his name was and is revered within the RLDS Church to this day, there are still those within the LDS Church who would deny him his rightful place in its history.

20

STORM CLOUDS

The month of July 1976 was doubly significant for James Allen and Glen Leonard. As U.S. citizens they would join in celebrating their country's bicentennial, and as authors they would celebrate the publication of their church's first comprehensive history since its own centennial in 1930.

THE STORY OF THE LATTER-DAY SAINTS

The impetus for a new history followed the death in 1972 of Joseph Fielding Smith, whose *Essentials in Church History*, first published in 1922 and then in its twenty-seventh edition, was outdated and unreflective of current scholarship. A week after the celebration of the bicentennial, the two authors—"about as faithful as any guys that walked"[1]—gave to each of the executives of the Historical Department a signed copy of their new book, *The Story of the Latter-day Saints*, "just off the press."[2]

The foreword, written by Leonard Arrington, made it clear that the book had been authorized at the highest level: "With the approval of the First Presidency, we asked two of our finest historians, James B. Allen and Glen M. Leonard, to undertake the task of preparing this history."[3] Written for the Latter-day Saint audience, it was intended as the text for church history classes in the Church Educational System as well as the general church membership.

The two authors enumerated in the preface the themes around which the history was written. First was their own conviction "that the Latter-day Saints were basically a religious people and not, as sometimes has been asserted, motivated largely by personal economic or political considerations. . . . They genuinely believed in the authenticity of their faith and were deeply concerned with sharing it with their fellowmen. From the time of Joseph Smith's first vision, the Saints bore constant testimony that the Church was divinely inspired, directed by revelation from God."

Second, although the church was "divinely inspired," it "was always influenced to some degree by the events of the world around it. We think it important to see the institution in the context of its environment, and where appropriate we have tried to demonstrate that relationship."

Third, the story of a church that began in 1830 with six members and, a century and a half later, claimed international membership in the millions, "is one of the essential themes of its history."

Finally, "we are impressed with the dynamics of change within the Church. We have tried to suggest how and why new programs were adopted, old policies reevaluated and changed, and new doctrinal information presented to the Saints."[4] The authors gave no indication of the potential problem of this fourth theme. Although the historical record made it abundantly clear that virtually every doctrine, policy, and practice of the church had evolved significantly since the church's founding and, by inference, was likely to continue to evolve, conservative senior apostles did not take kindly to the notion of change—either real change in the church, or change in the way its story was told. Since that was the issue with them, it hardly mattered how devout the authors were, or how carefully they had written their narrative of change.

The response of readers was overwhelming, with ten thousand copies distributed or sold within the first month.[5] Published reviews in LDS-related journals were very positive, even verging on enthusiastic in some cases. *Sunstone*, a liberal-leaning magazine founded by BYU undergraduates earlier that year, praised the willingness of the authors to allow the reader to draw conclusions: "For too long the LDS Church has weathered the charge that it would not voluntarily endure objective scrutiny. . . . But this one volume by two prominent LDS historians goes a long way toward refuting that charge. . . . The book does lead the reader to the conclusion that the Saints' basic driving force was indeed their faith in Jesus Christ as their redeemer. But we are not led by the nose."[6]

Dialogue called it "the most important volume yet produced in the new Mormon history. . . . As professional historians and active Mormons, the authors have achieved a remarkable blend of the scholarly approach and the religious story. . . . *The Story of the Latter-day Saints* must be judged as a milestone—a refreshing, readable narrative which every Latter-day Saint should not only own, as an indispensable addition to his library, but should read with enthusiasm."[7]

BYU Studies, notable for being published by the church's own university, praised the book for having achieved a delicate balance. "While it does well in educating the reader to a broader and truer view of the Latter-day Saint past, yet the treatment has been softened to accommodate delicate feelings. Many accounts fall short of telling the whole truth, and subjects controversial in some minds are handled with tact and a certain gentleness, softened rather frequently with concluding expressions of confidence, faith, and moral lessons to be drawn from the telling."[8] Given subsequent actions by two senior apostles, one wonders if they ever read this review.

Finally, the *Utah Historical Quarterly*, which, though sponsored by the State of Utah generally treated Mormon subjects with friendliness, began by working both sides of the street. Calling it *"far* superior in scholarship to *Essentials [in Church History]*, it is nevertheless an unabashed apologia for Mormonism," it praised the authors for their willingness to contextualize Mormonism's narrative. "Perhaps the most important lesson Mormons can learn from *The Story of the Latter-day Saints* is that history—yes, even Mormon history—operates in space and time. Taking advantage of important recent scholarship, the authors show that Mormonism arose within a social, intellectual, and cultural environment." It also welcomed the authors' "recognition that Mormonism evolved. . . . In spite of my reservations, I wish to emphasize that given the dilemma imposed upon the authors by the nature of their assignment, their achievement deserves more than just faint praise."[9]

And even though the book was written for LDS audiences, non-LDS reviewers publishing in non-LDS-oriented journals gave it praise. *Arizona and the West* praised the authors, who "have consciously tried to be fair and evenhanded—and their efforts, understandably difficult for church scholars at times, show this approach."[10]

And *Church History*, in a review that reached the broadest audience of non-Mormons, welcomed Mormon history into the larger church tent, and used effusive language in doing so:

> For the first time in Mormon history, an analysis published under semi-official Mormon Church auspices, and covering the entire sweep of Latter-day Saint development, can be judged as serious history. . . . The Mormon experience is placed within history, not outside it, as in all previous such accounts. Allen and Leonard portray Mormonism as a product of sincere religious commitment, influenced by its time and place, subject to internal dynamics of change, and moving toward becoming a genuine world church. . . . To present one's own faith sympathetically yet objectively is always difficult, especially for a literalistic group such as the Mormons. . . . Nevertheless, this account provides a generally objective and fair-minded narrative, free of religious chauvinism. . . . As a path-breaking attempt to understand both the Mormon past and future, this fine product of the revitalized Church Historical Department deserves our most serious consideration.[11]

Decades later, coauthor Glen Leonard commented on the philosophy that drove the writing of the book, and on the popular reaction to it. "The *Story*'s perspective was, 'Let's give them the ground-up meat so they can digest it, and help them put it in a context that they can deal with it, so they don't have to find it first somewhere where it has spikes in it, and they bite, and they get bloodied.' That's the way faithful Latter-day Saint historians write now. They tell it, and they tell it in ways that it is helpful to those who are dealing with it for the first time, so they can have reliable sources that they can turn to, that they can trust."

The reaction, he said, was overwhelmingly positive. "I only had one person who said, 'It's cold.' Everyone else said, 'It's about time the Church did this! Why haven't they done it before? This is wonderful. This helps us.' And that was the purpose. And it worked. It sold a lot. It was a book that church members were ready for."[12]

Against a backdrop of near-unanimous acclaim for the new book, Leonard Arrington was unprepared for a backlash that was swift and overwhelming. Although Boyd Packer's reaction to Dean Jessee's *Brigham Young's Letters to His Sons* should have been an early warning, Leonard had read it as an aberration, and thus failed to see it as a signal of the beginning of the end of the History Division.

Ezra Taft Benson, who saw the hand of God as both the proximate and ultimate cause of the founding and development of the United States of America and of the Church of Jesus Christ of Latter-day Saints, was outspoken not only in delivering that message but also in criticizing any who suggested that other factors might also have been consequential. Just three months prior to the release of *The Story of the Latter-day Saints*, Benson spoke to the students and faculty of Brigham Young University on "God's Hand in Our Nation's History."[13] Citing a plethora of Latter-day Saint scriptures as proof of God's direct influence in establishing the United States, he then turned on those who dared to contextualize what he saw as sacred history. "Today, students are subjected in their textbooks and classroom lectures to a subtle propaganda that there is a 'natural' or a rational explanation to all causes and events. Such a position removes the need for a faith in God, or belief in His interposition in the affairs of men. Events are *only*—and I stress that—*only* explained from a humanistic frame of reference. . . . Why is it that the references to God's influence in the noble efforts of the founders of our republic are not mentioned?"

After spending several minutes to describe "intellectual trends defaming the Founding Fathers," he continued his denunciation, using demeaning and even insulting language. "All too often those who subscribe to this philosophy are not hampered by too many facts. . . . Some have termed this practice as 'historical realism' or moderately call it 'debunking.' I call it slander and defamation. I repeat, those who are guilty of it in their writing or teaching will answer to a higher tribunal."

Benson then turned his attention to his own front yard: "humanistic trends in church history." Here his wrath rose to new heights. "There have been and continue to be attempts made to bring this philosophy into our own Church history. Again the emphasis is to underplay revelation and God's intervention in significant events. . . . It is a state of mind and spirit characterized by one history buff, who asked: 'Do you believe the Church has arrived at a sufficient state of maturity where we can begin to tell our *real* story?' Implied in that question is the accusation that the Church has not been telling the truth."

Once one understands that Benson was speaking from his core beliefs, the sequence of events following the release of *The Story of the Latter-day Saints* may be viewed as not only understandable, but inevitable. When he gave that address, Benson was not even aware that the book was in press—but that was irrelevant, because the strategic issue for him had little to do with the book. Indeed, he did not even need to read the book (and he later acknowledged that he had never read it) in order to have it in his crosshairs, for the real issue was not a book but a philosophy of historiography.

Benson was twenty-three years old when *Essentials in Church History* first appeared, and he was called as an apostle in 1943 at age forty-four. For the next twenty-nine years, Joseph Fielding Smith was his senior in the hierarchy. Although Smith's patriotism never developed the paranoid streak that characterized Benson's, the two men saw eye-to-eye on what constituted a correct approach to history—and that philosophy had become embedded in the Church Historian's Office during the decades that Smith was church historian. *Story* inevitably became the poster child for Benson's campaign to eliminate "humanistic emphasis on history" from the department—a campaign that, in the short term, he won. It didn't even matter that some of the allegations against *Story* had no basis in fact, for if they weren't true for that book, they must have been true *somewhere*. Bill Hartley, one of Leonard's historians, reported an eye-opening conversation he had had with the editor of the *Church News*. When Hartley asked when the *Church News* was going to mention *The Story of the Latter-day Saints*, he was startled to have his query greeted with scornful dismissiveness:

> "Oh, *that* book. We're not going to ever talk about that book. Joseph Smith's 'alleged visions' here and Joseph Smith's 'alleged visions' there." I said, "What are you talking about? I read that last week. There's not a thing in there like that." "Oh, yes there is." Well,

that was evidence that some of the palace guards, as I irreverently call them, some of the staff members on General Authority staffs, who knew what buttons to push, or what would help their boss, or their boss would be interested in—here were some people up there that just did not like good, solid church history.[14]

While Benson had powerful allies in his campaign—most notably Mark Petersen and Boyd Packer—he was its undisputed leader. Had Leonard Arrington fully understood the implications of Benson's speech at BYU, he likely could have scripted the rest of the story.

Benson's campaign against *Story* began within days of when the book was published. Leonard recorded in mid-August that a friend told him that "one or two members of the Quorum of the Twelve had perused"—not read—*Story*, and "did not like it." Their primary gripe was precisely what the published reviews universally praised: "the absence of inspiration—descriptions of occurrences in Church history"—in other words, the environmental context that the authors put forward as one of the book's main themes. The men took their complaints to Benson, who "had a critique prepared by some person or persons and this resulted in a nine-page single-spaced critique. Again, the principal criticism was the lack of divinity in each episode of Church history described." One example related to Leonard would have been comical had it not served as the catalyst for the fierce backlash against *Story*: "Allen and Leonard mention the coming of the seagulls to swallow the crickets without saying the Lord caused the seagulls to come and eat the crickets."

The friend told Leonard that the book was going to be discussed the following day in the weekly meeting of the First Presidency and Quorum of the Twelve in the Salt Lake Temple. Always the optimist, Leonard recorded in his diary, "I feel confident that the book will have more advocates than detractors and that no attempt will be made to halt its sale or to interrupt the processes which are slowly placing it on required reading lists for seminaries, institutes, and classes at BYU. . . . that it will weather the criticisms that some persons are apt to make of it and that it will come to be a standard and well accepted one-volume history of the Latter-day Saints."[15]

His cheerfulness was buoyed several days after the meeting of the Quorum of the Twelve (which he did not attend), when apostle David Haight, who did attend, saw him at lunch. "He stopped me and said, 'Say, I have been thumbing through that new book of yours, *The Story of the Latter-day Saints*. It looks fine.'" Haight asked what the response from others had been. "I told him we had had dozens of responses, some personal visitations, some telephone calls, some letters, and every single person we have had a response from, whether Mormon or non-Mormon, was very enthusiastic about it."

Haight then went to the heart of Benson's issue with the book. "'Joseph Fielding Smith has an approach in which the Lord is responsible for all the things that brought about the growth of the Church and the devil is responsible for all things that interfere with that growth. You don't have that approach, do you?' I said, 'Well, when people experienced the influence of the Lord and said so, we have mentioned that and the devil as well. But there are a wide variety of things that bring about certain developments, economic, political, natural, and so on, and we bring those into the account.'" In a dramatic departure from Benson's criticism, Haight replied, "I am glad you do. . . . I realize that some of our history is controversial, but we can't avoid that nor do I think we can restrict our history to telling about things the Lord caused or the devil caused. We have to tell a straightforward story. I hope you will continue to do that."[16]

Leonard was greatly encouraged by this revelation of support from an apostle, but there is no evidence currently available that, when hostilities later began in earnest, Haight, who was the most junior apostle at the time, argued for his view of history or that he defended the History Division's approach.

The following day, Leonard wrote to his children with mixed news. "We understand Public Communications has ordered 5,000 copies of *Story of the Latter-day Saints* to place one in every library in the United States. On the other hand, there are a few people that think it is too secular—not spiritual enough. Well, we knew we'd have criticism from both sides. It's a tightrope we're walking."[17]

Four days later, in a meeting with Historical Department executives, Delbert Stapley, who had replaced Bruce McConkie as one of the department's two apostolic advisors, "reported that he had heard some criticism of the book in that some of the facts given in the book were inaccurate. Brother Arrington indicated that if we could obtain further information as to which statements were inaccurate, they would be happy to make corrections in the next edition."[18] But a list of inaccuracies was never forthcoming, for the reason that the real objections from Benson and his colleagues related not to the *substance* of the book, but to its *tone*.

At the same meeting, Leonard announced that another book, *Building the City of God*, which contained a history of the United Order in nineteenth-century Mormonism, would be off the press in a few days. "He explained that this book was not published under the sponsorship of the Historical Department but was one on which he had been working for a number of years and which should also be credited to two other authors."[19] It, too, came into Benson's crosshairs.

Three days later Leonard gave his children an upbeat status report in his weekly letter. "[Benson] has ordered it read and has scheduled a debate in the Twelve on whether we should have someone read all our stuff before it goes to the publisher. . . . I feel very confident that we will come out all right in the discussion of the Twelve. We've had many expressions of approval of our work, and think this will continue. . . . I saw the Prophet [Spencer Kimball] on Monday and he gave me a very warm handshake and patted me on the back and told me how much he appreciated what we are doing."[20]

Two days later, Leonard's mood was more somber as he wrote a lengthy and painfully perceptive diary entry that gave context to the criticisms being levied against *Story*. It began by noting that a friend had given Leonard "the complete critique" of *Story* that Benson had commissioned, which consisted of eight single-spaced, typewritten pages whose authorship Leonard attributed to William O. Nelson, a personal assistant to Benson. Specific criticisms and recommendations were:

- Joseph Fielding Smith's *Essentials in Church History* should be kept in print, rather than being phased out and replaced by *Story*.

- *Story* contained in its bibliography works that the commentator considered "anti-Church," including Fawn Brodie's classic *No Man Knows My History* and several articles from *Dialogue*.

- It did not bring "God into the picture" in relating the story of the crickets and seagulls.

- Its account of Zion's Camp implied that the expedition had been a failure.

- Its account of the 1911 firing of BYU professors for their belief in organic evolution was not "sufficiently anti-evolution."

- It did not contain the doctrinal contributions of Joseph Fielding Smith (although the critique failed to suggest what those were).

- It secularized the history of the church.

- All future publications from the History Division "should be routed through Correlation in order to insure that they were doctrinally and historically accurate, and had the right tone and impact."

The book had been discussed by the Quorum of the Twelve in their regular Thursday meeting on September 2, but was deemed a sufficiently important matter that a special meeting in the temple was held three days later, on a Sunday. At the time he wrote the diary entry, he had not heard the outcome of the Sunday meeting. "I have been hurt by this episode," particularly by the failure of any of the General Authorities to contact him, James Allen, or Glen Leonard and allow them to defend the book.

Feeling powerless in the face of Benson's attack on "real" history, he saw two options for his future. "Shall I retain the job (assuming they don't release me) and try to write history which will be approved by Correlation. Or shall I resign and continue to write 'real history.' . . . I am not clear in my own mind as to the best course to pursue, but feel discouraged, sad, shook. It has been a tough few days for me since I do not dare mention all this to a soul."[21]

Although he presented himself with only two options, they comprised a false dichotomy. There was a third option and that was the one that he ultimately chose, even though it was not successful in the long run: keep his job, continue to write candid history without trying to gain approval from Correlation, and hope that he could survive the balancing act.

The critique, which was the most detailed that Leonard would receive of *Story*, sidestepped completely his earlier request—"Show us the inaccuracies and we will fix them"—for the simple reason that inaccuracies (if indeed there were any) were not the issue. The real issue was that Benson was determined to terminate the History Division, and *Story* was simply the catalyst that initiated the process. While it took another six years for him and his allies to complete their work of disassembly, it was already "game over." Leonard's observation that Benson would not stand for "real" history and that Leonard and his coworkers were powerless in the face of his opposition was spot on, and one wonders how he could have operated subsequent to this time with such denial of the inevitable outcome—but he did.

The following day, Delbert Stapley summoned Leonard to his office for a wide-ranging discussion. Although the central subject of the meeting, as Leonard might have guessed, was *Story of the Latter-day Saints*, the request to meet with Stapley came with no indication of the details of the meeting, and hence no chance for Leonard to prepare for it or to bring relevant materials.

Stapley began the meeting by describing the Sunday temple meeting, apparently having been assigned to do so. One subject that had been discussed was the mandate that Leonard had been given when called to the position of church historian. "He asked me if at the time I was appointed Church Historian I was given a letter of appointment which outlined my duties. I told him no, that the call had been made by the First Presidency in January 1972 as the result of a personal interview and that subsequently my name was sustained in the April 1972 meeting of the general conference." His specific duties had never been written; instead, they "had been worked out under the direction of Brother Alvin Dyer during the four months he was our managing director until he had his stroke."

Stapley kept probing, wanting "to know specifically whether we had been counseled about having somebody read our manuscripts before they are published"—something that had not happened prior to the publication of *Story*. Leonard replied that Harold Lee and his counselors had approved Leonard's proposal that he, the two assistant church historians, and the department's editor be the screening committee for all publications.

Would Leonard agree to a new arrangement whereby one or more members of the Twelve would review manuscripts prior to publication? "I told him that we are at the service of the brethren and would not object to their wishes but that before such an arrangement was made I would like the opportunity of giving in some detail the reasons why the other screening committee seemed to be preferable." It was not the answer Stapley had hoped for, and his response "suggested that he had been directed by the Quorum of the Twelve to set up such a Quorum of the Twelve screening committee. So that matter was apparently decided on Sunday."

Stapley then relayed the sentiment of some within the Twelve that "we should not put anything in any of our histories that reflects badly on the Church. . . . I replied that if our picture is entirely rosy nobody, even members of the Church, will have confidence in what we write because members of the Church know that there are warts and blemishes and unless we acknowledge some of these they will not have confidence that we are writing the whole truth and nothing but the truth. His reply was again, we must leave the bad things out of our history."

Reflecting on the meeting in his diary entry, Leonard questioned his fitness for the position he held—"whether a professionally trained historian ought to be Church Historian since he will be called to submit the things he writes and approves to a committee of people who are not trained historians."[22] Whether or not it *ought* to be the case, Leonard's tenure was the only time in the nearly two-century history of the church when a professionally trained historian was church historian.

Never in his professional life had Leonard been presented with such a clear and painful dilemma: Would he continue to write history at the standards demanded by the norms of his profession, and thus disobey what essentially was a direct order from the ecclesiastical line; or would he write only good-news history that might satisfy the ecclesiastical line, but that would betray his professional norms as well as demolish his credibility with readers? He still held the Redd Chair at BYU, and thus would still have had an income if he had resigned as church historian; but he elected instead to try to achieve what would prove to be an impossible balancing act. He chose the *status quo*.

Ten days after Stapley met with Leonard, Benson spoke to Church Educational System employees gathered in the Assembly Hall on Temple Square. He picked up where he had left off with his BYU speech in March, referring directly to the speech as he continued to pummel the historians. "We would warn you teachers of this trend [to underplay revelation and God's intervention in significant events], which seems to be an effort to reinterpret the history of the Church so that it is more rationally appealing to the world. We must never forget that ours is a prophetic history."[23]

Then, without mentioning the title of either book, he lashed out at *The Story of the Latter-day Saints* and *Building the City of God*, the latter having been published by church-owned Deseret Book during the first week of September. He first took on *Story*'s account of the Word of Wisdom. "To suggest, for example, that the Word of Wisdom was an outgrowth of the temperance movement in America and that Joseph Smith selected certain prohibition and dietary features from that movement and presented them to the Lord for confirmation is also to pronounce an explanation contradictory to the one given by Brigham Young."

In fact, the Word of Wisdom *was* a direct outgrowth of the American Temperance Movement, which began in 1826 and swept across the country in response to epidemic drunkenness incident to a tripling in per capita consumption of distilled spirits over the prior three decades. Every detail in the Word of Wisdom can be found in temperance literature predating the revelation; a chapter of the American Temperance Society was organized in Kirtland, Ohio, in 1830, shortly before the fledgling church moved there from New York State; and a widely publicized, national day of temperance observance was held on February 26, 1833, just one day prior to the revelation.[24] But Leonard's foes in the Twelve never allowed data to shape or slow their attacks.

Benson next took aim at the second book, *Building the City of God*, which used the word "communal" in describing the United Order—which had been, by very definition, a utopian, communitarian society. "The Church never was, and under existing commandments never will be, a communal society, under the directions thus far given by the Lord. The United Order was not communal nor communistic. It was completely and intensely individualistic."[25] Benson, always the Cold Warrior, simply would not tolerate anything that even sounded like Soviet Communism, definitions notwithstanding.

Four days after Benson's speech, the First Presidency—Spencer Kimball, Eldon Tanner, Marion Romney—convened a meeting that included themselves, Ezra Taft Benson, Mark Petersen, Howard Hunter, Bruce McConkie, and Leonard. Leonard must have hoped for a strong statement of support, but he must also have felt considerable trepidation. He wrote in his diary a detailed account of the meeting.

Kimball began the meeting by noting the two books that had been the target of Benson's criticism, and asked Benson to explain his concerns. Benson admitted "that he had not read all of either book," but said that one member of the Twelve had read *Story* completely, and others had read portions of it. He then read aloud a two-page, singled-spaced typed letter from a church member that complained about *Story*. Lacking in specific criticisms, it nonetheless alleged that the book "would cause young people to lose faith; it tended to degrade or demean Joseph Smith; it did not give enough emphasis to important events such as the founding of the Church (only 16 lines and the names of the six persons not given); it had raised questions." Benson then offered his own assessment that *Story* should never have been published, "and that it would do great damage."

With Kimball's consent, Leonard responded to Benson's remarks. Mark Petersen then went on the offensive, after which Leonard responded to his remarks as well. Leonard's defense was that the responses the History Division had received to the book were "very enthusiastic and favorable"; that since the book also had a non-Mormon audience, "we tried to be careful in our statements, provide evidence, and so on"; that the contextualizing of the story was an attempt "to show that the Lord was preparing the people to receive the restored Gospel"; and that certain controversial subjects—the Mountain Meadows Massacre, differing versions of the First Vision, the ban on ordination of blacks—were already so well known that "they had to be put in their proper light."

Kimball then shifted the discussion to the sixteen-volume sesquicentennial history project, asking Leonard to review his understanding of how its volumes were to be screened and approved. Kimball read from minutes of meetings that had discussed the approval process, thus corroborating Leonard's account that the agreement had been that the manuscripts, after undergoing review by the History Division's internal committee, "were to be read also by a person assigned by President Kimball from the Quorum of the Twelve and the book was not to be published until approved at that level."

At this point in the meeting, Leonard asked that the ecclesiastical review step never be made public, "that whatever suggestions or changes were made by them would be suggested by me in my own name; this for the purpose of not diminishing our credibility as historians and raising the cry of censorship of our works." All present "seemed to agree to that arrangement."

Kimball then directed Leonard to submit the manuscripts to Howard Hunter, "who would then submit them to President Kimball for assignment of a reader to convey their reactions to me." While the tone of the meeting was positive, thanks to the implicit support of Kimball, the church president concluded with cautionary advice to Leonard: "He thought we should be concerned more with writing for a church audience than for the scholars, the professors, the students, the outside world. I bore my testimony as to my belief that a person could write for both audiences successfully, and he and specifically President Tanner expressed agreement with this and suggested that I continue under this assumption."[26]

In retrospect, it appears that Leonard's assumption rested on shaky ground, given the events that subsequently unfolded. However, he had the specific endorsement of the church president as well as Eldon Tanner, who had been in the First Presidency for over a decade. And although Kimball's eventual decline in health created a power vacuum that the senior apostles boldly filled, at this point in time he was in good health, and his most important and influential days lay ahead.

Leonard felt protected, and he continued his diary entry on an optimistic note. "I felt very good about the meeting: (a) in having the opportunity of responding personally to the criticisms that had been made of our publications; (b) that they did not require us to clear our things through Church Correlation; (c) that President Kimball seemed to be supportive and friendly as were his counselors. . . . I think I managed to quiet some of the criticism."[27] In fact, he did not quiet the criticism—not for lack of coherent argument, but because Benson and Petersen cared not a whit for *any* argument. In their minds testimony was no longer being taken because the judgment had already been made. All that remained was the execution of the penalty, and although it was delayed, it was not denied.

Meeting the next day with Davis Bitton and James Allen, Leonard summarized the meeting for them and then struck a realistic tone about the two senior apostles who had staked out oppositional positions.

> Elders Benson and Petersen will never accept books written by us, given our understanding of history. They want the glorious stories of the Restoration, unsullied by discussion of practical problems and controversial evidence. They want Prophets without warts, revelation direct from on High in pure vessels. They want faith-promoting stories and moral homilies. They feel strongly and will vigorously oppose all our books, written as we understand history. We must therefore write books which will be appreciated and defended by the other Brethren.[28]

Leonard's game plan rested on two assumptions, neither of which was true. First, he assumed that other General Authorities would jump to his defense on principle, the principle being that no matter what the political cost might be, the writing of candid, honest history must proceed. And second, he assumed that "the other Brethren," likely meaning more than two, would be able to overcome the opposition of the two most senior apostles in a system where seniority was of paramount importance, and where the gradual incapacitation of the sitting president, Spencer Kimball, would concede far more power to the two than they then held.

Two weeks later, Leonard reported the meeting with the First Presidency to his entire staff in upbeat language. He felt "very encouraged, in spite of some rumors. We have known all along that some of the Brethren don't favor the kind of history we write. But we have others in high places who are strong supporters." He saw the challenge as being more cosmetic than structural. "We should be more careful than we have been and should consult more often with our advisors [but] do not expect to be forced to compromise our basic integrity as historians. We're talking about questions of wording."[29]

But the upbeat language did not alter the essential message that trumped all others: Benson's position was immovable. It would only be a matter of time, given the gradual deterioration of Spencer Kimball's health, before he would win, especially since junior apostles with an eye to their own careers would take care not to oppose him.

The junior historians Leonard was mentoring must have left the meeting with a renewed commitment to continue writing the "best" history they could according to contemporary standards. To an acquaintance later in the month, Leonard painted an even rosier and less realistic picture. "Things continue to go well here. As we expected, there has been a little criticism of our one-volume history, *The Story of the Latter-day Saints* by Jim Allen and Glen Leonard, but it was only a momentary thing."[30]

On October 19, Stapley invited Leonard, Joseph Anderson, and Earl Olson to his office for a meeting whose subject was not indicated in advance. "When we got to Elder Stapley's office we discovered Elder [Howard] Hunter was there as well." The purpose of the meeting was to discuss the books that the History Division was publishing, especially *Story*. "Elder Stapley said in fairly strong terms that our primary goal must be to write for members of the Church, especially young people."[31]

Afterward, Hunter took Leonard aside and gave him an extraordinary assessment of the situation—extraordinary in that he freely acknowledged a deep division of opinion among the Quorum of the Twelve on matters of writing history, and was candid in criticizing the philosophy of historiography that Benson and others held:

> "Leonard, I want you to understand that while it is difficult for me to be at odds with certain of my brethren I am in complete agreement with your point of view and with your policies. I want you to know this so you will not feel you are alone in standing up against the views of some of the brethren. I agree completely that you must keep in mind the audience of professional historians and scholars.

You are doing a great work there in influencing their treatment of the Church and its leaders. I also agree completely that you must give a balanced view of our history. In the law it is not only unethical and immoral to misstate a fact; it is equally unethical and immoral to leave out a pertinent fact. We must surely be honest in our own history and we have nothing to fear from being honest and candid and pointing out some of the weaknesses and problems of some of the brethren. We must do it if our treatment is to be believed. I think you also ought to know that there are other brethren who agree with this."

Leonard's reaction revealed the stress he had been enduring and the relief that this kindly attorney-cum-apostle's personal support gave him: "I felt like crying. This seemed to relieve all of my anxiety and to settle the matter of the legitimacy of my call and my work. I once more felt completely confident of what I am doing and the role I am playing and also completely satisfied about what we have done in the past."[32]

In the aftermath of this and prior meetings, Leonard wrote a diary entry that acknowledged events of three days. "I began to doubt whether I was the right person to have this assignment and I began to consider seriously whether to offer my resignation and whether to consider seriously other employment. A new position in Western History will open up at the University of Utah in the next few months as they attempt to replace Dave Miller who is retiring. I thought this might be a logical place for me to go and that it was quite possible that I might be able to get the appointment."[33]

On the day before Thanksgiving, Leonard received a phone call from a friend, reporting a meeting earlier that day of the board of directors of Deseret Book Company. While the news was good on the surface, once again Leonard failed to appreciate that a long game was being played—a game that put the ultimate victory on Benson's side. "After the meeting, Deseret Book [board members] were told privately that President Kimball had just completed reading the book [*Story*] for himself, that he liked the book very much, that he couldn't understand those who objected to it, and that he thought it was a fine piece of work." To Leonard, this meant but one thing: "We were right, after all, in our judgment about the tone and contents of the book, and that the only mistake we had made was tactical—authorizing it under an introduction mentioning the approval of the First Presidency." He interpreted Kimball's approval of *Story of the Latter-day Saints* as assurance that other projects, most notably the sesquicentennial history, would succeed. He ended the diary entry with unbridled enthusiasm: "GLORY HALLELUJAH!!!"[34]

The end of 1976 essentially marked the end of the controversy over *The Story of the Latter-day Saints.* Leonard was able to declare a victory of sorts by the fact that the book was allowed to remain in print until the extraordinarily large first printing run of 35,000 copies was sold—having missed the shredder, according to one secondary source, by one, unspecified vote.[35] But it was only a tactical victory and a hollow one at that, for the primary factor that kept it in print was economic rather than philosophical: Deseret Book Company could not afford to lose its investment in the first printing.[36]

In 1980, when Spencer Kimball was suffering the effects of a subdural hematoma that was treated surgically, his brother-in-law, George Boyd, told him some of the details of the *Story,* particularly the treatment given to Leonard and to the book's authors, and Benson's stated determination to prevent a second printing. "President Kimball wept and declared that this was not a Christian way to treat somebody who had performed satisfactorily an assignment. . . . [He] told George that Elder Benson did not have the right to stop the reprinting of the book—did not have the authority."[37] Lack of authority notwithstanding, Benson and his allies succeeded in delaying a second printing until 1986,[38] four years after the History Division had been disbanded and moved to BYU. And Leonard's tactical victory was more than offset by his strategic defeat, for the *Story* episode marked a permanent downturn in the fortunes of the History Division.

Having vacillated for six months between optimism and pessimism with respect to *Story,* Leonard ended 1976 by writing an assessment that proved to be prophetic:

> I was shaken by the way in which these brethren [Benson and Petersen] had their way; by the failure of anyone to defend the book, to speak up for it, to explain why we felt it was a good book. The entire episode convinced me that there are some Brethren, including the two persons next in line to be president of the Church and president of the Quorum of Twelve, who would not approve of any of our work—not just this book but our methods, our goals, our approach and attitude toward the Church and its history. We have to reckon with the distinct possibility that, upon President Kimball's death, these brethren, if they are still alive, will probably replace us and greatly diminish and alter the work of studying and writing about church history.[39]

Kimball gave his last conference talk in April 1981, four and a half years before his death. The subdural hematoma he had suffered in September 1979 recurred in 1981, leading to a presidential limbo.[40] In the four years between 1981 and his

death in 1985, his intellectual and physical capacity diminished steadily. His counselors, Eldon Tanner and Marion Romney, were, respectively, eighty-three and
eighty-four in 1981. Gordon Hinckley's appointment to the First Presidency in 1981
meant that an astute and vigorous administrator was managing church affairs; but
clearly, Kimball's waning energies had to be directed only to issues of the highest
priority. The History Division was not on the list, and in 1982, thanks in large
part to Hinckley's role, Leonard and his colleagues were replaced.

G. HOMER DURHAM

On April 29, 1977, at age eighty-eight, Joseph Anderson was relieved of his duties as managing director of the Historical Department.[41] Eldon Tanner announced to the staff of the department that the new managing director, effective
immediately, would be G. Homer Durham, then sixty-six years old. Leonard
wrote to his children that night, with genuine enthusiasm, "We are very pleased
with the choice. He has been a good supporter, these many years."[42] "Many
years" referred to cumulative time of association, for at the time of his new appointment Durham had been a General Authority—a member of the First Quorum of the Seventy—for only four weeks, and this was his first assignment in his
new calling.

Durham had close ties to the hierarchy. His wife, Eudora, was a daughter of
John Widtsoe (1872–1952), a Harvard University–educated apostle with genuine
intellectual interests whose pre-apostolic career had included the presidency of
both Utah State University (1907–1916) and the University of Utah (1916–1921).
Lacking sons, Widtsoe had become deeply attached to the bright and devoted
Durham, who had served under him as a missionary while Widtsoe was president
of the European Mission (1926–1932).

That mission brought Durham into an equally close personal relationship with
another missionary, Gordon Hinckley. The two were companions at a time when
anti-Mormonism was flourishing in Great Britain.[43] Despite Durham's solid credentials as an educator (his degrees and appointment were in political science) and
historian, his personal allegiance—and perhaps his personal ambitions as well—
were to the ecclesiastical, rather than the professional.

A month after Durham assumed his duties within the Historical Department,
Leonard's pleasure had turned to ambivalence, and he wrote a mixed review that
assessed his new boss and compared him to his predecessor:

 1. He is very proud of his achievements and experiences.
 2. He likes to drop names of people and places he has been and
   experiences he has had.

3. He wants to *run* the department; that is, set goals and objectives and means of attaining goals and objectives.

4. He is sincerely respectful of me and of the staff of our division and wishes sincerely to help us in our mission.

In brief, he is very different from Elder Anderson, who made no attempt whatsoever to tell us what to do or enter into our professional decision-making. Every matter we took up with him, he simply said we should discuss it with our advisors or with the First Presidency. He did not run interference for us or attempt to protect us from the criticisms and brickbats of those who had reason to dislike or oppose what we had done or were doing. He was sweet and kind and helpful.[44]

Two days later, with his usual cheerfulness, Leonard wrote an upbeat reinterpretation to his children: "The department is going to be a more lively place. He wants to read all that we write, too, and that's going to take some doing on his part. He's a fast reader. He makes suggestions but he seems to have no desire to be a censor."[45] Writing two decades later, however, Leonard gave a much more nuanced report: "Durham sincerely believed he was protecting our best interests—or the best interest of church history. He said that shortly after his appointment he asked Joseph Anderson what land mines to avoid. Anderson assured him there were none, that things were going along very well with the department and with the manner in which the department was being received by others. But when Durham was called in by a few members of the Twelve who expressed grave concern about the History Division, he knew that there were plenty of land mines."[46]

"Grave concern" was one part of the message from the apostles; "tighten up procedures" was the other.[47]

ALTERED DIRECTION

The franchise that Durham inherited was unique within the entire church. The historians within the History Division were on "hard money"—academic parlance for salaries that came through line items in the institutional budget. "Soft money," which increasingly has become the norm within private universities and many public universities, requires the professor to obtain much or all of the salary through grants, contracts, and other means—a much more tenuous situation. While Leonard and his coworkers had the luxury of living on hard money, albeit with a salary scale that was not competitive with academe, their productivity was not subject to the kind of scrutiny that was standard in university departments, even for those living on soft money. Once Leonard's grand plan was approved by Harold B. Lee's First Presidency, he and his staff were largely left alone to work out the specifics, in terms both of what to write and how quickly to write it. For the History Division, it was a sweet deal—no wonder that Davis Bitton retroactively applied the label of "Camelot."

The other sweet spot that the History Division occupied was a special exemption from Correlation,[48] a movement that had gathered power over the previous decades until, by the 1970s, it constituted an internal kingdom that affected virtually every aspect of the church's work. Most significantly for Leonard, it had almost total control over official church publications. Though nominally under the management of a committee of General Authorities, its actual tasks were carried out by professional bureaucrats who brought with them their personal views and expertise, but also an intense desire to carry out the wishes of their General Authority supervisors as transmitted down the chain of command. Access was power, but access to General Authorities was limited.

The reorganization effected by the implementation of the Cresap study, though much needed for administrative efficiency, shrank the opportunities of midlevel management for access to top leaders and also greatly increased the number of links in the chain of communications. A further restriction was a basic fact of life of General Authorities: a pool of aging men who had to deal with colleagues who were also aging. Health problems were inescapable and increased from year to year. The smallness of the group of men at the top who could make decisions meant that they trusted and relied heavily on gatekeepers. As a result, for those each step further down in the communication chain, a great deal of energy went into attempts to intuit how a particular General Authority would decide a particular matter, and then act on the assumption that one's intuition was correct. Clear-cut public statements like Benson's greatly simplified the task.

Earlier attempts at establishing a firm hierarchy with line control over virtually every activity dated back to 1908 and had been periodically revived, but none succeeded to the extent originally envisioned. Prior to 1960, when the modern correlation movement had begun, each organization—Relief Society, Sunday School, Primary, Young Men's Mutual Improvement Association, Young Women's Mutual Improvement Association, the Primary Association, and the Church Education System (seminary and institute)—selected, wrote, and printed its own courses of study, generally with little or no cross-talk between organizations. Church president David O. McKay assigned Apostle Harold B. Lee to head Correlation in 1960 with the primary goal of eliminating overlap and contradiction.

As the movement evolved, however, it took on a larger and larger portfolio; and by the time Leonard was called as church historian, all church publications—including lesson manuals and magazines—required, first, passage through the church's internal editing division (with numerous opportunities for second-guessing whether a particular item was "acceptable" or not), and then reading by the respective correlation committee (adult, teen, or children) that had control over every item that appeared with the church's name on it: manuals, magazines, artwork, newsletters, and letters to the field. Examples in prior chapters of this book document instances when seemingly trivial items were denied publication because of correlation rulings.

As a prior university professor who had enjoyed twenty-six years of academic freedom in publishing books and articles, Leonard bristled at the thought of having nonhistorians in the Correlation Department review and correct what he and his coworkers would write—particularly when he was aware of the hassles surrounding pierced ears (described in chapter 14), or of the fact that the *Ensign* would not allow quotations from the twenty-six volume *Journal of Discourses* and even turned thumbs down on any reference to polygamy. "We were doing a series of articles on the families of Church presidents," recalled the editor assigned from the magazine to work with the history articles. "I heard, in a roundabout way, that the ban on the *Journal of Discourses* was because it included Brigham Young's sermons on Adam-God and blood atonement. The ruling against polygamy was left over, I think, from the attempt to make the church respectably monogamous in post-Manifesto days, and the fear that even mentioning the word would somehow give the fundamentalists ammunition. But I'm not sure. We didn't get reasons, just instructions. You can imagine what those two rules did to an article about Brigham Young. It was so exasperating!"[49]

In a diary entry in late 1973, Leonard was adamant about the subject: "If we had to go through correlation and get approval from higher ecclesiastical authority for all we publish, then we might as well close up shop. If history is going to be an aspect of doctrine and missionary work, then our department should not exist."[50]

The first time the issue of Correlation came up with Leonard, as noted in chapter 14, was in the context of the original approval of the Sesquicentennial History project in April 1972, just one week after Leonard was sustained in general conference as the new church historian: "It was noted that all writings that are produced should be submitted to the Correlation Committee for their approval."[51]

Leonard raised no objections at the time; but in later years neither he nor his associates made reference to this early decision—quite the opposite, in fact, for in the midst of the controversy over *The Story of the Latter-day Saints* in 1976, he was alarmed at the possibility that the sesquicentennial volumes might have to be submitted to Correlation. Either he had genuinely forgotten that he had agreed to exactly such conditions four years earlier or his exposure to its internal workings in the interim had solidified his alarm into concrete opposition. In mid-August 1976, when the magnitude of Benson's and Petersen's disdain for professional history was becoming apparent, he noted in his diary: "It is conceivable that sufficient concern will be expressed that we may be required to run all of our manuscripts through Church correlation. Even that tactic will probably not secure the approval of the First Presidency and the entire quorum. If it should, we will be in real trouble with our *History of the Latter-day Saints,* the 16-volume history being prepared in connection with the sesquicentennial."[52]

On several other occasions, both earlier and later, the issue of submitting History Division manuscripts to correlation prior to publication came up, and each time Leonard reacted aggressively to maintain the division's literary independence. In late November 1974, in the aftermath of Boyd Packer's letter to the First Presidency concerning Dean Jessee's *Letters of Brigham Young to His Sons,* the subject received serious consideration in a meeting of Leonard, Earl Olson, Howard Hunter, and Bruce McConkie. In response to a question from Olson as to whether Packer's letter meant that all History Division material was now to go through the Correlation Committee, McConkie spoke forcefully in favor of maintaining the division's *status quo.* "He said they [Correlation] were given their assignment to read manuscripts for manuals—for presentation in Sunday School and Priesthood classes. To be sure that the doctrine was right. Here, he said, we have something different. If one of our books was to be used as a manual then presumably they would go over it, and eliminate this and that and change, but for the uses we had in mind, he thought they had to be read and approved by people who knew history." Hunter, the senior of the two apostles, agreed.[53]

One month later, in spite of McConkie's and Hunter's stated aversion to correlation, Olson again raised the issue with Leonard. "Earl said something about clearing things through correlation. I said that would be the worst thing that could happen. How can they possibly judge us on what is good history and what is bad history?"[54]

In the midst of the fireworks over *The Story of the Latter-day Saints,* Delbert Stapley, one of the Historical Department's two apostolic advisors at the time, had, in reporting the Sunday meeting of the First Presidency and Twelve, wanted to see Leonard's "letter of appointment" outlining his duties. Leonard had reported the verbal authorization he had received and had also rebuffed Stapley's request/recommendation that he submit manuscripts to Correlation. Leonard had explained the internal screening committee he had set up with, as he stressed, First Presidency approval, that substituted for correlation. After Leonard met with the First Presidency, Benson, Petersen, Hunter, and McConkie on September 21, he declared victory on the main issue though acknowledging new limitations to balance his continued autonomy: "We shall not have to clear our books and articles through Correlation. We shall have to work more closely with our advisors. We shall have to go to them more often for counsel and clearance on problems, and they may take some of these to the quorum. This is the minimum alternative to Correlation Committee clearance."[55]

But the issue was never quite as simple as Leonard had made it out to be, and that was why it came up again and again. The History Division was an outlier; and to many within the hierarchy, the special status didn't make sense, especially when it was generating controversy. As a follow-up to the September meeting with the First Presidency, Stapley and Hunter, the Historical Department's advisors, asked that Leonard document the background of *Story*. In a lengthy written response, he justified the division's special exception on the basis of a conversation— not a document—with Church president Harold B. Lee in August 1973. He prefaced the report by writing, "Let me copy from my own diary record the consequent conversation":

> President Lee then began talking about the problem of having committees read books by General Authorities. He then told me some experiences, which I regard as confidential and am therefore not recording. I was somewhat surprised that he would speak to me so frankly about these matters.
>
> President Lee then talked to me about the histories we were writing. He expressed the feeling that I should establish a screening committee of professional historians who were loyal to the Church, and that this committee should help assure that our books were accurate and readable. He did not believe, he said, that the Correlation Committee was equipped to evaluate our history books. He thought this should be done by professionally trained historians.[56]

But there was a problem with that account: It did not square with Leonard's actual diary entry for that date, which read,

> He [Lee] began talking about the problem of having committees read books by Church authorities. He said that he had served as a member of a committee (I gather as chairman of a committee) to read works by the General Authorities. He said they had had problems only with two authors or books—one of them was a book by Brother Ezra T. Benson. The reading committee made a number of suggestions and President Lee said when the book came out it did not incorporate a single one of any of the suggestions.[57]

Perhaps Lee had discussed a Correlation Committee decision with Leonard, but the diary entry that recounts that conversation does not substantiate such a discussion. It appears that Leonard took literary license with the diary entry in writing to the two apostles in 1976, clearly for the purpose of strengthening his case that his division should be exempted from Correlation.

There is no indication that Homer Durham was aware of the entire sequence of discussions regarding the History Division and correlation—not surprising, since the sequence was not clear even to Leonard, who had been there at every step of the journey. One thing, however, was clear to Durham, and that was that he came into the new job with a mandate to reel in a group that, whatever its prior justifications and authorizations, was out of step with the rest of the bureaucracy. Whether through the Correlation Committee or through other means, Durham had a mandate to change the tone of the publications emerging from the History Division.

Durham's first meeting with the entire division on May 3, 1977, sent shock waves through the already nervous members of the History Division, though more for tone and nuance than substance. Jim Allen, interviewed almost three decades later, still remembered the essence of Durham's message: "The first talk that he gave to us . . . was, 'You have to be careful. You have to write your history in the image of Brother Benson.' I don't know whether he meant the same thing that it implied to me. I think what he meant was, 'You have to remember that Brother Benson and other people are going to be concerned about what comes out of the Historical Department.' I think that's what he was saying. But just that term frightened me, as a scholar, and I know it frightened other people, as scholars."[58]

THE NEW MORMON HISTORY

As had been the case three years earlier with Reed Durham's presidential address on Mormonism and Freemasonry at Nauvoo, Leonard was caught off-guard by an event over which he had no control, but that had a detrimental effect on the History Division. He called it "another land mine . . . that later exploded."[59] In May 1977, Richard Marshall wrote an honors thesis for his bachelor's degree at the University of Utah. He borrowed the title, "The New Mormon History,"[60] from a *Dialogue* article written by Robert Flanders and published three years earlier.[61] Leonard, already hypersensitive to the suspicion surrounding his division, was not pleased.

> He sought to show how much different we were from the traditional
> historians on whom the Church had long relied. He interviewed me
> and, without my knowledge or consent, made a tape of my responses
> to his questions. By choosing, out of context, phrases that seemed
> to be heretical and disloyal, he alleged we were betraying the Church.
> He was called in by the apostle I have mentioned previously [Mark

Petersen], pumped for information adverse to our interests, and required to turn over his paper, which was then circulated to the Twelve. Once again, all of this without anyone talking with us to learn our side of the story.[62]

Leonard wrote about this episode well over a decade later and overplayed both his role and Marshall's motives. Marshall, who interviewed him on April 11, 1977, quoted him only twice, and then in an appropriate context. Indeed, the reader will likely interpret Leonard's remarks as quite supportive of his employers. Marshall wrote, "Latter-day Saint Church Historian, Leonard Arrington, explained to this writer that to call this type of history a 'New History' 'gets us into trouble with the General Authorities.' He says they prefer to look at it as a reinforcement of the traditional history, emphasizing continuity."

Trying to downplay any conflict between scholars and General Authorities, Leonard "emphasized the continuity between present day historical activities and those practiced by Joseph Fielding Smith, former Church Historian. He did point out that whenever a new volume of Mormon history has appeared it has been criticized. He said Joseph Fielding Smith's *Essentials in Church History* came under sharp criticism when it was first published, as did B. H. Roberts' *Comprehensive History of the Church*. Arrington believes that faith can increase through a study of history. He believes that the trend is toward more openness. 'The direction is set,' he said." Leonard emphasized that "he does not believe that to humanize Mormon history is to secularize it."[63]

Nothing that Leonard was quoted as saying would have been problematic even to the conservative apostles who took issue with him on other matters. Nonetheless, Marshall did point out what should have been obvious then—and is obvious now—which is doubtless why Leonard, connecting the dots of the subsequent dismantling of the History Division, saw the Marshall paper as a significant next step on the slippery slope. "That the Mormon Church has gone through a type of 'naturalistic humanism' is evidenced by the treatment its history has been receiving in recent years by scholars both within and without the Church, as well as in the many doctrinal, political and social changes which the Church has undergone since its organization."[64]

In other words, with or without the work of Leonard Arrington and his colleagues in the History Division, Mormon historiography had shifted, irreversibly, away from the polemics that had characterized it for well over a century. But obvious or not, Marshall's paper was not helpful to a division struggling to position itself as being—or at least appearing—more orthodox. Davis Bitton complained to Marshall's advisor that the topic "should have been approached differently, especially with respect to the interviews, so that misquotation would be less likely. I am afraid this is a malicious piece of work. It damages people professionally, ecclesiastically, and perhaps even personally. It did us no good, for it puts the most unfavorable possible interpretation on our activities, showing no interest in or awareness of many things we do, and it lumps us together with fundamentalists and apostates."[65]

Three months after Homer Durham's arrival and Marshall's paper, Leonard noted his disappointment—not so much with *where* the History Division was heading, but *how*, including the creation by the Quorum of the Twelve of a sub-committee to " 'look into the affairs of the Historical Department.' And by that he meant only the History Division of the department. This sub-committee consisted of Elder Petersen, Elder Hinckley, and Elder Packer," two of them being openly hostile to the division. Durham had met with the subcommittee on at least two occasions, leading Leonard to complain in his diary, "It is a peculiar thing that there would be such a sub-committee to look into the affairs of our division and that they would not talk to anyone in the division. They have not talked to me, they have not talked to any of the assistant historians, they have not talked to anyone else in the division. . . . It's almost as it they are afraid of talking to us."[66]

In early December, Durham summoned Earl Olson and Leonard to his office, although his message was only for Leonard. It was not a gentle one. "First, that our division was very suspect, had very little standing with 'the Brethren,' and he was trying to 'save' us by keeping a tight rein on us. Our free wheeling style of operation, without strict control from above, would have to be curbed. We did not fit snugly enough into the church program."

Durham implied that Leonard and his colleagues would have to reduce the amount of writing and submit every proposed research project, every staff assignment, every article to him for approval. "In short, he wants to be the Church Historian. I am to be a supervisor of the history division."

Durham then wanted a detailed report on what each staff member was working on, and a note on every change in assignment or new assignment, "except for the vignettes." These vignettes were short, inspirational stories about historical persons that were published weekly in the *Church News* in an illustrated column on the back page, next to the unsigned editorials. They had proved popular with readers who were looking for lesson and talk illustrations. They were published without formal footnotes, which may have given Durham an idea that he proposed later in this unpleasant meeting.

Next, he wanted the Mormon History Trust Fund to be controlled by Earl Olson. At this, Leonard dug in his heels. He had established the fund, which came exclusively from private donors, at the beginning of his tenure, primarily to pay

Leonard Arrington as many remember him: smiling. Photo ©1983 by Kent Miles.

Leonard Arrington shortly after his
calling as church historian in 1972.

Leonard Arrington, as church
historian, in his first office in the
Church Administration Building, 1972.

Newly appointed church historian Leonard Arrington with his two assistant church historians, James Allen (left) and Davis Bitton (right), 1972.

Leonard Arrington in his office in the newly completed (1973) Church
Office Building.

When Alvin R. Dyer suffered a stroke a few months after Arrington was
called to be church historian, Joseph Anderson replaced him as the executive
director of the Historical Department. The 1973 administrative team,
shown here, included (from left) Earl Olson (Archives), Joseph Anderson,
Donald Schmidt (Library), and Leonard Arrington (History).

Leonard meets Brigham. In 1976, James Arrington played the role of Brigham Young in a one-man show that he wrote, *Here's Brother Brigham.*

On June 23, 1978, shortly after G. Homer Durham announced to the History Division employees that their franchise would be dismantled, Arrington and several of those employees climbed Ensign Peak, overlooking Salt Lake City, where Leonard spoke to them passionately about their mission to write honest history, regardless of current events. Seated, from left: Ronald Esplin, Ronald Walker, Jill Mulvay Derr, Carol Cornwall Madsen. Standing: James Allen, Leonard Arrington, Davis Bitton, Unidentified (partially hidden), William Hartley, Richard Jensen, Bruce Blumell, Gordon Irving.

Leonard and Grace Arrington at the wedding reception of their son Carl and Christine Rigby. February 12, 1975.

The last formal portrait of the Arrington family prior to Grace's death. 1981. From left: Leonard, Grace, James, Susan, Carl.

Leonard Arrington and his siblings, 1983. Front row: Doris, Leonard, LeRoy, Marie. Back row: Kenneth, Wayne, Ralph, Donald, Ross.

In November 1983, nearly two years after Grace's death, Leonard
Arrington married Harriet Ann Horne, who is shown here with
Leonard's granddaughter, Sarah Grace Madsen.

for transcribing oral histories and handwritten documents. Losing control of this fund would seriously curtail his flexibility in sponsoring a wide range of projects. After Leonard's strenuous objections, Durham backed down; but Leonard saw the episode as the death-knell of his hopes for a collegial working relationship. He confided, "I suppose I am most hurt by Elder Durham displaying a complete lack of confidence in my handling of this and other matters. Where is the brotherly encouragement? Where is the appreciation? Why the suspicion, the distrust?" But the meeting was not over.

The final item on the agenda was Durham's displeasure with the relatively open archival access that nonemployee researchers had been given. He also wanted to frustrate their process of discovery by having division employees cut down on their citations to primary materials in the archives. When Leonard said, "I thought we could not avoid citing our archives as the source of much material," Durham asked why they could not merely mention a document without noting its source. He wrote, incredulously, "That from a former University president! . . . In sum, the entire interview was a vote of no confidence."[67]

Late in February 1978, Durham again brought the division directors into his office, only minutes after he returned from meeting with the First Presidency. This time, the news was worse, even catastrophic from Leonard's point of view. First, Boyd Packer, who for years had attempted to reign in the work of the History Division, had been assigned as one of the two new apostolic advisors to the Historical Department (Gordon Hinckley being the other).

Next, Leonard was informed that he had been relieved of the title Church Historian. He would now function as "Director, History Division." Durham tried to assure him that "the title change is regarded as descriptive not substantive."

Finally, the function of the History Division would change. While Durham assured Leonard that "this does not mean any heroic change of direction but only a gradual redirection over time," it constituted authorization from the First Presidency for the eventual phasing out of narrative history writing, and a concentration on writing the "Journal History" of the church, essentially a day-by-day, unpublished scrapbook.

It was hardly necessary for Durham to clarify the message, but he continued to dish out the bad news, saying that the First Presidency had told him "that he is to regard himself, not as coordinator of the four divisions in the Historical Department, but as the Managing Director in the strictest and most responsible sense. He wants to be informed of all projects and wishes to authorize them and approve them."

Leonard mourned in his diary entry, "The titles Church Historian and Assistant Church Historian thus disappear and may they rest in peace. . . . Elder

Durham was feeling positively buoyant as the result of the conference, and he also seemed to have felt that we would accept all of these changes and that they would be regarded as desirable by us." Indeed, Durham had reason to feel buoyant, for he had been given carte blanche to restore the Old Order within the Historical Department. The History Division employees, by contrast, would be devastated by the change, Durham's rosy prediction notwithstanding.

In ending the meeting, Durham "said that he hoped the measures taken would help to quiet the controversy that was stimulated by the Marshall honors thesis at the University of Utah on 'The New Mormon History,'"[68] perhaps in an attempt to convince Leonard that the catastrophe that had just been announced had not really been his fault.

Leonard was not consoled when, two weeks later, Durham gave him faint praise for the accomplishments of the History Division. He recorded Durham's words in his diary without comment, likely unaware that they were prophetic: "I know you must feel that what you and your colleagues have done in the past six years is not appreciated; but that is not true. You have done good work and it is appreciated. And I am sure that fifty years from now when we look back at these events the work you have done and are doing will be regarded as a magnificent contribution."[69]

Prophetic or not, they did little to lift Leonard's spirits. They were followed in March by a First Presidency letter, addressed to Durham, that might as well have been handwriting on the wall in spelling out the future for Leonard and the History Division of an "altered direction." After giving faint praise to the accomplishments of the History Division over the past half-dozen years in writing the church's history, the letter noted, "we now feel that the need for this might be satisfied through the efforts of a growing number of LDS scholars throughout the Church, as well as by others. . . . We have felt that the Historical Department should likewise move in a somewhat altered direction."

The letter, which had the tone of input from Durham even though it was addressed to him, then went on to specify the job description of a once-proud group of historians who had just had their wings clipped: "(1) careful maintenance and refinement of the Journal History; (2) maintenance of the growing archives and the ever-increasing resources of historical data pertaining to the Church; (3) providing assistance to the First Presidency, General Authorities, and Church agencies as directed; and (4) undertaking such research and publication projects as may be directed or specifically authorized from time to time by the First Presidency."

The greatly reduced work scope of the department would obviously result in a reduction of workforce, a reality that the letter massaged by noting euphemistically, "We recognize that these changes may eventually involve the Department in budgetary and personnel adjustments. . . . [We] are hopeful that if changes may be deemed necessary they may be accommodated through normal retirements, voluntary transfers, or other arrangements acceptable to those concerned."

All of this was a bitter pill for Leonard to swallow, perhaps made even more bitter by a sentence in the final paragraph: "We commend [Leonard] and his associates on their faithful service."[70]

Leonard had had sufficient contact with First Presidencies over the years, either directly or through archival documents, to understand the genesis of the letter. He wrote in his diary, "I firmly believe that this letter was written by Elder Durham and presented first to Elders Hinckley and Packer and with their approval submitted to the First Presidency for them to sign as a letter of instruction to him from them. It is my belief that he did this with the hope that he could change the image which our division has in the minds of a few brethren of the Twelve."

Although it is difficult for a current reader to fathom, Leonard actually walked away from the incident thinking, "No harm, no foul." Despite having been presented with the blueprint for the dismantling of the History Division—a blueprint that soon was followed to the smallest detail—he managed to lapse into denial and concluded his diary entry, "Actually I do not see the letter as requiring us to do anything substantially different than what we have been doing all along."[71]

But the letter, in fact, changed *everything* for his department—if not immediately, then in his near future. By restricting "publication projects" only to those specifically authorized by the First Presidency, all other projects, including the ongoing Sesquicentennial History, could be put on the chopping block. Employees of the History Division would be shifted to a "history-writing" function, a euphemism for collecting records and maintaining the unpublished Journal History, rather than the cutting-edge narrative histories that they had been writing. Narrative history would, from then on, be written by "a growing number of LDS scholars throughout the Church, as well as by others"—but not by employees of the History Division. And finally, the door was opened to downsizing the History Division.

While Leonard remained in denial, it did not take long for others to understand the implications. If there was any residual doubt as to the direction in which things were headed, it was laid to rest one month later when, prior to the Mormon History Association's annual conference, Boyd Packer, now advisor to the History Department, addressed all department employees at length, among other things telling them, "We are required to tell the truth but we are not required to tell the whole truth."[72]

The following day, Durham convened the History Division employees and read the First Presidency letter to them. His manner, Leonard recorded, was "as if he were 'dropping a bomb.'" He implied that some employees would be transferred to other divisions, part-time employees would be terminated, and "some members of the staff might find it necessary or desirable to go into the Institute [of Religion] system. The staff were all shocked and taciturn."[73]

Durham also directed that they tell people at the MHA meeting "that (1) LJA [Leonard] not fired, (2) H. Div. not abolished, (3) sesquicentennial history not cancelled, (4) publication program not cancelled, (5) all publications not necessarily cleared by an apostle." Why the concern? "All these matters are current rumors."[74]

After Durham left the meeting, Leonard attempted damage control. "I pointed out that the letter of the First Presidency does not require any measures as heroic as Brother Durham indicated. They require only that the staff be reduced by attrition and they do not require elimination of any projects on which we are working that they approve of." Whether his efforts were successful is difficult to tell, and perhaps he was trying primarily to convince himself. His diary entry concludes with remarkable naiveté: "I am surprised that [Durham] injected such gloom unnecessarily. His remarks were far more negative than the facts and conditions justify."[75] In fact, they telegraphed exactly what he would do over the next few months.

Later in May, Durham interviewed each employee of the History Division, some of whom got the message that Leonard did not—or could not—receive. One of the first employees to leave, Bruce Blumell, described his transition. "Right away, they had a formal thing where we all went in for personal interviews to see if we had testimonies. I believe he found out that we all had very strong testimonies, but . . . I could see the trend of where things were going. . . . I said [to my wife], 'Jean, maybe it's time that we think of a move. Maybe we should go back to Alberta. I have to have a job, so maybe I can still go to law school.' So we made the decision."[76]

During the interviews, Durham told Leonard for the first time that "he is also toying with possibilities of moving us to BYU or setting us up as a separate group at arm's length from the Church but with full access to the archives. This way the Church will not be responsible for what we publish."[77]

The news got worse. In late June, Durham reported to Leonard that the department's two advisors, Hinckley and Packer, had told him in a recent meeting, "The Historical Department should function mainly so that the archives are constantly and carefully maintained, and maintained primarily as a resource for the First Presidency and the General Authorities to use."[78] In August, Durham "said he continued to feel impressed that one of his responsibilities was to reduce our staff, not this year, but to plan for its elimination in the years to come. That is, say, beginning in 1980."[79] The irony that the sesquicentennial anniversary of the church's organization would actually be celebrated by dismantling both the sesquicentennial history and the division that initiated it, seems to have passed without comment. And in October, "Elder Durham advised me that I was to devote more of my time to my personal projects—Brigham Young biography—and refer problems of the staff to him and Earl. That is surely one thing I will not do!"[80] In December one colleague wrote, "Leonard looks more and more like a powerless marker."[81]

By the end of 1978, Leonard finally admitted to himself what was already apparent to others, even though he managed to maintain a tone of optimism that would have shamed Pollyanna. "The truth is that Elder Durham himself wants to see our work liquidated and done, instead, by professors at BYU, U of U, USU, and the Institute of Religion staff, or dropped entirely. If he wished to defend us in our work, he could easily do so. He chooses not to do so. He has said a number of times that he hates to preside over the liquidation of the division, paraphrasing Churchill. I do not find this funny."

Then, as if he had any power to influence the outcome, he lapsed back into denial and wrote, "I am determined not to let him liquidate the division. . . . I firmly believe in what we are doing, that what we are doing is beneficial to the Church, and that future generations will call us blessed for doing what we are doing. Believing this firmly, I am determined not to 'let the Church down' by giving in to Elder Durham's whims."[82]

Denial notwithstanding, Leonard could not hide the reality from his colleagues who were dealing grimly with their own futures. A coworker said, "I sat at my desk in the corner of the Church Office Building, and I watched him just spiral downward. It was just a sense, not that he was showing it. It was wearing. His hair was graying, his face was falling, his weight was going up."[83] An outside historian added, "Camelot was over, and everybody began to know it."[84]

21

THE REVELATION

June 9, 1978, is to Mormons what December 7, 1941, and November 22, 1963, are to virtually all Americans who lived through those days: They remember not only what happened on the day, but also where they were and what they were doing when they first heard the news. The news for Mormons was that after more than a century of a policy that excluded black men of African ancestry from ordination to the otherwise-universal male lay priesthood, a revelation to church president Spencer Kimball banished the policy that increasingly had become a stumbling block and embarrassment for church members, and a wedge increasingly isolating Mormonism from the larger religious society.

LEONARD AND BLACKS: THE FORMATIVE YEARS

The town of Twin Falls, Idaho, in which Leonard spent his formative years, was essentially all white. People of color were an abstraction to Leonard; and like nearly all Mormons of his time, he accepted uncritically the Mormon doctrine—albeit one not confined at the time to Mormonism—that dark skin, and particularly black skin, was a sign of God's curse. Supporting this doctrine was a unique Mormon teaching, derived from the Book of Mormon, that the American Indian was similarly cursed, although in a way that did not proscribe priesthood ordination. As a teenager Leonard confidently noted in a speech, "Possibly you wish to know how their skin came to be red as the original Israelites were white. It was probably the same way that there came to be Negros, as recorded in the Bible. God colored their skin for becoming wicked & placed that curse upon them."[1]

Despite the scarcity of ethnic minorities in Twin Falls, and despite Leonard's racist beliefs as a boy, his father, Noah, held egalitarian viewpoints that he attempted to pass to his family. Leonard recollected, "My father was a very democratic man; that is, he treated every man equally. Regardless of color or nationality (black, Mexican, Finnish, Norwegian, Chinese, whatever). Regardless of social status (banker, hired hand, bum, whatever). Regardless of belief (LDS, non-LDS, radical, conservative, whatever). He treated everyone with respect, with dignity. . . . With that example, all of us in the family more or less imitated. I never had any prejudice against talking with, eating with, working with any person."[2]

While four years of college in Moscow, Idaho, broadened Leonard's horizons in many ways, it was not until his move to North Carolina in 1939 that exposure to the stereotypes and prejudices of the South obliged him to confront the realities of racism. Upon arriving in Chapel Hill, he had to learn an entirely new set of social behaviors, for which he was not prepared. First, he had to learn how to speak of blacks. Not having a clue, he asked a black woman who cleaned his room. "She replied that they prefer to be called coloreds. North Carolinians often called them Nigras. I do not recall anybody ever calling them niggers. Black was not used, and I suspected would have been an insult at that time." He learned "that you never refer to them as lady or gentleman, such as, that colored lady, or that colored gentleman." And he learned that he was never to eat a meal with a black person, nor was he ever to sit in the back of a bus or streetcar, because "that's where the coloreds sat."[3]

As he courted Grace Fort, however, he began to see a different, more benevolent side of race relations. "She talked about the colored girls she had employed to clean her shop and apartment. She became quite attached to several of them, spoke of them much as members of her family and personal friends. I remember during the Christmas season of 1941, shortly after we started going together, that she took me with her out to see a former maid that she was fond of and took a basket of fruit to. They hugged and kissed, much as a mother might do her daughter. I was impressed with this personal warmth."[4]

As Leonard progressed in his graduate studies, he came to realize that racist white society was all that kept blacks from achieving at the level of whites. A notable evening showed him that blacks were, at the very least, his intellectual equals. Kenneth Cameron, a professor at North Carolina State University, invited Leonard to a Sunday evening discussion with black professors and students from Raleigh colleges. It was Leonard's first exposure to black intellectuals, and he found them to be even more learned and intelligent than their white counterparts. Decades later he wrote to Cameron, "I was so grateful to be invited. Although I had met blacks in Chapel Hill, this was my first opportunity to meet black intellectuals, in an intellectual discussion of religion, history, etc. I was very much impressed with them, and with your effort to bring us into mutual dialogue."[5]

Eating, commingling, and even showering with black enlisted men did not resolve deep-seated prejudices among many white soldiers. Indeed, "Southern boys object like the devil & Northern boys tease them about [showering together]."[6] But Leonard's war experiences moved him into a positive direction of increasing inclusion of all races. "Everybody wonders what in hell we're fighting for if it isn't toleration of race, religion, & belief."[7]

It is likely that Leonard was not even aware of the church's exclusionary policy when he moved to Logan in 1946, nor that racism within Utah differed little from its counterpart in the South. In November 1954 W. Miller Barbour, a field director for the National Urban League, published a report that stated, "In large areas of Utah, Nevada, and southern Arizona, and in most of the smaller towns, the discrimination is almost as severe as in the south." Regarding trailer parks, "we encountered complete rejection in Utah."[8]

The same month, in a "Symposium on the Negro in Utah" held at Weber College in Ogden, Harmon O. Cole, who described himself as "a person of Negroid ancestry," confirmed Barbour's report: "We are not free to eat or to sleep where we want, nor, in a theater, can we sit where we choose; we are even, in some instances, refused the common courtesy of going openly to a hotel to see a Caucasian friend. . . . A few months ago, my wife was asked to come to a hotel in Salt Lake City to call on a Caucasian friend. She was asked at the desk to take the service elevator to her friend's room, since Negroes were not allowed to use the passenger elevator."[9]

Writing to a BYU professor that same year, Leonard complimented him on an attitude that went counter to the prevailing racism in the state. "Your paper on the religious status of the Negro in Utah was one of the finest things I have ever heard a scholar do. That magnificent stroke probably did more to elevate your university in the eyes of members of the Academy than any single work of scholarship by your faculty members in recent years. . . . Such probity on the part of one who was reared in Mormon culture almost atones for all the injustices and wrongs which Mormons may have done to colored people in the name of religion."[10]

In 1957 Leonard wrote to Roman Catholic scholar Thomas O'Dea about his recently published, landmark sociological study, *The Mormons,* and chided him gently for his failure to mention the exclusionary policy. "The one problem which seems to disturb many at this particular time, and which you did not mention, was the problem of the Negro and the priesthood. . . . [People] find this the biggest stumbling-block. Lowry Nelson, as you know, has published a criticism of the Church on this score. I am sure that you are aware of this problem, and I mention it only to emphasize that it is one of the biggest stumbling blocks for some of the 'liberals' in the Church."[11]

While the policy was indeed a stumbling block for some of the church's liberals, Leonard gave no indication that it served that function for him. However, a 1969 letter from a correspondent suggests that Leonard had at least mentioned the possibility of change in the future. His correspondent queried, "Where can I get a nicely balanced, yet sympathetic statement on the Mormon Church and the Negro? Last year when I came to the Mormons in my West class, it was clear that students wanted very much to talk about the subject and I felt unprepared. I remember that you told me once that you fully expected the Mormon Church's position to change in the years ahead, and I think you even predicted that it would change rather soon. Do you still feel that way?"[12] There is no record of Leonard's response to the letter.

CHALLENGING THE POLICY

Although Leonard did not challenge the policy, he was aware, as few other church members were, that others at a higher level had done so. Reflecting on the topic in his autobiography, he noted that "a special committee of the Twelve appointed by President McKay in 1954 to study the issue concluded that there was no sound scriptural basis for the policy but that the church membership was not prepared for its reversal. . . . Personally, I knew something about the apostolic study because I heard Adam S. Bennion, who was a member of the committee, refer to the work in an informal talk he made to the Mormon Seminar in Salt Lake City on May 13, 1954. McKay, Bennion said, had pled with the Lord without result and finally concluded the time was not yet ripe."[13]

Leonard's awareness of ongoing scholarship in the field was piqued by a manuscript written by Stephen Taggart, a graduate student at Cornell University who died of cancer before it could be published. Taggart's father, Glen, was president of Utah State University. Leonard volunteered to finish preparing the manuscript for publication.[14] In so doing, he became complicit in a firestorm within the highest levels of the Mormon hierarchy, the details of which he did not learn for another two years.[15]

Taggart, who incorrectly concluded that the exclusionary policy began with Joseph Smith in Missouri,[16] included in the manuscript a 1968 letter from Sterling McMurrin to Llewelyn McKay, son of church president David O. McKay. That letter became the subject of an acrimonious debate that ultimately led to the release of First Counselor Hugh Brown from the First Presidency following McKay's death in 1970.[17]

McMurrin's letter described his 1954 meeting with President McKay, in which McKay informed him that the exclusion of blacks from the priesthood was a policy rather than a doctrine, and that it would be changed someday. He kept McKay's confidence for fourteen years until, when McKay was ninety-four years old, McMurrin described the historic meeting in the letter to Llewelyn in order that the McKay family might have a record of it.

Taggart's manuscript came to the attention of the First Presidency only a month after Leonard volunteered to edit it, and from that point until shortly before McKay's death in January 1970 it was the subject not only of internal debate, but also of political intrigue.[18] McKay had never shared with his counselors or members of the Quorum of the Twelve Apostles his insight that the issue was policy rather than doctrine. Taggart's manuscript prompted Brown to attempt to change the policy administratively. Alvin Dyer, a counselor in McKay's First Presidency but not a member of the Twelve, and senior apostle Harold Lee blocked Brown's move, and Lee's inclusion in the First Presidency following McKay's death gave him the power to release Brown from that body, the first time since the death of Brigham Young that a counselor in the First Presidency was not retained by the new church president.

One month after Leonard became church historian, Dyer made him aware of the controversy that had emanated from Taggart's manuscript. "Elder Dyer discussed in detail the subject of the Negro and the Priesthood as it pertained to Sterling McMurrin, Llewelyn McKay, etc. Elder Dyer wrote an article and paper on this matter and presented it to the First Presidency. He feels that a copy of these two items should be on file in the archives and will see that this is done."[19] Whether at this meeting or elsewhere, Leonard was made aware that this was a topic that was hands-off for him and his new associates in the department. Bill Hartley remembers getting the message clearly: "There were three or four things that were off-limits when we first started: you could not write about the blacks and the priesthood; you could not write about plural marriage; and the temple endowment was another."[20]

THE BUSH MANUSCRIPT

After Lester Bush completed medical school at the University of Virginia, he served an internship at LDS Hospital in Salt Lake City during 1968–1969. On the side, he researched the history of the church's policy on black ordination, digging into places that others had carefully walked around or of which they were not aware.

Continuing his research on a subsequent trip to Utah, he found in the papers of Apostle Adam S. Bennion, housed at BYU, a folder containing the work of the 1954 committee referenced in Leonard's autobiography. Bush took his own documentary collection of several hundred pages, which included the Bennion material and his own research notes, on an overseas assignment in Cyprus, during which he gave a copy to Edwin ("Ted") and Janath Cannon. Ted was then president of the Swiss Mission, which had an international mandate that included the island nation. Janath, without consulting Bush in advance, subsequently showed the compilation to Apostle Boyd K. Packer during his autumn 1972 tour of their mission. In November, she wrote with some excitement to Bush, "It was most fortunate that the opportunity presented itself to bring your manuscript on the Negro to the attention of Elder Boyd Packer, as he not only has the scholastic background to appreciate the value of such a compilation, but has served on a committee to consider the problem of the Negro in relation to Church policy." Upon returning to Salt Lake City, Packer immediately took the matter to the First Presidency, and following that meeting he wrote to the Cannons, "asking if we would be willing to send our copy to him for their perusal."[21]

Within the same month of November 1972, Packer asked Leonard to investigate how Bush had been able to gain access to the Bennion papers. The implication was clear: the compilation should have been off-limits. Leonard made inquiries and then wrote the following careful response:

> The Adam S. Bennion Papers (ASB Papers) were placed in the BYU Library several years ago. When he accessioned them, Brother Chad Flake, Special Collections Librarian, noted a folder dealing with the question of the Negro and the Priesthood. Recognizing that this was a sensitive issue, and that it should not be made generally available to the patrons of the library, Brother Flake withdrew this folder from the collection. Two or three years ago, he did make the file available to one person, Brother Lester Bush. Brother Bush is the only person to have seen the file, Brother Flake thinks. About a year and a half ago, one of the General Authorities, Brother Flake thinks it was President Romney, asked for the file and Brother Flake gave it to him. And presumably it is still in his hands. At any rate, that file is not now in the BYU Library.[22]

The contents of the Bennion papers were problematic for church leaders who held that the exclusionary policy was doctrinal—that is, grounded in a purported nineteenth-century revelation—and therefore likely immutable. The fact that no documentary evidence of such a revelation had ever been found—nor even a second-hand claim of such a revelation—was in itself disturbing, since it led to the circular argument that such an important position could not have been taken without such a revelation.

Among those who defended this questionable assertion was Harold Lee, who became church president within weeks of Leonard's being sustained as church historian in the April 1972 general conference. In addition to deflecting Hugh Brown on the subject late in 1969, Lee had confided to his daughter, Maureen Wilkins, his intent to maintain the status quo. Interviewed in 1998, decades after

Maureen's tragic death during pregnancy, one of her closest friends recalled Maureen saying firmly, "My daddy said that as long as he's alive, they'll never have the priesthood."[23] Predictably, Lee was not pleased to learn of the Bush compilation. "President Lee said that unfortunately this study quoted from the minutes of the Quorum of the Twelve that had gotten into the papers of an apostle, and he had been unwise enough to let it go to BYU library."[24]

Still overseas, this time in Vietnam, Bush used his compilation to write a manuscript that, for the first time, documented that the exclusionary policy originated with Brigham Young and that it had never had the imprimatur of revelation. At some point during the spring of 1973, as he later reconstructed the chronology, "I had sent Packer a draft of my paper on blacks and the priesthood, and he had responded that the Historical Department had been consulted and there were some problems"[25]—problems that he did not specify.

In fact, although Packer may have talked to either Earl Olson or Don Schmidt, he definitely did not consult the professional historians. Davis Bitton, assistant church historian, wrote to Bush, "I have heard that Elder Packer and others have been reading it. But we in the Historian's Division of the Church Historical Department have not seen it. Could it be that the Authorities are consulting with the advisors to our Department rather than those of us who are historians? Leonard Arrington told me that he has not seen your manuscript, although I am sure he would be interested in reading it."[26] Bush responded by sending a copy of the manuscript, which had already been accepted for publication in *Dialogue: A Journal of Mormon Thought*, directly to Arrington and Bitton.[27]

Only a week later, an unexpected trip from Vietnam to Washington, D.C. allowed Bush to spend several days in Salt Lake City. Not knowing any of the historians, he went directly to the front desk of the archives. Leonard recorded the complicated sequence of events that followed. "As soon as he came to our archives and asked for material, they spotted his name and told him he would have to get the approval of Brother [Joseph] Anderson before he could use the material in the archives. He went to see Brother Anderson. Brother Anderson referred him to Brother Packer. He talked with Brother Packer. They both arranged later in the day to speak with him together. So most of his day was spent in interviews and conversations with these two brethren. Brother Anderson reported those to me."

The result of the meetings with Anderson and Packer was that Anderson directed Leonard "to allow Brother Bush to see anything in our archives, which is not restricted to other scholars. He also said that while they wish his piece would not be published as scheduled in *Dialogue*, they are interposing no obstacles and told him that as far as they were concerned they would not ask him not to publish. . . . They would not ask him not to publish it because they were more fearful of the result of a Church request not to publish than they were of the publication itself."[28]

What Anderson did not communicate to Leonard was that in Packer's meetings with Bush, he tried repeatedly to dissuade him from publishing it without directly asking him to withdraw it. Bush countered by expressing his willingness to correct any inaccuracies, but Packer could not cite any. Packer was no doubt accustomed to having the expression of his preference interpreted as authoritative instruction, but the young doctor firmly resisted "anticipating counsel," a phrase that Packer would later make famous. Interviewed in 2008, Bush recalled how that meeting ended: "He finally, grudgingly said that I actually knew more about it than they did. So they weren't really going to be able to debate that with me. This was after he had tried for a day-and-a-half. But it was the sort of thing they just didn't think should be put in the record."[29]

Far more affable were Bush's meetings with Leonard and his staff, who saw him as a surrogate dealing with a crucial historical issue that they were not allowed to touch themselves. Bush recalled, "My sessions with the historians were wonderful. They were very curious about me and my experiences on at least three counts: the subject of my paper was as important to many of them as it was to me; I represented a generic case study of the Church's response to someone tackling any of a number of potentially controversial subjects of historical importance; and the Historical Department was a relatively new development—with professional historians doing professional history, and they saw my case as the sort they reasonably should be asked to weigh in on."

Something between a curiosity and a celebrity, Bush immediately attracted a small group of professional historians as he took a seat in the archives reading room, led by Leonard. "It was clear that some of them knew at least the gist of my paper—which must have received some informal circulation—and that many were aware of my ongoing interviews. They were particularly interested in my discussions with Packer, and in individual conversations I recounted some of the experiences reported above, including the probing into who gave me the Bennion papers." While none presumed to know who gave him the lead to the papers, all were intrigued at the persistence of his questioners in attempting to ferret out the identity. To a person they said, "You didn't tell them, I hope?"

The comparison to Bush's earlier research experience in the archives was dramatic. "I was given virtually free access to all the things previously denied to me, plus recommendations on my paper. . . . I did ask Arrington why, for all their new professionalism, none of the heavyweight historians had undertaken a study of the Negro doctrine—so that amateurs like myself wouldn't have to try to work things out on our own. He said that my ongoing experience with the Authorities—meaning right then—provided the answer to the question."[30]

Bush met with Leonard on successive days. After the second meeting, Leonard recorded his observations. "It would appear that the purpose of these additional interviews [with Packer] was to attempt to sell him [Bush] on the idea that there is absolutely no doubt among the Brethren on the 'Negro Doctrine' of the Church, and that any research and writing on this subject is superfluous, wasteful, and potentially harmful. They do not see historical research on this question as making it easier for the Church to solve the 'Negro Problem'; the doctrine is solved and settled." Having had access to Bush's massive compilation on the subject, it is doubtful that Packer actually believed what he was attempting to sell to Bush, with the hope that Bush, believing the story, would withdraw the manuscript from publication. Indeed, the compilation made it clear, as did the *Dialogue* article that emerged from it, that the foundational argument that had been used to justify the priesthood ban for over a century was wrong—there had been no revelation. Packer likely realized that the effect of Bush's research would be to undermine the justification for the ban, and if that occurred, no one would be able to predict the outcome. Better, in his mind, to try to maintain the status quo.

Bush, while realizing that his research had already challenged the justification for the ban, felt "very depressed that there appears to be no possibility of a change on the Church's Negro doctrine within the next twenty years. There seems to be unanimity among all the brethren on this question and no desire to alter the Church policy and practice in this regard."[31] It turned out that both Packer and Bush were mistaken in their reading of the consequences of Bush's research, for Packer learned that the doctrine was not "solved and settled," and Bush learned that there was a possibility of change, and far sooner than twenty years.

After Packer failed to dissuade Bush, unnamed church authorities used a surrogate, BYU academic vice president Robert Thomas, to try to persuade Robert Rees, editor of *Dialogue*, not to publish the manuscript. Thomas, a bright and competent graduate of the famous liberal Reed College, had joined BYU's English faculty in 1951 but had soon been shunted into administration under BYU's president, Ernest Wilkinson. Whatever Thomas's personal feelings on the issue, he had received clear instructions to block publication, and he felt free to employ a variety of near-threats to achieve his purpose.

Since Rees was employed by the University of California at Los Angeles, he was relatively immune to personal warnings, so Thomas hinted that publication would certainly not improve *Dialogue*'s dangerous reputation as a liberal periodical. However, Leonard was also in Thomas's crosshairs. Rees immediately wrote a report of their phone conversation: "He indicated that another one of the ramifications of our publishing this article would be that innocent people would be affected by it. He thought that Leonard Arrington would probably lose his job. His statement was he is afraid of what would happen to Leonard Arrington. He felt that it was a very important step for Leonard to be made Church Historian but this could clearly affect that appointment."[32] Thomas's threat to Leonard proved to be groundless.

Back in Vietnam, Bush wrote appreciatively to Arrington: "It's impossible to say how encouraging a development your 'regime' has been for me (surpassing even the advent of *Dialogue*, if that is possible). I'm sure you are familiar with many Church-Historian's-Office-Stories, and, from my own experiences in 1968–9, many are true. By contrast, our conversations were easily the high point for me of my stay in Salt Lake, notwithstanding my other interviews, and your frankness provided me with a perspective and balance especially needed at that time."[33]

Two weeks after Bush's letter to Leonard, *Dialogue* published the article.[34] Leonard told Bush in February 1974[35] that it was "a relief (his [Leonard's] word) that it was finally out in print where it could be discussed, and made an analogy to the relief felt when *Mountain Meadows Massacre* was published by Juanita Brooks."[36]

A NEW PROPHET

Four months after Bush's article was published, the Mormon world was surprised by the sudden death of church president Harold Lee just before Christmas in 1973. Having assumed the presidency at the relatively young age of seventy-three, ten years younger than the average age of the five men who have since succeeded him in that office, he died less than two years later at an age eighteen years younger than the average of those same colleagues.

Succeeding Lee was Spencer Kimball, a cancer survivor five years Lee's senior who lived to the age of ninety. Leonard's immediate assessment of the new church president was not unusual: "I was told this afternoon that President Kimball was a traditionalist, very conservative as to doctrine and as to procedures. A prediction was made that he would most likely choose Elders [Ezra Taft] Benson and [Mark] Petersen, as the senior members of the Quorum after him, to be his counselors. He has great compassion for ordinary persons and their problems, but his approach is that of a traditionalist rather than an innovator."[37]

The assessment was wrong on all counts. Kimball retained Eldon Tanner and Marion Romney, Lee's counselors; and although he had been a traditionalist, he turned out to be the most progressive church president of the twentieth century.

His innovations reached into many realms of Mormon life, but his most significant was to abolish the policy on ordination of blacks.

The day after Kimball's first press conference, Leonard noted Kimball's response to one of the questions asked by a reporter: Will there be any change in the policy on blacks and priesthood, now or in the future? "President Kimball said that this is a matter which depends upon the Lord. We ourselves have not said this policy. We are subject to the revelations of the Lord and if the Lord should dictate a change in this then it will occur."[38]

While Kimball did not intend initially to be proactive in challenging the policy,[39] for many years he had been uncomfortable with it and saw it as an impediment to the progress of the church. On one occasion more than a decade before he became church president, he voiced his concern to J. Thomas Fyans, an executive at the church-owned department store, ZCMI, who was then president of the Uruguayan Mission.[40] Interviewed in 1995, Fyans recalled a visit from Kimball, then a senior apostle, to Montevideo in about 1962. They met in "a little chapel, with a little balcony in it. We were holding meetings, and for some reason he and I happened to be up in the balcony, just the two of us. I don't remember the circumstances, but there were just the two of us there, and the chapel was empty. He said, 'Tom, some way we've got to solve this problem of "the blood." They are worthy people.'"[41]

Unlike the 1960s, when there was intense external pressure on the church to change its policy, by the time of Kimball's presidency the issues nudging him toward change came from within. The first was described by former U.S. Treasury Secretary David Kennedy, whom Kimball made a special ambassador at large, a position that had not previously existed. Kennedy spoke at a meeting of the Cannon-Hinckley Church History Club that Leonard attended and summarized in his diary: "Kennedy then talked about the central theme of President Kimball of taking the gospel to all the world. This is not a Utah church or an American church—it is a universal church. It is Christ's church and God's church. The gospel is for all men, as pointed out in the introduction to the first section of the Doctrine and Covenants."[42]

"All the world" included Africa. While Kimball was intent on moving in that direction, he was well aware of the abortive attempt of the church to begin a mission in Nigeria in the early 1960s, an attempt that failed largely because the priesthood ban had made a functional church organization that relied on a lay priesthood a practical impossibility.[43]

The second issue was the construction of a temple in São Paulo, Brazil, announced by the First Presidency in March 1975. Interracial marriage has long been common in Brazil, much of it involving blacks of African ancestry. Most of the ordinances performed in LDS temples require that the man be ordained to the priesthood, presenting the obvious conundrum of denying temple ordinances to worthy, but black, Brazilian church members. Leonard recorded one example that may have been a pivotal point in Kimball's thinking:

> In March 1976 Kimball was present at the laying of the cornerstone of that temple. There he was told about Helvécio and Rudá Martins, sincere black members converted in 1972. Helvécio was a prominent professor and businessman in Rio de Janeiro who had saved funds to send his son on a mission. Discovering that the young man couldn't go because he was black, the Martins gave the money to the church to send another person. Helvécio had donated for the construction of the temple, both in labor and money, knowing full well that under existing arrangements he could never enter. At the same time Rudá sold her jewelry and contributed the proceeds to the temple fund. All of this grieved Kimball.[44]

Another conundrum was that church policy forbade ordination of a man with *any fraction* of black African ancestry, and yet there was no objective means of verifying fractional ancestry. Heightened enforcement of this policy in the South African Mission in the 1940s had brought the mission to a near standstill, for six missionaries assigned full-time to do genealogical research to document all-European ancestry for white South African men were unable to clear enough men for ordination to staff the local churches. A visit to the mission by David O. McKay, the church president, resulted in abandonment of the research policy, but maintained the *status quo* on the larger issue of ordination.[45] The situation in Brazil was far more complex, for while South Africa's apartheid policy had made interracial marriage a rarity, it was common and well accepted in Brazil.

WEIGHING OPTIONS

Jack Carlson was a Utah native, but for years he had made his home in Washington, D.C., where he held high-ranking positions in the Office of Management and Budget and the Department of the Interior. A Washington insider who spoke candidly to power, Carlson became Kimball's confidant over the years. Several years after Jack's death his wife, Renee, described that relationship. "When we went in to talk to President Kimball, it was very informal, just like talking to a good friend. We'd just sit there and talk to him. The person who always got us in was Bishop [D. Arthur] Haycock [who was, at the time, Kimball's personal secretary]. He was a good buddy, and so all Jack would do is call Bishop Haycock and he'd get him right in. In all the times that we were there, we would just talk about what was going on, what was happening in Washington."

One topic that came up in their conversations was the Jimmy Carter Administration. Carter had visited Salt Lake City, he and Kimball rode together in a parade, and despite being politically conservative, Kimball liked the president on a personal level. He remarked to the Carlsons that he couldn't understand why Mormons had been shut out of the Carter Administration, and why the administration was "being so nasty to the Mormons." Jack, whose manner was always direct, cut to the chase immediately: "Don't you get it? It's the black issue and the women's issue. We're the only people now who are standing so rigid on those issues, and until you change some of those policies, we are going to be excluded."

Kimball responded, "Well, what do you think would happen if we changed the policy? Give us a scenario." Renee was in the meeting, "and we talked for maybe an hour. We just talked about what it would be like. . . . He was really serious about what the repercussions would be within the Church, what it would be within the Quorum of the Twelve, what he would have to do to get them to go along with it. He was very candid. There was no, 'I think I need to go pray.' It wasn't that at all. It was a very rational, political issue that he would have to steer through his committee. . . . He asked all the right questions. For instance, he asked what we thought would happen with the southern parts of the Church."

The meeting occurred in the spring of 1978, just months before Kimball announced the revelation that changed the church. While it was apparent to the Carlsons that Kimball had not yet made a decision, it was also clear that he had given the matter serious consideration for some time, and that he had walked down that road far enough to discuss tactics. "He was still searching, but he was seeing the writing on the wall. . . . They talked about how it should be done. Jack's advice was, 'You should do it fast. Take advantage of the fact that you are the Prophet.'"[46]

Carlson was not the only outsider providing input to Kimball. John Baker was an executive of the Mars Corporation who earlier had hired Merrill Bateman to head a cocoa research institute for the corporation. Early in 1978, Bateman contacted Baker, saying that the First Presidency had asked him to travel to the cocoa-producing countries in Africa where he had good contacts. "At this time, they did not want to call attention to the fact that someone was there for religious purposes. Would the Mars Corporation allow him to work on cocoa on his own, and at the same time check on the things that the Church was interested in? I went to the ownership of the company, and they said, 'Yes, there isn't any problem. He can still do some work there, and arrangements can be made.'"

Baker accompanied Bateman for part of the trip, the purpose of which "was to interview the members of the Church. I don't remember the words he used, but it was indicated that the Church was investigating the political situation and the strength of those that were likely to come into the Church, and assessing the whole situation."[47]

At the same time these outsiders were providing input to Kimball, Leonard had also been enlisted. On the day the revelation was announced, he added a notation in his diary of an episode that he had not recorded at the time it happened:

> Approximately six months ago Elder Neal Maxwell telephoned me on a confidential basis to ask if I could find for him the quote of Joseph Fielding Smith that "darkies are wonderful people." He said he understood Joseph Fielding had said something more in that interview about blacks ultimately being given the Priesthood. My memory was that this was in an article in *Time* about 1966, or 1967. I hunted through *Time* and through other publications and could not find it. I gave up. Then about a month ago, quite by accident, I learned that it was in an article in *Look* in 1963.[48] I hunted that article up, Xeroxed the article and sent it on to Elder Maxwell. He expressed his appreciation and asked for a Xerox of the *Deseret News* interview on which it was based. I sent that as well. He expressed appreciation for that as well. This suggests that Elder Maxwell, as chief planning officer, was actively working on a memorandum to President Kimball about the issue and wanted all the evidence he could find.[49]

That Leonard had not viewed Maxwell's request as a harbinger of significant change was indicated by his diary entry at the beginning of 1978: "I predict the Church will take a small step toward recognizing the dignity and worthiness of members of the Church of the black race."[50] It was not a small step. It was a gigantic leap.

THE LONG-AWAITED DAY

On June 1, 1978, Spencer Kimball met in the Salt Lake Temple with his counselors and ten of the twelve apostles. (Delbert Stapley was in the hospital and Mark Petersen was out of the country.) Eight days later, Kimball met again in the temple, this time with the church patriarch, the Presiding Bishopric, and the First Quorum of the Seventy, which, at this point, numbered about forty-six individuals. One of the Seventies described the life-changing event in great detail years later.

During the first week in June, these men received notice of a meeting to be held in the Salt Lake Temple on Friday, June 9. "That never happened. We always meet on Thursdays. So, that sent up a signal in our minds. General Authorities speculate too, you know–Black issues, Second Coming, Armageddon, back to Missouri? Everybody was saying, 'What are you thinking?' We do it, we kidded around with it. They said, 'Do not announce this. In fact, if you have any plans to go early to stake conference or special meetings, cancel all meetings.' That has never happened as long as I had been there, before or since." Adding to the suspense was the timing of the meeting. "They called the meeting at eight o'clock, and we always meet at nine. So that put a little more ammunition to it."

The meeting did not include the apostles, who had met with Kimball the previous week. Kimball asked his counselor, Marion Romney, to conduct the meeting. "He said, 'I feel impressed to have us sing We Thank Thee, Oh God, for a Prophet,' which was appropriate for what was going to happen. We sang it, then he said, 'Let us kneel, and I am going to ask President Tanner to pray.' They *never* do that. It's always one of us. The First Presidency has never opened or closed with prayer there in my whole tenure, except this time." Tanner's prayer contained words to the effect "that we will all be receptive to the things that the Lord has prompted our prophet." By that point, "everything was coming together." Tanner then turned the meeting over to Kimball.

Kimball began by telling of his childhood in rural Arizona, wondering why the Native Americans in the area were treated so badly. "One day, when I was 5, 6, or 7, I asked my father [Andrew Kimball, son of Heber C. Kimball] why do we do that? My dad put me on his knee and told me about prejudices and how terrible human beings can be toward other human beings. He said, 'Son, some day the Lord will make that right with the Indian.'"

Later, in his teens, when Kimball learned about the priesthood ban, he spoke again to his father. "'Dad, how come Blacks don't have the same privilege we do?' My father was the kind of father who would always sit me down when I had a question. My father said, 'The time will come when they will have full priesthood blessing and authority in the Church.' I believed my dad."

Later, while Kimball was a stake president, "a member of the Twelve came out and I said, 'Elder, why do we take the position that we do that the Black can't hold the priesthood?' The answer he gave was, 'We don't fully know all of the reasons, but the time will come, I promise you, President, when that will occur.' I believed that."

"Then," he said, "the mantle fell on me, and I wanted to know. . . . There were days when you brethren went home at night, and I had come over here night after night after night; and I have poured my heart out to the Lord to know why. Last week he answered me. He said, 'The time has come.' I called my counselors and told them and they said, 'It is right.' Then I said to my counselors, 'We should notify the Twelve.' They fully supported and sustained it, that the time had come."

There was one more step Kimball needed to take. "I will not announce this to the world, unless all of you feel comfortable. I would like to hear from you." Over the next two or three hours, each man spoke to the subject. With one exception, they endorsed it with enthusiasm and with emotion. That one exception was an unnamed man who said, "I had a suspicion when we walked over here that this might happen, and I was against it. But after getting the feeling of this meeting, it's right."

The Seventy continued his narrative: "Then he [Kimball] leaned over and put his hand on Eldon Tanner's knee, and he looked at him. I will never forget that look. He said, 'Eldon, go tell the world,' just like that."

By the time the men returned to their offices, the world knew. "For two days you couldn't get a call in or out of there. I mean it just lit up everything."

In a subsequent meeting, Kimball told his colleagues of his wife's response. "I went home and, boy, did my wife bawl me out! She said, 'It's a fine how-do-you-do, Spencer! You go over there and tell everybody about the Blacks, and I hear it on the radio.' "[51]

As Leonard began to write his weekly letter to his children on the morning of June 9, he noted, "Not much special news to report." But by the time he was completing the letter, the world had changed. "I just heard a few moments ago the news that President Kimball had announced that Church authorities are now permitted to ordain all worthy male members to the Priesthood, without regard to race or color. Within five minutes of my hearing it, Carl telephoned to say that he had heard it broadcast in the East. . . . I was in the midst of sobbing with gratitude for this answer to our prayers, and could hardly communicate with him."

He concluded the letter, "I know absolutely nothing about the background, but will let you all know if I learn anything."[52] He quickly shifted gears from grateful church member to historian, realizing the importance of documenting Mormonism's most momentous event of the twentieth century.

In his diary entry for the same day Leonard wrote: "I had no premonition of the announcement of this day revealing that the Lord will now permit blacks to hold the Priesthood and go to the temple." He also acknowledged his own uncritical acceptance of the policy over the years: "In talks to public groups, almost inevitably the question is asked 'Why . . . ?' My reply in such public discussions has been pretty much as follows: For the believing Mormon it is sufficient to know that the Lord's servants—those empowered to interpret His will—have said the Lord has not sanctioned giving the Priesthood to blacks. As to why, we don't know, nor do the Lord's servants know. We accept it as one of the inexplicables."[53] His task now, as church historian, was to attempt to explain.

CAPTURING THE HISTORY

On Monday, the first business day after the revelation was announced, Leonard held a meeting with his staff. The record that he made, capturing personal experiences and reconstructing the great event from small glimpses, forms a significant section of over fifty pages in his diary, much more comprehensive, though inevitably somewhat repetitious, than anything he said in a public speech or put in his autobiography. He wrote a preface to the lengthy compilation: "It occurred to me as Director of the History Division to convene the research-writers in the History Division in my office to give the circumstances under which they learned of the new revelation, to express their initial and subsequent reactions, and to repeat the reactions of others they had observed over the weekend. . . . We thought this record would be important for the historians of the future."

In addition to Leonard's quest to capture the details of events surrounding the revelation, he announced that Homer Durham "asked him to have a private meeting with staff members present to ask any of us if we have or could get within a day or two any instances in which any predecessors of President Kimball had made the statement that some day the Priesthood would be given to the blacks." The reason for the request was obvious: "The First Presidency, in the second paragraph of their letter, stated that 'our predecessors have looked forward to this day,' and 'aware of the promises made by our presidents and predecessors.'"[54]

Everyone in the meeting then related the circumstances of their hearing of the revelation, but the closest thing to inside information came from Maureen Beecher, whose Sunday School teacher was Don McConkie, son of Oscar McConkie who was a partner in the law firm that did most of the church's business, and the brother of Apostle Bruce R. McConkie who had been present in the meeting on June 1. "Apparently when he got the word, Oscar went to Bruce's office to ask him about it. Bruce said only: 'The revelation was presented on June 1 in a meeting between the First Presidency and ten members of the Quorum of the Twelve.' Bruce then said, 'I am very busy getting ready to fly to Latin America where I have been assigned to go and implement the revelation.' He said nothing further about it."[55]

Within a month, Leonard had a compiled a substantial database, consisting of first- and second-hand snapshots, that allowed the construction of an intriguing, albeit incomplete picture of the events leading up to and including June 9.

In a letter to his children a week after the announcement of the revelation, Leonard described, without indicating the sources of his information, two prior church presidents' attempts to change the policy. The first was David O. McKay. "It is my understanding that President McKay was disappointed that he was not permitted by the Lord to go any further than this, but he nevertheless went as far as the Lord would permit." The second, surprising in light of the comment of his daughter noted earlier in this chapter, was Harold B. Lee. "It is my understanding that President Harold B. Lee, shortly before his death, inquired earnestly of the Lord to rescind the exclusion rule. It is my understanding that President Lee spent three days and nights fasting in the upper room of the temple praying to the Lord for guidance on this matter and the only answer that he received was 'not yet.'"[56]

In his published autobiography, Leonard described Kimball's activism on the subject as having begun two years prior to the revelation. "In 1976, two years after he became president, Kimball began a systematic program of prayer, fasting, and supplication, asking the Lord to rescind the rule denying blacks the priesthood. Special emphasis was placed on this effort during the two-month period beginning in April 1978, when every day he put on his sacred clothes and went alone into the Holy Room of the temple for meditation, prayer, and supplication."[57]

Boyd Packer, when approached by a church member inquiring of the events surrounding the revelation, responded that "he could share part of the experience [but] part of it he could not share." He then related that before June 1, Kimball had requested that the Quorum of the Twelve be fasting prior to their scheduled meeting that morning. At the meeting, he told them that "for the past two months he has gone daily to an upper room in the temple to pray" for guidance on the priesthood ban. After an open discussion, Kimball asked if he might give a prayer on behalf of the group. The church member told Leonard, "At a certain point in the prayer, Elder Packer stated, all present became aware of what the decision must be. He did not say what happened; this is no doubt the part which he was forbidden to tell. But there was some kind of manifestation, presumably which was plain to all those present. As Brother Packer referred to this he sobbed—something which he does not commonly do." Packer said that the next to speak was Ezra Taft Benson, who said, "We all are aware of what has happened. Now what should we do about it?" Marion Romney responded, "Let's take a week to formulate a statement to announce it to the other general authorities and to the Church." The statement was written in the course of the week, presented to the Quorum of the Twelve on June 8, and then to the other General Authorities on June 9.[58]

Bruce McConkie, also a member of the Twelve, gave details of the revelation at a family gathering, an account of which he authorized to be quoted. He confirmed what Leonard wrote in his autobiography about the two-year period of intense focus that Kimball gave to the matter, and added details. "Great emphasis was focused on the question during the last three months especially in the upper room of the temple on the part of all the General Authorities. During this period of great emphasis the Prophet invited any of the Brethren to speak and/or write and share their feelings about the issue. Many of the Brethren responded with discussion and cross-examination following."

McConkie said that the June 1 meeting actually had two components. The first was the regular monthly meeting that included all General Authorities. At the conclusion of that meeting, "everyone was dismissed except the First Presidency and the Twelve (Elder Mark E. Petersen was in Colombia and Delbert Stapley was sick). President Kimball indicated he wanted another prayer circle commenting that he hoped to receive a revelation on the question of the Blacks and the Priesthood but that if no revelation were received he would defend the Church's position to his dying day." Just prior to Kimball's prayer, there was open discussion about the subject. "Elder McConkie spoke for about ten minutes as did Elder Packer and others."

"President Kimball then offered a magnificent prayer that lasted about ten minutes—the words of the prayer were indeed the words of the Lord. Elder McConkie compared the feeling and experience that transpired to the day of Pentecost and the beautiful experience that transpired in the Kirtland Temple at its dedication. (Several of the Brethren of the early days of this dispensation were there.)"[59]

An additional and lengthy account attributed to McConkie was provided by his son, Joseph Fielding McConkie, to Jay Todd, editor of the church's adult magazine, the *Ensign*. "The First Presidency had been interested in the topic for years, President Kimball especially, and 'had felt a message coming through.' Last June[60] several of the apostles were invited to submit memos on various implications of the question—historical, medical, sociological, doctrinal, etc., among them Elders Packer, [Thomas] Monson, and McConkie. The First Presidency had made the question a matter of formal prayer in the temple a number of times and had received no revelation, no answer."

Joseph Fielding McConkie said that his father told him "that at one meeting—unclear whether it was all the Twelve or just the First Presidency—that someone commented, 'The former presidents of the Church are here,' and President Kimball confirmed it. On a second occasion, one of the men said, 'President So-and-So is here,' and President Kimball again confirmed that impression."

In the second temple meeting on June 1, when Kimball asked for comments from the Twelve prior to leading the group prayer, McConkie "immediately arose and delivered a ten-minute lecture on why the blacks must receive the priesthood before the Millennium. He was followed by Boyd K. Packer, who spoke for ten minutes, bringing up different but equally persuasive reasons, and then by Elder

Monson." The junior apostles were followed by all remaining members of the Twelve. "All took totally different points, and all were highly persuasive."

When Kimball began to pray, according to McConkie, he phrased the question differently than on prior occasions, when the question was circumspect: "Would it be proper for us to ask this question?" This time, said McConkie, "he was direct, communicating on a different level."

"At the end of that prayer, a Pentecostal experience occurred. All thirteen experienced and saw 'just the way it was at Kirtland.'" Intrigued, McConkie's family asked him several questions for clarification of the Pentecostal experience, and each time he gave the same answer. "The rushing of a great wind? 'Just like Kirtland.' Angelic choirs? 'Just like Kirtland.' Cloven tongues of fire?[61] 'Just like Kirtland.' Visitors from across the veil? 'Just like Kirtland,'" although he declined, despite several entreaties from his family, to identify who came "from across the veil."

A family member asked McConkie, "Why did you all see it? Why didn't just President Kimball receive it and you receive confirmation of it?" He answered, "Because it will take all thirteen[62] to witness of it in the kinds of changes that will have to take place."

During the week after June 1, no further action was taken. At the meeting on June 8, the First Presidency and the Twelve discussed how to announce the revelation. "Some wanted to wait until October conference, others for the mission presidents' seminar the following week." McConkie argued strongly for immediate release, the rationale being that otherwise word of it would leak out, and then "we have to beat Satan. He'll do something between now and then to make it appear that we're being forced into it." McConkie and Boyd Packer were asked to write separate drafts of an announcement. "Elder Packer told Elder McConkie that 'they chose your draft.' Elder McConkie said, 'It was the First Presidency's letter.'" The implication of this report was that the statement was produced overnight, between the apostolic meeting on June 8 and the larger meeting on June 9.

Although the full Quorum of the Twelve was not present at the meeting on June 9, McConkie was asked to attend, and he gave "an impassioned extemporaneous lecture on the relevant scriptures." He was followed by Marion Romney, one of Kimball's counselors in the First Presidency, who made a statement that indicated why the force of revelation was necessary to change the policy—an observation that went back at least to church president Heber J. Grant in the early 1920s.[63] "I have a confession to make. Whenever we've discussed this question, I've assured President Kimball that I would support him fully, but if the decision had been left to me, I would have felt that we've always had that policy and we would stick to it no matter what the opposition. I have now changed my position 180 degrees. I am not just a supporter of this decision. I am an advocate."[64]

The final account in Leonard's compilation came from David Haight of the Quorum of the Twelve, and was relayed to Leonard by Davis Bitton. Bitton reported that at the monthly testimony meeting of his ward on July 5, 1978, Haight, who was a member of the ward, went to the pulpit shortly before the scheduled end of the meeting and said, "I should like to take the last ten minutes, if that will be all right, to share with you, with the members of my own ward, some of the circumstances surrounding the announcement on June 9."

The story that he told was substantially the same as the others in Leonard's diaries, but there were two new details. One was that in the weeks prior to the June 1 meeting, Kimball had met individually with each apostle, and again with some small groups of apostles, to discuss the implications of changing the policy. The other was that, in a variation of the story McConkie had told his children, all of the Twelve worked through the week following the June 1 meeting to draft the text of the announcement. "All of them had a hand in it. All of them had the opportunity to consider individually and collectively each word and each phrase so that the statement itself is not presumed to be dictated by the Lord but worked out by the Brethren to convey the answer which the Lord had revealed to them."[65]

Six weeks after the revelation, Leonard and Grace attended the Days of '47 luncheon and sat next to Camilla Kimball, Spencer's wife. Leonard took the opportunity to ask Sister Kimball about the revelation. "She said she did not learn of it until a friend of hers called her sometime after the announcement.[66] Said President Kimball had not said a word to her about it in advance. Said she knew he had great anxiety for several days before the announcement but didn't know what. He had great anxiety because he didn't know for sure how it would be received."[67]

A decade thereafter, Leonard added the final detail to his database after speaking with the daughter of LeGrand Richards, an apostle who had been present at the temple meeting on June 1, 1978, and who died in 1983. Leonard recorded:

> She told me that her father had told her about the revelation which permitted black men to hold the Priesthood. He told her that President Kimball had suggested, at the conclusion of the meeting of the First Presidency and the Quorum of the Twelve in the Temple, that he wanted them to join him in prayer. He prayed fervently, then an electric moment when he switched gears, so to speak. As if struck by a special vision he thanked the Lord for the revelation which made this addition possible. At that very moment, Elder Richards told his

daughter, he, Elder Richards, felt a presence in the room and opened his eyes and looked up and saw Wilford Woodruff looking at President Kimball and smiling. Elder Richards said it was not his imagination; it was, in fact, President Woodruff, who was easy to recognize. He, Elder Richards, was 12 years old when President Woodruff died, and he had seen President Woodruff several times as a boy, so he knew very well what he looked like. Elder Richards said that he suddenly realized why Elder Woodruff was there. He also (WW) had faced a problem of similar urgency (the abolition of polygamy) when he was President. And he was now there to reassure President Kimball and the Apostles that they were doing the right thing in granting the Priesthood to worthy blacks. LeGrand's daughter said this was not rumor, not hearsay, but she heard this from her own father, who told it to his family in a serious moment. So she knew it was an actual happening.[68]

This signal moment upon which the church pivoted during the rest of the twentieth century and into the future will be cited, celebrated, and reinterpreted for decades to come. Leonard chose to be restrained, writing a very condensed version of these events in his autobiography and prefacing it with a disclaimer even while he made his own desire for fuller disclosure part of his private record:

Although members of the Twelve and the First Presidency with whom I sought interviews felt they should not elaborate on what happened, I learned details from family members and friends to whom they had made comments. Some of these statements may have involved colorful, symbolic language that was taken literally. It is a common regret among Latter-day Saints that general authorities do not speak openly about their remarkable spiritual experiences in the way Joseph Smith and other early prophets used to do. Although they unquestionably do have such experiences, they have said little about this one. Such a sacred experience that affected us all calls for a sober recitation. Here was indisputable evidence of God's presence and direction in these latter days—divine reaffirmation of the faith and values of our church. The telling of the event expresses the profound wonder and enthusiasm that continues to grip Latter-day Saints in general and historians in particular. I need to emphasize that the following account is mine and might be different from another person's understanding.[69]

22

DISASSEMBLY

THE MORMON EXPERIENCE

Looking back at the end of 1979 on an otherwise dismal year for the History Division, Davis Bitton saw one piece of optimistic news. "The cloud has not filled the whole sky. Sunshine breaks through from time to time. While production of scholarly works may have declined slightly (I have not counted up the publications to make sure), we are still getting things out. The most important publication of 1979 was *The Mormon Experience*, the reception of which has been a happy, even exhilarating surprise."[1]

The project had been on again/off again for over a decade since Alfred Knopf originally requested in 1967 that Leonard write such a book, but the obstacles to its completion had been internal—that is, Leonard's own priorities and schedule—rather than any clamping down by the church. Indeed, given the flak over *The Story of the Latter-day Saints*, which had been published more than a year before the manuscript of *The Mormon Experience* had been completed, the internal review process was remarkably—almost astoundingly—smooth.

Leonard and Davis Bitton completed the draft of the book late in the summer of 1977 and sent it in two directions for review: Knopf and the First Presidency. By mid-autumn Knopf's reader recommended publication subject to revisions. Leonard then awaited word from the First Presidency, writing in his diary, "As favorable as the book is to the Church in our view, it has now been accepted by Knopf's reader and therefore it would put us in a very bad light to have the First Presidency recommend extensive revisions. I do not think either Rodman Paul or Knopf would publish a book which is more favorable than the present version."[2] Leonard's misgivings were not groundless. The First Presidency had assigned Boyd Packer to read it and "answer the question of whether he thought they should object to the publication of this manuscript."[3] Packer's views of the History Division to date had ranged from dim to hostile, even about History Division publications that were far less provocative than *The Mormon Experience*.

It was probably just as well for Leonard's already taut nerves that he and Davis did not know the identity of the designated reader until the review was finished.

In early November 1977, Leonard and Homer Durham met with Packer. Braced for the worst, they were not only relieved but astonished that Packer raised no serious issues regarding the manuscript and said his recommendation to the First Presidency would be that "they should not object to the publication of this book." On the way back to the office, Durham spelled out the meaning of the meeting, which Leonard, possibly thinking it was a battle that would need to be refought further down the road, recorded carefully: " 'Now you have had this read by one of the most critical of the members of the Quorum of the Twelve and he has approved it or at least has not disapproved it. You now have the go-ahead.' . . . He thinks this is a monumental book; he feels good about it."[4]

Two factors may have played into Packer's unexpected behavior. Knowing that the book was written for a non-Mormon audience and published by a national press—as contrasted to *The Story of the Latter-day Saints*, which was written for a Mormon audience and published by the church's own press, Deseret Book Company—he may have realized that the less apologetic tone of *The Mormon Experience* would give the book greater credibility among its targeted audience. But it is also possible that, having achieved his, Ezra Taft Benson's and Mark Petersen's strategic objective of beginning the dismantling of the History Division, he saw no need for further intervention.

Publication of the book was still a distant event, for Knopf required extensive revision of the manuscript, particularly the last chapters that were seen to be "too pro-Church." That created a dilemma for the authors. "The church people think we've leaned over backwards to accommodate the Gentile point of view; and Knopf thinks we've leaned forwards to accommodate the Church point of view," Leonard commented wryly to his children. "So we're clearly doing the impossible. Impossible to satisfy both groups. And whatever we do, both will be dissatisfied."[5]

Revision of the manuscript, which required a delicate balancing act to keep both Knopf and the church on board, required nearly a year of work. In September 1978, Leonard and Davis Bitton sent the final version to Knopf. To a friend Leonard wrote, "My one-volume history of the Mormons has been accepted by Alfred Knopf and is due to be published about April 1. Feel very good about it."[6]

Perhaps Leonard's greatest relief in seeing the book published was that his patron, Alfred Knopf, who "was becoming impatient and complained that he would die before my book appeared," was still alive and alert. *"The Mormon Experience: A History of the Latter-day Saints* came out when Alfred Knopf was in his eighty-seventh year. He was overjoyed with the publication and wrote one of the most heart-warming letters I have ever received, expressing his approbation and enthusiasm."[7]

A preview of the book in the January 29, 1979, issue of *Publishers Weekly* was glowing:

> This superb history of the Mormons is everything a religious history ought to be and seldom is. The authors, both historians, both Mormons, had unrestricted access to church archives. Their book, then, is solidly based on fact, and the fine research is tempered with their views as insiders and balanced by the writers' unfailing and admirable professional objectivity. The story they tell, beautifully written, begins with Mormonism's origins some 150 years ago, traces the early church and its development, moves to the "kingdom in the West" and goes on to an assessment of the modern church. In the course of the book Arrington and Bitton take up polygamy, the role of women, attitudes toward blacks, the Mormon ward, persecutions, [and] conflicts with the government. An outstanding and definitive study, a very model of religious-historical scholarship.[8]

Two months after the preview, *The Mormon Experience* came off the press. With *Publishers Weekly* having paved the way, the book was well received within the church hierarchy. Homer Durham, who had been so problematic for the History Division, set differences aside and cheerfully walked into Leonard's office to describe the reception the book had had in the meeting of the Seventy's Quorum, to which Durham belonged. Durham had taken a copy of the book to the meeting, held it aloft for all to see, and spent several minutes describing the book and its complex genesis. "[He] told them it was a splendid product, and he thought the Church should be proud of it." Noting the anti-Mormon books that until now had been the staples in public libraries, Durham told them "all of this should change gradually as the result of the publication of this book." As he concluded, "he told the Brethren that he hoped some of them would find time to read the book, as he thought they would enjoy it and learn from it."

The contrast to *Story of the Latter-day Saints* could hardly have been greater, a fact not lost on Davis Bitton, who was also in Leonard's office. After Durham left, Bitton remarked sardonically, "Too bad he couldn't have had the opportunity of selling this to the Quorum of the Twelve and the First Presidency."[9]

Durham's praise for *The Mormon Experience* was sincere and durable. Over a year after its publication, he passed along to Leonard the comment of a non-Mormon friend, Elmer Culp, to whom he had given a copy of the book. Culp's last sentence contained an irony that the writer could not have appreciated: "Having read many other books about Mormonism—both pro and con—it is a relief to find one that is both scholarly and objective in its treatment of the subject. *The Mormon Experience* surely meets the need for that kind of writing. Incidentally, the fact that the church condoned its publication shows how much progress your people have made in facing up to the real world of the present and its historical underpinnings."[10] By the time Culp wrote his letter, the History Division whose work he had praised was being dismantled.

THE SESQUICENTENNIAL HISTORY

The centerpiece of Leonard's activities as church historian was the Sesquicentennial Series, the first comprehensive history of the church in a half-century and a project that church president Spencer K. Kimball had called "one of the most important projects we have inaugurated in the Church in many years."[11] Although most volume authors were not employees of the History Division, the church's role as publisher and Leonard's position as series editor gave him a major stake in the outcome.

As momentum developed toward the dismantling of the History Division, Leonard became increasingly concerned about the future of the series. In March 1978 he spoke with Lowell Durham Jr., manager of Deseret Book Company and Homer Durham's nephew, about its status. "Lowell emphasized that it was not fair for us to be working away and yet be uncertain about the possibilities of publication. Marvin Ashton, president of Deseret Book, agreed to present the matter to the Quorum of the Twelve, which he did in their Sunday meeting—presumably the meeting of March 12, this past Sunday."[12] Gordon Hinckley was given the task of investigating the matter and making a recommendation to the Twelve, and instructed that he might recommend a range "all the way from publication of all to publication of nothing, with many options or alternatives in between."

Leonard, whose customary cheeriness was worn thin by the waning fortunes of the History Division, wrote a pessimistic commentary on the likely outcome of Hinckley's investigation. "I suppose I should be completely confident that we shall be vindicated, but remembering the arbitrariness of other decisions, made without consulting us, I feel a real terror that he might recommend they publish nothing." If he recommended terminating the project, "I should have to resign. . . . I feel discouraged that they should even consider the possibility of breaking the sesquicentennial contracts. I think the Lord is testing me to see how I will bear discouragement."[13]

A week later, the two men spoke again. Durham acknowledged rumors "that the General Authorities were opposed to publishing the sesquicentennial volumes" and confirmed that Hinckley "had contacted the Church Legal Department to see if there was any way they could get out of the contract." Wilford Kirton, the church's senior attorney at Kirton & McConkie, "said orally that he did not see any way that Deseret Book could get out of the contract." Nonetheless, Leonard considered possibilities in the event that the project was canceled. One was to create a private publishing firm and publish the books himself—an audacious thought that was totally at odds with his essentially nonexistent business skills, but that reflected the depth of his commitment to the project. "This experience helps to remind me that I still have an important responsibility in staying on this job until the sesquicentennial volumes are finally published. I can't quit on the job until that is done—at least until those which are submitted by 1980 are published."[14]

Kirton's oral report was followed by a lengthy written opinion that made it clear that the church—in this instance through Deseret Book—could not simply cancel the contracts for the volumes and walk away. Leonard's reaction to the memo was predictably jubilant, albeit naïve: "All of this to me means that we are exactly in the same status that we supposed we were all along and that the project must go ahead on exactly the same basis that it has been proceeding since the contracts were signed in 1973. In brief, what we have done is alive and legally defensible and legally required."[15]

News that Leonard received only one day later should have sobered him. "Jim Clayton [of the University of Utah's History Department] said he had heard from a friend of his, a bishop, that the sixteen-volume sesquicentennial history would never be published. The bishop said he was told this by Elder Hinckley." But Leonard responded optimistically, "I reassert in this diary that in my own mind there is absolutely no doubt that all of the histories which are turned in by the end of 1980 will be published by Deseret Book in the form in which they are approved by me, by Elder Durham, and by a reader from the Twelve."[16]

When the church, presumably through Hinckley, approached Kirton & McConkie to see if Deseret Book could cancel the contracts of authors who had not finished their respective volumes by the end of 1980, the law firm quickly rebuffed that possibility, explaining that, unless they had cancelled all other contracts for books that were submitted after the contract date, their cancellation of the Sesquicentennial Series would never hold up in court.

One month later, as members of the History Division were set to attend the annual meeting of the Mormon History Association, Homer Durham instructed them to spread the word at the meeting that the Sesquicentennial Series had not been cancelled, thus authorizing them to authoritatively quash the persistent—though far from groundless—rumors to the contrary.[17]

Four days later, Lowell Durham called to tell Leonard that he had encountered Gordon Hinckley over the weekend, who had told him "that the matter of the sesquicentennial history which he had been instructed to study had all been resolved. They had decided that the authors were to be encouraged to finish their manuscripts, the manuscripts were to go to me for suggestions and improvements and alterations, and when I was satisfied they were then to go to Elder Durham." If Durham approved the manuscripts, they would go the First Presidency for final approval, and then to Deseret Book for publication.[18]

Writing in September 1978 of "Things I Have Done as Church Historian Since 1972 That I Am Most Proud Of," Leonard listed "the 16-volume sesquicentennial history—that each of the sixteen persons we asked agreed to sign; and proud despite the cloud over the work of the History Division that these contracts have been reaffirmed and the work is proceeding satisfactorily."[19]

By mid-1979 four of the sixteen projected manuscripts had been completed, representing four periods of Mormon history: New York (Richard Bushman), Ohio (Milton Backman), the transitional period spanning the turn of the twentieth century (Thomas Alexander), and twentieth-century developments (Richard Cowan). Since every volume had to be approved by a General Authority,[20] Leonard was anxious for the process to move quickly and became apprehensive when, in July, he inquired about the status of the reviews and the identity of the reviewers. "[Durham] gave the impression that there may be interminable delays on some of the sesquicentennial histories; didn't sound like he had any interest in speeding up the processes, either."[21] In late November, still with no General Authority reviews forthcoming, a colleague "asked [Leonard] about the Sesquicentennial history. He didn't know if it would survive. DB [Deseret Book] has had three manuscript volumes for six months with no action taken. And these are the 'safe' volumes!"[22]

By the end of 1979 a fifth manuscript, the history of the Church in Polynesia and the Pacific Rim (Lanier Britsch), was completed and submitted for review, but the continued silence from the ecclesiastical side caused mounting apprehension for Leonard. The written account of a year-end family gathering, which Leonard included in his diary, said that he "most fears the future of the sesquicentennial volumes."[23] A month later, he admitted to a sympathetic History Division employee, "If they kill the Sesquicentennial series, I would be forced to resign."[24]

In April 1980, having heard nothing more about the fate of the manuscripts after almost nine months, Leonard's frustration compelled him to write a letter to Marvin Ashton—a letter that he did not send:[25]

This letter is being written without the knowledge of my immediate superior, Elder G. Homer Durham. I hope that you will treat it as a confidential matter and that you will recognize why I feel sincerely anxious and am forced to consider this direct message to you—and to you alone. . . .

Three complete manuscripts have been turned in. They have been examined by the reading committee designated and approved earlier—myself, Davis Bitton, and Maureen Beecher.[26] They have been read and approved, with a few suggestions for improvement, by Elder G. Homer Durham. Then they have been forwarded by Elder Durham to one or more of the Council of the Twelve for final approval.

There the wheels of progress have stopped. . . .

I am placed in a difficult position, having been provided with no information. Not wishing to say anything disrespectful about those above me, I am forced to say, "I don't know, but I am confident things are progressing satisfactorily." But even this is frustrating. The one person everyone supposes should know the exact status of this project is myself, as general editor of the series and as director of the History Division. . . .

As the months go on—month after month without so much as a word—it does look very much like a deliberate, silent shelving of a series of books that all of us have worked on for many years in good faith. If for some reason the Brethren do not have confidence in me as editor, and this is the stumbling block, I am fully prepared to resign. The project is too important to be held up by personal privilege.[27]

Two weeks later, Leonard received bad news from an unnamed source. "Elder Hinckley has asked the legal department to work out a legal opinion which would enable them to cancel the contracts on the sesquicentennial history."[28] The following day, Leonard met with Lowell Durham and showed him the letter he had drafted to Homer Durham, which, without referring to Hinckley's action, defended the Sesquicentennial Series. Lowell responded, "I don't think it will do any particular harm." He also added "that he [Lowell] had attended a meeting within recent days at which the sesquicentennial series was discussed. Although he did not give a complete list of all those in attendance, I gathered later that at least Elders G. Homer Durham, Hinckley, Packer, and Ashton were there." Although none of them advocated abandoning the project, they acknowledged that possibility. "The real obstacles are Elders Benson and Petersen. Lowell thinks he can win Elder Petersen over, but thinks Elder Benson has such a mind fix about historians that he will never budge."[29]

After reflecting on this information, Leonard chose not to send Homer Durham the letter he had shown Lowell, without indicating in his diary a specific reason. Instead, he poured his frustration into a diary entry. "I have myself mentioned the project to hundreds of groups I have met with in the past seven years. . . . It is hard to overemphasize the fact that any decision to retract on a solemn obligation would be a crushing blow to individual authors who have invested untold hours—in reality, years—in their project. An announcement of cancellation would also be read as a signal of reluctance on the part of the Church to bring out thorough, responsible treatments of its history. It would be taken by many in and out of the Church as an unwillingness to face the facts of our past."

Since all of the authors were both friends and colleagues of Leonard, he felt an enormous obligation to deal with them honestly; and yet, the unexplained silence from church officials left him unable to say anything definitive, either positive or negative. "I want to be in a position to explain to them with full confidence, 'The histories are going ahead. We are at such-and-such a stage with your manuscript. We expect to see it published by such-and-such a date.' It is not fair to the authors to make an agreement and then fail to hold up the Church's side of the bargain."[30]

About six weeks later, in mid-June, Homer Durham gave Leonard a progress report of sorts: "At a meeting with Elder Packer and Elder Hinckley yesterday, the arrangement for paying the authors of the sesquicentennial volumes was finalized. Presumably letters will be going out in the next few days. Nothing was said about publication."[31] The following week Leonard reported the ambiguous situation at a History Division retreat: "As to the sesquicentennial volumes, we are not sure whether the news is good or bad. On the one hand, the authors whose books we have approved (Bushman, Backman, and Britsch)[32] have received their payment. The others are promised theirs when their volumes are completed and approved. On the other hand, we have heard no word that the volumes have 'gone to press.' But we have been assured that *the volumes will be published.* It seems to be a question of *when.*"[33]

Several weeks later, frustration turned into depression for Leonard, who confided to his diary, "For the past day or two I have been quite depressed about the status and future of history in the Church. . . . The sesquicentennial history volumes which have been approved and paid for—those by Bushman, Backman, and Britsch—have not been released for publication, and it appears that they simply sit on the shelf 'until someone dies.'"[34]

The following week, Lowell Durham finally gave Leonard some insight into the impasse within the Quorum of the Twelve that had resulted in such mixed messages. "Lowell says that the Brethren of the Twelve have to meet side by side with each other for 50 or 60 years, and so they don't want to make one angry; they go out of their way not to ruffle or irritate one of them. . . . Lowell also said he felt that his Uncle Homer had been more frustrated over the sesquicentennial controversy than any other."[35]

By December, Leonard was exasperated by the back-and-forth news that, by now, had dragged on for well over a year. In a letter to the authors of the series volumes that he did not send, he unveiled his frustrations:

> After exerting patience beyond the ordinary, I now must say that I am placed in a false position which is not fair to me and to you. I am not informed of the status of the manuscripts; no consultation is taking place that would allow me to know when or whether the three manuscripts received will be published. This is disconcerting, frustrating, and unprofessional. But rather than hide the truth of the matter and pretend that I know that the wheels are still turning, I must confess to you that as general editor of this series I am in the dark along with the rest of you. You know me well enough to know that I do not discourage easily. But I do not wish to bear the brunt of responsibility for something over which I have no apparent control.
>
> I do not know what to advise you. You have invested untold hours (years!) in the project and it is impossible for me to believe that the Church would fail to honor its commitment. We can all hope for some evidence of good faith. And it would be reassuring to have the project placed back where it was—on track, with a suggested timetable for publication, so many per year, as the manuscripts come in. I still believe in the project and envision it as a great constructive demonstration of the importance we Latter-day Saints place in our history. For the present, however, you should know that the matter is not in my hands. Now you know everything I know. Let us all pray for a fair resolution of the matter.[36]

Writing letters that he later chose not to send was highly unusual for Leonard and likely reflected the frustration that nearly paralyzed him as he attempted vainly to bring the Sesquicentennial Series to completion. Later the same month, Leonard received the phone call that he had been dreading. "Lowell Durham telephoned to say that he will try to set up an appointment with G. Homer Durham and myself tomorrow or Wednesday to discuss the sesquicentennial history. I asked him if the news was basically good or bad. He said it was not nearly as good as he hoped."[37]

The following day, the three men met. Homer Durham began the meeting by asking that Leonard be "understanding and supportive" of the difficult role that his nephew was about to play. Lowell spoke from a yellow pad filled with notes, a departure from his usual manner of speaking with Leonard, and a tip-off "that he had been coached as to what he was to say and that this outline would help guide him in doing it the way he'd been directed."

Lowell said that there was not a consensus among "the Brethren" as to what should happen to the sesquicentennial history. He indicated that Gordon Hinckley, Thomas Monson, and Marvin Ashton had "recently supported it vigorously in the deliberations," and Howard Hunter had supported it, but with reservations. On the other hand, there were those who were "strongly opposed to publishing any of the books"—Leonard assumed them to be Ezra Taft Benson, Mark Petersen, and Boyd Packer—and by virtue of being the two most senior apostles, Benson's and Petersen's opinions carried far more weight than those of the junior members of the quorum. Some of those who opposed publication had suggested that Deseret Book buy all the manuscripts and put them in a safe.

Division within the Quorum of the Twelve was not unprecedented, and while in this case it had led to a paralysis, in others it had been resolved by firm directions from the First Presidency. However, Lowell explained, "No member of the First Presidency felt strongly enough about it to counteract the very strong statements of opposition made by Elders Benson and Petersen and Packer." Therefore, Lowell had been directed to pursue a middle road that "would involve an individual conference between Lowell, myself, and the author in which the author would indicate his status on the project, and he would be reimbursed for some portion of the total sum due him."[38]

While Lowell hoped that some of the volumes might eventually be published by Deseret Book,[39] he was certain that one of them—the one covering the earliest period of Mormonism—would not be and that, indeed, its content was the basis of the divided opinions among the Quorum of the Twelve. "He cannot publish Richard Bushman's within the foreseeable future, because his was the one which has been the focal point of all the deliberation about the whole series and it will be politically naive for him to propose within two or three years the Bushman manuscript for publication."[40]

With the plug pulled on the series for lack of consensus, what remained was to settle with the individual authors, a task in which Leonard was expected to be present, the hope being that he would be able to persuade the authors to accept the cancellation of their work instead of defending it and arguing for it. Beyond expressing personal sympathy and sharing their resentment and discouragement, there was virtually nothing he could do. Those who had completed their manuscripts were paid $20,000 and allowed to shop their manuscripts elsewhere, with the proviso that Deseret Book share in royalties and rights, while those with partially completed manuscripts were paid on a *pro rata* basis.[41] The centerpiece of Leonard's franchise was dead.

Decades later, his son Carl recalled what that period felt like from the perspective of a child who had had to watch the suffering of a beloved but helpless parent. "I think that he knew that he could be pretty straight with me. . . . I never heard him say to anybody else the sense of betrayal he felt, and the lack of support by the Brethren. . . . When they pulled the plug on [the series], that was really kind of a knife in the heart. It was unfair, and it was shortsighted, and maybe fully understandable. If your goal is the retelling of the myth, all you needed was a screen at the Hotel Utah to do that."[42]

ARCHIVAL ACCESS

The disassembly of the History Division occurred incrementally, with one of the first straws in the wind being the limitation of access to archival materials. "One of the first things that I noticed was that we did not have free access to the documents anymore," recalled Carol Cornwall Madsen, who accepted a half-time position with the History Division in the fall of 1977. "We had to go through the process that everybody else did to request them. We previously had only had to sign for them. In fact, before I came all the staff members had free access . . . going up to the stacks and getting what they wanted. That changed just about the time I got there."[43]

The first genre of manuscripts to be restricted was presidential papers. In January 1979, Scott Kenney, one of Leonard's staff who was working on a biography of church president Joseph F. Smith, wrote in his journal, "Church Archivist Don Schmidt informs me that a month ago a new policy was established prohibiting photocopying any presidency papers without special permission."[44] Kenney, seeing the handwriting on the wall, worked feverishly in an attempt to complete his research while he still had access. "My main concern is will I be able to get everything I need out before restrictions are tightened? Will [Ezra Taft] Benson be content with this victory, or will he be able to implement even tighter measures?"[45] His redoubled efforts notwithstanding, he was never able to complete the biography, and a professional-quality biography of this important president remains to be written.

The circle of restriction gradually broadened to cover nonpresidential records. Linda King Newell, who was working on a biography of Emma Smith, "also sees things getting worse at the Archives," Kenney noted. "Within the past two weeks she was denied access to Relief Society minutes—just typescript. Relief Society presidency restricting now."[46]

In March 1980 the restrictions were extended still further to cover family diaries. For example, although prior policy had allowed for direct descendants of church president Wilford Woodruff to obtain copies of his diaries, Homer Durham instructed Leonard, "We're not going to give copies of diaries to anybody. I said that seems to me foolish, because the anti-Mormon crowd already have copies of these and they are apt to publish them in the anti-Mormon context; and to deny them to the families is to omit the possibility of their being published in a favorable context. He said to go ahead with the Wilford Woodruff project but not try to rush it, just simply cooperat[e] with the family to the minimum extent necessary."[47]

Three months later, Leonard commented on the gradual closing of archival access, even to the insiders in the History Division. "Elder Durham is becoming increasingly strict with the Archives—about allowing the use of materials to reputable scholars and even to us. The spirit of freedom is not quite as prevalent as it once was. I have been able to do some things on my own authority and at my own risk. . . . Exceptions to rules are now not considered except in very rare instances. He will not usually forward requests to the First Presidency."[48]

In late 1981, not long before the entire History Division was transferred to BYU, Leonard described the very grim situation for scholars of all types: "Elders Benson and Petersen are very much in the saddle and they do not want archival material made available to anybody."[49]

ATTRITION OF PERSONNEL

As the first winds of change blew in with Homer Durham's appointment in the spring of 1978, it became apparent to Leonard not only that the History Division would not grow beyond its current size, but also that it would likely begin to shrink. In October 1978, Durham gave Leonard an ultimatum on staffing: "Elder Durham is adamant—he will not allow us to replace anybody who leaves."[50] A week later, Leonard asked for clarification of the new policy: did it mean that there would be a reduction-in-force by attrition, or would there be forced reduction?[51] Durham did not give an immediate answer; but within a few months, he was employing both passive and active means to trim the size of the History Division.

On the passive side, Bruce Blumell left to attend law school in Canada; Glen Leonard transferred to the Arts and Sites Division of the Historical Department; and Jill Mulvay Derr left "to devote more time to her family [her son had been born in 1980] and to work with the Relief Society and Deseret Book Co. on a history of LDS women."[52] James Allen, one of the two assistant church historians, was "encouraged" to return to his fulltime professorship in the BYU History Department. As he put it in an interview in 2006, "At about that time I began to wonder if it was time for me to go back to BYU fulltime. Martin Hickman, who was the dean of social sciences, was encouraging me to come back. In talking with him, I sensed that Elder Durham was encouraging him to encourage me to come back. Nothing was said specifically like that, but that was the sense that I had. When I went to Elder Durham and said, 'I'm thinking of resigning and going back to BYU,' there was nothing but encouragement to do that."[53]

Durham wanted to reduce the size of the division as much as possible prior to the move to Provo, and so he began to meet one-on-one with employees. Glen Leonard's experience was fairly typical of the approach Durham used with the other staffers. "He called me in and said, 'Glen, you are from the University of Utah. You got a PhD from there. I think maybe I could get you a position there. Would you like me to see if I could find you a position at the University of Utah?' I knew that people were leaving, but people had left before, on their own. . . . As soon as they decided that we had to leave . . . they started helping people to find positions."[54]

Leonard characterized Durham's role quite succinctly: "He served as a midwife to get some of them transferred."[55] None of the former staffers interviewed later characterized Durham as a mentor or facilitator in advancing their careers. Perhaps that would have been too much to expect, given their love for and loyalty to Leonard; but perhaps they also saw their own love for and commitment to Mormon history being trampled by the new downsizing and de-emphasis policy.

OUTSOURCING HISTORIOGRAPHY

The outsourcing of the writing of church history carried two advantages for the church. One was that it could distance itself from the assumption by church members that what was written by the History Division represented the official voice of the church, this being a major concern of the senior apostles who were inimical to the division. Outsourcing would establish an arm's-length relationship that would allow the church to say, "This author speaks for himself/herself only." The other advantage was that it was easier to control archival access if the researcher was not a church employee.

Durham told division employees that apostle Gordon Hinckley had directed the outsourcing. "He said Elder Hinckley, though sympathetic with what we are doing, feels strongly that we ought to turn over the research and writing of Church history to independent scholars not in the employ of the Historical Department."[56] At the same time, "the First Presidency endorsed in writing a proposal of the Quorum of the Twelve (especially by Benson and Petersen) which in effect rescinds the Historical Department's 1973 charter,"[57] the charter having been to write history.

Part of the new order was a policy that previously approved projects that had been initiated by staff members, while technically still permissible, were effectively choked off by a new layer of restrictions that precluded even after-hours research. Durham specified that "the archives would not be open to them either at noon or after 5:00 P.M." Having dropped the bombshell, he closed the meeting without discussion and announced that he was leaving immediately on a five-week vacation and would not be available for comment.[58]

For the group of PhD historians, the dilution of mission was beyond the pale. One staff member commented to another, "It is clear that our purpose is to promote faith ONLY. Everything else is out. Just look for anecdotes."[59] At one department meeting in particular, emotions boiled over when Leonard reacted to Earl Olson's refusal to remodel the dysfunctional office space by saying, "What some of my staff are doing is important—is, in fact, more important than what you or I are doing." Olson countered that what the History Division was doing was not important and began to suggest that even those activities would soon be curtailed. "Leonard interrupted, 'Yes, and you would have us twiddle our thumbs. But we won't do it!' At this, Earl revealed his real feelings: 'They should just get rid of all of you right now.'"[60]

CHURCH HISTORIAN NO MORE

At a time when the essence of the History Division was being changed dramatically, a powerful symbol also changed. In late 1978, without warning or explanation, Homer Durham "made his position clear by putting up a series of photos of Church Historians over the years. Mine was excluded, and his own was included."[61] At a meeting of the Utah Endowment for the Humanities shortly thereafter, Sterling McMurrin took Leonard aside and commented: "I understand that there is a line-up of pictures in the Historical Department and it does not include your picture but instead has the photo of Homer Durham." It was a golden opportunity for venting, or at least candor, with McMurrin, the former U.S. Commissioner of Education in the Kennedy administration.[62] Instead, Leonard responded with almost superhuman loyalty to his administrators: "I said this was true and it didn't worry me in the least and I hoped it didn't worry him. I pointed out that the functions exercised by Joseph Fielding Smith and Howard Hunter and others had been divided up among several of us and that the managing director of the department might be seen as the heir to the Church Historian's position in a more accurate sense than myself as Church Historian or Director of the History Division." McMurrin didn't buy it and bluntly characterized this action as "reprehensible and wrong."[63]

Others thought so as well, one of them being a woman who was a member of the church library's book acquisition and cataloging staff under Earl Olson, who wrote to the First Presidency expressing her concern that Leonard's picture was not on the wall. "The First Presidency had replied to this sister that they would investigate the matter. The First Presidency then wrote a letter to Elder Durham which verified that I had been selected as a Church Historian, that I was a proper occupant of that office, and suggested to Brother Durham that either my picture ought to be put up or they would like a letter of explanation of why it shouldn't be."

Durham brought the letter to Leonard, and after reading it to him expressed his feeling "that in 1972 when the Historical Department was organized, that the managing director—a general authority—was regarded as the proper successor to Howard Hunter as Church Historian and Recorder." Durham was correct in his reading of history, and if the reorganization had either given the title of church historian to Alvin Dyer, the first managing director, or if it had dropped it entirely, which it did for many years after Dean Larsen held it, there would have been no controversy. Leonard understood this, as he had expressed to McMurrin weeks earlier, and when Durham asked him if agreed with his thinking, Leonard concurred. "He said he would then write a letter to the First Presidency explaining what they had done and justify it and tell them that of course I agreed with this."[64]

Although Leonard appeared not to be troubled by the photograph incident, the ongoing ambiguity over his title was troublesome enough that he took action. In December 1981 he wrote to Gordon Hinckley, then an extra counselor in the First Presidency due to the incapacitation of its other members, and asked for clarification.

"At the time of my 'call,' as Church Historian, President Tanner advised me that it was partly a Church call (and for the first two or three years my name was presented for a sustaining vote by the general conference), and partly a position in the Church group of headquarters employees, thus accompanied by a salary. I now feel that I should ask for a clarification. Have I been released from my Church call as Church Historian? If so, when?" He had a legitimate point, for the rule with church callings is that one serves until he or she is "released" from the calling. Leonard had never been released, and so there was confusion. "Many persons continue to refer to me as Church Historian, since there has been no public announcement of any release. Indeed, President Kimball only a few months before his recent operation introduced me to a friend of his by saying, 'This is Brother Arrington; he is our Church Historian.' On the other hand, other persons are referring to me as 'the former Church Historian.'"

Leonard emphasized to Hinckley that titles were not important to him. His concern was a practical one. "I still receive invitations to speak in Sacrament meeting and firesides almost every Sunday, and to study groups, civic clubs, and Sons of Pioneer and other organizations two or three times a week. I continue to receive a substantial body of mail and telephone calls from mission presidents, regional representatives, stake presidents, and others asking me to clarify issues of Church history that bother members and missionaries." In the absence of someone else in the History Division who could respond to the invitations and queries, he had continued to do so—"some of the letters contain earnest pleas for help because, as they say, they have written to other Church officials who have not been able to give them satisfying answers"—but he saw a need for clarification from Hinckley. He concluded by writing, "I am glad to do all of this if you wish me to do so, regardless of title."[65]

One month later a letter over the signatures of all four members of the First Presidency clarified the matter and, in the process, rewrote history:

> We are informed that on February 24, 1978, you were orally advised by Elder G. Homer Durham of the change in your title and status from Church Historian to Director of the History Division. That change was intended to constitute a release from your duties as the Church Historian. However, since you have asked for clarification, it is appropriate now formally to extend to you a release as Church Historian effective as of February 24, 1978. Also, in view of your transfer to the Brigham Young University to assume your full duties there, we also hereby extend to you an honorable release as the Director of the History Division.[66]

Leonard did not comment on the letter, either in his diary or his weekly letter to his children, for Grace's declining health preoccupied his attention. Two weeks later, in a diary entry backdated to February 2, he recorded but muted a second shock: "On this date, according to an entry in the Journal History of the Church kept by Ron Barney of the Historical Department, Elder G. Homer

Durham was set apart by the First Presidency as Church Historian and Recorder. Presumably his name will be presented in that capacity in the April Conference of the Church."[67] In fact, it was not (nor was Leonard's release announced); but Hinckley, who was conducting the conference session, slipped the information into a rather awkward sentence that was constructed, bizarrely, to give Durham's birthplace: "Elder G. Homer Durham, a member of the Presidency of the First Quorum of the Seventy and the Church Historian who, if I remember correctly, was born in Parowan, has now addressed us." Dwight Israelsen, a colleague from Utah State University days, remember how Leonard told him the news. "He said, 'I found out that I was not Church Historian by going down and reading the Journal History of the Church, down in the Church library.' . . . That did disturb him a lot. . . . He said, 'This is the way I found out. They didn't have the guts to come and tell me directly.' "[68]

DISASSEMBLY AND THE MOVE TO BYU

The possibility of the History Division—or, more accurately, its remnants—being moved to BYU had been floating in the air for some time, but as 1980 began it became more tangible, and Leonard's reaction was both prickly and a bit delusional. Even though the History Division was part of the church bureaucracy, he saw BYU as having less academic freedom than he then enjoyed at church headquarters. "Lodging us with BYU would ruin us," he complained. Even though he had received what should have been an unambiguous message, through Durham, that the sentiment among the Twelve was to remove history writing from direct church support (although allowing Leonard and his colleagues to continue research and writing under the auspices of BYU), Leonard still expressed denial. "It is not what we hear from General Authorities who talk with us. They appreciate what we do, they are glad we are doing it, and they think it is right and proper that the Church should be employing us for this purpose."

He continued to chafe at the manner in which Ezra Taft Benson and Mark Petersen were controlling the History Division, and although Benson was next in line for the church presidency and Spencer Kimball was in failing health, Leonard could not comprehend why people would not defer to Kimball. "Persons tell us that Elders Benson and Petersen do not like what we are doing and that if and when President Benson becomes president of the Church we might all be relieved of our positions. It's almost as if the decisions of the bureaucrats were being made, not on the basis of what the Prophet wants, but on the basis of what the next Prophet wants." It is difficult for anyone with even cursory knowledge of workings of the Mormon bureaucracy to comprehend Leonard's failure to see the writing on the wall. Yet, he wrote, "I refuse to believe that Elder Benson would fire us; I am convinced that we are doing what the Lord wants and that the Lord will not permit such a violent end to our work. I refuse to act on the basis of what might happen if Elder Benson became president."[69]

Five months later, in June, came a brief glimmer of hope that the transfer to BYU might be avoided. "Elder Durham says he will not abolish our Division unless ordered to do so. The chances of that being done are probably about 20 percent."[70] It is not clear what Durham was basing this prediction on; however, the enthusiasm was short-lived, for exactly one week later, on June 26, the First Presidency and Quorum of the Twelve, in an unusual joint action, informed Durham that the History Division would be dismantled and that staff members who wished it would be transferred to BYU, where they would become the Joseph Fielding Smith Institute of Church History.[71] On July 1 Scott Kenney, a staff member, wrote, "As of today, there is no longer a History Division." He continued, "The Institute will continue at the Church Office Building for another two years, and then move to one of the two new buildings now under construction." (That part turned out not to be true, as the JFSICH was housed in Knight-Mangum Hall, one of the older buildings on the campus.) Kenney continued, "My guess is that before the move is made, research will be closed except for those approved projects, and access to materials for other projects will be tightly restricted—as under Joseph F[ielding Smith]. . . . Starting immediately, everyone's paycheck will be coming from BYU."[72]

A month after the announcement dissolving the History Division, Durham wrote a conciliatory note to Leonard that tried to put a positive spin on things. "I am grateful for the decision of the Presidency and Twelve to shift the work of the division to the new Institute. In my opinion, that will guarantee permanence and continuation of the enterprise you launched under President Lee in 1972. The University auspices are highly appropriate for research and writing such as was your original 'charter.' When that charter was modified, it may have become possible for the work to have been phased out so far as headquarters are concerned, in my opinion."[73]

Though doubtless sincere, and likely accurate that without the BYU option the employees of the History Division may simply have been cut loose, the letter did little to assuage Leonard's damaged feelings. At the end of the year, his report in a family gathering had the tone of a broken man. "My third ambition, beginning in 1972, was to establish a research and writing division of the Historical Department. This was forcefully taken away from me in 1980, and so my present ambition is simply to finish up the Brigham Young book and then to do other studies on Church history. When the BY book is finished, I might well wish to complete my memoirs."[74]

Given the lack of transparency about the decision and the absence of a candid group discussion, rumors swirled in to fill the vacuum. Six months later, with the remnants of the History Division still housed in the Church Office Building, Leonard was confronted by rumors that he was released as church historian "to preserve his reputation," that "he had made some errors in judgment and rather than fire him they simply transferred him and his staff to BYU." He did not dignify the first with a response but commented curtly on the second, "My own feeling is that the biggest error in judgment was our decision to write history instead of propaganda."[75]

Many years later, several of Leonard's colleagues commented on various aspects of the disassembly of the History Division. Earl Olson, who began as Leonard's peer and ended up as his boss, defended the move without attempting to lessen the emotional toll that it extracted from Leonard. "It was a touchy thing. How do you change people from Church employment like that, down to BYU? That's where it more properly belonged, because their responsibility there is to publish . . . on their own, different from the Historical Department. So that took a lot of touchy manipulating, I think, in order to get the transfer made without offending. And yet, of course, it did offend. He had been Church Historian, you know, and that had a big meaning to him."[76]

Bob Flanders, a fellow historian from the Reorganized Church of Jesus Christ of Latter Day Saints, reflected on Leonard's heartbreak, which Leonard expressed to him with unusual candor:

> One day Leonard said, "I have to drive to Provo this afternoon, Bob. Would you like to ride with me?" I said, "Sure." I thought it a little unusual. Maybe it was the way he invited me, as though, "I want you to go with me, Bob."
>
> So we got out of town on the highway, and he said, "They are going to shut me down. I knew this would happen someday. I didn't know it would be this soon. But I have tried to get everything in print that I could get in print while there was time." He didn't say a whole lot more. . . . I don't think Leonard Arrington was capable of bitterness, but there was a depth of sadness. It was tragic, and you can't confront tragedy of that magnitude happily. Leonard was a joyous man as far as I could tell, but he was not joyful on that occasion.[77]

And George Daines, a former student of Leonard, suggested that Leonard was never fully satisfied with the explanation given for the move to BYU. " 'President Hinckley has decided to move the whole department to BYU. Is that to protect us from what he sees as a succession that will occur and it will be worse, and this is the best choice? Is it the choice he wants, or is it the best choice he can do?' I remember that discussion with Leonard, and Leonard basically talking about it in my presence, but not concluding what it was."[78]

G. Homer Durham as Disassembler

Once the disassembly of the History Division was a given, employees within the division readily pointed the finger at Homer Durham. In late 1978 Leonard had written, "I'm to keep smiling so that everybody will feel okay about what's going on; I'm to continue to be optimistic, but I must realize that his, Elder Durham's, job is to preside over the gradual liquidation of the History Division."[79] Despite Leonard's acknowledgment that "Brother Durham says he views himself as someone who is protecting my best interests,"[80] he would have been less than human if he had not seen it differently. "Leonard is very upset with G. Homer," Scott Kenney recorded sympathetically, "for he was in a position to speak up for the department, but instead went along with everything."[81] "This is a different G. Homer Durham," Leonard lamented to his diary, "than the one who wrote the series of articles for the *Improvement Era* many years ago."[82]

Despite Durham's claim that he was acting under instructions from members of the Quorum of the Twelve Apostles from the time he was assigned to supervise the Historical Department, Leonard put the blame squarely on his shoulders, claiming that "we know that the principal actions he took were on his own initiative. The First Presidency no doubt approved, based on information from him alone, but he himself wrote the basic memoranda, the basic policy letters."[83]

But Leonard's simplistic view, while understandable given that he was the victim, did not square with the complexity of the situation. At the beginning of the disassembly process, Durham opened up to Leonard with a candid acknowledgment: "He spent the whole time telling me that he had really worried, almost to the point of getting an ulcer, about our division and its future."[84] Most revealing of Durham's dilemma was his journal entry, written for himself only, at the end of 1979. In a lengthy and nuanced appraisal of the situation, which had not yet reached a conclusion, he showed that, in fact, he had been on the side of the History Division to a far greater extent than Leonard or anyone else in the division had been aware. It is regrettable that none of the division employees—or, for that matter, fellow General Authorities—ever saw the entry.

> The future, including the individual welfare and well-being of
> the staff of the History Division, has continued to occupy a major

portion of my thoughts throughout 1979, as it has since May 1977. Increasingly it has become clear that the desire of the Twelve is to have scholarly research published, researched, and written on the basis of individual initiative, and responsibility, both in the interests of the Church long-range, and of the individuals themselves. As the Church grows in size, there is increasing tendency for many to view anything that comes from Church Headquarters or Church staff members, as carrying official status, whereas the "simplification and reduction" process [which had rapidly become a major focus of the Correlation movement] aims at decreasing regulation, increasing individual family responsibility, and encasing the gospel in individual lives, not through increased "regulationism" but on the basis of pure principle. At the same time I recognize that Brother Arrington and his staff have been deeply in love with their unusual advantages since 1972. I have been very grateful for the fact that they have responded, if even slightly, to the "altered direction" indicated by the First Presidency on April 5, 1978. It has long been clear to me, and I presume to many of the Twelve, that a function such as obtained in the past in the History Division since 1972, is more properly the function of a university. It is my private view that such a function could flourish, both to the benefit of Brigham Young University, to the Church, to the world of scholarship, and the individuals concerned, had the project been launched at that point. The year 1980 may see further developments of some nature, for it is clear to me that the presiding brethren are clear in their desire, both on the basis of cost, and the basis of the advantages indicated above, to encourage scholarship individually, rather than at Church Headquarters. We will see what 1980 brings in this regard.[85]

Durham's journal entry is fully consistent with his actions throughout the process of disassembly and with the fact that he was the messenger, but not the architect, of the process. He was not specific, in this entry or any other, about who those architects were. His son, George H. Durham, a well-respected pediatrician in Salt Lake City, commented decades later, "I think my father was a very loyal Latter-day Saint, and obedient to directions from above. I do not think that he was the architect to the demise of the History Department as it then existed. I think he tried very hard to salvage it as best he could, and yet still meet the concerns that the Presiding Brethren, as he refers to them, had."

With respect to the hot-button issue of *The Story of the Latter-day Saints*, George noted:

At one point during his service as a member of the Seventy, Elder Petersen and Elder Benson had asked my father to read [*The Story of the Latter-day Saints*]. It is just full of pencil marks and notations. I think my father found himself in a position of trying to justify the ways of scholarship and scholarly independence and historical authenticity, to an institution that was concerned about building faith. I think the solution that he talks about in the [journal entry in 1979] is that you need to preserve scholarly independence and you need to respect what the institutional needs are, and they probably are best separated. I think he worked very hard to get that Joseph Fielding Smith Institute of [Church] History established.[86]

Parting Thoughts

Shortly before the move of the Joseph Fielding Smith Institute to Provo, Leonard wrote a lengthy and bittersweet valedictory in his diary, "Reflections on Leaving the Church Office Building." In its first paragraph, after describing the physical layout of the History Division's first home in the Church Administration Building, and its second in the new Church Office Building, he noted, "We are now forced to leave all of our offices in the Church Office Building."

He then described the various, and unsuccessful attempts he had made to hold onto even a vestige of the "real estate" that he had occupied for a decade. "I requested the privilege of holding on to my office for another year, but this was denied. I requested the privilege of my secretary holding on to her office for another year, in order to have a 'headquarters' office in Salt Lake City for the staff. This was denied. I requested one of the little anterooms in the Archives Search Room. This was denied. I then requested a table or desk for my secretary in one corner of the Archives Search Room. This was denied." A final request, for a vacant desk on the fifth floor of the building in which the division had first been housed, was under consideration, but it was later denied. He interpreted all of these denials as symbolic of the leaders' decision to move the division out of church headquarters. "It means lack of confidence in our loyal historians. It means no Church-approved research, writing, and publishing. . . . It means our great experiment in church-sponsored history has proven to be, if not a failure, at least not an unqualified success."

Perhaps most painful of all to read, and likely most painful for Leonard to write, was an admission that others who had not shared his optimism had been right. "One aspect that will be personally galling to me will be the gibes of my non-Mormon and anti-Mormon friends: 'I told you so.' Some scholars, Mormon and non-Mormons alike, have contended that skeptical and critical methods of historical research and writing are incompatible with the maintenance of a firm testimony of the Gospel. I have felt confident that they were wrong, and I have said so publicly many times—in professional papers, talks, books, and private conversations."

The grand experiment that Leonard had undertaken but never completed was to show that Mormonism, which is intimately attached to its own history as are few other religious traditions, would be strengthened, and not weakened by rigorous and honest exploration of the historical record. "I have contended that a Mormon can examine the truth of these and other facts connected with Mormon history with the same detachment and objectivity he would manifest toward other phenomena. If his faith is strong enough—and my own faith is certainly strong enough—he will take it for granted that, whatever the outcome of his research, he is not digging the grave of his own Church but, in the long run, is bolstering its structure by uncovering the truth."

Although he did not complete the grand experiment, he did take satisfaction in the fact that, at least in his own assessment, he and his colleagues had discredited the cover-up of history in which his predecessors had engaged, notwithstanding the fact that they were attempting, in their own way, to "defend the Kingdom." "What did the Church gain by the order of one General Authority to the BYU Library to lock up and prevent the circulation of Robert Woodford's Ph.D. dissertation on changes in the Doctrine and Covenants?[87] How was the faith of members preserved by the decision of Deseret Book Company, as influenced by the Quorum of Twelve, not to publish a second and revised edition of *Story of the Latter-day Saints?*"

Then, he extolled the virtues of a religious tradition that "has presupposed itself to be a progressive revelation of truth. Far from being inhibited by his loyalty to the Church from pursuing historical truth, the Mormon historian is committed to the discovery and unveiling of truth. He ought to be freer than the non-Mormon or doubting Mormon, who are already committed to a rejection of the Gospel, or at least to many of its claims."

Finally, after venting about the move to BYU—"On the face of it, the move to BYU seems stupid. Why move to BYU, where there are only limited materials on Church history, when we are already located on the Mother Lode?"—he acknowledged that there were, in fact, some significant advantages to the change in venue. The thought of teaching bright undergraduate students suddenly appealed to him. "Moreover, in the classes we teach at the 'Y' we can communicate our findings to students and thus help to educate Church members about our history." And not to be overlooked, especially for a man who never felt that he had enough money, "We are also in a setting which enables us to earn higher salaries than would be possible under Church employment." His concluding sentence was reminiscent of the 1963 hit song by Allan Sherman, "Camp Granada," wherein the camper who had been nothing but pessimistic while it was raining outside, saw his world change with the weather: "Wait a minute! It's stopped hailing. Guys are swimming. Guys are sailing." He wrote, "If some of the denials of our requests for certain holdover privileges seem petty and humiliating, we are certainly being welcomed and treated generously at BYU."[88]

The era of Leonard Arrington and the History Division, an era that had begun with great promise and that produced unprecedented scholarship and publications, ended with resounding silence, not even punctuated with a formal closing. On August 31, 1982, the packing and moving process was completed. Before noon the following day, the sign on the doorway was gone. "Earl Olson was standing in front of the directory on the main floor of the Church Office Building, rearranging the lines and letters to remove the name of the Joseph Fielding Smith Institute, Leonard J. Arrington, Director. A ten-year experiment in church-sponsored historical research and writing had ended."[89]

23

WHAT WENT WRONG?

In the autumn of 1981, before the final move to BYU but as the doors were closing on the History Division, Leonard wrote a candid self-assessment that began, "What did us in?" He then listed three factors that had combined to lead to the demise of the division. "First, the Tanners, Marquardt et al., and Fred Collier et al., 'borrowed' things from the archives, duplicated them, and used some of the material against the Church.[1] Although this had nothing to do with our unit, with our mismanagement or activities, we were blamed for it. Somehow, our image was tarnished by the stealings and sensationalizing of the anti-Mormons."

Second was the "jealousy and diligence of our John Bircher 'spy,' Tom Truitt [a longtime employee in the LDS Church History Library], who picked up everything he could find that would incriminate us and reported it regularly to Elder Petersen and Benson."

And third, he had depended on Elder Durham to arrange what was best for them, rather than taking Eldon Tanner up on his initial offer of an open door. "I should have been more pushy. . . . I should have insisted on some means of educating the First Presidency and Council of the Twelve about our Church history. I should have written them a regular newsletter or some other device of keeping them up-to-date on our work and our findings. I was too preoccupied with keeping the profession behind me."[2]

He was correct in the three factors that he named, yet he failed to mention a fourth that perhaps was more decisive than all of the others: the worldview of the New Mormon History's opponents that came directly from the period in which they had come of age, a worldview that simply could not accommodate the new history.

THE "UNDERGROUND"

Leonard accurately identified one source of the mistrust: an active attempt to break down the walls of secrecy that had been standard operating procedure in dealing with historical documents during the first three-quarters of the twentieth century. Part of this drive was energized by sheer human curiosity. Being told that something is secret automatically generates the desire to know more, and some of the curious figured out ways to work around the admittedly primitive security measures employed by the archives under Joseph Fielding Smith's regime.

But part of the attack on the church's policy of secrecy was genuine hostility to its truth claims, the classic motive of anti-Mormons that has accompanied Mormonism since its earliest days. Such an approach has produced dichotomy of good-versus-evil that has made genuine dialogue difficult. Significantly, the commitment of Leonard Arrington and the New Mormon Historians to "tell the truth" about Mormon history exacerbated the fears of General Authorities who were only one generation away from the protective strategy termed "lying for the Lord" (in B. Carmon Hardy's memorable phrase),[3] and who were, in general, so ill-informed about the facts of Mormon history that they were genuinely alarmed at the possible damage of "telling the truth." For church leaders with this attitude, faithful and believing historians could—and frequently did—fall into the same category as those Leonard saw as trying to embarrass the church.

Chief among them were Jerald and Sandra Tanner, both born into Mormon families and raised in Utah. Sandra reflected on their initial interest in Mormon history, and the subsequent development of the "Mormon Underground." When Jerald was eighteen, his bishop suggested that he begin preparing for a mission. "This got him thinking about the whole truth of the Church," Sandra said. "He had always assumed the Church was true. He just liked to smoke behind the ward house, but the Church was true. So he read the Book of Mormon and decided he couldn't believe all of that. One thing led to another, and he was challenged to determine why he believed Mormonism."

Jerald began to dig deeply, seeking out early imprints on Mormonism that were almost inaccessible, in addition to standard references such as *History of the Church*. "How many kids, at nineteen, are going to sit down and read the whole documentary history? I don't know why, but he did. Then he got a set of the *Journal of Discourses*. So there was this drive to get to the bottom of the whole thing. . . . How do you put the pieces together? He kept feeling the Church was controlling the pieces of the puzzle, so that you wouldn't come up with the right picture. He wanted to find the missing pieces that gave the full picture."

Finding the "missing pieces" and making them available to all interested parties became Jerald's passion—and after their marriage, Sandra's as well. "So Jerald becomes this super-dedicated Sherlock Holmes. For years, that's how he saw himself, as Sherlock Holmes trying to put together all the pieces. It made life very exciting, because there was always something going on. It was a race to get out the latest information on stuff." A loose network of document traders became known as the Mormon Underground. "You start making these connections of people that have been able, through the years, to get photos [microfilms] of documents. Then, you start having this behind-the-scenes thing of, 'I've got two documents on this topic. What will you give me for them?' 'Well, I'll give you one on this topic. But two isn't enough. You need to have three of something.' You get this trading going on. When someone comes up with a hot new deal, he can ask for so many things. Or he knows someone else has some hot deal, and you get this trading going on behind the scenes. . . . No matter who you are, you ought to have a right to see the documents, the same as somebody else."[4]

Although the Tanners also published narrative histories, their stock-in-trade became reprints of early Mormon publications, decades before the Internet made them available digitally. They also dealt actively in unpublished documents that circulated through the Underground. Michael Marquardt and Fred Collier, working independently, followed in the tradition of the Tanners.

The problem for Leonard and his colleagues was guilt by association. Davis Bitton described their dilemma. "Those ex-Mormons had begun their publishing activity before the History Division was ever created, and they would continue it long after. But the two activities were going on simultaneously. Some of the documents they published left the archives in unethical ways. We were not responsible for that. We did not sympathize with the Tanners. But in a very vague and general way one can imagine how 'the troubles with our Church history' could be seen in terms of both fronts. . . . Guilt by association is a devastating thing, as we discovered."[5]

Misplaced blame is also a devastating thing. While employees of the History Division had access to documentary material, they did not control it. That function belonged to the Archives Division, another part of the Historical Department, with its own director, Don Schmidt. Ronald Esplin, an employee of the History Division, gave an insider's perspective. "There [was] all sorts of stuff going out, but the perception was that Leonard was responsible: 'We had a closed shop. We brought in a professional historian, and all hell has broken loose!' But it wasn't fair, because Leonard was not responsible for the policy, he wasn't responsible for the management of the Archives, and he couldn't have controlled most of this."

Three times in eight years, by Esplin's count, documents from the archives got out to the Mormon Underground. In one case of which Esplin had first-hand knowledge, a seminary teacher—employed by the Church Educational System—was the culprit. "When I realized what had happened, I confronted this person and said, 'That is dishonest and unethical.'" The response surprised him: "If the Church is going to hide things, it's my heritage, as a Seminary teacher, as much as theirs. I need it for my students. It will bless their lives. If the Church won't let me have it, I know that So-and-so has it, and if I trade him this, I can get it."

So as was the case with the Tanners and other ex-Mormons, the History Division was blamed for documents that exited the archives via active Mormons. "One of the Brethren saw this as the 'Parable of the Toxic Gardener': The historians were allowed into the garden. They rummaged around, and everything that seemed to be sensational and dangerous and toxic, they threw over the wall. That was the perception that hurt us."[6]

Although Leonard was not privy to the extent of document swapping in the Underground, he was keenly aware of its harmful effects on his History Division. Since he did not control access to the documents, his response to the information that they contained, as well as the often-slanted narrative histories that devolved from them, was to provide nuanced, contextualized narratives from the History Division. "The solution to the publication of one-sided views by the Tanners, it seems to me, is not to deny that their view has any basis," which had been the standard approach by Joseph Fielding Smith and Mark E. Petersen.

Their reaction to little-known but revisionist information was to dismiss the information as lies, if they engaged it at all, and to blacken the reputation of those who published it as anti-Mormons and apostates. For example, flat denials by some apostles that Brigham Young taught blood atonement or the Adam-God doctrine created shattering cognitive dissonance for those who read his sermons in the *Deseret News* or the *Journal of Discourses*. Leonard's approach was predictably scholarly. The corrective to bad information was good information—"to show the whole picture, to provide context, to show that their view is misleading. The church's history may not have been unblemished, but it has survived and flourished because its members understand that any 'error' is a minor brush stroke in a very large painting."[7]

Leonard's best efforts notwithstanding, the perception in the minds of the only people who ultimately mattered, the Quorum of the Twelve Apostles, was not favorable to the History Division. "The best way to conceptualize this, in my view," explained Esplin, "is that members of the Quorum of the Twelve came to believe that they had a historians problem—that the historians didn't respect confidentiality, they didn't respect sensitivity, they didn't respect the sources. In fact, they didn't have a historians problem nearly so much as they had an archives problem."[8] Esplin's analysis was astute, and events bore out the truth of this observation.

SPIES

"Spy" is a word with strong connotations, whether used as a noun or a verb. The fact that Leonard and his coworkers used it to describe those around them who, for whatever reason, reported their activities to ecclesiastical officers says much about the atmosphere that came to pervade the Historical Department.

With the benefit of over three decades of hindsight, Davis Bitton speculated charitably about the root cause of the "spying," although apparently minimizing its total significance. "I think almost from the beginning I sensed, maybe 'resentment' would be the word, on the part of the older staff. Here were these new professionals brought in—I don't know that we strutted around like little peacocks, but maybe that impression could have been given, that [we thought] they were not doing things right or up to standard. On the surface, relations were always polite, and I think as good as could be expected. This little resentment on the part of some of them, if it was there, may have been just a natural thing."[9]

Viewed from the vantage point of the older staff, the new historians would have inevitably been seen as threatening. Whereas all of the senior people whom Leonard brought in had doctorate degrees, the carry-overs in the archives and library lacked college degrees and specialized training at the time they were hired. Some, such as Earl Olson, were the beneficiaries of nepotism, his grandfather having been Andrew Jenson, assistant church historian. Others had come to the job thanks to patronage—a friend-of-a-friend in many cases.

But for whatever they may have lacked, they were the institutional memory and, perhaps more important, they were totally invested in the culture that had characterized the Church Historian's Office for many decades, a culture that looked at history solely as a means for building faith. When their new colleagues ignored them—or at least failed to find ways to include them in the new mission— they did so at a price. Bill Slaughter, an active researcher and writer in the archives who became something of a master of the church's photograph collections, put much of the responsibility for the culture of subterfuge on the shoulders of the new historians, including himself:

> We really didn't take time to listen to them or learn from them. I'm kind of ashamed of it now. These guys may have known something that could have been useful, and had they been befriended they may not have become antagonists. I don't think people are aware of it, and at the time I wouldn't have thought that was going on, that they were active antagonists to the point where they were feeding information.

They were marginalized by the historians, by the archivists and by the librarians. Part of it is being in this position now, where I am a couple of years away from retirement. You get new people coming in and you hear them make statements, and you think, "That's really stupid!" They don't have any corporate memory. That idea of corporate memory is needed. There always needs to be an appreciation of those who came, and those who are about to leave need to be mentoring those who are taking over. . . .

I think we just kind of rolled in there and wondered when they were going to leave. [Our attitude was:] "You guys don't know what you're talking about," and yet they owned this place.[10]

Feeling minimized and ignored, on the one hand, and then sensing that the new historians were undermining the kind of devotional history that had been the goal of their office for decades, some of the older employees resisted. Being in a different division (usually the library) and receiving a much lower pay grade than Leonard and his staffers, they fought back by using the contacts they had built over the years to their patrons in the ecclesiastical line. There they found receptive ears and eyes. Writing a decade after the History Division was dissolved, Leonard described how disgruntled colleagues combined with a larger culture of increasing fear and distrust to undermine his division:

Many of the employees had begun working there when they had finished high school and were not the bright, imaginative, inquisitive people we had been accustomed to working with in the university. Many of the employees had a suspicion of university people; they did not trust "hot shots" who were interested in new ideas, new ways of doing things. These were years when, for security reasons, officers of the Church employed a number of former FBI men to watch for disloyalty. Trained by J. Edgar Hoover, they began to accumulate files on suspected individuals, files that incidentally still exist (1992). Perhaps encouraged by them, or perhaps on his own initiative, one employee of the Church Archives took personal offense to our trained historian newcomers, read everything we wrote, underlined in yellow questionable statements we had written, and forwarded these to a receptive apostle (one of the two mentioned previously)[11] who periodically read these statements, out of context, to the Council of the Twelve in an attempt to discredit us in the minds of "The Brethren." An active member of the John Birch Society, this employee also supplied church authorities with everything potentially questionable about us or our background, leading to the creation of files on us to add to those on other "liberals" who worked for the church or held church offices. He succeeded in raising questions about us in the minds of church authorities, so that there was something of a "police state" atmosphere.[12]

The active search for incriminating statements—which were made to sound incriminating by taking them completely out of context—and the atmosphere of hostile "tattling" were more than a minor personality difference with a disgruntled employee or two. Leonard wrote, "What is most disturbing is the apparent feeling on the part of some that we are letting some historical cats out of the bag. What they ought to realize is that the cats have been out of the bag long before we came in, in 1972, and that our efforts have been to try to minimize the historical impact of those unfavorable facts and to put the lid on other facts that can be found by intense study of Archival material that would damage the Church and all its officers."[13]

Making things worse for Leonard was the fact that the ecclesiastical officers to whom the information was funneled never sought independent confirmation or context. "Elder [Mark] Petersen never once talked to me, interviewed me, asked me about the things I wrote, but he complained in meetings of the Twelve."[14] Being ignored in this way hurt Leonard's feelings and, worse, made him feel disrespected as a professional. But perhaps most dangerously, Leonard was not fully aware that the terrain was being sown with landmines. His son Carl recalled, "I don't think my dad really realized, 'They're going to have spies in your class, reporting back what you will say. They're going to have somebody poring over every draft that they see, and underlining the stuff and giving it to Brother Benson and Brother Petersen.' I just don't think his imagination was that profound for what was really going on there. I don't know if he was naïve, or willfully ignorant, or just hopeful in a bad situation. It's hard to distinguish between those."[15]

Virtually any document can be taken out of context and made to appear different than its author intended, in some cases even the opposite of the intention. Once the History Division's detractors from within decided that Leonard and his colleagues were the enemy, they found abundant grist for their own mills. Not only did they freely link the History Division with those who, in Larry Foster's phrase, were "career apostates,"[16] but they constructed a conspiracy theory that provided a powerful interpretative model for the History Division's activities. Davis Bitton commented on the resulting headache. "It is my guess that some of our detractors had the mental picture of us as a conspiratorial, anti-Church cabal that sat around trying to figure out ways to cause trouble, to embarrass the

Church, to undermine and destroy. I can state categorically that such a picture was a nightmare reflecting fears and suspicion but did not bear any resemblance to the facts."[17]

Administrative Challenges and the Twelve

Third on Leonard's "What did us in?" list was the realization that he had been too passive when Homer Durham assumed the leadership of the Historical Department. Instead of assuming that the gentle amiability and explicit support of Joseph Anderson would continue, Leonard realized that he should have been proactive in reaching out to Eldon Tanner and, eventually, to the Quorum of the Twelve Apostles. The situation was more complicated than his self-assessment indicated, and really consisted of two parts: his own lack of administrative skills and experience, sadly by his own choice; and his failure to understand the primacy of the Twelve, thinking instead that his relationship to Eldon Tanner of the First Presidency ensured his division's success.

At a History Division retreat in 1980, after the fate of the division had been determined by others, Leonard acknowledged to his colleagues, "I spent most of my professional life avoiding administrative responsibilities, and managed to do so until this one. And I hold onto this one simply because I feel that if I'd step down from it, the consequences might not be in the best interest of the History Division."[18] Where others would likely have used his former position in academe as a stepping stone to higher things, Leonard saw it as his chosen destination where he could do what he most enjoyed doing: research and writing. "On two occasions," he wrote, "I turned down the opportunity of being department chairman. I will also confess something I have never told anyone else, that I turned down the opportunity of serving in the Tenth Ward bishopric for the same reason. I do not regret any of these decisions."[19] A colleague in the History Division noted, "He didn't want to get encumbered. He wanted to do his scholarship. He avoided all of those assignments like the plague, and then here he was, responsible for it."[20]

One of his first bureaucratic mistakes was to cede seemingly mundane administrative responsibilities to Earl Olson. When called to be church historian, Leonard accepted with the thought that he would research, write, and speak. "I left Earl Olson to do the administering, handle budgets, personnel, and housekeeping. . . . I do not regret this, even though, in afterthought, it might have been helpful if I had created a power-base at the Historical Department that might have been helpful in the long run. Certainly, Elder Durham demonstrated what could be done by using the Historical Department as a power base instead of a center for research, writing, and publishing."[21]

As a result Olson, who was Leonard's peer in 1972, became his boss and exerted control over the History Division. Olson's background, lack of professional training, and unquestioning loyalty to the devotional model of church history meant that he viewed with misgivings the reorganization creating the History Division. This uneasiness meant that instead of being an ally for the New Mormon History, Olson worked against Leonard's plans.

Leonard was bright and affable. Enthusiastically, he embraced a vision of this job as church historian where "everybody would be following church standards, everybody would be pleasant and cheerful, and there would be a 'Christian' atmosphere," as he put it.[22] In such an environment, almost certainly he would have thrived. But his vision was illusory, and his affability—and even lack of guile—were insufficient to deal with the challenges of reality, particularly when the going got tough. A fellow historian at the University of Utah commented on his skill set. "I think he was a very optimistic person. I think a person more calculating, more critical, even cynical would have avoided some of those missteps. On the other hand, they probably wouldn't have tried some things that he tried. And maybe there wouldn't have been as many people who would have come into the area of the New Mormon History and worked with him. They wouldn't have been as willing to, because he was so encouraging. But I think his strengths were also his weaknesses."[23]

Not only would a different skill set have allowed Leonard to avoid some of the missteps that he took, but it also would have given him a better defense when his adversaries moved to disassemble the History Division. In the words of one colleague, "I think Leonard was disappointed at who would come out with knives against him. I think he was unprepared for that. And they were some kind of knives."[24]

The other piece of the bureaucratic mix was Leonard's lack of understanding of the primacy of the Quorum of the Twelve Apostles and their priorities. Perhaps because the focus of his historical research had favored economic history, he appeared unaware of a dramatic and recent change in church governance that was in full bloom at the time he became church historian.

For much of the late nineteenth century and all of the twentieth century, the Quorum of the Twelve Apostles had served largely as staff to the First Presidency. Auxiliary organizations and church departments reported directly to the First Presidency. For the first half of the twentieth century, church presidents and their counselors had been generally active, vigorous, and above all accessible. Because of the relatively small size of the church, such a system of governance generally worked well.

David O. McKay's lengthy final illness of slowly diminishing capacity (he died in 1970) ushered in a period where, with the exception of Harold B. Lee's unexpected death in 1973 at the relatively young age of seventy-four, church presidents generally experienced periods ranging up to several years of partial-to-complete loss of physical or intellectual function. While the initial objective of the correlation movement was to eliminate overlap between organizations that previously had had minimal cross-talk, a more important long-term objective, of which Harold B. Lee was the architect, was to reorganize the hierarchy in a manner more suited to governing a multimillion-member church—a task that was becoming increasingly difficult so long as all organizations continued to report directly to the three-person First Presidency.

Although Lee did not say as much, it is clear in retrospect that his actions also addressed the problem of an incapacitated church president by shifting the power base away from the First Presidency. He began a process of structural revision so that virtually all components of the church eventually reported to the Twelve—essentially transforming the church from a monarchy to a constitutional monarchy. The church president remained the head of state, but the president of the Quorum of the Twelve became the prime minister, overseeing most aspects of church governance.

One who fully appreciated the supremacy of the Twelve was Hugh B. Brown, who served David O. McKay as a counselor in the First Presidency from 1960 to 1970. When McKay died in 1970, Brown was released from the First Presidency and returned to his position as a junior member of the Quorum of the Twelve—the first time since the death of Brigham Young in 1877 that a counselor in the First Presidency was released. Brown was reported to have said, "Even if you were in the First Presidency at one point, if you ignore the Twelve, eventually it's at your peril."[25]

Thus, the position of counselor in the First Presidency became more tenuous as power shifted to the Twelve, particularly when counselors were junior to several members of the Twelve, for in the "Q15"—the fifteen men who constitute the two leading councils of the church—seniority in tenure is all-important. When Leonard became church historian, his patron was Lee, who was then second-senior member of the hierarchy and shortly thereafter church president. He was an assertive leader whose influence was unchallenged, and he retained Eldon Tanner as one of his counselors. Because of Lee's assertiveness Tanner, although one of the most junior of the apostles at the time, had great influence.

Had Lee remained church president for the fifteen or even twenty years that were confidently expected of his presidency, it is unlikely that any of the three apostles who worked to dismantle the History Division—Ezra Taft Benson, Mark Petersen, and Boyd Packer—would have succeeded. However, Lee's untimely death in 1973 resulted in the ascension of Spencer Kimball to the presidency; and Kimball's primary priority was the church's missionary program. Even though his personal contacts with Leonard were unfailingly encouraging and warm, they were irregular and infrequent, and almost never involved any kind of systematic discussion about the History Division's agenda.

Lacking a church president who championed the History Division as Lee had done, Tanner's influence was greatly reduced. "[Leonard] didn't realize that a call from President Tanner was not all you needed," commented Richard Sadler, a historian at Weber State University and a future president of the Mormon History Association.[26] What you needed was buy-in from the Twelve, where a consensus would carry forward and prevail even with a change in church president. But what seems clear in retrospect was not clear to Leonard at the time. One colleague said, "I've sometimes wondered how you can be such a great Church Historian, and not see how powerful and important the Quorum of the Twelve has been in our history."[27]

But Leonard didn't see it, and thus he moved boldly to implement an entirely new approach to the writing of church history without laying the groundwork that would first build trust from and consensus within the Twelve. With the clarity of hindsight, Ron Esplin articulated in 2012, when he had major responsibility for the gigantic Joseph Smith Papers project, the arc of the History Division's development, spelling out the first stirrings of unease that he felt at the time:

> What happened [after Harold B. Lee's death] was that we began to get a number of public statements by members of the Twelve, especially Elder Benson and Elder Packer, but not only them. . . .
>
> It seemed to some of us eventually, through the mid-70s, that if Leonard could only open up some space to talk with some of these folks so that they didn't have to go public with all of their concerns, that it would be healthier for everybody. There was even some discussion internally that we pressed in staff meetings: "Shouldn't we have some conversation? You tell us about what President Tanner thinks and you tell us about President Lee, but the public conversation is this and this and this. Can we influence that at all?" His position was, "We have our marching orders," even after President Lee was gone. "It came from the First Presidency. We have an agreement. I have a vision, we have a plan, and we are going to go forward." He consciously decided not to engage the Twelve. . . .

Today there is conversation going all of the time, and regularly scheduled meetings with the advisors. That has been in place for a long time. Even from BYU, we had access to the church history advisors periodically. I didn't ever see that Leonard had that, and certainly if he had it, he chose not to use it.

So he could, in our view, have experimented with trying to reach across the aisle and hopefully work out a little bit of an understanding, or at least help them understand better why we think it works.[28]

By going it alone—that is, without the expressed consent of the Twelve in spite of his nod from the First Presidency—Leonard had mobilized no allies within the Twelve to offset the opponents of the History Division. Earl Olson pinned the ultimate decision to disband the division on Leonard's insistence on independence. "He wanted to be on his own. He published and wrote. Because of that decision to publish and write more on his own, he didn't get counsel from the Brethren as to what should be printed and written. They decided that [the History Division] was no place for a lot of publications to be written and published."[29]

William Slaughter, whose tenure in the archives spanned several decades reaching back to the Arrington years, reflected on the absolute need to bring the Quorum of the Twelve on board, and the fruits of such a strategic approach:

If you are going to get the respect of the Brethren, you must first come through for them. You must follow the agenda they give you. Correctly or not, many of us felt at that time that they [the History Division] weren't fulfilling what they were supposed to do, and they were going off and doing these things they wanted to do. . . .

We had all these young historians who were smart and capable, and the potential was there; but they were naïve in many ways, including what they thought the Brethren would think about this. They agreed among themselves, "They're going to go along with what we are doing." Having been here for thirty-five years, I have learned that it's *their* show. We are here at their behest. . . .

Once the Brethren understand that we are needed, that we are useful, then you can start to do some things. . . .

Like any new employee, I was trying to figure out the lay of the land. I do remember, probably within that first year, a realization that there were problems. The boys back there like to talk about "Camelot," and those who were never in the department like to talk about Camelot. But a lot of us archivists and librarians didn't think it was so "Cameloty," because we knew they could take us down.[30]

While it is only conjecture what Leonard and his colleagues might have produced if they had gained the approval of the Twelve, later experience provides some guidance, as noted by Ronald Esplin, who succeeded Leonard as director of the Joseph Fielding Smith Institute of Church History and who became one of the three general editors of the highly influential Joseph Smith Papers project. While he was institute director, he and his colleagues published a history of the LDS Relief Society, *Women in Covenant* (1992). In many respects it was a much bolder book than *The Story of the Latter-day Saints*, with many more sensitive areas that could have attracted criticism from church leaders. Esplin commented, "We got that published and had no flak. That's not to say that everybody loved it, but there was no pushback, and no administrative or institutional repercussions of any sort."

So why did *Women of Covenant* succeed where *The Story of the Latter-day Saints* got into trouble? "Because nobody had a chance to comment on [*Story*] ahead of time. . . . They are not going to tell you what to do. They want you to make the decisions, but they don't want to be blindsided. They want to be able to see it, comment, think about it, maybe give counsel." In order to give them that space, the institute personnel informed their advisors what they planned to do, what the timetable was, and, "By the way, there are drafts if you want to read them."

In response to reading the draft, general Relief Society president Elaine Jack, acting in behalf of unnamed General Authorities, sat down with Esplin and said, "We're not asking you to remove anything that is in here, any of the controversial stuff. But you could have a few fewer instances. We would be okay with that." With that kind of interaction, the book was published seamlessly.

By contrast, with *The Story of the Latter-day Saints* there was no conversation, no space for the supervisors to weigh in. While Leonard rightly felt that nonhistorians should not be given authority to edit history books, soliciting input from ecclesiastical leaders who were paying the bills and setting the overall agenda for the church would not have had a major effect on the content of the books—and it would likely have salvaged the reputation of *Story* and perhaps the life of the History Division.

"So from their perspective," Esplin continued, "I think it looked like, 'We are doing our best here to make our concerns known'—even though it had to be public, we knew who they were talking to on some of these pretty specific cases—'but they are not listening.' Then, when *The Story of the Latter-day Saints* came out, some staff people went through it and marked the passages that could possibly rile somebody up, and passed it on. And then, there was pushback."[31]

TIMING IS EVERYTHING

To have been complete, Leonard's "What Did Us In?" list would have needed a fourth item: timing. Part of the timing problem was unforeseen and uncontrollable by Leonard: the Mark Hofmann forgeries and murders, which had no direct connection to the History Division, but by being coincident in time with the turbulent years of the division had an effect detrimental to its operations. Hofmann heightened already troubling tensions surrounding Mormon history, a story discussed in chapter 28; but the timing was critical.

The other part of the timing issue was more problematic and might have been seen and reacted to at the time, but it went unaddressed and probably unnoticed by Leonard and his coworkers. While it is true that later historians employed by the church were able to write histories far edgier than *The Story of the Latter-day Saints* and to do so without the repercussions that Leonard and his group suffered, getting buy-in from the Quorum of the Twelve was only part of their successful equation. The other part was timing. One of the two primary antagonists of the History Division, Mark Petersen, died in 1984, not long after the division was disbanded. The other, Ezra Taft Benson, became church president in 1985; but despite having all of the "keys of the kingdom," he shifted his attention to matters other than church history and became a pastoral figure who kindly urged church members to read and assimilate the Book of Mormon.[32] Absent the adverse influence of these two men, the arc of historiography—*any* kind of historiography—continued to curve toward objectivity, bringing along with it a new generation of apostles conditioned by such objectivity. But neither of those factors had worked to Leonard's advantage.

In 1973, Leonard attended a banquet and sat next to Wendell Ashton, chairman of Public Communications for the church, and his wife Belva, who served on the Relief Society general board. The two men discussed historical writing, and Leonard "talked frankly to Wendell about the problems we had in writing good biographies, regretting that we had not produced better ones. I said that I doubted we could do very much about it as long as family members and church officials were so sensitive about realistic treatments." At that point, Belva broke into the conversation, saying that church employees should not even attempt to write biographies and histories—a harsh message for a Church Historian who was still in the honeymoon phase of his new career, brief though it was. Rather, she contended, such books should be written by independent persons "who could write honestly. She asked me if in writing history and biography we had to consider what the church leaders and members would think. I replied affirmatively. She countered that our work would always be compromised because we had to do this.

She greatly preferred to rely on Juanita Brooks, a fiercely independent writer with acknowledged probity. She remarked that if she wanted to get a straightforward account of something, she would read Juanita's publications instead of the church historian's accounts."

Belva had reached the same conclusion in 1973 that senior apostles reached almost a decade later, but for a different reason. Whereas they preferred to control the message by distancing the official church from its telling, an end that could be accomplished by outsourcing the writing of the history, she preferred unfiltered history, something she saw as impossible for a church-employed writer.[33]

For that time and place, Belva probably was correct in her assessment—and for reasons that seem to have escaped Leonard. Indeed, at the time of the conversation he had barely entered his second year of service as church historian and was still in a starry-eyed phase when every day brought new details to revise and flesh out traditional narratives. Even more significantly, his staff were frequently discovering major records whose very existence had been unknown. It seems likely that Leonard didn't even see the risk of his new venture. Ross Petersen, whose career lay in the History Department at Utah State University, reflected on the same point—that Leonard's strength was also his weakness:

> There was a side of Leonard that, I think, at that stage of his life and earlier, was a bit naïve. He felt good history would stand on its own merits, and he felt the process of encouraging people to do history and to do it well would stand on its own merits. So you're going to have a *Dialogue*, a *Journal of Mormon History*, a *Western Historical Quarterly*—you're going to have a lot more outlets for people to publish. And so, consequently, that's a risk. But he didn't think it was a risk. He thought it would just further enlighten, further clarify things, make it a lot easier for everybody if you didn't have to deal with some of the old myths. You'd just put them behind you and move on.[34]

One point that Leonard missed was the generation gap between himself and his two apostolic adversaries, Ezra Taft Benson and Mark Petersen. Petersen and Benson were contemporaries—Petersen was only sixteen months Benson's junior—but both were two decades Leonard's senior. They had grown up at a time when some of the original pioneers who arrived in the Salt Lake Valley in 1847 were still alive—and still telling their stories of persecution. Furthermore, Benson served an LDS mission in the British Isles in the early 1920s, a time when anti-Mormonism sold newspapers, books, and the new genre of silent movies (*Trapped by the Mormons* was released in 1922), packed lecture halls, and surrounded elders on the street with jeering hecklers. To the two apostles, religion was still an us-versus-them contest, a theological war—and in warfare one does not concede anything to the enemy. For them, history served but one purpose and that was to win the war, both by glorifying one's own side and by demonizing the other.

Leonard, by contrast, grew up outside the Great Basin, had no contact during his youth with the pioneers and their stories, and by not serving a proselytizing mission was never the object of persecution or even derision. David Whittaker, a historian and long-time archival administrator in BYU's library, recalled asking Leonard if he had received any persecution during his formative years because of his Mormonism. "He said, 'The only memory I have that would be negative would be this parade. In this parade was a flatbed trailer being pulled by some horses. There was straw on it, and wooden cages with chickens in them. Up front was a rooster, and along the side was written, "Mormon Patriarch and his Harem."'" He said that was the only thing he remembered that, visibly in his community, could be seen as anti-Mormon." Thinking about that, Whittaker put the puzzle together. "That's why he writes the kind of history he does. His generation had come to move beyond the prior period. But the problem was that the General Authorities that Leonard had to work with were of the prior generation."[35]

The worldview of the apostles, which Leonard failed to appreciate fully, was one of heroic history where the Saints always prevailed because of their righteousness, and the enemies of the church ultimately failed because of their iniquity—thereby "proving" Mormonism to be the One and Only True Church. One historian who spent most of his career in the Historical Department archives spoke to the continuing nature of this quest, even among some of today's younger generation of scholars. "We will do everything we possibly can to be 'provers.' That's why many of the BYU faculty, bright, brilliant guys, are in this proving mode. I don't mind the idea that they are apologists, but everything that they put out has to have some feature of proof to it; and if you are not proving, you are an antagonist, you are an iconoclast, you are trying to undermine."

While this kind of apologetic approach to history is seen occasionally today, it was the rule when Leonard became church historian. "It was just building momentum after the 1950s and 1960s. I don't have a better word than 'hardliners.' Some of the names are very easy to list, because they were public about their discontent with people like Leonard who tried to naturalize history. They couldn't understand that he could tell a story in an environmental setting, and still allow it to drip with faith. If he wasn't explicitly stating that the Hand of God did this, it was, in effect, a denial of the things that we profess to believe."[36]

In fairness to Leonard, his optimism about the power of the New Mormon History and his failure to appreciate its danger were natural outgrowths of the trajectory of American historiography, and more particularly of American religious historiography. Whereas earlier scholars had tended to disparage religion in general, post–World War II historians gave religion a second and respectful look, as described by Richard Bushman:

> After the war [World War II], Perry Miller at Harvard redeems Puritans. He depicts them as a powerful intellectual system that has to be taken seriously as one way of coping with the problems of human life. And then that continued all through that period. It was a time when Paul Tillich is hired at Harvard Divinity School, and Reinhold Neibuhr is a major voice in American intellectual history. So religion can no longer be dismissed as it had been in the '30s and '40s. That made it possible to treat even a far-out religion like Mormonism seriously. But what I see as also important is this growing love for young Mormons to get PhDs in the '50s and '60s, because up to that point most of our writing had either been directed in the form of debate with our critics, or instruction for our people, especially our young. . . .
>
> When you go back and start writing a dissertation in a graduate school, that your committee will certainly read and you imagine your peers read it, you have to get a different tone of voice. You have to measure up to a certain standard. You have to admit errors. You just can't get away with apology. We had that generation that went away in the '30s to Chicago, and they came back not with the intention of writing for the world at large, but of instructing the Saints and bringing them out of their naiveté. So they sort of moved in thinking, "We are now going to liberalize Mormons." Of course, they got into huge trouble. So that, in a way, was a failure in terms of our graduate work.
>
> But after the war, Jim Allen . . . just wants a job as a historian. It becomes a career path. . . . So that evokes a new kind of history, which requires speaking across the divide. You have to find a tone of voice and an interpretive stance that will work in both worlds. And that is really what defines the New Mormon History, to find a way of speaking broadly and not just to a single audience.[37]

Imbued with a sense of mission as the vanguard of a new approach to history that was certain to move the church forward, Leonard plunged in headlong without stopping to consider either that he might be biting off more than he could chew, or that his elders, particularly the Twelve, might be getting more than they could swallow. There was a huge gap between where Benson and

Petersen stood and where Leonard wanted to move them, and the gap could not possibly have been closed quickly. In fact, it could not have been closed at all without a careful transition program designed to educate those tribal elders about the virtues of the new history. They knew that their history had been neglected for decades, and they agreed in principle that having a professional historian as church historian was a step in the right direction—hence their approval of the recommendation of the Cresap report to professionalize the Church Historian's Office.

But no one was sure, at first, where that direction would take them. Rather than consider the nuances of his task, Leonard moved quickly and broadly to write and publish Mormon history in quantity, with the goal of merging it into the mainstream of American—and particularly Western American—historiography, rather than continuing the tradition of devotional history of his predecessors. Jan Shipps, a non-Mormon historian of Mormonism whose acquaintanceship with Leonard stretched back to the early 1960s at Utah State University, commented on Leonard's goal. "When he went to talk to the Brethren—when they called him to talk to them—he was talking about merging Mormon history with the history of the West, not concentrating on the sacred history. He hadn't dealt with that. Here you have a man who is a profoundly religious man, even a mystic; but he separates that off on one side, and the history is the history of the West. It's just like Civil War history. It was *history*. It was not religion."[38]

But religion was what his patrons expected, and he failed to demonstrate to them why the new approach was better, and how it could tell the history without jettisoning the religion. Richard Howard, Leonard's counterpart in the RLDS Church, sympathized with Leonard's plight, for he was dealing with the same dilemma. "He could see connections between culture and institution, culture and church, culture and person. I think probably some of that was what got some of the Brethren a little bit anxious. The minute you start humanizing your religious icons, your religious leaders, you start to show them with their human traits as well as their spiritual traits. . . . It's a threat to people who feel like theirs is the One True Church. . . . He could make his people believable because they were human beings living in a culture. They weren't just one-dimensional figures walking down some illuminated track, and beyond them was darkness. That's just such a false image."[39]

False though that image was, any attempt to modify it to one more closely aligned with historical data was fraught with peril, and Leonard seems not to have been fully aware of the depth of that peril. Lester Bush, author of the game-changing article on blacks and priesthood, had a keen, almost intuitive, grasp of the strategy, public relations, and political maneuvering. He reflected:

I think Leonard actually believed he was going to pull it off, that the Church was going to be willing to embrace this new history. . . . It suggested that he was very naïve; but sometimes I even wondered if he understood exactly where all that history was going. Honestly, I think he probably did and didn't think about it, because it was hard to imagine a person in his position not being much more aware. But he always talked like a man of pretty simple faith, at least to me. It was as though it wasn't people he was dealing with, and that maybe things hadn't been as unfortunate as it would appear from the historical record.

I can remember being somewhat in a related camp in those years, where my simplistic statement of it was, "If it was good enough for the Lord for it to happen this way, why do we choose to express it differently?" It's that faith of a fundamental believer that says, "Why would God ask us to put it down differently than what He actually did?" Of course, that assumes that He did anything. But one misses the fact that it is an organization, with all of that dimension of self-preservation.[40]

And self-preservation, in the worldview of the church leaders of Leonard's era, was contingent upon maintaining a carefully burnished image not only of past events, but also of the leaders of that past. After more than a century of inspirational heroics, that image could go only in one direction with the kind of history that Leonard and his colleagues were writing. Bush continued,

It always seemed to me like tolerating the evolution of thinking undermined the stature of the leaders: First, what they thought they knew, they didn't, so they became lesser authorities. Second, if you demonstrate fallibility or humanity or whatever you want to call it in the history, that cuts forward as well as backwards. So you take these guys down a few notches because the organization, if you look at its history, doesn't suggest that God personally came down and picked them out of the millions or billions of people to run this unique thing. And if you didn't have it already in your mind, if the icons of the past made mistakes, then how about this one at present? So they have a problem of self-esteem and a problem of governance.[41]

David Whittaker put it most succinctly when he said, "Historians, by nature, are the enemies of memory."[42] And when that memory is tinged with the sacred, the historians will always fight an uphill battle with the ecclesiastics. Nonetheless it is a winnable battle, as the current Church History Department has shown with books such as *Massacre at Mountain Meadows* that have gone beyond Leonard's wildest dreams in dealing candidly with the darkest shadows of Mormonism's past, while at the same time gaining buy-in from the top.[43] Part of the success of the current generation of historians employed by the LDS Church has been a greater appreciation of the hazards in retelling the story, and greater patience and skill in negotiating those hazards; but perhaps the most important difference from Leonard's era has been the passage of time. His most formidable foes have long since departed this life, replaced by men with markedly different appreciation of the changed world of historiography, and particularly of the influence of the Internet on telling the entire story lest well-informed critics immediately discredit it. Even with the kind of care that he did not demonstrate as church historian, the response from the ecclesiastical side may still have been, "We are not yet prepared to do this."

$$24$$

GRACE'S DECLINE

Grace Arrington was deeply contented with her life in Logan, with her southern friendliness and charm drawing around her a circle of loyal friends; but she never fully adapted to Salt Lake City. The house that they purchased was ill-suited both to their advancing age and to their cohabitation with Grace's mother, who lived with them from 1963 until her death in 1980. But the most unfortunate aspect of the move had to do with Grace's health: "The day we moved I got a terrible cold," she wrote, "which turned out to have far-reaching effects. The doctors now think I had a virus which affected my heart."[1] For the following decade, until her death in 1982, congestive heart failure—weakness of the heart muscle resulting in inadequate blood circulation and the accumulation of liquid in the extremities, particularly the legs—defined Grace's health.

Congestive heart failure is a progressive disease. By 1976 Grace's health had deteriorated to the point where she required medication—diuretics—to address edema in her extremities. In his weekly letter to his children in January, Leonard summarized her condition, including her medications, and then stated optimistically, "With all of this clear, both to the doctor and to Mamma, and with her now recognizing and able to recognize each of the different pains, the doc thinks she will have 20 more good years."[2] He missed the mark by fourteen years.

With this diagnosis and a medication regime that targeted her symptoms, her quality of life improved markedly. One month later Leonard noted, "Yesterday was Grace's 62nd birthday. She awoke yesterday morning with no pain in her arm, none in her back, none in her leg, none in her stomach—feeling good, she says, for the first time in many months."[3]

"Feeling good," however, was a relative term, for several weeks later Leonard commented on the larger picture of Grace's health, noting somberly that she had not been physically well since the move to Salt Lake City four years earlier. "She has had to have a hysterectomy, she also fell down the stairs and had a shoulder separation—a very painful thing, her arthritis is more advanced, she has had some stomach troubles; she really has not felt well even half the time. She has felt poorly day after day, week after week to the extent that she could do things she desired to do only perhaps two or three days a week." Although her health problems might have occurred at the same age if she had remained in Logan, their occurrence in Salt Lake City "contributed to her depression and sense of hopelessness here."[4]

Six months later, Leonard wrote an update to his children: "Mamma, while basically better, and feels she is going to be better still, has had some bad days, or nights. But none of the deep depression she was having months ago."[5] Her condition stabilized enough that Leonard mentioned it only infrequently during the next four years.

Intermixed with Grace's physical problems, however, was the emotional toll of the turmoil in the History Division. Maureen Beecher, who worked with Leonard daily, linked the two: "During all that time, it is my belief that Leonard did not talk to Grace about it. . . . My own feeling is that that is what brought Grace down. She could see what was going on in him, and he wasn't talking to her about it. You could see her wearing down bit by bit. She always hosted our Christmas gatherings and attended other sessions with him, and I could see her wearing down. But that's my thought, and that's because that's how I would feel under those circumstances."[6]

Grace's daughter agreed with Beecher's assessment. "It's much more difficult having your husband criticized than it is to have them criticizing you. So Mom was having a very bad time with these things that were happening to Dad. He realized that pretty quick, and so he stopped telling her—which was worse. . . . Carl [Susan's brother] thinks that Mom passed away much earlier than she may have died, because of the effect this was having on her."[7]

Only rarely did Leonard either bring his problems home or let his coworkers know of Grace's dilemma, but on at least one occasion he blew off steam at work. When coworker Bill Hartley mentioned in a division meeting the discouragement and insecurity among the spouses of the historians, Leonard shot back, "Nobody has been more bitter about it all than Grace Arrington."[8]

By early 1981, Grace's condition deteriorated to the point that she only infrequently felt like leaving their home. In April, Leonard wrote to his children: "Since Christmas I have gone to most things alone, and it looks like I'll have to continue to go alone or not go at all. And one doesn't hear Mamma's usual laughter and enthusiastic talk around the house. Things are more solemn, grave, long-faced, sad, words of concern, some moaning and occasional crying. I still am hopeful; I still have faith she'll get better, but it's more faith and less reasonable expectation than it used to be."[9]

Two weeks later, following a visit to her physician, Leonard gave his children the most pessimistic assessment yet. "Mamma will never get over her heart condition. She will never get well, in the sense of being restored to where she was 20 years ago. Her heart will forever be inadequate to a full, busy life. Her heart's performance will vary, between 'good' and 'bad.' That is, there will be weeks and months when the heart will enable her to function reasonably well; other times when she will have to spend much of every day in bed."[10]

In January 1982, Grace's condition worsened significantly. In an attempt to control her edema, her physician first doubled, and then quadrupled her dose of diuretics.[11] In mid-February, most of the family members were able to gather in Salt Lake City. Leonard gave a somber and yet reassuring account of the meeting. "We had a pretty serious family meeting that evening. Grace told them she didn't think she had much longer to live, that she was fully reconciled to it, that she had accomplished all her important goals, that she had received a manifestation in the temple that caused her to feel at peace and fully reconciled."[12] Leonard later expanded on his account of that meeting and other family gatherings when writing to friends after Grace's death:

> Perhaps the most helpful thing is that Grace was aware of her condition and on occasions when we had the family together during the last several months—James's wedding, Christmas, a family meeting in February—she told us all that she knew we loved her, that she had accomplished all of her goals in life (seeing each one married in the temple, having the opportunity of showing each one North Carolina, knowing that her husband's work was fully appreciated, etc.), and that she was fully reconciled to what might happen. She had had a couple of spiritual experiences in the temple which added to this feeling of reconciliation and reassurance.[13]

The temple experiences that were so meaningful to Grace in reconciling her to her approaching demise must have had a similar blessing in strengthening Leonard for the demise of his professional dreams. As authorized by President Spencer W. Kimball, Leonard and Grace received their second anointings on April 1, 1979.[14] This ultimate Mormon ritual assured them of salvation and eternal union.[15]

Early in March, Grace's condition plummeted. March 7 was "the worst night she had ever spent. She could sleep only in five-minute intervals. She was very pale and cold all over." The next morning, after conferring with Grace's doctor, Leonard had her taken to the hospital in an ambulance. On the morning of March 10, Leonard visited her in the hospital. "I asked Grace whether I should go ahead and accept my appointment to speak to the Ogden Rotary that noon. She said yes. I couldn't remain there during the noon period in any case."

When he returned to the hospital later in the afternoon, Grace's condition was worsening quickly. By early evening, Grace's doctor told Leonard that "the cause seemed hopeless," and suggested that he call his children. Within the hour, and before any of the children were able to reach the hospital, "her spirit left her."[16]

What Leonard's account of Grace's last days, written a week after her death, did not portray was a sense of denial on his part of her imminent death. Many years later, daughter Susan recalled her mother's last hours. "[Dad] called me up the morning of the 10th and said, 'I just wanted to let you know that Mama has been put in the hospital. I think by the weekend she'll be stabilized and she'll be better. So go ahead and make your plans to come on the weekend. But I just wanted to let you know she is in the hospital.'" With that assurance, Susan and her family planned to visit Grace on the weekend, not knowing that she had been transported to the hospital in an ambulance, "with the red lights going. [Dad] didn't convey that to us. He just sounded almost casual about it." Nor did he tell them that when Grace was admitted, her doctor told Leonard that she probably would not recover. "So red lights flashing, ambulance, doctor saying she was not going to come out of it; and he told us not to come."

Leonard's phone call on the evening of March 10 was the first Susan knew about her rapidly deteriorating condition. She recalled, with considerable anguish, the hours following the phone call:

> We threw the kids in the back seat and drove as fast as we dared, to Salt Lake. About in the Bountiful area as we were going in the car, Spence Craney, who is the mortician in Logan who had done two funerals for our family, passed us on the freeway going pretty lickety-split. I looked over and I recognized him, and I knew she was gone. She probably died within 20 or 30 minutes of Dad's phone call to us. I remember not saying anything; I didn't lose it, but I said, "Dean, did you see who that was?" There was just silence.
>
> We got to LDS Hospital and went up the elevator to the intensive care unit. When the elevator door opened Dad was standing right there, and he said, "She has died. She's gone."
>
> I think about that, especially that he went and gave a talk. He was in denial of some pretty important things in his life.[17]

Indeed, as Leonard went through Grace's papers, particularly the diary that she had kept for several years, he implicitly acknowledged that he had often paid far more attention to his career than to her life. "Her diary reflects her innermost thoughts and it is sometimes painful for me to read, since she did not always feel that I understood her. . . . I have read some in the diaries and I have been surprised at the large amount of space given to 'I don't feel well today'; 'I wonder if I can go on like this.' Clearly, she suffered a long time."[18]

Leonard was, by nature, reticent to show the kinds of emotion that relate to sorrow and grief. Grace's funeral was a cathartic experience for him, and a dramatic contrast to his usually stoic temperament. Susan was startled at his unrestrained emotion. "That funeral of Mom's, in March of 1982, was the only time I ever saw my dad cry. He never showed that kind of emotion." She recalled how her father and mother, while courting in North Carolina in 1942, attended a Christmas Eve mass. As the choir began to sing "O Holy Night," Leonard slipped a ring on Grace's finger. "[He] held his hand over it until the song was over. When it was over, he took his hand off, and it was a diamond ring. So that was the occasion at which they got engaged. At the funeral, there was a couple who sang 'O Holy Night,' even though it was March. That was why the song was chosen, and Dad just broke down. I was sitting next to him. That song was their song. That was the first and last time I saw him really shed tears."[19]

For their entire married life of thirty-nine years, Grace had run interference for Leonard so that he could devote himself, single-mindedly, to his professional life. With her death, he had to confront things that others take for granted.

25

TRANSITIONS

The year 1982 brought major transitions to Leonard: first, the loss of Grace that left him a widower, and second, reconfiguring a career after the disbanding of the History Division and the move to BYU.

DOMESTIC SKILLS

Leonard was the equal of his father in his complete bafflement when faced with a domestic task. Noah Arrington demonstrated his personal skills a decade after Leonard's birth, as Leonard recalled wryly. "In September 1927 Mom was taken to Montooth Maternity Home in Twin Falls to have her first baby delivered away from home. Dad did not know how to cook. While she was gone, Dad was simply incapable of managing the household, though he was well intentioned. He tried once to make tomato soup; we all got sick and haven't been able to stand tomato soup since. He once brought home cans of sardines and hominy that we couldn't stand and can't bear to have them in the house to this day."[1]

Grace was a superb homemaker and cook, famous for her pecan pies. As Leonard's wife, she had so thoroughly taken care of all of Leonard's domestic needs that her death left him, in many ways, helpless. The month of Grace's funeral he confessed to friends, "The children all know that I have never cooked or kept house, so Carl stayed here an additional week to teach me how to cook for myself."[2] The cooking lessons began with a basic: "He literally didn't know how to boil water." But that lesson, though it took, was not the foundation for a new culinary career. "When he learned about frozen dinners, boy! He was cool with that. He could get through the supermarket faster than anybody I've ever seen. He would go in there, and he was running! He'd run right down to the frozen aisle, throw frozen dinners in his cart, run out, and that was it. He'd get seven, and go."[3]

Several weeks after Carl left, Leonard noted triumphantly in his dairy, "I'm back at a normal pace of eating Stouffer's for dinner."[4] With cereal for breakfast and lunch out, either at the Lion House or across the street in the ZCMI food court, he managed to keep himself fed. However, in a letter to his children the following month he complained, with unintended comedy, about his struggle to master new skills.

> From time to time I have referred to various problems which confront me. Let me mention the biggest in recent months. And that is the indefiniteness of instructions that I am supposed to follow in keeping house.
>
> My Stouffer's instructions say: Place chicken pouch on non-metallic plate and puncture top three to four times with fork to vent. Well, is it three or four? If I puncture it three, what might happen? What if I puncture it four? Would it get too much air on four? Would it explode if only three? Why don't they say what they mean? Then it says heat three to four minutes. O.K., should it be three or should it be four? Will it be undercooked if three? Or overcooked if four? Or does it depend on the altitude? And if I'm at 4,000 feet, should it be three or four? I simply can't stand this indefiniteness; it's driving me crazy, making these decisions when I am so ignorant and inexperienced. I wish somebody would tell me what to do. . . .
>
> Now when I was in the Army there was none of this. And I presume there will be none of this in the United Order, or even in Heaven. When you give the blessing on the food it has to be said precisely—not one extra word and not one word omitted. And in the temple everything is precise. Why can't ordinary life be like that?[5]

Somehow he managed to learn just enough to fend for himself, and in September, six months following Grace's death, Leonard, who had turned sixty-five in July, reassured his children that he was in no hurry to remarry: "Certainly, I'm not looking for someone now. Women my age look too old, and women that look good are too young & cannot be happy marrying someone who has no more years ahead than I am likely to have."[6] Only two days later he went on his first date.

THE UPSIDE OF THE MOVE TO BYU

Tucked amid Leonard's protests, denials, and attempts to work around the fiat, he also occasionally acknowledged an upside to the move to BYU that went beyond the essential fact that the history-writing franchise had been saved. In July 1980, shortly after the decision to move to BYU had been made, Leonard wrote to his children: "I suppose I am most hurt by the failure of anyone to consult with me in advance of the action, and by the insistence that Davis [Bitton] not go with us to BYU if he preferred. On the other hand, I certainly will enjoy being in an academic setting once more, responsible to academic administrators rather than ecclesiastical officials."[7]

Several months later, he became far more expansive in enumerating to his children the move's benefits. First on the list, and given Leonard's lifelong sense that he never had sufficient money, probably foremost in his mind, was a 25 percent raise, from $40,000 to $50,000. He noted that his staff would also be well paid "in comparison with other BYU faculty. Nobody can say that the Church is not investing a lot in us."

Next, having faculty status would give him "the opportunity of being more professional. We won't have to sign time cards, worry about taking annual leave (vacation time) every half day we decide to stay home and work, and so on. We'll have time to do some professional improvement, be eligible for sabbaticals, have a full month vacation each year, and so on."

Third, and curious in light of the long, unsuccessful fight he had waged to retain his job at church headquarters, was an acknowledgement that "we'll probably have better status professionally by being connected with a university. Fewer people will be apt to think 'He/she is just a Church employee; doing what the Church wants done.'"

And finally, he and his coworkers would have far greater freedom in writing and publishing, being "one step removed from ecclesiastical control. . . . I'm sure the Lord must get impatient with the overprotective recommendations of some of the bureaucrats at Church headquarters. We'll now be one step removed from them."

He concluded the letter, "There is one other aspect that is extremely important in our present stage. The First Presidency authorized, by letter, the Brigham Young project. This means that no one has a right to deny me any materials I want to use; it also means that I may use the staff to help with the project." He saw the Young project as a free pass to the archives, at least until the book was published. With no apparent awareness of the huge contradictions he represented, he exulted to his children, "You must imagine how exciting, how exhilarating, how inspiring, it is to work in depth in these materials. I have the most exciting job in the historical world, and I'm trying to make the most of it. . . . I thank the Lord for my appointment and for my work."

The final sentence of the letter makes one wonder how introspective, how honest with himself Leonard was: "I am neither cynical nor discouraged."[8] The lack of cynicism and discouragement proved to be short-lived.

THE MOVE TO PROVO: PUNISHMENT OR PRESERVATION?

Gordon Hinckley and Homer Durham had been close friends for decades, dating back to having served as missionary companions in the British Mission in the early 1930s. The two men understandably worked closely together once Durham became managing director of the Historical Department since Hinckley was advisor to the department. Their highest priority was to address the conflict between Ezra Taft Benson and Mark Petersen, on the one hand, and the History Division on the other. Since neither Hinckley nor Durham communicated directly to Leonard or his coworkers exactly what went on behind the scenes, and since no written record of such is currently accessible to scholars, it is not possible to know, with certainty, the entire story behind the creation of the Joseph Fielding Smith Institute, although the basic outline is quite clear.

In 1993, when Davis Bitton was critiquing an early draft of Leonard's autobiography, he recalled that the creation of the Smith Institute and the move to BYU were actually a contingency plan that was pursued when the original plan was abandoned. The first plan was to disband the group, with Dean Jessee returning to the archives, where he had worked prior to Leonard's arrival; Ron Walker and Ron Esplin moving to the Church Educational system; James Allen returning to BYU, where he still had an academic appointment; Davis Bitton returning to the University of Utah, where he, too, still had an academic appointment; and Leonard working full-time at BYU as occupant of the Charles Redd Chair. With Dean May already having announced his departure from the History Division, and Gene Sessions and Bruce Blumell likely to leave soon on their own initiative, there would be little to dismantle. "It seems that Elder Durham had an interview with Carol Madsen, urging her that she should be at home. (To which she responded that her position was a result of prayer.) If I am right, then the move-to-BYU was a contingency plan, chosen when the other one didn't work and was not enthusiastically accepted."[9]

Leonard agreed with Bitton's recollection; and in the published version of the autobiography he attributed "Plan A" to Durham. When that plan proved impractical, "Durham worked out an alternative plan with Gordon B. Hinckley, one of the Historical Department advisors. They moved our trimmed-down division to Brigham Young University, where we would be less tied to the church and the Archives and still be in a position to write sound history. Although I had been warned of this possibility as early as 1978, this action was taken without consulting me."[10]

Writing of "Plan B" contemporaneously—in 1980—Leonard hypothesized that Hinckley had taken a hand in the proposal, likely as part of a broader and proactive move to cushion two institutions—the History Division and BYU—from possible repercussions in the event that Ezra Taft Benson became church president—an event that many saw as not only likely but also imminent, given the serious health challenges that Spencer Kimball was confronting:[11]

> Having heard from several sources earlier that Elder Gordon Hinckley appears to have orchestrated the acceptance of Dallin Oaks['s] resignation as president of BYU and appointed Jeff Holland to take his place, in order to remove any possibility that Elder Benson upon succession to the Presidency might have appointed a John Birch-type to that position, it now occurs to me that perhaps the creation of the Joseph Fielding Smith Institute of Church History, the abolition of the History Division, and the transfer of our division to BYU may similarly have been orchestrated by Elder Hinckley in consultation with Elder Durham in order to keep our work alive, in order to avoid a situation in which the History Division may have been eliminated and the functions discontinued. That is a positive interpretation to place on the actions of last week—that Elder Hinckley and Elder Durham felt that they were doing us a favor and the Church a favor by assuring that by this transfer we will not be touched by a subsequent action of the next President of the Church.[12]

While his observation about the Holland-for-Oaks substitution at BYU was more speculative, his explanation of the creation of the Joseph Fielding Smith Institute appears to have been remarkably accurate. Yet despite the benignity of the move, Leonard gradually gave it a dark spin.

A week later Leonard mused again on the topic, this time speculating on a larger role for Homer Durham. "Whether the initiative in the move was taken by Elder Hinckley or Elder Durham, one cannot be sure; it was probably the result of a joint discussion."[13] Regardless of the relative roles of the two men, the move to BYU as an act to preserve the History Division in the face of an uncertain future if Benson became church president was inferred in a one-on-one meeting that Leonard had a few weeks later with one of his former students at Utah State University, L. Tom Perry, who had become a member of the Quorum of the Twelve Apostles in 1974, just junior to Packer. "He said that when this proposal came to the Twelve he was very much delighted because it offered a means of 'preserving the professionalism of our historians.' He said that he had recognized the problem that we have of speaking for the Church as well as for history. Placing our historians within an academic atmosphere would help to preserve our professionalism and preserve the professional respect for the work that they do."[14]

The two assistant church historians were also inclined to see the move to BYU as preservative, albeit painful. In an interview a quarter-century later, Davis Bitton reminisced:

> Maybe it should come out of a university setting. I think that was the thinking behind G. Homer Durham's recommendation. I believe he thought he was doing everybody a favor. Here was a group of historians that had irritated some people, and there was this bad blood between the historians and some members of the Twelve. Solution: just move them right out of the Church Historian's Office and let them function as a research institute attached to BYU, and let the BYU administrators deal with them. That way, the Church could say, "They don't represent the Church. They are university people."[15]

James Allen, interviewed the same year, held similar views:

> Everybody who moved down just felt hurt, not trusted, even though Brother Durham, I am sure, felt he was doing the right thing. As I understand it, in his mind he felt that by moving Leonard and the professional historians down here, they would be able to do what they were doing anyway, but without having the fear of always being looked at over the shoulder because they were fulltime employees of the Church. "As someone who is not a fulltime employee of the Church"—that was the reasoning he would use—"you can be much more free in what you say. You won't have to feel like the Brethren are constantly looking over your shoulders." I think he was sincere in that, but I also think that he was trying to figure out a way to please Brother Benson and others who were upset about some of the things that they felt might be coming out of the Historical Department.[16]

One other factor that likely played a part was Durham's own family experience with church employment. William Hartley, a member of the History Division who remained on the payroll by moving to BYU, noted: "The fear was in us, and Brother Durham said, 'I remember when my father worked for the Church and they laid him off, and what a tough thing that was. So you get ready.' And then all the sudden we got transferred—the ones that were left—to BYU, and I just said, 'Hallelujah!' "[17]

FIGHTING THE MOVE

Even though Leonard was a congenital optimist, he had mixed feelings about the move and strenuously resisted it, despite its inevitability. Shortly after the 1980 announcement that the move would take place two years later, a diary entry suggested that a move delayed was a move denied: "Another positive thought is that we'll remain here at our desks doing the same work under essentially the same conditions for the next two years and perhaps by then authorities will be willing to allow us to continue to remain here indefinitely. It may well be that in two years we could retain the services of Davis [Bitton] and Dean Jessee for an indefinite period. Indeed, it may well be that within a few years the History Division could be reinstated as a division of the Historical Department."[18]

Two weeks later, while accepting the move, he reacted with a spirit of passive aggression. "I shall never expect to move our home to Provo. We expect to remain in our present home in Salt Lake City until other circumstances necessitate a change." Furthermore, he would not do the daily commute from Salt Lake City to Provo. "At the most, I would expect to go to the office there three days a week—possibly as few as two days a week." Why the resistance to the move? Again, it was his continual optimism, supported by a wish but not by reality. "At an appropriate time—say, the spring of 1981 when they are beginning to think about the 1982 budget—I expect to ask the president of BYU to write the managing director of the Historical Department, asking him to continue to provide indefinitely office and desk facilities for me and for Richard Jensen."[19]

In early February 1982, only a few months away from the move and at a time when Grace's rapidly deteriorating health cast a pall over everything in his life, Leonard appealed to Martin Hickman, the BYU dean under whose supervision the Smith Institute would function, hoping to avoid at least his own move to Provo. While he might well have cited Grace's condition as the reason for requesting a delay in the move—she died only three weeks after Leonard wrote the letter—instead he appealed on a different level: personal inconvenience. Alleging that "nobody has paid any attention to my feelings about the inconvenience of it all," he argued logistics. Grace, he said, would only allow him to move two of his eleven filing cabinets from the Church Office Building to the house, and the remaining nine were the problem. "If I take them to BYU they will not be available to me as I do my research and writing here. If I try to do research and writing at BYU I will have nothing to work with but files and books and precious little manuscript materials."

Knowing that even a desk in the Church Historical Department was no longer a possibility, he had already requested of Henry Eyring an office in the Church

Educational System suite in the same building, but to no avail.[20] "I think Elder Durham has told him he can't spare one." There was one last option, and that was a request for space in the BYU Continuing Education branch campus in Salt Lake City. Would Hickman approach BYU president Jeffrey Holland with a request?[21]

Learning of Leonard's continuing resistance to the move, Holland extended an olive branch that nonetheless left it clear that the move was a done deal that Leonard was simply going to have to swallow. First, the firm message: "I know you have been anxious to have office space there. You approached me on that matter in a Salt Lake street corner conversation once and I understand you have more formally approached the First Presidency directly. It is my understanding from the Trustees, the officers of which are the members of the First Presidency, that they would not like to arrange space for the Joseph Fielding Smith Institute in Salt Lake City and that they clearly see it as a BYU function physically and professionally."

Then, the olive branch: "We do want you to feel comfortable here and in spite of the recent controversies swirling around historical issues we are determined to have a first-rate professional climate for you here. We will, of course, need everyone's help to earn that. If you, Dean Hickman, President Ballif and I need to get together to chart out this new chapter in the life of the Institute, I would be glad to do so. In any case we do hope you will feel comfortable about making BYU your professional home."[22]

Having been cut off at the pass, Leonard wrote to his children on February 27 acknowledging Holland's instructions: "I have been told that I must definitely move out of my office August 31."[23] The following week, Martin Hickman responded equally decisively to Leonard's plea for intervention. "I recognize the force of the arguments you advance for having an office in SLC, but there are some compelling reasons why I believe your office ought to be at BYU." He then listed the reasons:

- As director of the Joseph Fielding Smith Institute, Leonard had a responsibility to establish a sound brand for the institute, something that could hardly be done without his physical presence on campus.

- Throughout the process of creating the institute, all parties had made it clear that the BYU campus would be the sole home of the institute and its staff. "The future of the Institute will be advanced by graceful acceptance of that decision with all of its implications."

- The sheer mass of Leonard's collection—the eleven filing cabinets— made it a practical impossibility to bring them to a single place except the institute.

- Other BYU faculty members with offices in Provo had managed to use the Church Archives. "While that does make it more inconvenient to do research, they seem to survive. I should imagine that given the cooperation between the BYU Library and the Church Archives some arrangement to your benefit could be worked out."[24]

Hickman's logic was sound, and while Leonard accepted the ultimatum—he really had no choice—he did so begrudgingly. A month prior to the final move, he again lamented: "We are now forced to leave all of our offices in the Church Office Building."[25]

The "Black List"

Leonard's standing as a church member in full fellowship was of utmost importance to him. Throughout his career he carried a valid temple recommend, a credit-card–sized form signed by him, his bishop, and his stake president, and laminated to protect it from being damaged by frequent use and also to facilitate temple record-keeping, which by then had been computerized. Possession of such a recommend not only gave him (or any holder) entry to any of the church's temples, but also signified that he was a member in good standing. However, the decision to disassemble the History Division caused him to wonder if he was now being seen as out of favor, on a personal level, with the church hierarchy.

In mid-1980, at a low point for the History Division, he received two speaking invitations that reassured him. The first was "a ten minute talk in a series of religious messages, half by Mormons, half by non-Mormons. To give one of these, the Latter-day Saints must be approved by the Council of the Twelve. That I should have been invited to give one shows that I am no longer (if I ever was) on anybody's black list." The second, and the more substantive, came from BYU, inviting him "to give a devotional address at BYU [to the full student body] in July on 'Our Pioneer Heritage,' or some aspect of Church History. That means I am no longer (as I believe I was for a while) on Bob Thomas' black list.[26] I think maybe the series in the *Church News* helped people to understand we are believers, just as others are, and that we are capable of writing faithful history. Which of course we have been all along."[27]

Despite the affirmation of the speaking invitations, two later episodes demonstrated that he was still viewed with suspicion by at least some men who held high ecclesiastical positions. One was the invitation to become a guest columnist for the *Church News*, a weekly supplement to the church-owned *Deseret News*, which initially he greeted with enthusiasm in a weekly letter to his children: "I have been asked to write an article once a month for the *Church News*, so I have finished the first one, presumably to appear the first Sunday in April. I'll try to remember to send you copies of each one as they appear. Shows they don't have any prejudice against me, and have confidence that I can write faith-promoting history as well as analytical history."[28]

The vote of confidence—if that's what it was—was short-lived, however. Seven months later, he wrote in his diary, "Perhaps as a result of Chris Arrington's name being attached as 'Reporter' to the piece on *Time* about [Ezra Taft] Benson, some General Authority, perhaps President Benson, instructed *Church News* not to carry further articles by me once each month. I had published one on the organization of the Church and one on Women."[29]

The more damaging episode that had fueled his concerns about being on a black list had taken place years earlier at BYU. Shortly after *The Mormon Experience* was published, Leonard was invited to teach a new class at BYU, "Mormonism in American History." The students "were very bright and knowledgeable and intensely interested," and so he began to introduce "topics in LDS history not often covered in conventional treatments." In each instance he allowed for class discussion time, and the reception from the students was, overall, very positive. "Several of the students have since told me how much they gained from the class and how much more meaningful our history was when pursued in some depth."

However, Leonard was unaware at the time of something sinister going on in the classroom. He later learned that the infamous Committee for Strengthening [Church] Members, which kept files on church members who were felt to be suspect, "approached two registered students to spy on me and report to him weekly on what transpired in class. One of them has confessed to me that he reported twice and then gave up the assignment. The other, however, continued to make reports throughout the semester." While the spying never resulted in actions averse to Leonard, the whole episode left a bitter taste in his mouth. "That spying of this nature was going on in 1979 suggests the determination of some people to build a strong case against any BYU instructor who tried to look upon Mormon history as professional historians would do."[30]

Leonard's colleague Michael Quinn later commented on the toll that the spying exacted—a toll greater than his own record had suggested. "Leonard was just devastated when he learned this. . . . [He] had a sense that students were innocent, and that they were completely trustworthy because they were innocent. They were guileless. After he found out about this, at the end of the semester, that three or more students had been spying on him and reporting back anything he said that they thought was non-faith-promoting, I really don't know if he taught a BYU class after that. But I know it devastated him. . . . I think that this was a rude introduction to human behavior in the Church that he never got over."[31]

THE INNER RESPONSE

Given the differing messages that Leonard sent to different constituencies, and the differing messages that he received from the same constituencies, it is difficult to ascertain what his innermost thoughts were concerning the move and his subsequent professional life. Again, it appears that his inner feelings were ambivalent, shifting in response to varying events; but for the most part the combination of a strong sense of self and a continual input of affirmation led to a generally upbeat mood interspersed with moments of depression, discouragement, and—surprisingly rarely—anger.

In the spring of 1982, just weeks before the final move out of the Church Office Building, Leonard was notified that he would be receiving an honorary doctorate degree from Utah State University. Since such a degree required the approval of the Board of Regents that oversaw all of the state's universities and colleges, he justifiably saw it as a vindication of his entire career, including that as church historian:

> My honorary [degree] may have been intended to thank me for my long period of teaching and publishing, but it may also have been a way of making a statement to the community and church on the issue of history. I am a kind of symbol, to many people, of "honest" LDS history; of the necessity of giving a forthright and impartial look at our history. USU and Stan Cazier were telling the state, the culture, the church, that the university favors this kind of history, as opposed to the defensive, missionary-type of history previously approved. In granting me the honorary they were making a statement, taking a position, putting themselves on record.[32]

The official program for the commencement contained one sentence, in particular, that affirmed Leonard's feelings: "Professional historians agree that under Dr. Arrington's leadership the History Division of the Church of Jesus Christ of Latter-day Saints made phenomenal forward strides."[33]

Several weeks later, and just two days before the final move, Leonard wrote to his children about the affirmation he felt upon attending the Sunstone Symposium:[34] "I enjoyed especially a session of the Symposium on 'Closet Doubters,' in which there were interesting comments by one who was and one who wasn't. Very thoughtful and indeed, inspiring. I realized more than ever that I have become a kind of symbol to many people—people I do not know but people who know me from my writings. In a way, my life is not my own. Everything I do is watched and read and listened to by many people that I am not aware of."[35]

The following year, in 1983, he received a high compliment from Marion D. Hanks, a member of the third-ranked First Quorum of the Seventy, who was well known for championing objective scholarship and a liberal worldview—a worldview that, it was widely believed, kept him from advancing to the Quorum of the Twelve despite his obvious talents and ability. In his conversation with Leonard, which occurred as he performed Leonard's second marriage (detailed below), "among other things, he looked at me to say that he hoped I would continue to be a productive scholar, and continue to insist upon honesty and integrity in my work. I appreciated that."[36]

And Leonard did continue to write from the same perspective as before— which was a triumph of his vision, costly though it was, over the bruising messages he had been given about the problematic New Mormon History. As son James saw it: "My dad, as far as I can see, just took his typewriter, put it on another desk, and kept writing. And he kept writing the same stuff. He didn't change his point of view."[37]

Some compared him favorably to two church luminaries who, in earlier decades, had responded magnanimously to forced career changes. The first was J. Reuben Clark Jr., who was demoted from first counselor to second counselor in David O. McKay's First Presidency in 1951, an unprecedented move that no other church president had taken.[38] A correspondent wrote to Leonard: "As many of us have observed your transfer to Provo and the events leading up to it, I admired you for the serene and dignified manner in which you complied with this move, your reaction and your spirit free of any rancor, but instead showing forth great loyalty and devotion to the cause. Like President J. Reuben Clark in the spring of 1951, you have set an unforgettable and stirring example to all of us."[39]

The second was Lowell Bennion, who in 1962 had been punitively stripped of the directorship of the LDS Institute of Religion at the University of Utah because of his espousal of liberal causes and his continued resistance to Ernest L. Wilkinson, the heavy-handed president of Brigham Young University who was also Church Commissioner of Education during the closing years of the McKay presidency.[40] Emma Lou Thayne, a gifted poet and writer in Salt Lake City who had friends on both the liberal and conservative sides of the cultural divide, recalled: "I never heard any 'Poor me.' There was no victim mentality. Never any of that. He rose above it all. He was a lot like Lowell Bennion, in that Lowell, when he was dismissed from the University of Utah Institute of Religion—and no one ever told him why, but he knew—he told me once, . . . 'I'm not going to be defeated twice, once by circumstance and another time by myself.' He just rose above it and went past it. And Leonard was of the same kind."[41]

James Allen commented on the manner in which Leonard managed to rise above the fray, in spite of having taken hits. "In private conversations I could feel that that hurt was still there. . . . [but] publicly, he was on top of it all the time. . . . Even when he was dismissed as the Church Historian, and he said privately to us how disappointed he was, and we knew he was unhappy with Elder Durham, anything he would say publicly would be positive and upbeat. 'This is great. This is going to work.' That was the nature of Leonard. He did not want to hurt anybody; he did not want to embarrass anybody. And that's what made him what he was."[42]

But such magnanimity notwithstanding, it was clear to some of his closest associates, as well as family members, that the whole process of disassembly had taken a permanent toll on Leonard. Stan Cazier, who was president of Utah State University at the time of the transfer to BYU, recalled, "There was not that buoyancy, that sparkle in the eye, in Leonard after that. . . . I felt he had lost something. He was not the Leonard I knew in 1960, where he had the whole world in his arms, ready to embrace anybody in fellowship and support. He kind of withdrew into himself. . . . Never did he bad-mouth the Church. He stayed loyal. But in his room, by himself, I don't know what went through his mind. He did say he just felt that he could never get the message across. He was trying to help the Church, trying to give it an image of respectability in the world."[43]

Even the accolades that he received were something of a two-edged sword: on the one hand he was honored by his peers for authentic achievements; but on the other hand, such accolades too early in one's life tend to carry an overlay of finality, even eulogy—a sense that one has thus been consigned to irrelevance. His son Carl picked up on that theme. "I used to think of it as my dad going to his own funeral so many times, with these big gatherings where they would gather to honor him."[44]

Two things carried him through the tough years at the end of his career. The first was articulated by folklorist Bert Wilson, who stressed that one of Leonard's greatest strengths was the simple faith that had sustained him throughout his life. "I remember when his wife died and we went to her funeral. I was talking to him, just the way you do at funerals. There was absolutely no bitterness there. He said, 'Well, now we just have to decide what the Lord has in mind for us in the future.' I thought that was a good metaphor for his life in general. 'We have to decide what the Lord has in mind for us, and get to work and do it.'"[45]

The second was a new love.

HARRIET HORNE

Although Leonard had told his children that he was in no hurry to remarry after Grace's death, he was terribly lonely. Just two months after her funeral, he relayed to them some strong advice that a close friend, Russell Mortensen, had given to him at the mortuary. "[He] lost his first wife and had a family of five to raise. He grieved for years and rebelled for years. He was angry and could not become reconciled. Finally, after 18 years I think, he remarried. He confessed to me that it was the best thing he had done. He should have remarried earlier, he said. His grieving stopped and he was able to look at things in a better perspective. His parting word to me was, 'Leonard, don't wait too long to remarry!'"[46]

Leonard's son James described the gradual process by which Leonard first worked through mourning, and then reentered the dating scene:

> He waited, properly, for a year, and in that year, one of the things he did as part of his mourning was to go through all the family pictures. He put them in binders and separated them all out. He gave me my binders, and Carl his, and Susan hers. They are arranged methodically, and it was a way that he had of dealing with all of this.
>
> He gave himself one year of mourning, and then it was time to date, because he needed another path-clearer. He enjoyed being married. He liked being married. And it was very useful for him to be married, because he was not a man who liked to shop, or to take care of himself, or go to the laundry, or get his shirts starched, or anything like that. Somebody else does that. It wasn't that he was mean about it; it just slowed him down. He wanted to be intellectually going after things. That's what he liked, and that's what he was good at.
>
> So after that period, he started taking out women. He took out all these women, and each one of them, by our report, he proposed to. He did! I'm serious! On the first or second date. You can just see him, playing with his napkin and saying, "So, you're single and I'm single. What do you think? Should we get married?" The image of it is just hilarious to me. Most of them said, "Leonard, what are you talking about? We hardly know each other!" "Well, we can take care of that." I can just see him doing this. He just didn't have a clue. . . . But my father just wanted somebody to clear the way, and he was going to go until he found somebody.[47]

That "somebody" was Harriet Horne, whom Leonard first dated on September 1, 1983. Some minor matchmaking had cleared the way. During Sunstone, which was held at Hotel Utah that year, Leonard lunched in the Crossroads Mall with a group of other attendees that included Annette Sorensen Rogers, Harriet's daughter. Leonard recalled, "We happened to sit next to each other, and walked together at least part of the way back. . . . Annette asked me about my social life. I mentioned it briefly and my desire to have suggestions of others. Annette suggested her 'cute little mother.' . . . [She] said her mother might respond favorably if I asked her for a date. She had not dated for years, but had done so to some extent in the last year or two."[48]

Harriet gave her version of their courtship in an interview a decade after Leonard's death:

> He was at a [Sunstone] conference luncheon, and he had my daughter, Annette Sorensen Rogers, and Mary Bradford at his table. I think it was 1983. Leonard told them that he had proposed to four women, and that they had all turned him down. That was a real blow to him. Annette said, "My mother will go out with you. She knows the Arringtons." We all had been in Twin Falls with them. So she gave him my telephone number. I was divorced and was living in a condominium in downtown Salt Lake City. She called me up and said, "I just gave your telephone number to Leonard Arrington. Don't you dare turn him down! If he wants you to go to dinner, you go to dinner." I said, "Well, I'll go to dinner with him," but I did know that he had proposed to these women.
>
> We had to go to the [state] fair and see the chickens, the most important thing in his life. How do I know one chicken from another? Are you kidding? I don't. But we went to see the chickens, and then we went to lunch.[49]

Harriet, the daughter of Salt Lake physician Lyman M. Horne and Myrtle Swainston Horne, was the oldest of eight children. She married Frederick Sorensen, with whom she had three children. By her second marriage, to Gordon Moody, she had another child. The granddaughter of Alice Merrill Horne, a legendary patron of Utah artists, Harriet took an active interest in history (though not chickens), and it formed a bond between her and Leonard that Leonard had shared only tangentially with Grace.

They dated almost daily, and a week after their first date Leonard wrote enthusiastically to his children, "We have enjoyed each other and are beginning to get a little serious."[50] Four weeks later, Leonard again updated his children, "She is anxious to marry, and we are talking about the possibility."[51] In early November, just two months after their first date, Leonard and Harriet announced their engagement, and on November 21, 1983, they were married in the Salt Lake Temple, with Marion D. Hanks performing the ceremony.[52]

Lavina Fielding Anderson, who had worked closely with Leonard during his church historian years, described Harriet and the marriage. "She was well educated; a superb hostess, every bit as good as Grace; warm and welcoming like Grace. The families went to the temple, and the kids were giggling and talking and having a good time while they were waiting for Harriet and Leonard. Someone from the temple presidency came in and said, 'Can't you be more subdued?' That sent them off into total gales of laughter. So it got off to a good start. They were affectionate, and Harriet was fiercely loyal to Leonard. I think it was a compatible marriage, but unfortunately, the families didn't fit."[53]

The lack of compatibility between Harriet and Leonard's children and grandchildren was never completely resolved, much to the sorrow of the children.[54] James explained:

> He came from a generation of people that didn't easily say, "We've got to get this worked out, Harriet." They just lived the way they lived. I don't think he knew what to do. I don't think, for the most part, he regretted marrying Harriet, because they got along fine as long as the children weren't brought in. . . .
>
> My father was not a man who could live by himself. He just couldn't do it. And so he took the best shot at being happy that he could, and I think, for the most part, he was happy. . . .
>
> I don't think he regretted marrying her, but I do think he regretted the turn of events that alienated his family from being able to see him whenever they wanted to. He worked hard to overcome that, but he really kind of couldn't. In the end, he was just as sweet and kind and wonderful as he could be, but he was married to Harriet, and he was an honorable man, and he stayed married to her. He was caught between a rock and a hard place. He was married to her and he had his children.[55]

THE JOSEPH FIELDING SMITH INSTITUTE

Leonard was the spark plug of the History Division. Always present, always optimistic, always the mentor, he was the unquestioned leader. That he chose not to play the same role with the Smith Institute says much for why it never functioned at the same level as the History Division. By choosing to maintain his residence in Salt Lake City and by limiting his appearances on the BYU campus to once or twice a week, he practically ensured that the Smith Institute would never become a cohesive, vibrant organization. Jill Mulvay Derr mourned the difference. "Leonard was still connected, but he was slowly moving out. . . . The thing that struck me the most was that here, at the Church Office Building when we had been the Church History Division, there was very much a feeling of community. . . . When I reconnected at BYU, what really struck me was that people were in individual offices, and there wasn't the same, common meeting space."[56]

The contrast was also apparent to outsiders who happened to visit the institute. Elbert Peck, then the editor of *Sunstone* magazine, commented not only on the fragmentation within the institute, but also on Leonard's failure to integrate it thoroughly within the larger BYU community. "Leonard didn't really push his people to publish or to integrate. . . . I dropped in on the Smith Institute people a lot. They always were talking about their own little projects, but you never heard them talking about larger projects. When people talk about the times when they were at the Church Historian's Office, it *was* a larger project. . . . There was a master plan that they were going to do. But when they got to BYU, they were licking their wounds and hiding in their little caves."[57]

On its surface, the move to BYU should have resulted in greater productivity from the surviving employees than they had achieved in the History Division, given their higher salaries, absence of interference from ecclesiastical officers, commingling with academicians across the campus, and minimal or no teaching loads. Granted, the forty-five-mile separation from the Church Archives was a limiting factor, but those who were still working on approved projects continued to have archival access; and given the multiyear advance notice that the move would take place, they had laid up stores of photocopies—"squirreling away things to use when we make the change in offices," in Leonard's words.[58] And yet, productivity lagged.

Newell Bringhurst, an outside scholar, commented on the problem. "I never heard Leonard directly say this, but I think he expected the people under him to do much more than they did. I think, in a way, that that helped to set up what ultimately happened down at BYU, which is the other half of the tragedy. . . . I think that's one of the ironies of Mormon studies, that the people who were supposed to do the most productive, cutting-edge stuff, the Leonard Arrington students, didn't live up to his expectations."[59]

Even after the fact—the Joseph Fielding Smith Institute was dissolved in 2005, with its remaining historians then relocated back to Salt Lake City to work on the Joseph Smith Papers Project—Leonard missed both the cause and the effect. While writing his autobiography he sent an early draft to Davis Bitton for comment. Bitton reacted sharply to Leonard's praise for the productivity of the institute in a personal memo to him in February 1993: "'Splendid books and articles.' How many? Is this cost-effective? Multiply the annual payroll of the Institute by the number of years of its existence, and we must have over a million dollars. Count up the books and articles. Ask which of these might well have been produced anyway. This is not the line of thinking you will wish to push, but it is one that has to occur to some people."[60]

Leonard's tenure as director of the institute lasted for four years—which was four years longer than BYU policy at the time allowed. (BYU required all administrative personnel to step down at age sixty-five, and Leonard's birthday had come one month before the final move to Provo.) He was the one exception to the rule, and in 1986 the Church Board of Education decided that there would be no more exceptions. Never having enjoyed administrative duties, he was actually relieved. He wrote to his children, "I feel very good about the new arrangement. I lose nothing and gain two advantages—two years before I retire instead of one, and no more meetings or responsibilities in connection with the Institute with administrative officials."[61]

Leonard still maintained his salaried chair at the Redd Center, but his trips to Provo gradually tapered off until his mandatory retirement from the university at age seventy.[62] He viewed the second retirement in a different light than the first. "He was crushed that BYU made him retire at seventy," Ross Peterson recalled. "It was a standard thing that you retired at seventy, but he didn't want to give up the chair, he didn't want to give up the staff, he didn't want to give up the secretarial stuff."[63]

MEANWHILE, BACK AT THE CHURCH HISTORICAL DEPARTMENT

Moving the History Division to BYU was one part of a two-part initiative to tighten control over the church's history. Earl Olson commented on the effect of the move: "The function [Leonard] had been doing was writing and publishing books. That stopped. There was a redirection. Nobody was assigned to do any more writing of books. It mainly became the responsibility of the Archives and the Library and the Museum to carry on. It just eliminated that function."[64]

The other part was an increasingly strict policy controlling access to archival material. "I think it was a cumulative thing," noted James Allen, "but it seemed almost to be crashing down as we moved to Provo. Before I moved to Provo, I still had access to anything. After I moved to Provo, I didn't have access without special permission. . . . It was still possible, once they knew you and trusted you, to get the papers that were important to your topic, [but] you had to tell them what you were doing." And although the policy regarding access was stricter than when Allen had worked in the History Division, the doors had not slammed shut, rumors to the contrary notwithstanding. "I think that image of it crashing down was a distorted image. They did close, in terms of not just letting anybody take things like they had before. You needed to be known, and you had to be interviewed before you could start looking at stuff."[65]

Not all of the tightening occurred after the move to Provo. In August 1981, a year before the move, Leonard reported a conversation with Homer Durham: "Since the shift of the Historical Department to the Twelve, Elders Benson and Petersen are very much in the saddle and they do not want archival material made available to anybody. . . . So we are now back to the days of Joseph F. Smith and A. Will Lund."[66] Restrictions tightened further in early 1982: "The Church Archives have put all the papers of the General Authorities on a restricted basis. Lots of complaints about the restrictive policies of the Church and Elder Durham. . . . This will certainly hurt our image among scholars, who have lauded our ten-year effort to open things up."[67] Complaints were so vocal and so broadly based that Durham reversed field. Only a week later, Leonard wrote to his children, "Interesting to watch Elder Durham and Earl Olsen backtrack on the decision to close all papers of all General Authorities. We're not far from where we were a few weeks ago. Wish they'd consult with people who could give them good advice."[68]

However, the backtracking was a temporary measure. Newell Bringhurst, who was using breaks in his academic year to write a biography of Brigham Young, compared the archives before and after Leonard's departure. "They wouldn't let me look at anything in the Brigham Young papers, themselves. I remember talking to Jim Kimball, who was the gatekeeper at that time. I remember him telling me, 'We have to know exactly what you want to look at in this particular document or that particular document. We can't let you be going on a fishing expedition.' It was so different from what it had been under Arrington."[69]

Some coped with the restrictions in creative ways—for instance, branding one's research as something other than history. Dwight Israelsen, an economist from Utah State University, described his ingenious ploy to facilitate access for one of his doctoral students who wanted to do a study of the church's investment in education in the nineteenth century. "Elder Durham met with us, and the first question he asked, and the only real substantive question was the question I expected to be asked, because of what had been going on for several years when I was at BYU, when the History Department was always under scrutiny and the Economics Department never was. . . . 'Is this economics or history?' I said, 'Oh, this is economics.' And he said, 'Okay.' And that was it."[70]

Eventually the archival policy morphed into one consistent with other similar archives, which essentially is the policy that exists today. Bill Slaughter, a career archivist, watched the pendulum swing from unprecedented openness, which as noted earlier actually began before Leonard's tenure but blossomed under his stewardship; to near-impenetrability towards and after the existence of the History Division; and then back towards a middle ground.

> That's where they came up with this rather responsible and correctly professional way of saying, "Okay, we have these different kinds of records, and not all records are equal. Some have private information. Some have confidential information." Those are basically the same thing. And we have corporate records. We are not an archive, we are not a manuscript library, we are not a . . . photo library—we are all of them. We are a Special Collections Library, and we deal with all sorts of records. Most companies don't allow you into their corporate records. Their corporate archives are meant for those who come later, so they can see why you did what you did. The Church actually has been pretty generous in allowing people to look into those things.[71]

26

Brigham Young: American Moses

Brigham Young is arguably the second-most important figure in Mormon history; but until the 1970s, he had not been the subject of a definitive biography. The two most recent books represented the polemical extremes. Preston Nibley's *Brigham Young: The Man and His Work* (1936), despite being over five hundred pages in length, managed to avoid entirely the mention of polygamy, arguably a central theme in Young's presidency; and Stanley Hirshson, author of *The Lion of the Lord: A Biography of Brigham Young* (1969)—which Leonard called "that terrible book"[1]—managed to avoid entirely the LDS Archives.

In the early 1960s, Leonard and George Ellsworth proposed to the National Historical Publications Commission that they edit Young's papers for publication by that organization. The commission's prior projects had included the papers of several U.S. presidents. "They were enthusiastic and agreed to funding," Leonard recalled later. "We wrote to First Presidency, and they declined. I think the reason was that the papers had never been studied and they were fearful that we might find things that were prejudicial, incriminating."[2] In the aftermath of Hirshson's biography, the two men proposed again to the First Presidency that the Young papers be edited and published. They received no reply.

Shortly after Leonard became church historian, as noted in an earlier chapter, Michael Quinn discovered in the basement of the Church Administration Building tens of thousands of pages of manuscript material from the Brigham Young era that had sat undisturbed for over a century. The discovery was a catalyst for a different proposal: a multivolume biography. Leonard wrote to Wendell Ashton, then head of the Public Communications Department, "I myself would enjoy doing a biography of Brigham Young and have certain qualifications by way of acquaintanceship with materials, but my administrative duties are so onerous that I cannot see any possibility of getting to it in the next two or three years."[3]

Still, Leonard made his pitch to the First Presidency, receiving, in reply, instructions "to catalog the material and then return for further discussion. Because of other assignments and the large mass of Brigham Young–period manuscripts to be examined, we did not complete the cataloguing, even in a preliminary way, until 1977, the one-hundredth anniversary of Brigham Young's death. We then studied the materials for two years, trying to decide whether we should simply edit the papers, or at the rate of, say, one volume per year, write a multi-volume biography, and, if the latter, who should write it."[4]

Spencer Kimball approved a one-volume biography, rather than the seven-volume work that Leonard had requested, and asked that Leonard be its author. Still stung by the repercussions over *The Story of the Latter-day Saints*, yet eager to push forward, he confided his ambivalence to his children: "I guess what I am trying to say is that I'm not proceeding very fast to start on the Brigham Young biography. I know very well that it will create troubles for me if I get it to the stage of publication. Two of the brethren just do not want published the kind of biography which I would have to do, so maybe I'm just not in any hurry. Yet, in my bones, I know I must do it, sooner or later."[5]

The potential reaction of "two of the brethren" was not as daunting as the sheer magnitude of the literal mountain of Young manuscript material, "most of which has never before been examined." Leonard listed what the cataloguers had found:

- 4 diaries in Brigham Young's own hand
- 29 letterpress copybooks of letters, representing about 30,000 outgoing letters
- 6 telegraph books, representing about 800 telegrams
- 48 volumes of manuscript history kept by Brigham Young's clerks, representing about 50,000 pages
- 18 volumes of minutes of meetings in which Brigham Young participated, representing about 6,000 pages
- 9 office journals, with about 300 pages each

And, of course, there were thousands of incoming letters, diaries of those associated with him, and many other documents relating to the period—his papers as governor, his papers as superintendent of Indian affairs, the histories of the colonizing companies he sent out, and so on. Also several hundred business records of enterprises he founded and assisted.[6]

Leonard proposed to Kimball that the book be submitted to Alfred Knopf, which had published not only Leonard's *The Mormon Experience*, but also influential and unsympathetic biographies of Joseph Smith (Fawn Brodie's *No Man Knows My History*) and Hirshson's *The Lion of the Lord*. The First Presidency approved the proposal, specifying that its members must review the manuscript *before* it went to the publisher, a tighter control than had been the case with *The Mormon Experience*, which was submitted to the First Presidency and the publisher simultaneously.[7] Leonard contacted Knopf the same month and, according to a retrospective timeline he prepared in 1985, signed the contract in September 1979.[8]

It took Leonard more than a decade to research and write *Great Basin Kingdom*. He taught during the academic year but often had summers free, and he had no administrative responsibilities. Now, in 1979, when his time was largely devoted to being director of the History Division as it faced dissolution and the move to BYU, he faced a daunting deadline for the Young biography, for Spencer Kimball had told him, "I would like to see a really good, one-volume biography of Brigham Young before I die."[9] At a History Division summer retreat a month after the First Presidency approved the project, Leonard explained his dilemma: "Brother [Homer] Durham interprets our instructions as permitting only my name as author. I have asked at various times to permit a co-author or co-authors, but he consistently takes a legalistic position on this, so we're stuck with it. But I plan to involve all of you."[10]

He subsequently outlined to Martin Hickman, his dean at BYU, the division of labor he foresaw:

> It would be impossible for one person to cover all of this material, even in a lifetime, and so I've had Richard Jensen working through all of the material on immigration, Carol Madsen working through the material on women, Davis Bitton working through the sermons, and Bill Hartley working through the material on priesthood activities and government. All of this is important to Church history as well as to Brigham Young's personal history, and will eventuate in articles which may be published by *BYU Studies* and other magazines and journals. Ron Esplin has been studying Brigham Young and the Quorum of the Twelve in Nauvoo, and that will form a chapter in my biography and quite possibly a separate book authored by him.[11]

Because of the First Presidency approval of the biography, Leonard and his team continued to have access to the Young papers at the Church Archives. And the First Presidency alone, rather than the Correlation Committee or any other review body, including one or more apostles, would have the power to make binding recommendations regarding the manuscript. In a letter to his children,

Leonard used uncharacteristically blunt language to describe his disdain for the middle-level bureaucrats and his glee at being able to bypass them.

> I do not suppose that my Brigham Young biography would be approved by those idiots in the middle management. But, thanks to Elder Durham's switching us to BYU, I am independent enough that, while I am required to send them a copy of the manuscript, I am not required to pay attention to their suggestions. I also am entitled to personal revelation in connection with this assignment, and that revelation will be my primary guide, not the suggestions of the idiot fringe. I'm talking mighty brave, as you see, to keep up my courage.[12]

With an impressive cadre of assistants doing most of the actual research, Leonard began writing on May 23, 1981, and completed the entire first draft in seven months. After having three colleagues read and critique the manuscript, he sent it to Knopf in February 1982, just one month before Grace's death.

After two years of working back and forth with Knopf on revisions, he shipped the final version in the summer of 1984[13]—minus a whimsical "Dedication" that he had written for his own amusement: "To Elder Rameumptum J. Moriancumr who, by his stupid regulations and irritating bureaucratic pronouncements, has helped me understand Brigham Young's impatience with self-important people of his own day, thus provoking some of the colorful language which I am delighted to reproduce in this biography."[14]

Brigham Young: American Moses was released in the spring of 1985.[15] While it sold well and was listed by the History Book Club, it garnered no awards outside of Mormon historical organizations, and never gained the critical acclaim of *Great Basin Kingdom*.

REVIEWS

American Moses represented a major leap forward from prior Brigham Young biographies, and many published and verbal reviews made that observation the centerpiece of their critiques. The dust jacket blurbs were, predictably, effusive: "This is without a doubt the definitive Mormon History." "A work long needed . . . An important book." "An outstanding and definitive study, a very model of religious-historical scholarship." "A remarkably intelligent and open-minded official history."

One coworker, Maureen Beecher, was similarly effusive. "His Brigham Young book, I think, was his masterpiece, even better than *Great Basin Kingdom*, in that he developed a personal relationship with a man that he really admired."[16] And Howard Lamar, an eminent historian of Western America and former president of Yale University, gave it a strong thumbs-up. "I think that Leonard's masterful biography, *American Moses*, just can't be beat. It was so full of understanding. It made Brigham so believable. No matter what he did, there was a kind of ratio-nale to it, even very emotional responses." He saw Leonard's achievement as pushing beyond the common view "that Brigham Young was a partisan of the Church so strongly that, in a sense, he couldn't be taken seriously. Because [Leonard] wrote for understanding, not conversion, he made Young so much more believable."[17]

But other reviewers dug more deeply and, while generally giving an overall affirmative critique, took the book to task for significant shortcomings. One con-tentious issue was "turf"—that he relied too heavily on the research of others while giving them minimal attribution and, in one significant instance, appeared to have impeded another scholar's attempt to write a Brigham Young biography.

Although the First Presidency had mandated that Leonard be designated the author of the book, "doing the Brigham Young biography is one of the things that caused a degree of conflict between him and his staff at the Church. Some of them felt it was theirs," that given the amount of work they had contributed, "they should have been listed as co-authors."[18] One historian whose contribution was felt to be greatly underacknowledged was Ronald Esplin, whose doctoral disser-tation, "The Emergence of Brigham Young and the Twelve to Mormon Leader-ship," was a key component of the biography.[19] Jan Shipps pointed out this debt in her review published in the *Journal of American History*[20] and recalled Leon-ard's displeasure with the disclosure: "Leonard said, 'You can give us honest re-views of the materials that we publish.' And when I gave him an honest review of his book on Brigham Young, he was so hurt! It just killed him. He was really up-set! But what I did in that review was to say that a lot of it came straight out of Ron Esplin's dissertation, which it did. Leonard said, 'Ron helped me. Ron works for me.' He didn't say, 'I took all of Ron's work and published it so he cannot publish anything.'"[21] Leonard's response to Shipps did not directly address Esp-lin's contribution. "Leonard told me this in this same conversation that the Breth-ren wanted him to put his name on everything that came out of the Historical Department."[22]

Even more troubling was the suggestion that Leonard had taken measures to limit another scholar's access to the Brigham Young papers at the same time that Leonard was working on his biography. According to Gene Sessions, who had been employed by the History Division before he joined Weber State's History Department, "Arrington wasn't letting [Don Moorman] see the material he

wanted to see. Don figured it was all selfishness. Don wanted to write the definitive biography of Brigham Young." Moorman's interest in a biography predated
the History Division, and he had a handwritten directive from Joseph Fielding
Smith, who stepped up from church historian to church president in 1970, to prove
it. While the directive gave him access, it didn't give him cooperation from Leonard. "Leonard refused to let him use the copying machines. He said, 'You can see
the Young stuff as long as you hand-copy it.' So Don spent hours and hours and
hours sitting in a room in the back of the archives search room. Leonard was
letting other people use the copying machine but Don couldn't, because he
was working on Brigham Young and Leonard had already announced that
he was going to write the definitive biography of Brigham Young."[23]

With respect to the content of *American Moses*, a general critique was that
Leonard had pulled too many punches. "He was just too nice a guy to get into
real controversy," commented Leo Lyman, whose hard-hitting doctoral dissertation about Utah's quest for statehood did not stop short of disclosing church bribes
to national newspapers in exchange for their support—or at least their silence. "It
was not his nature. And everybody that knew and loved him knew that and accepted it. But most of us who do, don't value that book as much as we would
have a book that had not pulled punches."[24] Although Shipps conceded that "Arrington includes more than enough information to fill out a 'warts and all' portrait that clarifies Young's position in Mormon and American history,"[25] there was
a feeling that he had overemphasized the positive while underemphasizing the
negative. Assistant Church Historian James Allen said, "I think one of the criticisms of the Brigham Young biography may be that it doesn't point out all the
problems and all the negatives. He has some in there, but he was an admirer of
Brigham Young, and because he was an admirer, that's the kind of biography he
wrote. But that was Leonard."[26] Leonard's son Carl agreed, noting, "I think that
my dad was basically quite conservative about people's personal lives, their private
lives, as he was circumspect about his own."[27] And indeed, Leonard himself had
noted in his diary, as he began to write the biography, "I am of course finding
many things about Brigham Young that would be better left unsaid."[28]

Brigham Young was an enormously powerful and enormously complex man
who presided over the LDS Church longer than any other leader in its history,
and yet many readers bemoaned the lack of complexity portrayed by the biography. Shipps was one reviewer who chided Leonard for having missed the inner
complexity:

> Something is missing from these pages. Where is the man more
> concerned with "making Saints" than with the comfort of his people,

the leader who spoke in tongues and who remained a visionary long after the first flush of religious enthusiasm was past, the believer who exhibited Joseph Smith's "seer-stone" in Salt Lake City in 1857 and consecrated it during the dedication of the St. George Temple in 1877? Leonard's *Brigham* offers a reasonable, straightforward, less than authoritarian religious leader whose theology and religious life were, above all, rational. In short, here is a Latter-day Saint leader who would appeal to today's Mormon liberals. As otherwise informative and valuable as is this work, in that area it presents a serious misreading of the life *and times* of the "Lion of the Lord."[29]

Picking up on the same theme was Newell Bringhurst, whose own biography of Brigham Young was published a year after *American Moses*.[30] "I had gotten to know Brigham Young very well, and I had done a lot of research, not only reading secondary stuff, but going through all the Donald Moorman stuff at Weber State, which gave me a pretty good feeling for Brigham Young and the complexity of him. . . . I was interested in all the family dynamics that were going on with Brigham Young, going back all the way to his childhood, and then how he dealt with the issue of his [first] wife being an invalid, and what impact that would have on the development of a personality; and the dynamics of him becoming involved with polygamy. Arrington really glossed over that." It's one thing to drill down into controversial aspects that are present in anyone's life, but that was not Bringhurst's complaint. "Arrington didn't like confrontation. I'm not going out to provoke confrontation, but I'm not afraid to deal with controversial issues. I'll let the chips fall where they may. If people don't like it, I won't care. I feel we want to tell the true story, get as close to the truth as possible, without being sensational or salacious."[31]

One colleague who brought the matter up directly with Leonard was Floyd O'Neil, a professor of history at the University of Utah. Not long before *American Moses* was published, the two men chanced to be on the same flight back to Salt Lake City, and Leonard asked to be reseated so they could sit together. "He was just about to finish his biography of Brigham. I will admit, on top of it, that I think that Brigham Young could often times be a dictator, and sometimes cruel. Very cruel at some times. . . . Then we got off onto the subject of the character of Brigham Young. While Leonard could be mildly critical, he could not go very far. I talked about some of the economic enterprises, and he said, 'You may be too harsh.' I said, 'All right, Leonard, let me put it down bluntly. Could you have worked for Brigham Young?' He wouldn't answer."[32]

Publicly, Young was even a more complex and controversial figure. Melvin Smith, who directed the Utah State Historical Society from 1971 to 1986, identified in a published review Leonard's superficial treatment of that aspect of Young's life, particularly the first decade in the Salt Lake Valley, when Young was both church president and territorial governor. "Young's methods, his power, and his objectives were, during that decade, not subject to either scrutiny or challenge. During that first free-handed decade, Young's leadership produced public endorsement of polygamy, the Reformation, the doctrine of blood atonement, treasonous political rhetoric, and the Mountain Meadows massacre. These issues receive inadequate treatment, especially the massacre."[33]

The massacre at Mountain Meadows, on September 11, 1857, was the largest white-on-white mass murder in the history of the United States up until the 1995 bombing of the Alfred P. Murrah Federal Building in Oklahoma City. It dogged the LDS Church and Brigham Young for the last two decades of Young's life and remained a millstone around the church's neck until a decade into the twenty-first century. While Leonard did not have access to all of the documents that eventually enabled a comprehensive treatment of the massacre,[34] he had sufficient access to have allowed him to write a more nuanced account of the event and its ripples. Instead, he gave minimal treatment to it, devoted only a single sentence to the "Reformation" of 1856, which by raising spiritual fervor to a fever pitch arguably set a tone that facilitated the massacre, and completely passed over Young's doctrine of "blood atonement," which postulated that the shedding of blood may actually be the victim's ticket to eternal redemption. Writing for the RLDS *John Whitmer Historical Association Journal*, Harold Muir took the biography to task for these omissions. While he agreed with Leonard's assertion that Young did not order the massacre, "the charge that he knew about it shortly after it happened and participated in a cover-up is much more serious and at least merits consideration. It would be one thing to present the evidence on both sides and argue forcefully for his innocence. But Arrington makes no mention whatever of John Doyle Lee's memoirs or Lee's bitter claim that Young conspired in the cover-up."[35]

The omission was intentional, as Leonard acknowledged to Robert Kent Fielding, a colleague who wrote on the Mountain Meadows Massacre as well as a preceding and related event, the Gunnison Massacre. "At a symposium that I attended just before he published his book on Brigham Young, I asked him if he was going to include the Mountain Meadows Massacre in his account, and give us a good understanding and explanation of it. He said no, he was not going to deal with that. He was going to leave that for other scholars."[36]

Leonard also passed over some theological issues that, while not part of current Mormon belief, were of great importance to Young—notably his doctrine of "Adam-God," another significant omission that Muir pointed out.[37]

"The theological peculiarities, such as Adam-God worship, that Brigham introduced to Mormonism and which currently have difficulty competing in the religious marketplace are played down and almost brushed aside with the explanation that 'he occasionally got carried away and expressed himself more strongly or less thoughtfully than he might have done if he had given carefully planned sermons.'"[38]

At least in the case of Adam-God, Leonard's oversight may have been due to general ignorance of the subject. In 1979, only a year and a half before he actually began to write the biography, he wrote to his children, "At the office we held our staff meeting and Ron Esplin gave a lecture on Brigham Young and the so-called Adam-God theory. He gave an understandable explanation of the thing, which is the first time I understood what the controversy was all about."[39] Adam-God, for all the emphasis that Young gave to it, did not survive Young himself as a serious component of Mormon theology.

Much more egregious was Leonard's slanted treatment of racial issues. Again, Muir underscored Leonard's problematic approach:

> A much more serious omission, which could only have resulted from a desire to avoid embarrassing the church, is Arrington's failure even to touch on the exclusion of Blacks from the priesthood, a Young legacy that has caused the church more grief than any issue since polygamy. He quotes Young as telling Horace Greeley that he wanted Utah admitted to the Union as a free state, saying, "Slavery here would prove useless and unprofitable. I regard it generally as a curse to the masters." Yet it is quite out of context to end the quotation there, for Young also told Greeley, "We consider [slavery] of divine institution and not to be abolished until the curse pronounced on Ham shall have been removed from his descendants." Nor does he mention that Young did in fact legalize slavery in Utah in 1852, making it the only territory west of the Mississippi and north of the Missouri Compromise line to do so. Nor does he mention Young's invitation to Southerners to use Utah as a refuge from "the domination of negroes and negro worshippers" during Reconstruction. Nor does he mention that Young, in endorsing Andrew Johnson's Reconstruction policies, stated, "I do not know that there is any President who could swallow all the niggers there are, without bolting." The above quotations are found in [Newell] Bringhurst's biography. Although he [Bringhurst] does not dwell at length on the subject, and he does place Young's attitude in the context of those unenlightened times, he does not avoid it as Arrington does.[40]

Leonard was more aware than most members of the LDS Church of the history of the policy that prohibited males of black African ancestry from ordination to the priesthood. Indeed, he had been at the forefront of the paradigm shift caused by Lester Bush's monograph on the subject. The omission of Young's role as instigator of the policy thus was not inadvertent. Perhaps Leonard felt that the 1978 revelation that eliminated the exclusionary policy made any discussion of it moot. However, such reasoning would also have rendered moot any treatment of polygamy, which the church had disavowed in 1890. A more likely explanation is that Leonard simply chose to take a pass on an episode of history that was, for one who had lived through it, still too painful to deal with in print.

To be sure, *American Moses* was an important biography of a seminal figure in Mormon history, and certainly it was a great improvement on the several biographies of Brigham Young that had preceded it. But it never garnered the critical acclaim that remains attached, for over a half-century, to *Great Basin Kingdom*. Muir wrote with a note of genuine wistfulness, "One would like to read the book that Arrington *could* have written if he had allowed his objectivity precedence over his religion."[41] Richard Bushman, whose personal struggle to write a biography of Joseph Smith extended throughout his professional career, said, simply, "It didn't go anywhere."[42] Perhaps the overall shortcoming of the book was due to Leonard's inability to address head-on an essential question that continues to confront the LDS Church today: How do you deal with flaws in a prophet? Neither Leonard then nor the church hierarchy today has fully answered that question.

27

CONTROLLING THE STORY

The quest by the church hierarchy to control the story of Mormonism extended beyond the History Division. However, control of individuals and groups not employed by the church proved far more problematic than control of its employees.

FEMINISTS

As detailed in chapter 17, the Equal Rights Amendment was a pivotal issue for the church. Sonia Johnson became a lightning rod for advocates of the ERA as her public remarks put a bright and unwanted spotlight on the all-male Mormon hierarchy that opposed it. The church was on the defensive, and a growing chorus of Mormon feminists sought to keep it there. Indeed, Johnson essentially created a community consisting of women whose feminism previously had lived in solitude. Nadine Hansen, a young mother and attorney in California, recalls the electric moment when she realized she was not alone:

> When the Equal Rights Amendment was at issue, I was young. I didn't know a single other feminist in my whole Mormon world. . . . I bought a newspaper one day, because there was something in particular in the news that I wanted to have more depth in than there was on television. As I thumbed through it, I came across this article that talked about an exchange between a Mormon woman and Senator Orrin Hatch. . . . He said that she was insulting his wife by the things she was saying. As she described it, "He put on his priesthood voice to do it." This sleepy little hearing that was going on without much fanfare went as viral as things could go viral in those days. So I found out, "My gosh! There are some other Mormon women who support the ERA."[1]

Even as Johnson's ecclesiastical court was proceeding, church leaders were working to control the larger story of the ERA. Two months after her December

1979 excommunication, a twenty-three-page booklet entitled *The Church and the Proposed Equal Rights Amendment: A Moral Issue* was sent to all church members in the United States who subscribed to the church's monthly magazine, *The Ensign*. No author was identified, but its placement communicated its strongly authoritative aura—though it stopped short of having the imprimatur of the First Presidency or the Twelve. In strong and unambiguous terms it explained the church's opposition to the ERA, painting the issue as one of morality rather than civil rights. It also responded indirectly to Johnson's excommunication by reassuring church members, "Church membership has neither been threatened nor denied because of agreement with the proposed amendment. However, there is a fundamental difference between speaking in favor of the ERA on the basis of its merits on the one hand, and, on the other, ridiculing the Church and its leaders and trying to harm the institution and frustrate its work."[2]

Indeed, there were no further excommunications directly related to the ERA; however, Mormon feminism had moved to a new plateau that it would never again completely abandon.

INTELLECTUALS

There was not a single event that either defined the intellectual movement within the LDS Church or brought it into direct conflict with the church hierarchy. Rather, it was a process that was occasionally punctuated with notable events such as the beginning of the Mormon History Association in 1965, the founding of *Dialogue: A Journal of Mormon Thought* in 1966, *Exponent II*'s beginning in 1974, and *Sunstone*'s publication in 1975. The blossoming of the independent Mormon press overlapped the Arrington years in the Church Historical Department, and the latter part of the 1970s saw a steady stream of articles and books containing new and often edgy data and interpretations, particularly in *Dialogue* and *Sunstone*. Although the combined subscriber base of the two publications never amounted to even one percent of the church's membership total, the potential reach of the publications was substantial—Lester Bush's 1973 *Dialogue* article on blacks and priesthood being a case in point.

In 1979, as Sonia Johnson galvanized the Mormon feminist movement, a number of articles appeared in the two periodicals that were both authoritative in their scholarly stance and threatening to the status quo of the institutional church:

- "Campus in Crisis: BYU, 1911" described the threats of "higher criticism" of the Bible and biological evolution at BYU, which resulted in the firing of four of the university's brightest professors.[3]

- "Mormon Women and Depression" brought to the forefront a half-hour documentary whose broadcast on church-owned television station KSL originally had been cancelled by church leaders but, in the face of public pressure, was expanded to one hour and then broadcast.[4]

- "Faith and History: The Snell Controversy" described the firing from the Church Educational System of Heber Snell, largely over his liberal interpretations of the Bible.[5]

- "Mixed Messages on the Negro Doctrine: An Interview with Lester Bush" explored the unfinished business of dealing with over a century of erroneous explanations for the exclusionary policy.[6]

- "Elijah Abel and the Changing Status of Blacks within Mormonism" refocused attention on Brigham Young's role in having initiated the ban on ordination of blacks and the absence of any recorded revelation.[7]

- "The Book of Abraham Facsimiles: A Reappraisal" strongly challenged the narrative that the Book of Abraham in the Church's Pearl of Great Price was a literal translation of an Egyptian papyrus.[8]

- "The New Biology and Mormon Theology" discussed some of the ethical and theological challenges that modern reproductive medicine and molecular biology posed, including artificial insemination, sperm banking, and cloning.[9]

Then, in the summer of 1979, the Sunstone Foundation, publisher of *Sunstone* magazine, sponsored in Salt Lake City the first Sunstone Theological Symposium (later renamed the Sunstone Symposium). Unlike the Mormon History Association, whose conferences since 1965 had focused on Mormon history and generally had showcased serious historians giving papers targeted for publication in scholarly journals, the symposium covered a wide range of topics and invited as participants virtually anyone who had something to say and who would follow the usual academic format of proposal presentation, response, and audience Q&A. It quickly became an annual gathering place for the fringe as well as the center—and a threat to the institutional church because its format encouraged open debate and dissent.

The cumulative effect of the articles and the symposium was an implicit challenge to the largely uncontested primacy of the church hierarchy in matters historical, theological, and temporal. In February 1980, Ezra Taft Benson, president of the Quorum of the Twelve Apostles, responded to this perceived threat in a speech at a BYU devotional that some interpreted as setting the stage for his own course of action upon becoming church president and prophet, which occurred five years later.[10] First, he defined unambiguously the priority of the prophet in dealing with *any* issues:

> The prophet will never lead the Church astray. . . .
>
> The prophet is not required to have any particular earthly training or credentials to speak on any subject or act on any matter at any time. . . .
>
> The prophet does not have to say 'Thus saith the Lord' to give us scripture. . . .
>
> The prophet tells us what we need to know, not always what we want to know. . . .
>
> The prophet is not limited by men's reasoning. . . .
>
> The prophet can receive revelation on any matter—temporal or spiritual. . . .
>
> The prophet may be involved in civic matters."[11]

Then, to make sure that there was no misunderstanding about the target of his remarks, he said, "The two groups who have the greatest difficulty in following the prophet are the proud who are learned and the proud who are rich."

Leonard, who was a charter subscriber to *Dialogue* and *Sunstone* and kept up with the scholarship, had an inside track to some behind-the-scenes information about Benson's controversial speech. Four months thereafter he spoke with George Boyd, a Church Educational System employee whose wife, Maurine, was Spencer Kimball's sister:

> George also said that he had learned that President Kimball in particular and the First Presidency in general were very angry about Elder Benson's talk at BYU in which he made the statement that every word spoken by the current prophet must be regarded as from the Lord. They called Elder Benson in and scolded him and caused him to apologize to the First Presidency for those remarks. President Kimball declared that when the Lord spoke to him, that was one thing, but that the Lord did not speak to him on every topic and therefore it was Spencer Kimball talking, not the Lord.[12]

Firm though Kimball was in chastising Benson, the rebuke remained private. As a result, Benson's message, rather than Kimball's, was the one that predominated among church members. Furthermore, Kimball's ability to control Benson and the other apostles who were aligned against the intellectuals was being compromised by a series of serious health challenges that began with two emergency brain operations in late 1979 to remove subdural hematomas, "marking the midpoint of his twelve years as president and the beginning of steep decline."[13]

Dialogue and *Sunstone* continued to publish provocative articles that challenged the church's politicized activities, the traditional versions of the First Vision, and the origin of the Book of Mormon. In the first half of 1980 they included:

- "Church Politics and Sonia Johnson: The Central Conundrum"[14]
- "The Book of Mormon—A Literal Translation?"[15]
- "Scholarship and the Future of the Book of Mormon"[16]
- "The Orson Pratt–Brigham Young Controversies: Conflict within the Quorums, 1853 to 1868."[17]

In addition to the articles, several books were published in 1980 that challenged the traditional narrative of Mormonism:

- *Mormon Answers to Skepticism: Why Joseph Smith Wrote The Book of Mormon*, written by a non-Mormon, challenged in a nonpolemical manner the official narrative that the Book of Mormon is a literal translation of an ancient record.[18]
- *The Words of Joseph Smith* gathered all known accounts of Joseph Smith's discourses during the Nauvoo period, thus making them readily available to scholars—including revisionist scholars—for the first time.[19]
- *Thus Saith the Lord* challenged the conventional understanding of the process of revelation as it has occurred within the LDS tradition.[20]
- *The Changing World of Mormonism*, an updated version of Jerald and Sandra Tanner's privately published *Mormonism, Shadow or Reality?*, for the first time facilitated national distribution of their foundational work exploring and exposing the weaknesses in traditional claims.[21]

In June, Apostle Bruce McConkie took up where Ezra Taft Benson had left off and, in a fourteen-stake fireside at BYU, responded to the cumulative scholarship by lashing out at the "Seven Deadly Heresies" that he saw in many of the controversial articles.[22] Back and forth the skirmishes went, always through surrogates because the Mormon intellectuals never comprised a planned, coordinated movement. That is, there was never a center for the LDS hierarchy to comprehend, control, or even engage in ongoing dialogue—although there is no evidence that church leaders attempted to initiate such a dialogue.

The flow of publications continued through the remainder of 1980 and into 1981:

- "The Reconstruction of Mormon Doctrine: From Joseph Smith to Progressive Theology."[23]
- "The Mormon Concept of Mother in Heaven."[24]
- "The Fuhrer's New Clothes: Helmuth Hübener and the Mormons in the Third Reich."[25]
- "Personal Conscience and Priesthood Authority."[26]
- "All that Glitters: Uncovering Fool's Gold in Book of Mormon Archaeology."[27]
- "A New Climate of Liberation: A Tribute to Fawn McKay Brodie, 1915–1981."[28]

In the summer of 1980, just weeks after McConkie's "Seven Heresies" speech, Leonard attended the first meeting of a new society of Mormon intellectuals, named after one of their heroes, Brigham H. Roberts. Truman Madsen, a BYU professor and Roberts's biographer, lectured on the society's namesake. Leonard recorded, "An enormous crowd overflowed the building. Perhaps four or five hundred people. The cream of Salt Lake's intellectual community. The purpose of the B. H. Roberts group, organized more or less by Grethe Peterson, is to provide intellectual evenings for Mormon intellectuals, all positively oriented, of course, but stimulating and thoughtful rather than doctrinaire. Young Mormon intellectuals need this."[29]

Again, there was no organized intellectual movement that was attempting to usurp or even challenge the church's ecclesiastical authority. However, the piecemeal reevaluation of an increasingly broad array of historical and doctrinal topics became a *de facto* assault on that authority—or at least it was interpreted as such by ecclesiastical officers.

In the summer of 1981, this time using the annual Religious Educators' Symposium at BYU (for Church Educational System administrators and teachers), Boyd Packer drew a deep line in the sand in "The Mantle Is Far, Far Greater Than the Intellect."[30] Lavina Fielding Anderson, in an early draft history of Leonard's years as church historian, called it "a dismaying anti-scholarly manifesto," the strongest rebuke yet to the Mormon intellectuals. Initially published in a pamphlet for CES personnel, it later appeared as the lead article in *BYU Studies*. Anderson continued, "Despite a few disclaimers and qualifications, Elder Packer basically set scholarship and faithfulness in opposition to each other and con-structed his address around a list of cautions to teachers of history. Academic competence, he stressed, did not qualify a teacher of the Church. It was difficult not to read the speech as a major anti-intellectual statement by denying faithful-ness to scholars; it was even more difficult not to read it as a continuation of the attack that had begun with Elder Benson's denunciation of *The Story of the Latter-day Saints* in 1976, four years earlier, at the same forum."[31]

Packer used apocalyptic terminology to describe a "war with the adversary"—a thinly veiled shot at intellectuals whose research and writings went contrary to his own views:

> There is a temptation for the writer or the teacher of Church history to want to tell everything, whether it is worthy or faith promoting or not. Some things that are true are not very useful. . . .
>
> In an effort to be objective, impartial, and scholarly, a writer or a teacher may unwittingly be giving equal time to the adversary. . . .
>
> There is much in the scriptures and in our Church literature to convince us that we are at war with the adversary. We are not obliged as a church, nor are we as members obliged, to accommodate the enemy in this battle. . . .
>
> I think you can see the point I am making. Those of you who are employed by the Church have a special responsibility to build faith, not destroy it. If you do not do that, but in fact accommodate the enemy, who is the destroyer of faith, you become in that sense a traitor to the cause you have made covenants to protect.[32]

In the immediate aftermath of Packer's speech, another publication began, one that became the biggest thorn yet in the side of the hierarchy, the *Seventh East Press*. Leonard enthusiastically wrote to his children about the new publication, pointing out that its literary independence came at an impressive monetary price. "The founders, Elbert Peck and Ron Priddis, are both students at BYU. One of them sold his car to get the money; the other got a loan with his car as security."

The cover story of the paper's first issue had the headline, "Elder Packer Counsels Historians." Although published in early October, *Seventh East Press* "broke" the story of Packer's speech: "Not a word has appeared about it in the press until this." The twelve-page newspaper carried a wide variety of articles and commentary in addition to the article on Packer. To Leonard, it was "a pretty important development. Of course, it may not pay financially and may go the way of many such papers. But in the meantime, we're getting some fresh air at BYU, and it will be interesting to this historian to see what is revealed next."[33]

While taking note of Packer's speech, Leonard put an optimistic spin on it, in a subsequent letter to his children, that differed markedly from the alarmed reaction of others. "Without naming anybody in particular he says we have not built faith enough. . . . Frankly, it didn't bother me and I do not think it will have any effect on us. We're sailing right along doing what we've always done and what we expect to continue to do. Elder Packer's admonitions, in my judgment, should not cause any alteration in our work. If they embarrass anybody, they embarrass him."[34]

One of Leonard's former coworkers, D. Michael Quinn, by this time a professor of history at BYU and director of its graduate program, reacted quite differently and, in an unprecedented move, went public with a direct response not only to Packer's speech, but also to Ezra Taft Benson's 1976 speeches, "God's Hand in Our Nation's History" and "The Gospel Teacher and His Message." In a lecture to the BYU Student History Association on November 4, 1981, Quinn said, "Elder Packer has created an enemy that does not exist,"[35] and then went on to rebut, point by point, the anti-intellectual allegations made by both apostles. He concluded by redefining the "enemy" to which Packer had referred:

> The central argument of enemies of the LDS church is historical, and if we seek to build the Kingdom of God by ignoring or denying problem areas of our past, we are leaving the Saints unprotected. As one who has received death threats from anti-Mormons because they perceive me as an enemy historian, it is discouraging to be regarded as subversive by those I sustain as prophets, seers, and revelators. Historians did not create problem areas of the Mormon past, but most of us cannot agree to conceal them, either. We are trying to respond to those problem areas of Mormon experience. Attacking the messenger does not alter the reality of the message.[36]

Seventh East Press carried a report of Quinn's speech in a front-page article, and the story then gained national traction.[37] Now realizing that Packer's speech carried substantial baggage, Leonard wrote to Gordon B. Hinckley, a member of the First Presidency. "Elder Packer's recent BYU address concerning Church history has produced some results that perhaps were not intended. The effect has been to isolate intellectually some of our fine LDS people from their Church leaders. The possibilities of creating a negative and difficult-to-manage image for the church are rather serious. Some of those consequences can be minimized or avoided, and if I can assist in this I would be pleased to do so."[38]

The First Presidency took a pass. In a letter signed by all four members they counseled, "As to the concerns you expressed in your letter, we suggest that you discuss them with Elder G. Homer Durham when his health will permit and that you follow his counsel."[39]

Coincident with the First Presidency's letter to Leonard was the preparation of an article in *Newsweek*, which appeared in early February under the title, "Apostles vs. Historians." It noted, in part:

> In a stirring defense of intellectual integrity, historian D. Michael Quinn of Brigham Young University recently warned his school's student history association that the "so-called 'faith-promoting' Church history which conceals controversies and difficulties of the Mormon past undermines the faith of Latter-day Saints who eventually learn of the problems from other sources." Defying the demands of Benson and Packer, Quinn argued that Mormon historians would be false to church doctrine, human conduct and the documentary evidence "if they sought to defend the proposition that LDS prophets were infallible in their decisions and statements." Such a history of "benignly angelic Church leaders . . . would border on idolatry," declared Quinn, who at 37 is the most accomplished of the Church's younger historians.[40]

Leonard sent a copy of the article to his children, along with a note. "My own feeling is that it was fair and balanced, accurate, well-worded, with no low blows. It could have been much worse. In other words, it was responsible, informative journalism. And if Elder Packer didn't like it, he shouldn't have given the talk in the first place. I do not see the article as damaging to the Church, to Mike Quinn, or to our historical efforts. So I'm relieved, if not pleased. It gives due credit to Mike for 'standing up' on a question very important to all of us."[41]

The *Newsweek* article led to a meeting at the Church Administration Building, arranged by Mark Petersen, that included Quinn, Petersen, Ezra Taft Benson, and Boyd Packer, but not Leonard. Quinn described the meeting: "The apostles were careful not to ask me a single direct question. In order of seniority (Apostle Benson first, me last), each of us expressed his own views of the *Newsweek* article, the 'problems' of writing Mormon history, and the effects of all this on the faith of LDS members. The meeting was congenial and supportive."[42]

For nearly a year thereafter, an uneasy calm prevailed, but it was asymmetrical. On the one hand, none of the apostles made any public statements averse to intellectuals, while on the other hand *Dialogue* and *Sunstone* continued to publish articles practically guaranteed to antagonize not only Benson, Petersen, and Packer, but also even some of the more moderate members of the church hierarchy:

- "The Word of Wisdom in Early Nineteenth-Century Perspective."[43]
- "A Gift Given, A Gift Taken: Washing, Anointing, and Blessing the Sick Among Mormon Women."[44]
- "Women and Ordination: Introduction to the Biblical Context."[45]
- "Process Philosophy and Mormon Thought: Two Views on a Progressing God."[46]
- "Religion and the Denial of History."[47]
- "The Adam-God Doctrine."[48]
- "A Further Inquiry into the Historicity of the Book of Mormon."[49]
- " 'The Fulness of the Priesthood': The Second Anointing in Latter-day Saint Theology and Practice."[50]

Seventh East Press, with an audience that now reached well beyond the BYU campus, took on equally charged issues including the "Mormon Underground," evolution, sex education, unreported sex crimes at BYU, the Book of Abraham controversy, dissent at BYU, Wilkinson's employment of student spies to report on what liberal faculty said in the classroom, homosexuality at BYU, and plural marriage. Perhaps emboldened by the silence from the hierarchy since Packer's 1981 speech, the editors published a lengthy interview with Sterling McMurrin in January 1983 that proved to be their undoing—and likely was the catalyst for what followed shortly thereafter.[51] McMurrin's expressed doubts about Joseph Smith's First Vision and the historicity of the Book of Mormon were the final straw. Shortly after the interview appeared in print, Paul Richards, BYU Public Communications director, informed the editor that the newspaper could no longer be sold at the campus bookstore or on campus newsstands. Its lifeline severed, it ceased publication on April 12, only days after the calm was shattered.[52]

WITCH HUNT

On March 28, 1983, Lester Bush, author of the landmark 1973 *Dialogue* article on blacks and priesthood, received a phone call from the executive secretary of the Washington DC Stake, scheduling a meeting with stake president J. Willard Marriott Jr. and his counselor. Bush reported, "[It] became a two-hour discussion of my research and writing on all subjects. At the conclusion, Marriott simply thanked me for coming in, and said something to the effect that he didn't see any cause for concern in my record. No further explanation was given." But while Bush's experience was benign, over the next few weeks he learned that other scholars, also called in for interviews with stake presidents, had not been so fortunate.

Hearing of the other meetings, Bush asked Marriott for a follow-up meeting. "He said he had received a telephone call from Elder Mark E. Petersen, who had spoken 'very harshly' about me over my publications on the 'Negro Doctrine' and instructed Marriott to call me in and take some appropriate action. After talking with me, though, Marriott felt that no action was warranted, so just let the matter drop."[53]

Increasingly bothered by publications by Mormon intellectuals, Petersen had engaged the services of two of his assistants, Tom Truitt, an employee in the Church Library, and Roy Doxey, a BYU professor of religion who was the first chairman of the adult Correlation Reading Committee, to compile a list of problematic authors. Petersen then telephoned these individuals' stake presidents.[54] Marriott may have been the first stake president to receive a phone call from Petersen. Over the following weeks, the contacts broadened. By the first of May the list had grown to eight, all of whom had written for or had some association with *Dialogue, Sunstone,* or *Seventh East Press.* Outcomes of the meetings ranged from the congenial atmosphere of Marriott's meeting with Bush, to a hostile meeting with one employee working in the Church Office Building who was subsequently fired.[55]

At the annual Mormon History Association meeting in early May, Leonard, knowing that Lester Bush and I were in the same ward (congregation), asked me, "What do you know about the rumors we've heard about Lester?" For his part, Leonard shared the information that Petersen was "upset at *Seventh East Press* for publishing an interview with Sterling McMurrin" and had had Truitt and Doxey compile a list that initially was restricted to people associated with the *Press.* When he saw that it contained only four names, he sent the two men back to expand it to include "other suspicious characters."[56]

The list continued to grow until "at least fourteen stake presidents" had been apprised of "suspicious" writers in their stakes, according to Spencer Kimball's son.[57] One of the later-added names was Leonard's. "Leonard was on the list," confirmed Elbert Peck, "and his stake president was told to talk to him. He came over and visited Leonard and said, 'I feel like I would just like to give you a blessing. Would that be okay?' So he put his hands on Leonard's head and gave him a blessing of counsel and comfort. That was his way of dealing with the problem of having to talk to Leonard."[58]

A meeting in mid-May between *Sunstone* editor Peggy Fletcher and Gordon Hinckley of the First Presidency suggested that Petersen had acted on his own in conducting what was then being termed the "witch hunt," for Hinckley said he had known nothing about it, and apparently he brought the interviews to an abrupt end.[59]

A footnote to the unsavory episode was given at the Sunstone Theological Symposium three months later when Frederick Buchanan, a professor in the Graduate School of Education at the University of Utah, analyzed Mormonism's educational philosophy and twice invoked Leonard's name. Buchanan first asserted that both intellectual and spiritual growth come at the cost of dissonance, tension, and struggle. "To avoid the struggle by making sure that faculty do not disturb testimonies is to deny a basic element of human growth and development—as my weight-lifting teenage son's T-shirt proclaims, 'No Pain—No Gain.' Leonard Arrington has referred to this necessary tension as 'creative tension,' but admirable as this might be, it is well to remember that creativity also has risks."

Buchanan went on to say that if stability and institutional efficiency were the desired outcomes of the church's educational system, "of course it would be hard to fault those who want to promote a no-risk party line for B.Y.U. On the other hand, as I understand Mormon theology, 'risk' seems to be what this mortal existence is all about. To paraphrase a Mormon aphorism—'for it must needs be that there be risk in all things.'" He then invoked Leonard's name a second time. "The tensions on the tightrope at the Brigham Young University *can* be creative and fulfilling as Arrington suggests, if they are produced by the open clash of ideas in the academic market place where the antidote for poor reasoning is better reasoning, not suppression of 'false' ideas."[60]

PUNCTUATED EQUILIBRIUM

In September 1983, Leonard learned of a short-lived initiative on the part of Boyd Packer. In a meeting of the First Presidency and Quorum of the Twelve early that month, "Elder Packer commented that the Church ought to do something to prevent the Sunstone Symposium; it was damaging because it generated criticism of the General Authorities. No person picked up on the comment, however, so there was no discussion and no action taken. . . . Elder Packer, in this instance, seems to have been a lone crusader."[61]

Aside from that, Leonard's world settled down. His marriage to Harriet in November 1983 filled a major void in his life, and he quietly, if reluctantly, eased into retirement upon turning seventy. Life for Mormon intellectuals continued to be fraught with occasional peril,[62] but Leonard was in a good place. Commissioned histories and biographies, particularly a two-volume history of Idaho, largely consumed his attention. Only occasionally did he comment on higher-profile issues, such as Eugene England's startling allegation during a Q&A following a paper presentation in the Sunstone Symposium of 1992 that a church committee kept track of intellectuals. "There've been articles in the paper on the First

Presidency committee on strengthening the members of the church that keeps files on us intellectuals and occasionally asks stake presidents to call us in to check on our loyalty," Leonard commented to his children. "I'm glad it's out in the open. The church's activity in this regard has been indefensible, and I hope this public outcry will cause them to be more circumspect in their intimidation of historians and other writers."[63]

28

MARK HOFMANN

THE "MAGIC MAN"

In 2002 Simon Worrall wrote a book about an episode of contemporary history that shook the Mormon Church and left two people dead.

> Over a five-year period, starting in 1980, [Mark] Hofmann would "find" nearly four hundred and fifty Mormon documents, which he would sell to the Church for hundreds of thousands of dollars. Nearly all of them were sensational documents that shed important new light on Mormon history. To other dealers working in the field it appeared that Hofmann had almost magical powers. "I called him the Magic Man," confided Rick Grunder, a rare documents dealer who specializes in Mormon manuscripts and knew Hofmann in Salt Lake City. "He was like a nondescript Richard Cory, fluttering pulses when he said, 'Good morning,' glittering when he walked. Not by his appearance or by his manner. He didn't stand out. I never heard him raise his voice or exhibit any kind of bravado. The charisma he enjoyed was because of what we thought he had. He convinced us that he knew something we did not, that he had access to things we could otherwise never hope to find. There I was, grubbing around in piles of old paper, and not getting very far. Mark seemed to just wave his wand and this amazing stuff turned up. He was the Mormon Indiana Jones who could lead us to impossible treasures of information and wealth."[1]

THE ANTHON MANUSCRIPT

Leonard should have been skeptical, but wasn't. Dean Jessee, the church's foremost handwriting expert and Leonard's coworker in the History Division, should have been even more skeptical, but wasn't. Instead, Leonard gushed as he wrote to his children of Hofmann's first "discovery":

> Yesterday was an exciting day at the office. A returned missionary-student at USU, Mark Hofmann, had acquired an old Smith family Bible in which, between two pages partially glued together, he had found a document in the handwriting of Joseph Smith, which was THE DOCUMENT the Prophet made for Martin Harris to take to Professor Anthon in 1828. The earliest holograph writing of Joseph Smith! What a miraculous find for this sesquicentennial year. After Dean Jessee and I studied it for a while and decided, tentatively of course, that it was genuine, we showed it to Elder Durham; he arranged a meeting with Elders Hinckley and Packer. We spent sometime [*sic*] with them. They then arranged a meeting with the First Presidency. President Kimball had to change a doctor's appointment and cancel a meeting with the President of General Electric, but he did so, and the full First Presidency were there. We spent about 30 minutes or so with them. They were fascinated; a number of photos were taken by the Church photographer, and Elder Hinckley asked me to write up a news release which ought to go out this weekend. Quite a thing.[2]

Prior to showing the document to Leonard, Hofmann had taken the bible, published in England in 1668, to Jeff Simmonds, head of Special Collections at Utah State University where Hofmann was an undergraduate student. Simmonds "helped him open the glued document"[3]—thereby securing for Hofmann an eye-witness to the coming to light of what became known as the Anthon Manuscript.

Still functioning as church historian and under Hinckley's mandate, Leonard quickly wrote a narrative describing the discovery—which, remarkably, coincided with the sesquicentennial anniversary of the LDS Church. The story, which came from Hofmann, was that he had obtained the bible from an unnamed source who, in turn, purchased it at an estate sale of a descendant of Katharine Smith, a sister of Joseph Smith. The purchaser was intrigued with the book because of handwriting in it by Samuel Smith, a great-grandfather of Joseph.

Hofmann purchased the book from the source "on approval" in order to be able to verify its authenticity. In leafing through it, he came across two pages in the book of Proverbs that were stuck together. Rather than separate those pages immediately, he took them to Simmonds. Upon separating them, the two men found lodged between them a document "which had been folded four times so that it was approximately two and a half or three inches in width."[4]

Hofmann's discovery not only coincided with the church's sesquicentennial year, but also fit neatly within the calendar of the Mormon History Association, which was having its annual meeting the following week near Palmyra, New York, the site of Mormonism's origins. Arrangements were quickly made to add a special presentation to the opening plenary session of the conference. Most of the attendees had no advance notice of the Anthon Manuscript and were in awe as Danel Bachman, an Institute of Religion teacher in Logan who acted as Hofmann's surrogate, gave a hastily assembled slide show.

The Mormon historical community was immediately abuzz, in part because the manuscript was the earliest known holograph of Joseph Smith, and in part because many felt that its characters could be translated and thus vindicate Smith's claims as a translator of ancient languages. Herm Olson, an attorney in Logan, Utah, quickly sent a photocopy to Barry Fell, a professor of invertebrate zoology at Harvard University whose book *America BC* claimed that many pre-Columbian inscriptions in the Americas constituted proof of contact with Old World civilizations.[5] Within weeks, Fell wrote to a colleague in Saudi Arabia, a copy of the letter subsequently being included in Leonard's diary.[6] Fell's suggestion that part of the translation was the "apocryphal book of Nefi" raised historical chatter to a fever pitch, but the subsequent failure of scholars of ancient languages to verify any of Fell's translations quickly quieted the chatter—for a year.

JOSEPH III

The death of Joseph Smith Jr. in 1844 caused an immediate leadership crisis because Smith never made an unambiguous statement about how his successor would be chosen. Muddying the water still further were at least eight ambiguous precedents that could be gleaned from the historical record, two of which led to the two largest "Restoration" churches claiming Smith as their founder.

The Church of Jesus Christ of Latter-day Saints claimed that rightful succession came through the Quorum of the Twelve Apostles, which jointly presided over that church for three years following Smith's death, at which time Brigham Young became its president and prophet. That church moved to the Great Salt Lake Valley in 1847, where it established its permanent headquarters.

Many who chose not to follow Young eventually coalesced around Joseph Smith's oldest son, Joseph III, and formed the Reorganized Church of Jesus Christ of Latter Day Saints. Their claim of authority was that Smith had designated one of his sons to be his successor. In 1976, D. Michael Quinn, summarizing the eight succession possibilities Joseph Smith initiated over the years, noted, "Whether, in fact, Joseph Smith officially designated his son Joseph III to be his successor has been debated for more than a century."[7] Hofmann's second "find" put an end to the debate—at least temporarily—as Leonard recorded in his diary. "Apparently a week ago, on February 25, Wednesday, Mark Hofmann went to Don Schmidt [LDS Archivist] and said that he had acquired some manuscripts from the Bullock family in Coalville and that they included a 'minute' from Thomas Bullock saying that Joseph Smith had set apart his son Joseph the 3rd on January 17, 1844, to succeed him as president of the Church." Schmidt, to Hofmann's dismay, "said he really wasn't interested."

Hofmann then telephoned RLDS church historian Richard Howard, "who expressed great interest, was very eager and wanted to discuss the purchase of it." Sight unseen, Howard offered in trade a copy of the Book of Commandments, the rarest of all Mormon books. When word of the phone call "got back" to Schmidt and Earl Olson, they suddenly took great interest and arranged a meeting with Gordon Hinckley.

Hinckley thought the LDS church should buy it, but deferred action until consulting with Eldon Tanner of the First Presidency. Tanner's response was immediate and unambiguous: "By all means, we must have it. We must have it in our library. It must be our property." Knowing that the document would fetch a high price, Hinckley implied to Durham that "it would have to come out of their budget, and they decided that the only budget they had anything to play with was the Arts & Sites. It would have to come out of the Arts & Sites acquisitions budget."[8]

Dean Jessee, the church's acknowledged handwriting expert, was then called into the deliberations. In his own diary account, which he gave to Leonard, he noted that Earl Olson asked a crucial question: "Earl asked where all of this new Ms [manuscript] material was coming from—amazed that there was so much important material still being found. I told him I thought there was a lot of stuff still lying around in people's attics, and if my experience with the Brigham Young family was any indication, a person or organization with any acquisition ability at all could pick up all kinds of new material."[9]

In a meeting on March 2, 1981, that included Hofmann and Richard Howard, Jessee examined the manuscript and told Howard: "I felt it was Bullock's hand and that I could see no evidence of a forgery."[10]

The LDS Church purchased the document, and Leonard attempted to leverage its purchase to gain access to one of the few documents that he had never been allowed to see while church historian. In a letter to Gordon Hinckley he made his case:

In anticipation of the inevitability that the blessing pronounced by the Prophet Joseph Smith on his son Joseph III will become public knowledge, we assume that it is to the interest of the church to be able to place it in the proper context.

Our historians can be of help in responding to this challenge. They can do so most effectively if they are allowed access to the relevant documents. Otherwise they are seriously handicapped.

From all we can learn, the Council of Fifty minute book contains the last charge of Joseph Smith to the Twelve given some time after the [a]forementioned blessing. Would it be possible for me, or Dean Jessee, to examine this book, which is in the vault of the First Presidency? This should help us respond to some of the inevitable questions.[11]

Leonard's request was declined. Instead, church leaders—but not the historians—made an unsuccessful search among manuscript records to try to ascertain the authenticity of the document and the date of the purported ordination. Leonard reacted to their actions in his diary, "It would have been so simple for them to have consulted any one of our historians, who could have given them the right date. That they would pursue this without calling in a single historian is almost unbelievable—it certainly isn't the Spirit of the Kingdom. It makes one a little resentful, even a little angry."[12]

Eventually realizing that the document was of far greater value to its Missouri cousin, LDS Church leaders agreed to give it to the RLDS Church, in return for which they received an original Book of Commandments (1833).

LUCY'S LETTER

A year and a half elapsed before the next Hofmann document surfaced. Leonard wrote to his children, "The big professional news of the week is the public announcement of the Lucy Mack Smith letter to her sister-in-law, dated Jan. 23, 1829, telling about the glorious new work about to begin, and the completion of the first 116 pages of the Book of Mormon. . . . It's the earliest dated document in Church history. A marvelous addition to our history and good proof of the sincerity of our historical claims."[13]

Once again, Dean Jessee was asked to weigh in. "Dean Jessee, a distinguished writer of Church history and a handwriting authority, has examined closely a copy of the letter and has indicated the handwriting is 'definitely that of Lucy Mack Smith.' "[14]

Again followed a year and a half of quiet from Hofmann's Mormon document franchise.

The Salamander Letter

In February 1984, Leonard wrote "a highly confidential memo" to his daughter-in-law, journalist Christine Rigby Arrington, to assist her with a professional assignment to write a story about a most unusual document that quickly came to be known as the "Salamander Letter." This was the most sensational "find" of Hofmann to date—"sensitive enough that it ought to be presented in a fuller context, where the sensationalistic aspect will be minimized. How can we be protected from sanctions from above if we participate in publishing so explosive a document?"[15]

A small group knew about the existence of the letter, and a still-smaller group was aware of the content that might cause some, in Leonard's words, to be "thrown for a loop." One of these individuals was Jerald Tanner who, in the minds of many at church headquarters, was the personification of "Enemy of the Church." He was the person who perhaps had the most to gain by *not* being skeptical, yet he was the *most* skeptical. He was also the first to raise a warning flag. In the March 1984 issue of the *Salt Lake City Messenger*, the newsletter of their Utah Lighthouse Ministry, Jerald and his wife, Sandra, broke the news of the latest document offered by Mark Hofmann:

> For a month or two there have been rumors circulating that an extremely important letter written by Book of Mormon witness Martin Harris has been discovered. Although there has been an attempt to keep the matter quiet until the document has been published, we have been able to piece together the story and to learn of the remarkable contents of this letter. The document was apparently purchased by Mark Hofmann, a Mormon scholar who has made a number of significant discoveries in the last few years. . . .
>
> In this letter, written just after the Book of Mormon was published, we find these revealing statements concerning how Joseph Smith obtained the gold plates from which the Book of Mormon was translated:
>
> ". . . I found it 4 years ago with my stone but only got it because of the enchantment the old spirit come to me 3 times in the same dream & says dig up the gold but when I take it up the next morning the spirit transfigured himself from a white salamander in the bottom of the whole . . ."[16]

Jerald Tanner had much to gain from the letter. Having devoted his entire adult life to discrediting the truth claims of the LDS Church, he now confronted a document that linked a salamander—and not an angel—to the origin point of the Book of Mormon. Setting aside the sensationalism that had characterized most of his writings over a quarter-century, he proceeded in a reasoned and cautious tone:

> At the outset we should state that we have some reservations concerning the authenticity of the letter, and at the present time we are not prepared to say that it was actually penned by Martin Harris. The serious implications of this whole matter, however, cry out for discussion. If the letter is authentic, it is one of the greatest evidences against the divine origin of the Book of Mormon. If, on the other hand, it is a forgery, it needs to be exposed as such so that millions of people will not be mislead [*sic*]. . . .
>
> While we would really like to believe that the letter attributed to Harris is authentic, we do not feel that we can endorse it until further evidence comes forth.[17]

Tanner was thus the first to go public in challenging the authenticity of the Salamander Letter—or, for that matter, any of the documents that came through the hands of Mark Hofmann. Decades later his wife, Sandra, reflected on the ironies. "Jerald had a very keen, analytic mind to recognize a person's style, although he was a totally untrained guy. Before the Salamander Letter came out, when we just got rumors of it, it was really exciting. Then, when he finally got the typescript of it, which I assume came from Mike Marquardt, he was all excited. He was going to try to find all of the supportive evidence to show why this had to be a genuine document."[18]

After he studied what he assumed would be supportive evidence, including the 1834 book by E. D. Howe[19] that contained the earliest affidavits from Mormonism's detractors, Jerald said to his wife, "It's a forgery!" Her response probably surprised him: "Jerald, you can't just go around accusing someone of fraud." He responded, "I know this is a fraud, because someone has read the Newel Knight article in *BYU Studies,* and has read E. D. Howe, and has come up with the Salamander Letter."[20]

For months, Jerald Tanner was a lone voice of skepticism. In August 1984 an article in the *Los Angeles Times* pointed out the irony of his position: "The Tanners' suggestion of forgery has surprised some Mormons, who note that the parallels in wording also could be taken as evidence for authenticity."[21] And in an entirely unexpected and unprecedented move one week later, the LDS Church–owned *Deseret News,* apparently reflecting a growing realization by church leaders that a forged Salamander Letter would make their own lives easier, interviewed and quoted Jerald:

> Outspoken Mormon Church critics Jerald and Sandra Tanner suspect the document is a forgery, they told the *Deseret News.* Jerald Tanner has not seen the actual letter but says similarities between it and other documents make its veracity doubtful. Tanner said he studied a typescript of the document and wanted to believe it. But when he compared it to the 1834 book *Mormonism Unvailed* by E. D. Howe, he found highly similar stories about Smith viewing a toad that turned itself into a man or a spirit. Another disturbing aspect, Tanner said, was [that] the letter seemed out of character for Harris. "In the entire text of the letter, there is no mention of religion in the sense of religion as we know it," Tanner said.[22]

In May 1985 the plot took an even more bizarre twist. At the opening session of the Mormon History Association annual meeting, a panel of four historians that included handwriting expert Dean Jessee gave a presentation in a plenary session, announcing "that an 1830 letter written by Martin Harris, Mormonism's first follower, was authentic in spite of Harris' seemingly bizarre report that Smith told him a 'white salamander' guarding the golden plates (later the basis for the Book of Mormon) in 1823 turned into an old spirit who fended off Smith, striking him three times." The really bizarre part—not to minimize the whole salamander-turned-spirit business—was that the newspaper article that reported the panel presentation mentioned it only in passing, its headline reading, "Mormon Church Releases Letter Revealing Founder's Belief in Cult." It described an 1825 letter, in Joseph Smith's hand, that gave guidance on finding treasure, complete with cautions about spirits that might be guarding the treasure—a hand-in-glove companion to the Salamander Letter. The article read, in part:

> The Mormon Church Friday released photographic copies of an 1825 letter written by church founder Joseph Smith Jr. in which he suggests occult methods for finding treasure guarded by "some clever spirit." The letter, the oldest ever found in his hand, thus adds new evidence that the origins of Mormonism were interwoven with magical lore. Church leaders acknowledged only this week that they own the letter, whose contents were rumored as long as a year ago. . . .
>
> After a previous denial that the church owned it, Jerry Cahill, the church's spokesman, said he was called into the office of Gordon Hinckley, second counselor to Mormon President Spencer Kimball,

on May 3 and told that the First Presidency had the letter in its vault and that it might eventually be available for study.[23]

Both the nature of the letter and the timing of its release were fortuitous for proponents of the letter's authenticity—including the four panelists, one of whom was quoted in the article, "With Smith himself writing matter-of-factly in 1825 about a 'clever spirit' guarding buried treasure, the later Harris letter also gains credibility."[24]

Two problems were beginning to emerge, although few at the time saw them as such. One was that the 1825 letter served to shore up claims of the authenticity of the 1830 letter—too conveniently. The other was that, for the first time, the church leadership acknowledged that it had purchased a document from Hofmann without disclosing it to anyone publicly. If Hofmann's documents were forgeries—and Jerald Tanner now was not the only one warning of the possibility—then nothing could better serve his purposes than a client who bought and then sequestered.

Rick Grunder, the book dealer who termed Hofmann the "magic man," recalled the frustration in some quarters over this very issue when the Anthon manuscript first surfaced. Speaking to Craig Jensen, the book conservator at the BYU Library, Grunder described just having seen and handled the Anthon Transcript, the earliest of Hofmann's finds, which had been shown to him by church archivist Don Schmidt. Jensen's reaction caught him off-guard. "Craig was angry, and he said, 'Why isn't anyone trying to authenticate these things better?' He was really upset that more wasn't being done to authenticate them. Well, when you want it to be true—or if, like the Salamander Letter, you don't want it to be true but you're afraid it is—you probably don't want to bring a lot of experts in. And they didn't."

With the benefit of hindsight, Grunder acknowledged that all of the church people, both historians and ecclesiastics, would likely have solved the puzzle earlier if they had only bothered to look carefully. "He often got himself in financial binds and had to forge things quickly, and he thought, 'It's just going to the Church anyway, and they are going to hide it, so I don't have to make this too good. It's good enough to satisfy them, and it will be locked up until long after I die'—not realizing that all he had to do was slip once and it would all come out."[25]

Indeed, at a press conference shortly after Hofmann's house of cards collapsed, Gordon Hinckley of the First Presidency acknowledged that "the LDS Church has acquired some 40 documents from Hofmann,"[26] nearly all of which had been unknown even to the church's own historians.

The Mormon History Association panel notwithstanding, a small but persuasive group of naysayers went public with their allegations of forgery. Rhett James of Logan did a syntax analysis that compared the Salamander Letter to the few letters known to have been written by Martin Harris. "Known Harris letters averaged 30 words a sentence as contrasted to 13 words a sentence in the 1830 letter, James said. Technical details aren't consistent, he said—participles and noun clauses as direct objects were nine times more plentiful in the known Harris letters than in the salamander letter. Appositives, dependent clauses and infinitives appeared twice as often in established Harris correspondence than in the 1830 letter, he said." By applying quantitative analysis to the letter, James was able to say, with confidence, "There is no way it could be the same author. It would be impossible."[27]

Some voiced their suspicions privately, and among them was Eudora Widtsoe Durham, G. Homer's wife. Their son, George Durham, recalled in 2011, "I remember at a Sunday dinner my mother inquiring of [my father] where these were all coming from. He explained how Mark Hofmann was interested in philately, supposedly, and was looking at old stamps, and was trying to get into stamp collections. My mother looked at him rather quizzically and she said, 'Homer, are you sure he's not doing these in his basement?' I remember when the whole thing unraveled, *Mother was right!*"[28]

Leonard was well aware of the allegations that the Salamander Letter was a forgery, for he pasted the newspaper clippings in his diary. Nonetheless, even after the collapse late in 1985 of Hofmann's empire, his exposure as a forger, and his eventual confession to being a murderer who had killed two people in an attempt to cover his tracks, Leonard clung to the belief that at least one of the documents he produced—the Salamander Letter—was not a forgery. "I feel that the letter is authentic," he told a correspondent in November 1985. "The account Martin Harris gives of the finding of the gold plates parallels that of Joseph Smith, but he explains it in terms of the folk culture of his day."[29] He wrote this letter only two weeks after a double murder that, fifteen months later, led to a plea bargain that spared the LDS Church from a public trial that undoubtedly would have exposed embarrassing actions by its leaders at the highest level, and spared Hofmann from the death penalty but committed him to prison for life.

THE BOMBINGS

On October 15, 1985, as skepticism mounted about Hofmann's "magic" and pressures intensified for him to produce a legendary collection of revealing documents created by William McLellin, one of the original Mormon apostles, Mark

Hofmann, in an apparent attempt to deflect attention, murdered Steven Christensen and Kathleen Sheets using two sophisticated package bombs. The next day, Hofmann was injured by a third bomb that detonated in his own car—thought to be an attempt both to portray himself a third victim and to destroy evidence that was found in the remains of the car.

Writing to his children the week after the bombings, Leonard was still in a state of considerable denial:

> There was speculation that the killing was done by some investor in [Coordinated] Finance Security, the business firm of Christensen and Sheets. But the media also introduced what I regarded as some rather silly speculation about Christensen's role in the so-called Salamander letter of Martin Harris to W. W. Phelps. . . .
>
> All of the important documents we have been aware of (the Anthon transcript, the Lucy Mack Smith 1829 letter, the Joseph Smith blessing on his son, the Joseph Smith 1825 letter, and the Martin Harris letter to W. W. Phelps) are, according to our opinion, enforced by scientific studies, authentic. . . .
>
> Those of us who have known Mark Hofmann have had no reason to suspect his honesty and integrity until the events of the past week have cast an ugly and tragic shadow.[30]

After the third bombing, Hofmann immediately became a suspect. Even then, Leonard gave him the benefit of the doubt. In February 1986, four months after the bombings and at the time when Hofmann was formally charged with twenty-seven felony counts but was free on bond,[31] Leonard wrote to his children, "Of those I have personally seen, the Anthon transcript, Lucy Mack Smith letter, the Joseph Smith blessings letter, the Salamander letter, I do not believe any were forged."[32]

Finally, on January 7, 1987, Hofmann pled guilty to second-degree murder. As part of a plea bargain, he submitted to fourteen interviews between January 7 and May 27, 1987, in which he systematically confessed that *all* of the documents relating to Mormonism that had passed through his hands were his own forgeries.[33] Once Hofmann made his complete confession, there was no more denial on Leonard's part. But once again, he put an optimistic face on events, writing to his children, "For the rest of us, we'll just keep writing what we've been writing all along. I don't see that the Hofmann forgeries made that much difference, at least in what the most of us were writing."[34]

Although Hofmann's forgery scheme had little direct effect on the History Division, since it was disbanded well before the bombings, it cast a dark shadow on the entire field of Mormon history for years to come by reinforcing biases of senior church leaders that nothing good could come from Mormon historians, regardless of who signed their paychecks. Soon, independent scholars became suspect, and "writing what we've been writing all along" became highly problematic.

29

THE SEPTEMBER SIX

THE COMING FURY

There was no truce between certain church leaders and intellectuals, outward appearances of uneasy calm notwithstanding. While Mark Petersen did not attempt to repeat his bold 1983 "witch hunt," his inaction may have been due as much to age and declining health as to Hinckley's instructions or the bad publicity. Indeed, after a long bout with cancer, Petersen died in January 1984, less than a year later. But actions averse to intellectuals continued to occur, among them being:

- June 1985: Linda Newell and Val Avery were banned from speaking at any church gatherings because of their authorship of *Mormon Enigma*, a candid biography of Emma Smith.[1] The ban, which was widely publicized, remained in effect for nearly a year, during which the authors' speaking invitations and book sales tripled.[2]

- August 1985: Boyd Packer, speaking at a regional priesthood leadership conference, lashed out at magazines "which defame and belittle the brethren."

- August 1985: Dallin Oaks, a member of the Quorum of the Twelve Apostles since the prior year, warned church members not to criticize church officials. "It does not matter that the criticism is true"—a message that he repeated publicly the following year.

- November 1987: David Wright, a BYU assistant professor, was terminated from the university because of his unorthodox views about biblical and LDS canon, despite never having voiced those views in the classroom.

- April 1989: Three General Authorities, speaking in the annual general conference, issued warnings to LDS intellectuals.

- August 1991: Two weeks after the annual Sunstone Symposium, the First Presidency and Quorum of the Twelve Apostles issued an unprecedented statement that condemned "recent symposia," without mentioning any by name, and strongly discouraged church members from participating in them in the future.

- August 1992: Despite the previous year's statement on symposia, 1,500 people attended the Sunstone Symposium. One of them, Eugene England, spoke out against the Strengthening Church Members Committee, which he said was keeping files on Mormon intellectuals. One week later, the First Presidency acknowledged and defended the existence of the committee.

- August 1992: Apostle Neal Maxwell, speaking to some 30,000 people at BYU Education Week, called out those who "become critics instead of defenders."

- Late 1992: BYU's board of trustees vetoed an invitation to Laurel Thatcher Ulrich, Mormon feminist and winner of the 1991 Pulitzer Prize for History for *A Midwife's Tale*, to speak at the 1993 BYU/Relief Society Women's Conference. The board gave no explanation for its vote. Ulrich later won a MacArthur "genius" award and was appointed the 300th Anniversary University Professor at Harvard University in its History Department.

- May 1993: Boyd Packer, in a speech to the All-Church Coordinating Council, singled out "the gay-lesbian movement, the feminist movement (both of which are relatively new), and the ever-present challenge from the so-called scholars or intellectuals" as "dangers" to the church.

- August 1993: The Sunstone Symposium drew its largest crowd to date.

Six Disciplinary Councils

In retrospect, and viewing in a few paragraphs events that spanned nearly a decade, one sees a virtual tsunami quickly approaching the shore. But in fact, it was the action of one man, Boyd Packer, rather than a broadly based, coordinated assault on intellectuals, that broke through the event horizon—and thus, it caught most people off-guard.

On September 12, 1993, Leonard received a devastating letter from Lavina Fielding Anderson, an editor and former church employee with whom he had worked for years and whom he had hired a decade earlier to prepare a draft autobiography covering his years as church historian.[3] The following day he broke the distressing news to his children: "We learned yesterday that Lavina Fielding Anderson had received a notice from her stake president to report for a trial of her membership, 'for conduct unbecoming a Latter-day Saint' for her collection and publication of spiritual abuses by church authorities toward individual members. I do not know of anything we can do to show our support for her and to express our abhorrence of this action. After all, she is a believer but simply wants people to stop this spiritual abuse, which the revelations warn against anyway."[4]

Anderson was one of six intellectuals who were summoned to appear before disciplinary councils in their wards and stakes. Within nineteen days, the September Six—a name already being used by the media—had been subjected to harsh church discipline. The first to be tried, Lynne Kanavel Whitesides, received the lesser punishment of "disfellowshipment," which restricted her privileges as a church member but did not eject her from the church. The remaining five—Lavina Fielding Anderson, Avraham Gileadi, Maxine Hanks, D. Michael Quinn, and Paul J. Toscano—were excommunicated.

As the councils were proceeding, Leonard lamented to his children, "Looks like a pattern of purging militant feminists and vocal intellectuals. Very silly and wrongheaded, I think. It will only harm the church's image and lessen the loyalty of the many active intellectuals."[5]

Anderson's excommunication occurred late in the month and caused Leonard particularly deep pain, which he conveyed to his children in his weekly letter. "Yesterday was one of the saddest days in my life. Lavina Fielding Anderson, one of our closest friends since 1972, was notified that she had been excommunicated for apostasy. Here is a person that we know personally to be one of the most devout, believing Mormons, who was excommunicated because she is compiling a list of incidents in which Mormons, especially women, were badly treated by bishops, stake presidents, regional representatives, and/or general authorities. And publishing the list without names."[6]

He not only lamented Anderson's fate, but also feared that a similar one may await him, "because in my own memoirs I record some instances of my own run-ins with church authorities, and if I should publish it they will probably excommunicate me."

The rumor mill had been busy with suppositions about the origin of the disciplinary councils, it being roundly rejected that six such councils could have occurred simultaneously without some kind of signal from church headquarters. Leonard pointed a finger: "Our information is that Elder Packer is behind this purge. Why don't the older Brethren speak out to halt this business."[7]

Leonard's "information" turned out to be accurate, although in the short term there was a denial that anyone at church headquarters had been involved in the process. But a syndicated Associated Press article on October 12 quoted Steve Benson, who was not only the Pulitzer Prize–winning political cartoonist for the *Arizona Republic* but also the grandson of the sitting church president, Ezra Taft Benson. Steve Benson reported that a member of the Quorum of the Twelve acknowledged to him that Packer had, in fact, initiated at least one of the disciplinary councils. The original *Arizona Republic* article "quoted Packer as admitting he had met with [stake president Kerry] Heinz about Toscano's case, but he denied having pressured the stake president to excommunicate Toscano."[8] Leonard included the entire article in his diary, and at the end wrote his own commentary under the heading "Added by LJA": "Let me here record that I was told by an 'insider' that Elder Packer, some time ago, had told Jon Huntsman, president of Monument Park Stake, that he must excommunicate a certain person. President Huntsman said he would not like to do it. They argued a little. Finally, insistent on having his way, Elder Packer told him, 'Excommunicate that person or I will excommunicate you.' President Huntsman held the trial and excommunicated him."[9]

The following week, in his regular letter to his children, Leonard described having reached out to Michael Quinn, one of his brightest protégés who, at one time, Leonard had hoped would succeed him as church historian.[10] "We had Mike Quinn for dinner at our house last evening and were assured that he will continue to work on his two books and on articles dealing with Mormon history. He did not seem to be upset particularly; he seemed to think it was inevitable. These excommunications are the worst examples of blaming the messenger for the message. . . . I feel like singing, 'Oh Say What Is Truth?' "[11]

On October 18 one of Leonard's friends wrote to him words that echoed the sentiments of many for whom the efforts and writings of Leonard and his colleagues had long been a lifeline. "It appears that some senior members of the church leadership have tried to severely curtail the independent pursuit of some church members as a kind of LDS McCarthyism. It does not feel like the same church as the one that existed in the late seventies, when I discovered *Dialogue* as a young missionary in Canada. . . . I realize that there has always been a tension between 'liberals' and 'conservatives' in the church, but it looks like open season has been declared on people who only want the church to be honest about its history." Rather than throw in the towel, the friend stated what many church members felt. "I love the church; I cannot imagine what my life would have been without it. But how can I merely shrug off the deeply hurtful atmosphere that has been created around the intellectual sphere of the Church?"[12]

Leonard's response mirrored his friend's feelings: "Your puzzlement is the same as mine. I do not know how to explain the actions of the past few weeks. My wife and I continue to pray for the Church and its leaders, and for those who have been disciplined. We continue to make positive contributions toward the writing of good Church history, and we continue to give talks that will help to remind us of our wonderful heritage of truth-seeking and professional excellence. As I say, we pray for enlightenment and greater understanding."[13]

To his own children, Leonard was more expansive in his comments. Citing examples where prior church presidents had been incapacitated—which currently was the situation with Ezra Taft Benson—he inferred that the current purge of intellectuals was occurring in a power vacuum. "Right now the most outspoken apostle seems to be Boyd Packer, who seems to want to purge the church of outspoken feminists and intellectuals. My own view is that they have gone over the line and the Church will tarnish its image of being compassionate, encouraging scholarship, and living with diversity. . . . When we've had a president that was fully functioning, he has taken a balanced and kind-hearted approach."

Then, with characteristic optimism, he looked forward to better days. "Of course, these things are temporary—they pass. I just hope we will pass the vindictive stage when I submit my memoir for publication—sometime next year. May the Lord have mercy on those stalwart members who are committed but still searching, who wish the Church well and are still growing in understanding and commitment. Faith is not an anchor to hold us back in safe harbors, but the sail of the ship that catches the breath of the Spirit and moves us out into broader seas."[14]

One lasting effect of the excommunications, hinted at in his letter to his children, was explicit in a letter to one of his brothers: "We continue to be saddened by our friends Mike Quinn, Lavina Anderson, and the Church. I feel more strongly about publishing my Memoir."[15]

30

Adventures of a Church Historian

Leonard's first initiative in autobiography began at age ten with these words: "In Jan. 1919 I took down with the flue and had it very badly, to add to the grief of my mother I took down with pneumonia at the same time! I came very near passing away but by the work of the Lord and a dear old nurse named Mrs. Hanna Bowen I lived."[1] He continued writing his diary sporadically throughout his life, the last entry being a letter to his children written on March 30, 1998, less than a year before his death. Because he inserted printed materials and important correspondence, which increased in volume after his transfer to the Joseph Fielding Smith Institute of Church History, his diaries amount to over twenty thousand pages and formed the foundation of the several topic-focused autobiographical volumes that he wrote and self-published.

The first attempt by the mature Leonard at a well-seasoned autobiography came in 1975, three years after he became church historian and had already published three biographies of other historical figures. Since his duties in the office would not allow sufficient time to write the book himself, he enlisted Rebecca Cornwall, who was working with him on a biography of Edwin Woolley.[2] As with the Woolley book, Leonard's autobiography would carry his name as sole author. He offered Cornwall $3.50 per hour and a split of royalties from the sale of the proposed book by Deseret Book Company.[3]

The plan was for Cornwall to ghostwrite the autobiography. He instructed her, "Write as if in first person using, where appropriate and suitable, my own words, either in quotes or in text. . . . I suggest you start first with World War II and my service overseas. I wrote Grace a letter *every* day that I was overseas. This means about a thousand letters. I think it would be emotionally impossible for me to write up this period."[4]

After working sporadically on the manuscript, Cornwall eventually decided to pursue other interests.[5] The autobiography became biography, and rather than covering Leonard's life to that point, it was limited to the period from 1931 until his return from World War II in 1946, with a four-page epilogue describing the three subsequent decades. "Just what we will do with it," he wrote to his children, "I'm not sure. I doubt it has general enough interest to be published."[6] In fact, Leonard decided against publication and had a few copies of the typescript bound for family and close friends.[7]

Five years later, in 1981, he again turned to autobiography, this time focusing on his years as church historian, which were then winding down. Again, he turned to a ghostwriter, Lavina Fielding Anderson, paying her an hourly wage with the understanding that it was a work for hire in which she would have no proprietary interest. She had just been fired from the *Ensign*,[8] so this project was one she greatly enjoyed. Leonard had long been one of her heroes, so she particularly cherished the daily contact with a man she respected and loved:

> I thought at first that he was just making a project for me out of the goodness of his heart. It did turn out that he really did want an autobiography; he'd done the first volume about growing up in Idaho, being on the chicken farm, going to graduate school, being in the army and meeting Grace.
>
> It was a documentary history, because what he gave me to work with were his weekly letters to his kids, and occasionally minutes from the historical department meetings, or a newspaper clipping or an official letter of some sort.
>
> I'm still not sure that it was what Leonard had in mind. I was writing with a real head of steam, I thought he'd gotten a bum rap, and I didn't like Elder Durham at all. I wasn't too fond of the Church in general, but I was having a good time working there in Leonard's division.

Anderson worked for one year—"This was pre-computer days, too, but I did have an electric typewriter. Leonard was still using a manual typewriter at that point"—and produced a 1,280-page typescript that, like Cornwall's earlier work, was biographical rather than autobiographical. Leonard approved the provocative title suggested by Anderson: *Doves and Serpents: The Activities of Leonard Arrington as Church Historian, 1972–1982*. The primary source throughout was Leonard's diary. "The materials were not right up to the date, and I handed everything over to him. I never saw what he did with them and I don't know how much he edited them."[9]

It appears that Leonard's sole literary contribution was a one-page biographical note describing Anderson's role, which concluded, "After she set up her own editing company in 1981, she was a logical choice for this biographical project and has written this long documentary history that should commend itself to my children and to future historians."[10] As with Cornwall's biography, several copies of the typescript of *Doves and Serpents* were bound for family members and close friends, but it was never published commercially. Indeed, Leonard did not want it to be circulated beyond that small circle. He wrote to his children a disclaimer that, characteristic of Leonard throughout his career, gave the benefit of the doubt to church leadership, his own pain at their hands notwithstanding:

> It's a pretty intimate history, and MUST NOT BECOME PUBLIC KNOWLEDGE because it essentially gives the story of THE GOOD GUYS and THE BAD GUYS. The General Authorities, in that work are the Bad Guy, and it would have been a far more fair approach [than] to have made it a story of the Good Guys v. the Good Guys. After all, one must consider the point of view of the Defenders of the Faith. Good men, betrayed to some extent by their own limitations. The book gives no sense of the struggles that are endemic in any religious organization. The book also does not give our own failures— the missed deadlines, the misplaced emphasis, our own limitations in writing and scholarship.[11]

After Grace's death in 1982, Leonard went through diaries, letters, photographs, and other scrapbook items and began to write a series of autobiographical vignettes. Taking advantage of desktop publishing technology, which had not existed when the earlier volumes were written, and with the assistance of technology-savvy Harriet (he never did learn to use a computer), Leonard wrote nearly a dozen photographically illustrated vignettes, beginning with *Magic Valley Pioneers: A Photographic Record of N. W. and Edna Arrington* in 1991. As with *From Chicken Farm to History* and *Doves and Serpents*, they were published privately in very small press runs.

While Leonard was beginning work on the vignettes, his son Carl was egging him on to write a full-scale autobiography. In April 1988 Carl wrote, "I fear you are spending precious years organizing the facts of lives so much less interesting than your own. If you don't leave a frank assessment and summing up and simply leave it as a mosaic to be pieced together then you will have left your great work purposefully undone. . . . You stand at the fulcrum of the intellectual mind of a major religious movement. . . . I think you need to shrug off the traumas and wounds of the end of Camelot and the Hofmann bombing and finish the work."[12]

Six months later, Carl returned to the subject with renewed urgency:

> Why was your life miraculously spared during the influenza epi-
> demic? Was it to write a history of the Steiner Corporation or Char-
> lie Redd's biography? I do not doubt the historical value of those
> worthy projects, but there are others who could do them. And yet
> there are some projects that *only* you could accomplish. The most
> crucial of these, I believe, would be a kind of spiritual autobiogra-
> phy—a story of your faith. As a descendant of Noah, Brigham, Edna
> and Clio I believe you are in a unique position to fashion a lasting
> gift for your children (physical, intellectual, spiritual). I believe the
> Mormon culture is hungry. They need some refreshing water in the
> baptismal fonts, someone who can properly bless the sacrament, a
> man with power to name and bless a child. The Army needs a leader
> with charisma to awaken and mobilize them. I say this not to flatter
> you, but perhaps to plant a seed.[13]

The seed fell on fertile soil, and Leonard began to write his own story in his
own voice. In 1993 he gave a draft of the manuscript to his trusted colleague, Davis Bitton, asking that he provide a critique. Bitton responded with a lengthy assessment that, surprisingly, had serious reservations about the project, including
a stern warning against publishing it in the form Leonard was intending:

> I'm sure it will be frustrating for you, assuming that you had wanted
> a simple recommendation, but I have to play Tevye and refer to both
> "hands."
>
> On the one hand, it is a refreshing self-portrait of one aspect of
> your life. . . . On the other hand, I have to say that I don't think the
> time is ripe for going public with a naming of names. (And for you to
> shield them with phrases like "a certain general authority" would
> take the punch out of it.) Despite all your careful laying of a founda-
> tion by talking of the fact that prophets are humans, the real world
> we are in is still one in which this would be seen as an "attack." And
> although that may be insular and narrow-minded, the brethren
> would probably be right in suspecting that it would be the anti-
> Mormons who would greet your work with glee. I can just imagine
> the Tanner[s] romping through it, underlining the sentences they
> wanted to sensationalize.
>
> What you say about the writing of church history may strike you
> and some others as eminently sound, but I think we can safely pre-
> dict, too, that it will be the Midgleys who will pounce on those

sections.[14] I can imagine what he would do with "we must be rela-
tivists." If it reaches the hands of formidable intellects like Peter
Novick for review, you might find the criticism very painful.[15]

So having summarized the general considerations on each side,
my recommendation is to do this up for your family and a few others.
(I would be honored to be on the list of recipients.) But even in this
form if you distribute it too widely, it will reach the hands of the
Tanners.

Naturally I will understand if you decide to go with those who
would urge you to go big time with your "confessions." As I told
Mike Quinn once, in giving him advice he chose to ignore, I am
quite aware of the fact that one can find other recommendations. I
would be delighted to be proved wrong about the response in high
Church circles.[16]

Cautions notwithstanding, Leonard pushed forward with the manuscript.
Nine months after Bitton's critique, he spoke with poet and playwright Carol Lynn
Pearson, a longtime friend, who remembered that she "asked him if anybody had
come after him in all this stuff and he said no, but they will. I asked when. He
said, 'When I publish my memoirs. I'm about finished now and am looking for a
publisher.' He said he tells everything like it was, recounts run-ins with Boyd
Packer and others. He said they won't like that."[17]

Initially Leonard thought to have the book published by church-owned Deseret Book Company—an unlikely prospect given the sometimes-brutal candor
of the autobiography. He changed direction in 1995. In an after-hours meeting
at the Mormon History Association's annual conference, Leonard acknowledged
that he was having second thoughts about submitting the manuscript to Deseret. "There are certain things that I want to say in this book that they don't
want me to say. I don't know why I can't say what I want in my own book."

Liz Dulany, an editor with the University of Illinois Press, replied, "Gee,
Leonard, if you published with us, we'd let you say anything you wanted
to." Nothing more was said that evening, but about a year later Dulany received
a letter from Leonard that said, "I've got it finished, and I remembered that we
had this conversation."

Dulany put it on a fast-track, referring it to only one outsider reviewer, Jan
Shipps, rather than the usual two. Dulany recalled, "Because of the stature of both
Leonard and Jan, I made an argument that that was all we needed. She did have
some suggestions to make, and Leonard made them. . . . He delivered the revised
manuscript to me personally at the MHA convention in Omaha in May of 1997,
and it was published in May of 1998."[18]

The book, while candid, rises above vindictiveness, petty complaints or self-pity. Leonard's daughter-in-law later described her reaction to it. "*Adventures of a Church Historian* is a diplomatic telling of the story. But it is so emblematic of him, that he just is insisting that this was not a tragedy. It was how he maintained his emotional and intellectual balance, his sanity. Just like [Barack] Obama: racist remarks are made, and he doesn't take the bait. That's how Leonard was."[19]

But even though Leonard pulled some punches, exercised tact, and employed his historical expertise to present the story fairly, as he saw it, he was genuinely concerned that the autobiography would backfire and cause him grief. D. Michael Quinn, one of Leonard's closest friends, heard a remarkable message from Leonard shortly before the book reached the bookstores:

> One time he invited me out for a birthday dinner. It was as he was just about to publish *Adventures of a Church Historian*, with the University of Illinois Press. . . . He told me that he was expecting to be excommunicated because of what he had published in the book. He said he thought that this would be enough for Packer to marshal enough influence to do it. Of course, by that time there had been the September Six, and it had been continuing. There had been others. And Leonard thought he was going to be the next example that Packer was going to trumpet. He told me that at my birthday dinner. He said—not that it was a certainty, and he didn't claim that he had an impression about it—he just said, "I think it is possible that I will be excommunicated because of that book."
>
> I didn't read the book until after he died, and when I read it, I thought that Leonard was so kind! He was so kind! He pulled so many punches! He was so circumspect in how he presented those controversies. I thought, "This is an ultimate comment on the environment of the late '90s, that he would think a book of such circumspection, of such mild criticism could be the grounds for him being excommunicated!" He was so circumspect. And for him to think, seriously, that this could result in his excommunication, that's something that weighed down on him. That last year of his life, he was, I think, waiting for the anvil to fall. It was a terrible thing.[20]

Leonard did not confide this fear only to Quinn. A surprisingly large number of people, including his son James, heard a similar message from him. "When he was writing *Adventures of a Church Historian*, I remember overhearing him on the phone, 'Will they excommunicate me if I put that in? Do you think they will excommunicate me? What do you think they will do? Do you think that's okay to put in?' He was worried."[21]

He needn't have worried. The autobiography was well received and he suffered no official repercussions from it. One colleague, in a letter of appreciation to Leonard, spoke for many. "You have indicated uneasiness with how certain officials in the Church will receive your book. . . . If anything, you are overly generous to certain individuals as you recount your story. But as a whole, the recipe of your restraint, honesty, personal and institutional loyalty, and openness to spiritual realities while insisting on respect for the verifiable historical record is a model for all Mormondom, and for those outside as well. If we as a Church cannot deal with the gentle and careful account you have offered, then it is we who are unworthy of you—not the reverse."[22]

The only tragedy attached to the autobiography was Leonard's death less than a year after it was published. Yet, even in so brief a time he garnered abundant accolades from the wide audience of admirers whose trust and loyalty he had gained over the decades. Emma Lou Thayne, perhaps the best-known Mormon poet and essayist of her generation, hosted a study group and invited Leonard to come talk about his autobiography. It was the last time she saw him before his death. "I can just see him sitting there in our living room and talking to all of us. . . . He was articulate, but also humble in really wonderful ways. He would talk about what had happened, but never with bitterness, never with any animosity toward people who had been responsible for having him leaving his job at the Church, which we all were sorry for. But he always could move ahead and get on with things and see things the way they were. And that's the way his book was."[23]

While Leonard was concerned about the reception *Adventures* might have among the church hierarchy, the book avoided the mud-wrestling genre of tell-it-all memoirs that have become a staple of the national political scene. Decidedly more candid than any of his previous publications, it also was decidedly less candid than his diary entries, letters to his children, and conversations with friends and colleagues as reflected in subsequent interviews.

At 249 pages, *Adventures*, which was the last book that Leonard published, is less than half the length of *Great Basin Kingdom*, his first book. Although autobiographical, it does not purport to be a complete autobiography. Instead, as suggested by the title, it focuses on Leonard's tenure as church historian, with 153 pages devoted to that time period, 74 pages to antecedent events, and the remainder to his post–church historian career. His personal life barely enters the narrative: the first three decades of his life, including his ancestry, childhood, education, courtship, marriage, and experiences in World War II, occupy less than two pages; and while his immediate family members are not totally excluded, they are not the focal point of any of the chapters. Indeed, his wife Grace is referenced in the index in only thirteen pages and his second wife, Harriet, in only six, while assistant church historians James Allen and Davis Bitton are listed on twenty-five and twenty-nine pages, respectively.

The most unusual aspect of *Adventures* is the candor with which Leonard described the decline and eventual dismantling of the History Division. In contrast to the tradition of self-censorship (or institutionally imposed censorship) that long had characterized historical, biographical, and autobiographical narratives written by church insiders, Leonard named names as he described in considerable detail the fading of Camelot. In particular, he called out apostles Ezra Taft Benson, Mark Petersen, and Boyd Packer for their adversarial roles; and devoted an entire chapter, with the ominous title "A New Pharaoh and New Directions," to describing the demise of the History Division.

Of historical significance aside from autobiography is chapter 11, "The Long-Promised Day," which gives hitherto unpublished insights into the 1978 revelation and the context in which it occurred. Here, Leonard wrote as both historian and participant, beginning the chapter with the words, "The most exciting single event of the years I was church historian occurred on June 9, 1978, when the First Presidency announced a divine revelation that all worthy males might be granted the priesthood."[24]

Although Leonard's pain is evident through much of the book, he characteristically rose above it in the valedictory that comprised its final paragraphs:

> I have tried in this memoir to bear witness to the loyalty of my colleagues and associates to the Latter-day Saint ideals of professional competence, sincere truth-seeking, and unquestioned integrity, trustworthiness, and dedication. Our historical scholarship was accompanied by firm convictions of the truth of Mormonism. If we did not measure up, we can at least say that we sincerely tried.
>
> May Latter-day Saint historians lengthen their stride as they strive to develop capacities that will enable them to write histories worthy of the marvelous work and the wonder that is their heritage.[25]

31

Legacy

Bypass Surgery

Coronary artery disease is a gradual, cumulative process that sometimes leads to sudden, unexpected death, while at other times gives advance notice of trouble. The winter of 1983–1984, one of the most severe in Utah's history, was Leonard's wake-up call. It produced the second-largest snowfall in Logan in the twentieth century. The snow pack in the mountains was twice the normal depth. There were more continuous days without sunshine than any prior period in the history of the state. The absence of sunshine meant that snow tended to accumulate on roofs, rather than melting or sliding off.

Many buildings had in excess of four feet of snow on their roofs, enough to cause the roof of one of Leonard's neighbors to collapse. That was a call-to-action for Leonard, at least to clear the snow from around his car, which was parked in the driveway. "Just a few movements of my arms and I felt a tightening in my chest and a feeling that I couldn't breathe. I went in the house and after a few moments everything was back to normal. I informed Harriet of this experience when she returned from an errand, and she recommended I telephone my doctor, A. Hamer Reiser." Since the symptoms had subsided, Dr. Reiser told Harriet to bring Leonard to the office the following Monday. In an essay that he wrote two months later, he allowed that the experience was jolting. "I was sixty-six years old and to that moment had enjoyed a lifetime of excellent health."[1]

He kept the appointment with his physician, and the initial portion of the exam went well. In his weekly letter to his children he described the visit: "The doc found my blood pressure all right, my lungs fine, my pulse good, and my general health very good. He decided, for the first time, to give me an EKG, and an X-Ray of my lungs and heart and found everything normal." Then, the clincher: a stress EKG, with Leonard on a treadmill rather than resting. "I failed that one! I am overweight, I can't run very far without breathing difficulties, and I get a

445

constriction in my chest when I engage in vigorous exercise. He diagnoses this as the beginning of warning stage of angina."

In addition to prescribing medication, Dr. Reiser scolded him about the unnecessary weight he was carrying. "Lose at least a couple of pounds a month. Harriet agrees to do the same. We have each gained 10 pounds since our marriage." Then, he injected a bit of humor: "You will not say anything about this to *anyone*, of course. Nor about my hemorrhoids, nor about my prostate, nor about my sneaking some food on Fast Day, nor anything else affecting my soul or body."[2]

A week later he went to the hospital for a follow-up examination and angiogram, which disclosed severe coronary artery disease. Ever the optimist, Leonard initially tried to put a positive spin on his condition: "Sounds worse than it is. . . . It is common among people my age."[3] One of the three physicians who examined him that day was Russell Nelson, a cardiac surgeon. While the other two suggested medication and a wait-and-see posture, Nelson advised Leonard to prepare for a bypass operation within two to three weeks. Leonard chose medication.

Six weeks later, shortly after the church's annual general conference, Leonard returned to his primary care physician, who asked what the patient thought. "I am not getting any better as the result of the medication. I am not getting any worse either. Harriet would be glad to look after me for the rest of my life in this condition, I'm sure, but I do not wish to remain this way when there is a good chance I can improve it substantially. I want to be able to walk to the corner if I wish. I want to be able to lecture without fear of overdoing it. I do not want to live under the haunting fear of a heart attack some day."[4]

They decided that bypass surgery was the best option, and that Russell Nelson was the best surgeon for the procedure. There was, however, a complication: in the general conference only a few days earlier, Nelson had been called to the Quorum of the Twelve Apostles and was in the process of retiring from his surgical practice. When Leonard telephoned Nelson, "he said 'the Brethren' told him to take care of all his commitments, but not to make any new ones. He said he did regard my case as a commitment and would be glad to do it."[5]

On April 22, 1984, Leonard checked into the hospital. That evening, in addition to his wife Harriet, he was visited by Jan and Michael Quinn, and Maureen Beecher. In a scene reminiscent of the time more than six decades earlier when his mother and Hannah Bowen had blessed him as he lay suffering from influenza, "I asked Mike to join hands on my head with Maureen, Jan, and Harriet and ask a special prayer. It was a beautiful prayer and very much appreciated by each of us."[6]

The following day, Dr. Nelson performed sextuple bypass surgery on Leonard. As Leonard was convalescing in the hospital, Nelson came to see him. "Leonard, your operation has marked the end of an era. I have done thousands of these bypasses, some of them history making in themselves, but this is the last. And I am so pleased that I have been able to perform this historic operation on a historian!"[7]

FINAL DECLINE

The bypass surgery added several good years to Leonard's life. Seven years later he wrote a progress report for his children. "I still feel good, although not quite as good as the year after the operation. My breath is shorter, and I'm not quite as sharp in my movements. I have not followed the doctor's instructions very religiously. I exercise, but not as much or as regularly as he recommended. I have gained as least ten pounds in weight, which is a no-no, and I keep working on it to bring it down, but not too successfully. But I lead a happy life, mostly because of the creative work I do writing."[8]

A month later he attempted to inject some humor into the weekly letter to his children. "I'm at the prime of life; but it not only takes longer to get primed, I have also lost the percussion cap."[9] As his health gradually continued to deteriorate, his productivity in writing—the centerpiece of his life—tailed off. In 1993 he wrote, "I cannot do as much in a day as I used to do. Working on the Idaho [history] and previous projects, I could turn out five to seven pages a day. But no more. Three to four pages is about the limit. My typing is not as accurate, I sometimes have to stop and look up names, and, though I am still imaginative and creative, the result is more modulated, less sharp."[10]

The following year, 1994, he received more bad news. "Dr. Preece said that a main artery to the heart, one that had been a by-pass ten years ago, is gone. Occluded. Also a diagonal artery is 80% occluded. This accounts for my occasional chest pain and arm numbness when exercising. They can't use the balloon treatment, because they're by-passes. They don't like to consider operating because of my age and my diabetes."[11]

On Independence Day 1997, he wrote another update to his children, still managing optimism in the face of what now was inevitable: "I feel grateful to be in good health at age 80. I have diabetes, irregular heart, very high white blood count that borders on leukemia, prostate cancer, and high blood pressure. Anyone of these could do me in. And yet here I am, enjoying life, writing books, enjoying children and grandchildren, and doing interesting things with friends. The Lord is blessing me, even if there is no reason to deserve it!"[12]

During the final year of his life, Leonard's strength gradually ebbed. His closest colleague, Davis Bitton, described one of his final visits:

> I do remember this one occasion when they pulled up in the car and Harriet came to the door.
>
> "Is Leonard coming in?"
> "No, he's sitting in the car."
> I went out and talked to him. "How are you, Leonard?"
> "Tired as poop!"
> I said, "What can I do to help you, Leonard?"
> "I've got this article that I've been assigned."
> I said, "Let me take that on for you. I'll produce something for you and it will go out in your name. You read it over and make sure it represents what you want to say, and if you want me to revise it, I'll do it." I did that for him. . . . That was near the very end, in the last year of his life.[13]

Ross Peterson, one of Leonard's long-time colleagues at Utah State University, spoke of Leonard's demeanor as the end of his life approached. "The last few times I talked to him, it was pretty obvious. He was very calm, and talked openly about it. He had circulation problems that had hassled him for a long time that kept him from doing a lot of things. Not being able to travel and do some of the things he enjoyed so much, like going to the conferences, he was reaching the point where he wasn't afraid of it at all."[14]

Though not afraid of death, Leonard nonetheless lost his cheery disposition as it approached. Michael Quinn recalled a phone conversation just a few months before his death. "I asked how he was doing, and he said, 'If the rest of my life is going to be the way it has been the last week, I do not want to continue on.' He was so demoralized. I had never heard him that way. . . . My heart just sank. I just said, 'Oh, Leonard, you're still making such contributions. You have so much to live for.' But he was in a funk. He was down, as I had never heard him before. To hear that over the phone in late 1998 was just devastating."[15]

Leonard died at home on February 11, 1999. He had two funerals: one in Salt Lake City, and the second in Logan, where he was buried. James Arrington recalled: "Dad left directions about his funeral, and he updated it once in a while. He said, 'I don't want any General Authorities speaking at my funeral.' He said that many times."[16] But one phone call changed the program. "The Prophet [Gordon Hinckley] came to his funeral. He called up—I think it was Harriet that he talked to, if I remember right. It was out of the blue. 'I'm coming. Can I say a few words?' 'Sure.' The *New York Times* published his obituary, without anybody asking them to."[17]

A LEGACY OF PUBLICATIONS

The *New York Times* obituary, written by someone who did not know Leonard personally, focused on his publications, yet failed to mention the publication that remains both his best known and most respected, *Great Basin Kingdom*.[18] In a special section on Mormonism published in the *Christian Century* during the 2012 presidential campaign of Mitt Romney, prominent Mormon historian Richard Bushman, in an article entitled "Essential Books on Mormonism," listed only eight books, one of which was *Great Basin Kingdom*.[19] Nonetheless, others saw *Great Basin*'s legacy as mixed, including BYU historian and bibliographer David Whittaker:

> Leonard in some ways can be seen as the culmination of historical writing up to his lifetime. We've tended to see him as the person who begins everything, but in a sense *Great Basin Kingdom* is the culmination of the kind of history that was being written up to the 1950s. I think Leonard was wise enough not to re-edit that book, but to let it stand as a monument to that early, regional kind of history. I think Chas Peterson's essay in the Arrington Symposium is a good look at the strengths and weaknesses of *Great Basin Kingdom*. The bibliography of *Great Basin Kingdom* is a wonderful benchmark watershed of Mormon studies. He had conquered Mormon studies, everything that had been done, I think, up to the time that book was published in 1958. I think that book opened up a lot of things. But negatively, it may have kept Mormon historians still focused pretty much on themselves and their regional history. I think Leonard pushed those boundaries in time, but his public persona may have reinforced our inability to get outside. That's unfair to Leonard, but I think that's one way to view *Great Basin Kingdom*.[20]

Leonard's other books were of very mixed quality, with the quality of the writing depending on the ghostwriter. Those that were written by him or had the greatest input from him—*Adventures of a Church Historian, Brigham Young: American Moses, The Mormon Experience*—have had staying power, but others have faded. Stan Cazier, at one time a colleague of Leonard at Utah State University and later president of the same university, put it this way: "I would say that some of the stuff Leonard wrote is just impossible to read, it's so dull. Some of the biographies he's done, some of the institutional histories. A lot of these little commissions. He gave me copies of all of them, and I just can't read them."[21]

If, however, one steps back and looks at the larger landscape of publications that his "franchise" produced, particularly during the History Division years, a much more positive and durable effect is seen. Sandra Tanner, a professional critic of Mormonism, paid tribute to his lasting contribution, which she tied to the dismantling of the History Division:

> I think there is a sense in which having the plug pulled on Arrington's department was the best thing that could have happened, because then I think the different authors had more freedom to write their books, that they may not have had if they had had to go through a church audit committee. So ultimately, the research may have flowed out in a better form for not having come out under an official church imprint. But it has certainly been an amazing flow of research that has come out, and I think Arrington certainly set that in motion.[22]

A LEGACY OF COLLEGIALITY

Earlier chapters of this book have described multiple instances where Leonard's collegial persona won over individuals and groups. Two tributes, both given posthumously and both from members of the Community of Christ (formerly the RLDS Church), summarize well that portion of his life. The first was from Paul Edwards. "Since Leonard Arrington first extended himself to make me feel accepted, this man has been the example by whom I have been encouraged in my efforts and chastised in my inability. He always seemed to be there to promote my efforts, to expand my professionalism. He easily acknowledged my desire to understand. But far more than that, he was a friend who was present even when I was most unlovable, and he cared for me when I most needed care."[23]

The second, from William Russell, placed Leonard within the Pauline tradition of Christian love. "A true Christian loves people, and loves truth much more than he or she loves an institution. Leonard was that kind of person. I always felt unconditionally loved by Leonard. To draw upon chapter 2 of Ephesians, he has broken down the walls that have divided the Mountain Mormons from the Prairie Mormons. Leonard Arrington embodied that spirit more than anyone."[24]

In addition to projecting a benign countenance to individuals, Leonard was able to foster the coalescence of communities—sometimes communities of disparate elements, such as the LDS and RLDS alluded to above; and sometimes communities of like elements that hitherto had not been able to coalesce on their own. An example of the latter was described by Elbert Peck: "A decade earlier you had few people just writing and bonding together, Juanita Brooks and her friends, but there weren't many. In the '60s you had more people coming out. There is some correspondence between her and Dale Morgan where they are commiserating about their lonely plight as historians. But there was not this boostering sort of thing. I would say that was Leonard's greatest contribution."[25]

Perhaps the most productive means by which Leonard fostered the development of a community of historians was through the summer fellowships that he funded during the History Division years. Ron Esplin, one of the recipients who turned into a full-time History Division employee, recalled, "Lots of folks that are not connected in any way to the enterprise right now still trace their roots back to being inspired by, taught by, mentored by, encouraged by him. All of those things. He did more with a little bit of fellowship money than you will ever count. He had $10,000 a year, and he divided it up into 10 fellowships of $1,000 each. . . . It changed lives and increased the body of people who cared about this stuff."[26]

Perhaps even more important than sharing money was sharing information. Whereas many scholars guard jealously their research notes, particularly those derived from manuscript sources, Leonard gave freely, as noted by his close associate Glen Leonard. "You would go to the MHA meetings, or the Western History Association meetings, and he would meet in a room and go around and say, 'Tell us what you are doing.' That made you feel like what you were doing was of interest to him—which it was—and important to him. He was looking for people, and he was feeding ideas to people, sharing information with people. His philosophy was that you don't hoard it to be the first one to write it; you share it to see that it gets done. You facilitate the creation of new work."[27]

After Leonard retired from the Smith Institute, Ron Esplin, who succeeded him as director, spoke of his legendary selflessness that created a lasting culture. "He was the academic who said, 'Let's share. I'll share with you, you share with me.' That was unheard of. So that got lots of people working on their own, and that's the philosophy they have at the Historical Department now: open the sources and encourage people to write. Like Leonard said, 'Multiple biographies of Brigham Young are good for us. It's good for us to have these different perspectives. Within the Mormon spectrum there are all kinds of perspectives, and outside there are others. They are good for us.'"[28]

A LEGACY OF INDIRECT MENTORSHIP

As is generally the case with those whose achievements are authentic, the effect of the ripples radiates well beyond the pebble. Jaded by the frequent, and yet deserved accolades that Leonard received in his later years, those who had known him long were sometimes caught short by the effect he had on those who knew him not at all. Elbert Peck recalled an incident from a history meeting. "I remember being there once with a very young Bryan Waterman. He was bright and had read everything about Mormon history almost by the time he left his mission. It was his first Mormon History Association meeting, and Leonard was just like George Washington for him. He stood up and tears were streaming from his eyes, and he was applauding enthusiastically, because Leonard was a living symbol for the history."[29]

Since Leonard's release as church historian in 1982, an entirely new generation of scholars has populated Mormon studies, many of them not even born by that year. Most of them never met Leonard, much less had him as a mentor. Nonetheless, they continue to be the beneficiaries of his influence. Ronald Barney, who spent most of his career in the Church Archives, reflected, "Leonard influenced a generation of thinking. His person will be forgotten. I can remember Leonard's voice as we are here talking, but a generation from now nobody is going to remember that. But they will remember the stuff that Leonard produced. And there is a lore about Leonard Arrington, and it will never dissipate."[30]

A LEGACY OF RESPECT FROM NON-MORMON SCHOLARS

Serious Mormon readers didn't require conversion to the New Mormon History. Indeed, they were its most avid consumers, having lived so long on a low-calorie diet of apologetic history. Far more difficult to win over were the non-Mormon readers, and of those, most difficult of all were the non-Mormon scholars of Western America who, because of the steady diet of apologetic history spanning decades, were reluctant to take seriously any books written by Mormon scholars. It was here that Leonard made a crucial contribution, for he, more than any other author, moved Mormon historiography from the backwaters into the mainstream. Charles Peterson, a Mormon historian, recalled, "I think he was a true friend with the people in the Organization of American Historians and the Western History Association. If you look through the list of the first ten presidents, which include him, you won't find a one who wouldn't go right to the bar in fighting for Leonard Arrington, because of his personal charm and their conviction that he was shooting square."[31]

Of historians of the American West who are not LDS, one of the most respected is Howard Lamar, who in addition to being an eminent historian was also president of Yale University. He gave unqualified praise to Leonard for making Mormon history respectable and accessible:

Leonard made everybody be serious about Mormon history, because they felt that he would tell them more about it than they had been getting. His being appointed [church historian] just changed the whole image of how seriously you should take the Mormon story. . . .

I would say if you listed the five or six best historians, with a national reputation, who were Western historians, that Leonard is up there with the best. I would put him in the category with Frederick Jackson Turner, Martin Ridge, Ray Billington—he was in that top category. . . .

I got Gerry Nash, who is the twentieth-century historian of the West, at New Mexico, to do the biographies of 400 prominent Western historians to include in my encyclopedia. I read his account of Leonard this morning, and it is just totally full of praise and respect. Gerry Nash was not used to giving anybody praise that didn't deserve it.[32]

Equally respectful was the posthumous tribute paid to Leonard by Martin Marty, an emeritus professor at the University of Chicago Divinity School and one of the world's most esteemed figures in the field of religious studies:

My times in person with Leonard Arrington were few—a visit in Utah, a time together at the Mormon Historical Association, brief chats at the American Historical Association. But my times with his writings were many and long. Not only was he the most consistent source on Latter-day Saint history for the Saints but also for the rest of us. He was respected in the American Historical Association and the Organization of American Historians as someone who would give an accurate accounting of Mormon history in the larger context.

When historians belong to groups that sociologists call "cognitive minorities," they have the opportunity to (a) kick over the traces and show anger to the place from which they come, (b) turn apologist, (c) equivocate on controversial points, or (d) do a public relations job, glib from start to finish. Leonard avoided all of these ways of being. These days few historians give much credence to the theme of "objectivity." But there are many of us who think historians can be "fair-minded" and be "disinterested" where that matters. In respect to a religious group, this means: critical loyalty and loyal criticism. There was never any doubt but that Arrington loved the tradition that often inspired and too often frustrated him. . . .

When a faith relies as much on story as the Mormon version does, there are more risks than when the origins of faith lie in mythical pasts. Arrington knew how to take risks and when to show love—and he showed love for the tradition!—and when to be restrained.[33]

A LEGACY OF FOUNDATION

The final pages of Leonard's autobiography contain his credo:

> Speaking for myself and, I think, for most of the historians who have worked with me, some tension between our professional training and our religious commitments seems inevitable. Our testimonies tell us that the Lord is in this work, and for this we see abundant support-ing evidence. But our historical training warns us that the accurate perception of spiritual phenomena is elusive—not subject to unques-tionable verification. We are tempted to wonder if our religious be-liefs are intruding beyond their proper limits. Our faith tells us that there is moral meaning and spiritual significance in historical events. But we cannot be completely confident that any particular judgment or meaning or significance is unambiguously clear. If God's will can-not be wholly divorced from the actual course of history, neither can it be positively identified with it. Although we see evidence that God's love and power have frequently broken in upon the ordinary course of human affairs, our caution in declaring this is reinforced by our justifiable disapproval of chroniclers who take the easy way out and use divine miracles as a short-circuit of a causal explanation that is obviously, or at least defensibly, naturalistic. We must not use history as a storehouse from which deceptively simple moral lessons may be drawn at random.[34]

Leonard's commitment to the pursuit of knowledge was the foundation of his own life, as it was and is of many of his coreligionists. Laurel Thatcher Ulrich of Harvard University expressed that kinship to him. "His commitment to knowl-edge, which I associate with my father as well—that's the way I was raised, even though my dad was pretty right wing. Even my siblings, my brothers, are very conservative Republicans, but they are intellectually curious and they believe in knowledge. There is that strand of Mormonism that goes back to the beginning, and it is part of my heritage."[35]

Leonard's embrace of the truth—and of the necessity of telling the truth in publications—was an issue of personal integrity. Later, for others, it became an issue of necessity as the Internet became all-pervasive. There are no more secrets, and any attempt to gloss over inconvenient truths from our past is quickly exposed by those who have open access to the data. Richard Bushman, one of the most respected elder statesmen of Mormon history, told folklorist Bert Wilson, "The day has passed when we can keep things private and to ourselves. With the Internet, with the widespread availability of all kinds of information on different aspects of Mormon history, we can't hide it any longer. It's there. We either have to deal with it, or be made fools of." Wilson agreed, and added, "[Leonard] was the one person more responsible than anybody else that started this New Mormon History approach, an objective rather than just a subjective approach. It was not a critical approach in that you try to denigrate or run down the Church, but it was not an apologetic approach, and so much of Mormon history before then had been an apologetic approach. He wanted to tell the story as it was, and in doing that, I think he created the whole discipline in Mormon historical research that we know today."[36]

Telling the truth, and particularly telling the truth to power, has always been fraught with risk, and Leonard willingly took that risk, even if somewhat naively at times. Emma Lou Thayne commented, "He wanted to inject into any kind of history the 'why,' not just the 'what.' That was a great gift, but the 'why' became suspect. . . . How often are we asked to consider something? We are *told*. To be asked to consider is the greatest kind of compliment. When were you ever asked to consider something in a church manual or a church setting? To me, that is the sort of thing that Leonard capitalized on, and why he was such a treasure to all of us."[37]

But the treasure came at a cost and Leonard bore the brunt of that cost—more because of timing than because his cause was unjust. Jim Clayton, a long-time historian and administrator at the University of Utah, reflected, "When I look back on Leonard, I think he was a great guy with a noble purpose, and he suffered grievously and publicly for trying to achieve that purpose. In the long run, I think he may achieve that purpose. There may be a coming together; I don't know. But in the short run, I think we were naïve in expecting the other side to move a little bit more toward the middle. . . . He took some chances and he took a lot of abuse, and he did some very good things; and for that, he should be praised."[38]

When viewed in hindsight, the actions that church leaders took to dismantle the History Division appear overreactive and even draconian, particularly with the perspective of the Internet's subsequent effect on historical candor. But when viewed in the context of American society during those years, their actions are actually reflective of the mainstream. Laurel Ulrich positioned Leonard's contribution in the national context of the profession. "I guess the question has to be whether someone who is buoyant and optimistic and has such an abiding faith that 'the truth and nothing but the truth is good enough for my church' may not have seen that some people can't handle complex historical arguments. It's a kind of thinking, and not everybody has it. It's not transparent: history is dangerous. I think it might be important to think of that." What Leonard encountered as he attempted to present complex historical arguments to church leaders who couldn't handle the news was similar to the reaction of larger American society to arguments they couldn't handle, particularly those dealing with the Vietnam War. Ulrich continued, "Certainly in American history, the turmoil of the '60s produced a dramatic transformation of the profession that continued into the '70s and '80s. The pushback from the right wing was immense. I think the Mormon story is probably a smaller manifestation of a larger national story about revisionist history."[39]

Although there was disappointment and hurt as a result of the disassembly of the History Division, in its aftermath there were changes, both in the short term and the long term, that went against merely returning to the former status quo of apologetic history. These changes devolved directly from the experience of the History Division. Perhaps the most important in the short term was a long-overdue change in archival policy: "When this all got out of control and the historians got blamed and moved off," commented Ronald Esplin, "one of the things they did was not just to close down—in other words, the pendulum was too far on the open side, and now we were going to go too far the other way—it was to say, 'We now understand. We have an archives problem, and we are going to put in place professional archives procedures, and we are not going to open back up until we get these in place.'"[40] Thus, rather than being at the whim of whomever sat at the front desk of the archives, researchers were presented with an archival policy comparable to that of other scholarly institutions.

In order to appreciate fully the long-term effect of Leonard's franchise, it is useful to employ the metaphor of the construction of the Salt Lake Temple, which began, with tremendous enthusiasm, in 1853. Only four years later, the approach of federal troops and the ensuing "Utah War" resulted in a decision by church leaders to cover completely the emerging foundation of the temple so that if the army invaded the Salt Lake Valley, it would have no indication of where the temple was being constructed. The foundation remained covered for several years after the war, at which time it was uncovered and the magnificent temple was built upon it.

The parallel to the disassembly of the History Division is quite appropriate, for the foundation that Leonard and his coworkers constructed with such enthusiasm was, upon their departure to BYU, so completely covered that most outsiders would not have known that it was there—that there had been any departure from the status quo that had reigned for decades. But when the time came to uncover the foundation, it proved to be fully adequate of supporting whatever structures were to be built upon it.

What changed in the interim? For one thing, Leonard's two strongest adversaries, Ezra Taft Benson and Mark Petersen, passed from the scene—Petersen in 1984 and Benson in 1994—and the bureaucrats who had assisted them in their efforts to dismantle the History Division retired. For another, the Internet made it increasingly difficult—almost impossible—to conceal, and hence control data. "Even those who may still be there who had some question about it could see that this was inevitable, that we have to have a scholastically respectable history written," observed Carol Madsen. "We can't keep doing the eulogistic biographies and histories that we had before and expect anybody to take us seriously."[41]

Arguably the most compelling force for lasting change has been the Joseph Smith Papers Project, a monumental task equivalent to that of the papers of some U.S. presidents, and one whose success required the foundation that Leonard constructed. Ronald Esplin considered:

> It's ironic in a sense, but one of the realities is that had Leonard not had the History Division, had not much of that survived at BYU, had not 25 years later a good part of it come back here,[42] and had the [Larry] Miller family not come in with resources to allow us to triple that, we would probably never have had the resources to have the Publications Division they are building right now. So what they view as their destiny, their future of being the center for Mormon scholarship is absolutely built on what Leonard started. Without that seed that has survived, and then the additional resources that the Millers provided, it wouldn't have happened.[43]

Leonard was never able to produce the multivolume Brigham Young biography that he proposed, and one can only wonder what his reaction would be to the Joseph Smith Papers, which has now published twelve volumes out of a projected twenty-four, all of them published in-house by the Church Historian's Press that was created specifically to ensure a high quality of editing and publishing. Less well known but equally important is a mammoth digitalization project of all kinds of personal papers and correspondence of other figures—all available, as are the Joseph Smith Papers themselves, online.

And one can only imagine what Leonard's response would have been to the publication of a 2008 history of the Mountain Meadows Massacre—a subject largely off-limits during his tenure—by three historians employed by the church, one of them being the assistant church historian, Richard Turley.[44] Indeed, *Massacre at Mountain Meadows* provided the final link in a completed circle, as witnessed by Leonard's daughter Susan:

> I heard Rick Turley a year-and-a-half ago when he came to Utah State. That man got up there to the microphone, and I think the first sentence out of his mouth was something like, "My name is Richard Turley, and I'm here to talk to you about one of the darkest chapters in the history of the Church of Jesus Christ of Latter-day Saints." Then, he started to build on that. There was a student sitting by me, a young man who was not a member of the Church. He was the reporter from the USU student newspaper, *The Statesman*, and he was there to cover it. I was enthralled by Richard's talk, and at the end of it, I turned to this kid and said, "You have no idea what you have just witnessed here tonight." He said, "What do you mean?" I said, "This would never have happened even ten years ago. Fifteen years ago, twenty years ago, a person talking that way and telling the information that he was telling would probably be disfellowshipped for exposing negative things that had taken place."[45]

GALILEO?

Elbert Peck recounted a moving scene that took place in Leonard's home a short time before his death:

> A few weeks before he died, Jan Shipps and I went to visit him at his house. He was feeble but alert, and came out and talked to us for about an hour. But then he got tired, and had to go back to sleep. His autobiography had just come out. I had read it, and I said to him, "Leonard, everyone is looking for you to score all these points against the people who did you wrong, but you really downplayed that in your autobiography. The point you seem to be making again and again and again is the possibilities that Mormon history can contribute to the Kingdom." His face really lit up and he said, "Yes! Yes! Yes! That's the point I wanted to make, that it is a positive contribution!" I think that really was Leonard.[46]

The totality of any person's lasting effect on the world does not become apparent until years, decades, even centuries after his or her death. Leonard's counterpart in the RLDS Church, Richard Howard, put it eloquently: "Sometimes you can say, 'Here is a historical event, and we can finally say it's in the past, and it won't have any more ripples or reverberations into the present.' But I don't think you can justify saying that about Leonard's life and career. The continuing impact through the people he was associated with and trained and brought along is going to live forever."[47]

How far Leonard's ripples will extend and what their ultimate effect will be are questions to be addressed by future generations of historians, but one current historian, James Clayton, sets the bar high: "I am not optimistic that there will be, in my lifetime or even soon thereafter, any real appreciation for what he did. But eventually, I think his name will go down in the church records as someone like Galileo, who made a point and took a position that was unpopular at the time, but eventually the church came around."[48]

EPILOGUE

THE LEONARD ARRINGTON PAPERS

By any measure, Leonard Arrington was a packrat. Just the materials that comprise his collection at the Merrill-Cazier Library at Utah State University, which do not represent the entirety of the paper trail that he left, amount to 319 linear feet—one of the most important collections of personal papers relating to Mormon history. A decade before he died, Leonard began to give serious consideration to the permanent home of his papers. To poet and friend Carol Lynn Pearson, he described in general terms his paper legacy. "My papers include a diary of perhaps fifty large notebooks, the most sensitive part of which is that kept from 1972 to 1982 when I was in the Church Office Building. I record many conversations, perhaps even some with you! They also include, besides books and pamphlets, magazines, and other published material, a large number of typescripts of things I have copied, or things others have copied and given me Xeroxes or carbons of."

The dilemma that he described to her was where the collection should be housed. "I can't very well leave them with the Historical Department of the Church because they are so fussy about who can use the archival material and what can be used by anybody. Why place it where it will never be used?" That left him with three choices: Brigham Young University, the University of Utah, and Utah State University, where he spent over two decades of his career. "Leaving the papers [at USU] would mean the most to them because their holdings are smaller. But who would go to Logan to use them? I have many loyalties to USU because I was there so long (26 years) and our children all graduated from there."[1]

His loyalty to USU won out, and his papers became the largest and most important collection at the library. The process of cataloging the collection took over a year. In October of 2001, just one month after the 9/11 attacks on the World Trade Center and Pentagon, it was opened to the public. Among the first patrons was a group of employees of the Church Historical Department, laptops in hand. Ross Peterson, then on the USU history faculty, picked up the story from there:

I wasn't in Logan when it opened. I came back the next Monday and I got a frantic call from Bob Parson, who works in Special Collections. He said, "You wouldn't believe what is over here." I went over there, and there were eight people, many of whom I had taught, who worked for the Church Historian's Office, who were going through the 710,000 items. They stayed there, working nine hours a day, five days a week. We didn't open on weekends, and we didn't want those people, especially, to break the Sabbath! For about three and a half weeks—and you can count the hours, and I don't know how much they make—this is a considerable investment; . . .

I went over there and said, "What are you doing?" It was too late for me to change their grades or revoke their master's degrees. They said, "We have been asked to go through this." I said, "Why?" I have no authority over the library, but we were going through a number of transitions, we had a new president, and my brother [Max] is over the library, and they were really concerned.[2]

The "why?" began to become apparent when the leader of the group made a phone call. Ross Peterson continued his account:

One afternoon, just after this "inquisition" began at Utah State, Steve Sorensen, an administrator in the Church Historical Department, went outside the search room of USU Special Collections and used a [public] phone to call someone at Church headquarters. He apparently used phrases during this phone conversation such as "church ownership," "controversial," and "censorship." While Steve was talking on the phone, a USU student was standing behind him, listening to every word. Apparently the conversation fell on the wrong ears and this student recognized something fishy was going on. He went straight to the student newspaper, *The Statesman*, and told them that there was a group of LDS Church employees looking through this valuable collection in the library. The student newspaper then ran an article about it, questioning what the Church was looking for and why, and the whole controversy then exploded into virtually every newspaper in the state of Utah.[3]

The story also went beyond Utah, being picked up by the Associated Press and the *Chronicle of Higher Education*. Peterson continued his narrative:

Then, when they left, the next Monday the university got a letter from a legal firm in Salt Lake City, Kirton, McConkie, that they perceived that the Church owned over 60% of those items—about

400,000 or so of the 710,000. The university response, immediately, was, "This was a gift given to us by a donor. We own it, and that's the way it is going to be."

Then, they [Kirton & McConkie] filed an injunction against it being used. I want to separate something very, very clearly. I had to do this at the time, and I still do it. I never felt, for a minute, that it was the university against the Church. It was the university's Special Collections against the Church Historical Department and their attorneys. It was bureaucrats vs. bureaucrats, in many respects, and academics vs. lawyers, and a variety of other versus. But it suddenly became very tense, because it became a major item in the newspapers.[4]

The initial response of USU to the church action was cautious: "Until a review of the materials is completed, the university has agreed to temporarily sequester a portion of the documents until the central ownership issues are clarified."[5] Church officials continued to contend that they had "an 'ironclad' document"[6] giving the church full ownership of as much as 60 percent of the Arrington papers; and by early November a lawsuit appeared possible and tempers were flaring. An interview of Lavina Fielding Anderson, published in the *Salt Lake Tribune*, underscored some of the relevant issues. "The matter has been cast as a question of control and possession. But that conceals a whole set of deeper questions. . . . Who owns a people's history? What happens to a history-based faith if the primary message about its history is that it's scary and dangerous and has to be so carefully controlled? Where's the line between preserving documents and suppressing the information they contain?"[7]

At that point, a phone call brought the temperature down and moved things towards a negotiated solution. "President [Gordon] Hinckley called Kermit Hall, president of Utah State, and said, 'We are *not* going to sue you. Just forget about these threats of court cases. We would like to settle this really quickly. There are some things that we are concerned about that we would like returned.'"[8] The two men agreed that an eight-person board, with four representatives from each side, would work out a settlement. "The board's objective," the *Salt Lake Tribune* reported, "is to recommend to Hinckley and Hall 'documents that may not have been intended for the extensive collection of papers, research notes and other documents passed to the university by Arrington.'"[9]

The board then got down to the specifics of what items would stay in the USU collection and what items would be returned to the church. Ross Peterson described the next step:

We asked specifically for them to tell us which items made up the 400,000. "We're not bending until we look at the items." Then, they came up with a much-shortened list, which was published in the *Salt Lake Tribune*. . . .

The second list was a hundred-and-some thousand, and they wanted a response within four days. We just went full-bore, went through all the things that they felt had been stolen, or that they really owned. I said basically to our university, and to the university attorneys, that I didn't think we should give back anything at this point. But, if we had to give back something, the only things I could see were the Council of the Twelve minutes, some from Nauvoo and the ones between 1877 and 1951, because I felt that because of the way the Church is structured, they were more corporate minutes, private minutes; and the other thing, because I knew from my own experience the sensitivity over issues relative to exact details, were the earliest temple ceremonies.[10]

The minutes of the Council of the Twelve combined with the material on the temple ceremonies amounted to about eight linear inches[11]—well less than one-half of 1 percent of the total collection and a far cry from the 60 percent over which the Church Archives claimed ownership. That would likely have been a very hard sell to the church representatives, but suddenly the negotiations took an entirely unexpected turn. Peterson continued:

As we were concluding things on the Friday night before Thanksgiving, all of a sudden our people on the other side of the table said, "Now, there are some things in Leonard's journals that we are not very comfortable with, and we think ought to be taken out." I said, "Have you read the journals?" They said, "Well, when we receive things, we have to read them." I said, "Well, have you read the journals? And how many of you have read them?" Then, all of a sudden, George Daines, the lawyer for the Arringtons, said, "This meeting is over."[12]

Daines walked out of the meeting and immediately called Susan Madsen, Leonard's daughter, who remembers that tense exchange. "He said, 'Do you have a copy of the agreement that the Church made with your father concerning his journals?' I said, 'I know right where it is.' He said, 'Can you be here in 20 minutes?' So I took that document down. He basically said, 'It's over. With that, in and of itself, it's over.'"[13]

The dilemma for the church representatives was that when Leonard allowed the Historical Department to make a microfilm of his diaries up to the time that he was released as church historian—1982—he explicitly forbade any church official from reading them for a period of twenty-five years past his death, which would have been 2024. On the "Acquisition Sheet and Instrument of Gift," under the section conveying "legal title and all literary property rights," he wrote, "No. I assign no rights to the Hist. Depart. LJA."[14] By acknowledging in the meeting that they had violated the terms of the agreement, the church representatives had placed themselves not only in a very awkward position, but also one of potential legal liability.

At the next meeting, Daines produced a photocopy of the document, showed it to the church attorneys, and informed them that the Arrington family had grounds for legal action against them.[15] With that, the negotiations came to a quick conclusion. Daines, acting on behalf of the Arrington family, wrote to Rolfe Kerr and Quentin Cook, two of the four board members representing the church. "With this letter, the Arrington Family returns to the Church certain materials that were mistakenly delivered to Utah State University. These materials comprise approximately one half box and include all documents known to be within the Arrington Archives which are temple sacred or which constitute Minutes of meetings of the Quorum of Twelve Apostles or First Presidency."[16]

That should have been the end of the story, but a month later it went public via the *Salt Lake Tribune*, in an article entitled "Was Deed to Arrington Journal Ignored?"[17] The article began, "Despite Mormon historian Leonard Arrington's explicit instructions that only his children have access to his personal diaries until 2024, an LDS Church historian read, copied and circulated portions of the diaries among church officials." In a final public note, the Logan *Herald Journal* editorialized stingingly the following week, "It would appear the right to privacy does not apply equally to everyone in the eyes of the LDS Church. . . . It seems pretty clear to us what Arrington's intentions were. Odd that the church, so concerned with its own privacy, can't understand an individual's claim to a private life."[18]

Shortly before Leonard's death, his children discussed with him the embargo time on the diaries. He agreed that twenty-five years was too long and shortened it to ten years for the originals housed in the Merrill-Cazier Library at Utah State University, with the proviso that his children had flexibility in determining the actual opening date. In September 2010, the diaries were made available to researchers, without restrictions, thus completing the opening of the entire Arrington collection. It is, without question, one of the most important archival sources on twentieth-century Mormon history.

Notes

Abbreviations

LJAD. Leonard J. Arrington Diaries, Leonard J. Arrington Historical Archives, Special Collections and Archives, Merrill-Cazier Library, Utah State University, Logan

LJAHA. Leonard J. Arrington Historical Archives, Special Collections and Archives, Merrill-Cazier Library, Utah State University, Logan

LJA. Leonard J. Arrington

Preface

1. All of these publications are detailed in the bibliography section.

2. Leonard J. Arrington, *Adventures of a Church Historian* (Urbana: University of Illinois Press, 1998), 5.

Prologue

1. Robert B. Flanders, interview, May 18, 2005.

2. Prior to 1972, all documents and functions relating to church history came under the Church Historian's Office. In 1972 the name was changed to Church Historical Department, with three new divisions created within the department: Archives, Library, and History Division. Arrington had two titles, director of the History Division and church historian. Chapter 14 describes the unintended consequences of his being church historian, which in prior years was the title given to the ecclesiastical leader who oversaw all historical issues.

3. LJAD, April 1, 1974.

4. Ibid., May 29, 1974.

5. Paul Edwards to Gregory A. Prince, August 10, 1980.

6. Carol Lynn Pearson diary, April 4, 1973.

Chapter 1—Ancestry

1. An excellent overview is Patrick Q. Mason, *The Mormon Menace: Violence and Anti-Mormonism in the Postbellum South* (New York: Oxford University Press, 2011).

2. Remarks at the funeral service for LeRoy Madison Arrington, LJAD, August 16, 1946.

3. Ibid., August 23, 1989. Beginning in the mid-1970s, Leonard included in his diaries occasional accounts of his ancestry and his own upbringing.

4. Ibid., September 28, 1986.

5. Ibid., January 17, 1977.

6. Marie Arrington Davidson interview, January 16, 2006.

7. Susan Arrington Madsen interview, July 29, 2012.

8. LJAD, December 11, 1987.

9. Bud Davidson interview, January 16, 2006.

10. LJAD, December 11, 1987.

11. Ibid., January 17, 1977.

12. Ibid., April 9, 1975.

13. Leonard J. Arrington, *Magic Valley Pioneers: A Photographic Record of N. W. and Edna Corn Arrington* (Salt Lake City: Historian's Press, 1991), 8.

14. Noah Arrington to Leonard J. Arrington, September 20, 1926.

15. Leonard J. Arrington, *Growing Up in Twin Falls County, Idaho* (Hyde Park, UT: Historian's Press, 1996), 34.

16. LJAD, July 4, 1994.

17. Ibid., November 23, 1976.

18. Ibid., November 1, 1976.

19. Ibid., July 4, 1994.

20. Ibid., November 1, 1976.

21. Ibid., November 23, 1976.

22. Ibid., January 3, 1973.

23. Ibid., January 10, 1975.

24. Ibid., January 17, 1977.

25. Ibid., July 4, 1994.

26. Ibid., November 1, 1976.

27. Ibid., November 23, 1976.

28. LJA, untitled typescript, August 28, 1984, LJAHA, Series X, Box 2, fd. 3.

29. A "temple recommend" is a certificate that allows a church member to attend one of the LDS temples. It is issued by the bishop or his assistant following an interview to ascertain worthiness.

30. LJA, untitled typescript, August 28, 1984; LJAHA, Series X, Box 2, fd. 3.

31. LJAD, November 26, 1979.

32. Ibid., November 1, 1976.

33. Ibid., November 26, 1979.

CHAPTER 2—A CHILDHOOD WITH CHICKENS

1. LJAD, November 14, 1976.

2. Ibid., May 30, 1988.

3. Ibid., May 12, 1973. Note that Leonard was the recipient of blessings from two midwives: one when he had influenza, and one when he had smallpox.

4. Ibid., copied verbatim from a handwritten diary started in 1927 when he was ten years old.

5. LJA letter to Grace Arrington, in ibid., May 12, 1944. Leonard included letters, among other documents, in his diaries.

6. Ibid., November 14, 1976.

7. Ibid. The family eventually numbered ten children: LeRoy W. (b. 1914), Thelma (b. 1916), Leonard J. (b. 1917), Marie (b. 1919), Kenneth (b. 1923), Asa (b. 1925), Doris (b. 1927), Donald (b. 1929), Ralph (b. 1930), and Ross (b. 1934).

8. LJA to Noah Arrington, January 8, 1925, in ibid.

9. LJAD, March 30, 1975.

10. Ibid.

11. Marie Arrington Davidson interview, January 16, 2006.

12. Leonard J. Arrington, *Growing Up in Twin Falls County, Idaho* (Hyde Park, UT: Historian's Press, 1996), 55.

13. Ibid., 101.

Chapter 3—Enchanted by Economics

1. LJAD, May 13, 1976.

2. Leonard J. Arrington, "On Going to College," LJAHA, Series X, Box 4, fd. 10.

3. LJAD, May 13, 1976.

4. Leonard J. Arrington, "The Founding of the LDS Institute of Religion," *Dialogue: A Journal of Mormon Thought* 2 (Summer 1967): 138–47. See also Kenneth W. Godfrey, "Institutes of Religion," in *Encyclopedia of Latter-day Saint History*, ed. Arnold K. Garr, Donald Q. Cannon, and Richard O. Cowan (Salt Lake City: Deseret Book, 2000), 541–42.

5. Gary Anderson, "A Historical Survey of the Full-Time Institutes of Religion of the Church of Jesus Christ of Latter-day Saints, 1926–1966," EdD diss., Brigham Young University, 1968, 58.

6. Bill Johnston, "Student Cooperatives at the University of Idaho," *Improvement Era* 43, no. 1 (1942): 21, 57–58.

7. LJAD, May 13, 1976.

8. LJAD, April 9, 1975.

9. Leonard J. Arrington, *Farm Boy at the University of Idaho, 1935–39* (Hyde Park, UT: Historian's Press, 1996), 2.

10. LJAD, May 13, 1976.

11. Ibid.

12. Ibid., March 25, 1975.

13. Ibid.

14. Ibid.

15. Arrington, *Farm Boy at the University of Idaho*, 4.

16. Leonard J. Arrington, interview, June 6, 1995.

17. "Religious Differences on the Question of Evolution," February 4, 2009, Pew Research Center, www.pewforum.org.

18. LJAD, November 26, 1935.

19. Ibid., December 1, 1935.

20. George S. Tanner's Master of Arts degree, awarded in 1931, included the thesis, "The Religious Environment in which Mormonism Arose" (M.A. thesis, University of Chicago, 1931).

21. Arrington, *Farm Boy at the University of Idaho*, 5.

22. Tanner, "The Religious Environment in which Mormonism Arose," 4, 85, 97–98, 105.

23. George S. Tanner, interviewed by Rebecca Cornwall, June 15, 1976, in LJAD of the same date.

24. LJAD, April 22, 1936.

25. Arrington, *Farm Boy at the University of Idaho*, 7–8. There was one notable exception to this statement, and that was the Book of Mormon. As discussed in chapter 12, Arrington was never able to shift from an ancient to a metaphorical, nineteenth-century Book of Mormon.

26. LJAD, March 25, 1975.

27. Ibid.

28. Ibid.

29. Ibid., May 13, 1976.

30. "The Beginnings of My Interest in Mormon Scholarship," in LJAD, Christmas 1984.

31. Ibid.

32. LJAD, May 13, 1976.

33. Ibid.

CHAPTER 4—IDAHO BOY IN GRADUATE SCHOOL

1. LJAD, June 22, 1988.
2. Ibid., May 25, 1976.
3. Ibid.
4. "The Beginnings of My Interest in Mormon Scholarship," LJAD, Christmas 1984.
5. Ibid., May 25, 1976.
6. LJA to Lowry Nelson, copy in LJAD, May 1, 1975.
7. "The Beginnings of My Interest in Mormon Scholarship," LJAD, Christmas 1984.
8. *Harper's Monthly Magazine* 106 (April 1903): 667–78.
9. LJA, Remarks for *Great Basin Kingdom* symposium, LJAD, May 4, 1988.

CHAPTER 5—A WOMAN NAMED GRACE

1. LJAD, August 30, 1974.
2. Ibid.
3. Leonard topped out at slightly under five feet six inches in height—four inches shorter than Grace's first husband. According to Leonard's sister, "He always used to say that he started growing when he was 16, and quit the next day." (Marie Arrington Davidson interview, January 16, 2006.)
4. Rebecca F. Cornwall and Leonard J. Arrington, eds., *I'm Glad My House Burned Down: The Personal Story of Grace Fort Arrington* (Salt Lake City: Privately Distributed, 1977), 47–48.
5. Ibid., 48–49.
6. LJAD, August 30, 1974.
7. LJAD, November 14, 1976. In writing the diary entry titled "Recollections, Response to Suggestions of Carl," Leonard alternately cast himself in both first *and* third persons.
8. The *Home Mission Monthly*, published by the Women's Executive Committee of Home Missions of the Presbyterian Church, published diatribes against the Mormon Church from its first volume in 1886 through the early 1920s. For many of those years, the entire October issue was devoted to a critique of the Mormons.
9. Cornwall and Arrington, *I'm Glad My House Burned Down*, 47.
10. LJAD, August 30, 1974.
11. Ibid., May 6, 1976.
12. Cornwall and Arrington, *I'm Glad My House Burned Down*, 50–51.
13. Marie Arrington Davidson interview, January 16, 2006.
14. Susan Arrington Madsen interview, October 17, 2005.
15. Carl Arrington interview, September 24, 2009.
16. Cornwall and Arrington, *I'm Glad My House Burned Down*, 37–41, 50.
17. There is no first-hand record of what Noah Arrington, "who had never written a single letter to anyone since his mission," thought about Leonard and Grace's relationship. LJAD, March 28, 1982. Although Leonard's memory of his father as a noncorrespondent is essentially correct, Noah had, in fact, written Leonard one known letter describing plans for their chicken farm. See chapter 1.
18. LJAD, July 1942.
19. Ibid., November 14, 1976.
20. Ibid., December 7, 1971.
21. Ibid., August 30, 1974.
22. Susan Arrington Madsen interview, July 29, 2012.
23. Cornwall and Arrington, *I'm Glad My House Burned Down*, 180–81.
24. LJAD, October 31, 1976.
25. Ibid., February 8, 1985.

26. Maureen Beecher interview, July 11, 2009.

27. Chris Rigby Arrington to Leonard J. Arrington, LJAD, March 21, 1982.

28. Susan Arrington Madsen interview, October 17, 2005.

29. James Arrington interview, April 12, 2009.

CHAPTER 6—WORLD WAR II

1. LJAD, December 7, 1979; August 30, 1974.

2. Ibid., August 30, 1974.

3. Ibid.

4. Ibid., December 7, 1971.

5. Ibid., May 31, 1975.

6. Ibid., December 7, 1971.

7. Ibid., April 7, 1976.

8. LJA to Grace Fort, April 2, 1943, LJAD.

9. LJA to Grace Fort, April 6, 1943, LJAD.

10. LJAD, March 9, 1976.

11. Ibid.

12. Ibid., December 7, 1971.

13. Ibid., March 9, 1976.

14. LJA to Grace Arrington, July 10, 1945, LJAD.

15. LJAD, March 9, 1976.

16. LJA to Grace Arrington, August 13, 1943, LJAD.

17. Ibid.

18. Ibid., September 7, 1943.

19. LJAD, December 7, 1971.

20. Arrington, *A Soldier in North Africa and Italy, 1943–1946*, 17.

21. LJA to Grace Arrington, July 11, 1944, LJAD.

22. LJAD, December 7, 1971.

23. LJA to Grace Arrington, September 17, 1944, LJAD.

24. Ibid., October 19, 1944, LJAD.

25. LJAD, March 9, 1976.

26. Ibid., December 7, 1971.

27. LJA to Grace Arrington, November 29, 1944, LJAD.

28. Ibid., December 4, 1944, LJAD.

29. LJAD, December 7, 1971.

30. Ibid., March 9, 1976. Mussolini and Petacci had been shot on April 28, 1945.

31. Ibid., November 21, 1996.

32. Ibid., May 8, 1995.

33. LJA to Grace Arrington, August 10, 1945.

34. "Award of Disability Compensation or Pension (Service Connected)," LJAD, April 27, 1946, LJAHA.

35. LJA to Children, March 14, 1991.

36. Ibid., October 22, 1997.

CHAPTER 7—BECOMING DR. ARRINGTON

1. LJA to Grace Arrington, September 9, 1943.

2. Ibid., October 24, 1943.

3. LJA to John A. Widtsoe, July 30, 1945, LJAD.

4. Grace Arrington to LJA, August 8, 1945, LJAHA Series X, Box 10, fd. 5.

5. John A. Widtsoe to LJA, August 7, 1945, LJAD.

6. LJA to John A. Widtsoe, February 21, 1946, LJAD.

7. John A. Widtsoe to LJA, March 19, 1946, LJAD.

8. LJAD, November 13, 1946.

9. Newell G. Bringhurst, *Fawn McKay Brodie: A Biographer's Life* (Norman: University of Oklahoma Press, 1999), 110, citing "Appraisal of the So-Called Brodie Book," *Church News*, May 11, 1946, 1, 6, 8. According to Bringhurst (*Fawn McKay Brodie*, 289n113), "The article was written by a church committee of which Apostle Albert E. Bowen was apparently the principal author."

10. Leonard J. Arrington, *Life in Happy Valley: Early Years in Logan and Our First Sabbatical* (Hyde Park, UT: Historian's Press, 1996), 14.

11. LJAD, May 23, 1973.

12. Ibid., November 24, 1976. Leonard's account of being a camel in the archival tent completely ignores the logistics of how he got to Salt Lake City, how long he typically stayed and where, how he managed such mundane chores as meals and laundry, whether he avoided teaching summer classes and, if so, what the loss of income did to the family budget. No letters between him in Salt Lake City and Grace in Logan during this period survive.

13. LJA, Remarks for *Great Basin Kingdom* symposium banquet, May 4, 1988, LJAD. Unfortunately, his papers contain no records, contemporary or reminiscent, of these conversations.

14. LJAD, June 22, 1988.

15. Ibid. His brother Ross, in recognition of Leonard's longtime affection for mockingbirds, played a piano rendition of "Listen to the Mockingbird" at Leonard's funeral.

16. LJAD, Christmas 1984.

17. LJAD, June 22, 1988.

CHAPTER 8 — GREAT BASIN KINGDOM

1. LJAD, May 23, 1973.

2. Ibid., May 4, 1988.

3. Ibid., March 22, 1976.

4. Ibid., May 4, 1988.

5. Leonard J. Arrington interview by F. Ross Peterson, April 12, 1988. Transcript provided to me by Peterson.

6. LJAD, March 22, 1976.

7. Ibid., March 8, 1992.

8. Ibid., March 22, 1976.

9. Reid L. Neilson and Ronald W. Walker, eds., *Reflections of a Mormon Historian: Leonard J. Arrington on the New Mormon History* (Norman: Arthur H. Clark Company, an imprint of the University of Oklahoma Press, 2006), 77.

10. Arrington interview by Peterson, April 12, 1988.

11. Leonard J. Arrington, *Adventures of a Church Historian* (Urbana: University of Illinois Press, 1998), 31–32.

12. Douglas L. Alder interview, March 1, 2007.

13. The tone of the book was made clear in its complete title: *Mormonism Unvailed: or, A Faithful Account of That Singular Imposition and Delusion from Its Rise to the Present Time. With Sketches of the Characters of Its Propagators, and a Full Detail of the Manner in Which the Famous Golden Bible Was Brought before the World. To Which Are Added, Inquiries into the Probability That the Historical Part of the Said Bible Was Written by One Solomon Spalding, More Than Twenty Years Ago, and by Him Intended to Have Been Published as a Romance* (Painesville, OH: E. D. Howe, 1834).

14. Leonard J. Arrington, *Great Basin Kingdom An Economic History of the Latter-day Saints 1830–1900* (Cambridge, MA: Harvard University Press, 1958), ix.

15. LJA to A. R. Mortensen and Everett Cooley, June 3, 1959, LJAHA, Series X, Box 11, fd. 12.

16. *Great Basin Kingdom*, 119.

17. Ibid., 127.

18. Ibid., 128–29.

19. Ibid., 129.

20. Ibid., 131.

21. Ibid., 195.

22. Ibid., 244. The quotation is from E. L. T. Harrison, "An Appeal to the People," *Utah Magazine* 3 (October 30, 1869): 406–8, in which he described his excommunication. Harrison attributed the words to Brigham Young and George Q. Cannon and said they were spoken at his excommunication trial.

23. *Great Basin Kingdom*, 380.

24. Floyd O'Neil interview, June 16, 2008.

25. LJAD, May 4, 1988.

26. Bruce Blumell interview, June 30, 2012.

27. LJAD, May 4, 1988.

28. Ibid.

29. Ibid.

30. Everett Cooley interview, January 13, 2006.

31. LJAD, March 8, 1992.

32. Howard Lamar interview, February 23, 2007.

33. LJAD, March 8, 1992.

34. Ibid.

35. Gary Topping, *Leonard J. Arrington: A Historian's Life* (Norman: Arthur H. Clark Company, an imprint of the University of Oklahoma Press, 2008), 69.

36. Alder interview, March 1, 2007. William Mulder was a professor of English at the University of Utah and a historian. His most notable book was *Homeward to Zion: The Mormon Migration from Scandinavia* (Minneapolis: University of Minnesota Press, 1957). Mulder's 1969 anthology, *Among the Mormons: Historic Accounts by Contemporary Observers*, coedited by A. Russell Mortensen and published by Alfred A. Knopf, gained a broad, national readership, but it was a compilation of documents written by others, rather than the interpretive history of *Great Basin Kingdom*. Eugene Campbell was a professor of history at Brigham Young University. His most notable books were *Hugh B. Brown: His Life and Thought* (Salt Lake City: Bookcraft, 1975), which he coauthored with Richard D. Poll; and *Establishing Zion: The Mormon Church in the American West, 1847–1869* (Salt Lake City: Signature Books, 1988).

37. John Hughes to LJA, October 7, 1975, LJAHA, Series V, Box 5, fd. 2.

38. James B. Allen, "Since 1950: Creators and Creations of Mormon History," in Davis Bitton and Maureen Ursenbach Beecher, eds., *New Views of Mormon History: Essays in Honor of Leonard J. Arrington* (Salt Lake City: University of Utah Press, 1987), 423. On page 438, Allen added this note: "Professor Ellsworth never published the results of his quest, but he has graciously shared his data with me, with permission to use it as it seemed appropriate."

CHAPTER 9—THE ACADEMIC YEARS AND THE MOVE TO GREENER PASTURES

1. LJA to "Lois," LJAD, November 30, 1939. Leonard's papers do not mention Lois's last name or his relationship to her.

2. LJA to Grace Arrington, October 8, 1943, LJAD.

3. LJA to Grace Arrington, April 1, 1944, LJAD.

4. LJA to Grace Arrington, October 2, 1944, LJAD.

5. LJA to Grace Arrington, October 18, 1944, LJAD.

6. LJA to Grace Arrington, October 29, 1944, LJAD.

7. LJA to Grace Arrington, April 15, 1945, LJAD.

8. Arrington, *Life in Happy Valley*, 1.

9. LJAD, September 6, 1976.

10. LJAD, October 22, 1997.

11. Arrington, *Life in Happy Valley*, 14.

12. LJAD, September 6, 1976.

13. Ibid.

14. Max J. Evans interview, November 26, 2007.

15. F. Ross Peterson interview, September 17, 2007.

16. LJAD, September 8, 1976.

17. Gary B. Hansen, "Two Unique Contributions of Leonard J. Arrington to USU and the Economics Department," unpublished manuscript, 2009, 1; photocopy in my possession.

18. Arrington, *Life in Happy Valley*, 24. U-4 grants came from discretionary university funds and did not require application to outside organizations.

19. Hansen, "Two Unique Contributions of Leonard J. Arrington," 4.

20. Douglas D. Alder interview, March 1, 2007.

21. Econometrics is a branch of economics that employs mathematics, statistics, and computer science to quantify what had largely been qualitative observations.

22. Dwight Israelsen interview, January 15, 2006.

23. Robert P. Collier, Dean, College of Business and Social Sciences, to LJA, April 29, 1961; LJAD.

24. LJAD, October 10, 1976.

25. Cliometrics is also known as econometric history.

26. Arrington, *Life in Happy Valley*, 35.

27. Leonard J. Arrington, "The Beginnings of My Interest in Mormon Scholarship," no date. LJAHA, Series X, Box 3, fd. 1.

28. Arrington, *Life in Happy Valley*, 35.

29. Robert B. Flanders interview, May 18, 2009.

30. Leonard did acknowledge the assistance of Ellsworth, but in a sentence that also acknowledged ten other colleagues and gave no special attribution to Ellsworth. *Great Basin Kingdom*, x.

31. LJAD, December 28, 1997.

32. David J. Whittaker interview, May 22, 2008. Ellsworth's carefully constructed high school text was *Utah's Heritage* (Layton, UT: Peregrine Smith Publications, 1972).

33. Max J. Evans interview, November 26, 2007.

34. LJAD, March 22, 1973.

35. LJAD, December 28, 1997.

36. Susan Arrington Madsen interview, January 16, 2006.

37. Leonard J. Arrington, *Years of Achievement and Pleasure in Logan: 1958–72* (Hyde Park, UT: Historian's Press, 1996).

38. Gary B. Hansen interview, January 15, 2006.

39. C. Hardy Redd interview, August 9, 2008.

40. Ernest L. Wilkinson to LJA, May 17, 1971; LJAHA, Series IV, Box 19, fd. 1.

41. LJA to D. B. Gardner, January 5, 1972; LJAHA, Series IV, Box 19, fd. 1.

CHAPTER 10—THE CHURCH HISTORIAN'S OFFICE

1. Alan Blodgett to Prince, September 9, 2009.

2. Lynn S. Richards interview, January 15, 1996.

3. Jeffery O. Johnson interview, February 8, 2012.

4. Ibid.

5. Davis Bitton, "Ten Years in Camelot: A Personal Memoir," *Dialogue: A Journal of Mormon Thought* 16, no. 3 (Fall 1983): 10.

6. Edward Leo Lyman interview, October 8, 2008.

7. Lauritz G. Petersen, Research Supervisor, to Dean Jessee, April 8, 1969; LJAHA, Series V, Box 2, fd. 5. The article was Jessee's "The Early Accounts of Joseph Smith's First Vision," *BYU Studies* 9, no. 3 (1969): 275–300.

8. Dean C. Jessee, "The Original Book of Mormon Manuscript," *BYU Studies* 10 (Spring 1970): 259–78.

9. Bernard ("Bud") Kastler interview, June 3, 1997.

10. Neilson and Walker, *Reflections of a Mormon Historian*, 111.

11. N. Eldon Tanner to LJA, June 15, 1966, in LJAD.

12. LJA to N. Eldon Tanner, January 11, 1967, in LJAD.

13. Leonard J. Arrington interview by F. Ross Peterson, April 12, 1988; LJAHA.

14. Neilson and Walker, *Reflections of a Mormon Historian*, 113.

15. Arrington, *Adventures of a Church Historian*, 76. Davis Bitton wrote, "I was one of those fortunate enough to receive such a letter—now no longer operative but glued in my scrapbook as proof of an attitude that one prevailed." "Ten Years in Camelot: A Personal Memoir," 10.

16. Max J. Evans interview, November 26, 2007.

17. D. Michael Quinn interview, December 5, 2005.

18. Richard E. Bennett interview, May 29, 2010.

19. Evans interview, November 26, 2007.

20. LJA to Howard W. Hunter, "on behalf of James B. Allen, LaMar C. Berrett, R. Davis Bitton and Reed C. Durham Jr.," August 31, 1970, in LJAD.

21. Davis Bitton interview, August 11, 2006.

22. Davis Bitton to Howard W. Hunter, October 21, 1970, in LJAD.

23. LJA to Carl Arrington, April 4, 1971; LJAHA, Series X, Box 15, fd. 6.

24. LJA to Carl Arrington, September 27, 1971, in LJAD.

25. LJA to Carl Arrington, November 14, 1971, in LJAD.

26. LJAD, November 23, 1971.

27. James B. Allen and Glen M. Leonard, *The Story of the Latter-day Saints* 2d ed. (Salt Lake City: Deseret Book, 1992), 603–6.

28. L. Brent Goates, *Harold B. Lee: Prophet & Seer* (Salt Lake City: Bookcraft, 1985), 436–37.

29. Richard L. Bushman interview, January 16, 2009.

30. Stanford O. Cazier interview, January 15, 2006.

31. Neilson and Walker, *Reflections of a Mormon Historian*, 113.

Chapter 11—A Portrait of Leonard

1. LJAD, "Recollections, Response to Suggestions of Carl," written in third person in Diary, November 14, 1976.

2. LJAD, "Great Basin Kingdom Revisited," March 8, 1992. The nephew is not named or referred to in any of Arrington's papers.

3. Lavina Fielding Anderson interview, March 3, 2008.

4. Maureen Ursenbach Beecher interview, July 11, 2009.

5. Richard L. Bushman interview, January 16, 2009.

6. Armand L. Mauss interview, January 14, 2006.

7. Robert B. Flanders interview, May 18, 2009.

8. LJA to Children, December 12, 1995, in LJAD.

9. Mary L. Bradford interview, July 24, 2009.

10. Chris Rigby Arrington interview, September 24, 2009.

11. Elbert E. Peck interview, June 17, 2008.

12. Anderson interview, March 3, 2008.

13. Original lyrics written by Jill Mulvay (Derr) for a Historical Department appreciation dinner, May 6, 1977, and resurrected and modified for Leonard Arrington's retirement dinner, April 23, 1987, by Jill Mulvay Derr and Paul L. Anderson.

14. LJA to Children, July 21, 1989, in LJAD.

15. "My Dream," LJAD, November 18, 1984. "Iron Rodders" and "Liahonas" were terms derived from the Book of Mormon and used by historian Richard D. Poll to describe the manner in which two distinctly different kinds of church members approached their religious life. "Iron Rodders" comes from Nephi's dream of travelers in the wilderness, striving to reach the luminous and lovely "tree of life," despite dangers, a "mist of darkness," and other hazards. If they clung to the iron rod which paralleled a treacherous body of "filthy" water, they could reach the tree safely on a "strait and narrow path" (1 Nephi 8:1–20). The image of the "Liahonas" came from the family's journey after leaving Jerusalem when a brass ball "of curious workmanship" mysteriously appeared outside Lehi's tent one morning. It contained two spindles, one of which "pointed the way whither we should go" but which was operational only through the exercise of "faith and diligence" (1 Nephi 16:10, 28). The travelers' personal agency was critical in implementing the direction and working out the details. Richard D. Poll, "What the Church Means to People like Me," *Dialogue: A Journal of Mormon Thought* 2 (Winter 1967): 107–17.

16. Davis Bitton interview, August 11, 2006.

17. Mary L. Lythgoe Bradford interview, July 24, 2009.

18. Richard P. Howard interview, May 27, 2010.

19. Beecher interview, July 11, 2009.

20. D. Michael Quinn interview, December 5, 2005.

21. Bradford interview, July 24, 2009.

22. Jill Mulvay Derr interview, August 7, 2008.

23. G. W. Willson interview, May 23, 2008.

24. Howard R. Lamar interview, February 23, 2007.

25. James B. Allen interview, January 12, 2006.

26. Alma P. Blair interview, May 20, 2009.

27. Paul L. Anderson interview, March 3, 2008.

28. Martha Bradley-Evans interview, August 6, 2008.

29. Lavina Fielding Anderson, email to Prince, May 8, 2014.

30. Robert B. Flanders interview, May 18, 2009.

31. See Robert B. Flanders, "Nauvoo on My Mind," *John Whitmer Historical Association 2002 Nauvoo Conference Special Edition*; and "MHA after Forty Years," address delivered at the Mormon History Association, June 2006, Casper, Wyoming.

32. Elizabeth Dulany interview, May 28, 2010.

33. Juanita Brooks, a St. George schoolteacher of steely integrity and amazing historical persever-ance, faced down threats of being excommunicated to publish her landmark study *The Mountain Meadows Massacre* (1950; 2d ed., Norman: University of Oklahoma Press, 1962). For additional explorations, see Will Bagley, *Blood of the Prophets: Brigham Young and the Massacre at Mountain Meadows* (Norman: University of Oklahoma Press, 2002); Ronald W. Walker, Richard E. Turley Jr., and Glen M. Leonard, *Massacre at Mountain Meadows: An American Tragedy* (New York: Oxford University Press, 2008); and Shannon A. Novak, *House of Mourning: A Biocultural History of the Mountain Meadows Massacre* (Salt Lake City: University of Utah, 2008).

34. Blair interview, May 20, 2009.

35. LJA to Children, March 9, 1996, in LJAD.

36. Cornwall and Arrington, *I'm Glad My House Burned Down*, 182.

37. For example, Joseph Fielding Smith, president of the Quorum of the Twelve Apostles and the second-highest ranking church official in the 1950s and 1960s, condemned caffeinated soft drinks in

strong language, while at the same time church president David O. McKay said, "I don't care what it says *on* the cup, as long as there is a Coke *in* the cup." Edward Barner interview, October 1, 1996.

38. Jan Shipps interview, December 7, 2009.

39. Paul M. Edwards interview, May 19, 2009.

40. Beecher interview, July 11, 2009.

41. Flanders interview, May 18, 2009.

42. A controversial statement by a church member in an NBC "Rock Center" special on Mormonism, broadcast on August 23, 2012, led quickly to the first official stand of the LDS Church on caffeinated soft drinks: they were okay. They are now available for purchase on church properties.

43. Susan Arrington Madsen interview, July 29, 2012.

44. LJA, undated typescript; LJAHA, Series X, Box 2, fd. 2.

45. David J. Whittaker, "Leonard James Arrington (1917–1999): A Bibliography," *Journal of Mormon History* 25, no. 2 (Fall 1999): 11–45.

46. James Arrington interview, April 12, 2009.

47. Madsen interview, January 16, 2006.

48. Douglas D. Alder interview, March 1, 2007.

49. Cornwall and Arrington, *I'm Glad My House Burned Down*, 182.

50. Richard L. Bushman interview, January 16, 2009.

51. LJAD, February 17, 1979.

52. LJA to Children, December 9, 1987, in LJAD.

53. Madsen interview, January 16, 2006.

54. LJA to Children, November 10, 1989, in LJAD.

CHAPTER 12—WALKING A SPIRITUAL PATH

1. LJAD, November 1 and 14, 1976.

2. Ibid., April 26, 1975.

3. Ibid.

4. "Family Experiences," undated document, LJAHA, Series X, Box 1, fd. 4.

5. LJA to Children, LJAD, February 11, 1990.

6. "The Influence of College upon Tolerance," essay for high school English 4; LJAD, May 23, 1936.

7. LJAD, January 28, 1978.

8. Ibid., November 29, 1975; capitalization standardized.

9. Ibid.

10. "Why I Am a Believer," August 26, 1983.

11. LJA to Children, November 24, 1987, in LJAD. Leonard's use of the term "Higher Orientation" seems to be the broader, more all-encompassing approach that now is generally called historical/critical methodology. Higher criticism, or its specific application to the Bible, had erupted into controversy at Brigham Young University in about 1911 when BYU professors were fired for teaching evolution and this scriptural approach.

12. LJAD, July 15, 1977.

13. The literalistic interpretation of all scripture continues to be prevalent among all "religions of the book"—Judaism, Christianity, and Islam. The challenge that a data-based understanding of the world poses to scriptural literalism within the Latter-day Saint tradition was highlighted by a front-page article in the *New York Times* that described the faith crisis of a high-ranking Mormon official in Sweden who almost left the tradition after being confronted with discomfiting data. (Laurie Goodstein, "Some Mormons Search the Web and Find Doubt," *New York Times*, July 21, 2013, A1.) In response to the article, Rabbi Harold Kushner, author of *When Bad Things Happen to Good People*, wrote a letter to the editor suggesting the value of a worldview that can accommodate both literal and

figurative truth: "It will be interesting to see how the leaders of the Church of Jesus Christ of Latter-day Saints deal with the apparent coming to light of facts to cast doubt on the validity of its founding narrative. Might I suggest that they use the tactic used by many modern Jews dealing with biblical narratives that defy credulity, from a six-day story of creation to Jonah living inside a large fish. We distinguish between left-brain narratives (meant to convey factual truth) and right-brain narratives (meant to make a point through a story; the message will be true even if the story isn't factually defensible)." (Rabbi Harold Kushner, untitled letter to the editor, *New York Times*, July 27, 2013, A18.)

14. "My Most Influential Teacher," LJAD, November 3, 1978.

15. Leonard J. Arrington, "Why I Am a Believer," (delivered at the Sunstone Symposium), August 26, 1983; LJAHA, Series X, Box 3, fd. 1, published under the same title in *Sunstone* 10, no. 1 (January 1985): 36–38.

16. Ibid.

17. LJAD, November 29, 1975.

18. LJA to Children, October 21, 1987, in LJAD.

19. LJA to Grace Arrington in LJAD, September 26, 1943.

20. In a 1976 reminiscence (LJAD, May 13, 1976), he wrote, "I had had a dream as a youth of becoming a United States Senator from Idaho."

21. Arrington, *A Soldier in North Africa and Italy*, 11–12.

22. All of the quotations are from LJAD on the indicated dates.

23. Arrington, *Life in Happy Valley*, 9–11.

24. Carl Arrington interview, September 24, 2009.

25. This local quorum, which mirrored the third-ranked body of General Authorities, was generally assigned missionary responsibilities but became increasingly irrelevant until, in 1986, local quorums of the Seventy were disbanded altogether and its members were reassigned to either the ward elders' quorum or high priests' quorum, dependent largely on the man's age.

26. LJAD, September 8, 1976.

27. LJA to Children, LJAD, October 29, 1988.

28. "Pillars of My Faith," (delivered at the Sunstone Symposium), August 1, 1998, LJAHA, Series XII, Box 174, fd. 22.

29. LJA to Jan Shipps, November 14, 1972, LJAHA, Series V, Box 6, fd. 3. His reference to "The Mormon Experience" was a shaping image that became the title for the one-volume history designed for a non-Mormon audience that he coauthored with Davis Bitton and published with Alfred A. Knopf in 1979.

30. James Arrington interview, April 12, 2012.

31. Carol Lynn Pearson diary, June 2, 1983. Copy of entry in my possession, courtesy of Pearson.

32. LJA, undated and untitled typescript, LJAHA, Series XII, Box 121, fd. 3.

33. James Arrington interview, April 12, 2012.

34. LJA to Carol Lynn Pearson, July 27, 1978; LJAHA, Series II, Box 13, fd. 10.

35. James B. Allen interview, January 12, 2006.

36. Gene A. Sessions interview, August 7, 2011.

37. N. George Daines interview, January 16, 2006.

38. Ibid.

39. F. Ross Peterson interview, September 17, 2007.

40. D. Michael Quinn interview, December 5, 2005.

41. Jan Shipps interview, December 8, 2009.

42. Maureen Ursenbach Beecher interview, July 11, 2009.

43. "Proof of the Book of Mormon," LJAD, ca. 1933.

44. LJAD, July 15, 1977.

45. The first published attack, written by Alexander Campbell, founder of the Disciples of Christ tradition, was published in February 1831 in Campbell's magazine, *Millennial Harbinger*, and the following year as a pamphlet entitled *Delusions: An Analysis of the Book of Mormon*.

46. See chapter 21.

47. Lester E. Bush Jr., "The Spalding Theory Then and Now," *Dialogue: A Journal of Mormon Thought* 10, no. 4 (Autumn 1977): 42—71.

48. B. H. Roberts to "Heber J. Grant and Counsellors, the Quorum of the Twelve Apostles, and the First Council of the Seventy," December 29, 1921, in B. H. Roberts, *Studies of the Book of Mormon*, edited by Brigham D. Madsen (Urbana: University of Illinois Press, 1985), 46.

49. Brigham D. Madsen, "Introduction," in *Studies of the Book of Mormon*, 22.

50. LJAD, September 19, 1978.

51. LJAD, April 21, 1981.

52. LJA to Children, in LJAD, November 13, 1978.

53. LJA to John Sorenson, November 13, 1978, LJAHA, Series II, Box 16, fd. 8.

54. LJA to Children, in LJAD, March 16, 1987.

55. Pearson diary, October 10, 1988.

56. "Thoughts about Religion, for the Family," in LJAD, February 11, 1982.

57. LJA to Children, in LJAD, March 28, 1982.

58. Official opposition did not name *Sunstone* but left no doubt by citing "recent symposia"— the Sunstone Symposium at the time being the only such symposium. In November 1991 the Council of the First Presidency and the Quorum of the Twelve Apostles issued a "Statement on Symposia." The statement is still listed on the church's website, http://www.lds.org/ensign/1991/11/news-of-the -church/statement-on-symposia?lang=eng&query=symposia.

59. Arrington, "Why I Am a Believer," 36–38.

60. LJAD, February 4, 1985. William O. Nelson had been associated with Benson as an aide when Benson had served as U.S. Secretary of Agriculture in the Eisenhower administration and continued to carry out Benson's assignments, whether formally or informally, but which demonstrated Benson's political and ecclesiastical conservatism.

61. LJAD, July 9, 1985.

62. LJA to Terry Allen, January 9, 1986; LJAHA, Series X, Box 81, fd. 4.

63. LJA to Children, in LJAD, September 18, 1989.

64. LJAD, August 17, 1992.

65. LJA to Children, May 14, 1998; LJAHA, Series X, Box 103, fd. 11.

CHAPTER 13—PROMOTING MORMON HISTORY

1. Notes of a discussion between LJA, Robert Flanders, and George Ellsworth in Philadelphia, PA, April 18, 1969; LJAHA, Series X, Box 2, fd. 2.

2. LJAD, September 20, 1972.

3. Notes of a discussion between LJA, Robert Flanders and George Ellsworth in Philadelphia, PA, April 18, 1969. LJAHA, Series X, Box 2, fd. 2.

4. LJAD, March 23, 1976.

5. Arrington, *Adventures of a Church Historian*, 58.

6. Robert Kent Fielding interview, May 6, 2009.

7. Leonard J. Arrington, "An Economic Interpretation of 'The Word of Wisdom,'" *Brigham Young University Studies* 1, no. 1 (Winter 1959): 37–49.

8. Arrington, *Adventures of a Church Historian*, 58.

9. LJAD, March 23, 1976.

10. Alfred L. Bush to LJA, June 18, 1964; LJAHA, Series X, Box 74, fd. 5.

11. LJA to Hugh B. Brown, July 6, 1965; LJAHA, Series IV, Box 29, fd. 1.

12. Douglas D. Alder interview, March 1, 2007. Stan Cazier and Blythe Ahlstrom were both faculty in the History Department. Ahlstrom became Cazier's executive assistant when Cazier was president of Chico State and, later still, returned to USU as its president.

13. LJA interviewed by F. Ross Peterson, April 12, 1988. Transcript provided to me by Peterson.

14. LJA to Joseph Fielding Smith, October 25, 1965; LJAHA, Series X, Box 79, fd. 6.

15. LJA to Hugh B. Brown, November 8, 1965; LJAHA, Series X, Box 74, fd. 4.

16. LJA to John Sorenson, October 26, 1965; LJAHA, Series IV, Box 29, fd. 1. While Leonard shrugged off the possibility of a trial—now known within the LDS Church as a disciplinary council, whose most extreme outcome is excommunication—he later feared that his soon-to-be-published autobiography would result in just such discipline.

17. LJAD, March 23, 1976.

18. Armand L. Mauss interview, January 14, 2006.

19. Robert B. Flanders interview, May 18, 2009.

20. Leonard J. Arrington interview by F. Ross Peterson, April 12, 1988. In response to steadily increasing productivity among scholars of Mormonism, the Mormon History Association began publishing the *Journal of Mormon History* nine years later, in 1974.

21. LJA untitled remarks at *Dialogue* anniversary banquet, LJAD, August 27, 1987.

22. LJA Diary, March 29, 1981.

23. A comprehensive history of *Dialogue* was written by Devery S. Anderson and published in four installments: "A History of *Dialogue*, Part 1: The Early Years, 1965–1971," *Dialogue* 32, no. 2 (Summer 1999): 15–67; "A History of *Dialogue*, Part 2: Struggle toward Maturity, 1971–1982," *Dialogue* 33, no. 2 (Summer 2000): 1–96; "A History of *Dialogue*, Part 3: 'Coming of Age' in Utah, 1982–1987," *Dialogue* 35, no. 2 (Summer 2002): 1–71; "A History of *Dialogue*, Part 4: A Tale in Two Cities, 1987–92," *Dialogue* 41, no. 3 (Fall 2008): 1–54.

24. LJA to Joseph H. Jeppson, August 6, 1965; LJAHA, Series IV, Box 29, fd. 1.

25. Joseph H. Jeppson to LJA, August 13, 1965; LJAHA, Series IV, Box 29, fd. 1.

26. Arrington, *Years of Achievement and Pleasure in Logan: 1958–72*, 41.

27. LJAD, March 29, 1981.

28. Richard Bushman to Wesley Johnson, November 7, 1965, quoted in Anderson, "A History of *Dialogue*, Part 1," 24.

29. Richard Bushman and Eugene England to First Presidency, November 20, 1965, quoted in ibid., 26.

30. David O. McKay, Diary, December 8, 1965.

31. Ibid.

32. "Mormon Scholars Plan a Journal: Independent Quarterly Will Be Issued in February," *New York Times*, December 12, 1965, p. 80.

33. Wallace Turner, "Mormons Gain Despite Tensions," *New York Times*, December 27, 1965, p. 18.

34. This statement appears on the page facing the inside front cover of each issue.

35. LJA to G. Wesley Johnson, February 1, 1966; LJAHA, Series IV, Box 29, fd. 2.

36. Anderson, "A History of *Dialogue*, Part 1," 28–29. England wrote his letter to Hinckley on March 7, 1966. Hinckley responded on March 9.

37. Editors, "In This Issue," *Dialogue: A Journal of Mormon Thought* 1, no. 2 (Summer 1966): 2.

38. LJAD, August 27, 1987.

39. LJA to John R. T. Hughes, May 24, 1966; LJAHA, Series IV, Box 29, fd. 2.

40. LJA to Rodman W. Paul, June 20, 1966; LJAHA, Series IV, Box 1, fd. 1.

41. "Mormons: For Ruffled Believers," *Time Magazine*, August 26, 1966, 61. The "unruffled Mormon" is a quotation from Frances Lee Menlove's essay in that inaugural issue, "The Challenge of Honesty." The quotation is on page 4 of her collected essays.

42. J. D. Williams, "The Separation of Church and State in Mormon Theory and Practice," *Dialogue: A Journal of Mormon Thought* 1, no. 2 (Summer 1966): 30–54.

43. Arrington, *Adventures of a Church Historian*, 89. In a diary entry, Leonard noted, "From that time my name has been on his [Benson's] black list." LJAD, March 29, 1981.

44. Alvin R. Dyer Diary, December 1, 1967; quoted in McKay, Diary, December 1, 1967.

45. LJAD, September 20, 1972.

46. "*Dialogue* Magazine," *The Priesthood Bulletin* 3, no. 2 (March–June 1967): 1.

47. Stewart L. Udall, Letter to the editor. *Dialogue* 2, no. 2 (Summer 1967): 5–7.

48. Wallace Turner, "Udall Entreats Mormons on Race; Bids Church Remove Curbs on Its Negro Members," *New York Times*, May 19, 1967.

49. Turner's syndicated article was republished in the *Salt Lake Tribune* the same day as its publication in the *New York Times*, under the title "Udall Asks LDS to Reexamine Negro Doctrine." The "no comment" remark was an addendum in the *Tribune* version, without authorship. *Salt Lake Tribune*, May 19, 1967, B-1.

50. McKay, Diary, May 24, 1967.

51. Gregory A. Prince and Wm. Robert Wright, *David O. McKay and the Rise of Modern Mormonism* (Salt Lake City: University of Utah Press, 2005), chapter 4, "Blacks, Civil Rights, and the Priesthood."

52. Dyer, Diary, September 10, 1969, quoted in McKay, Diary, September 10, 1969.

53. First Presidency Minutes, September 17, 1969, quoted in McKay, Diary, September 17, 1969.

54. Stephen G. Taggart, *Mormonism's Negro Policy: Social and Historical Origins* (Salt Lake City: University of Utah Press, 1970).

55. Lester E. Bush, "A Commentary on Stephen G. Taggart's *Mormonism's Negro Policy: Social and Historical Origins*," *Dialogue: A Journal of Mormon Thought* 4, no. 4 (Winter 1969): 86–103. For Bush's 1973 article and the events surrounding it, see chapter 21.

56. LJA to Richard Bushman, October 28, 1967; LJAHA, Series X, Box 74, fd. 4.

57. LJA to Dr. Lindsay Curtis, June 23, 1968; LJAHA, Series X, Box 75, fd. 2.

58. Charles D. Tate to Eugene England, August 22, 1967, quoted in Anderson, "A History of *Dialogue*, Part 1," 15.

CHAPTER 14—CHURCH HISTORIAN

1. Bitton, "Ten Years in Camelot," 9–19.

2. Lund had served for sixty years as assistant church historian.

3. LJAD, January 7, 1972.

4. LJA to Carl Arrington, January 8, 1972, LJAHA, Series X, Box 15, fd. 6.

5. B. Z. ("Bud") Kastler interview, June 3, 1997.

6. Russell M. Nelson, April 3, 1993, *Official Report of the One Hundred Sixty-third Annual General Conference of the Church of Jesus Christ of Latter-day Saints* (Salt Lake City: Church of Jesus Christ of Latter-day Saints, 1993), 52.

7. Joseph Fielding Smith also authored *Church History and Modern Revelation*, 4 vols. (Salt Lake City: Council of the Twelve Apostles of the Church of Jesus Christ of Latter-day Saints, 1946–1949), but despite the title it was a compilation of Joseph Smith's teachings with some theological commentary, rather than a history per se, and was written as a course of study for the adult male priesthood quorums. He also published a biography of his father: *Life of Joseph F. Smith: Sixth President of the Church of Jesus Christ of Latter-day Saints* (Salt Lake City: Deseret News, 1938), which contains some historically important material—i.e., quotations from his father's diary which was otherwise (and still is) unavailable to researchers.

8. Prince and Wright, *David O. McKay and the Rise of Modern Mormonism*, chapter 10.

9. David O. McKay, in 1961, also had called Hugh B. Brown as an "additional counselor," largely to help carry the administrative load during the time when First Counselor J. Reuben Clark Jr.'s health was declining. Upon Clark's death just three months later, Brown became second counselor in the First Presidency.

10. Salt Lake City: Deseret Book, 1968.

11. L. Brent Goates interview, May 20, 1996.

12. Arrington, *Adventures of a Church Historian*, 107.

13. Carl Arrington interview, September 24, 2009.

14. LJAD, December 17, 1979.

15. Ibid., December 12, 1972.

16. Leonard J. Arrington, "Church Historian, 1972–1982," written in 1992; LJAHA, Series X, Box 16, fd. 1.

17. LJA to Children, May 7, 1977, LJAD.

18. The change in name occurred in 1972 as part of a larger reorganization of the church bureaucracy (see Prologue, note 2).

19. Earl E. Olson interview, January 17, 2006.

20. The Language Training Mission was established in the early 1960s to teach Spanish to missionaries prior to their departure for their assigned countries rather than having them pick the language up from scratch after arriving in-country. Eventually it expanded to teach dozens of foreign languages and was renamed the Missionary Training Center (MTC), with several additional centers in Europe, South America, Asia, and Africa.

21. LJA to Carl Arrington, January 15, 1972, in LJAD.

22. LJA to Carl Arrington, January 23, 1972, in LJAD.

23. Lee Bickmore was an informal advisor to the church on administrative matters. In mid-1971 he recommended to the First Presidency that they engage the services of the consulting firm Cresap, McCormick, and Paget, Inc. "to begin a comprehensive study of Church operations to establish more objective administration guidelines." Goates, *Harold B. Lee: Prophet & Seer*, 436.

24. A significant analysis of the Tanners' activities and motivations was written by Lawrence Foster, a non-Mormon, an early beneficiary of Arrington's summer fellowship program, and the author of one of the most important early studies of polygamy. See his "Career Apostates: Reflections on the Works of Jerald and Sandra Tanner," *Dialogue: A Journal of Mormon Thought* 17 (Summer 1984): 35–60. His prize-winning book was *Religion and Sexuality: Three American Communal Experiments in the Nineteenth Century* (New York: Oxford University Press, 1981).

25. The publication of the Council of Fifty minutes for the Nauvoo period by the Church Historian's Press was announced with considerable fanfare at a plenary session of the Mormon History Association in San Antonio in June 2014.

26. LJAD, January 26, 1972.

27. LJA to Carl Arrington, January 8, 1972, LJAHA, Series X, Box 15, fd. 6.

28. Arrington, "Church Historian, 1972–1982."

29. LJAD, August 9, 1972.

30. Ibid., March 13, 1972.

31. Olson interview, January 17, 2006.

32. Jan Shipps interview, December 8, 2009.

33. LJA to Carl Arrington, March 11, 1972, in LJAD.

34. William A. Linn's *The Story of the Mormons: From the Date of Their Origin to the Year 1901* (New York: Macmillan, 1902), was highly critical of the Mormons—and widely read. Shortly after its publication, Assistant Church Historian and General Authority B. H. Roberts began to write *History of the Mormon Church*, which appeared serially in *Americana Illustrated* magazine from 1909 to 1915. Roberts later updated it and published it as the church's centennial history in 1930, *A Comprehensive History of the Church of Jesus Christ of Latter-day Saints, Century I*, 6 vols. (Salt Lake City: Deseret Book, 1930).

35. LJA to George Ellsworth, October 22, 1956, in LJAD. The "documentary history" he refers to is the seven-volume history attributed to Joseph Smith but actually prepared by rephrasing records, letters, and notes made by others such as Wilford Woodruff so that they appeared in first person, as though Smith had written it himself. See *History of the Church of Jesus Christ of Latter-day Saints*, ed. B. H. Roberts, 2d ed. rev. (Salt Lake City: Deseret Book, 6 vols., 1902–1912, Vol. 7, 1932). For an analysis of its preparation, which was not unusual for nineteenth-century documentary procedures though misleading by modern historical standards, see Dean C. Jessee, "The Reliability of Joseph Smith's History," *Journal of Mormon History* 3 (1976): 23–46, and Jessee, "The Writing of Joseph Smith's History, *BYU Studies* 11 (Summer 1971): 439–73.

36. Robert Glass Cleland and Juanita Brooks edited the diaries, which were published by the Huntington Library in 1955 as *A Mormon Chronicle: The Diaries of John D. Lee, 1848–1876*, 2 vols.

37. Leonard J. Arrington, Address to the Timpanogos Club of Salt Lake City, January 7, 1960, in LJAD.

38. Leonard J. Arrington, Address to Phi Alpha Theta and history majors at Brigham Young University, May 17, 1961, in LJAD.

39. LJA to Rodman W. Paul, June 20, 1966; LJAHA, Series IV, Box 1, fd. 1.

40. LJA to Richard Bushman, October 28, 1967; LJAHA, Series X, Box 74, fd. 4.

41. LJAD, February 24, 1972.

42. Ibid., February 25, 1972.

43. James B. Allen interview, January 12, 2006. James B. Allen and Glen M. Leonard, *The Story of the Latter-day Saints* (Salt Lake City: Deseret Book, 1976); Leonard J. Arrington and Davis Bitton, *The Mormon Experience: A History of the Latter-day Saints* (New York: Alfred A. Knopf, 1979).

44. This account was reminiscent. The idea for the one-volume history for church members actually arose in the weeks following this meeting.

45. Neilson and Walker, *Reflections of a Mormon Historian*, 122.

46. LJAD, August 8, 1972.

47. Ibid., September 14, 1972.

48. Brown was first counselor in the First Presidency. Crockett, who had been academic vice president of Brigham Young University, was acting president of BYU at this time while Ernest Wilkinson was on a leave of absence to run for the U.S. Senate.

49. LJA to Richard L. Bushman, May 25, 1964; LJAHA, Series X, Box 74, fd. 5.

50. Richard L. Bushman to Hugh B. Brown, July 22, 1964; LJAHA, Series X, Box 74, fd. 5.

51. Antone K. Romney to Harold B. Lee, September 3, 1964; LJAHA, Series X, Box 74, fd. 5.

52. Boyd K. Packer, "The Mantle Is Far, Far Greater Than the Intellect," *BYU Studies* 21, no. 3 (Summer 1981): 259–78.

53. Romney to Lee, September 3, 1964.

54. Harold B. Lee to Richard L. Bushman, September 3, 1964; LJAHA, Series X, Box 74, fd. 5.

55. Richard L. Bushman to LJA, September 29, 1964; LJAHA, Series X, Box 74, fd. 5.

56. LJAD, March 13, 1972.

57. "Plan of Operations of the Church History Division of the Historical Department of the Church," April 10, 1972, in LJAD.

58. Minutes of the Executives of the Historical Department of the Church of Jesus Christ of Latter-day Saints meeting, April 11, 1972, in LJAD.

59. LJAD, May 29, 1974.

60. LJAD, June 10, 1974. Even though the series was ultimately canceled, the authors were allowed to publish their books independently. Those published to date are: [I] Richard L. Bushman, *Joseph Smith and the Beginnings of Mormonism* (Urbana and Chicago: University of Illinois Press, 1984); [II] Milton V. Backman, *The Heavens Resound: A History of the Latter-day Saints in Ohio, 1830–1838* (Salt Lake City: Deseret Book Company, 1983); [IV] Glen M Leonard, *Nauvoo: A Place of Peace, A People of Promise* (Salt Lake City and Provo: Deseret Book Company and Brigham Young University Press, 2002) [Glen Leonard completed the Nauvoo history that T. Edgar Lyon, who died in 1978, had initiated]; [VI] Eugene E. Campbell, *Establishing Zion: The Mormon Church in the American West, 1847–1869* (Salt Lake City: Signature Books, 1988); [VIII] Thomas G. Alexander, *Mormonism in Transition: A History of the Latter-day Saints, 1890–1930* (Urbana: University of Illinois Press, 1986); [IX] Richard O. Cowan, *The Church in the Twentieth Century* (Salt Lake City: Bookcraft, 1985); [XII] R. Lanier Britsch, *Unto the Islands of the Sea: A History of the Latter-day Saints in the Pacific* (Salt Lake City: Deseret Book Company, 1986), and *From the East: The History of the Latter-day Saints in Asia, 1851–1996* (Salt Lake City: Deseret Book Company, 1998); [XIII] F. LaMond Tullis, *Mormons in Mexico: The Dynamics of Faith and Culture* (Logan: Utah State University Press, 1987).

61. LJAD, May 29, 1974.

62. Richard L. Bushman interview, January 16, 2009.

63. "Recollections of 1972–1973," in LJAD, October 13, 1981.

64. James B. Allen, "Some Accomplishments of the History Division of the Historical Dep't," LJAD, January 1973.

65. LJAD, November 19, 1975.

66. "Report of the Historical Department, 1976–1980," in LJAD, January 1, 1981.

67. Reid L. Neilson, Managing Director, Church History Department, to Gregory A. Prince, January 21, 2014.

68. LJAD, August 23, 1972.

69. F. Ross Peterson interview, September 17, 2007.

70. Arrington, *Farm Boy at the University of Idaho*, 24.

71. LJAD, September 12, 1972.

72. Ibid., June 11, 1973.

73. Richard L. Jensen interview, August 8, 2008.

74. Lavina Fielding Anderson interview, March 3, 2008.

75. George D. Smith interview, June 30, 2012.

76. LJA to Charles D. Tate Jr., October 11, 1974; LJAHA, Series II, Box 17, fd. 2.

77. LJA to Wallace R. Bennett, July 12, 1976; LJAHA, Series II, Box 2, fd. 6.

78. Howard Lamar interview, February 23, 2007. Quinn's dissertation was "The Mormon Hierarchy, 1832–1932: An American Elite" (PhD diss., Yale University, 1976).

79. Ronald K. Esplin interview, June 30, 2012.

80. Cheryll Lynn May interview, August 4, 2011.

81. F. Ross Peterson interview, September 17, 2007.

82. LJAD, May 22, 1974.

83. James Arrington interview, April 12, 2009.

84. The most high-profile example of this was Hans Mattsson, a former Area Seventy in Sweden, whose faith crisis was triggered by the same questions that Arrington sidestepped. See Laurie Goodstein, "Some Mormons Search the Web and Find Doubt," *New York Times*, July 20, 2013.

85. Dwight Israelsen interview, January 15, 2006.

86. Earl E. Olson interview, January 17, 2006.

87. Untitled manuscript, LJAHA, Series X, Box 16, fd. 1; dated 1992.

88. LJA to Joseph Anderson, May 14, 1973, in LJAD.

89. LJA to N. Eldon Tanner, January 11, 1967, in LJAD.

90. William J. Whalen, *The Latter-day Saints in the Modern Day World: An Account of Contemporary Mormonism* (New York: John Day Company, 1964); Wallace Turner, *The Mormon Establishment* (Boston: Houghton Mifflin Company, 1966).

91. First Presidency Minutes, January 17, 1967, in David O. McKay Diary, Special Collections, Marriott Library, University of Utah, Salt Lake City.

92. N. Eldon Tanner to LJA, January 18, 1967, in LJAD.

93. LJA to Evan Murray, March 6, 1967; LJAHA, Series II, Box 12, fd. 4.

94. LJA to Milton R. Merrill, March 6, 1967, in LJAD.

95. Roberts, *A Comprehensive History*.

96. Alvin R. Dyer Journal, March 8, 1968; photocopy in McKay, Diary.

97. LJAD to Joseph Anderson, May 14, 1973, in LJAD.

98. First Presidency to Joseph Anderson, July 2, 1973, in LJAD.

99. Joseph Smith et al., *History of the Church of Jesus Christ of Latter-day Saints: Period I*, 6 vols. B. H. Roberts, 2d. ed. rev. (Salt Lake City: Deseret News Press, 1902–1912).

100. LJAD, April 10, 1972.

101. First Presidency Minutes, September 5, 1969, in McKay Diary.

102. Dean C. Jessee, ed., *Letters of Brigham Young to His Sons* (Salt Lake City: Deseret Book Company, 1974).

103. LJAD, September 14, 1972.

104. *The Church in Action—1971* and *The Church in Action—1972* were replaced in 1973 by the *Deseret News Church Almanac*. The *Church Almanac* was published through 2012 when, without announcement or explanation, its publication ceased.

105. Floyd O'Neil interview, June 16, 2008.

106. LJA to Anthony Cluff, Director of Research, Security Industries Association, October 24, 1972; LJAHA, Series II, Box 4, fd. 5.

107. LJAD, January 30, 1973.

108. Published later as Thomas G. Alexander, *Mormonism in Transition: A History of the Latter-day Saints, 1890–1930* (Urbana: University of Illinois Press, 1986).

109. Thomas G. Alexander interview, January 12, 2006.

110. Jill Mulvay Derr interview, August 7, 2008.

111. Peggy Fletcher Stack interview, January 13, 2006.

112. Richard E. Bennett interview, May 29, 2010.

113. LJAD, July 28, 1972.

114. Paul L. Anderson interview, March 3, 2008.

115. Carl Arrington interview, September 24, 2009.

116. Patricia Bennett interview, May 29, 2010.

117. Veda Tebbs Hale, "In Memoriam: Maurine Whipple," *Sunstone* 16, no. 2, August 1992, 13–15.

118. Maurine Whipple to LJA, November 21, 1972; LJAHA, Series V, Box 11, fd. 24.

119. Allen, "Accomplishments of the History Division for 1974."

120. LJAD, March 31, 1976.

CHAPTER 15—THE BUREAUCRACY

1. LJAD, January 1, 1975.

2. "Appointment to Church in 1972," undated typescript, LJAHA, Series X, Box 2, fd. 4.

3. LJAD, June 15, 1972.

4. Ibid., June 19, 1972.

5. Ibid., January 30, 1973.

6. Ibid., July 18, 1972.

7. Ibid., December 5, 1973.

8. Ibid., November 2, 1976.

9. One example of this attitude was given by a now-deceased General Authority: "I don't hear an Apostle ever quote anybody in public lower than himself." Paul H. Dunn interview, March 21, 1997.

10. LJAD, November 2, 1976.

11. LJA to Susan and James Arrington, February 17, 1973; LJAHA, Series X, Box 102, fd. 2.

12. LJAD, December 12, 1976.

13. Leonard's diary documents eight meetings with Harold B. Lee between the time of his calling as church historian and Lee's unexpected death less than two years later: February 24, August 8, and December 15, 1972; and January 30, March 8, June 26, August 9, and September 21, 1973. The number of formal meetings between a church employee and a senior apostle is unusual.

14. "Church Historian, 1972–1982," 1992, LJAHA, Series X, Box 16, fd. 1.

15. LJAD, December 12, 1976.

16. Doctrine and Covenants 42:88.

17. LJAD, December 19, 1976. For this complaint about Leonard's Word of Wisdom article, published in *BYU Studies*, see chapter 13.

18. "Appointment to Church in 1972."

19. Ibid.

20. Ronald K. Esplin interview, June 30, 2012. Leonard's papers contain no reference to this controversy about employee salaries, leaving the question open about how much, if anything, he knew.

21. LJAD, October 10, 1976.

22. Ibid., November 2, 1976.

23. Esplin interview, June 30, 2012. Esplin did not comment further on these steps.

24. Robert D. Hales was sustained as a member of the Quorum of the Twelve Apostles on April 2, 1994.

25. James L. Clayton interview, August 8, 2008.

CHAPTER 16—PROMOTING MORMON HISTORY

1. LJA to Howard W. Hunter, December 1, 1972, in LJAD of the same date.

2. First Presidency (signed by N. Eldon Tanner and Marion G. Romney) to LJA, September 13, 1972, in LJAD of the same date.

3. Meeting minutes, in LJAD, September 21, 1972.

4. LJAD, November 20, 1972.

5. Paul H. Dunn interview, March 22, 1997.

6. LJAD, November 30, 1972.

7. Ibid.

8. LJAD, December 1, 1972.

9. LJA to Howard W. Hunter, December 1, 1972, in LJAD of the same date.

10. LJAD, December 4, 1972. Briton and Bruce McConkie were brothers. At that point, Packer was a junior apostle (ordained in April 1970), while Bruce McConkie was the most junior member of the Twelve, ordained only two months earlier in October 1972.

11. LJAD, December 8, 1972.

12. Ibid., January 11, 1973.

13. Minutes of the meeting of the Executives of the Historical Department, January 18, 1973, in LJAD.

14. LJAD, January 30, 1973.

15. Ibid., June 26, 1973.

16. Ibid., September 14, 1978.

17. Arrington, *Adventures of a Church Historian*, 97.

18. Everett L. Cooley interview, January 13, 2006. Cooley mistakenly remembers that the meeting convened in the Church Office Building auditorium, which would have held several hundred people in theater-style seating. It was actually held in the Historical Department reading room which was set up with tables, microfilm readers, and chairs, and, as Leonard described, was rearranged for the meeting to allow the maximum number of chairs.

19. James B. Allen interview, January 12, 2006. Allen's memory that one or two meetings followed the inaugural gathering is mistaken.

20. Sandra Tanner interview, August 8, 2008.

21. Doctrine and Covenants 93:36.

22. Dallin H. Oaks, currently a senior member of the Quorum of the Twelve Apostles, was a charter member of the *Dialogue* board of editors in 1966, and served in that capacity until 1970.

23. As chapter 21 will document, a 1973 *Dialogue* article on the historical basis of denying priesthood ordination to black males of African descent challenged a longstanding belief about the origins of the policy, thereby opening the door to overt questioning of it and, five years later, its reversal.

24. The Church College of Hawaii was founded in 1955 as a two-year school catering primarily to church members in Hawaii and Polynesia. It received four-year accreditation in 1961. In 1974 church president Spencer W. Kimball announced that it would become a campus of Provo-based Brigham Young University, whereupon it was renamed BYU–Hawaii.

25. LJAD, May 21, 1972.

26. LJA to Children, October 9, 1972, in LJAD of the same date. Leonard's article was "Joseph Fielding Smith: Faithful Historian," *Dialogue: A Journal of Mormon Thought* 7, no. 1 (Spring 1972): 21–25. This short essay was part of a seven-item memorial to Smith, who had died in July of that year. The mismatch in publication dates and actual appearance would frequently plague the quarterly. The rest of the issue, which Allen had guest-edited, dealt with "Challenge, Constancy, and Change: Samples of the Mormon Experience in the Twentieth Century." Alexander's article was titled "Reed Smoot, the L.D.S. Church, and Progressive Legislation, 1903–1933," ibid., 47–56.

27. LJAD, January 30, 1973. "Jack Mormon" was a commonly used nickname for lapsed Mormons.

28. LJAD, April 19, 1973.

29. Ibid., April 27, 1973.

30. Ibid., May 1, 1973.

31. Ibid., June 24, 1974.

32. Ibid., November 27, 1974.

33. Ibid., December 17, 1974. *Exponent II* is a quarterly newspaper established by LDS women in Massachusetts in 1974. It is discussed at length in chapter 17.

34. LJA to Robert A. Rees, May 13, 1975; LJAHA, Series II, Box 14, fd. 10.

35. "Recollections, Religion and Life Week at the University of Idaho," in LJAD, October 31, 1976.

36. Ibid., February 18, 1978.

37. The Washington Bullets—now the Washington Wizards—won the National Basketball Association championship in 1978.

38. Mary L. Bradford to LJA, June 29, 1978; LJAHA, Series IV, Box 29, fd. 4.

39. LJAD, September 14, 1978.

40. Scott G. Kenney interview, December 2, 2012.

41. Susan Arrington Madsen interview, January 16, 2006.

42. Carl Arrington interview, September 24, 2009.

43. Meeting minutes, February 8, 1972 in LJAD.

44. LJAD, May 24, 1973.

45. James B. Allen interview, January 12, 2006.

46. Douglas D. Alder interview, March 1, 2007.

47. Thomas G. Alexander interview, January 12, 2006.

48. Stanford Cazier interview, January 15, 2006.

49. Glen M. Leonard interview, July 27, 2012.

50. William A. ("Bert") Wilson interview, August 12, 2009.

51. F. Ross Peterson interview, September 17, 2007.

52. Ferron Losee was president of Dixie College (St. George, Utah) from 1964–1976. In the late 1960s Losee overruled the recommendation of faculty advisors that Smith, head of the Social Science Department, be granted academic tenure. Smith sued unsuccessfully to retain his faculty position. Peterson's reminiscence captures the residual animosity between Losee and Smith.

53. Charles S. Peterson interview, November 9, 2006.

54. Jill Mulvay Derr interview, August 7, 2008.

55. Edward Leo Lyman interview, October 8, 2008.

56. Allen interview, January 12, 2006.

57. D. Michael Quinn interview, December 5, 2005. The article was "Utah's Education Innovation: LDS Religion Classes, 1890–1929," *Utah Historical Quarterly* 43 (Fall 1975): 379–89.

58. Alma R. Blair interview, May 20, 2009.

59. Ronald K. Esplin interview, June 30, 2012.

60. Lester E. Bush Jr. interview, October 24, 2008.

61. Jan Shipps interview, December 7, 2009.

62. Leonard J. Arrington, "Historian as Entrepreneur: A Personal Essay," *BYU Studies* 17, no. 2 (1977): 1–15.

63. David J. Whittaker interview, May 22, 2008.

64. Everett L. Cooley interview, January 13, 2006.

65. N. George Daines interview, January 16, 2006.

66. Charles S. Peterson interview, November 9, 2006.

67. D. Michael Quinn, contribution in "Remembering Leonard" (compilation of reminiscences), *Journal of Mormon History* 25, no. 1 (1999): 27–28.

68. N. George Daines interview, January 16, 2006.

69. Linda King Newell interview, October 25, 2009.

70. LJA to Harold Cannon, November 9, 1977; LJAHA, Series II, Box 3, fd. 10.

71. Linda King Newell and Valeen Tippetts Avery, *Mormon Enigma: Emma Hale Smith, Prophet's Wife, "Elect Lady," Polygamy's Foe* (New York: Doubleday & Company, 1984).

72. Linda King Newell interview, October 25, 2009.

73. Richard L. Bushman interview, January 16, 2009.

74. Richard E. Bennett interview, May 29, 2010.

75. Christine Rigby Arrington interview, September 24, 2009.

76. Cazier interview, January 15, 2006.

77. Robert B. Flanders interview, May 18, 2009.

78. Paul M. Edwards interview, May 19, 2009.

79. Armand L. Mauss interview, January 14, 2006.

80. Edward Leo Lyman interview, October 8, 2008.

81. Maureen Ursenbach Beecher interview, July 11, 2009.

82. Lavina Fielding Anderson interview, March 3, 2008.

83. LJA, interviewed by F. Ross Peterson, April 12, 1988.

84. Ronald O. Barney interview, October 26, 2009.

CHAPTER 17—BLESSED DAMOZELS

1. Marie Arrington Davidson interview, January 16, 2006.

2. Ibid.

3. Leonard J. Arrington, "FFA and Women," ca. November 1934, in LJAD.

4. Susan Arrington Madson, telephone conversation, May 31, 2014.

5. Leonard J. Arrington, "The Economic Role of Pioneer Mormon Women," *Western Humanities Review* 9, no. 2 (1955): 145–64.

6. The Female Relief Society was organized in Nauvoo, Illinois, in 1842, where it functioned during the remainder of Joseph Smith's lifetime, but it was disbanded at the time of the exodus from Nauvoo in 1846.

7. Carol Cornwall Madsen, contribution in "Remembering Leonard" (compilation of reminiscences), *Journal of Mormon History* 25, no. 1 (Spring 1999): 100–101.

8. LJA to Royal Eccles, July 7, 1969; LJAHA, Series X, Box 76, fd. 1.

9. Robert B. Flanders interview, May 18, 2009. The image of Martha Hughes Cannon, a trained physician and the fourth wife of Angus Cannon, president of the gigantic Salt Lake Stake, running successfully against him, was journalistically irresistible at the time and still is; but the reality is slightly more nuanced. The candidates were running in an open field that included a number of other candidates—not just "Mattie versus Angus."

10. *Dialogue: A Journal of Mormon Thought* 6, no. 2 (Summer 1971): 22–31. A special issue that focused on Mormon women, its nickname came from its pink cover.

11. Eugene England, contribution in "Remembering Leonard," (compilation of reminiscences), *Journal of Mormon History* 25, no. 1 (Spring 1999): 25.

12. Arrington and Bitton, *The Mormon Experience*, chapter 12, "Mormon Sisterhood: Charting the Changes," 220–40.

13. LJAD, November 14, 1978.

14. Arrington and Bitton, *The Mormon Experience*, 238–39.

15. Jill Mulvay Derr interview, August 7, 2008.

16. Leonard J. Arrington, "The Search for Truth and Meaning in Mormon History," *Dialogue: A Journal of Mormon Thought* 3, no. 2 (Summer 1968): 56–66.

17. LJA to Milton Backman, January 18, 1979; LJAHA, Series II, Box 2, fd. 1.

18. LJAD, October 15, 1974.

19. LJA to Paul E. Dahl, LDS Institute of Religion, Tucson, Arizona, February 7, 1973; LJAHA, Series II, Box 5, fd. 1.

20. LJAD, June 17, 1975. Mary Whitmer, mother of David Whitmer, one of the three witnesses, and also mother of Christian, Jacob, Peter Jr., and John Whitmer (four of the eight witnesses), was shown the plates by an angel as a blessing for assuming the extra chores of hosting Joseph Smith and Oliver Cowdery, who lived with the Whitmers while finishing the translation of the Book of Mormon. The second woman was Emma Smith, who did not see the plates but who touched them as they lay, wrapped in cloth, on the table, moved them about as she worked, and remembered the rustling sound their edges made as she ran her thumb down them.

21. Ibid., August 23, 1972.

22. Maureen Ursenbach Beecher interview, July 11, 2009.

23. She was married in 1974 to Dale Beecher but used both her maiden and married surnames in her publications.

24. Derr interview, August 7, 2008.

25. Ibid.

26. Madsen interview, June 17, 2008.

27. Beecher interview, July 11, 2009.

28. The first issue of *Exponent II*, carrying the subtitle "Am I Not a Woman and a Sister?," was published in July 1974. The periodical remains in print.

29. Claudia L. Lauper Bushman interview, January 16, 2009.

30. Claudia L. Bushman, ed., *Mormon Sisters: Women in Early Utah* (Cambridge, MA: Emmeline Press Limited, 1976).

31. Claudia L. Bushman interview, January 16, 2009.

32. Ibid. Her doctoral dissertation at Boston University, "Harriet Hanson Robinson and Her Family: A Chronicle of Nineteenth Century New England Life," was completed in 1978.

33. Cheryll Lynn May interview, August 4, 2011.

34. Mormon.org/faq/relief-society.

35. LJAD, December 31, 1973.

36. Maureen Ursenbach Beecher diary, April 4, 1978, in LJAD, April 4, 1978.

37. LJAD, May 3, 1976.

38. Carol Cornwall Madsen and Susan Staker Oman, *Sisters and Little Saints: One Hundred Years of Primary* (Salt Lake City: Deseret Book Company, 1979). Susan reverted to her birth name, Staker, after a divorce.

39. LJAD, August 18, 1978.

40. Madsen interview, June 17, 2008.

41. LJA to Children, March 22, 1981, in LJAD. As of January 2014, the BYU website, www.byu .edu, listed sixty-seven full-time faculty in the College of Religious Education, six of whom were women.

42. LJAD, January 9, 1979. Leonard does not give the source of this information, but he did not hear it directly from Dennis, who added clarifying details in June 2014. As bishop of Hingham Ward, Dennis proposed to Brent Lambert, president of the newly organized Hingham Stake and a former bishop of Hingham Ward, that he call a woman as Sunday School president. Lambert "immediately encouraged" Lythgoe, since the handbook did not specify that a man must hold the position and because "routinely new male converts served in that position even without the priesthood." The woman called "was Bonnie Brackett (now Bonnie Canfield) and she served very, very well." Dennis Hawley bishop of Foxboro Ward in the same stake, "thought it was an excellent idea, so he also called a woman as Sunday School president." A complaint from someone in his ward went to "someone at 47 E. South Temple," and Lambert was soon called to pass on the message from Elder Rex Pinegar, a Seventy, that "the Brethren thought the call in both wards was inappropriate and that both bishops should release their Sunday School presidents." He added that "the next handbook would state clearly that women should not be Sunday School presidents." Lythgoe was "very disappointed" but released Brackett as instructed. The other details in Leonard's account mystified him. Neither Lythgoe nor Hawley wrote to Elder Perry and, consequently, received no replies. Lythgoe had never heard of a discussion at the level of the Twelve. The Elder Hales in question was not Apostle Robert D. Hales, who had moved from the area before these appointments and had no connection with the Hingham Stake. Nor does Lythgoe recall saying, "We have taken a step backwards." When Dennis and his wife, Marti, moved to Salt Lake City, they belonged to the Lowell Bennion Study Group, of which Leonard was a member; the two men were good friends, and Dennis describes Leonard as consistently "warm, complimentary, and talkative." Dennis Lythgoe, email to Lavina Fielding Anderson, June 15, 2014, copy in Prince's possession. Used by permission; capitalization and abbreviations standardized. Either Leonard heard this story from an insider source who had learned independently about the involvement of General Authorities or the story had been passed on through more than one person, losing nothing in the retellings.

43. Jeff McClellan, "A Lingering Influence: Top 10 BYU Professors," *BYU Magazine*, Winter 1999, http://magazine.byu.edu/?act=view&a=172.

44. Beecher interview, July 11, 2009.

45. President Spencer W. Kimball announced the change to this policy on September 29, 1978, three months after the landmark announcement that worthy black men could be ordained to the priesthood.

46. Although Alice remembered this modest level of permission as being available on request, by the early 1980s it was strictly forbidden. In fact, before this period, nonmember fathers or LDS fathers who lacked either worthiness and/or office in the Melchizedek Priesthood to perform the blessing had been allowed to stand in the circle and help hold the baby (or, in the case of confirmations of children baptized at or over the age of eight, to likewise stand in the circle and lay hands on the child's head). However, the policy changed so that only Melchizedek Priesthood holders could participate in these ceremonies in any role, leading women to observe that church leaders would rather restrict the participation of men than allow even the limited participation of women.

47. In a 2012 Pew Research Center survey only 8 percent of LDS women thought that women should be ordained to the priesthood. http://www.pewforum.org/2012/01/12/mormons-in-america -family-life/.

48. LJAD, August 17, 1978.

49. Ibid., September 18, 1978.

50. Ibid., September 19, 1978.

51. LJA to Children, January 9, 1980, in LJAD.

52. LJAD, March 15, 1979.

53. Ibid., March 23, 1979. John M. Madsen served on the Melchizedek Priesthood MIA general board and Young Men general board prior to being called to the Second Quorum of the Seventy on June 6, 1992.

54. For a discussion of this policy, see Prince and Wright, *David O. McKay and the Rise of Modern Mormonism*, epilogue.

55. LJAD, December 26, 1973.

56. Beecher interview, July 11, 2009.

57. Meeting minutes, May 13, 1975 in LJAD.

58. LJAD, May 23, 1975.

59. Minutes of the Executives of the Historical Department, June 10, 1975, in LJAD.

60. LJAD, June 25, 1975.

61. In 1982 Durham was appointed an associate justice of the Utah Supreme Court, where she continues to serve at this date. She served as the chief justice and chair of the Utah Judicial Council from 2002 to 2012.

62. Beecher interview, July 11, 2009.

63. "Reminiscences," LJAD, September 14, 1978.

64. Beecher interview, July 11, 2009.

65. *United States Statutes at Large* 86:1523–4.

66. Neil J. Young, "'The ERA Is a Moral Issue:" The Mormon Church, LDS Women, and the Defeat of the Equal Rights Amendment," *American Quarterly* 59, no. 3 (September 2007): 623–44. The quotation is on p. 626.

67. "Equal Rights Amendment," untitled editorial by Mark E. Petersen, *Church News*, January 11, 1975, 16.

68. Ezra Taft Benson. See Young, "The ERA Is a Moral Issue," note 39.

69. LJA to Children, June 29, 1977, in LJAD.

70. LJA to Children, December 1, 1979, in LJAD.

71. LJAD, December 3, 1979.

72. Esther W. Eggertsen Peterson was perhaps the most prominent Mormon woman ever to serve in the federal government. She was appointed Assistant Secretary of Labor and Director of the United States Women's Bureau under John F. Kennedy; Special Assistant for Consumer Affairs under Lyndon B. Johnson; and Director of the Office of Consumer Affairs under Jimmy Carter. On January 16, 1981, Carter awarded her the U.S. Presidential Medal of Freedom for her work as national consumer rights advocate and consumer affairs, the first Latter-day Saint so honored and still the only LDS woman. Gordon B. Hinckley received the award in 2004.

73. Jeffrey Willis, the LDS bishop who presided over the church court, was a personnel officer with the Central Intelligence Agency at the time.

74. "Further Reflections on the Sonia Johnson Case," LJAD, December 13, 1979.

75. LJAD, January 17, 1980.

76. LJA to Children, January 23, 1980, in LJAD.

Chapter 18—First Fruits

1. LJAD, January 7, 1973.

2. James B. Allen and Thomas G. Alexander, eds., *Manchester Mormons: The Journal of William Clayton, 1840 to 1842* (Santa Barbara, CA: Peregrine Smith, 1974).

3. Dean C. Jessee, ed., *Letters of Brigham Young to His Sons* (Salt Lake City: Deseret Book, 1974).

4. Leonard J. Arrington, *Charles C. Rich: Mormon General and Western Frontiersman* (Provo, UT: Brigham Young University Press, 1974).

5. Davis Bitton, "Reflections on 1974," in LJAD, January 1, 1975.

6. LJAD, January 1, 1975.

7. Bitton, "Reflections on 1974."

8. Arrington, *Adventures of a Church Historian*, 121.

9. Lucile C. Tate, *Boyd K. Packer: A Watchman on the Tower* (Salt Lake City: Bookcraft, 1995).

10. Ronald K. Esplin interview, June 30, 2012.

11. Jeffery O. Johnson interview, February 8, 2012.

12. Boyd K. Packer, "I Say Unto You, Be One," BYU Devotional address, February 12, 1991. In *Brigham Young University 1990–91 Devotional and Fireside Speeches* (Provo, UT: Brigham Young University, 1991).

13. LJAD, July 10, 1972.

14. William G. Hartley, "The Priesthood Reform Movement, 1908–1922," *BYU Studies* 13, no. 2 (1973): 137–56.

15. LJAD, April 27, 1973.

16. Joseph Anderson to Howard W. Hunter and Bruce R. McConkie, May 1, 1973, in LJAD.

17. LJAD, December 1, 1973.

18. D. Michael Quinn, answer to "I Have a Question," *Ensign* (December 1973): 32.

19. Meeting minutes, January 22, 1974, in LJAD.

20. LJAD, February 6, 1974.

21. LJA to D. Michael Quinn, February 7, 1974; LJAHA, Series II, Box 14, fd. 7.

22. Reed C. Durham Jr. "Is There No Help for the Widow's Son?," Mormon History Association presidential address, 1974, in *Mormon Miscellaneous* 1, no. 1 (October 1975): 11–16.

23. Ibid.

24. A subsequent author was not so discreet. See David John Buerger, *The Mysteries of Godliness: A History of Mormon Temple Worship* (San Francisco: Smith Research Associates, 1994).

25. Michael W. Homer, *Joseph's Temples: The Dynamic Relationship between Freemasonry and Mormonism* (Salt Lake City: University of Utah Press, 2014), 319, 341.

26. Barbara Higdon interview, May 20, 2009.

27. Photocopy of letter, n.d., provided to me by Barbara Higdon, who, as one of the attendees, received a copy of the apologetic letter.

28. Reed C. Durham Jr. and Steven H. Heath, *Succession in the Church* (Salt Lake City: Bookcraft, Inc., 1970).

29. LJAD, December 12, 1974.

30. Response to questions from Lavina Fielding Anderson, December 7, 1981, in LJAD.

31. Sandra Tanner interview, August 8, 2008.

32. Jessee, *Letters of Brigham Young to His Sons.*

33. "Excavating the Great Basin: A Conversation with Leonard Arrington," Sunstone Symposium, Salt Lake City, August 12, 1993. Transcription of audiocassette.

34. Boyd K. Packer to First Presidency, October 24, 1974, in LJAD, attached to entry of November 27, 1974.

35. https://history.lds.org/event/three-fold-mission-of-church?lang=eng. Church president Spencer W. Kimball formalized this statement on April 3, 1981, but other church leaders had articulated it years earlier.

36. Packer, "The Mantle Is Far, Far Greater Than the Intellect," 259–78.

37. LJAD, December 3, 1974.

38. Minutes of the Executives of the Historical Department, December 3, 1974, in LJAD.

39. LJAD, December 18, 1974.

40. Ibid., December 17, 1974.

41. Ibid., December 31, 1974.

42. Minutes of the Executives of the Historical Department, January 23, 1975, in LJAD.

43. LJAD, January 1, 1976.

44. Susan Arrington Madsen, email to Gregory A. Prince, June 7, 2014.

45. Ibid.

46. Arrington, *Adventures of a Church Historian*, 88.

47. Madsen, email to Prince, June 7, 2014.

48. Cornwall and Arrington, *I'm Glad My House Burned Down*, 128, 131.

49. Carl Arrington interview, September 24, 2009.

50. Susan Arrington Madsen interview, July 29, 2012.

CHAPTER 19—RLDS

1. William Smith's ventures included a series of overtures to Brigham Young (ignored) such as rebaptism, and brief affiliations with George J. Adams, James J. Strang, Lyman Wight, Isaac Sheen, at least a half-dozen other dissidents, and founding his own church, which quickly dissolved over the issue of polygamy. Finally, in 1878, he was received into the RLDS Church on his original baptism with the office of a high priest; but his nephew Joseph III deftly kept him attached while deflecting his open lobbying for higher office, until his death fifteen years later. Kyle R. Walker, "William B. Smith and the 'Reorganites,'" *Journal of Mormon History* 39, no. 1 (Fall 2014): 73–129; Kyle R. Walker, *William Smith: In the Shadow of a Prophet* (Salt Lake City: Greg Kofford Books, 2015).

2. Edmund C. Briggs, Journal, No. 2, 1863–1864, August 11, 1863; quoted in Newell and Avery, *Mormon Enigma*, 281. Chapter 21, "Josephites and Brighamites," describes in detail the early years of the feud between the two churches.

3. Ibid., 285.

4. Paul M. Edwards interview, May 19, 2009.

5. David O. McKay, Diary, June 9, 1949, Special Collections, Marriott Library, University of Utah.

6. A. Merlin Steed to David O. McKay, January 12, 1956, in McKay Diary.

7. F. Henry Edwards to David O. McKay, in McKay Diary, April 12, 1957.

8. David O. McKay to RLDS Church, c/o Wilford Wood, June 16, 1958, in McKay Diary.

9. Ibid., March 11, 1960.

10. Ibid., December 6, 1967.

11. Ibid., September 17, 1969.

12. Richard P. Howard interview, May 27, 2010.

13. McKay, Diary, November 22, 1968.

14. *The "Reorganized" Church vs. Salvation for the Dead*, first published in 1905, and *Origin of the "Reorganized" Church and the Question of Succession*, first published in 1907. Both were reprinted numerous times over many decades as tracts used by LDS missionaries.

15. McKay, Diary, February 18, 1969.

16. Howard interview, May 27, 2010.

17. LJA to G. Wesley Johnson, October 21, 1965; LJAHA, Series IV, Box 29, fd. 1.

18. Alma R. Blair interview, May 20, 2009.

19. William D. Russell interview, May 26, 2006.

20. Executive meeting minutes, February 22, 1972 in LJAD.

21. LJAD, September 18, 1973.

22. Ibid., January 30, 1973.

23. Earl Olson to Howard W. Hunter and Bruce R. McConkie, April 1, 1974, in LJAD.

24. Paul L. Anderson interview, March 3, 2008.

25. Maureen Ursenbach Beecher interview, July 11, 2009.

26. Leonard referenced the unpublished 1831 revelation in Arrington and Bitton, *The Mormon Experience*, 195. Although there is not a consensus on the authenticity of the revelation, the fact that McConkie assumed it to be authentic adds credibility to Leonard's acceptance of it.

27. LJAD, May 29, 1974.

28. W. Grant McMurray interview, May 19, 2009.

29. Richard P. Howard interview, May 27, 2010.

30. *Courage* was published from 1970 to 1973.

31. Russell interview, May 26, 2006.

32. Edwards interview, May 19, 2009. The First Presidency's authorization of two-piece temple garments in the late 1970s allowed much more comfortable fitting options.

CHAPTER 20—STORM CLOUDS

1. F. Ross Peterson interview, September 17, 2007.

2. Minutes of the Executives of the Historical Department, July 13, 1976, in LJAD.

3. James B. Allen and Glen M. Leonard, *The Story of the Latter-day Saints* (Salt Lake City: Deseret Book, 1976), vii. The second revised edition, much expanded and updated, was issued, also by Deseret Book, in 1992.

4. Ibid., ix–x.

5. LJAD, August 18, 1976.

6. John N. Drayton, Review of *The Story of the Latter-day Saints*, by James B. Allen and Glen M. Leonard, *Sunstone* 1, no. 4 (Fall 1976): 86–88.

7. Dennis L. Lythgoe, "Artful Analysis of Mormonism," *Dialogue: A Journal of Mormon Thought* 10, no. 4 (Autumn 1977): 134–37.

8. S. George Ellsworth, Review of *The Story of the Latter-day Saints*, by James B. Allen and Glen M. Leonard, *BYU Studies* 17, no. 2 (Winter 1977): 241–46.

9. Klaus J. Hansen, Review of *The Story of the Latter-day Saints*, by James B. Allen and Glen M. Leonard, *Utah Historical Quarterly* 46, no. 1 (Winter 1978): 82–86.

10. William P. MacKinnon, Review of *The Story of the Latter-day Saints*, by James B. Allen and Glen M. Leonard, *Arizona and the West* 19, no. 3 (Autumn 1977): 272–74.

11. Lawrence Foster, Review of *The Story of the Latter-day Saints*, by James B. Allen and Glen M. Leonard, *Church History* 46, no. 3 (September 1977): 403–4.

12. Glen M. Leonard interview, July 27, 2012.

13. Ezra Taft Benson, March 28, 1976, http://speeches.byu.edu/index.php?act=viewitem&id =1148.

14. William G. Hartley interview, May 28, 2010.

15. LJAD, August 18, 1976.

16. Ibid., August 27, 1976.

17. LJA to Children, August 28, 1976, in LJAD.

18. Meeting minutes, September 1, 1976, in LJAD.

19. Ibid.

20. LJA to Children, September 4, 1976, in LJAD.

21. LJAD, September 6, 1976.

22. Ibid., September 7, 1976.

23. Ezra Taft Benson, "The Gospel Teacher and His Message," September 17, 1976, http://www .ldsces.org/content/talks/general/1976-benson-the-gospel-teacher-and-his-message__eng.pdf.

24. The *Journal of Health*, published in Philadelphia from 1830 to 1833, was the most prominent journal of the movement. It, alone, contains every aspect of the Word of Wisdom, all having been published prior to February 1833. Several speeches given on the day of national temperance observance, February 26, 1833, were published in pamphlet form, one being Thomas S. Grimke, *Address on the Patriot Character of the Temperance Reformation* (Charleston, SC: Observer Office Press, 1833).

25. Benson, "The Gospel Teacher."

26. LJAD, September 21, 1976.

27. Ibid.

28. Ibid.

29. Meeting minutes, October 5, 1976, in LJAD.

30. LJA to Mr. and Mrs. Gerald [and Carol Lynn] Pearson, October 21, 1976; photocopy in author's possession.

31. LJAD, October 22, 1976.

32. Ibid.

33. Ibid.

34. Ibid., November 24, 1976.

35. Jan Shipps interview, December 7, 2009.

36. David J. Whittaker interview, May 22, 2008.

37. George and Maurine Boyd—Maurine being Camilla Kimball's sister—met with Kimball. LJAD, June 17, 1980.

38. Glen Leonard, one of the authors, described the changes in the second printing: "The editor at Deseret Book, Lowell Durham Jr., approached us and said, 'I have worked it out with 47 East that we can go in and do a second printing, and you may make any subtle changes and corrections you want to.' Jim wanted to fix some of those words, and there were some typos and some factual errors that we corrected. So that second printing tweaked it so that the most offensive items were dealt with." Glen M. Leonard interview, July 27, 2012.

39. LJAD, January 1, 1977.

40. Kimball's deteriorating health is described in detail by his son in chapters 37 and 38 of Edward L. Kimball, *Lengthen Your Stride: The Presidency of Spencer W. Kimball, Working Draft* (Salt Lake City: Benchmark Books, 2009), 581–625.

41. The position of Emeritus General Authority was created the following year, whereupon members of the First Quorum of Seventy—of which Anderson was one—have generally been placed on emeritus status, effective at the first general conference after they reach the age of seventy.

42. LJA to Children, April 29, 1977, in LJAD.

43. A description of conditions affecting the church in Great Britain at this time is contained in Alan K. Parrish, *John A. Widtsoe: A Biography* (Salt Lake City: Deseret Book, 2003).

44. LJAD, May 26, 1977.

45. LJA to Children, May 28, 1977, in LJAD.

46. Arrington, *Adventures of a Church Historian*, 165.

47. William W. Slaughter interview, April 19, 2012.

48. For an in-depth discussion of this topic, see Prince and Wright, *David O. McKay and the Rise of Modern Mormonism*, chapter 7.

49. Lavina Fielding Anderson, interview, May 30, 2014.

50. LJAD, December 1, 1973.

51. Minutes of the Executives of the Historical Department, April 11, 1972, in LJAD.

52. LJAD, August 18, 1976.

53. Ibid., November 27, 1974.

54. Ibid., December 31, 1974.

55. Ibid., September 21, 1976.

56. LJA to Delbert L. Stapley and Howard W. Hunter, December 3, 1976, in LJAD.

57. LJAD, August 9, 1973.

58. James B. Allen interview, January 12, 2006.

59. Arrington, *Adventures of a Church Historian*, 154.

60. Richard Stephen Marshall, " 'The New Mormon History': A Senior Honors Project Summary," May 1, 1977, Department of History, University of Utah, Special Collections, Marriott Library, University of Utah; photocopy in my possession.

61. Robert B. Flanders, "Some Reflections on the New Mormon History," *Dialogue: A Journal of Mormon Thought* 9, no. 1 (Spring 1974): 34–41.

62. Leonard J. Arrington, *An Illustrated History of the History Division of the LDS Church, 1972–82* (Salt Lake City: Historian's Press, 1994), 8–13.

63. Marshall, "The New Mormon History," 13, 82–83.

64. Ibid., 3, 18.

65. Davis Bitton, "Reflections on the Historical Department," in LJAD, January 1, 1978.

66. LJAD, August 11, 1977.

67. Ibid., December 8, 1977.

68. G. Homer Durham, quoted in ibid., February 24, 1978.

69. LJAD, March 14, 1978.

70. First Presidency, by Spencer W. Kimball and N. Eldon Tanner, to G. Homer Durham, April 5, 1978, in LJAD.

71. LJAD, April 5, 1978.

72. Ibid., May 4, 1978.

73. Ibid., May 8, 1978.

74. Staff Meeting Minutes, May 4, 1978, in LJAD.

75. LJAD, May 8, 1978.

76. Bruce Blumell interview, June 30, 2012.

77. LJAD, May 26, 1978.

78. Minutes of the Executives, June 29, 1978, in LJAD.

79. LJAD, September 6, 1978.

80. Ibid., October 9, 1978.

81. Scott Kenney Journal, December 14, 1978.

82. Leonard J. Arrington, "Reflections on History Division During 1978," in LJAD, January 1, 1979.

83. Maureen Ursenbach Beecher interview, July 11, 2009.

84. Jan Shipps interview, December 8, 2009.

CHAPTER 21—THE REVELATION

1. Leonard J. Arrington, "Proof of the Book of Mormon," speech given ca. 1933 in LJAD. Leonard inserted the typescript of the speech at the beginning of records for 1933.

2. LJA to Children, August 10, 1989, in LJAD.

3. Undated and untitled document, LJAHA, Series X, Box 5, fd. 13.

4. Ibid.

5. LJA to Kenneth W. Cameron, March 19, 1984; LJAHA, Series X, Box 6, fd. 1.

6. LJA to Grace, August 22, 1944, LJAD.

7. LJA to Grace, August 11, 1945, LJAD.

8. Lester E. Bush, "Compilation on The Negro in Mormonism" (unpublished manuscript, 1973), 262. Copy in the Lester E. Bush Papers, Special Collections, Marriott Library, University of Utah.

9. Ibid., 261–62.

10. LJA to Gaylon Caldwell, Department of Political Science, BYU, November 22, 1954; LJAHA, Series IV, Box 16, fd. 5.

11. LJA to Thomas O'Dea, October 7, 1957; LJAHA, Series V, Box 3, fd. 6.

12. Bob Hine to LJA, December 12, 1969; LJAHA, Series X, Box 77, fd. 1.

13. Arrington, *Adventures of a Church Historian*, 183.

14. LJA to Carl Arrington, August 3, 1969, in LJAD. Also Taggart, *Mormonism's Negro Policy.*

15. For a detailed analysis of this episode, see Prince and Wright, *David O. McKay and the Rise of Modern Mormonism*, chapter 4, "Blacks, Civil Rights, and the Priesthood."

16. The policy began with Brigham Young following the death of Joseph Smith. See Lester E. Bush Jr., "Mormonism's Negro Doctrine: An Historical Overview," *Dialogue: A Journal of Mormon Thought* 8, no. 1 (Spring 1973): 11–68. The groundbreaking position paper posted on the LDS Church's website, www.lds.org, in December 2013 is unprecedented in the candor with which it treats this subject. And yet, while it acknowledges the findings of Bush's *Dialogue* article, it does not reference his article, nor any article published in *Dialogue*. Given the fact that the article was the definitive work on the subject and is still hailed as a turning point in LDS history, one must conclude that the church has a formal policy against quoting *anything* published in *Dialogue*.

17. Edwin B. Firmage interview, June 6, 1995. Firmage is Brown's grandson.

18. See entries in the David O. McKay Diaries beginning September 10, 1969. The diaries are in the Special Collections division of the J. Willard Marriott Library, University of Utah.

19. LJAD, February 17, 1972.

20. William G. Hartley interview, May 28, 2010.

21. Janath Cannon to Lester Bush, November 14, 1972; quoted in Lester Bush, "Writing 'Mormonism's Negro Doctrine: An Historical Overview' (1973): Context and Reflections, 1998," *Journal of Mormon History* 25, no. 1 (Spring 1999): 229–71; the quotation is on p. 247.

22. LJA to Boyd K. Packer, November 14, 1972, in LJAD.

23. Ramona Bernhard interview, December 5, 1998.

24. LJAD, January 30, 1973.

25. Lester E. Bush to Gregory A. Prince, October 25, 2008.

26. Davis Bitton to Lester E. Bush, May 15, 1973. This and subsequent Bush correspondence from 1973 are contained in Bush's October 25, 2008, letter to Gregory A. Prince.

27. Lester E. Bush to Davis Bitton, May 22, 1973.

28. LJAD, May 31, 1973.

29. Lester E. Bush Jr. interview, October 24, 2008.

30. Bush to Prince, October 25, 2008.

31. LJAD, June 1, 1973. Twenty-five years later, Bush complied with Leonard's request. See Bush, "Writing 'Mormonism's Negro Doctrine: An Historical Overview,'" 229–71.

32. Robert Rees, notes of a conversation with Robert K. Thomas, June 28, 1973; quoted in Bush, "Writing 'Mormonism's Negro Doctrine: An Historical Overview,'" 262.

33. Lester E. Bush to Leonard J. Arrington, August 16, 1973.

34. Bush, "Mormonism's Negro Doctrine: An Historical Overview," 11–68. Significantly, this single article was so important that, even after the issue sold out, it was reprinted as a monograph and stayed in print until *Dialogue* back issues became available on the Internet.

35. Bush to Prince, December 6, 2013.

36. Bush to Prince, October 25, 2008.

37. LJAD, December 30, 1973.

38. Ibid., December 31, 1973.

39. Edward L. Kimball (Spencer W. Kimball's son), "Spencer W. Kimball and the Revelation on Priesthood," *BYU Studies* 47, no. 2 (Spring 2008): 5–78.

40. Kimball called Fyans as an assistant to the Twelve in April 1974, only four months into Kimball's presidency.

41. J. Thomas Fyans interview, June 3, 1995. The term "the blood" was commonly used by LDS missionaries in Latin America at the time. It referred to the church policy wherein "one drop" of "Negro blood" would disqualify a man from ordination to the priesthood.

42. LJAD, September 18, 1974.

43. See Prince and Wright, *David O. McKay and the Rise of Modern Mormonism*, chapter 4, for a description of the Nigerian initiative.

44. Arrington, *Adventures of a Church Historian*, 182. Arrington does not mention how he learned about the Martins' sacrificial obedience.

45. See Prince and Wright, *David O. McKay and the Rise of Modern Mormonism*, chapter 4, for a description of the South African trip.

46. Renee Pyott Carlson interview, June 2, 1994.

47. John Baker interview, October 26, 1994.

48. *Look* published an article by Jeff Nye, "Memo from a Mormon: In Which a Troubled Young Man Raises the Question of His Church's Attitude Toward Negroes," in the October 22, 1963, issue, pages 74–79. On page 79 is an "Editor's Note" that quotes Joseph Fielding Smith, then president of the Quorum of the Twelve Apostles, as having said, "'Darkies' are wonderful people, and they have their

place in our Church." Smith said nothing in the article about blacks ultimately being given the priesthood.

49. LJAD, June 9, 1978.

50. Leonard J. Arrington, "LJA Predictions for the year 1978, made January 1978," in LJAD, January 1, 1978.

51. Paul H. Dunn interview, January 11, 1997.

52. LJA to Children, June 9, 1978, in LJAD.

53. LJAD, June 9, 1978.

54. "Meeting with Staff Members," Ibid., June 12, 1978.

55. Ibid.

56. LJA to Children, June 15, 1978, in LJAD.

57. Arrington, *Adventures of a Church Historian*, 176.

58. Account provided by Gil Warner to LJA, in LJAD, June 18, 1978. Leonard's diary entry states that Gil and his wife Nedra "had ridden a bus to St. George to attend a meeting of the board of some corporation. Along on the trip also, for the same purpose, were Boyd Packer and his wife. For a part of the trip, Gil was able to sit next to Brother Packer. Gil asked him if he could share some of the experiences which led up to the announcement of the revelation on the priesthood for blacks."

59. Typescript prepared by George Pace and given to LJA, in LJAD, June 18, 1978. Pace was recounting what William Pope, president of the BYU 7th Stake, had said at a Sacrament meeting of the Oak Hills 5th Ward on June 18, 1978, the same day that Pace wrote the account. "President Pope indicated he had permission to quote Elder McConkie and that Elder McConkie had shared this information at a family gathering."

60. Apparently 1977.

61. Leonard inserted this note in the narrative: "Elder McConkie reportedly said that during this experience he came to understand, for the first time, just what was meant by 'cloven tongues of fire.' "

62. The First Presidency consisted of three men. The absence of Mark Petersen, who was out of the country, and Delbert Stapley, who was in the hospital, accounted for the total of thirteen.

63. See Prince and Wright, *David O. McKay and the Rise of Modern Mormonism*, chapter 4, for the statement by Grant, which came in response to a question from McKay.

64. Conversation between Jay Todd and Joseph Fielding McConkie, LJAD, June 27, 1978. Dunn's account, as one of the Seventies in attendance, explicitly states that the apostles were not present; however, this account from Joseph Fielding McConkie based on his father's version in the family meeting, reports the presence of at least Bruce R. McConkie. I have not found any record documenting who was present at either and/or both meetings, so the discrepancy remains. Perhaps President Kimball asked McConkie to be present and to speak to the issue because of his well-known writings supporting a racist position. His fervent support of the revelation, like President Romney's, almost certainly contributed to the emotional intensity of the experience.

65. LJAD, July 5, 1978.

66. "While Camilla was working in the garden in the late morning, she heard the telephone ring and came in to answer it. Her daughter, Olive Beth, asked excitedly, 'Have you heard the news?' 'What news?' 'About the revelation that all worthy men can receive the priesthood!' " Kimball, *Lengthen Your Stride*, 364.

67. LJAD, July 25, 1978. Ed Kimball wrote, "Her first thought was that Spencer's anxiety had arisen from fear of possible schism." Ibid.

68. LJA to Children, September 26, 1987, in LJAD. Arrington does not give the daughter's name.

69. Arrington, *Adventures of a Church Historian*, 176–77.

CHAPTER 22—DISASSEMBLY

1. Davis Bitton, "Report on 1979," in LJAD, January 1, 1980.

2. LJAD, October 11, 1977. Rodman Paul (1912–1987) was a historian specializing in the American West. He served as a press reader of Leonard's manuscript for Knopf.

3. Ibid., November 4, 1977.

4. Ibid.

5. LJA to Children, November 19, 1977, in LJAD.

6. LJA to JoAnn Bair, September 7, 1978; LJAHA, Series II, Box 2, fd. 1.

7. Leonard J. Arrington, "The Founding of the LDS Church Historical Department," in Neilson and Walker, *Reflections of a Mormon Historian*, 114–15. Unfortunately, Knopf's letter is not among Leonard's papers and may no longer be extant.

8. "Review of *The Mormon Experience*," *Publishers Weekly*, January 29, 1979, unpaginated clipping in LJAD.

9. LJAD, March 23, 1979.

10. Elmer J. Culp to G. Homer Durham, August 1, 1980. The paragraph was contained in a letter from G. Homer Durham to LJA, August 5, 1980, in LJAD, under the same date.

11. LJAD, May 29, 1974.

12. At the time, Marvin J. Ashton was also a member of the Quorum of the Twelve Apostles.

13. LJAD, March 15, 1978.

14. Ibid., March 23, 1978.

15. Ibid., April 5, 1978.

16. Ibid., April 6, 1978.

17. Ibid., May 4, 1978.

18. Ibid., May 8, 1978.

19. Ibid., September 14, 1978.

20. Scott G. Kenney Journal, October 23, 1979; photocopy in my possession courtesy of Kenney. Kenney was working under Leonard's direction at the time and wrote contemporaneous diary entries.

21. LJAD, July 31, 1979.

22. Kenney Journal, November 22, 1979.

23. Family Meeting held the night of December 25, 1979, in LJAD January 1, 1980.

24. Kenney Journal, January 21, 1980.

25. A later diary entry noted that Ashton was among a group of apostles who met to discuss the fate of the Sesquicentennial Series.

26. Although two more manuscripts had been turned in, apparently they were still being reviewed and revised at the level below that of the General Authority reader.

27. LJA to Marvin Ashton, April 10, 1980, in LJAD.

28. LJAD, April 21, 1980.

29. Meeting with Lowell Durham Jr., April 22, 1980, in LJAD, April 24, 1980.

30. LJAD, April 24, 1980.

31. Ibid., June 12, 1980.

32. Leonard gave no reason why the other two completed manuscripts, by Thomas Alexander and Richard Cowan, had not yet been approved.

33. Ibid., June 19, 1980; emphasis his.

34. Ibid., August 9, 1980.

35. Ibid., August 14, 1980.

36. Ibid., December 1, 1980.

37. Ibid., December 29, 1980.

38. Ibid., December 30, 1980.

39. Deseret Book Company eventually published three of the volumes: Milton V. Backman Jr. *The Heavens Resound: A History of the Latter-day Saints in Ohio 1830–1838* (1983); R. Lanier Britsch,

Unto the Islands of the Sea: A History of the Latter-day Saints in the Pacific (1986); and Glen M.
Leonard, *Nauvoo: A Place of Peace, A People of Promise* (2002).

40. LJAD, December 30, 1980.

41. Ibid., February 8, 1981.

42. Carl Arrington interview, September 24, 2009.

43. Carol Cornwall Madsen interview, June 17, 2008.

44. Kenney Journal, January 18, 1979.

45. Ibid., October 23, 1979.

46. Ibid., November 28, 1979.

47. LJAD, March 27, 1980. After being denied access to the Joseph F. Smith papers, Kenney
arranged with representatives of the Wilford Woodruff family to publish a nine-volume typescript
edition in 1983.

48. Ibid., June 19, 1980.

49. LJA, Untitled typescript, August 7, 1981; LJAHA, Series XII, Box 121, fd. 3.

50. LJAD, October 3, 1978.

51. Ibid., October 9, 1978.

52. "Annual Comment on the History Division," in LJAD, January 1, 1980.

53. James B. Allen interview, January 12, 2006.

54. Glen M. Leonard interview, July 27, 2012. Glen became the assistant director of the Museum of
Church History and Art (now the LDS Church History Museum), which had been constructed under
the direction of Florence Smith Jacobsen, the former general president of the Young Women's Mutual
Improvement Association and first director of the church's Historic Sites and Arts Division. When she
retired in 1985, Glen succeeded her as the museum's director, a position he held until his retirement.

55. LJAD, August 6, 1981.

56. Ibid., July 31, 1979.

57. Kenney Journal, October 23, 1979.

58. Lester E. Bush to Gregory A. Prince, July 19, 1981.

59. Kenney Journal, November 27, 1979.

60. "Staff Journal," August 9, 1979, quoted in Lavina Fielding Anderson, *Doves and Serpents: The
Activities of Leonard Arrington as Church Historian, 1972–1982* (Salt Lake City: Privately Published,
1982), 683.

61. LJAD, August 6, 1981.

62. McMurrin served prior to the creation of the Department of Education. As Commissioner of
Education, he held the position that today would be the Secretary of Education.

63. Ibid., February 23, 1979.

64. Ibid., May 22, 1979.

65. LJA to Gordon B. Hinckley, December 21, 1981, in LJAD.

66. First Presidency to LJA, January 25, 1982, in LJAD.

67. LJAD, February 2, 1982.

68. L. Dwight Israelsen interview, January 15, 2006. Leonard had, in keeping with his list of
"approved projects," personally carried on the updated Journal History of the Church—the
chronological scrapbook-like compilation that Andrew Jenson had reconstructed from 1830. In late
1979, this project was reassigned, presumably as part of Elder Durham's shifts, to Ronald O. Barney
of the archival staff. Although Leonard's diary and correspondence clarify that he did not learn of his
official "release" as church historian until the scrambled backtracking of the First Presidency letter of
February 1982, the psychologically important point communicated in Israelsen's memory is that the
change violated church protocol and tradition—not to mention common respect—by imposing the
earlier "release" date on Leonard and by requiring that he agree publicly with the cobbled-up
version.

69. "Annual Comment on the History Division," LJAD, January 1, 1980.

70. LJAD, June 19, 1980.

71. "Report of the Historical Department, 1976–1980," LJAD, January 1, 1981.

72. Kenney Journal, July 1, 1980.

73. G. Homer Durham to LJA, August 5, 1980.

74. Family meeting held December 22, 1980, in LJAD, January 1, 1981.

75. LJAD, July 6, 1981.

76. Earl E. Olson interview, January 17, 2006.

77. Robert B. Flanders interview, May 18, 2009.

78. N. George Daines interview, January 16, 2006.

79. LJAD, October 9, 1978.

80. Ibid., July 31, 1979.

81. Kenney Journal, October 23, 1979.

82. LJAD, December 29, 1980. From 1961 to 1970, Durham wrote a monthly article for the *Improvement Era*, generally on world events, under the series title "These Times." The column was discontinued in 1971 when the *Ensign* replaced the *Improvement Era* as the church's magazine for adults.

83. Ibid., August 6, 1981.

84. Ibid., October 9, 1978.

85. G. Homer Durham Journal, "Closing Thoughts," December 1979. I am indebted to his son, Dr. George Durham, for providing me a copy of the journal entry.

86. George H. Dunham II interview, January 25, 2011.

87. Robert J. Woodford, *The Historical Development of the Doctrine and Covenants* (PhD diss., Brigham Young University, 1974).

88. LJAD, July 27, 1982.

89. Anderson, *Doves and Serpents*, 963.

CHAPTER 23—WHAT WENT WRONG?

1. Jerald and Sandra Tanner, founders of Modern Microfilm, later renamed Utah Lighthouse Ministry; H. Michael Marquardt, author of several books on Mormon history and biography with a particular specialty in the Joseph Smith period; and Fred C. Collier, author of several dozen books and pamphlets on Mormon history and theology.

2. Leonard J. Arrington, "Appraisal of My Service as Church Historian," in LJAD, September 4, 1981.

3. B. Carmon Hardy, *Solemn Covenant: The Mormon Polygamous Passage* (Urbana: University of Illinois Press, 1992). In an appendix, "Lying for the Lord," Hardy discusses dishonesty as the defensive strategy of Latter-day Saints who were under intense federal and judicial pressure against plural marriage and who went "on the underground" to avoid prosecution. Men and women created false identities, taught their children to lie about who their parents were, and otherwise broke the law (of man) to enable them to keep the "higher law" (of God). Part of the pattern was internal misrepresentations, with public statements made by some General Authorities contradicting the private counsel they gave in other settings, leading to intense confusion about what constituted "obedience" and feelings of betrayal and abandonment. It is ironic that the term "the underground" (meaning hiding from law officers in the 1880s) was revived to describe the circulation of otherwise unavailable manuscripts in the 1960–1970s).

4. Sandra Tanner interview, August 8, 2008.

5. Bitton, "Ten Years in Camelot," 17.

6. Ronald K. Esplin interview, June 30, 2012.

7. Arrington, *Adventures of a Church Historian*, 63–64.

8. Esplin interview, June 30, 2012.

9. Davis Bitton interview, August 11, 2006.

10. William W. Slaughter interview, April 19, 2012.

11. Ezra Taft Benson and Mark Petersen.

12. Leonard J. Arrington, untitled document, 1992, in LJAHA, Series X, Box 16, fd. 1.

13. LJAD, July 6, 1981.

14. Untitled, undated entry, in LJAHA, Series X, Box 11, fd. 5.

15. Carl Arrington interview, September 24, 2009.

16. Foster, "Career Apostates," 35–60.

17. Bitton, "Ten Years in Camelot," 16–17.

18. LJAD, June 19, 1980.

19. LJA to Children, July 28, 1989, in LJAD.

20. Esplin interview, June 30, 2012.

21. LJA to Children, July 28, 1989, in LJAD.

22. Leonard J. Arrington, untitled document, 1992, LJAHA, Series X, Box 16, fd. 1.

23. James L. Clayton interview, August 8, 2008.

24. Richard E. Bennett interview, May 29, 2010.

25. Hugh B. Brown, quoted in Esplin, interview, June 30, 2012. Esplin does not explain whether he heard this comment directly from Brown or second-hand.

26. Richard W. Sadler interview, August 5, 2011.

27. David J. Whittaker interview, May 22, 2008.

28. Esplin interview, June 30, 2012.

29. Earl E. Olson interview, January 17, 2006.

30. Slaughter interview, April 19, 2012.

31. Esplin interview, June 30, 2012.

32. Another factor that worked to the advantage of those writing objective history was Benson's lapse into dementia, which, according to a grandson, robbed him completely of intellectual functioning during the final years of his life. See http://www.lds-mormon.com/benson1.shtml.

33. Arrington, *Adventures of a Church Historian*, 163.

34. F. Ross Peterson interview, September 17, 2007.

35. David J. Whittaker interview, May 22, 2008.

36. Ronald O. Barney interview, November 10, 2011.

37. Richard L. Bushman interview, January 16, 2009.

38. Jan Shipps interview, December 8, 2009.

39. Richard P. Howard interview, May 27, 2010.

40. Lester E. Bush Jr. interview, October 24, 2008.

41. Ibid.

42. Whittaker interview, May 22, 2008.

43. Walker, Turley, and Leonard, *Massacre at Mountain Meadows*.

Chapter 24—Grace's Decline

1. Cornwall and Arrington, *I'm Glad My House Burned Down*, 129.

2. LJA to Children, January 8, 1976, in LJAD.

3. LJAD, February 10, 1976.

4. Ibid., March 31, 1976.

5. LJA to Children, September 4, 1976, in LJAD.

6. Maureen Ursenbach Beecher interview, July 11, 2009.

7. Susan Arrington Madsen interview, July 29, 2012.

8. Anderson, *Doves and Serpents*, 676.

9. LJA to Children, April 15, 1981, in LJAD.

10. LJA to Children, April 29, 1981, in LJAD.

11. LJAD, January 20 and 29, 1982.

12. LJAD, February 13, 1982.

13. LJA to Col. P. J. and Mrs. Mary Lacey, May 13, 1982; LJAHA, Series II, Box 10, fd. 4.

14. Both Leonard and Grace referred to this experience in their diary entries for that date, albeit tangentially. Grace's biographer elaborated on the ceremony. Rebecca F. Cornwall, *The Grace of Our Lord Was With Her: Grace Fort Arrington, 1943 to 1946 and 1977 to 1982* (Salt Lake City: Privately distributed, 1982), 44.

15. Instituted in Nauvoo by Joseph Smith himself, the administration of this ritual at a time when Leonard was overwhelmed personally and humiliated professionally was a quiet but compelling reminder that the church's prophet, seer, and revelator viewed him and Grace as fully worthy of exaltation, not—like some of that same prophet's associates—as a danger to the church. See David John Buerger, " 'The Fulness of the Priesthood': The Second Anointing in Latter-day Saint Theology and Practice," *Dialogue: A Journal of Mormon Thought* 16 (Spring 1983): 10–44.

16. LJAD, March 16, 1982.

17. Madsen interview, March 25, 2010.

18. LJAD, March 28 and April 7, 1982.

19. Madsen interview, July 29, 2012.

CHAPTER 25—TRANSITIONS

1. Arrington, *Magic Valley Pioneers*, 14.

2. LJA to "Morris and Frances," in LJAD, March 31, 1982.

3. James Arrington interview, April 12, 2009.

4. LJAD, June 18, 1982.

5. LJA to Children, July 30, 1982, in LJAD.

6. LJA to Children, September 10, 1982, in LJAD.

7. LJA to Children, July 4, 1980, in LJAD.

8. LJA to Children, October 22, 1980, in LJAD.

9. Davis Bitton to LJA, February 9, 1993; LJAHA, Series X, Box 121, fd. 1.

10. Arrington, *Adventures of a Church Historian*, 214.

11. For a complete narrative of Kimball's health challenges, see Kimball, *Lengthen Your Stride.* Although for lengthy stretches Kimball was incapable of acting in his office, he lived for five years following Leonard's diary entry.

12. LJAD, June 30, 1980. The institute's name underwent minor changes, ending up the Joseph Fielding Smith Institute for Latter-day Saint History. Further, despite Leonard's speculation about Oaks's replacement by Holland, Oaks's resignation was awkwardly managed, coming abruptly and leaving him without a job until the BYU Law School hastily supplied an office and a position. The situation was resolved more gracefully later the same year when Governor Scott Matheson appointed Oaks to the Utah Supreme Court, a position that he assumed on January 1, 1981. He was still holding the position when the ailing Spencer W. Kimball appointed him to the Quorum of the Twelve in 1984. Kimball died the next year.

13. Ibid., July 7, 1980.

14. Ibid., August 25, 1980.

15. Davis Bitton interview, August 11, 2006.

16. James B. Allen interview, January 12, 2006.

17. William G. Hartley interview, May 28, 2010.

18. LJAD, June 30, 1980.

19. Ibid., July 15, 1980.

20. Henry B. Eyring was then serving as Commissioner of Church Education for the LDS Church, a position that oversaw the church's three universities—now BYU–Provo, BYU–Idaho, and BYU–Hawaii—in addition to the seminaries and institutes of religion.

21. LJA to Martin Hickman, February 18, 1982; LJAHA, Series II, Box 8, fd. 4.

22. Jeffrey R. Holland to LJA, February 23, 1982; LJAHA, Series III, Box 15, fd. 7. Jae Ballif was BYU provost.

23. LJA to Children, February 27, 1982.

24. Martin B. Hickman to LJA, March 5, 1982; LJAHA, Series III, Box 15, fd. 7.

25. LJAD, July 27, 1982.

26. Robert Thomas was then BYU's academic vice president.

27. LJA to Children, May 23, 1980; LJAHA, Series X, Box 102, fd. 9.

28. LJA to Children, March 10, 1985, in LJAD.

29. LJAD, November 18, 1985. Christine Rigby Arrington was married to Leonard's son Carl at the time.

30. Arrington, *Adventures of a Church Historian*, 193–94. The functional chair of the Committee for Strengthening Members was William O. Nelson, Benson's personal aide, although this committee technically functioned under the direction of two apostles.

31. D. Michael Quinn interview, December 5, 2005.

32. LJAD, June 5, 1982. Stanford Cazier, who began his academic career at Utah State University, had been president of Chico State in California, then returned to USU as its president.

33. *The Eighty-Ninth Annual Commencement Ceremonies, Utah State University, June 5, 1982*, p. 11.

34. Initially called the Sunstone Theological Symposium and begun in 1979, the main symposium is held each summer in or near Salt Lake City, attracting hundreds of participants and dozens of speakers on a wide range of topics relating to Mormonism.

35. LJA to Children, August 29, 1982, in LJAD. The term "closet doubter" was the term coined by Jeff Burton, an engineer in Bountiful, who devoted more than two decades to helping troubled Mormons find ways of negotiating a relationship that allowed them to remain authentic yet attached and contributing members, on their own terms. He presented frequently at Sunstone and also self-published *For Those Who Doubt*, suggesting helpful approaches and scenarios that would reduce tensions for more orthodox family members and church leaders.

36. LJAD, November 21, 1983.

37. James Arrington interview, April 12, 2009.

38. See Prince and Wright, *David O. McKay and the Rise of Modern Mormonism*, chapter 1.

39. Max B. Zimmer to LJA, June 11, 1985, in LJAD.

40. See Mary Lythgoe Bradford, *Lowell L. Bennion: Teacher, Counselor, Humanitarian* (Salt Lake City: Dialogue Foundation, 1995), chapter 8.

41. Emma Lou Thayne interview, April 11, 2009.

42. James B. Allen interview, January 12, 2006.

43. Stanford O. Cazier interview, January 15, 2006.

44. Carl Arrington interview, September 24, 2009.

45. William A. ("Bert") Wilson interview, August 12, 2009.

46. LJA to Children, May 11, 1982, in LJAD.

47. James Arrington interview, April 12, 2009.

48. LJAD, September 1, 1983.

49. Harriet Horne Arrington interview, June 15, 2008.

50. LJA to Children, September 8, 1983, in LJAD.

51. LJA to Children, October 10, 1983, in LJAD.

52. LJAD, November 21, 1983.

53. Lavina Fielding Anderson interview, March 3, 2008.

54. When the author interviewed Harriet, she was circumspect about discussing her relationship with Leonard's children, limiting her remarks to, "They have given me so much difficulty. But I didn't know any of them." Harriet Horne Arrington interview, June 15, 2008.

55. James Arrington interview, April 12, 2009.

56. Jill Mulvay Derr interview, August 7, 2008.

57. Elbert E. Peck interview, June 17, 2008.

58. LJA to Children, October 22, 1980, in LJAD.

59. Newell G. Bringhurst interview, May 22, 2008.

60. Davis Bitton to LJA, February 9, 1993; LJAHA, Series X, Box 121, fd. 1.

61. LJA to Children, June 21, 1986, in LJAD.

62. After Leonard retired from BYU, his long-time associate Thomas Alexander took his place as the Lemuel Hardison Redd Jr. Professor of Western American History.

63. F. Ross Peterson interview, September 17, 2007.

64. Earl E. Olson interview, January 17, 2006.

65. James B. Allen interview, January 12, 2006.

66. LJAD, August 7, 1981.

67. LJA to Children, February 27, 1982, in LJAD.

68. LJA to Children, March 5, 1982; LJAHA, Series X, Box 102, fd. 11.

69. Bringhurst interview, May 22, 2008. It took several years, but Bringhurst published *Saints, Slaves, and Blacks: The Changing Place of Black People within Mormonism* (Westport, CT: Greenwood Press, 1981) and *Brigham Young and the Expanding American Frontier* (Boston: Little Brown & Co., 1986), plus numerous articles on these topics and on Fawn Brodie.

70. L. Dwight Israelsen interview, January 15, 2006.

71. William W. Slaughter interview, April 19, 2012.

CHAPTER 26—BRIGHAM YOUNG: AMERICAN MOSES

1. LJA to Martin Hickman, February 17, 1981; LJAHA, Series II, Box 8, fd. 4.

2. LJAD, May 3, 1985.

3. LJA to Wendell Ashton, February 22, 1973; LJAHA, Series II, Box 1, fd. 9.

4. "Statement on the Brigham Young Biography," LJAHA, Series X, Box 3, fd. 1.

5. LJA to Children, January 27, 1978; LJAHA, Series X, Box 102, fd. 7.

6. LJA to Spencer W. Kimball, May 1, 1979; LJAD.

7. Francis M. Gibbons, Secretary to the First Presidency, to LJA, May 11, 1979, in LJAD.

8. LJAD, May 3, 1985.

9. LJAD, June 11, 1989. It was published several months before Kimball's death. Kimball's son Edward, in his definitive biography of his father, wrote, "Camilla [Spencer's wife] told Arrington that she had read the book to Spencer and he was pleased with it." Kimball, *Lengthen Your Stride . . . Working Draft*, 297.

10. LJAD, June 29, 1979.

11. LJA to Hickman, February 17, 1981.

12. LJA to Children, April 15, 1981, in LJAD.

13. LJAD, May 3, 1985.

14. Ibid., June 1, 1983.

15. Leonard J. Arrington, *Brigham Young: American Moses* (New York: Alfred A. Knopf, 1985).

16. Maureen Ursenbach Beecher interview, July 11, 2009.

17. Howard R. Lamar interview, February 23, 2007.

18. F. Ross Peterson interview, September 17, 2007.

19. Ronald K. Esplin, "The Emergence of Brigham Young and the Twelve to Mormon Leadership" (PhD diss., Brigham Young University, 1981).

20. Jan Shipps, Review of *Brigham Young: American Moses*, by Leonard J. Arrington, in *Journal of American History* 73, no. 1 (June 1986): 190–91.

21. Jan Shipps interview, December 7, 2009.

22. Ibid.

23. Gene A. Sessions interview, August 7, 2011. Donald Moorman was a professor at Weber State College in Ogden, Utah. He died in 1980, never having published a Brigham Young biography.

24. Edward Leo Lyman interview, October 8, 2008. Lyman's revised dissertation was published as *Political Deliverance: The Mormon Quest for Utah Statehood* (Urbana: University of Illinois Press, 1986); a revised edition is forthcoming at this writing.

25. Shipps, Review of *Brigham Young: American Moses*, 191.

26. James B. Allen interview, January 12, 2006.

27. Carl Arrington interview, September 24, 2009.

28. LJAD, July 6, 1981.

29. Shipps, Review of *Brigham Young: American Moses*, 191; emphasis hers.

30. Bringhurst, *Brigham Young and the Expanding American Frontier*.

31. Newell G. Bringhurst interview, May 22, 2008.

32. Floyd A. O'Neil interview, June 16, 2008.

33. Melvin T. Smith, Review of *Brigham Young: American Moses*, by Leonard J. Arrington, in *Dialogue: A Journal of Mormon Thought* 20, no. 3 (Fall 1987): 171–72.

34. Ronald W. Walker, Richard E. Turley Jr., and Glen M. Leonard, *Massacre at Mountain Meadows: An American Tragedy* (New York: Oxford University Press, 2008). The church now maintains the site of the massacre, with a monument dedicated by Gordon B. Hinckley; but the subject continues to be controversial. See also Will Bagley's indictment of Brigham Young in *Blood of the Prophets: Brigham Young and the Massacre at Mountain Meadows* (Norman: University of Oklahoma Press, 2002); the follow-up documentary history by Will Bagley and David L. Bigler, eds., *Innocent Blood: Essential Narratives of the Mountain Meadows Massacre* (Norman: Arthur H. Clark, an imprint of the University of Oklahoma Press, 2008), and Shannon A. Novak, *House of Mourning: A Biocultural History of the Mountain Meadows Massacre* (Salt Lake City: University of Utah, 2008), which documents that uneasiness and possible cover-ups are not a thing of the past. Also relevant in establishing the mood of fear and zealotry in Utah is William P. MacKinnon, *At Sword's Point, Part 1. A Documentary History of the Utah War to 1858* (Norman: Arthur H. Clark, an imprint of the University of Oklahoma Press, 2008).

35. Harold T. Muir, Review of *Brigham Young: American Moses*, by Leonard J. Arrington, in *John Whitmer Historical Association Journal* 6 (1986): 77–80.

36. Robert Kent Fielding interview, May 6, 2009.

37. A scholarly treatment of the subject is David John Buerger, "The Adam-God Doctrine," *Dialogue: A Journal of Mormon Thought* 15, no. 1 (Spring 1982): 14–58.

38. Muir, Review of *Brigham Young: American Moses*, 80.

39. LJA to Carl and Chris Arrington, September 28, 1979, in LJAD.

40. Muir, Review of *Brigham Young: American Moses*, 78.

41. Ibid., 80.

42. Richard L. Bushman interview, January 16, 2009.

CHAPTER 27—CONTROLLING THE STORY

1. Nadine Hansen interview, October 22, 2013. Almost thirty-five years after Sonia Johnson's excommunication, Kate Kelly, a Washington, D.C., attorney who was encouraging the priesthood ordination of Mormon women, was excommunicated June 2, 2014. Hansen drafted a brief critiquing the procedural errors in her disciplinary council. See Nadine R. Hansen, "Statement in support of Kathleen Marie Kelly, to: Mark M. Harrison, Kent Stevenson, Steve Moffit, Vienna Ward, Oakton Stake, Church of Jesus Christ of Latter-day Saints, June 18, 2014, http://ordainwomen.org/wp-content/uploads/2014/06/Brief-Submitted-by-Nadine-Hansen-in-Defense-of-Kate-Kelly.pdf.

2. *The Church and the Proposed Equal Rights Amendment: A Moral Issue*, 3; center insert in February 1980 *Ensign* with its own cover so that it could be removed from the staples.

3. Richard Sherlock, "Campus in Crisis: BYU, 1911," *Sunstone* 4 (January/February 1979): 10–16.

4. Louise Degn, "Mormon Women and Depression," *Sunstone* 4 (March/April 1979): 16–26.

5. Richard Sherlock, "Faith and History: The Snell Controversy," *Dialogue: A Journal of Mormon Thought* 12 (Spring 1979): 27–41.

6. Thane Young (interviewer), "Mixed Messages on the Negro Doctrine: An Interview with Lester Bush," *Sunstone* 4 (May/June 1979): 8–15.

7. Newell G. Bringhurst, "Elijah Abel and the Changing Status of Blacks within Mormonism," *Dialogue: A Journal of Mormon Thought* 12, no. 2 (Summer 1979): 22–36.

8. Edward H. Ashment, "The Book of Abraham Facsimiles: A Reappraisal," *Sunstone* 4, nos. 4–5 (May/June 1979): 33–48. In 2014 the church posted on its official website a position paper entitled "Translation and Historicity of the Book of Abraham." Without ever mentioning Ashment's *Sunstone* article, the paper steps back from the literal translation model, while still affirming that the church "embraces the book of Abraham as scripture." It acknowledges that "none of the characters on the papyrus fragments mentioned Abraham's name or any of the events recorded in the book of Abraham," and that "these fragments date to between the third century B.C.E. and the first century C.E., long after Abraham lived," and concludes by positing an allegorical, rather than literal definition of "translation": "Joseph's study of the papyri may have led to a revelation about key events and teachings in the life of Abraham . . . This view assumes a broader definition of the words *translator* and *translation*. According to this view, Joseph's translation was not a literal rendering of the papyri as a conventional translation would be." This view, unprecedented in an official statement of church policy, is consistent with Ashment's article. See https://www.lds.org/topics/translation-and-historicity-of-the-book-of-abraham?lgng=eng.

9. James L. Farmer, William S. Bradshaw, and F. Brent Johnson, "The New Biology and Mormon Theology," *Dialogue: A Journal of Mormon Thought* 12, no. 4 (Winter 1979): 71–75.

10. Lavina Fielding Anderson, "The LDS Intellectual Community and Church Leadership: A Contemporary Chronology," *Dialogue: A Journal of Mormon Thought* 26, no. 1 (Spring 1993): 13.

11. Ezra Taft Benson, "Fourteen Fundamentals in Following the Prophet," http://speeches.byu.edu/?act=viewitem&id=88.

12. LJAD, June 17, 1980.

13. Kimball, *Lengthen Your Stride*, 454.

14. Linda Sillitoe, "Church Politics and Sonia Johnson: The Central Conundrum," *Sunstone* 5 (January/February 1980): 35–42.

15. Edward H. Ashment, "*The Book of Mormon*—A Literal Translation?" *Sunstone* 5 (March/April 1980): 10–14.

16. Mark Thomas, "Scholarship and the Future of the Book of Mormon," *Sunstone* 5 (May/June 1980): 24–29.

17. Gary James Bergera, "The Orson Pratt–Brigham Young Controversies: Conflict within the Quorums, 1853–1868," *Dialogue: A Journal of Mormon Thought* 13, no. 2 (Summer 1980): 7–49.

18. Robert N. Hullinger, *Mormon Answers to Skepticism: Why Joseph Smith Wrote The Book of Mormon* (St. Louis, MO: Clayton Publishing House, 1980). Revised and reprinted under the title of *Joseph Smith's Response to Skepticism* (Salt Lake City: Signature Books, 1992).

19. Andrew F. Ehat and Lyndon W. Cook, eds., *The Words of Joseph Smith: The Contemporary Accounts of the Nauvoo Discourses of the Prophet Joseph Smith* (Provo, UT: BYU Religious Studies Center, 1980).

20. Duane S. Crowther, *Thus Saith the Lord . . . The Role of Prophets and Revelation in the Kingdom of God* (Bountiful, UT: Horizon Publishers, 1980).

21. Jerald and Sandra Tanner, *The Changing World of Mormonism* (Chicago: Moody Press, 1980).

22. McConkie, Bruce R. "The Seven Deadly Heresies." *1980 Devotional Speeches of the Year.* Provo, UT: Brigham Young University Press, 1981, 74–80. The speech was given at BYU on June 1, 1980.

23. Thomas G. Alexander, "The Reconstruction of Mormon Doctrine: From Joseph Smith to Progressive Theology," *Sunstone* 5 (July/August 1980): 24–33.

24. Linda Wilcox, "The Mormon Concept of Mother in Heaven," *Sunstone* 5 (September/October 1980): 9–15.

25. Alan F. Keele and Douglas F. Tobler, "The Fuhrer's New Clothes: Helmuth Hübener and the Mormons in the Third Reich," *Sunstone* 5 (November/December 1980): 20–29.

26. L. Jackson Newell, "Personal Conscience and Priesthood Authority," *Dialogue: A Journal of Mormon Thought* 13 (Winter 1980): 81–87.

27. Martin Raish, "All That Glitters: Uncovering Fool's Gold in Book of Mormon Archaeology," *Sunstone* 6 (January/February 1981): 10–15.

28. Sterling M. McMurrin, "A New Climate of Liberation: A Tribute to Fawn McKay Brodie, 1915–1981," *Dialogue: A Journal of Mormon Thought* 14 (Spring 1981): 73–76.

29. LJA to Children, August 22, 1980, in LJAD.

30. Packer, "The Mantle Is Far, Far Greater," 259–78.

31. Anderson, *Doves and Serpents*, 875.

32. Packer, "The Mantle Is Far, Far Greater," 263, 267, 268, 269.

33. LJA to Children, October 10, 1981, in LJAD.

34. LJA to Children, November 25, 1981, in LJAD.

35. D. Michael Quinn, "On Being a Mormon Historian (and Its Aftermath)" in George D. Smith, ed., *Faithful History: Essays on Writing Mormon History* (Salt Lake City: Signature Books, 1992), 69–111.

36. Ibid.

37. "Historian Responds to Apostle," *Seventh East Press*, November 18, 1981, 1.

38. LJA to Gordon B. Hinckley, December 21, 1981, in LJAD.

39. First Presidency to LJA, January 25, 1982, in LJAD. At the time the First Presidency consisted of Spencer W. Kimball as president, N. Eldon Tanner as first counselor, Marion G. Romney as second counselor, and, because of the declining health of those three men, Gordon B. Hinckley as an extra counselor.

40. Kenneth L. Woodward, "Apostles Vs. Historians," *Newsweek*, February 15, 1982, 51.

41. LJA to Children, February 10, 1982, in LJAD.

42. Quinn, "On Being a Mormon Historian," 90.

43. Lester E. Bush Jr., "The Word of Wisdom in Early Nineteenth-Century Perspective," *Dialogue: A Journal of Mormon Thought* 14, no. 3 (Autumn 1981): 46–65.

44. Linda King Newell, "A Gift Given, A Gift Taken: Washing, Anointing, and Blessing the Sick among Mormon Women," *Sunstone* 6 (September/October 1981): 16–25.

45. Anthony A. Hutchinson, "Women and Ordination: Introduction to the Biblical Context," *Dialogue: A Journal of Mormon Thought* 14 (Winter 1981): 58–74.

46. Floyd H. Ross, "Process Philosophy and Mormon Thought: Two Views on a Progressing God," *Sunstone* 7 (January/February 1982): 16–25.

47. Sterling M. McMurrin, "Religion and the Denial of History," *Sunstone* 7 (March/April 1982): 46–49.

48. David John Buerger, "The Adam-God Doctrine," *Dialogue: A Journal of Mormon Thought* 15, no. 1 (Spring 1982): 14–58.

49. William D. Russell, "A Further Inquiry into the Historicity of the *Book of Mormon*," *Sunstone* 7 (September/October 1982): 20–27.

50. David John Buerger, "'The Fulness of the Priesthood': The Second Anointing in Latter-day Saint Theology and Practice," *Dialogue: A Journal of Mormon Thought* 16 (Spring 1983): 10–44.

51. Blake Ostler, "7EP Interviews Sterling M. McMurrin," *Seventh East Press*, January 11, 1983, 5–7, 10–11.

52. Anderson, "The LDS Intellectual Community," 20. The following month, at the Mormon History Association annual meeting, Thomas Alexander "said that the decision to kill *Seventh East*

Press was made at the General Authority level, but the BYU administration was told by the General Authorities that BYU was to announce the decision as its own, and to take the blame for it. Salt Lake was not to be implicated." Gregory A. Prince Diary, May 5, 1983.

53. Lester E. Bush Jr., "Writing 'Mormonism's Negro Doctrine: An Historical Overview' (1973): Context and Reflections, 1998," *Journal of Mormon History* 25, no. 1 (Spring 1999): 267.

54. LJAD, January 13, 1984. This diary entry was written shortly after Petersen's death. Leonard concluded: "I have had a real concern that he might become President of the Twelve or, eventually, President of the Church. Now, at least, that will not happen. The Lord has preserved us from that kind of leadership."

55. Lester E. Bush Jr. in Prince diary, May 1, 1983.

56. Prince diary, May 5, 1983.

57. Kimball, *Lengthen Your Stride*, 290–91.

58. Elbert E. Peck interview, June 17, 2008.

59. Lester Bush reported to me his conversation with Fletcher establishing this point. Prince diary, May 18, 1983.

60. Frederick S. Buchanan, "The Ebb and Flow of Academic Freedom at Brigham Young University," a response to "Walking a Tightrope: The Duality of Mormon Educational Philosophy," by Gary James Bergera, Sunstone Theological Symposium, August 26, 1983; photocopy of Buchanan's paper in LJA's diary, courtesy of Buchanan.

61. LJAD, September 9, 1983.

62. For a comprehensive summary of the issue through 1992, see Anderson, "The LDS Intellectual Community."

63. LJA to Children, August 15, 1992, in LJAD.

CHAPTER 28—MARK HOFMANN

1. Simon Worrall, *The Poet and the Murderer: A True Story of Literary Crime and the Art of Forgery* (New York: Dutton, 2002), 114–15.

2. LJA to Children, April 23, 1980, in LJAD.

3. LJAD, April 22, 1980.

4. LJAD, April 24, 1980.

5. Barry Fell, *America B.C.: Ancient Settlers in the New World* (New York: Quadrangle, 1976).

6. Barry Fell to Ali-Akbar Habib Bushiri, May 27, 1980, in LJAD, June 10, 1980.

7. D. Michael Quinn, "The Mormon Succession Crisis of 1844," *BYU Studies* 16, no. 2 (Winter 1976): 223.

8. LJAD, March 6, 1981. Dean Jessee's diary account of the money coming from the Arts and Sites budget quoted Hinckley as saying, "I'd rather have a manuscript than a rocking chair." Dean Jessee diary, February 27, 1981. I have found no indication that this decision was discussed with Florence Jacobsen, managing director of the Arts and Sites Division.

9. Dean Jessee diary, February 27, 1981, in LJAD, March 9, 1981.

10. Ibid., March 2, 1981, in LJAD, March 9, 1981.

11. LJA to Gordon B. Hinckley, March 9, 1981, in LJAD.

12. LJAD, March 17, 1981.

13. LJA to Children, August 24, 1982, in LJAD.

14. Press Release written by L. Don LeFevre, Church Spokesman, August 23, 1982, in LJAD.

15. LJA to Christine Rigby Arrington, February 26, 1984.

16. [Jerald and Sandra Tanner], "Moroni or Salamander?," *Salt Lake City Messenger*, Issue No. 53 (March 1984): 1.

17. Ibid.

18. Sandra Tanner interview, August 8, 2008.

19. E. D. Howe published the first complete book that challenged the claims of Mormonism: *Mormonism Unvailed: or, A Faithful Account of That Singular Imposition and Delusion . . .* (Painesville, Ohio: E. D. Howe, 1834). The statements referred to by Tanner were affidavits from residents of the Palmyra, New York, region regarding the earliest days of Mormonism.

20. Sandra Tanner interview, August 8, 2008.

21. John Dart, "Mormons Ponder 1830 Letter Altering Idealized Image of Joseph Smith," *Los Angeles Times*, August 25, 1984, A14.

22. " 'Martin Harris Letter' Won't Be Released to Public Until Next Year, Owner Says," *Deseret News*, September 1, 1984.

23. John Dart, "Mormon Church Releases Letter Revealing Mormon Founder's Belief in Spirits, Occult Released," *Los Angeles Times*, May 10, 1985. Wire service printout in LJAD, May 10, 1985.

24. Ibid.

25. Rick Grunder interview, August 11, 2013.

26. "Pres. Hinckley Discloses that Hofmann Offered to Donate McLellin Papers," *Deseret News*, October 23, 1985, A1.

27. Tim Gurrister, "Is Harris Letter Fake?" *Logan Herald Journal*, April 30, 1985, 1.

28. George H. Durham II interview, January 23, 2011.

29. LJA to Ronald W. Weber, November 1, 1985; LJAHA, Series X, Box 81, fd. 3.

30. LJA to Children, October 23, 1985, in LJAD.

31. Linda Sillitoe and Allen D. Roberts, *Salamander: The Story of the Mormon Forgery Murders* (Salt Lake City: Signature Books, 1988), 361.

32. LJA to Children, February 9, 1986, in LJAD.

33. Office of the Salt Lake County Attorney, *Mark Hofmann Interviews* (Salt Lake City: Office of Salt Lake County Attorney, 1987).

34. LJA to Children, August 13, 1987, in LJAD.

Chapter 29—The September Six

1. Linda King Newell and Valeen Tippetts Avery, *Mormon Enigma: Emma Hale Smith, Prophet's Wife, "Elect Lady," Polygamy's Foe* (Garden City, NY: Doubleday & Company, 1984).

2. For details on bulleted events through August 1992, see Anderson, "The LDS Intellectual Community and Church Leadership," 7–64.

3. Lavina Fielding Anderson, *Doves and Serpents: The Activities of Leonard Arrington as Church Historian, 1972–1982* (Salt Lake City: Privately Published, 1982).

4. LJA to Children, September 13, 1993, in LJAD.

5. LJA to Children, September 18, 1993, in LJAD.

6. This was a misstatement by Leonard. Anderson did publish names, times, and places.

7. LJA to Children, September 25, 1993, in LJAD. The court was held on September 23, but the stake president didn't notify Anderson of the verdict until September 24.

8. Vern Anderson, "Cartoonist Says Oaks Lied to Protect Fellow Apostle," *Salt Lake Tribune*, October 12, 1993, B-1, B-2.

9. LJAD, October 12, 1993.

10. Quinn related a conversation with Leonard at the time he was contemplating attending graduate school at Yale University: "Leonard said, 'Mike, when the time comes for me to retire, and me to be replaced as Church Historian, the Brethren will be very persuaded and influenced by a nomination of somebody with a Ph.D. from Yale. If you get your Ph.D. at the U of U, or if you have a master's, they will never consider you as my replacement.' I was speechless! I didn't say another word. And that was his last comment. We went the rest of the way to my house in silence. I was just stunned that he would say that; that he would *think* of it. I didn't even have my master's at that point. And that's what he was planning for." D. Michael Quinn interview, December 5, 2005.

11. LJA to Children, October 15, 2005, in LJAD attending graduate school at Yale University. LJA to Children, October 15, 2008, in LJAD.

12. R. W. Rasband to LJA, October 18, 1993, in LJAD.

13. LJA to R. W. Rasband, October 20, 1993, in LJAD.

14. LJA to Children, October 1, 1993, in LJAD.

15. LJA to Ross Arrington, October 18, 1993; LJAHA, Series IV, Box 18, fd. 3.

Chapter 30—*Adventures of a Church Historian*

1. LJAD, "Copied Verbatim from a Diary and History Started by Leonard Arrington in 1927 When He Was Ten Years Old," in LJAD.

2. Leonard J. Arrington, *From Quaker to Latter-day Saint: Bishop Edwin D. Woolley.* (Salt Lake City: Deseret Book Company, 1976).

3. LJAD, March 27, 1975.

4. Undated and untitled typescript, LJAHA, Series X, Box 80, fd. 10.

5. A skilled researcher and evocative writer, Rebecca Cornwall published essays on Susa Young Gates and Brigham Young, then an anthology, *Audacious Women: Early British Mormon Immigrants* (Salt Lake City: Signature Books, 1995). In addition to her yeoman's labor on Leonard's biography, she also coauthored with him "Perpetuation of a Myth: Mormon Danites in Five Western Novels, 1840–1890," *BYU Studies* 23 (Spring 1983): 147–65; and *Rescue of the 1856 Handcart Companies* (Provo, UT: Brigham Young University Press, 1981).

6. LJA to Children, September 12, 1976, in LJAD.

7. Rebecca F. Cornwall, *From Chicken Farm to History: The Life of Leonard Arrington* (Salt Lake City: Privately distributed, 1976).

8. Hugo Olaiz posted a biographical article on Wikipedia, and she also discusses this episode briefly in her 1993 *Dialogue* article, "The LDS Intellectual Community and Church Leadership."

9. Lavina Fielding Anderson interview, March 3, 2008.

10. Anderson, *Doves and Serpents*, 1281.

11. LJA to Children, November 30, 1982; LJAHA, Series X, Box 102, fd. 11.

12. Carl Arrington to LJA, April 14, 1988, in LJAD.

13. Carl Arrington to LJA, October 6, 1988, in LJAD.

14. Louis Midgley, a professor of political science at BYU, was one of the most outspoken apologists within the church and did not stop short of *ad hominem* attacks in his excessive moments, accusing some of the New Mormon Historians of lacking faith.

15. Peter Novick was a professor of history at the University of Chicago. Bitton gave no context for mentioning Novick as a potential reviewer.

16. Davis Bitton to LJA, February 9, 1993; LJAHA, Series X, Box 121, fd. 1.

17. Carol Lynn Pearson diary, November 13, 1993.

18. Elizabeth Dulany interview, May 28, 2010. Leonard J. Arrington, *Adventures of a Church Historian* (Urbana: University of Illinois Press, 1998).

19. Christine Rigby Arrington interview, September 24, 2009.

20. D. Michael Quinn interview, December 5, 2005.

21. James Arrington interview, April 12, 2009. James was within earshot of his father when the phone call occurred. When I asked if he knew who was on the other end of the line he responded, "No, I don't. I have no idea whether it was one of the Brethren, or another historian."

22. Philip Barlow to LJA, May 28, 1998; LJAHA, Series X, Box 103, fd. 11.

23. Emma Lou Thayne interview, April 11, 2009.

24. Arrington, *Adventures of a Church Historian*, 175.

25. Ibid., 237.

Chapter 31—Legacy

1. "My Heart By-Pass Operation," LJAD, April 23, 1984.
2. LJA to Children, February 13, 1984, in LJAD.
3. LJA to Children, February 22, 1984, in LJAD.
4. LJA to Children, April 9, 1984, in LJAD.
5. Ibid.
6. LJAD, April 22, 1984.
7. Ibid., April 24–27, 1984.
8. LJA to Children, May 23, 1991, in LJAD.
9. LJA to Children, June 21, 1991, in LJAD.
10. LJA to Children, March 5, 1993, in LJAD.
11. LJA to Children, May 8, 1994, in LJAD.
12. LJA to Children, July 4, 1997, in LJAD.
13. Davis Bitton interview, August 11, 2006.
14. F. Ross Peterson interview, September 17, 2007.
15. D. Michael Quinn interview, December 5, 2005.
16. Susan Arrington Madsen interview, November 16, 2005.
17. James Arrington interview, April 12, 2009.
18. Wolfgang Saxon, "Leonard J. Arrington, 81, Mormon Historian," *New York Times*, February 13, 1999, B20.
19. Richard L. Bushman, "Essential Books on Mormonism," *Christian Century*, August 22, 2012, 27.
20. David J. Whittaker interview, May 22, 2008.
21. Stanford O. Cazier interview, January 15, 2006. Gary Topping, in *Leonard J. Arrington: A Historian's Life*, gives a detailed analysis of Leonard's books.
22. Sandra Tanner interview, August 8, 2008.
23. Paul F. Edwards, contribution in "Remembering Leonard," (compilation of reminiscences), *Journal of Mormon History* 25, no. 1 (1999): 11.
24. William D. Russell interview, May 20, 2009.
25. Elbert E. Peck interview, June 17, 2008.
26. Ronald K. Esplin interview, June 30, 2012.
27. Glen M. Leonard interview, July 27, 2012.
28. Esplin interview, June 30, 2012.
29. Peck interview, June 17, 2008. Bryan Waterman coauthored with Brian Kagel, *The Lord's University: Freedom and Authority at BYU* (Salt Lake City: Signature Books, 1998) and a number of articles documenting BYU's official crack-down on liberal faculty members that resulted in the firings or departures of such faculty members as D. Michael Quinn, Cecilia Konchar Farr, Eugene England, David C. Knowlton, Sam Rushton, Scott Abbott, and Gail Turley Houston.
30. Ronald O. Barney interview, October 26, 2009.
31. Charles S. Peterson interview, November 9, 2006.
32. Howard R. Lamar interview, February 23, 2007.
33. Martin E. Marty, contribution in "Remembering Leonard," (compilation of reminiscences), *Journal of Mormon History* 25, no. 1 (1999): 15–16.
34. Arrington, *Adventures of a Church Historian*, 236–37.
35. Laurel Thatcher Ulrich interview, June 30, 2012.
36. William A. "Bert" Wilson interview, August 12, 2009.
37. Emma Lou Thayne interview, April 11, 2009.
38. James L. Clayton interview, August 8, 2008.
39. Ulrich interview, June 30, 2012.
40. Esplin interview, June 30, 2012.
41. Carol Cornwall Madsen interview, June 17, 2008.

42. Esplin referred to the Joseph Fielding Smith Institute at BYU. In 2005, twenty-five years after its creation, the institute was dissolved, with some of its members joining the regular faculty at BYU and others moving back to church headquarters in Salt Lake City to work on the ongoing Joseph Smith Papers Project, which is being funded by the Miller family.

43. Esplin interview, June 30, 2012.

44. Ronald W. Walker, Richard E. Turley Jr., and Glen M. Leonard, *Massacre at Mountain Meadows: An American Tragedy* (New York: Oxford University Press, 2008).

45. Susan Arrington Madsen interview, March 3, 2009.

46. Peck interview, June 17, 2008.

47. Richard P. Howard interview, May 27, 2010.

48. James L. Clayton interview, August 8, 2008.

EPILOGUE

1. LJA to Carol Lynn Pearson, December 26, 1987; LJAHA, Series II, Box 13, fd. 10.

2. F. Ross Peterson interview, September 16, 2007.

3. Susan Arrington Madsen to Gregory A. Prince, April 1, 2009.

4. Peterson interview, September 16, 2007.

5. USU Press Release, Logan *Herald Journal*, October 25, 2001.

6. Peggy Fletcher Stack and Kirsten Stewart, "Church Calls Its Claim to Papers of Late USU Professor 'Ironclad,'" *Salt Lake Tribune*, October 26, 2001, http://www.sltribune.com/10262001 /utah/143394.htm.

7. Kirsten Stewart, "Documents Debate May Go to Court," *Salt Lake Tribune*, November 2, 2001. Photocopy without pagination.

8. Susan Arrington Madsen interview, October 17, 2005.

9. Kirsten Stewart and Peggy Fletcher Stack, "Board Seeks Truce in Document Fight," *Salt Lake Tribune*, November 10, 2001, http://www.sltribune.com/2001/nov/11102001/utah/147552.htm.

10. Peterson interview, September 16, 2007.

11. Madsen interview, October 17, 2005.

12. Peterson interview, September 16, 2007.

13. Madsen interview, July 29, 2012.

14. "Acquisition Sheet and Instrument of Gift," signed by Leonard J. Arrington on August 19, 1982; photocopy of original in my possession courtesy of Susan Arrington Madsen.

15. Susan Arrington Madsen interview, May 27, 2006.

16. N. George Daines to "Elder Kerr and Elder Cook," November 23, 2001; photocopy of original in my possession courtesy of Susan Arrington Madsen.

17. Peggy Fletcher Stack and Kirsten Stewart, "Was Deed to Arrington Journal Ignored?" *Salt Lake Tribune*, January 8, 2002, http://sltribune.com;01082002/utah/165522.htm.

18. "Ignoring Arrington Wish Shows Double Standard," editorial, Logan *Herald Journal*, January 13, 2002, http://news.mywebpal.com:80/partners/672/public/news237585.htm.

BIBLIOGRAPHY

ABBREVIATIONS

LJAD. Leonard J. Arrington Diaries, Leonard J. Arrington Historical Archives, Special Collections and Archives, Merrill-Cazier Library, Utah State University, Logan. Cited as LJAD by date in the notes.

LJAHA. Leonard J. Arrington Historical Archives, Special Collections and Archives, Merrill-Cazier Library, Utah State University, Logan. All correspondence to and from LJA is identified in the notes by addressee and date, file and folder, but not separately listed here. Other documents are identified by title (if available), date (if available), box, and folder, and are listed as separate items in this bibliography. Documents that LJA included in his diary are not separately identified.

"Acquisition Sheet and Instrument of Gift," signed by Leonard J. Arrington on August 19, 1982. Photocopy of original in author's possession, courtesy of Susan Arrington Madsen.

Alexander, Thomas G. *Mormonism in Transition: A History of the Latter-day Saints, 1890–1930.* Urbana: University of Illinois Press, 1986.

———. "The Reconstruction of Mormon Doctrine: From Joseph Smith to Progressive Theology." *Sunstone* 5 (July/August 1980): 24–33.

Allen, James B. "Accomplishments of the History Division for 1974." Unpublished memorandum from James B. Allen to LJA, January 1, 1975. Photocopy in LJAD of the same date.

———. "Since 1950: Creators and Creations of Mormon History." In Bitton and Beecher, *New Views of Mormon History: Essays in Honor of Leonard J. Arrington*, 407–38.

Allen, James B., and Thomas G. Alexander, eds. *Manchester Mormons: The Journal of William Clayton, 1840–1842.* Santa Barbara, CA: Peregrine Smith, 1974.

Allen, James B., and Glen M. Leonard. *The Story of the Latter-day Saints.* 2nd ed., Salt Lake City: Deseret Book, 1992.

Anderson, Devery S. "A History of *Dialogue*, Part 1: The Early Years, 1965–1971." *Dialogue: A Journal of Mormon Thought* 32, no. 2 (Summer 1999): 15–67.

———. "A History of *Dialogue*, Part 2: Struggle toward Maturity, 1971–1982." *Dialogue: A Journal of Mormon Thought* 33, no. 2 (Summer 2000): 1–96.

———. "A History of *Dialogue*, Part 3: 'Coming of Age' in Utah, 1982–1987." *Dialogue: A Journal of Mormon Thought* 35, no. 2 (Summer 2002): 1–71.

———. "A History of *Dialogue*, Part 4: A Tale in Two Cities, 1987–92." *Dialogue: A Journal of Mormon Thought* 41, no. 3 (Fall 2008): 1–54.

Anderson, Gary. "A Historical Survey of the Full-Time Institutes of Religion of the Church of Jesus Christ of Latter-day Saints, 1926–1966." EdD diss., Brigham Young University, 1968.

Anderson, Lavina Fielding. *Doves and Serpents: The Activities of Leonard Arrington as Church Historian, 1972–1982.* Salt Lake City: privately published, 1982.

———. "The LDS Intellectual Community and Church Leadership: A Contemporary Chronology." *Dialogue: A Journal of Mormon Thought* 26, no. 1 (Spring 1993): 7–64.

Arrington, Leonard J. *Adventures of a Church Historian*. Urbana: University of Illinois Press, 1998.

———. "The Beginnings of My Interest in Mormon Scholarship." No date. LJAHA, Series X, Box 3, fd. 1.

———. *Brigham Young: American Moses*. New York: Alfred A. Knopf, 1985.

———. *Charles C. Rich: Mormon General and Western Frontiersman*. Provo, UT: Brigham Young University Press, 1974.

———. "Church Historian, 1972–1982," manuscript 1992. LJAHA, Series X, Box 16, fd. 1.

———. "An Economic Interpretation of 'The Word of Wisdom.'" *Brigham Young University Studies* 1, no. 1 (Winter 1959): 37–49.

———. "The Economic Role of Pioneer Mormon Women." *Western Humanities Review* 9, no. 2 (1955): 145–64.

———. "Family Experiences." Undated. LJAHA, Series X, Box 1, fd. 4.

———. *Farm Boy at the University of Idaho, 1935–39*. Hyde Park, UT: Historian's Press, 1996.

———. *From Quaker to Latter-day Saint: Bishop Edwin D. Woolley*. Salt Lake City: Deseret Book Company, 1976.

———. "The Founding of the LDS Church Historical Department." In Neilson and Walker, *Reflections of a Mormon Historian*, 111–28.

———. "The Founding of the LDS Institute of Religion." *Dialogue: A Journal of Mormon Thought* 2 (Summer 1967): 138–47.

———. *Great Basin Kingdom: An Economic History of the Latter-day Saints 1830–1900*. Cambridge, MA: Harvard University Press, 1958.

———. *Growing Up in Twin Falls County, Idaho*. Hyde Park, UT: Historian's Press, 1996.

———. "Historian as Entrepreneur: A Personal Essay." *BYU Studies* 17, no. 2 (1977): 1–15.

———. *History of Idaho*. 2 vols. Moscow: University of Idaho Press, 1994.

———. *An Illustrated History of the History Division of the LDS Church, 1972–82*. Salt Lake City: Historian's Press, 1994.

———. "The Influence of College upon Tolerance." Essay for English 4, May 23, 1936, LJAD.

———. *Life in Happy Valley: Early Years in Logan and Our First Sabbatical*. Hyde Park, UT: Historian's Press, 1996.

———. *Magic Valley Pioneers: A Photographic Record of N. W. and Edna Corn Arrington*. Salt Lake City: Historian's Press, 1991.

———. "On Going to College." Undated. LJAHA, Series X, Box 4, fd. 10.

———. "Pillars of My Faith." August 1, 1998. LJAHA, Series XII, Box 174, fd. 22.

———. "Proof of the Book of Mormon." LJAD, 1933.

———. "The Search for Truth and Meaning in Mormon History." *Dialogue: A Journal of Mormon Thought* 3, no. 2 (Summer 1968): 56–66.

———. *A Soldier in North Africa and Italy, 1943–1946*. Salt Lake City: Historian's Press, 1995.

———. "Thoughts about Religion, for the Family." LJAD, February 11, 1982.

———. "Why I Am a Believer." August 26, 1983. LJAHA, Series X, Box 3, fd. 1. Published as "Why I Am a Believer." *Sunstone* 10, no. 1 (January 1985): 36–38.

———. *Years of Achievement and Pleasure in Logan: 1958–72*. Hyde Park, UT: Historian's Press, 1996.

Arrington, Leonard J., and Davis Bitton. *The Mormon Experience: A History of the Latter-day Saints.* New York: Alfred A. Knopf, 1979.

Ashment, Edward H. "The Book of Abraham Facsimiles: A Reappraisal." *Sunstone* 4, nos. 4–5 (May/June 1979): 33–48.

———. "*The Book of Mormon:* A Literal Translation?" *Sunstone* 5 (March/April 1980): 10–14.

Bagley, Will. *Blood of the Prophets: Brigham Young and the Massacre at Mountain Meadows.* Norman: University of Oklahoma Press, 2002.

Bagley, Will, and David L. Bigler, eds. *Innocent Blood: Essential Narratives of the Mountain Meadows Massacre.* Norman: Arthur H. Clark, an imprint of the University of Oklahoma Press, 2008.

Benson, Ezra Taft. "Fourteen Fundamentals in Following the Prophet." February 26, 1980. http://speeches.byu.edu/?act=viewitem&id=88.

———. "The Gospel Teacher and His Message." September 17, 1976. http://www.ldsces.org/content/talks/general/1976-benson-the-gospel-teacher-and-his-message_eng.pdf.

Bergera, Gary James. "The Orson Pratt–Brigham Young Controversies: Conflict within the Quorums, 1853–1868." *Dialogue: A Journal of Mormon Thought* 13, no. 2 (Summer 1980): 7–49.

Bitton, Davis. "Ten Years in Camelot: A Personal Memoir." *Dialogue: A Journal of Mormon Thought* 16, no. 3 (1983): 9–19.

Bitton, Davis, and Maureen Ursenbach Beecher, eds. *New Views of Mormon History: Essays in Honor of Leonard J. Arrington.* Salt Lake City: University of Utah Press, 1987.

Bradford, Mary Lythgoe. *Lowell L. Bennion: Teacher, Counselor, Humanitarian.* Salt Lake City: Dialogue Foundation, 1995.

Bringhurst, Newell G. *Brigham Young and the Expanding American Frontier.* Boston: Little, Brown and Company, 1986.

———. "Elijah Abel and the Changing Status of Blacks within Mormonism." *Dialogue: A Journal of Mormon Thought* 12, no. 2 (Summer 1979): 22–36.

———. *Fawn McKay Brodie: A Biographer's Life.* Norman: University of Oklahoma Press, 1999.

———. *Saints, Slaves, and Blacks: The Changing Place of Black People within Mormonism.* Westport, CT: Greenwood Press, 1981.

Brooks, Juanita. *The Mountain Meadows Massacre.* San Marino, CA: Huntington Library, 1950; 2d ed., Norman: University of Oklahoma Press, 1962.

Buchanan, Frederick S. "The Ebb and Flow of Academic Freedom at Brigham Young University." A response to "Walking a Tightrope: The Duality of Mormon Educational Philosophy," by Gary James Bergera, Sunstone Theological Symposium, August 26, 1983; photocopy of Buchanan's article in LJAD, September 9, 1983, courtesy of Frederick S. Buchanan.

Buerger, David John. "The Adam-God Doctrine." *Dialogue: A Journal of Mormon Thought* 15, no. 1 (Spring 1982): 14–58.

———. "'The Fulness of the Priesthood': The Second Anointing in Latter-day Saint Theology and Practice." *Dialogue: A Journal of Mormon Thought* 16 (Spring 1983): 10–44.

Bush, Lester E. "A Commentary on Stephen G. Taggart's *Mormonism's Negro Policy: Social and Historical Origins.*" *Dialogue: A Journal of Mormon Thought* 4, no. 4 (Winter 1969): 86–103.

———. "Compilation on the Negro in Mormonism." Unpublished manuscript, 1973. Copy in author's possession. Other copies in the LDS Church History Library and in the Lester E. Bush Jr. Papers, Special Collections, J. Willard Marriott Library, University of Utah, Salt Lake City.

———. "Mixed Messages on the Negro Doctrine: An Interview with Lester Bush." By Thane Young. *Sunstone* 4 (May/June 1979): 8–15.

———. "Mormonism's Negro Doctrine: An Historical Overview." *Dialogue: A Journal of Mormon Thought* 8, no. 1 (Spring 1973): 11–68.

———. "The Spalding Theory Then and Now." *Dialogue: A Journal of Mormon Thought* 10, no. 4 (Autumn 1977): 42–71.

———. "The Word of Wisdom in Early Nineteenth-Century Perspective." *Dialogue: A Journal of Mormon Thought* 14, no. 3 (Autumn 1981): 46–65.

———. "Writing 'Mormonism's Negro Doctrine: An Historical Overview' (1973): Context and Reflections, 1998." *Journal of Mormon History* 25, no. 1 (Spring 1999): 229–71.

Bushman, Claudia L. "Harriet Hanson Robinson and Her Family: A Chronicle of Nineteenth-Century New England Life." PhD diss., Boston University, 1978.

———, ed. *Mormon Sisters: Women in Early Utah.* Cambridge, MA: Emmeline Press, 1976.

Bushman, Richard L. "Essential Books on Mormonism." *Christian Century*, August 22, 2012, 27.

———. RLB to Hugh B. Brown, July 22, 1964. LJAHA, Series X, Box 74, fd. 5.

———. RLB to Leonard J. Arrington, September 29, 1964. LJAHA, Series X, Box 74, fd. 5.

Campbell, Eugene. *Establishing Zion: The Mormon Church in the American West, 1847–1869.* Salt Lake City: Signature Books, 1988.

Campbell, Eugene, and Richard D. Poll. *Hugh B. Brown: His Life and Thought.* Salt Lake City: Bookcraft, 1975.

"The Church and the Proposed Equal Rights Amendment: A Moral Issue." Center insert in *Ensign* (February 1980).

Cleland, Robert Glass, and Juanita Brooks, eds. *A Mormon Chronicle: The Diaries of John D. Lee, 1848–1876.* San Marino, CA: Huntington Library, 1955.

Cornwall, Rebecca F. *Audacious Women: Early British Mormon Immigrants.* Salt Lake City: Signature Books, 1995.

———. *From Chicken Farm to History: The Life of Leonard Arrington.* Salt Lake City: privately distributed, 1976.

———. *The Grace of Our Lord Was With Her: Grace Fort Arrington, 1943–1946 and 1977–1982.* Salt Lake City: privately distributed, 1982.

Cornwall, Rebecca F., and Leonard J. Arrington, eds. *I'm Glad My House Burned Down: The Personal Story of Grace Fort Arrington.* Salt Lake City: privately distributed, 1977.

———. "Perpetuation of a Myth: Mormon Danites in Five Western Novels, 1840–1890." *BYU Studies* 23 (Spring 1983): 147–65.

———. *Rescue of the 1856 Handcart Companies.* Provo, UT: Brigham Young University Press, 1981.

Council of the First Presidency and the Quorum of the Twelve Apostles. "Statement on Symposia," November 1991. http://www.lds.org/ensign/1991/11/news-of-the-church/statement-on-symposia?lang=eng&query=symposia.

Crowther, Duane S. *Thus Saith the Lord: The Role of Prophets and Revelation in the Kingdom of God.* Bountiful, UT: Horizon Publishers, 1980.

Daines, N. George. Letter to "Elder Kerr and Elder Cook," November 23, 2001. Photocopy of original in author's possession, courtesy of Susan Arrington Madsen.

Degn, Louise. "Mormon Women and Depression." *Sunstone* 4 (March/April 1979): 16–26.

Derr, Jill Mulvay, Janath Russell Cannon, and Maureen Ursenbach Beecher. *Women of Covenant: The Story of Relief Society.* Salt Lake City: Deseret Book, 1992.

"*Dialogue* Magazine." *Priesthood Bulletin* 3, no. 2 (March–June 1967): 1.

Drayton, John N. Review of *The Story of the Latter-day Saints*, by James B. Allen and Glen M. Leonard. *Sunstone* 1, no. 4 (Fall 1976): 86–88.

Durham, Reed C. "Is There No Help for the Widow's Son?" Mormon History Association presidential address, 1974. In *Mormon Miscellaneous* 1, no. 1 (October 1975): 11–16.

Durham, Reed C., and Steven H. Heath. *Succession in the Church*. Salt Lake City: Bookcraft, Inc., 1970.

Dyer, Alvin R. Journal. Selected entries photocopied into David O. McKay, Diary. Special Collections, J. Willard Marriott Library, University of Utah, Salt Lake City.

Editors. "In This Issue." *Dialogue: A Journal of Mormon Thought* 1, no. 2 (Summer 1966): 2.

Edwards, Paul F. Contribution in "Remembering Leonard" (compilation of reminiscences). *Journal of Mormon History* 25, no. 1 (1999): 11.

Edwards, Paul M. Letter to Gregory A. Prince, August 10, 1980.

Ehat, Andrew F., and Lyndon W. Cook, eds. *The Words of Joseph Smith: The Contemporary Accounts of the Nauvoo Discourses of the Prophet Joseph Smith*. Provo, UT: BYU Religious Studies Center, 1980.

Ellsworth, S. George. Review of *Story of the Latter-day Saints*, by James B. Allen and Glen M. Leonard. *BYU Studies* 17, no. 2 (Winter 1977): 241–46.

———. *Utah's Heritage*. Layton, UT: Peregrine Smith Publications, 1972.

England, Eugene. Contribution in "Remembering Leonard" (compilation of reminiscences). *Journal of Mormon History* 25, no. 1 (Spring 1999): 25.

Esplin, Ronald K. "The Emergence of Brigham Young and the Twelve to Mormon Leadership." PhD diss., Brigham Young University, 1981.

"Excavating the Great Basin: A Conversation with Leonard Arrington." Sunstone Symposium, Salt Lake City, August 12, 1993. Audiocassette.

Farmer, James L., William S. Bradshaw, and F. Brent Johnson. "The New Biology and Mormon Theology." *Dialogue: A Journal of Mormon Thought* 12, no. 4 (Winter 1979): 71–75.

Fell, Barry. *America B.C.: Ancient Settlers in the New World*. New York: Quadrangle, 1976.

———. Letter to Ali-Akbar Habib Bushiri, May 27, 1980. In LJAD, June 10, 1980.

Flanders, Robert B. "MHA after Forty Years." Address delivered at the Mormon History Association, June 2006, Casper, Wyoming.

———. "Nauvoo on My Mind." *John Whitmer Historical Association 2002 Nauvoo Conference Special Edition*. Independence, MO: John Whitmer Historical Association, 2003.

———. "Some Reflections on the New Mormon History." *Dialogue: A Journal of Mormon Thought* 9, no. 1 (Spring 1974): 34–41.

Foster, Lawrence. "Career Apostates: Reflections on the Works of Jerald and Sandra Tanner." *Dialogue: A Journal of Mormon Thought* 17 (Summer 1984): 35–60.

———. *Religion and Sexuality: Three American Communal Experiments in the Nineteenth Century*. New York: Oxford University Press, 1981.

———. Review of *Story of the Latter-day Saints*, by James B. Allen and Glen M. Leonard. *Church History* 46, no. 3 (September 1977): 403–4.

Goates, L. Brent. *Harold B. Lee: Prophet and Seer*. Salt Lake City: Bookcraft, 1985.

Godfrey, Kenneth W. "Institutes of Religion." In *Encyclopedia of Latter-day Saint History*, edited by Arnold K. Garr, Donald Q. Cannon, and Richard O. Cowan, 541–42. Salt Lake City: Deseret Book, 2000.

Hale, Veda Tebbs. "In Memoriam: Maurine Whipple." *Sunstone* 16, no. 2 (August 1992): 13–15.

Hansen, Gary B. "Two Unique Contributions of Leonard J. Arrington to USU and the Economics Department." Unpublished manuscript, 2009. Photocopy in author's possession.

Hansen, Klaus J. Review of *Story of the Latter-day Saints,* by James B. Allen and Glen M. Leonard. *Utah Historical Quarterly* 46, no. 1 (Winter 1978): 82–86.

Hardy, B. Carmon. *Solemn Covenant: The Mormon Polygamous Passage.* Urbana: University of Illinois Press, 1992.

Harrison, E. L. T. "An Appeal to the People." *Utah Magazine* 3 (October 30, 1869): 406–8.

Hartley, William G. "The Priesthood Reform Movement, 1908–1922." *BYU Studies* 13, no. 2 (1973): 137–56.

"Historian Responds to Apostle." *Seventh East Press*, November 18, 1981, 1.

Homer, Michael W. *Joseph's Temples: The Dynamic Relationship between Freemasonry and Mormonism.* Salt Lake City: University of Utah Press, 2014.

Howe, Eber D. *Mormonism Unvailed: or, A Faithful Account of That Singular Imposition and Delusion from Its Rise to the Present Time. With Sketches of the Characters of Its Propagators, and a Full Detail of the Manner in Which the Famous Golden Bible Was Brought before the World. To Which Are Added, Inquiries into the Probability That the Historical Part of the Said Bible Was Written by One Solomon Spalding, More Than Twenty Years Ago, and by Him Intended to Have Been Published as a Romance.* Painesville, OH: E. D. Howe, 1834.

Hullinger, Robert N. *Mormon Answers to Skepticism: Why Joseph Smith Wrote the Book of Mormon.* St. Louis, MO: Clayton Publishing, 1980. Revised and reprinted as *Joseph Smith's Response to Skepticism.* Salt Lake City: Signature Books, 1992.

Hutchinson, Anthony A. "Women and Ordination: Introduction to the Biblical Context." *Dialogue: A Journal of Mormon Thought* 14 (Winter 1981): 58–74.

Jessee, Dean. Diary. Excerpts in LJAD by Jessee's permission.

———. "The Early Accounts of Joseph Smith's First Vision." *BYU Studies* 9, no. 3 (Spring 1969): 275–300.

———, ed. *Letters of Brigham Young to His Sons.* Salt Lake City: Deseret Book, 1974.

———. "The Original Book of Mormon Manuscript." *BYU Studies* 10, no. 3 (Spring 1970): 259–78.

———. "The Reliability of Joseph Smith's History." *Journal of Mormon History* 3 (1976): 23–46.

———. "The Writing of Joseph Smith's History." *BYU Studies* 11 (Summer 1971): 439–73.

Johnston, Bill. "Student Cooperatives at the University of Idaho." *Improvement Era* 43, no. 1 (1942): 21, 57–58.

Keele, Alan F., and Douglas F. Tobler. "The Fuhrer's New Clothes: Helmuth Hübener and the Mormons in the Third Reich." *Sunstone* 5 (November/December 1980): 20–29.

Kenney, Scott G. Selected diary entries in author's possession, courtesy of Scott Kenney.

Kimball, Edward L. *Lengthen Your Stride: The Presidency of Spencer W. Kimball.* Salt Lake City: Deseret Book, 2005. This printed volume includes, attached to the inside back cover, a CD-ROM of the longer "working draft" and several other items of Kimball material.

———. "Spencer W. Kimball and the Revelation on Priesthood." *BYU Studies* 47, no. 2 (Spring 2008): 5–78.

Lee, Harold B. Letter to Richard L. Bushman, September 3, 1964. LJAHA, Series X, Box 74, fd. 5.

Linn, William A. *The Story of the Mormons: From the Date of Their Origin to the Year 1901.* New York: Macmillan, 1902.

Lythgoe, Dennis L. "Artful Analysis of Mormonism." Review of *Story of the Latter-day Saints*, by James B. Allen and Glen M. Leonard. *Dialogue: A Journal of Mormon Thought* 10, no. 4 (Autumn 1977): 134–37.

MacKinnon, William P. Review of *Story of the Latter-day Saints*, by James B. Allen and Glen M. Leonard. *Arizona and the West* 19, no. 3 (Autumn 1977): 272–74.

———. *At Sword's Point*. Part 1, *A Documentary History of the Utah War to 1858*. Norman: Arthur H. Clark, an imprint of the University of Oklahoma Press, 2008.

Madsen, Carol Cornwall. Contribution in "Remembering Leonard" (compilation of reminiscences). *Journal of Mormon History* 25, no. 1 (Spring 1999): 100–101.

Madsen, Carol Cornwall, and Susan Staker Oman. *Sisters and Little Saints: One Hundred Years of Primary*. Salt Lake City: Deseret Book, 1979.

Marshall, Richard Stephen. "The New Mormon History." Senior Honors Project Summary, May 1, 1977, Department of History, University of Utah. Special Collections, J. Willard Marriott Library, University of Utah. Photocopy in author's possession.

Marty, Martin E. Contribution in "Remembering Leonard" (compilation of reminiscences). *Journal of Mormon History* 25, no. 1 (1999): 15–16.

Mason, Patrick Q. *The Mormon Menace: Violence and Anti-Mormonism in the Postbellum South*. New York: Oxford University Press, 2011.

McClellan, Jeff. "A Lingering Influence: Top 10 BYU Professors." *BYU Magazine*, Winter 1999, http://magazine.byu.edu/?act=view&a=172.

McConkie, Bruce R. "The Seven Deadly Heresies." *1980 Devotional Speeches of the Year*, 74–80. Provo, UT: Brigham Young University Press, 1981.

McKay, David O. Diary. Special Collections, J. Willard Marriott Library, University of Utah, Salt Lake City.

McMurrin, Sterling M. "A New Climate of Liberation: A Tribute to Fawn McKay Brodie, 1915–1981." *Dialogue: A Journal of Mormon Thought* 14 (Spring 1981): 73–76.

———. "Religion and the Denial of History." *Sunstone* 7 (March/April 1982): 46–49.

Menlove, Frances Lee. "The Challenge of Honesty." *Dialogue: A Journal of Mormon Thought* 1, no. 1 (Spring 1966); reprinted in *The Challenge of Honesty: Essays for Latter-day Saints by Frances Lee Menlove*, edited by Dan Wotherspoon. Salt Lake City: Signature Books, 2013: 1–19.

"Mormons: For Ruffled Believers." *Time Magazine*, August 26, 1966, 61.

Muir, Harold T. Review of *Brigham Young: American Moses*, by Leonard J. Arrington. In *John Whitmer Historical Association Journal* 6 (1986): 77–80.

Mulder, William. *Homeward to Zion: The Mormon Migration from Scandinavia*. Minneapolis: University of Minnesota Press, 1957.

Neilson, Reid L., and Ronald W. Walker, eds. *Reflections of a Mormon Historian: Leonard J. Arrington on the New Mormon History*. Norman: Arthur H. Clark, an imprint of the University of Oklahoma Press, 2006.

Nelson, Russell M. *Official Report of the One Hundred Sixty-Third Annual General Conference of the Church of Jesus Christ of Latter-day Saints*, April 3, 1993, 49–53. Salt Lake City: Church of Jesus Christ of Latter-day Saints, 1993.

Newell, L. Jackson. "Personal Conscience and Priesthood Authority." *Dialogue: A Journal of Mormon Thought* 13 (Winter 1980): 81–87.

Newell, Linda King. "A Gift Given, A Gift Taken: Washing, Anointing, and Blessing the Sick among Mormon Women." *Sunstone* 6 (September/October 1981): 16–25.

Newell, Linda King, and Valeen Tippetts Avery. *Mormon Enigma: Emma Hale Smith, Prophet's Wife, "Elect Lady," Polygamy's Foe*. New York: Doubleday & Company, 1984.

Novak, Shannon A. *House of Mourning: A Biocultural History of the Mountain Meadows Massacre*. Salt Lake City: University of Utah Press, 2008.

Office of the Salt Lake County Attorney. *Mark Hofmann Interviews*. Salt Lake City: Office of Salt Lake County Attorney, 1987.

Official Report of the One Hundred Sixty-Third Annual General Conference of the Church of Jesus Christ of Latter-day Saints. Salt Lake City: Church of Jesus Christ of Latter-day Saints, 1993.

Ostler, Blake. "7EP Interviews Sterling M. McMurrin." *Seventh East Press*, January 11, 1983, 5–7, 10–11.

Packer, Boyd K. "I Say Unto You, Be One." BYU Devotional address, February 12, 1991. In *Brigham Young University 1990–91 Devotional and Fireside Speeches*. Provo, UT: Brigham Young University, 1991.

———. "The Mantle Is Far, Far Greater Than the Intellect." *BYU Studies* 21, no. 3 (Summer 1981): 259–78.

Petersen, Lauritz G. Letter to Dean Jessee, April 8, 1969. LJAHA, Series V, Box 2, fd. 5.

Peterson, F. Ross. Interview of Leonard J. Arrington, April 12, 1988. Typescript in author's possession.

Poll, Richard D. "What the Church Means to People like Me." *Dialogue: A Journal of Mormon Thought* 2 (Winter 1967): 107–17.

Prince, Gregory A., and Wm. Robert Wright. *David O. McKay and the Rise of Modern Mormonism*. Salt Lake City: University of Utah Press, 2005.

Quinn, D. Michael. Contribution in "Remembering Leonard" (compilation of reminiscences). *Journal of Mormon History* 25, no. 1 (Spring 1999): 27–28.

———. "I Have a Question." *Ensign* (December 1973): 32.

———. "The Mormon Hierarchy, 1832–1932: An American Elite." PhD diss., Yale University, 1976.

———. "The Mormon Succession Crisis of 1844." *BYU Studies* 16, no. 2 (Winter 1976): 187–233.

———. "On Being a Mormon Historian (and Its Aftermath)." In *Faithful History: Essays on Writing Mormon History*, edited by George D. Smith. Salt Lake City: Signature Books, 1992: 69–111.

———. "Utah's Education Innovation: LDS Religion Classes, 1890–1929." *Utah Historical Quarterly* 43 (Fall 1975): 379–89.

Raish, Martin. "All That Glitters: Uncovering Fool's Gold in Book of Mormon Archaeology." *Sunstone* 6 (January/February 1981): 10–15.

Roberts, B. H. *A Comprehensive History of the Church of Jesus Christ of Latter-day Saints, Century I*. 6 vols. 1930. Reprint, Provo, UT: Brigham Young University Press, 1965.

———. *Studies of the Book of Mormon*. Urbana: University of Illinois Press, 1985.

Romney, Antone K., Letter to Harold B. Lee, September 3, 1964. LJAHA, Series X, Box 74, fd. 5.

Ross, Floyd H. "Process Philosophy and Mormon Thought: Two Views on a Progressing God." *Sunstone* 7 (January/February 1982): 16–25.

Russell, William D. "A Further Inquiry into the Historicity of the Book of Mormon." *Sunstone* 7 (September/October 1982): 20–27.

Sherlock, Richard. "Campus in Crisis: BYU, 1911." *Sunstone* 4 (January/February 1979): 10–16.

———. "Faith and History: The Snell Controversy." *Dialogue: A Journal of Mormon Thought* 12 (Spring 1979): 27–41.

Shipps, Jan. Review of *Brigham Young: American Moses*, by Leonard J. Arrington. *Journal of American History* 73, no. 1 (June 1986): 190–91.

Sillitoe, Linda. "Church Politics and Sonia Johnson: The Central Conundrum." *Sunstone* 5 (January/ February 1980): 35–42.

Sillitoe, Linda, and Allen D. Roberts. *Salamander: The Story of the Mormon Forgery Murders*. Salt Lake City: Signature Books, 1988.

Smith, Joseph Fielding. *Church History and Modern Revelation*. 4 vols. Salt Lake City: Council of the Twelve Apostles of the Church of Jesus Christ of Latter-day Saints, 1946–1949.

———. *Life of Joseph F. Smith: Sixth President of the Church of Jesus Christ of Latter-day Saints*. Salt Lake City: Deseret News, 1938.

Smith, Melvin T. Review of *Brigham Young: American Moses*, by Leonard J. Arrington. *Dialogue: A Journal of Mormon Thought* 20, no. 3 (Fall 1987): 171–72.

Sorenson, John L. *An Ancient American Setting for the Book of Mormon*. Salt Lake City: Deseret Book; Provo, UT: Foundation for Ancient Research and Mormon Studies, 1985.

Taggart, Stephen G. *Mormonism's Negro Policy: Social and Historical Origins*. Salt Lake City: University of Utah Press, 1970.

Tanner, George S. "The Religious Environment in which Mormonism Arose." M.A. thesis, University of Chicago, 1931.

Tanner, Jerald, and Sandra Tanner. *The Changing World of Mormonism*. Chicago: Moody Press, 1980.

———. "Moroni or Salamander?" *Salt Lake City Messenger*, Issue No. 53 (March 1984).

Tate, Lucile C. *Boyd K. Packer: A Watchman on the Tower*. Salt Lake City: Bookcraft, 1995.

Thomas, Mark. "Scholarship and the Future of the Book of Mormon." *Sunstone* 5 (May/June 1980): 24–29.

Topping, Gary. *Leonard J. Arrington: A Historian's Life*. Norman: Arthur H. Clark, an imprint of the University of Oklahoma Press, 2008.

Turner, Wallace. *The Mormon Establishment*. Boston: Houghton Mifflin, 1966.

Udall, Stewart L. Letter to the editor, *Dialogue: A Journal of Mormon Thought* 2, no. 2 (Summer 1967): 5–7.

Utah State University Press Release. *Herald Journal* (Logan, Utah), October 25, 2001.

Walker, Kyle R. *William Smith: In the Shadow of a Prophet*. Salt Lake City: Greg Kofford Books, 2015.

———. "William B. Smith and the 'Reorganites.'" *Journal of Mormon History* 39, no. 1 (Fall 2014): 73–129.

Walker, Ronald W., Richard E. Turley Jr., and Glen M. Leonard. *Massacre at Mountain Meadows: An American Tragedy*. New York: Oxford University Press, 2008.

Waterman, Bryan, and Brian Kagel. *The Lord's University: Freedom and Authority at BYU*. Salt Lake City: Signature Books, 1998.

Whalen, William J. *The Latter-day Saints in the Modern Day World: An Account of Contemporary Mormonism*. New York: John Day Company, 1964.

Whittaker, David J. "Leonard James Arrington (1917–1999): A Bibliography." *Journal of Mormon History* 25, no. 2 (Fall 1999): 11–45.

Wilcox, Linda. "The Mormon Concept of Mother in Heaven." *Sunstone* 5 (September/October 1980): 9–15.

Williams, J. D. "The Separation of Church and State in Mormon Theory and Practice." *Dialogue: A Journal of Mormon Thought* 1, no. 2 (Summer 1966): 30–54.

Woodford, Robert J. "The Historical Development of the Doctrine and Covenants." PhD diss., Brigham Young University, 1974.

Woodward, Kenneth L. "Apostles vs. Historians," *Newsweek*, February 15, 1982, 51.

Worrall, Simon. *The Poet and the Murderer: A True Story of Literary Crime and the Art of Forgery.* New York: Dutton, 2002.

Yocom, David E. *Mark Hofmann Interviews.* Salt Lake City: Office of Salt Lake County Attorney, 1987.

Young, Neil J. " 'The ERA Is a Moral Issue': The Mormon Church, LDS Women, and the Defeat of the Equal Rights Amendment." *American Quarterly* 59, no. 3 (2007): 623–44.

INTERVIEWS

Note: All interviews in this section (with the exception of F. Ross Peterson's interview of Leonard J. Arrington) were conducted by the author on the date indicated, digitally recorded, and full-length transcripts prepared. All transcripts are in the possession of the author and will eventually be deposited in the Gregory A. Prince Papers, Special Collections, J. Willard Marriott Library, University of Utah.

Aird, Mary ("Polly"). May 22, 2008. Historian.

Alder, Douglas D. March 1, 2007. Historian; president, Dixie College, 1986–1992; president, Mormon History Association, 1977–1978.

Alexander, Thomas G. January 12, 2006. Historian; president, Mormon History Association, 1974–1975.

Allen, James B. January 12, 2006. Historian; assistant church historian, 1972–1979; president, Mormon History Association, 1972–1973.

Allen, Renee. May 29, 2010. Friend of Leonard Arrington.

Anderson, Lavina Fielding. March 3, 2008. Historian and editor; excommunicated from the LDS Church in 1993 as one of the "September Six."

Anderson, Paul L. March 3, 2008. Architectural historian, museum curator, and hymn writer; president, Mormon History Association, 2007–2008.

Arrington, Carl. September 24, 2009. Writer; son of Leonard Arrington.

Arrington, Christine Rigby. September 24, 2009. Writer and educator; former daughter-in-law of Leonard Arrington.

Arrington, Harriet Horne. June 15, 2008. Writer; wife of Leonard Arrington, 1983–1999.

Arrington, James. April 12, 2009. Actor, professor; son of Leonard Arrington.

Arrington, Leonard J. Interviewed by F. Ross Peterson, April 12, 1988, and June 6, 1995. Founder and president, Mormon History Association, 1966–1967.

Arrington, Ross. December 2, 2009. Brother of Leonard Arrington.

Baker, John. October 26, 1994. Vice president, Mars, Inc.

Barney, Ronald O. October 26, 2009, and November 10, 2011. Historian.

Beecher, Maureen Ursenbach. July 11, 2008. Historian; president, Mormon History Association, 1984–1985.

Bennett, Patricia. May 29, 2010. Historian.

Bennett, Richard E. May 29, 2010. Historian; president, Mormon History Association, 2013–2014.

Bergera, Gary J. June 16, 2008. Historian and publisher.

Bernhard, Ramona. December 5, 1998. Prince family friend.

Bitton, Davis. August 11, 2006. Historian; assistant church historian, 1972–1979; president, Mormon History Association, 1971–1972.

Blair, Alma R. May 20, 2009. Historian.

Blumell, Bruce. June 30, 2012. Historian.

Bradford, Mary L. July 24, 2009. Writer; editor, *Dialogue: A Journal of Mormon Thought*, 1977–1982.

Bradley, Martha Sonntag. August 6, 2008. Historian; editor, *Dialogue: A Journal of Mormon Thought*, 1993–1998; president, Mormon History Association, 2003–2004.

Bringhurst, Newell G. May 22, 2008. Historian; president, Mormon History Association, 1999–2000.

Bush, Lester E., Jr. October 24, 2008. Historian.

Bushman, Claudia L. January 16, 2009. Historian.

Bushman, Richard L. January 16, 2009. Historian; president, Mormon History Association, 1985–1986.

Carlson, Renee Pyott. June 2, 1994. Family therapist.

Cazier, Stanford O. January 15, 2006. President, Utah State University, 1979–1992.

Clayton, James L. August 8, 2008. Historian.

Cooley, Everett L. January 13, 2006. Historian, archivist.

Daines, N. George. January 16, 2006. Attorney, banker.

Davidson, Marie Arrington. January 16, 2006. Sister of Leonard Arrington.

Derr, Jill Mulvay. August 7, 2008. Historian; president, Mormon History Association, 1998–1999.

Dulany, Elizabeth. May 28, 2010. Publisher.

Dunn, Paul H. January 11, 1997. LDS General Authority.

Durham, George H., II. January 25, 2011. Pediatrician and son of Homer Durham.

Dushku, Judith Rasmussen. February 29, 2012. Professor of government.

Edwards, Paul M. May 19, 2009. Historian; president, Mormon History Association, 1976–1977.

Esplin, Ronald K. June 30, 2012. Historian; president, Mormon History Association, 2006–2007.

Evans, Max J. November 26, 2007. Archivist.

Fielding, Robert Kent. May 6, 2009. Historian.

Flanders, Robert B. May 18, 2009. Historian.

Goates, L. Brent. May 20, 1996. Harold B. Lee's son-in-law.

Grunder, Rick. August 11, 2013. Antiquarian book dealer.

Hansen, Gary B. January 15, 2006. Economist.

Hansen, Nadine. October 22, 2013. Attorney.

Hartley, William G. May 28, 2010. Historian; president, Mormon History Association, 2000–2001.

Higdon, Barbara M. May 20, 2009. Historian.

Howard, Richard P. May 27, 2010. RLDS church historian, 1966–1994; president, Mormon History Association, 1990–1991.

Israelsen, L. Dwight. January 15, 2006. Economist.

Jensen, Richard L. August 8, 2008. Historian.

Johnson, Jeffery O. February 8, 2012. Archivist.

Kastler, Bernard ("Bud"). June 3, 1997. CEO, Mountain Fuel.

Kenney, Scott G. December 2, 2012. Historian.

Kimball, Thomas. May 22, 2009. Publisher.

Lamar, Howard R. February 23, 2007. Historian; president, Yale University, 1992–1993.

Leonard, Glen M. July 27, 2012. Historian; president, Mormon History Association, 2012–2013.

Lyman, Edward Leo. October 8, 2008. Historian.

Madsen, Carol Cornwall. June 17, 2008. Historian; president, Mormon History Association, 1989–1990.

Madsen, Susan Arrington. October 17, November 1, 16, and 18, 2005; January 16, 2006; July 28, 2008; March 3 and October 27, 2009; March 25, 2010. Historian; daughter of Leonard Arrington.

Marquardt, H. Michael. August 9, 2008. Historian.

Mauss, Armand L. January 14, 2006. Sociologist; president, Mormon History Association, 1997–1998.

May, Cheryll Lynn. August 4, 2011. Museum curator.

McMurray, W. Grant. May 19, 2009. Historian; prophet-president, Community of Christ, 1996–2004.

Mehr, Kahlile B. June 16, 2008. Historian.

Midgley, Louis C. April 12, 2009. Professor of political science.

Newell, L. Jackson. October 25, 2009. Historian; president, Deep Springs College, 1995–2004.

Newell, Linda King. October 25, 2009. Historian; president, Mormon History Association, 1996–1997.

O'Neil, Floyd A. June 16, 2008; August 13, 2009. Historian.

Olson, Earl E. January 17, 2006. Assistant managing director, LDS Historical Department.

Peck, Elbert E. June 17, 2008. Publisher and writer.

Peterson, Charles S. November 9, 2006. Historian; president, Mormon History Association, 1975–1976.

Peterson, F. Ross. September 16 and 17, 2007. Historian.

Quinn, D. Michael. December 5, 2005. Historian; excommunicated from the LDS Church in 1993 as one of the "September Six."

Redd, C. Hardy. August 9, 2008. Rancher.

Richards, Lynn S. January 15, 1996. Counselor in the General Superintendency of the LDS Sunday School.

Russell, William D. May 26, 2006; May 20, 2009. Historian; president, Mormon History Association, 1982–1983.

Sadler, Richard W. August 5, 2011. Historian; president, Mormon History Association, 1986–1987.

Sessions, Gene A. August 7, 2011. Historian.

Shipps, Jan. December 7 and 8, 2009. Historian; president, Mormon History Association, 1979–1980.

Slaughter, William W. April 19, 2012. Historian.

Smith, George D. June 30, 2012. Historian.

Smith, Melvin T. February 26, 2009. Historian; president, Mormon History Association, 1981–1982.

Stack, Peggy Fletcher. January 13, 2006. Journalist.

Tanner, Sandra M. August 8, 2008. Historian.

Thayne, Emma Lou. April 11, 2009. Writer and poet.

Ulrich, Laurel Thatcher. June 30, 2012. Historian.

Watt, Ronald G. April 9, 2009. Historian.

Whittaker, David J. May 22, 2008. Historian; president, Mormon History Association, 1995–1996.

Willson, G. W. May 23, 2008. Historian.

Wilson, William Albert ("Bert"). August 12, 2009. Folklorist.

INDEX

Note: Abbreviations used in the index are as follows: Brigham Young University (BYU), Church of Jesus Christ of Latter-day Saints (LDS), Leonard James Arrington (LJA), Reorganized Church of Jesus Christ of Latter Day Saints (RLDS)

526   INDEX

Arrington, Carl (son): (*continued*)
on Grace's first marriage and divorce, 33;
and invitation to author to write biography
of LJA, ix; on Kimball's support for LJA as
church historian, 157; on LJA and church
decision on Sesquicentennial Series, 338; on
LJA as mentor, 212; on LJA's autobiography,
439–40; on religion and family's early years
in Logan, 116; on response to LJA's
appointment as church historian, 160; on
spying at BYU, 358
Arrington, Edna Corn (mother), 3–4, 5, 9, 10, 14,
32, 33–34, 224
Arrington, Glenn (uncle), 11
Arrington, Grace Fort (wife): autobiography of,
x, 30, 33, 99; conversion of to Mormonism,
71, 116–17; decline in health and death of,
129, 372–76; gender stereotypes and life of,
225; letters of, 50; and life in Logan, 263–64;
and life in Salt Lake City, 264–66; on LJA's
work ethic, 102; meeting with and early
years of marriage to LJA, 29–37; and race
relations, 307; and underground church
group, 136
Arrington, Harriet Horne (wife), 390–92, 418,
439, 445, 502n54
Arrington, James (son): and *Adventures of a
Church Historian*, 509n21; and author's
service in Brazilian South Mission, xi; birth
of, 58; and invitation to author to write
biography of LJA, ix; on Grace's support for
LJA's professional life, 37; on LJA and New
Mormon History, 388; and LJA as public
speaker, 119–21; and LJA on role of truth in
church history, 179–80; on LJA's work ethic,
101; on second marriage of LJA to Harriet
Horne, 390, 392
Arrington, Leonard James (LJA): and access to
church archives, 81–82; ancestry and family
history of, 3–9; assessment by of reasons for
demise of History Division, 352–71; and
Brigham Young: American Moses, 397–406;
and bureaucracy of church, 192–200;
author's meetings with, xi; autobiography
of, 437–44; childhood of, 10–13, 105–7;
and church policy on ordination of black
men, 306–27; and church response to *The
Mormon Experience*, 328–31; conflicts with
LDS hierarchy in early years as church
historian, 250–66; and controversy on New
Mormon History, 298–305; and controversy

on *The Story of the Latter-day Saints*,
276–92; description of, 89–104; diaries of,
ix–x, 437, 438, 465n3, 483n13; and disassembly
of History Division, 338–51; disposition of
papers following death of, 460–64; and
Durham as managing director of Historical
Department, 292–98; education in
economics at University of Idaho, 14–24;
final years and legacy of, 445–59; and
graduate school at University of North
Carolina, 25–28, 49–55; and intellectual
movements within church, 412, 413–14,
417–19, 432–36; and Mark Hofmann
documents, 420–31; meeting with Grace
and early years of marriage, 29–37; military
service of during World War II, 38–48;
physical stature of, 30, 31, 39, 89–90, 468n3;
place of women in life of, 224–49; primary
sources for biography of, ix–x; and
promotion of Mormon history, 135–51,
201–23; research for and writing of *Great
Basin Kingdom*, 56–67; and resolution of
conflict between LDS and RLDS, 1–2,
267–75; role of Mormonism in life of,
105–34; and September Six, 432–36; and
Sesquicentennial Series, 331–38; as
subscriber to *Dialogue* and *Sunstone*, 151,
410; transitions in life of after death of
Grace, 377–96. *See also* church historian
Arrington, LeRoy (ancestor), 3
Arrington, LeRoy (brother), 14, 22, 26
Arrington, Marie (sister), 13, 32, 224
Arrington, Noah (father), 3–9, 12, 71, 103, 105,
306–7, 377, 468n17
Arrington, Susan (daughter): and author's
access to papers of LJA, x; birth of, 58;
and disposition of LJA's papers, 463; on
emotional toll on Grace of turmoil in
History Division, 373; on Grace's final
illness and death, 375, 376; on Grace's first
marriage and divorce, 32–33; on Grace's
life in Salt Lake City, 263–64, 265–66; on
Grace's support for LJA's professional life,
36–37; on implications of Turley's talk
about Mountain Meadows Massacre at
Utah State University, 458; invitation to
author to write biography of LJA, ix; on
LJA and caffeinated soft drinks, 100; on
LJA as mentor, 212; on LJA's life at Utah
State University, 76–77; on LJA's work
ethic, 101–2; and portrait of Grace, 35